English

Writing and Skills

CORONADO EDITION

HOLT, RINEHART AND WINSTON
FOURTH COURSE

Critical Readers and Contributors

The authors and the publisher wish to thank the following people, who helped to evaluate and to prepare materials for this series:

Charles L. Allen, Baltimore Public Schools, Baltimore, Maryland
Kiyoko B. Bernard, Huntington Beach High School, Huntington Beach, California
Sally Borengasser, Rogers, Arkansas
Deborah Bull, New York City, New York
Joan Colby, Chicago, Illinois
Phyllis Goldenberg, North Miami Beach, Florida
Beverly Graves, Worthington High School, Worthington, Ohio
Pamela Hannon, Kirk Middle School, Cleveland, Ohio
Carol Kuykendall, Houston Public Schools, Houston, Texas
Wayne Larkin, Roosevelt Junior High School, Blaine, Minnesota
Nancy MacKnight, University of Maine, Orono, Maine
Catherine McCough, Huntington Beach Union School District, California
Kathleen McKee, Coronado High School, Coronado, California
Lawrence Milne, Ocean View High School, Long Beach, California
Al Muller, East Carolina University, Greenville, North Carolina
Dorothy Muller, East Carolina University, Greenville, North Carolina
Arlene Mulligan, Stanley Junior High School, San Diego, California
John Nixon, Santa Ana Junior College, Santa Ana, California
Jesse Perry, San Diego City Schools, California
Christine Rice, Huntington Beach Union School District, Huntington Beach, California
Linda C. Scott, Poway Unified High School District, Poway, California
Jo Ann Seiple, University of North Carolina at Wilmington, Wilmington, North Carolina
Joan Yesner, Brookline, Massachusetts
Seymour Yesner, Brookline Education Center, Massachusetts
Arlie Zolynas, San Diego State University, San Diego, California

Classroom Testing

The authors and the publisher also wish to thank the following teachers, who participated in the classroom testing of materials from this series:

David Foote, Evanston High School East, Evanston, Illinois
Theresa Hall, Nokomis Junior High School, Minneapolis, Minnesota
Carrie E. Hampton, Sumter High School, Sumter, South Carolina
Pamela Hannon, Proviso High School East, Maywood, Illinois
Wayne Larkin, Roosevelt Junior High School, Blaine, Minnesota
Grady Locklear, Sumter High School, Sumter, South Carolina
William Montgomery, Hillcrest High School, Jamaica, New York
Josephine H. Price, Sumter High School, Sumter, South Carolina
Barbara Stilp, North High School, Minneapolis, Minnesota
Joseph Thomas, Weymouth North High School, East Weymouth, Massachusetts
Travis Weldon, Sumter High School, Sumter, South Carolina

Teachers of the Huntington Beach Union High School Writing Program

Cassandra C. Allsop	Carol Kasser	Catherine G. McCough
Eric V. Emery	Patricia Kelly	Kathleen C. Redman
Michael Frym	Stephanie Martone	Christine Rice
Barbara Goldfein	Lawrence Milne	Michael D. Sloan
Joanne Haukland	Richard H. Morley	S. Oliver Smith
Don Hohl	John S. Nixon	Glenda Watson
Sandra Johnson		

Dorothy Augustine, District Consultant in Writing

English
Writing and Skills

CORONADO EDITION

W. Ross Winterowd
Patricia Y. Murray

HOLT, RINEHART AND WINSTON

AUSTIN NEW YORK SAN DIEGO CHICAGO TORONTO MONTREAL

The Series:

English: Writing and Skills, First Course

English: Writing and Skills, Second Course

English: Writing and Skills, Third Course

English: Writing and Skills, Fourth Course

English: Writing and Skills, Fifth Course

English: Writing and Skills, Complete Course

Also available for each title:

Teacher's Edition

Workbook

Test Book

Teacher's Resource Binder

Computer Test Generator

Computer Scoring Program

W. ROSS WINTEROWD is the Bruce R. McElderry Professor of English at the University of Southern California. Since 1975, Dr. Winterowd has traveled widely as a writing consultant for numerous schools in North America.

PATRICIA Y. MURRAY is Director of Composition at DePaul University in Chicago. Dr. Murray taught junior and senior high school English in the Los Angeles city schools. She is also a consultant in curriculum development and teacher training.

Copyright © 1988, 1985 by Holt, Rinehart and Winston, Inc.

Printed in the United States of America

ISBN 0-03-014652-6

Contents

1   *Writing*

3 The Paragraph

4 Expository Writing

5 Research Writing

6   Persuasive Writing

7   Imaginative Writing

8   Business Writing

2   *Grammar and Usage*

9 Nouns

10 Pronouns

11 Verbs

12 Adjectives

20 Clauses

21 Sentence Structure

3   *Mechanics*

22 Punctuation

23 Capitalization

4   *Language Resources*

24 Library Skills

25 Reference Books

1
Writing

1 Discovering the Writing Process

The Writing Process

Writers," said the American poet William Stafford, "have more than space and time can offer. They have the whole unexplored realm of human vision." These are the rewards of the *writing process*, the process by which thoughts are translated into words and words are fashioned into sentences and paragraphs, poems and compositions.

The writing process involves three stages: *prewriting, writing,* and *postwriting*.

Prewriting is the stage of generating ideas and gathering information to write about—a crucial step in preparing to write. Writing is the stage of transforming your ideas into words on paper. As you write, you may discover new ideas or better ways to express your thoughts. For this reason, rewriting may be necessary. During the writing stage, you focus on *what* you are saying. In the postwriting stage, you examine *how* you expressed your ideas. Postwriting is the stage for revising and proofreading, for clarifying language and correcting mistakes, for sharing and responding.

Even famous authors struggle to find words that will adequately express what they want to say. Ernest Hemingway, for example, rewrote the last page of *A Farewell to Arms* thirty-nine times. He knew that writing is a process and that rewriting and revising are vital steps in that process.

The diagram on page 4 shows the kinds of activities that the writing process may include. Although the writing process has identifiable stages, it is not always a straightforward, orderly process. Some stages may be repeated; others may be skipped and then worked on at a later point. For example, sometimes you may begin writing and then realize you need to use a prewriting technique to gather more information. In this chapter you will practice using several prewriting methods, including brainstorming, clustering, free writing, and questioning. Other prewriting activities not introduced in this chapter will be included throughout the book. By the time you have completed your writing course, you will have learned to use the writing process for all types of compositions.

Prewriting

The most important part of prewriting is discovering ideas for writing. The best methods of discovering ideas vary for each individual. Albert Einstein, for example, said that some of his best ideas occurred to him while he was shaving in the morning. Agatha Christie, a famous mystery writer, often discovered ideas for writing while eating apples in the bathtub.

The most effective prewriting techniques not only help you discover ideas but also help you focus on a topic and inspire you to begin writing about it. The nature of each writing assignment can help you decide which type of prewriting technique will be most useful. For example, before writing a short report, you may need to read magazine articles, take notes, and make an outline. In contrast, prewriting activities for writing a poem might include different skills, such as observing, imagining, clustering, or using your senses to see, hear, smell, taste, or touch something. You will discover the prewriting methods that work best for you by experimenting with various ones.

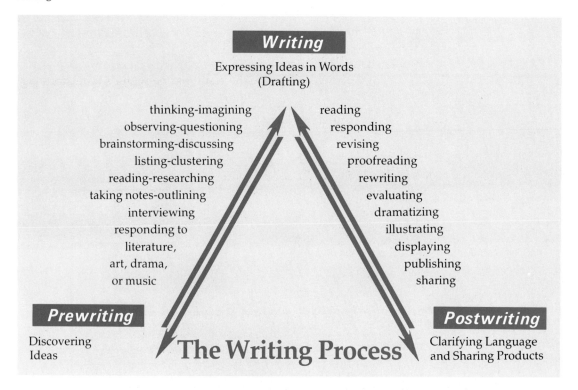

The Writing Process

Writing

Expressing Ideas in Words
(Drafting)

thinking-imagining
observing-questioning
brainstorming-discussing
listing-clustering
reading-researching
taking notes-outlining
interviewing
responding to
literature,
art, drama,
or music

reading
responding
revising
proofreading
rewriting
evaluating
dramatizing
illustrating
displaying
publishing
sharing

Prewriting

Discovering
Ideas

Postwriting

Clarifying Language
and Sharing Products

Writing Practice 1: *Listing Prewriting Methods*

Look at the diagram of the writing process above and read the prewriting methods listed on the left side of the triangle. Either individually or as a class, list the prewriting methods you have used to discover ideas for writing. Include any that are not on the list. Then circle the prewriting techniques that have been most effective for you.

Brainstorming

A *brainstorm* is a sudden idea. *Brainstorming* means generating as many ideas as you can without stopping to judge them.

To brainstorm, focus your thoughts on one subject and let ideas come into your mind. Do not stop to decide which ideas are useful and which are not. Accept *all* ideas; free your mind to play creatively during brainstorming. You can sift through your ideas later and select the most useful ones.

Brainstorming can be done alone or in a group. If you brainstorm alone, sit in a quiet place with some blank paper and a pen or pencil. Write your subject in large letters on a sheet of paper. Then let your thoughts roam freely on the subject, writing down ideas in words, phrases, or sentences as they come to you.

The following ideas are the result of one writer's brainstorming on the subject *The car of the future:*

The Car of the Future

Smaller than cars today
May hold only one person
Lighter
Aluminum
Styrofoam
Fuel crisis
Fuel efficient
Gasohol
Alcohol
Water-powered
Solar energy
Electric battery
Perfectly safe car

Electric cars will be used for
   short-distance driving.
Recharging stations will spring
   up all over the country.
Can fly like a helicopter
James Bond
Goes in water also
Supersonic
Moves on tracks
Shaped like a bullet
Silver bullet
Rubber bumpers
Rubber everything

This writer's thoughts wandered over all aspects of the subject —from the type of engine to the design of the car to safety features. The writer might later dismiss some ideas—building a car of styrofoam or powering a car with water—as impractical. The purpose of brainstorming, however, is to accumulate creative ideas, and this writer has gathered many.

Brainstorming in a group gives you access to other people's thoughts as well as your own.

The thoughts of others may also stimulate your own thinking, helping you come up with new ideas. To brainstorm in a group, select one person—a recorder—to announce the topic and write down ideas

as group members state them. If your group gets stuck, have the recorder read over the list of ideas. The entire process should not take more than fifteen minutes.

Writers who brainstorm often discover that they know more about a subject than they thought. They also may discover aspects of the subject they need to learn more about. The writer who brainstormed on the car of the future, for example, might decide to find out more about alternate fuels for tomorrow's cars. On the other hand, brainstorming may reveal the aspect the writer knows most about and so suggest a way of limiting the subject.

Writing Practice 2: *Brainstorming*

Either alone or in a group, select one of the following subjects or make up one of your own. Write the subject in large letters on a sheet of paper. (In a group, ask one member to serve as recorder.) Then brainstorm on your subject for about ten minutes, gathering as many ideas as possible without stopping to evaluate them.

1.   Part-time jobs

2.   Ideas for inexpensive birthday gifts

3.   Reducing traffic accidents

4.   The ideal vacation

5.   New ideas for conserving energy

6.   New courses for high schools

7.   Space travel in the year 2500

8.   Themes for a Homecoming float or dance

9.   Making good grades

10. Increasing attendance at school-sponsored events, such as games and dances

Clustering

Clustering is a prewriting method in which you brainstorm on a subject and write your ideas in *clusters*, or groups.

You can cluster ideas by yourself, with a small group, or with the entire class. To make a *word cluster*, begin by writing your subject in the middle of a blank page and circling it. Then let your mind wander freely on the subject. Write new ideas around the circled word, and draw lines to connect words and phrases that are related to each other.

An initial cluster for writing about the car of the future might look like the following one.

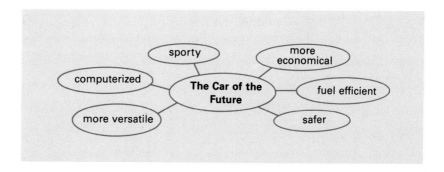

As ideas begin to flow, the word cluster expands. One word or phrase leads to another. Related ideas begin to form branches that show connections in the writer's mind.

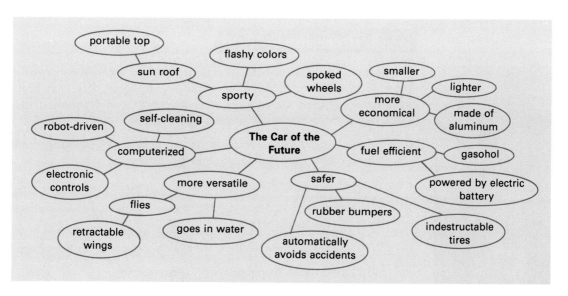

Clustering is also valuable in focusing ideas and narrowing a topic. If the writer who made the previous word cluster tried to include all the details from the cluster in a composition, the composition would be too general.

The following word cluster shows how the writer chose one branch from the original cluster and developed a specific topic for writing.

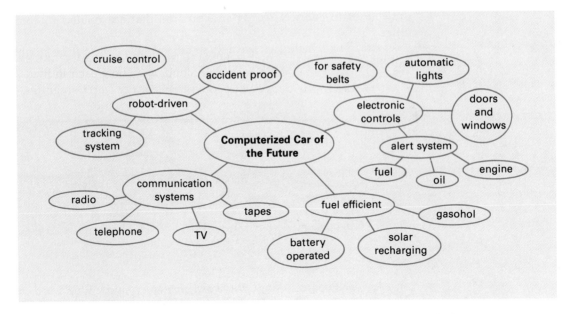

Writing Assignment I: *The High School of the Future*

A. Prewriting

Clustering: As a class, create a word cluster on the chalkboard using *The high school of the future* as your subject. Imagine how your high school will be different twenty years from now. Consider some of the following questions in making your word cluster.

1. What changes might occur in the appearance of buildings and classrooms in the high school of the future?

2. What new classes might be offered?

3. What new ways of teaching might exist? How might they affect the way students learn?

4. What changes might occur in the way people look, dress, or act?

5. What inventions would you like to see used?

B. Writing

Select one part of the word cluster and write a paragraph about *The high school of the future*. Focus your paragraph on one aspect, such as building design, classes of the future, or educational inventions. Clarify the focus of your paragraph by writing a topic sentence that introduces your main idea.

C. Postwriting

Responding in Groups: Share your composition with a small group of classmates. As compositions are read aloud, note how each individual used a part of the class cluster to write his or her own paragraph.

Free Writing

Free writing is the spontaneous flow of ideas from mind to paper.

The purpose of free writing, like that of brainstorming and clustering, is to tap the reservoir of thoughts in the mind and capture these ideas on paper. Free writing is done individually. The writer gets down ideas on paper as rapidly as possible. The focus is on *ideas* rather than on correct form. After transcribing thoughts onto paper, the writer then may choose some of the ideas to use in a composition.

Free writing can help uncover ideas that you may not be aware of having. Free writing can also help you discover writing topics that are meaningful to you. The quality of your writing will improve when you write about subjects of interest to you.

Writing Practice 3: *Free Writing*

Think back to the end of your last year in junior high or middle school. Recall some of the feelings and questions you had about going to high school. Perhaps you were unsure about how to register for classes or what activities or clubs to join. Free write about how you felt about going on to high school. Concentrate on getting your thoughts and memories down on paper.

Writing Practice 4: *A Letter to a New Student*

After completing the free writing exercise in Writing Practice 3, write a letter to someone who plans to attend your high school next year. Select some of the information from your free writing to use in your letter. For example, if you were anxious about registering for classes, explain the registration process to the prospective student. If you were unsure about which sports or club activities to join, inform the new student about the kinds of activities that are available. Try to anticipate the basic needs and questions an incoming student might have and address these needs in your letter.

Audience

In the previous Writing Practice you were asked to write to a specific audience—a new student who plans to attend your high school. Your audience affected the information you included and the kind of language you used. For example, you may have given instructions for registering for classes or suggestions on the kinds of classes to take.

Suppose you write another letter about registering for classes, this time to a different audience. Perhaps when you registered, you were unable to get a computer programming class that you wanted. As a result, you decide to write a letter to the principal, describing your problem and requesting a change in your class schedule. Or suppose you write an article for the school newspaper, informing students of a registration problem. Each time your audience changes, the contents, the language, and the tone (or attitude) of your letter also changes.

Purpose

Every writing assignment has a purpose. In the last Writing Practice, your purpose in writing the letter to a new student was to *inform* the student about some aspect of your high school. If you had written the letter to your principal about registration, your purpose may have been twofold—to *inform* the principal about your problem and to *persuade* the principal to change your class schedule. If you had written an article about class registration for your school newspaper, your purpose may have been to *tell* students about your experience and to *explain* how they might avoid similar difficulties. In each case, your purpose for writing guides what you say and how you say it.

Modes of Writing

Think about the variety of writing you do in your everyday life. You might make shopping lists, fill out job applications, write thank-you notes, write laboratory reports for a science class, or write in your diary.

In addition to paying attention to audience and purpose, you must also consider the mode, or kind, of writing you are doing. Most

writing falls into one of four categories: *description, narration, persuasion,* and *exposition.* You would use description in a letter to a new student if you wanted to tell what your high school looks like. If you witnessed a car accident, you would use narration to tell the officer what happened. You would use persuasion in a letter to the editor of your school paper if you wanted to convince readers of the need to lengthen the lunch period. You would use exposition—writing that explains or informs—to explain how to load a disk into a computer.

Not every piece of writing can be categorized into a single mode, however. For example, if your expository essay on loading a computer disk were written for a person who knew nothing about computers, you would need to include a description of both a disk and a disk drive. Much of the writing you will do throughout this book will involve some combination of the four modes of writing—description, narration, exposition, and persuasion.

Writing Practice 5: *Audience, Purpose, and Writing Modes*

Look through newspapers, magazines, or other written materials to find the kinds of writing listed below. Either cut out or copy a part of each example. Indicate the audience to whom the writing is directed and the purpose for which it is written. Possible audiences include teenagers, young children, adults, and members of a profession or specific group. The purposes for writing include *to describe, to entertain, to inform, to explain,* and *to persuade.*

1. Find an example of an article written to inform teenagers about a particular topic.

2. Find a story written to entertain young children.

3. Find a set of directions that explains how to do something.

4. Find an editorial in a newspaper written to persuade someone to adopt an opinion or to take an action.

5. Find an example of description used in combination with another mode of writing (perhaps in your favorite book or novel).

Share at least one example from the preceding list with your class or a small group. Read a paragraph of the example aloud, and ask the members of your group to specify the writer's purpose, the audience to whom it is directed, and the mode of writing used.

Questioning

For more information on interrogative pronouns and adverbs, see pages 328, 347-348, 420.

Questioning is another effective prewriting technique. Reporters often use the basic *Who? What? Where? When? Why?* and *How?* questions to gather information.

The following set of questions is called the *Pentad*.[1] It consists of five basic questions that focus on action, actors, scene, method, and reason. These basic questions can lead to other questions. For example, imagine that you plan to write a descriptive essay about a concert you attended last week. Although you want to make your readers feel as though they were at the concert, you are having trouble remembering details. You could use the following Pentad questions to gather the details you need.

The Action: What happened?

What did the group do on stage?

What was the audience's reaction?

What songs did they play?

What musical instruments or special effects were used?

The Actors: Who caused the action?

Who performed on stage? (List details to describe performers' appearance.)

Who attended the concert with you?

The Scene: Where and when did the action take place?

Where was the concert held? (List details to describe the setting.)

---

[1]This section is based on ideas in *Rhetoric: Discovery and Change* by Richard E. Young, Alton L. Becker, and Kenneth E. Pike (New York: Harcourt Brace Jovanovich, 1971).

Where were the performers?

Where did you sit?

When was the concert? (What time, day of week, and date was it?)

The Method: How was the action done?

Did the performers stand still, or did they move about the stage?

How was the concert organized?

How did the performers interact with the audience?

The Reason: Why did the action occur?

Do you know why this group performed here? Are they on a national tour? Are they a local group?

Why did you attend? Did someone invite you? Is this your favorite musical group?

Writing Practice 6: *The Pentad*

Using the Pentad, write a list of questions about an event you have recently attended, such as a concert, a sports activity, a rally, an

assembly, or a dance recital. Write your questions following the Pentad format. Answer your questions using specific words, phrases, or sentences.

A Student Profile

I n the preceding Writing Practice, you used a questioning system and answered the questions based on your own knowledge and information. Some writing assignments may require you to gather information from another person by interviewing. Newspapers and television reporters use carefully thought-out questions to interview people. The answers to these questions form the basis for their reports.

Writing Assignment II: *A Student Profile*

A. Prewriting

Composing a List of Questions: Make a list of specific questions you can use to interview a classmate, using the *Who? What? Where? When? Why?* and *How?* questioning method. Interview someone you do not know very well. (Later you will write a profile to introduce this person to members of a small group.) Include questions that help you discover the most interesting details about this person's life. Avoid questions that are too personal and may not be appropriate for a general audience. During the interview you may need to ask follow-up questions to clarify points or to acquire additional information. (You may want to brainstorm a list of questions with a small group or as a class before writing your own.)

Conducting an Interview: Before the interview, write each set of questions on separate cards. Arrange the cards in the order in which you want to ask the questions.

As your teacher directs, interview your classmate, taking brief notes on the cards as you ask each question. You, in turn, will be interviewed by this classmate. Each interview should take approximately fifteen to twenty minutes.

B. Writing

Read through your interview notes and mark the most interesting information. Using these details, write a personal profile that introduces this student. As you write, you may want to include elements of description, narration, and exposition. For example, you might describe this person's favorite meal; narrate his or her funniest experience; or inform the audience about the student's hobbies, interests, or special activities.

C. Postwriting

Partner Response: Ask the student you wrote about to read your composition and comment on the following points:

What part is the most interesting?

Is all the information correct?

What information could be added?

What information could be taken out?

You will also read and comment on the composition your interviewer wrote about you.

Revising and Rewriting: Reread your profile with the following questions in mind. Using your responses to these questions and the comments from your partner, make the necessary changes in your draft. Then rewrite your profile to share with your classmates.

1. Does the first sentence catch the interest of my audience?

2. Do I show what this person is like?

3. Do I avoid unnecessary repetition?

4. When I read the composition aloud, are all the sentences clear and smooth?

5. Does my composition have a real conclusion, rather than just an abrupt end?

Sharing Student Profiles: As your teacher directs, divide into groups of four to six students. Introduce your partner to your group by reading your profile aloud.

Revising

Revising means making changes in the content of writing.

The word *revision* literally means "seeing again." While revising, you may decide to change words, rewrite sentences, omit unnecessary information, add specific details, reorganize paragraphs, or write a new introductory paragraph. Revision may mean making a few minor changes, or it may involve rewriting the entire piece on a more specific topic. While revising, focus on communicating ideas clearly and organizing them logically. Try to improve the expression of ideas and the organization.

Because revision is the messy stage of writing, you will find it helpful to use the following editing marks for making changes. These marks will guide you in rewriting your final draft.

Editing Symbols

≣	Use a capital letter.	∧	Add something.
/	Use a lower-case letter.	ℓ	Remove or delete something.
⊙	Add a period.	↜⊃	Move a section.
⋀	Add a comma.	¶	Indent a paragraph.
⋁	Add quotation marks.	◯	Spell correctly.

Model: A Revised Composition

The following paragraph uses editing marks. Read the paragraph and note how the writer made changes to improve it. Then answer the questions that follow.

Of all my posessions my baseball glove is probably my favorite posession. I've been through an awfull lot with my baseball glove. I've had that glove for about seven years. It's a big glove, a tan color with Pete Rose's signature on it. I first got it when I started out *playing* in little league. I had a rough start in baseball, but my glove really helped me out. I've caught *many* a lot of balls with *my* that glove, but then I've missed some too. I can remember the time *playing* when I was out in center field, *when* and a great *came* *smacked* *so hard* hitter was up to bat. He hit that ball, and I thought it was *as* going out of the park. I ran back toward the fence. The ball *soared into* was way up in the air. When I got to the fence, I jumped up, and my glove and I caught that ball. ~~I've been through alot of~~ *e*

~~other good times with my glove too.~~ My baseball glove will always be special to me.

My baseball glove is my favorite possession. It's a big, tan glove with Pete Rose's signature. I got it when I started playing in Little League. I had a rough start in baseball, but my glove really helped me out. I've caught many balls with my glove. I remember playing center field when a great hitter came up to bat. He smacked that ball so hard I thought it was going out of the park. I ran towards the fence as the ball soared into the air. When I reached the fence, I jumped up, and my glove and I caught that ball. My baseball glove will always be special to me.

Think and Discuss

1. Look at the rough draft and reread the first sentence. Compare this sentence with the first sentence in the revised draft. What changes did the writer make? How do these changes improve the introduction?

2. What error does the writer correct in the fourth sentence?

3. Sentences 10 and 11 are combined in the revised draft. How does this change help create a variety of sentence patterns and sentence lengths? How was the word choice improved?

4. Which ending sentence is more effective? Why? Can you think of another sentence that would end the paragraph effectively?

Writing Practice 7: *A Special Object*

Think about an object that is special to you. Make a word cluster, including memories or feelings about the object and details that describe it.

Using some of the ideas in your word cluster, write a paragraph describing the object and telling why it is special to you. Save your draft for the next Writing Practice.

Using a Checklist for Revision

In the prewriting section, you learned how asking questions can help you gather information for writing. Asking questions can also help you evaluate your writing after you have completed a first draft. The following checklist, which also appears at the back of this book, can be used for revising most compositions.

Checklist for Revision

1. Have I clearly stated my central topic?

2. Should I add more details or examples?

3. Have I taken out irrelevant or repetitive information?

4. Does each paragraph include one main idea developed with several supporting sentences?

5. Have I used a variety of sentence patterns and lengths?

6. Are my sentences complete and smooth?

7. Did I use transitional words and phrases to show how ideas relate to each other?

8. Can I improve the word choices?

9. Does the style of my writing reflect my own ideas and thoughts?

10. Does my writing show the relationship between the introduction, the body of the composition, and the concluding statement?

Writing Practice 8: *Revising a Composition*

Using the preceding checklist, revise the composition you wrote in Writing Practice 7. Be sure you have accurately described the object and explained why it is special to you. Use editing marks to make changes. Save your revised draft for a later Writing Practice in which you will make final corrections in grammar, mechanics, and spelling.

Student Response Groups

Have you ever written a composition that is perfectly clear to you but not to someone else? This may happen because you, as the writer, know what you mean to say; your audience does not. For this reason, someone else can often help identify both the strengths and the weaknesses of your composition. Others' comments and suggestions can be used in revising a piece of writing.

To get reader response, you can ask a friend, classmate, parent, or teacher to read and comment on your writing. In the classroom, you can respond to one another's drafts in small groups. Ideally, a student response group has four or five students.

When responding to another person's writing, it is important to be sensitive to the person's feelings. Be considerate and make constructive comments. Observe the following guidelines when working together in student response groups.

Student Response Guide

Be positive:	First look for and comment on the positive features of a composition.
Be polite:	Make only constructive suggestions; ask questions if something is unclear.
Be specific:	Select one or two areas that need improvement and make specific suggestions that will help the writer make changes.

Writing Practice 9: *Working in a Student Response Group*

As your teacher directs, form a student response group or work with a partner to read and revise the composition you wrote in Writing Practice 7. Follow the standards in the Student Response Guide. After a composition is read, each member should first comment on a special feature he or she liked. Then each person can make a constructive suggestion for improving the composition.

Note areas in your draft that you want to change based on student comments.

Proofreading

Proofreading, the final step in the writing process, means checking a piece of writing for errors in spelling, grammar, and mechanics.

Although you can improve a composition throughout the entire writing process, when you proofread, you focus on correctness.

Besides proofreading your own writing, you may want to ask another person to proofread your composition because someone else may catch errors that you miss. Use the checklist on the next page, which is reprinted at the back of the book, to proofread your compositions.

Proofreader's Checklist

1. Have I indented each paragraph?

2. Did I capitalize the first word of each sentence, all proper nouns, and the word *I*?

3. Did I punctuate each sentence correctly?

4. Are there any sentence fragments or incomplete sentences?

5. Do related verbs, nouns, or pronouns in each sentence show agreement in kind and number?

6. Are all words spelled correctly?

7. Is my writing easy to read?

Writing Practice 10: *Proofreading a Final Draft*

Proofread the composition you wrote and revised in the last few Writing Practices. Using the preceding Proofreader's Checklist, make final corrections in grammar, mechanics, and spelling. You may also have another person proofread your paper.

Sharing Final Products

The final stage of writing can be the most pleasurable. You have taken your composition through many stages, and now you have a draft you can be proud of. Now is the time to share your writing for enjoyment.

Writing Practice 11: *Responding to a Final Draft*

Share your final draft with a small group of classmates (perhaps the same group that helped you revise it). The purpose of the response group is to enjoy the compositions and learn about your classmates. As each composition is read, the writer may also want to show the special object he or she wrote about.

Sentence Combining:
Using Connectors

Achieving Sentence Variety

As you read the following paragraph, think about how you might make changes to improve it.

> The tired custodian pushed his ragged mop down the hall. The hall was dirty. The hall had been neglected for months. Classes were not in session. The custodian was working nights. The custodian was paying for his oldest daughter's schooling. He wanted his daughter to have a bright future. He wanted his daughter to be happy. The mop moved slowly. It moved carefully. It covered every crack in the floor. It left a gleaming trail behind on the floor of the dimly lit corridor.

Although there are no errors in the paragraph, the writing seems immature. Each sentence is isolated from the others; there is no flow from one sentence into the next.

If you were to rewrite the paragraph by combining some of the sentences, you might produce the following paragraph.

> The tired custodian pushed his ragged mop down the dirty hall, which had been neglected for months since classes were not in session. He was working nights to pay for his oldest daughter's schooling, because he wanted her to have a bright, happy future. Slowly, carefully, the mop moved, covering every crack in the floor, leaving a gleaming trail behind on the floor of the dimly lit corridor.

The joined sentences or parts of sentences in the preceding example give the paragraph smoothness and fluency and make the paragraph more interesting for readers.

Throughout this text, you will learn several ways to write more interesting sentences, using a method called *sentence combining*. In the sentence-combining exercises you will use a model, or pattern, to combine two or more sentences. You will also complete some exercises that will allow you to use your own patterns and combinations. If you are unfamiliar with any of the grammatical terms used in these exercises, refer to the definitions in the Grammar and Usage part of this book.

Joining Sentences with Connectors

For information on conjunctions, see pages 452-463.

Several words in the English language may be used to make effective connections between sentences. The first group of *connectors* joins two statements of equal importance by indicating a relationship between the two:

and connects two similar ideas

but connects opposing ideas

for provides a reason

nor indicates a negative

or indicates a choice

so shows a cause and its effect

yet connects opposing ideas

Note: The grammatical term for these connectors is *coordinating conjunctions*.

The following models show how connectors are used to combine two sentences into one. The word in parentheses, called a *signal*, indicates which connector to use. Unless the two combined sentences are very brief and closely related, a comma precedes the connector.

Sentences: Maria repaired the broken fence.
I washed the grimy storm windows. (*and*)

Combined: Maria repaired the broken fence, *and* I washed the grimy storm windows.

Sentences: Jennifer didn't boast when she succeeded.
She didn't cry when she failed. (*nor*)

Combined: Jennifer didn't boast when she succeeded, *nor* did she cry when she failed.

Notice that *nor* follows the same pattern as other connectors but causes a change in word order. In addition, the word *not* (in the form of the contraction *n't*) is removed from the second sentence because *nor* already indicates a negative.

Exercise 1: Joining Sentences with Connectors

The following sentences can be combined with one of the sentence connectors in the previous section. In the first five sentences you are given a signal in the form of a connecting word in parentheses; for the last five sentences choose the connector you think makes the most sense. Study the example first and then write each newly combined sentence on a sheet of paper.

Example

a. The teens have organized a campaign to save the big oak. It is the oldest tree in La Salle County. (*for*)
The teens have organized a campaign to save the big oak, for it is the oldest tree in La Salle County.

1. Do you want to go out Saturday evening?
   Do you already have plans? (*or*)

2. Ryan was injured in yesterday's soccer tournament.
   He will be unable to attend tonight's rehearsal. (*so*)

3. Mrs. Romero was confined to a wheelchair for six months.
   She never missed a day of work. (*yet*)

4. A month ago Anita stopped eating rich desserts.
   She has lost six pounds. (*and*)

5. Dad always helps with the housework.
   My mother is working full time. (*for*)

6. Saturday's picnic was canceled because of the heavy rain.
   We have rescheduled it for next Sunday afternoon.

7. Mrs. Alvarez works at the lumberyard.
   On Saturday she serves as a volunteer at the art center.

8. My brother loves to cook.
   I would rather help with yardwork.

9. I had to leave early for an appointment.
   I missed the lecture on African art.

10. My great-aunt grows all her own vegetables.
    She freezes half of what she raises.

Writing Practice: *Revising for Sentence Variety*

For Writing Practice 7 of Chapter 1, you wrote a composition about an object of importance to you. Reread your composition for effective use of sentence connectors. Also note whether you have used a variety of sentence patterns and lengths. If you have many short, choppy sentences, combine a few by using coordinating conjunctions.

2 Personal Writing: Description and Narration

The Purpose of Personal Writing

Writing about your own experiences is called *personal writing*.

The purpose of personal writing is to write about what you know and to share your thoughts, ideas, and experiences with readers.

Personal writing may take many forms, including the diary, Writer's Notebook, personal letter, autobiography, and personal narrative. The skills necessary for personal writing include the ability to observe yourself and the physical world carefully and to record these observations in an interesting way. Other essential skills are the ability to organize and develop your thoughts. Each of these skills is also basic to many other kinds of writing.

In this chapter you will read about and practice three forms of personal writing: the Writer's Notebook, description, and the personal narrative.

The Language of Personal Writing

Every person who talks has a *speaking voice* made up of such features as words, the way words are pronounced, and the way words are arranged in sentences. Depending on the situation, a person's speaking voice may change. In conversation with good friends, for example, speakers tend to use simpler words and shorter sentences than they might on more formal occasions.

When you write, you have a *writing voice*. Your writing voice is largely determined by the words you choose and by the way you use them. One sign of a good writer is the ability to change writing voices according to the situation. When you write a letter to a friend, you want a writing voice that sounds friendly, but when you write a science report, you want a writing voice that sounds authoritative.

Personal writing calls for a natural writing voice.

Personal writing should sound almost as though you are talking with your reader. One way to ensure such a voice is to write about

yourself in the first person, using such words as *I, my,* and *me.* These first-person words let you make the simple, direct statements that are often a part of your personal speaking voice. A sentence such as *The writer thinks his (or her) first ambition was to be a circus clown* sounds more natural when written as *I think my first ambition was to be a circus clown.*

Another way to promote a natural speaking voice is to use words that are a natural part of your vocabulary. This does not mean, however, limiting your writing vocabulary to short, simple words. If a longer word says precisely what you want to say, then use that word, but do not use longer words just to sound more important. State or city park signs may ask you to "extinguish" campfires, but your personal writing will sound more natural when you write that you "put out" your campfire. In personal writing would you "terminate your employment" or "quit your job"?

An important part of personal writing is choosing *specific* words —words that will help the reader to understand exactly what you feel, think, observe, and experience. Used properly, specific words help recreate the feeling, thought, observation, or experience. *Sensory* words—words about sights, sounds, tastes, smells, and textures—are specific, as are words of dialogue, proper nouns, and figures or numbers.

Model: Personal Writing

Emancipation Day, January 1, 1863, was the day slavery officially ended in the United States. At Camp Saxton, South Carolina, a young woman named Charlotte Forten watched the ceremony marking the occasion. Having lived in the North, Charlotte Forten was never a slave herself, but the ceremony had a special meaning for her, and her excitement comes through in her writing. As you read the following passage in which Charlotte Forten describes her personal experiences on Emancipation Day, look for ways she achieves a natural writing voice. What specific sensory words does she use to help the reader share her experiences?

New-Year's Day, Emancipation Day, was a glorious one to us. General Saxton and Colonel Higginson had invited us to visit the camp of the First Regiment of South Carolina Volunteers on that day, "the greatest day in the nation's history." We enjoyed perfectly the exciting scene on board the steamboat *Flora*. There was an eager, wondering crowd of the freed people, in their holiday attire, with the gayest of headkerchiefs, the whitest of aprons, and the happiest of faces. The band was playing, the flags were streaming, and everybody was talking merrily and feeling happy. The sun shone brightly, and the very waves seemed to partake of the universal gayety, for they danced and sparkled more joyously than ever before. Long before we reached Camp Saxton, we could see the beautiful grove and the ruins of the old fort near it.

Some companies of the First Regiment were drawn up in line under the trees near the landing, ready to receive us. They were a fine, soldierly looking set of men, and their brilliant dress made a splendid appearance among the trees. It was my good fortune to find an old friend among the officers. He took us over the camp and showed us all the arrangements. Everything looked clean and comfortable; much neater, we were told, than in most of the white camps.

An officer told us that he had never seen a regiment in which the men were so honest. "In many other camps," said he, "the Colonel and the rest of us would find it necessary to place a guard before our tents. We never do it here. Our tents are left entirely unguarded, but nothing has ever been touched." We were glad to know that. It is a remarkable fact, when we consider that the men of this regiment have all their lives been slaves; for we all know that Slavery does not tend to make men honest.[1]

Think and Discuss

Even though the preceding passage was written over one hundred

---

years ago, it sounds modern because Charlotte Forten writes with a natural voice. She writes in the first person, makes short and direct statements, and uses specific details. Look back over the passage and find at least three examples of each of the following items.

1. Sentences where Charlotte Forten writes in the first person about herself and her companions
   Example: We enjoyed perfectly the exciting scene on board the steamboat *Flora*.

2. Sentences that are short and direct statements
   Example: New-Year's Day, Emancipation Day, was a glorious one to us.

3. Sentences that have specific details
   Example: There was an eager, wondering crowd of the freed people, in their holiday attire, with the gayest of headkerchiefs, the whitest of aprons, and the happiest of faces. [Details of sight]

Writing Practice 1: *Preparing to Write*

Make a list of several important events in your life, such as winning an award, starting your first part-time job, taking your driver's test, or preparing for the opening night of a play. Select one event as the topic for a composition.

To begin the assignment, use the *Who? What? When? Where? Why?* and *How?* system to gather information about your topic. Using specific details, take notes to answer the following questions: (1) Who was involved in the event? (2) What happened? (3) When did it happen? (4) Where did it happen? (5) Why did it happen? (6) How did it happen? Save your notes for the next assignment.

Example

Event: Taking My Driver's Test

1. *Who was involved in the event?*
   The license examiner, Officer Susan Williams
   Looked like every picture I have ever seen of a Marine drill sergeant
   Seemed to be about eight feet tall, but was probably five feet
   Wore dark sunglasses that covered half her face

2. *What happened?*
   Smooth ride to highway for road test
   Made proper stop at every stop sign and stoplight
   Turned around to come back to patrol office
   Car ran out of gas
   Examiner told me to get gas and come back next week.

3. *When did it happen?*
   On a bright spring morning in April
   On my sixteenth birthday

4. *Where did it happen?*
   In the parking lot of the highway patrol office and the highway

5. *Why did it happen?*
   I took the test to get my driver's license. The car ran out of gas because my brother had used the car the night before, and I forgot to check the gauge.

6. *How did it happen?*
   Just as I was ready to turn the car around and return to the

patrol office, I felt the car begin to lurch forward. The engine sputtered slightly, and the car lurched a few more feet, then completely died.

Notice that the preceding notes include specific details about when and where the event happened; they also tell what the day and place were like.

Another important question to ask yourself is what you felt and thought during the event. Writing about your thoughts and feelings helps readers to share the event with you, as you can tell from the following description of the writer's thoughts and feelings when the car ran out of gas.

> "The test is over!" I thought. "Nothing can stop me now." I leaned back confidently in my seat, turning to glance at the examiner sitting beside me. Just at that moment I felt the car begin to lurch forward. The engine sputtered slightly, and the car moved forward a few more feet and then completely died. I knew the worst had happened. The car was out of gas!

Keeping a Writer's Notebook

A *Writer's Notebook* consists of a series of personal writing pieces called *entries*.

The content of entries varies, depending on the reason for keeping the notebook. You may know that, by law, ship captains must keep a notebook, called a *log*, in which they record such information as the ship's position; the type of cargo it carries; weather conditions; and circumstances surrounding illnesses, injuries, and deaths on board. Writers often keep notebooks as well, and they do so for several reasons: to record and comment on personal experiences, to practice writing, and to collect a source of ideas for other kinds of writing. As a writer you should consider keeping a notebook for the same reasons. This text contains frequent suggestions for Writer's Notebook entries; notebook writing is an enjoyable way to increase your writing fluency.

In this chapter you will write several entries for your Writer's Notebook. Periodically, you may be asked to share entries with your classmates and teacher. For this reason, part of what you write in your notebook will be intended for an audience. Thus, you will not want to include thoughts, feelings, or experiences that you do not wish to share. Such topics can best be written about in a private notebook kept at home. You can also practice using your personal writing voice in your Writer's Notebook.

Model: A Writer's Notebook Entry

Kodoku: Sailing Alone Across the Pacific is the journal of a young Japanese man named Kenichi Horie, who crossed the Pacific Ocean alone in a small sailboat. The Japanese word *kodoku* means roughly "solitude." As you read the following entry, look for examples of both factual and personal details.

Sailing on the *port tack* means "sailing to the left of the wind's direction."

Starboard is the right side; *portside* is the left side.

The *companionway* is the stairway.

Fo'c'sle, short for forecastle, is the forward part of the upper deck.

14th day out: May 25th, Friday

5:00 a.m. Wind has dropped a good deal. Take in the "sea anchor." Winds from the north. Sail her on the port tack, course ENE. High seas, little wind. I don't like it. The storm is up and we're still afloat. But this is just the beginning. What's it going to be like in the long days ahead? My confidence is shaken.

The whole boat is a soaking mess. Gear all over the place. Things stored starboard are now portside. Looks as though a wizard had been through, making things jump into opposite places. Too tired to do much about it, though.

The way the gear in the cabin got mixed up was fantastic. It was almost unbelievable. The stuff in the port shelf went right across the cabin and landed in the starboard shelf. The port shelf was full of things from the starboard one. And I was sure it wasn't *me* that was mixed up. I had carefully fixed places for each item I had carried, and each had its proper place. The medical supplies went on the starboard shelf towards the bow. Books belonged to the port shelf on the side near the cabin entrance. But after the storm everything was completely jumbled.

The shelves are fixed on the cabin walls just above the berths. If anything dropped from either of the shelves, it would land on the berths or on the cabin floor. It would be impossible for it to crawl back on the shelf it dropped from, much less the *opposite* shelf. The only way anything could land on the opposite shelf would be for it to *fly!* But, how? Wings? What wings? Well, then, magic. That's all it could be—magic.

The motion must have been so violent during the storm that everything inside the cabin was sent off in a mad whirlwind of a high trapeze. The most acrobatic was the stuff in the toolbox. I had fixed it by the steps at the companionway. It was a fairly deep box with a simple lid on its top. The only way anything could get out of that box was straight up. But that's just what all my tools must have done, because they all ended up in the fo'c'sle!

During the storm I was too busy trying to hold myself down. I had no time to worry about the mad circus that was going on in the cabin. But when I think about it now, it must have been those curling, breaking seas that had done it. Those crests were terribly steep. Most even had an overhang as they came crashing down. As the *Mermaid* was lying to her stern anchor, she would climb, stern first, these steep walls of sea. She would almost flip over ends-on as she came up to the crest. But then her "sea anchor" would yank her stern down into the valley of the next sea as the first one went roaring past.[1]

Think and Discuss

Kenichi Horie's entry has many factual details, including the date and the time of day. The entry also has personal details, such as the comment that the cabin "Looks as though a wizard had been through. . . ." What other examples of factual and personal details do you find?

Writing Practice 2: *A Notebook Entry*

Using the details and notes you wrote in Writing Practice 1, write an entry in your notebook about the important event you previously selected. Write in a natural voice using the first person. Include specific details about the event. Keep in mind your audience—your classmates and your teacher—as you write.

Writing Descriptions

For information on developing vocabulary, see pages 662-675.

A *description* is a word picture that helps the reader form a mental image of the subject.

The ability to write good descriptions is important in notebook writing. Descriptions can help recreate important moments in your life; furthermore, you may want to use the details you have recorded for other kinds of writing.

Descriptions may include either *factual details* or *personal details.*

Factual details are used in objective description that does not include the writer's thoughts and feelings. For example, think of a person you know and forget for a moment how you feel about him or her. Then look for factual details about the person that almost anyone would agree on, such as the following five.

1. She is about five feet, six inches tall.

2. She weighs 120 pounds.

3. She has brown eyes and brown hair.

---

[1] From *Kodoku: Sailing Alone Across the Pacific* by Kenichi Horie, translated by Takuichi Ito and Kaoru Ogimi. Copyright © by Charles E. Tuttle Company, Inc. Reprinted by permission of the publisher, Tokyo, Japan.

4.   She is wearing blue jeans and a yellow sweater.

5.   She is carrying four books.

An important part of factual detail is *accuracy*. Factual details can be checked in reference books or through observation, and careful writers make certain their details are accurate.

Personal details are shaped by the writer's thoughts and feelings and are used to describe the subject as it appears to the writer. Often the writer selects details that help convey a main, or central, impression he or she has about the subject.

Model: Describing a Scene

The following short passage is from a letter written by Laura Ingalls Wilder while on a train in Nevada. What is her central impression about the Great Salt Lake? What details help to convey this central impression?

> I crossed Great Salt Lake in the moonlight last night and it was the most beautiful sight I've seen yet. Miles and miles of it on each side of the train, the track so narrow that it could not be seen from the window. It looked as though the train was running on the water. I undressed and lay in my berth and watched it, the moonlight making a path of silver across the water and the farther shore so dim and indistinct and melting away into the desert as though there was no end to the lake.[1]

Laura Ingalls Wilder's central impression was that the Great Salt Lake was "the most beautiful sight I've seen yet." The details about the train running on water, the moonlight, and the shore "melting away" help support the impression.

Writing Practice 3: *Describing a Scene*

Recall a scene you observed that left a special impression on you. Perhaps it was a river churning with white rapids, a volcanic mountain peak, a giant skyscraper, a pond full of quacking ducks, or a garbage dump tumbling with debris. Make a word cluster in your Writer's Notebook and include both the factual and personal details of the scene. Then use some of these details to write a notebook entry describing what you saw and experienced. Select details that support your central impression of the scene. For example, if you felt a sense of sadness about a scene, supporting details might include the

[1]Specified excerpt (p. 20) from *West From Home: Letters of Laura Ingalls Wilder, San Francisco 1915* edited by Roger Lea MacBride. Copyright © 1974 by Roger Lea MacBride.

sad expressions on the faces of people or the rundown appearance of houses.

Describing with Sensory Details

To recreate an experience with words, writers use *sensory details*—details of *sight, sound, taste, smell* **and** *touch.*

Good writers are especially aware of the importance of observation. They can remember sights, sounds, tastes, smells, and textures of their environment and are also able to recall memories of their thoughts and feelings about the experiences. One way to train yourself to be observant is to concentrate on each sense separately. Think first about what you see. Imagine for a moment that everything around you is frozen in space and carefully study details of shapes and colors in your environment. Then allow movement to begin and study the movements. Exactly how do people move? What objects move in your environment? (A moving object might be a clock's hands.) How do the objects move?

Next, concentrate on hearing individual sounds. If you cannot distinguish one sound from another, close your eyes as you listen. In the modern world there is seldom anything approaching total silence; a place that appears silent probably has many sounds. At 4 A.M. on a deserted city street, the rain hits the tops of garbage cans, and a prowling cat pushes aside loose rubble in its search for prey. In the distance a muted siren wails.

You can sometimes have the experience of tasting something even though you may not be eating or drinking at the time. Some

observers say, for example, that fear has a taste; others taste the salt in the air at the seashore. Be alert for tastes such as these. In a situation where you are not tasting something, imagine what you would like to be eating or drinking and how it would taste.

As you concentrate on smells, try to identify the source of the odor. Ask yourself whether the smell is pleasant or unpleasant and try to decide why it has that effect on you. Perhaps the smell is pleasant because it reminds you of a food you enjoy, or perhaps it is unpleasant because it reminds you of a bad experience.

Textures are things in your environment that you can physically feel. Textures most often noticed are the ones most extreme—very rough textures (such as sandpaper) or very soft textures (such as a kitten's fur). In your environment you are constantly being touched— by the air flowing over you, by the grass flickering against you as you walk, by rain and snow. Learn to be alert to these textures that may not be so obvious.

Your thoughts and feelings about sensory experiences are also important. Does your experience make you think anything in particular? How does it make you feel? Human emotions are complex and may range from extremes, such as grief or rage, to less powerful emotions, such as boredom or a sense of calmness. Writing about these inner experiences helps recreate your world for readers.

Model: A Description Using Sensory Details

In the following excerpt from his book *The Names*, N. Scott Momaday uses sensory details to describe his home.

> There is moonlight on the Southern Plains. I see the black trees in the north, where the river runs and my father has set out poles on the bank. When he goes before daylight with the lantern to take them up, there will be catfishes on the lines, their heads flat and green and shining, and their wide mouths grinning under their whiskers. There is a whole silence on the earth—only here and there are surfaces made of sound, frogs purring at the water's edge, a rooster crowing across the distance, the river running and lapping. And the plain rolls like water in the low light; the light is like chalk on the ripples of the land; the slow, warm wind seems to ruffle the soft light, to stir it up like dust. Oklahoma shines like the moon.[1]

Think and Discuss

N. Scott Momaday's description has details about sights, sounds, and touch. Details of sight include the "flat and green and shining" heads

[1]From *The Names* by N. Scott Momaday. Copyright © 1976 by N. Scott Momaday. Reprinted by permission of Harper & Row, Publishers, Inc.

of the catfish. "Frogs purring at the water's edge" is a detail of sound, and the writer uses a detail of texture (touch) when he writes about the warm wind. What other sensory details do you find? These details support the central impression of magic and peace.

Writing Practice 4: *Recording Sensory Detail*

For this assignment take your notebook to a quiet place, such as a bench in the park or an empty football stadium. Divide your paper into five columns, giving each column one of these labels: Sights, Sounds, Smells, Tastes, and Textures. As you sit, concentrate on observing details about the place with each of your senses. Write your observations under the appropriate headings, as in the following example. When you have finished, write about the place in your Notebook. Choose details that support one central impression.

Example

Place: Empty lot of old service station

Sights	*Sounds*	*Smells*
Tail fins of deserted old car from an earlier generation Broken gas pumps	Whine of diesel truck on nearby highway	Faint oily smell Humidity in the air

Tastes	*Textures*
Salted peanuts I used to buy on family trips	Flicker of ant crawling across bare feet

Describing People and Places

The purpose of describing people and places is to recreate them for readers.

Use of specific sensory detail is important in recreating the sights, sounds, tastes, smells, and textures of the places you describe, but recreating people in writing involves more than simply describing their physical appearance. Effective description of people also must include details about their inner characteristics and personalities.

Model: Describing a Person

Notice how Nora Ephron, in the following selection from *Crazy Salad*, describes the physical appearance and personality of Bernice Gera, the first woman to become an official baseball umpire.

> Mrs. Gera is a short, slightly chunky woman who wears white socks and loafers; her short blondish-brown hair is curled and lacquered. Around her neck is a gold charm decorated with a bat, mitt, and pearl baseball which she designed and had made up by a local jeweler. Her voice is flat and unanimated, unless, of course, she is talking about baseball: She can describe, exultantly, one of the happiest days of her life, when she had a tooth extracted and was able to stay home from work to see the Pirates win the World Series in 1960. Bernice Gera is, more than anything, a fan, an unabashed, adoring fan, and her obsession with baseball dates back to her childhood, when she played with her older brothers on a sandlot in the Pennsylvania mining town where she was raised. "I have loved, eaten, and lived baseball since I was eight years old," she says. "Put yourself in my shoes. Say you loved baseball. If you love horses, you can be a jockey. If you love golf or swimming, look at Babe Didrikson and Gertrude Ederle. These are great people and they had an ability. I had it with baseball. What could I do? I couldn't play. So you write letters, begging for a job, any job, and you keep this up for years and years. There had to be a way for me. So I decided to take up a trade. I decided to take up umpiring."[1]

Think and Discuss

To recreate Bernice Gera for readers, Nora Ephron provides details about the umpire's physical appearance, the way she dresses, how excited she sounds when describing a baseball experience, and how

---

[1]From "Bernice Gera, First Lady Umpire" in *Crazy Salad: Some Things About Women* by Nora Ephron. Copyright © 1975 by Nora Ephron. Reprinted by permission of Alfred A. Knopf, Inc.

she sounds when not talking about baseball. Finally, the actual words of the first woman umpire tell readers that this is not a person who gives up easily. The central impression is of an "adoring fan."

When describing people, you can simply tell readers about the person's appearance as Nora Ephron does when she writes "Mrs. Gera is a short, slightly chunky woman who wears white socks and loafers." Another way to describe people is to *show* readers what people are like through their words and actions, and then let readers draw their own conclusions. How does the writer *show* the character and personality of Bernice Gera?

Writing Practice 5: *Describing a Person*

First, select an important person in your life or use yourself as the subject of a description. Decide what your central impression is, and then gather details that will help support that impression. If, for example, you want to describe the courage of a friend with a severe physical disability, you might use more details about the person's personality, character, and behavior than about his or her appearance.

Using the following questions, note specific details for your description in your Writer's Notebook.

1. What is the person's physical appearance? (Shape of face and specific facial features; color of eyes and hair; hairstyle; markings on face, such as freckles; body build; posture; height)

2. How does the person dress?

3. How does he or she walk and talk?

4. Does he or she have any unusual mannerisms or gestures?

5. Does he or she have a distinctive behavioral characteristic?

6. What are the inner qualities of this person?

7. How does he or she behave when angry? When happy?

8. What places does this person enjoy the most? What do these places reveal about him or her?

9. In what ways is this person different from other people?

10. How has the person changed over time?

Then, using the specific details that answer some of the preceding questions, write a notebook entry describing both the physical features and inner qualities of the person.

Model: Describing a Place

In the following short essay, "Freedom to Breathe," Alexander Solzhenitsyn, the exiled Russian writer, describes an experience he had while standing in a small garden. What are the sensory details he uses to recreate this experience?

A shower fell in the night and now dark clouds drift across the sky, occasionally sprinkling a fine film of rain.

I stand under an apple tree in blossom and I breathe. Not only the apple tree but the grass round it glistens with moisture; words cannot describe the sweet fragrance that pervades the air. I inhale as deeply as I can, and the aroma invades my whole being; I breathe with my eyes open, I breathe with my eyes closed—I cannot say which gives me the greater pleasure.

This, I believe, is the single most precious freedom that prison takes away from us: the freedom to breathe freely, as I now can. No food on earth, no wine, not even a woman's kiss is sweeter to me than this air steeped in the fragrance of flowers, of moisture and freshness.

No matter that this is only a tiny garden, hemmed in by five-story houses like cages in a zoo. I cease to hear the motorcycles backfiring, radios whining, the burble of loudspeakers. As long as there is fresh air to breathe under an apple tree after a shower, we may survive a little longer.[1]

Think and Discuss

1. Details such as "dark clouds drift across the sky" help readers visualize the setting of Alexander Solzhenitsyn's experience. From details such as "motorcycles backfiring," readers can hear the sounds that surround the writer. What other sensory details does the writer use?

2. Sometimes the central impression is a particular mood or feeling created by a description. The mood of Alexander Solzhenitsyn's description, for example, is solemnity and thoughtfulness. By selecting only details that help to establish this mood, the writer maintains it throughout the description. Point out other sensory details that help create this mood.

People may be an important part of a place. A writer could not recreate a truck stop for readers without a description of the men and women who sit hunched on stools over greasy cups of coffee, trading jokes and information about roads and weather conditions. In some

---

[1]From "Freedom to Breathe" in *Stories and Prose Poems* by Alexander Solzhenitsyn, translated by Michael Glenny. Copyright © 1970, 1971 by Michael Glenny. Reprinted by permission of Farrar, Straus & Giroux, Inc., The Bodley Head, and Claude Durand as agent for the author.

cases the place itself may seem changed by the people who are there. An empty high school seems a much different place from one filled with jostling students. A shopping center during a busy season is different from a shopping center at other times of the year.

Writing Assignment I: *Describing a Place with People*

A. Prewriting

For this assignment select an important place in your life where there are people, such as a sports stadium, shopping mall, grocery store, your school cafeteria, or the waiting room in a dental office. If possible, observe the place and the people and record sensory details of sight, sound, smell, taste, and touch. As you observe, notice how the people in the place help create a certain feeling or mood. For example, the mood of a sports stadium would be entirely different when it is filled with cheering fans than when it is silent and empty. Use the following questions to record specific details about the place and the people there.

1. What are the special features of this place?

2. What sights, sounds, smells, tastes, and textures can be experienced here?

3. Who are the people that are part of this place?

4. How do they help make the place what it is?

5. How does the nature of the place create a certain mood or feeling?

6. What are my personal thoughts and feelings about the place and the people?

B. Writing

Using some of the specific details you gathered in the prewriting exercise, write a notebook entry describing the place and the people there. Recreate the scene for your readers by including sensory description and personal details that show the mood or central impression. As you write, concentrate on using natural language that is appropriate for your audience. For this assignment, your audience will be your classmates and your teacher.

C. Postwriting

Revising Your Draft: As you read over your paper, you may want to add or delete words or sentences, rearrange parts, or make substitutions. The changes you make when revising depend on your original purpose for writing. The purpose of writing a notebook entry is to share something of yourself—your ideas and impressions—with readers. Reflecting your flow of ideas and impressions, your writing should sound natural, as if you were talking. With this purpose in mind, use the following checklist to revise your entry.

Checklist for Revising

1. The composition reflects a natural writing voice with vocabulary appropriate for the intended audience.

2. Specific words help readers understand the writer's thoughts, feelings, observations, and experiences.

3. Details of factual description are accurate.

4. Details of personal description reflect how the writer thinks and feels about his or her subject.

5. Sensory details help readers see, hear, taste, smell, and feel what the writer describes.

6. Details are chosen to establish the mood the writer wishes to communicate.

Proofreading Your Draft: When you have completed your revision, check your writing for errors in grammar and mechanics by using the Proofreader's Checklist at the back of the book. Check your writing carefully against each item on the list. If you can correct your finished draft neatly, do so; if not, copy your paper over.

Sharing Your Draft: Share your experiences with a small group of classmates. After reading each paper aloud, listeners may comment on specific details that helped them to visualize the place and the people described.

Ideas for Your Writer's Notebook

The following suggestions will help you with ideas for keeping a Writer's Notebook of your own.

1. If you live in the city, keep a notebook in which you write about people, places, and experiences that are an important part of city life. If you live in the country or a small town, record your thoughts and observations about rural or small town life.

2. Keep a seasonal notebook in which you write about people, places, and experiences that are an important part of summer, winter, spring, or fall.

3. Write a series of entries that catalogue and describe a trip you have taken or would like to take.

4. Write one or more entries about current events, describing an event and your reactions to it.

5. Write about a moment when you felt particularly good or bad. Try to capture the moment in words and try to explain why it affected you the way it did.

6. Write an entry with unusual ideas about a common subject, such as a garbage can, a fog, or worms.

7. Write an entry describing the person you were five years ago.

8. Write an entry describing your favorite place five years ago.

9. Write an entry describing the person you would like to be ten years from now.

10. Write an entry telling about a story or poem that made you think or feel.

The Personal Narrative

To *narrate* means to tell a story, either true or imagined.

In writing a *personal narrative*, the writer presents a detailed account of a personal experience in narrative form. The purpose of a personal narrative is to share an interesting or unusual incident in your life with readers. The incident does not have to be of great significance to be interesting, but it should be one that is important to you, perhaps one that taught you something or changed you in some way. As a writer, your purpose is to show readers how the episode affected you and why it was important in your life.

Because the personal narrative is essentially a story, it has characters and a setting, but the emphasis is mostly on the action. Descriptive details about the characters and setting are usually brief. The action of the narrative may involve a single incident or a series of episodes. For example, suppose you write a narrative about conquering your fear and killing a dangerous snake in your backyard. Because it is important for readers to understand your fear of snakes, you describe this part of your personality, perhaps telling how you acquired the fear and about some earlier experiences with reptiles. To establish the setting, you would not need to describe your entire backyard, but a description of the tangled weeds and underbrush hiding the snake would be appropriate.

Thoughts and feelings are important details that help build a personal narrative.

Unless readers know your reactions to events, they cannot share the experience with you. One way to reveal thoughts and feelings in a narrative is to state them directly. You may say, for example, "I have never been more afraid in my life." Another way is to show behaviors that reveal your thoughts and feelings. A sentence such as "My hands were icy, and I could barely feel myself breathing" shows your physical reactions to an emotion.

Conflict and *suspense* are important elements in a personal narrative.

Conflict is a struggle either within a person or between one person and some other person or force. Conflict within a person, or *inner conflict*, is the internal struggle people have when making difficult decisions or regretting wrong actions. *Outer conflicts*, conflicts between people or between a person and some outside force would include an argument, a fight to save victims from a burning building, or a campaign by a disabled person to end society's discrimination.

Suspense, which keeps readers involved by making them wonder what will happen next, is often the result of conflict. Suspense may also be created if the writer describes a setting so that readers know something will happen there, or if a character description makes readers wonder what the character will do next.

Events in a narrative are usually arranged *chronologically* in the order in which they actually happened. For example, a personal narrative about getting lost in a shopping mall at age six might begin at the point when the writer left home for the shopping trip. The experience of becoming lost might follow, and the narrative might end with the writer's returning home. Writers sometimes scramble the order, perhaps beginning with the final event and then relating the first ones, to capture the reader's interest early.

Model: Personal Narrative

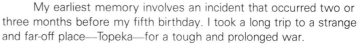

The following excerpt is from the autobiography of Dwight David Eisenhower, who was the thirty-fourth President of the United States, serving two terms between 1953 and 1961. As you read the selection, notice how President Eisenhower describes an incident that might have seemed small to others but that was important to him. Also, look for the elements of personal narrative you read about in the previous section.

My earliest memory involves an incident that occurred two or three months before my fifth birthday. I took a long trip to a strange and far-off place—Topeka—for a tough and prolonged war.

My mother's sister, Aunt Minnie, was visiting us. We lived in a little cottage on Second Street in Abilene. It was decided that I would return with her to Topeka where a considerable number of Mother's relatives lived.

It was a day trip and during the course of the morning the heat of the railroad car and the monotony of the noise made me very sleepy. "Does this train have a sleeping car?" I asked her, using a scrap of worldly knowledge I had presumably picked up while listening to a family conversation. "It's not really necessary to go to a sleeping car," my aunt replied. "Just lie down on the seat and I'll make sure you have a good nap." I did and she was right.

After leaving the train, we next had to take a long ride by horse and buggy to my relatives' farm out beyond the northern outskirts of Topeka. I can remember looking down through the floorboards, watching the ground rush past and the horses' feet, which seemed to slide. When we arrived, life became even more confusing. It was peculiar to be surrounded by so many strangers. It seemed to me that there were dozens or hundreds of people—all grownups—in the house. Even though they were, somehow, my family, I felt lonesome and lost among them.

I began to wander around outside. In the rear of the house was an old-fashioned well, very deep, with a wooden bucket and a long rope threaded through a pulley. My uncle Luther found me, fascinated by the well, and he offered a long story about what would happen to me if I fell in. He spoke in such horrible terms that I soon lost any ambition to look over the fearful edge into the abyss below. Looking around for less dreadful diversion, I noticed a pair of barnyard geese. The male resented my intrusion from our first meeting and each time

43

thereafter he would push along toward me aggressively and with hideous hissing noises so threatening my security that five-year-old courage could not stand the strain. I would race for the back door of the house, burst into the kitchen, and tell any available elder about this awful old gander.

Thus the war began. In the early parts of the campaign, I lost a skirmish every half hour and invariably had to flee ignominiously and weeping from the battlefield. Without support, and lacking arms of any kind, it was only by recourse to distressing retreat after retreat to the kitchen that I kept myself from disaster.

Ignominiously means "shamefully."

My enemy was that bad-tempered and aggressive gander. I was a little boy, not yet five years old, who was intensely curious about the new environment into which he was thrust and determined to explore its every corner. But the gander constantly balked me. He obviously looked upon me as a helpless and harmless nuisance. He had no intention of permitting anyone to penetrate his domain. Always hopeful that he would finally abandon his threatened attacks on my person, I'd try again and again, always with the same result.

An *adversary* is an enemy.

Uncle Luther decided that something had to be done. He took a worn-out broom and cut off all the straw except for a short hard knob which he probably left so that in my zeal, if I developed any, I might not hurt my odd adversary. With the weapon all set, he took me out into the yard. He showed me how I was to swing and then announced that I was on my own.

The gander remained aggressive in his actions, and I was not at all sure that my uncle was very smart. More frightened at the moment of his possible scolding than I was of aggression, I took what was meant to be a firm, but was really a trembling, stand the next time the fowl came close. Then I let out a yell and rushed toward him, swinging the club as fast as I could. He turned and I gave him a satisfying smack right in the fanny. He let out a most satisfactory squawk and ran off. This was my signal to chase him, which I did.

Belligerent means "quarrelsome."

From then on, he would continue his belligerent noises whenever he saw me (and the stick). He kept his distance and I was the proud boss of the back yard. I never made the mistake of being caught without the weapon. This all turned out to be a rather good lesson for me because I quickly learned never to negotiate with an adversary except from a position of strength.[1]

Think and Discuss

1. The third and fourth paragraphs of the preceding excerpt tell about President Eisenhower's trip from Abilene to Topeka, Kansas, to visit relatives. When he writes about "the heat of the railroad car and the monotony of the noise," he uses specific details to describe the experience. What are other descriptive details he uses in the two paragraphs?

[1]From "Sauce for the Gander" from *At Ease* by Dwight D. Eisenhower. Reprinted by permission of Doubleday & Company, Inc. and Robert Hale, Ltd.

2. Thoughts and feelings are important details in personal narrative. In the fourth paragraph President Eisenhower says that he felt "lonesome and lost." At what other times in the narrative does the writer reveal thoughts and feelings?

3. This narrative involves both an inner and outer conflict. What are they?

4. The narrative begins with President Eisenhower reflecting on an episode from his childhood. He relates the series of events in this episode in chronological order. In your own words relate this sequence of events.

5. Autobiographies involve writers' looking back on earlier parts of their lives. In looking back, you often see an experience in a different way than when it occurred. How do you think President Eisenhower's looking back affected the way he remembered the event?

Writing Assignment II: *Recapturing a Memory*

A. Prewriting

Selecting a Topic by Clustering: Think back over your early childhood years and recall certain memories that were significant to you—perhaps taking your first trip away from home, learning how to swim, getting a new pet, visiting a special friend or relative, moving to a new town, or leaving the home where you were born. In your Writer's Notebook, make a word cluster that includes all the memories that come to mind. Give a few details about each memory. Then select one childhood memory from your word cluster to use as the topic for a personal narrative.

Sequencing Events and Recalling Details: Focus on your topic and make a list of events that occurred during the incident. Sequence the events in chronological order (as they actually occurred in time). To help recall specific details about the event, answer the *Who? What? When? Where? Why?* and *How?* questions. These six questions can be posed in the following way.

1. *Who* was involved in the incident?

2. *What* do I remember about it?

3. *When* did the event happen?

4. *Where* did it take place?

5. *Why* was it important?

6. *How* did it affect my life or the lives of the people involved?

B. Writing

Using your list of events and details, compose a draft of a personal narrative that recaptures your childhood memory. Use your natural writing voice to tell your story. Use specific details, and let your reader know by the way you tell the story how the incident affected you (what you learned from it, how you felt, or in what way it changed your life). Begin with an introduction that entices your readers and end with a concluding statement that summarizes the significance of the event in your life.

C. Postwriting

Revising Your Personal Narrative: The purpose for writing your personal narrative is to share a significant childhood memory with readers. To learn whether or not you have achieved this purpose, you may want to ask a partner or a student response group to read your first draft and make suggestions for improving it. Use the following checklist in evaluating your draft. After you have finished your revision, check your writing for errors in grammar, mechanics, and spelling by using the Proofreader's Checklist at the back of this book.

Checklist for Revising a Personal Narrative

1. The topic concerns a childhood memory.

2. The details about characters and setting help readers understand the action.

3. Important details about the writer's thoughts and feelings are included.

4. The events in the narrative are arranged in the order in which they happened. If the order is changed, there is a reason for doing so.

5. The narrative is written in a natural voice.

6. The narrative includes an interesting beginning and a conclusion that summarizes the significance of the incident.

Sharing Your Draft: After you have completed your revision and proofread your final draft, share your composition by reading it aloud to a small group of classmates as your teacher directs.

Sentence Combining: The Semicolon and Paired Connectors

Connecting Sentences with a Semicolon

For more information on commas and semicolons, see pages 577-589.

When two sentences of equal importance are also closely related in thought, they can be combined with a semicolon. The signal (;) indicates that two related sentences can be combined in this way.

Sentences: Monday we visited your cousin in the country. Tuesday we went to a folk concert in Adams Park. (;)

Combined: Monday we visited your cousin in the country; Tuesday we went to a folk concert in Adams Park.

Sentences: Anita has already finished writing her science report. She plans to type it tonight after school. (;)

Combined: Anita has already finished writing her science report; she plans to type it tonight after school.

Exercise 1: Connecting Closely Related Sentences

Combine each of the following sets of sentences. The first five sets give you the signal (;). For the last five sets, decide whether to use a

47

connector and a comma, or a semicolon. (Some sentences can be combined in more than one way.) Study the example before you write your new sentences on a sheet of notebook paper.

Example

a. Mr. Ortiz leaves for the hospital at 5 o'clock every morning. He doesn't mind getting up that early.

Mr. Ortiz leaves for the hospital at 5 o'clock every morning, but he doesn't mind getting up that early.

or

Mr. Ortiz leaves for the hospital at 5 o'clock every morning; he doesn't mind getting up that early.

1. Granville I. Hicks was an electrical genius.
   He applied for over thirty-five different patents. (;)

2. Mr. Chang is a salesman for a furniture company.
   Mrs. Chang is a dental hygienist. (;)

3. Leon doesn't like his red sweater.
   He prefers to wear his new blue sweater. (;)

4. My sister and her husband have a four-year-old daughter.
   They plan to adopt another child within the next four months. (;)

5. Please lend me that novel you were reading.
   I'll return it within a week. (;)

6. Carlotta saves almost all the money she earns at the gas station.
   She plans to study at the university next year.

7. My grandmother can't afford to call us very often.
   She writes my brother and me a long letter every week.

8. Our new neighbors are very friendly.
   My little brother is still too shy to speak to them.

9. Commuting to the university involves a two-hour trip.
   Juanita has learned to study on the bus.

10. Very few people could attend the meeting on Thursday.
    It was rescheduled for a week from Monday.

Using Paired Connectors

For information on correlative conjunctions, see pages 456-457.

Paired connectors can also be used to make a connection between two sentences of equal importance. *Either . . . or* indicates a choice between alternatives. *Not only . . . but also* indicates an additional idea in the second sentence. When sentences are combined with paired connectors, a comma precedes the second connector.

Sentences:	Clean your room now.
	Set aside time on Saturday morning to clean it. (*either . . . or*)
Combined:	*Either* clean your room now, *or* set aside time on Saturday morning to clean it.
Sentences:	My grandmother refinished her dining room chairs.
	She caned the seats on the chairs. (*not only . . . but also*)

Combined: *Not only* did my grandmother refinish her dining room chairs, *but* she *also* caned the seats on the chairs.

Note: The grammatical term for these paired connectors is *correlative conjunctions.*

Sometimes, you will want to change the word order of sentences when you combine them with paired connectors. For example, in the preceding example, *refinished* was changed to *did refinish.* Word order in sentences combined with *either . . . or* may also change slightly.

Sentences: You can write your report in longhand.
                   You can double-space your typing. (*either . . . or*)
Combined: You can *either* write your report in longhand, *or* you can doublespace your typing.

Exercise 2: Using Paired Connectors

After studying the example, combine the following sets of sentences, using paired connectors. Write each newly combined sentence on a sheet of paper. (Remember to insert a comma before the second connector.)

Example

a. We must learn to use less of our energy resources.
   We must explore safe, new energy sources. (*not only . . . but also*)
   Not only must we learn to use less of our energy resources, but we must also explore safe, new energy sources.

1. This class teaches us to create new ideas.
    It teaches us how to express our ideas effectively. (*not only . . . but also*)

2. Sam should turn down that noisy stereo.
    He should save his money for a set of earphones. (*either . . . or*)

3. Keeping your school free from litter does promote an attractive environment.
    It saves the school a great deal of money. (*not only . . . but also*)

4. We toured the city fire department.
    We watched a demonstration of rescue techniques by city fire fighters. (*not only . . . but also*)

5. You can study cardiopulmonary resuscitation in health class.
    You can take a one-day course about it from the Red Cross. (*either . . . or*)

Writing Practice: *Using Given Sentence Patterns and Connectors*

In the preceding chapter on personal writing, the following excerpt by N. Scott Momaday was included to show the writer's use of sensory detail. As you reread the excerpt, note the writer's use of connectors.

> There is moonlight on the Southern Plains. I see the black trees in the north, where the river runs and my father has set out poles on the bank. When he goes before daylight with the lantern to take them up there will be catfishes on the lines, their heads flat and green and shining, and their wide mouths grinning under their whiskers. There is a whole silence on the earth—only here and there are surfaces made of sound, frogs purring at the water's edge, a rooster crowing across the distance, the river running and lapping. And the plain rolls like water in the low light; the light is like chalk on the ripples of the land; the slow, warm wind seems to ruffle the soft light, to stir it up like dust. Oklahoma shines like the moon.[1]

Use the sentence patterns from this excerpt to write a paragraph describing something you have observed. Create your own topic and sensory details, but follow Momaday's paragraph structure, using the same sentence connectors in your composition.

[1]From *The Names* by N. Scott Momaday. Copyright © 1976 by N. Scott Momaday. Reprinted by permission of Harper & Row, Publishers, Inc.

3 The Paragraph

Paragraph Writing

A paragraph can fulfill several functions. Special paragraphs may serve as introductions or conclusions, while long pieces of writing often contain brief transitional paragraphs that help the reader move from one idea to another. In exposition (writing that explains a topic), an important kind of paragraph is one which focuses on a central idea or thought. In this chapter you will learn to write such paragraphs.

The TRI Paragraph Pattern

The *TRI* (*Topic-Restriction-Illustration*) *pattern* is the framework for many paragraphs. The first two parts of the pattern (*topic* and *restriction*) identify the central idea of the paragraph. *Illustration*, the third part of the pattern, further develops the central idea with examples, comparisons, or other specific statements.

The *topic sentence* of a paragraph introduces the central idea or *topic* that the rest of the paragraph develops.

Since the topic sentence covers everything that will be discussed in its paragraph, it will be more general than the other sentences. Assume that a writer chooses the subject *Women's rights*. A single paragraph cannot develop every idea about women's rights, so the writer must limit the subject to a topic: *Women's rights in ancient Greece*, for instance. This one idea can now be stated in a topic sentence:

In ancient Greece women did not have the same rights as men.

The writer's next step is to *restrict* the topic so that it can be developed in a single paragraph:

Greek women were barred from participating in certain ceremonies and from taking part in important government activities.

Once the topic is restricted, the writer can add *illustrations*—specific statements that support, explain, or expand the main idea

more clearly and completely through facts, examples, reasons, comparisons and contrasts, or other methods of development.

Topic: In ancient Greece women did not have the same rights as men.

Restriction: Greek women were barred from participating in certain ceremonies and from taking part in important government activities.

Illustration: For example, women were not allowed even as spectators at the famous Olympiad, the ceremony known today as the Olympics.

Illustration: Neither were they permitted to sit on the Council of Five Hundred, which was the major governing body in Greece.

Illustration: Even their future husbands were selected for them in a special ceremony—one which they were not allowed to attend.

The finished paragraph—a topic sentence, a restriction sentence, and three sentences illustrating the restricted topic—would have the following form.

Model: The TRI Pattern

Topic
Restriction

Illustrations

In ancient Greece women did not have the same rights as men. Greek women were barred from participating in certain ceremonies and from taking part in important government activities. For example, women were not allowed even as spectators at the famous Olympiad, the ceremony known today as the Olympics. Neither were they permitted to sit on the Council of Five Hundred, which was the major governing body in Greece. Even their husbands were selected for them in a special ceremony—one which they were not allowed to attend.

Writing Practice 1: *The TRI Pattern*

On a sheet of paper, develop each of the following paragraphs by supplying the missing elements. In some of the paragraphs, you are given the topic and restriction sentences; in others you must supply the restrictions. In each paragraph write appropriate illustration sentences. For the last paragraph you are asked to use your own topic.

1. **Topic:** Music is often called "the universal language."

   Restriction: One kind of music that appeals to a large number of people is country and western.

   Illustration:

   Illustration:

2. **Topic:** Volunteer youth organizations provide essential services to the community.

   Restriction:

   Illustration:

   Illustration:

3. **Topic:** Sports can be dangerous.

   Restriction:

   Illustration:

   Illustration:

   Illustration:

4.   **Topic:**

     Restriction:

     Illustration:

     Illustration:

     Illustration:

The TI Paragraph Pattern

One way to vary the Topic-Restriction-Illustration pattern is to combine the topic and restriction parts into one sentence. When you combine these parts, you limit your topic in the first sentence. Then, to develop your paragraph, you need only add illustration sentences.

Model: Combined Topic-Restriction (TI) Pattern

The topic-restriction sentence is shown in the following paragraph about the *commedia dell'arte*, an Italian comedy that was popular from the sixteenth through the eighteenth century. The topic and restriction are stated in the first sentence: "Of all the *commedia dell'arte*'s contributions to the theatre, perhaps the greatest is its legacy of stock characters." Here, the general topic is *the contributions of the commedia dell'arte;* the restriction is *the specific contribution of stock characters.* Remaining sentences illustrate the topic-restriction sentence:

Of all the *commedia dell'arte*'s contributions to the theatre, perhaps the greatest is its legacy of stock characters. It created *Arlecchino*, the acrobatic clown or harlequin whose job it was to keep the crowd laughing. He wore a black mask, motley clothes, and carried a wooden sword, forerunner of the slapstick. The *commedia dell'arte* also created the stock character of the sophisticated rogue—a coward at heart—who would do anything for money. *Brighella* was his original name in the *commedia*. Then there was the rich, complacent merchant, always miserly and mean, who spent his time counting money and guarding his beautiful young wife or daughter. He was called *Pantalone*. The list continues with caricatures of the pompous, learned doctor (known as *Il Dottore*), the boastful but easily cowed professional soldier (*Il Capitano*), and the gossipy old woman (*La Ruffiana*) who takes pleasure in trying to keep the lovers apart. As for the lovers, he was the handsome *Inamorato* and she the exquisite *Inamorata*, eternally in love and destined for one another, a destiny often thwarted but always eventually fulfilled in the turnings and comic upheavals of each *commedia dell'arte* plot.

Writing Practice 2: *The TI Pattern*

Each of the following items is a combination topic-restriction sentence. Select two of these. On a separate sheet of paper, write three or four illustration sentences for each combined topic-restriction sentence you select.

1.   The sidewalks were full of people on the first warm day in spring.

2.   Despite all our efforts the car simply would not start.

3.   Training for athletic competition is a long and painstaking job.

4.   Everyone had a reason for not finishing the assignment.

5.   The telephone has easily been one of modern science's most important contributions to improve our lives.

Varying the Basic Paragraph Patterns

Using variations of the TRI (Topic-Restriction-Illustration) pattern gives the writer more options and greater flexibility.

Models: Variations of a TRI Paragraph

In the following paragraph, the topic is introduced in the first sentence and restricted in the second sentence.

> Today meteorologists provide day-by-day information about the approach of harsh winter weather. (TOPIC) A hundred years ago, however, rural families depended on folk superstitions to predict the winter's severity. (RESTRICTION) For example, heavy coats on spring buds were thought to be an omen of a harsh winter. (ILLUSTRATION) Tough, thick skins on the apples harvested in early autumn were another sign that the winter would be severe. (ILLUSTRATION) The paper nests of white-faced hornets were also closely observed, for nests placed unusually high suggested deep snow. (ILLUSTRATION) Cutting into the Thanksgiving turkey was exciting not only for the hungry children gathered at the table, but also for their parents, who believed a dark breastbone in the turkey meant long winter storms. (ILLUSTRATION) Unusually thick feathers on that same turkey would have been noted during butchering as another indication of rough weather ahead. (ILLUSTRATION) On the other hand, an extra-wide brown band on a woolly bear caterpillar was a sign of a mild winter. (ILLUSTRATION)

The TRI pattern can also be varied by reversing the order, placing the illustrations at the beginning of the paragraph and the restriction at the end, as in the following paragraph.

A hundred years ago cutting into the Thanksgiving turkey was exciting not only for the hungry children gathered at the table, but also for their parents, who believed a dark breastbone in the turkey meant long winter storms. (ILLUSTRATION) Unusually thick feathers on that same turkey would have been noted during butchering as another indication of rough weather ahead. (ILLUSTRATION) Heavy coats on spring buds and tough, thick skins on the apples harvested in early autumn were thought to be omens of a severe winter. (ILLUSTRATION) On the other hand, an extra-wide brown band on a woolly bear caterpillar was a sign of a mild winter. (ILLUSTRATION) Even the paper nests of white-faced hornets were closely observed, for nests placed unusually high suggested deep snow. (ILLUSTRATION) Today meteorologists provide day-by-day information about the approach of harsh winter weather. (TOPIC) A hundred years ago, however, rural families depended on folk superstitions to predict the winter's severity. (RESTRICTION)

In the next paragraph (another variation of the TRI pattern), the topic and restriction appear in the middle of the paragraph.

A hundred years ago cutting into the Thanksgiving turkey was exciting not only for the hungry children gathered at the table, but also for their parents, who believed a dark breastbone in the turkey meant long winter storms. (ILLUSTRATION) Unusually thick feathers on that same turkey would have been noted during butchering as another indication of rough weather ahead. (ILLUSTRATION) Today meteorologists provide day-by-day information about the approach of harsh winter weather. (TOPIC) A hundred years ago, however, rural families depended on folk superstitions to predict the winter's severity. (RESTRICTION) For example, heavy coats on spring buds were thought to be an omen of a harsh winter. (ILLUSTRATION) Tough, thick skins on the apples harvested in early autumn were another sign that the winter would be severe. (ILLUSTRATION) On the other hand, an extra-wide brown band on a woolly bear caterpillar was a sign of a mild winter. (ILLUSTRATION) Even the paper nests of white-faced hornets were closely observed, for nests placed unusually high suggested deep snow. (ILLUSTRATION)

Writing Practice 3: *Varying Paragraph Patterns*

Use the following topic, restriction, and illustration sentences as a basis for rewriting two paragraphs. In the first paragraph begin with illustrations and end with a combined topic-restriction sentence. For the second paragraph place the topic and the restriction sentences in the middle. Change words or add *for example, also, another,* or similar words to connect the statements in your paragraphs.

After you finish, look closely at the structure of your paragraphs. Each paragraph should have a clear central idea either in the restriction or the topic-restriction sentence. Each illustration sentence should develop the central idea. If a sentence does not present new information that relates to the central idea, rewrite or omit it.

Topic: People have not always dressed sensibly.

Restriction: The history of fashion shows that people have often worn clothing that was not only uncomfortable but also harmful.

Illustration: A knight's armor in the fourteenth century was so heavy and unwieldy that he could not stand up without help, making him an easy target once off his horse.

Illustration: During the nineteenth century it was popular for women to wear whalebone corsets so tight that breathing was difficult.

Illustration: Both men and women in different eras have favored shoes with exaggerated toes or heels that made walking awkward and even dangerous.

For Your Writer's Notebook

What folk superstitions are common in your family or the area where you live? Is spilling salt bad luck, for example? Does anyone you know predict the weather or the change of seasons by looking at signs of nature? In your notebook write about superstitions and what they mean or describe someone you know who takes superstitions seriously. You might want to formulate a class list of superstitions or use the library to find information about how certain superstitions originated.

Question–Answer Paragraphs

Another paragraph pattern you will find useful begins by asking a question and then suggesting an answer. Sometimes, the question will appear in the same paragraph with its answer. At other times, especially when the answer is a long one covering several paragraphs, the question or questions come in a separate paragraph.

Model: Question–Answer Paragraphs

The following paragraphs from Simone de Beauvoir's *All Said and Done* show how this pattern works.

Question:
Answer: Topic

Restriction

Illustrations

I love travelling as much as ever I did. In 1962 I had lost my appetite for it, but the taste has come back to me. During these last ten years I have visited and revisited a great many places. What have these explorations brought me?

In the first place they form an integral part of a much wider project that still means a great deal to me—the project of knowing. To be sure, seeing is not enough: one can pass through towns and countryside without understanding anything about either. I need conversation and reading to give me a clear notion of a country, but they alone cannot provide me with the equivalent of the flesh-and-blood presence of things. When I walk about the streets, mingling with the crowd, a town and its inhabitants begin to exist for me with a fullness that words cannot possibly convey. And then I am far more interested in places that have a connection with my actual life than in those that I have called to mind only by means of words.

To the question "What have these explorations brought me?" the writer begins to answer by telling what, "In the first place," visiting and revisiting towns and countryside mean to her. The reader can expect that subsequent paragraphs will continue with "In the second place" and "In the third place."

The question-answer pattern often presents a *problem* in question form, followed by several sentences that offer the *solution* to the problem.

Model: Problem–Solution Paragraph

Notice in the following example that the paragraph begins with introductory sentences that explain the situation. Then the question "What was causing this drop in water pressure?" is asked, followed by an explanation that gives the solution to the problem.

Problem:
Solution: Illustrations

Topic

Restriction

In the late 1940s city water department engineers in a large American city noticed that water pressure began to drop suddenly at regular thirty-minute intervals during the evening hours. Never having experienced this situation before, the engineers were puzzled. What was causing the drop in water pressure? In order to answer this question, the department made an intensive investigation to find the reasons behind the problem. By questioning a large number of people in the city, investigators found that about every thirty minutes between 7 and 10 o'clock in the evening, many faucets were being turned on and toilets flushed. From these facts the water department reasoned that television, at that time a new form of evening entertainment, was the cause of the phenomenon. Viewers were leaving their sets during station breaks and program changes—about every half hour—to use their kitchens and bathrooms. Of course, not everyone had television sets, nor did all those who had them leave as programs changed. But enough television viewers did to account for the problem.

Writing Practice 4: *A Question–Answer Paragraph*

Choose a topic from the following suggestions or use one of your own. Then restrict the topic, phrase it as a question, and write a short paragraph that uses the question-answer pattern. Your question may present a problem, if you wish. If it does, be sure your answer gives a solution to the problem.

1. Explaining a game such as hockey to a student from another country

2. Training an animal

3. Providing care for the elderly or for preschool children

4. Communicating with hearing impaired or visually impaired persons

5. Maintaining a bicycle, motorcycle, or car

Before you begin writing your question-answer paragraph, write the topic you chose and the question you have phrased. Then jot down several facts, reasons, or other types of illustrations you can use in the answer to the question. Study the following example.

Topic	Question	Answer
Money for vacation	What is the best way for me to make enough money for summer vacation?	Get a part-time job at the local market.
		Do neighborhood chores.
		Tutor summer school students.
		Make and sell artificial flowers.

Unity in the Paragraph

An effective paragraph has *unity*—that is, the sentences combine to produce a single, complete unit of thought.

A paragraph is unified when it states only one central idea that is developed by all other statements in the paragraph.

Models: Unity in the Paragraph

The following paragraph from Donald Sandner's *Navaho Symbols of Healing* is unified because it has one central idea. Can you identify the central idea?

Restricted Topic
Illustrations

The position of women in Navaho culture is important in several ways. For one thing, they own most of the property. For another, lineage is reckoned through the mother: a Navaho *belongs* to his mother's clan, and is said to be merely "born for" his father's. Furthermore, the women have a strong and decisive voice in family affairs and are responsible for much of the work, including crop raising, care of the animals, weaving (a major source of income), and household chores.[1]

This paragraph is unified because it presents information about one central idea: "The position of women in Navaho culture is important in several ways." All the other sentences relate to the central idea, providing more information and giving specific examples verifying it.

Even when the central idea appears at the end or in the middle of a paragraph, all the sentences illustrating that idea should relate to that main theme. In the next example, from Rachel Carson's *Silent Spring*, the writer introduces the topic (dependence of animal life on water, soil, and plants) in the first sentence but does not restrict it until the middle of the paragraph: "Our attitude toward plants is a singularly narrow one." As you read the following selection, consider the relationship of sentences to the central idea and how they help to develop that central idea.

Topic

Water, soil, and the earth's green mantle of plants make up the world that supports the animal life of the earth. Although modern man seldom remembers the fact, he could not exist without the plants that harness the sun's energy and manufacture the basic foodstuffs he depends upon for life. Our attitude toward plants is a singularly narrow one. If we see any immediate utility in a plant we foster it. If for any reason we find its presence undesirable or merely a matter of indifference, we may condemn it to destruction forthwith. Besides the various plants that are poisonous to man or his livestock, or crowd out food plants, many are marked for destruction merely because, according to our narrow view, they happen to be in the wrong place at the wrong time. Many others are destroyed merely because they happen to be associates of the unwanted plants.[2]

Restriction
Illustrations

[1]From *Navaho Symbols of Healing* by Donald Sandner. Reprinted by permission of Harcourt Brace Jovanovich, Inc.

[2]From "Earth's Green Mantle" in *Silent Spring* by Rachel Carson. Copyright © 1962 by Rachel Carson. Reprinted by permission of Houghton Mifflin Company, Laurence Pollinger Limited, and the Estate of the late Rachel Carson. Published in Great Britain by Hamish Hamilton, Ltd.

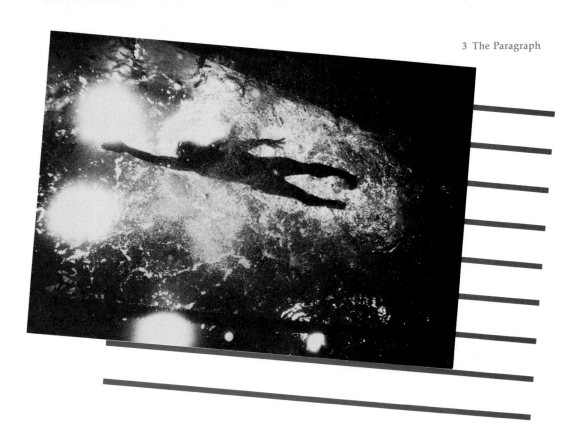

You can test the unity of a paragraph by checking the relationship between each sentence and the central idea. Be certain that each statement relates to the restriction of the topic. The following paragraph, for example, lacks unity because the writer has included sentences that do not relate to its restricted topic: "The origin of most sports is a mystery." Notice how the two underlined sentences distract the reader from the central idea.

The origin of most sports is a mystery. We do know that some sports had their beginnings in the necessities of survival: hunting, fishing, and swimming—all were at one time skills people needed to live. I myself enjoy fishing very much, but I don't believe in killing larger animals. Other sports originated with the nobility. Court tennis, falconry, and archery (although the latter certainly had its roots in necessary skills) were at one time enjoyed only by members of the royal family and by the nobility. On the other hand, games such as football and boxing originated with the masses. Football may look wild and uncontrolled, but much skill goes into planning and executing the maneuvers. Nonetheless, we do not know if these sports developed gradually, or if one person was instrumental in inventing them. One exception is basketball, which we know was invented by James Naismith of Springfield, Massachusetts, in 1891. The other great inventors of games, if there are any, remain anonymous.

Writing Practice 5: *Unity in the Paragraph*

Write both a topic sentence and then a restriction sentence or a combined topic-restriction sentence for one of the following broad subjects. Then write a paragraph that illustrates your topic. Remember that the topic and restriction sentences or the topic-restriction sentence may appear at the beginning, middle, or end of your paragraph. Be sure that every sentence in your paragraph relates to your restricted topic.

1. Being the eldest (middle/youngest/only) child

2. Finding a job

3. Inventing a much-needed product

4. The ideal school

5. The major problems of teenagers today

Using a Concluding Sentence for Unity

You can improve the unity of some paragraphs by adding a *concluding sentence* that restates the central idea in a new and interesting way or that sums up the information presented.

Model: Using a Concluding Sentence for Unity

The following paragraph about the role of air power in World War I develops the central idea in the first sentence. As you read, notice how the writer restates this idea at the end of the paragraph.

Restricted Topic

Illustrations

      With the passage of time, legends have arisen over the accomplishments of some of the World War I aces, but most historians agree that the role played by air power during this struggle was more romantic than decisive. The most important missions the airplane carried out were reconnaissance and artillery fire control. And when the war bogged down into static front-line trench warfare and increasingly effective camouflage techniques evolved, aerial reconnaissance became less and less significant. No airplane or Zeppelin sank or even seriously disabled any major naval vessel. No war industry was halted by strategic bombing. No major battle's outcome was decided by either control of the air or lack of its control. And so, even though vast technical progress was made in aviation development during World War I, what one celebrates are the men and not so much the machines.[1]

[1]From *The National Air and Space Museum* by C. D. B. Bryan. Copyright © 1979 by the Smithsonian Institution, published by Harry N. Abrams, Inc. Reprinted by permission of the publisher.

The central idea of the paragraph is that although World War I flying aces became legendary, the role of the airplane during the war was not significant. Notice how the concluding sentence returns to that idea: "And so, even though vast technical progress was made in aviation development during World War I, what one celebrates are the men and not so much the machines." This final sentence accomplishes two things: (1) it gives more information about the topic, telling readers that during World War I technical progress was made in aviation; and (2) it restates the central idea in a new and interesting way.

Writing Practice 6: *Using a Concluding Sentence for Unity*

After selecting one of the following subjects or a subject of your own, write both a topic and restriction sentence or a topic-restriction sentence on a sheet of paper. Then write a paragraph based on your sentence, paying close attention to paragraph unity and ending with an effective concluding sentence.

1. Why conflict sometimes occurs between teenagers

2. How the "inner you" differs from the image others have of you

3. A memory about a person who is special to you

4. The advantages (or disadvantages) of a part-time job

5. Why you like a particular sport or hobby

Coherence in Paragraphs

In *coherent paragraphs* (paragraphs that make sense and are easy to follow), the illustration sentences are organized in a clear way.

In a paragraph that describes a person, place, or thing, writers may organize the illustration sentences by their location in space (*spatial order*). In a paragraph about an event or a series of actions, writers often use *chronological order*, discussing what happened first, what followed, and what happened last. In a paragraph illustrated with reasons, writers often arrange the reasons from least important to most important, using *order of importance*.

Model: Chronological Order

In the following paragraph Arthur M. Schlesinger, Jr., uses *chronological order* to describe the unhappy progression of events during the Great Depression.

Restricted Topic

Illustrations

      Across the country the dismal process was beginning, ushering in a new life for millions of Americans. In the twenties wage earners in general found ample employment, satisfaction in life, hope for the future. Now came the slowdown—only three days of work a week, then perhaps two, then the layoff. And then the search for a new job—at first vigorous and hopeful; then sober; then desperate; the long lines before the employment offices, the eyes straining for words of hope on the chalked boards, the unending walk from one plant to the next, the all-night wait to be first for possible work in the morning. And the inexorable news, brusque impersonality concealing fear: "No help wanted here" . . . "We don't need anybody" . . . "Move along, Mac, move along."[1]

Think and Discuss

1. What was the first sign that "the dismal process"—the Depression—was beginning?

2. What chain of events followed the first indication that there was a Depression?

3. What words in the paragraph show chronological order?

---

[1]From *The Crisis of the Old Order 1919–1933* by Arthur M. Schlesinger, Jr. Copyright © 1957 by Arthur M. Schlesinger. Reprinted by permission of Houghton Mifflin Company.

Model: *Spatial Order*

In the following paragraph from "A Scottish Childhood" by Christian Miller, notice how the writer uses a *spatial order* based on the physical relationships among items to give readers a clear picture of the towers and chimneys on a Scottish castle.

Topic
Restriction

Illustrations

The top of the tower was flat. It was divided into two parts. Where the stairs ended, a trapdoor led to the higher part, an enclosed area a few yards square, carrying only the flagstaff. At one side, a heavy, nail-studded door opened onto a lead-covered rooftop, surrounded by iron railings. Here were the chimneys of the central tower—the big one, which plunged straight down to the dining room, and the smaller ones leading to the library, schoolroom, and other rooms in the tower. Here, too, were the mystery chimneys, from fireplaces in rooms that nobody could find. We tied a bell on the end of a rope and lowered it down these chimneys. Yard after yard of rope vanished over the edge of the chimney pot. One of us jerked the end while others ran round the rooms below, listening for the sound of the bell; it rang, muffled, in the thickness of a wall. What was there? We listened from every angle in the passages and nearby rooms, and measured the walls. Yes, there was space for a room. But where was the door? Where were the windows? We searched the outside walls, but two hundred years previously a tax had been imposed on windows, and many had been bricked up; some of these bricked-up windows were painted on the outside to look as if they were still in use, and some were not. We never found the hidden rooms.[1]

[1]From "A Scottish Childhood" by Christian Miller. Copyright © 1979 by Christian Miller. Reprinted by permission of Wallace & Sheil Agency, Inc., and Anthony Sheil Associated, Ltd. Published in Great Britain under the title "A Childhood in Scotland."

Think and Discuss

1. Where is the nail-studded door in relationship to the enclosed area?

2. Where are the iron railings in relationship to the rooftop?

3. Where are the mystery chimneys?

4. What words show the relationships among other objects in the castle?

Model: *Order of Importance*

In an expository paragraph developed with reasons or examples, the illustration sentences are often arranged in *order of importance*. In the following paragraph from Arthur C. Clarke's *Report on Planet Three,* notice how the sentence order progresses from least to most important. What idea does the author consider most important?

Restricted Topic

Illustrations

Ours is the century in which all of man's ancient dreams—and not a few of his nightmares—appear to be coming true. The conquest of the air, the transmutation of matter, journeys to the Moon, even the elixir of life—one by one the marvelous visions of the past are becoming reality. And among them, the one most fraught with promise and peril is the machine that can think.

Writing Practice 7: *Using Order of Ideas for Coherence*

Each of the following sentences states a central idea that can be developed into a paragraph. First select the kind of paragraph you want to write from example *A*, *B*, or *C*. Then choose one statement to write about in a paragraph, and develop sentences to illustrate it. You may want to restrict the central idea further in a restriction sentence. Use whatever order is indicated to arrange your sentences. If you prefer, think of your own central idea and organize your sentences with one of the three methods discussed in the preceding section.

A. Use chronological order with the following central ideas.

1. The summer passed so slowly I felt suspended in time.

2. From the minute I woke up I knew the day was going to be a lost cause.

3. The place had changed dramatically over the last years.

B.   Use spatial order with the following central ideas.

   1. My room may look like a disaster area, but I can find everything I need there blindfolded.

   2. As I opened the door to the alien spacecraft, I noticed a panel of blinking red lights.

   3. On my first day of high school, just finding the way from one class to another was confusing.

C.   Use order of importance with the following central ideas.

   1. There are three things I value most in another person.

   2. Most of the time I'm easy to get along with, but a few things drive me crazy.

   3. I know just what I want from a good (book/movie/other entertainment or sport).

Transition Words

You can also increase the coherence of paragraphs by using *transition words*—words or phrases that help the reader move smoothly from one sentence to another and that make the relationships between sentences clear.

The following are some common transitions and their uses.

Transitions	Uses
For example, for instance	To introduce illustrations
And, also, in addition, besides, another, moreover, furthermore	To add details, facts, examples
But, nevertheless, on the other hand, however, on the contrary, yet, still, despite, similarly, in the same way	To show comparison
First, second, third, next, then, later, meanwhile, eventually, finally	To show chronological order
At the top, above, below, behind, near, far away, on the right, on the left, about	To show spatial order
Least, most, least important, more importantly, most important	To show order of importance
So, for this reason, thus, in conclusion, therefore, finally	To make a conclusion

Model: *Transition Words*

For information on
phrases, see pages
512-523.

Notice how the underlined transitions in the following paragraph, adapted from Jacques Cousteau's *The Ocean World*, improve coherence by showing the relationships between ideas. (How does *For example* relate the second sentence to the beginning sentence?)

Restricted Topic

Illustrations

A *sonic device* is a machine that can send sound signals (through water).

Several marine laboratories are studying the shark-dolphin relationship with the hope of making the dolphin's behavior useful to man. For example, experiments with lemon sharks and bottle-nosed dolphins show that if given the choice, sharks will avoid dolphins. Therefore, the researchers have been training dolphins to be used for shark control. For instance, one dolphin has been taught to ward off sharks in captivity on a command from a sonic device. The dolphin, on cue, will chase and hit the shark. Soon the scientists will conduct these experiments in the open sea, with the hope of employing dolphins to defend divers from sharks. Someday such trained dolphins may help oceanauts by acting as watchdogs around undersea habitats. In addition, they may police coastal beaches, warding off sharks and protecting swimmers.[1] [underscores added]

Other Ways to Increase Coherence

Pronouns, paraphrase, and *repetition* contribute to coherence.

Pronouns are effective in linking sentences and ideas in a paragraph because they refer to nouns mentioned earlier. In the

---

[1]From *The Ocean World* by Jacques Cousteau. Copyright © 1979 Jacques-Yves Cousteau, published by Harry N. Abrams, Inc.

following example the pronoun *he* refers to *Muhammad Ali* and helps link the two sentences.

> *Muhammad Ali* came in third in the People's Almanac Poll listing the fifteen greatest male athletes from 1900 to 1977. *He* is ranked behind Jim Thorpe and Babe Ruth.

When you *paraphrase* words, you restate them in a different way without changing the meaning. Paraphrasing adds variety to your writing and also helps the reader move smoothly from idea to idea. In the following example the words *difficult journey* are a paraphrase of *trip.*

> The *trip* progressed westward across rivers, steep canyons, and barely defined trails. The *difficult journey* demanded courage and stamina.

Repeating the same word over and over can make writing dull; however, careful *repetition* of a key word or phrase often helps the reader move smoothly from sentence to sentence, as illustrated by the following model.

Model: *Repetition for Coherence*

In the following paragraph from Nora Ephron's *Scribble, Scribble,* notice how repetition of the key word *Double-Crostic* (a difficult crossword puzzle) gives the paragraph coherence.

Restricted Topic

Illustrations

It is one of the great surprises of my adult life that I am not particularly good at doing the Double-Crostic. When I was growing up, I thought that being able to do the Double-Crostic was an adult attribute, not unlike buying hardcover books, and that eventually I would grow into it. My mother, who was indirectly responsible for this misapprehension, was a whiz at Double-Crostics and taught me how to do them. In those days, the Double-Crostic was available through three sources: every week in the *Saturday Review,* every other week in the *New York Times Magazine* and twice a year in a Simon and Schuster anthology containing fifty or so new puzzles. The first two puzzles in each anthology were geared to beginners—to idiots, to be more precise—and I could usually solve one of them in about a month, using an atlas, a dictionary, a thesaurus, a Bartlett's and an occasional tip from my mother, who would never have been caught dead using any source material at all. There are many things I will never forgive my mother for, but heading the list is the fact that she did the Double-Crostic in ink.[1] [underscores added]

[1]From "Double-Crostics" in *Scribble, Scribble: Notes on the Media* by Nora Ephron. Copyright © 1975 by Nora Ephron. Reprinted by permission of Alfred A. Knopf, Inc.

Model: Using Several Techniques for Coherence

The following three paragraphs are taken from an essay on waste disposal in New York City titled "Garbage." Notice how the writer uses all four methods (transition devices, pronouns, paraphrase, and repetition) to give the passage coherence.

After the garbage has been burned, the cooled residue is dumped onto barges, which are towed off by tugboats to one of five landfill sites around the city. The largest of these is the 3,000-acre Fresh Kills site on Staten Island.

Topic
Restriction
Illustrations

Fresh Kills, which daily receives about 11,000 tons of garbage, is a strange place. Much of this former swampland resembles the ash heaps of *The Great Gatsby*. Vast, forlorn, endless. A vision of death. In the foreground, a discarded funeral wreath. A doll with outstretched arms. A man's black sock. A nylon stocking. And, beyond, refrigerators, toilets, bathtubs, stoves.

Restricted Topic
Illustrations

Yet Fresh Kills is also—in places and in its own way—unexpectedly beautiful. Thousands of gulls wheel in the air. Banking sharply, they dip down one by one to settle in for a good feast. In areas where the garbage is fresh, there is an overpowering stench, but where it is older, its blanket of earth is covered with grass, bushes, shrubs, trees. Summertime in Fresh Kills is a time of flowers and birdsong. A volunteer vegetable garden flourishes in the landfill. Here, in the world's largest compost heap, the seeds and sprouts of kitchen scraps thrive. Come fall, offices all around New York's City Hall are decorated with gourds and pumpkins harvested at Fresh Kills. In the fall, too, quail and pheasants scurry through Fresh Kills' underbrush, creating a problem for the Department of Sanitation: Hunters try to poach on this municipal game preserve.[1] [underscores added]

Think and Discuss

Tell what coherence technique is represented by each underlined word or phrase in the model.

Writing Practice 8: *Using Several Techniques for Coherence*

Write a well-developed paragraph about one of the following topics or about a topic of your choice. Use the techniques you have learned (transitions, pronouns, paraphrase, and repetition) to make your paragraph coherent. Your teacher may ask you to underline the words or phrases that add coherence.

1. My best friend and I couldn't be more alike or more different. (Suggestion: Use pronouns and the words *but, nevertheless, on the other hand, for example, despite, similarly,* and *in the same way.*)

2. When I became lost, the first thing I did was retrace my steps. (Suggestion: Use *first, second, third, next, then, later, meanwhile, eventually,* and *finally.*)

3. Across the field we saw a strange scene taking place. (Suggestion: Use pronouns and the words *at the top, above, below, behind, near,* and *far away.*)

4. Every morning I got up early and went down to the sea. (Suggestion: Use repetition of *sea* as a key word.)

5. For the first time in my life, I knew what fear really meant. (Suggestion: paraphrase *fear.*)

Developing a Paragraph Using Descriptive Details

The illustration sentences in a paragraph develop the central idea by providing additional detailed information about it. When a paragraph is not developed effectively, readers may misunderstand or reject the writer's central idea.

Writers often use specific, descriptive details to create images of people, scenes, and events. Sensory details are often used to describe the look, sound, feel, taste, or smell of something. These details help illustrate the central idea.

Model: Descriptive Details

The following paragraph from Bruce Chatwin's *In Patagonia* is about a writer who has been walking for two days and is hoping that a truck will pick him up. What specific details are used to describe the road or the sound of the wild animal called the guanaco?

> Walked all day and the next day. The road straight, grey, dusty, and trafficless. The wind relentless, heading you off. Sometimes you heard a truck, you knew for certain it was a truck, but it was the wind. Or the noise of gears changing down, but that also was the wind. Sometimes the wind sounded like an unloaded truck banging over a bridge. Even if a truck had come up behind you wouldn't have heard it. And even if you'd been downwind, the wind would have drowned the engine. The one noise you did hear was a guanaco. A noise like a baby trying to cry and sneeze at once. You saw him a hundred yards off, a single male, bigger and more graceful than a llama, with his orange coat and white upstanding tail. Guanacos are shy animals, you were told, but this one was mad for you. And when you could walk no more and laid out your sleeping bag, he was there gurgling and snivelling and keeping the same distance. In the morning he was right up close, but the shock of you getting out of your skin was too much for him. That was the end of a friendship and you watched him bounding away over a thorn bush like a galleon in a following sea.[1]

Think and Discuss

1. Is there a specific topic sentence in the model paragraph?

2. What method of organization does the writer use in describing his experience: chronological order, spatial order, or order of importance?

For Your Writer's Notebook

Perhaps the paragraph from *In Patagonia* reminds you of being alone in a strange place. In your notebook write your impressions of that place. Try to recall such details, as sounds, sights, smells, tastes, or the way things felt. If you were alone in an attic, for example, perhaps you remember the feel of dust on the tops of old boxes. Including descriptive details helps readers share your experience.

---

[1]From *In Patagonia* by Bruce Chatwin. Copyright © 1977 by Bruce Chatwin. Reprinted by permission of Summit Books, a Simon & Schuster division of Gulf & Western Corporation, and Deborah Rogers, Ltd., Literary Agency. Published in Great Britain by Jonathan Cape, Ltd.

Writing Assignment I: *A Paragraph with Descriptive Details*

Write a paragraph using one of the following topic-restriction sentences or make up one of your own. Develop your topic with at least four sentences that include good descriptive details by completing the prewriting, writing, and postwriting activities that follow on this page and the next.

1. The day before the holiday the department store was jammed with shoppers struggling to get to the counters.

2. I could feel a storm building in the air as I made the long trip by bicycle.

3. No shopping trip to a modern supermarket can surpass the fun of shopping in an old-fashioned general store.

4. The old car stood on cinder blocks in the front yard waiting to be fixed.

5. Magazine and newspaper advertisements often picture a "better world" that will supposedly be created if readers buy certain products.

A. Prewriting

One way to find ideas for writing assignments is to draw on your own experience. For example, suppose that you chose the following central idea for your paragraph: "The day before the holiday the department store was jammed with shoppers struggling to get to the counters." If you have had a similar experience of being in a crowded place, recall how it felt to push your way through the crowd. Ask yourself what sights, sounds, tastes, and smells you would find in a crowded department store during a holiday. Perhaps you will think of decorations or displays of merchandise. Then use the *Who? What? Where? When? Why?* and *How?* questions to give your readers a clear, specific picture of the merchandise display. *What* smells came from the perfume counter? *How* were the hats and gloves arranged? *Whom* did you see? *How* did these people act?

You can combine the details into descriptive sentences: "The counters were covered with bottles of perfume and tiny jewelry boxes. Shoppers rummaging through trays of woolly hats and gloves had thrown one salesperson into confusion. By the children's counter I heard shrieks of laughter as one little boy propelled a wind-up monkey down the aisle." Remember to ask yourself questions about all your senses.

B. Writing

Using your prewriting notes, write a first draft of your paragraph. You may put the topic and restriction sentences either at the beginning or in the middle of your paragraph. (Note that in a paragraph with many descriptive details, saving the topic and restriction sentences for the end may confuse the reader.)

Arrange your descriptive details in chronological order, spatial order, or order of importance. Use transitional words or other devices you have learned to clarify the relationships between sentences in your paragraph. If appropriate, end your draft with a clincher sentence—a sentence stating your main idea in a novel way.

C. Postwriting

Use the following Checklist for Revising Paragraphs as a guide in revising your paragraph. When you have completed your revision, check your writing for grammar and mechanics by using the Proofreader's Checklist at the back of the book.

Checklist for Revising Paragraphs

1. The paragraph has a clear central idea.

2. The central idea is sufficiently restricted to be developed in a paragraph.

3. The central idea is adequately developed with descriptive details.

4. Each detail in a sentence relates clearly to the central idea and presents new information.

5. The writer uses some method of organization to arrange the sentences in a clear way.

6. Transition words, pronouns, paraphrase, and repetition are used to improve paragraph coherence.

Developing a Paragraph Using Facts and Statistics

Many expository paragraphs can be developed effectively with *facts* and *statistics* that support the central idea.

A *fact* is information that has been or can be proved true. For example, the statement "Bats are the only flying mammals" is a fact science has proved. A *statistic* is a fact containing a number: "There are *1,000* living species of bats."

When you develop a paragraph with facts and statistics, use enough information to make your point but avoid using facts and statistics that are not related to your central idea. Using the *Who? What? When? Where? Why?* and *How?* questions will help you decide what information you need to develop the paragraph's central idea.

Model: Facts and Statistics

As you read the following paragraph from Barbara Ward's essay "Triage," identify the facts and statistics the writer uses to develop her point about the world supply of food.

Restricted Topics

Illustrations

     In the last ten years, at least one-third of the increased world demand for food has come from North Americans, Europeans and Russians eating steadily more high-protein food. Grain is fed to animals and poultry, and eaten as steak and eggs. In real energy terms, this is about five times more wasteful than eating grain itself. The result is an average American diet of nearly 2,000 pounds of grain a year—and epidemics of cardiac trouble—and 400 pounds for the average Indian.[1]

Think and Discuss

1. The first sentence gives a statistic: one-third of the increased demand for food worldwide in the last ten years has come from North Americans, Europeans, and Russians. What other facts does the paragraph present to show the problems with the food supply?

2. What statistics does it give about these facts?

[1]From "Triage" by Barbara Ward. Copyright © 1976 by the New York Times Company. Reprinted by permission.

Writing Practice 9: *A Paragraph with Facts and Statistics*

Select one of the following sentences to use as a topic or topic-restriction sentence for a paragraph developed with facts and statistics, or write a similar sentence of your own. Using a dictionary, encyclopedia, or other reference work, make a list of at least four facts or statistics by asking yourself the *Who? What? When? Where? Why?* and *How?* questions. Once you have collected your information, write a paragraph developing your central idea. Use the Checklist for Revising Paragraphs on page 76 as a guide in revising this assignment.

1. Yearly contracts for sports superstars total in the millions of dollars.

2. Many animals have highly developed ways of communicating.

3. Smoking is dangerous.

4. Martial arts for young people are increasingly popular.

5. Preparing for a long hiking (sailing/cross-country skiing) trip can be expensive.

Developing a Paragraph with Examples

An *example* is a specific case that illustrates a general idea or statement.

Examples can make a writer's meaning clear by answering the question "What do you mean by that?" Key words or phrases such as *for example*, *for instance*, *that is*, and *for this reason* are often used to introduce a specific example.

Model: Developing a Paragraph with Examples

In the following paragraph, what examples does the writer use to prove that the ancient Chinese depended on intuition and experience to warn them of earthquakes?

Topic

        Today professional quake-watchers in China use modern scientific methods and equipment such as "tiltmeters" and "creepmeters" that trace and record the shifting movement of the

Restriction

earth's crust. However, before such advanced technology was available, the Chinese depended more upon intuition, keen observance

Illustrations

of nature, and experience to predict earthquakes. For instance, rural Chinese who lived in areas where earthquakes were likely to occur claimed to know something was wrong because their animals acted strangely before an earthquake. Horses reared, cows would not enter their pens, fish and frogs leaped out of their ponds, snakes came out of their holes, and even pandas in the zoo acted differently. People noticed changes in the level and smell of well water as well as the eerie noises in suddenly swelling ground. These signs were clues to the people of the past that helped them predict and prepare for an earthquake.

Writing Practice 10: *Developing a Paragraph with Examples*

Select one topic or topic-restriction sentence from the following list, or write one of your own. On a separate sheet of paper, list three or four examples that could be used to develop the central idea in your sentence. Finally, write a paragraph, using your topic or topic-restriction sentence and examples. Use the checklist on page 76 to revise your work.

1. It is hard for me to lose my temper.

2. Some cartoon characters are so popular they are practically national celebrities.

3. Nearly everything costs more today than ten years ago.

4. Several books (songs/films/people) have influenced my life.

5. A single room in a house can be furnished and decorated in many ways.

Developing a Paragraph with Reasons

Reasons explain an idea or opinion by answering the question *Why?*

Model: Use of Reasons

The following paragraph from Henry David Thoreau's *Walden* is developed with reasons that support the central idea: The writer prefers not to eat animal meat or fish. As you read, try to identify the particular reasons why the author has chosen to be a complete vegetarian.

Restricted Topic

Illustrations

I have found repeatedly, of late years, that I cannot fish without falling a little in self-respect. I have tried it again and again. I have skill at it, and, like many of my fellows, a certain instinct for it, which revives from time to time, but always when I have done I feel that it would have been better if I had not fished. . . . Having been my own butcher and scullion and cook, as well as the gentleman for whom the dishes were served up, I can speak from an unusually complete experience. The practical objection to animal food in my case was its uncleanness; and besides, when I had caught and cleaned and cooked and eaten my fish, they seemed not to have fed me essentially. It was insignificant and unnecessary, and cost more than it came to. A little bread or a few potatoes would have done as well, with less trouble and filth. Like many of my contemporaries, I had rarely for many years used animal food, or tea, or coffee, etc.; not so much because of any ill effects which I had traced to them, as because they were not agreeable to my imagination. The repugnance to animal food is not the effect of experience, but is an instinct. It appeared more beautiful to live low and fare hard in many respects; and though I never did so, I went far enough to please my imagination. I believe that every man who has ever been earnest to preserve his higher or poetic faculties in the best condition has been particularly inclined to abstain from animal food, and from much food of any kind. It is a significant fact, stated by entomologists—I find it in Kirby and Spence—that "some insects in their perfect state, though furnished with organs of feeding, make no use of them"; and they lay it down as "a general rule, that almost all insects in this state eat much less than in that of larvae. The voracious caterpillar when transformed into a butterfly . . . and the gluttonous maggot when become a fly" content themselves with a drop or two of honey or some other sweet liquid. The abdomen under the wings of the butterfly still represents the larva. . . . The gross feeder is a man in the larva state; and there are whole nations in that condition, nations without fancy or imagination, whose vast abdomens betray them.

Think and Discuss

1. Thoreau's first reason for not wanting to eat animal food is that it is unclean. How many other reasons does Thoreau mention? What are they?

2. Thoreau uses facts to back up one of his reasons. From what source does he get his facts? Which of Thoreau's reasons do the facts support?

Writing Practice 11: *Use of Reasons*

The following list suggests topics for paragraphs you can develop with reasons. On a separate sheet of paper, write three or four reasons in support of the topic you select or in support of a similar topic of your own. Then use these reasons to write a paragraph on your topic. Revise your paragraph using the checklist on page 76.

1. Why I do (or do not) believe large cars should be banned in the United States

2. Why I do (or do not) believe we should elect a woman President of the United States

3. Why I do (or do not) believe in UFOs

4. Why all public facilities should (or should not) provide for the safety and convenience of disabled people

5. Why I do (or do not) enjoy being alone

Developing a Comparison and Contrast Paragraph

When you develop a paragraph by comparison and contrast, you point out similarities and differences between people or places, ideas, opinions, points of view, and so on.

In using the comparison-and-contrast method, it is important to compare similar features of *both* items. For example, if you are comparing two books and discuss the exciting characters in one, you should also discuss the characters in the other. Listing the ways the two items to be compared are alike and different will ensure that you discuss the same features in both items. For example, the following lists are based on the differences between the human brain and the electronic computer.

The Human Brain	*The "Electronic Brain"*
1. Composed of trillions of cells	1. Composed of millions of electrical components
2. Can be used to create, exercise initiative, deduce, reach conclusions, doubt, reason logically	2. Can compute, compile, and recall information
3. Can solve a problem independently	3. Must be programmed—told all the steps in advance—to solve a problem
4. Spends the time in actual computation	4. Spends time locating steps and information stored in its memory bank

Writers use either the *block method* or the *point-by-point method* to arrange the sentences in a comparison-and-contrast paragraph.

In the *block method* all the sentences about one item are grouped together in one block. For example, a writer using the block method to discuss the differences between the computer and the human brain might discuss the computer first, mentioning that it is composed of 10 million electrical components, that it can only compute, that it must be programmed, and that it uses time in locating information in its memory bank. Then the writer would move on to discuss all the features of the human brain together in a second block. On the other hand, *point-by-point* comparison and contrast involves moving back and forth between the two items, discussing how both items compare in terms of one point before moving to a second point.

Model: Point-by-Point Method of Comparison and Contrast

In the following paragraph from Gene Stanford's *Steps to Better English,* the writer uses the point-by-point method to discuss the differences between the human brain and the computer.

> An electronic computer, while able to perform certain mathematical calculations more quickly than man's brain, does not have the brain's complex structure. While a human brain consists of trillions upon trillions of nerve cells, a so-called "electronic brain" contains only about 10 million electronic components. A human has the ability to create, to exercise initiative, to deduct, to reach conclusions, to doubt, to reason logically. A computer can only compute; it can multiply, divide, add, subtract, and perhaps extract roots. Also it must be carefully "programmed" in order to arrive at an answer; that is, it must be told in advance all the steps necessary to perform a particular operation. A man, however, can be given a problem and go on to solve it with no further instruction. Most of the time taken up by a computer for problem solving is in locating the appropriate steps and intermediate values stored in its massive memory banks. The human brain, on the other hand, uses most of its time in actual computations. In short, a human brain is vastly more complex and versatile than that of a computer and therefore far superior.[1]

After stating the restricted topic in the first sentence, the writer deals first with the human brain, then the "electronic brain," then the human brain, followed by the computer, and so on throughout the entire paragraph. A concluding sentence continues the pattern by stating that the human brain is superior to the computer.

Model: Block Method of Comparison and Contrast

In the following paragraph, Robert Palmer remembers a time during the 1950s when he belonged to a teen group called the Tweeds. He uses the block method to compare the Tweeds and another popular group, the Greasers.

> Our world was divided into Tweeds and Greasers, both wanting to be "tough" and irresistible. The Tweeds were would-be Ivy Leaguers who bought Hollywood's Tab Hunter-Robert Wagner hard-sell—white bucks, khaki pants, button-down shirt, red-striped tie. We were shiny, formal, and eager. We trusted our facade to work for us as successfully as it had worked for our film heroes. They wore

---

[1]From *Steps to Better English* by Gene Stanford, "Aspects of English" Series. Copyright © 1972 by Holt, Rinehart and Winston, Publishers. Reprinted by permission of the publishers.

make-up; we had Clearasil. We wanted to be perfect. The Greasers swallowed James Dean and Marlon Brando whole. They were big on silence and scruffiness. They were losers in life, and, what's more, they didn't care; they gloried in it. That's why they were dangerous—they had nothing to lose. With their leather jackets, DA's, T-shirts with cigarette packs rolled in the turned-up sleeves, they wanted to be left alone. We wanted to be accepted.[1]

After identifying the two groups, this writer first discusses the Tweeds—their looks, the movie stars they liked, and their desire to be perfect. Then he discusses the Greasers—the stars they admired, their lack of ambition, and their looks. (*DA's* are hairstyles combed straight back from the forehead and sides.)

Writing Practice 12: *Comparison and Contrast*

On a separate sheet of paper, write a topic or topic-restriction sentence for one of the following subjects, or choose a similar subject of your own. Next, list three or four ways in which the two items are alike or different. Then write a paragraph about your topic, using either the block method or the point-by-point method. You may emphasize similarities, differences, or both. Revise your work using the checklist on page 76.

1. Growing up today—Growing up in my parents' day

2. Animal behavior—Human behavior

3. Living in a small town (or rural area)—Living in a large city

4. Working at school subjects—Working at a part-time job

5. Air travel today—Air travel in the twenty-first century

For Your Writer's Notebook

How do you think the teenagers of the 1980s will be remembered? The writer of the paragraph about the Tweeds and the Greasers uses the details *white bucks, leather jackets,* and film idols *Tab Hunter* and *Marlon Brando* to describe the teens of the fifties. In your notebook write about the appearance, fads, heroes, and goals of your generation. Remember to use specific details that will help your readers picture today's teen generation.

[1]From the "Introduction" by John Lahr to *Baby, That was Rock and Roll* by Robert Palmer. Copyright © 1978 by John Lahr. Reprinted by permission of John Lahr and Georges Borchardt, Inc.

Developing a Paragraph Using a Combination of Methods

Many paragraphs, especially longer ones, are developed with more than one method, as shown in the following model.

Model: Combining Methods of Paragraph Development

The following paragraph about the history of denim, from Hazel Todhunter's book *Make It in Denim*, combines facts and statistics with descriptive details and reasons.

Restricted Topic
Illustrations

Denim is the fashion phenomenon of recent years, but it has a long history. Two hundred years ago the clipper ships sailing to trade with the Americas used sails made of a fabric developed in Nîmes, France. (FACT AND STATISTIC) Because the colonies grew the cotton for the fabric and had a growing textile industry, it was not long before the fabric itself was being produced in the New World. (REASONS) The material was strong, durable, cheap, and white. Settlers going west took it with them, they even covered their wagons with it. (DESCRIPTIVE DETAILS) They used it for overalls and dungarees, but since the color was not very practical, they dyed it blue, using a dye extracted from an indigenous plant—indigo. (FACTS) In California, men were trying to make fortunes digging gold out of the hills. Another enterprising young man, Levi Strauss, made waist overalls for them. (FACT) At first they were made of sailcloth, but later from *Tissus de Nîme,* now called denim.[1] (FACT) [parenthesized words added]

Indigenous means "native to that region."

---

[1]From *Make It in Denim* by Hazel Todhunter. Copyright © 1977 by Hazel Todhunter. Reprinted by permission of Taplinger Publishing Company, Inc., and B. T. Batsford, Ltd., London.

Think and Discuss

The first sentence of the paragraph on the preceding page states the central idea: "Denim is the fashion phenomenon of recent years, but it has a long history." To develop this idea the writer traces the beginning of denim fabric, gives a variety of reasons for its production in America, explains how it came to be used for clothing in the New World, and presents descriptive details of its use by the early settlers. What facts and statistics does the writer include about the history of denim?

Writing Assignment II: *Combining Methods of Paragraph Development*

Use one of the following subjects or think of your own subject to write about in a paragraph developed with a combination of methods. Use descriptive details and examples or any other two methods of development. Follow the steps for prewriting, writing, and postwriting to complete this assignment.

1. The experience of trying to repair something

2. An experience of succeeding at something

3. An experience with a friend or relative

4. An experience of being in charge of something

5. An experience of working for a goal

A. Prewriting

The first step in combining methods of paragraph development involves writing a clear topic or topic-restriction sentence for the subject you have chosen. Next, use clustering to gather ideas for your paragraph. In the center of a sheet of paper, write your topic or topic-restriction sentence, and circle it. Then cluster ideas around it for about ten minutes, writing every fact, detail, or related thought that occurs to you.

After finishing your cluster, choose the ideas that you want to include in your paragraph. Classify the ideas you have chosen: Are they facts and statistics, examples, reasons, descriptive details, or similarities and differences? Decide which methods of paragraph development to use based on the kinds of ideas you have. Finally, number the items in your cluster to show the order in which you will use them in your paragraph.

B. Writing

Decide where to place the topic or topic-restriction sentence in your paragraph. Then write a first draft, using your cluster as a guide.

Include many illustration sentences in your paragraph. When you revise, it is easier to cut extra sentences than it is to write new ones because you have too few. As you write, make sure each sentence relates to the topic sentence. Use transitions, pronouns, paraphrase, and careful repetition to improve coherence.

End your paragraph with a strong concluding sentence.

C. Postwriting

Use the Checklist for Revising Paragraphs on page 76 as a guide in revising your paragraph. Finally, proofread your paragraph, using the Proofreader's Checklist at the back of the book.

With your teacher's permission, exchange paragraphs with your classmates. Read one another's work for enjoyment.

Sentence Combining:
Using Adverbs and Subordinators

Using Adverb Connectors

For more information on adverbs, see pages 418-435.

Some adverbs can be used to connect sentences of equal importance. Adverb connectors such as those in the following list indicate special kinds of relationships between two sentences. When an adverb connector is used, a semicolon separates the connected sentences, and a comma follows the adverb connector.

however instead nevertheless on the other hand	connect opposites
consequently hence therefore thus	suggest a conclusion is being made
besides furthermore in addition moreover	signal that an additional point is being made
indeed in fact	give emphasis to the writer's ideas

Sentences: Many Americans are working hard to conserve energy. Our country still faces a critical shortage of energy resources. (*nevertheless*)

Combined: Many Americans are working hard to conserve energy; *nevertheless*, our country still faces a critical shortage of energy resources.

Sentences: Langston Hughes is noted both for his poetry and his fiction.
His book *Not Without Laughter* is an outstanding novel about a teenage boy. (*in fact*)

Combined: Langston Hughes is noted both for his poetry and his fiction; *in fact*, his book *Not Without Laughter* is an outstanding novel about a teenage boy.

Exercise 1: Using Adverb Connectors

Use an adverb connector to write a combined sentence from each of the following pairs of sentences. When a signal is not given, choose the connecting adverb that makes the most sense. Study the examples carefully before you begin, noticing the punctuation before and after the connecting adverbs.

Examples

a. The banks were closed.
    Tanya couldn't deposit her check. (*therefore*)

    The banks were closed; therefore, Tanya couldn't deposit her check.

b. If you want to borrow the car to go to the library, you may.
    Be sure to drive safely and watch the icy roads. (*however*)

    If you want to borrow the car to go to the library, you may; however, be sure to drive safely and watch the icy roads.

1. Kim wrote the best essay in the class.
    She was awarded a certificate of achievement. (*consequently*)

2. Ms. Espinosa did not think her client was well enough to testify.
    The evidence was clearly in their favor without his testimony.
    (*besides*)

3. Carl was severely reprimanded for his misbehavior.
    All privileges and freedoms were taken away from him for a month. (*in fact*)

4. I left home early this morning.
    I was caught in traffic and missed my appointment. (*however*)

5. Michael likes to read and write short stories.
    He enjoys teaching others to write. (*furthermore*)

6. Kim's father is concerned about energy conservation.
    He bought a car that averages thirty-five miles per gallon of gas.

7. Your idea sounds fabulous to me.
    Others may not be so enthusiastic.

8. Joey Montez has a hearing impairment.
    He is one of the top students in the class.

9. The school officials wanted to schedule homeroom in the morning hours.
    They decided on the afternoon.

10. A smoke detector is an essential safety device in the home.
    Having some type of burglar alarm is also a good idea.

Connecting Sentences with Subordinators

For more information on subordinate clauses, see pages 534-547.

To combine a major statement with one of lesser importance, connecting words called *subordinators* may be used. Subordinators link a lesser statement to a major statement by indicating the relationship between the two.

after	before	whenever
although	even though	where
as if	just as	wherever
as long as	just when	whether
as soon as	since	while
as though	so that	unless
because	when	until

Note: The grammatical term for the subordinators is *subordinating conjunctions*.

When a subordinator is placed in front of a statement, the resulting string of words cannot stand alone as a separate sentence; it becomes dependent on the major statement. For example, when the subordinator *because* is added to the statement *She was a star athlete*, a new structure called a *subordinate clause* is created. This clause cannot stand alone but is dependent on another sentence:

Sentences: Several scholarships were available to Elena.
                 She was a star athlete. (*because*)

Combined: Several scholarships were available to Elena *because* she was a star athlete.

Subordinate clauses do not always follow the sentence to which they are attached. In the following example the subordinate clause (a subordinator and statement) appears at the beginning of a combined sentence. A subordinate clause at the beginning of a sentence is usually separated from the rest of the sentence by a comma. A subordinate clause at the end of a sentence usually does not require a comma.

Sentences: You scrape the old paint off the porch railing. (*if*)
The new paint will be less likely to chip.

Combined: *If* you scrape the old paint off the porch railing, the new paint will be less likely to chip.

Sentences: Daniel vacuumed the living room this morning.
He left for the basketball game. (*before*)

Combined: Daniel vacuumed the living room this morning *before* he left for the basketball game.

Exercise 2: Connecting Sentences of Unequal Importance

On a sheet of paper, combine the following pairs of sentences by using subordinators. In the examples the signals appear at the end of the sentence that you are to make into the subordinate clause. When you combine the sentences, however, place the subordinator at the beginning of the clause. When no signal is given, choose the subordinator you think works best. (The sentences without signals can be written in more than one way.)

Examples

a. Jason walked into the room. (*as soon as*)
Everyone shouted "Happy birthday!"
As soon as Jason walked into the room, everyone shouted "Happy birthday!"

b. The survivors huddled together in the center of the lifeboat.
They feared a shark attack.
The survivors huddled together in the center of the lifeboat because they feared a shark attack.
or
Because they feared a shark attack, the survivors huddled together in the center of the lifeboat.

1. The night security guards at the highly restricted atomic energy plant heard a suspicious noise. (*when*)
They checked the grounds for intruders.

2. This mystery won't be solved.
Detective Columbo arrives. (*until*)

3. You will be sure to receive a good grade in any class you faithfully attend.
You do your best work. (*if*)

4. Plants grow best in fresh air outdoors. (*even though*)
Many can be grown quite successfully indoors if given good care.

5. I am afraid of heights. (*although*)
I will climb the ladder to fix the swag lamp.

6. Maria Santos is the best qualified candidate for the office of State Comptroller.
She will probably win the election.

7. Michelle tells an unexpected joke.
The class breaks out in laughter.

8. Mr. Ramirez typed the letter and left it for Ms. Parkins' approval.
   He left the office.

9. Max was a mere six years old.
   He first learned to ice-skate.

10. Ms. Conkle tutored her child every other evening.
    His reading would improve.

Writing Practice: *Times of Your Life*

Native Americans recorded a memorable event from each year of their lives by painting the event inside a buffalo robe. Suppose you were to create a picture-calendar of your life. Think about the pictures you would draw to represent the past two years. Perhaps you would draw yourself as an excited, wide-eyed freshman entering a new high school or show yourself on a lake learning to water-ski. Write about the two events you would choose for your calendar, painting a vivid word picture of them for your reader.

As you write, remember to use some of the sentence-combining skills you have learned.

4 Expository Writing

The Purpose of Exposition

The purpose of *expository writing*, or *exposition*, is to explain factual information.

In high school and college, two important kinds of expository writing are the expository composition, or essay, and the essay examination. In the following sections you will study and practice the steps involved in developing the expository essay: finding and focusing a subject, gathering and recording information, organizing the information, and writing and revising the essay. You will also learn to organize and to write the kinds of items you are most likely to find on essay examinations.

Planning the Expository Essay

The first step in writing an expository essay is the same as that for other kinds of writing—finding a subject. When you are not assigned a subject for an expository essay, the best way to find one is to take time to think over your own experiences. As you think, keep in mind that expository writing deals with information and explanations. It would not be appropriate, for example, to tell the story of the first day at your new job, since that would be narrative writing. You could, however, write an explanation of the steps in training for your job or a definition of your job. You might also find ideas in your Writer's Notebook or from subjects you have studied in school or read about on your own.

Writing Practice 1: *Finding Subjects for Exposition*

Make a list of five subjects on which you could base an expository essay. *Surviving freshman year; How not to catch a fish;* and *New computer games* are examples of subjects you might use. Remember—the purpose of exposition is to present information.

Focusing Your Subject

Focusing your subject means limiting it or narrowing it to the specific topic of your essay.

The purpose of limiting your subject is to produce a topic that you can write about interestingly and well in one paper. If your subject is too large, the information you present to the reader will be too general or vague to be interesting. Assume, for example, that you want to write about space exploration, a subject that could include earth-orbiting satellites, the space race between the U.S.S.R. and the United States, moon landings, space probes of other planets (such as Venus, Mars, and Saturn), and the data produced by *Skylab*. The range of this subject is so great that to write about it properly you would have to turn your composition into a book.

You can narrow the subject of space exploration to a specific topic by focusing on one of its parts, perhaps the space race or data produced by *Skylab*. Depending on the length of your composition, you may want to limit the boundaries of your topic even further. For example, you could write about one particular part of the space race, such as the first accomplishments of *Sputnik 1* in 1957 and *Explorer 1* in 1958. You could also write about practical uses of the data about earth produced by *Skylab*, such as information about mineral deposits, crops, and global pollution.

The following are other examples of limiting a general subject to a topic for an expository essay.

Subject: Communication in the animal world

Topic: How bees communicate by "dancing"

The preceding topic limits or narrows the *general* subject of animal communication to the *particular* kind of communication that bees express with their dances.

Subject: Musical instruments

Topic: How to play the *khora*

This topic limits the *general* subject of popular music to one *particular* instrument for making popular music, the African *khora*.

Writing Practice 2: *Limiting the Subject*

The six subjects that follow are too general and need to be limited for use in an expository essay. On a separate sheet of paper, write a limited topic for each subject, as the following example shows.

Subject: The Sierra Club

Topic: How the Sierra Club helps protect the environment in Yosemite Park

1. Consumer problems
2. Natural resources
3. The Olympics
4. Student government
5. Dolphins
6. Science fiction

For information on using the library, see pages 624-635.

Gathering Information for the Expository Essay

Gathering information is an important step because the information you present about a topic forms the basis of the entire essay. In addition to using your Writer's Notebook as a source of details, you can also use any prewriting methods. The example in this section shows how to find ideas by using the *changing viewpoints method.*

With the changing viewpoints method, you look at a topic from three different perspectives to discover information about it. The first point of view examines the features and characteristics of the topic; the second studies how the topic changes or varies; and the third looks at how the individual parts fit together and how the topic fits into a larger background. Imagine that you are interested in the general subject of unusual methods of travel and have narrowed this subject to the topic of ballooning. By using the changing viewpoints method, you can examine the topic in three different ways to gain a range of information about it.

The first viewpoint examines the features and characteristics of a topic, asking the question *What is it?* When you look at ballooning from this perspective, you pose the following sorts of questions.

What is a balloon?
What do balloons used for travel look like?
What materials are used to make them?
What air or gasses make balloons rise?

What is ballooning?
What is the purpose of ballooning?
How do balloonists control their balloons?
How is ballooning like similar means of travel?
What makes ballooning different from travel by similar means, such as airships?

This first viewpoint, in effect, freezes your topic in time: you look at it as you would a photograph of an object to learn about its features.

The second viewpoint examines a topic to learn how it changes over a period of time, asking the question *How has it changed or varied?* When you consider ballooning from this viewpoint, you ask the following sorts of questions.

How have balloons changed?
Are balloons made of different materials now from when they were invented in 1783?
How has the shape of balloons changed since 1783?
Has the use for balloons changed since they were invented?

How has ballooning changed?
Have people's attitudes toward ballooning changed over time?
Has ballooning changed since the first balloonist crossed the English Channel in 1785?

By investigating the topic from this second viewpoint, you learn about changes in the appearance, construction, use, and popularity of balloons and ballooning. This viewpoint observes your topic as a process of change: you learn about the variations that time or a change of place bring to your topic.

The third viewpoint examines how the parts of a topic relate to one another and how the topic itself relates to a larger background, asking the question *What are its relationships?* When you consider ballooning in this way, you ask the following questions.

How does a balloon work?
What is each necessary part in a balloon?
How do the parts of a balloon work together?
How does ballooning fit into other categories?
How does ballooning relate to other sports and hobbies?
How does ballooning relate to other attempts people have made to fly?
How does ballooning relate to other interests you have?
How does ballooning relate to other inventions with practical applications?

By investigating ballooning from this third viewpoint, you look at the topic as if you were examining it under a microscope; you learn what its parts are and how they function together. Then you look at the topic from a broader perspective so that you learn what larger categories it fits into and how it relates to them.

Writing Practice 3: *Changing Viewpoints Method*

Select one of the following topics to explore by the changing viewpoints method, or use a similar topic of your choice. Write a list of questions you would ask for each viewpoint, as in the preceding example on ballooning. When you have finished, write out the answers to your questions.

1. Hang gliding
2. Ghosts
3. Student government
4. Submarines
5. Saber-toothed tigers

6. Hockey
7. Blue jeans
8. Pyramids
9. Computer graphics
10. Space shuttle

Recording Information for the Expository Essay

As you explore your topic, you will find many ideas about it. You will probably remember the most relevant ideas, but other thoughts, impressions, and details will most likely be forgotten unless you record them as they occur to you.

Note-taking **is the simplest and most efficient way to record your ideas.**

A useful method of recording notes is to write each idea separately on a note card or a slip of paper. For example, assume that you have chosen the topic of the women's liberation movement. The first note you write might look like the following one.

> *Attitudes about women's liberation*
>
> *I have a different attitude about women's liberation than my sister because she is ten years older and things have changed a good deal since she was my age.*

As you write your notes, always put a heading on each note for easy reference later. Sometimes your notes will be words or phrases:

1. My talks with Mother about her childhood

2. The issue of using *Ms.* instead of *Miss* or *Mrs.*

3. The Equal Rights Amendment

Sometimes your notes will be complete sentences:

1. Why does my sister feel she was treated differently because she was a girl?

2. The most widely supported women's lib demand is the equal-pay-for-equal-work issue.

3. Some television shows still show women in stereotyped roles.

Sometimes your notes will be paragraphs:

> I think things are changing because of the women's liberation movement. When my grandmother was in school, everybody expected her to get married right away. Her father told her she could go to college if she wanted but that it was a waste of money. When my mother was in school, she did well in math but wasn't encouraged to be a mathematician because it was "a man's field." In my class, though, I know three girls who want to be engineers, and their families are very proud.

Writing Practice 4: *Recording Information*

Using a topic you have already selected, apply the changing viewpoints method, brainstorming, clustering, or any other prewriting technique to gather information. As you do, make notes on 3 × 5 note cards or on slips of paper. Save these notes to use in a later assignment.

Organizing Your Notes

One of the easiest ways to organize your notes is to separate them into stacks, making each idea a separate group and putting all the notes about one idea together. The following notes were collected for an expository essay titled "A Teenager Looks at the Women's Liberation Movement." The notes appear in the order in which they were written and have not yet been organized. As you read them, try to find some general ideas you could use to group notes together.

1. What is women's liberation? Does it mean the same thing now as when the movement began?

2. The history of the women's movement goes back to the nineteenth century when the suffragettes concentrated on getting the vote.

3. Talked with mother about her friends—they were all married before they were twenty.

4. Mother said she was brought up to believe that a woman's place was in the home.

5. Women on television and in movies not true to life.

6. The percentage of women in top-level jobs in this country is still low. Other countries, especially in Scandinavia, have higher rates of employed women in executive positions.

7. When grandmother was little, she wasn't allowed to play with boys because they were "too rough."

8. Organizations for women—what do they do?

9. Even though I'm strong, my brother is always the one who is asked to carry in the groceries or move the chairs around.

10. I know girls who ask boys for dates, but it's still mostly the other way around. When Mother was my age, she didn't know any girls who asked boys out.

11. My parents have always encouraged me to do whatever I was really interested in, such as going to college or getting a job or studying the subjects I wanted.

12. Talked about women's liberation with my friend Jim. He said, "Liberation from what?"

13. My parents have a traditional life. Dad works outside the house, and Mother works at home taking care of us and keeping house.

14. Girls' intramural sports are very popular today. My teachers say that when they were in school no one paid much attention to girls' sports.

15. Women artists.

16. Reading about "role models." A *role model* is someone to look up to and try to follow. In work situations boys have more role models than girls because there are more men in the professions than women. I think this is true. For instance, our next-door neighbor is an electrician, and the fathers of two of my friends are electricians. I don't know any women electricians.

17. My grandfather's attitude compared with my father's attitude about women.

18. When my English teacher was growing up, her brothers didn't have to help with the dishes because it was "women's work."

19. I've never been told, "You can't do that because you're a girl."

20. Statistics on the percentage of women who go on to college.

Some of the preceding notes are general, and some are specific. Each note deals with the same topic, but you would not try to incorporate all the notes into one composition. When you take notes, however, do not try to decide beforehand what you will use in your paper. Put down whatever thoughts, questions, or impressions come to you and later determine which ones you will use.

Writing Practice 5: *Organizing Notes*

Many of the thoughts and ideas expressed in the sample notes are related. For example, notes 7 and 18 both have to do with traditional attitudes about women. Read through the notes to find at least three other general categories into which the notes can be grouped. Write these categories on a sheet of paper and then list beneath these headings the notes that fit into these categories.

Writing the Thesis Statement

A *thesis statement* is a sentence that clearly states the thesis, or topic, of the composition.

Writing a thesis statement helps you to focus the main point of your essay and helps the reader understand exactly what will be covered in your paper. For example, imagine that you have decided to write a composition on the subject of black holes and have narrowed the subject to the topic *Formation of a black hole*. To develop a thesis statement look over the information you have gathered and decide on the main idea you want to express about the topic. On the subject of black holes, one possible thesis statement might be "Although scientists are not certain about the exact nature of black holes, they do agree about how black holes are formed." This thesis statement tells the reader that the composition will explain how black holes are formed.

Another way to narrow the subject of black holes is to define them. A possible thesis statement for defining a black hole is, "When some stars die, the force of gravity causes them to collapse inward; a star that keeps on collapsing is called a *black hole*." This thesis statement gives a brief definition and indicates that the purpose of the composition is to make a thorough definition of black holes.

Writing Practice 6: *Writing the Thesis Statement*

For this assignment, use a topic you have already developed. After reading the information you have gathered on the topic, write a thesis statement that expresses the main idea you will explain in your composition. Study the following example first.

Subject:	Movies
Topic:	Irritating behavior of movie audiences
Thesis statement:	Three kinds of behavior among movie audiences are particularly annoying: loud whispering and talking, constant moving up and down aisles, and finding seats before the previous showing has ended.

Making an Informal Outline

An *informal outline* is a plan for writing.

Begin making an informal outline by separating your notes into stacks according to categories, so that when you finish you will have perhaps four or five groups of notes with related information.

The stacks of notes and your thesis statement will suggest the form of your outline. (You can rearrange your notes until the order makes sense to you.) As you organize your thoughts, you will probably find that some of your notes will have to be discarded and that new ideas will occur to you as you go along. Always feel free to add more ideas or to delete any information that does not contribute to the main idea of your composition.

The following informal outline is developed from the sample notes. As you read, notice that each separate section represents a group of ideas.

A Teenager Looks at Women's Liberation

The Women's Liberation Movement
 Definition
 History
 Issues
  Issues about attitudes
  Issues about jobs

Mother's life before women's lib
 Traditional attitudes of her family
  Attitudes about college
  Attitudes about "a woman's place"
 Traditional attitudes of society
  Attitudes about dating
  Attitudes about "a woman's place"

My life after women's lib
 Traditional attitudes
  Stereotyping on radio and TV
  Lack of women in top-level jobs
 Changing attitudes
  Encouragement of parents
  More women in college
  More women in the work force

Notice that in the informal outline numbers are not used to designate headings; instead, divisions and subdivisions are shown by indentions and spacing. (The *formal outline,* which is most often used in preparing research papers, does have a definite numbering system.) The sample outline shows one way to plan an expository essay. However, you could use the same notes to organize the composition in other ways that would be equally effective. There are no strict rules for making an informal outline. Its purpose is simply to provide you with a guide for writing a clear and well-organized composition.

Writing Practice 7: *Making an Informal Outline*

Using notes you have gathered for an expository essay, write an informal outline. Discard any notes that do not fit into your plan for the composition.

Writing the Expository Essay

The basic form of an expository essay consists of the introduction, the body, and the conclusion.

The *introduction* identifies the topic and gives some information about it to interest the reader. The *body*, usually several paragraphs long, develops the topic stated in the introduction. The *conclusion* gives a brief summary of the main ideas, reemphasizes an important point, or restates the topic.

Model: An Expository Essay

In the following essay, "The Spider and the Wasp," Alexander Petrunkevitch explains how a certain species of wasp uses the tarantula spider as a source of food for its young. After you have finished reading, you should be able to identify the introduction, body, and conclusion of the essay, as well as the thesis statement.

The Spider and the Wasp

[1] To hold its own in the struggle for existence, every species of animal must have a regular source of food, and if it happens to live on other animals, its survival may be very delicately balanced. The hunter cannot exist without the hunted; if the latter should perish from the earth, the former would, too. When the hunted also prey on some of the hunters, the matter may become complicated.

[2] This is nowhere better illustrated than in the insect world. Think of the complexity of a situation such as the following: There is a certain wasp, *Pimpla inquisitor,* whose larvae feed on the larvae of the tussock moth. *Pimpla* larvae in turn serve as food for the larvae of a second wasp, and the latter in their turn nourish still a third wasp. What subtle balance between fertility and mortality must exist in the case of each of these four species to prevent the extinction of all of them! An excess of mortality over fertility in a single member of the group would ultimately wipe out all four.

[3] This is not a unique case. The two great orders of insects, Hymenoptera and Diptera, are full of such examples of interrelationship. And the spiders (which are not insects but members of a separate order of arthropods) also are killers and victims of insects.

[4] The picture is complicated by the fact that those species which are carnivorous in the larval stage have to be provided with animal food by a vegetarian mother. The survival of the young depends on the mother's correct choice of a food which she does not eat herself.

[5] In the feeding and safeguarding of their progeny the insects and spiders exhibit some interesting analogies to reasoning and some

crass examples of blind instinct. The case I propose to describe here is that of the tarantula spiders and their arch-enemy, the digger wasps of the genus Pepsis. It is a classic example of what looks like intelligence pitted against instinct—a strange situation in which the victim, though fully able to defend itself, submits unwittingly to its destruction.

[6] Most tarantulas live in the Tropics, but several species occur in the temperate zone and a few are common in the southern U.S. Some varieties are large and have powerful fangs with which they can inflict a deep wound. These formidable looking spiders do not, however, attack man; you can hold one in your hand, if you are gentle, without being bitten. Their bite is dangerous only to insects and small mammals such as mice; for a man it is no worse than a hornet's sting.

[7] Tarantulas customarily live in deep cylindrical burrows, from which they emerge at dusk and into which they retire at dawn. Mature males wander about after dark in search of females and occasionally stray into houses. After mating, the male dies in a few weeks, but a female lives much longer and can mate several years in succession. In a Paris museum is a tropical specimen which is said to have been living in captivity for 25 years.

[8] A fertilized female tarantula lays from 200 to 400 eggs at a time; thus it is possible for a single tarantula to produce several thousand young. She takes no care of them beyond weaving a cocoon of silk to enclose the eggs. After they hatch, the young walk away, find convenient places in which to dig their burrows and spend the rest of their lives in solitude. Tarantulas feed mostly on insects and millipedes. Once their appetite is appeased, they digest the food for several days before eating again. Their sight is poor, being limited to sensing a change in the intensity of light and to the perception of moving objects. They apparently have little or no sense of hearing, for a hungry tarantula will pay no attention to a loudly chirping cricket placed in its cage unless the insect happens to touch one of its legs.

[9] But all spiders, and especially hairy ones, have an extremely delicate sense of touch. Laboratory experiments prove that tarantulas can distinguish three types of touch: pressure against the body wall, stroking of the body hair and riffling of certain very fine hairs on the legs called trichobothria. Pressure against the body, by a finger or the end of a pencil, causes the tarantula to move off slowly for a short distance. The touch excites no defensive response unless the approach is from above where the spider can see the motion, in which case it rises on its hind legs, lifts its front legs, opens its fangs and holds this threatening posture as long as the object continues to move. When the motion stops, the spider drops back to the ground, remains quiet for a few seconds and then moves slowly away.

[10] The entire body of a tarantula, especially its legs, is thickly clothed with hair. Some of it is short and woolly, some long and stiff. Touching this body hair produces one of two distinct reactions. When the spider is hungry, it responds with an immediate and swift attack. At the touch of a cricket's antennae the tarantula seizes the insect so

swiftly that a motion picture taken at the rate of 64 frames per second shows only the result and not the process of capture. But when the spider is not hungry, the stimulation of its hairs merely causes it to shake the touched limb. An insect can walk under its hairy belly unharmed.

[11] The trichobothria, very fine hairs growing from disklike membranes on the legs, were once thought to be the spider's hearing organs, but we now know that they have nothing to do with sound. They are sensitive only to air movement. A light breeze makes them vibrate slowly without disturbing the common hair. When one blows gently on the trichobothria, the tarantula reacts with a quick jerk of its four front legs. If the front and hind legs are stimulated at the same time, the spider makes a sudden jump. This reaction is quite independent of the state of its appetite.

[12] These three tactile responses—to pressure on the body wall, to moving of the common hair and to flexing of the trichobothria—are so different from one another that there is no possibility of confusing them. They serve the tarantula adequately for most of its needs and enable it to avoid most annoyances and dangers. But they fail the spider completely when it meets its deadly enemy, the digger wasp Pepsis.

[13] These solitary wasps are beautiful and formidable creatures. Most species are either a deep shiny blue all over, or deep blue with rusty wings. The largest have a wing span of about four inches. They live on nectar. When excited, they give off a pungent odor—a warning that they are ready to attack. The sting is much worse than that of a bee or common wasp, and the pain and swelling last longer. In the adult stage the wasp lives only a few months. The female produces but a few eggs, one at a time at intervals of two or three days. For each egg the mother must provide one adult tarantula, alive but paralyzed. The tarantula must be of the correct species to nourish the larva. The mother wasp attaches the egg to the paralyzed spider's abdomen. Upon hatching from the egg, the larva is many hundreds of times smaller than its living but helpless victim. It eats no other food and drinks no water. By the time it has finished its single gargantuan meal and become ready for wasphood, nothing remains of the tarantula but its indigestible chitinous skeleton.

[14] The mother wasp goes tarantula-hunting when the egg in her ovary is almost ready to be laid. Flying low over the ground late on a sunny afternoon, the wasp looks for its victim or for the mouth of a tarantula burrow, a round hole edged by a bit of silk. The sex of the spider makes no difference, but the mother is highly discriminating as to species. Each species of Pepsis requires a certain species of tarantula, and the wasp will not attack the wrong species. In a cage with a tarantula which is not its normal prey the wasp avoids the spider, and is usually killed by it in the night.

[15] Yet when a wasp finds the correct species, it is the other way about. To identify the species the wasp apparently must explore the spider with her antennae. The tarantula shows an amazing tolerance to this exploration. The wasp crawls under it and walks over

it without evoking any hostile response. The molestation is so great and so persistent that the tarantula often rises on all eight legs, as if it were on stilts. It may stand this way for several minutes. Meanwhile the wasp, having satisfied itself that the victim is of the right species, moves off a few inches to dig the spider's grave. Working vigorously with legs and jaws, it excavates a hole 8 to 10 inches deep with a diameter slightly larger than the spider's girth. Now and again the wasp pops out of the hole to make sure that the spider is still there.

[16] When the grave is finished, the wasp returns to the tarantula to complete her ghastly enterprise. First she feels it all over once more with her antennae. Then her behavior becomes more aggressive. She bends her abdomen, protruding her sting, and searches for the soft membrane at the point where the spider's leg joins its body—the only spot where she can penetrate the horny skeleton. From time to time, as the exasperated spider slowly shifts ground, the wasp turns on her back and slides along with the aid of her wings, trying to get under the tarantula for a shot at the vital spot. During all this maneuvering, which can last for several minutes, the tarantula makes no move to save itself. Finally the wasp corners it against some obstruction and grasps one of its legs in her powerful jaws. Now at last the harassed spider tries a desperate but vain defense. The two contestants roll over and over on the ground. It is a terrifying sight and the outcome is always the same. The wasp finally manages to thrust her sting into the soft spot and holds it there for a few seconds while she pumps in the poison. Almost immediately the tarantula falls paralyzed on its back. Its legs stop twitching; its heart stops beating. Yet it is not dead, as is shown by the fact that if taken from the wasp it can be restored to some sensitivity by being kept in a moist chamber for several months.

[17] After paralyzing the tarantula, the wasp cleans herself by dragging her body along the ground and rubbing her feet, sucks the drop of blood oozing from the wound in the spider's abdomen, then grabs a leg of the flabby, helpless animal in her jaws and drags it down to the bottom of the grave. She stays there for many minutes, sometimes for several hours, and what she does all that time in the dark we do not know. Eventually she lays her egg and attaches it to the side of the spider's abdomen with a sticky secretion. Then she emerges, fills the grave with soil carried bit by bit in her jaws, and finally tramples the ground all around to hide any trace of the grave from prowlers. Then she flies away, leaving her descendant safely started in life.

[18] In all this the behavior of the wasp evidently is qualitatively different from that of the spider. The wasp acts like an intelligent animal. This is not to say that instinct plays no part or that she reasons as man does. But her actions are to the point; they are not automatic and can be modified to fit the situation. We do not know for certain how she identifies the tarantula—probably it is by some olfactory or chemo-tactile sense—but she does it purposefully and does not blindly tackle a wrong species.

[19] On the other hand, the tarantula's behavior shows only

confusion. Evidently the wasp's pawing gives it no pleasure, for it tries to move away. That the wasp is not simulating sexual stimulation is certain, because male and female tarantulas react in the same way to its advances. That the spider is not anesthetized by some odorless secretion is easily shown by blowing lightly at the tarantula and making it jump suddenly. What, then, makes the tarantula behave as stupidly as it does?

[20] No clear, simple answer is available. Possibly the stimulation by the wasp's antennae is masked by a heavier pressure on the spider's body, so that it reacts as when prodded by a pencil. But the explanation may be much more complex. Initiative in attack is not in the nature of tarantulas; most species fight only when cornered so that escape is impossible. Their inherited patterns of behavior apparently prompt them to avoid problems rather than attack them. For example, spiders always weave their webs in three dimensions, and when a spider finds that there is insufficient space to attach certain threads in the third dimension, it leaves the place and seeks another, instead of finishing the web in a single plane. This urge to escape seems to arise under all circumstances, in all phases of life and to take the place of reasoning. For a spider to change the pattern of its web is as impossible as for an inexperienced man to build a bridge across a chasm obstructing his way.

[21] In a way the instinctive urge to escape is not only easier but more efficient than reasoning. The tarantula does exactly what is most efficient in all cases except in an encounter with a ruthless and determined attacker dependent for the existence of her own species on killing as many tarantulas as she can lay eggs. Perhaps in this case the spider follows its usual pattern of trying to escape, instead of seizing and killing the wasp, because it is not aware of its danger. In any case, the survival of the tarantula species as a whole is protected by the fact that the spider is much more fertile than the wasp.[1]

Think and Discuss

1.   The general subject of Alexander Petrunkevitch's essay is *Animal species that use other animal species as sources of food*. What is the topic?

2.   The thesis statement of this essay is not given until the fifth paragraph. What sentence or sentences contain the thesis statement?

3.   In the introduction (paragraphs 1–5), the writer gives several examples of animals (mostly insects) that feed upon each other. What else does Alexander Petrunkevitch accomplish in this introduction? Why do you think this essay has such a long introduction?

4.   The body of the essay (paragraphs 6–17) is divided into two parts. In the first part (paragraphs 6–12), the writer explains information about the tarantula that helps readers understand its behavior. What does Alexander Petrunkevitch explain in the second part of the body?

5.   In the long conclusion (paragraphs 18–21), the writer attempts to explain why the tarantula behaves as it does. What explanation does he give for the tarantula's allowing the wasp to overpower it?

Writing the Introduction

The *introduction* is usually the first paragraph of a composition. The purpose of the introductory paragraph is to present the basic idea that will be discussed as well as to interest the reader.

You may choose to begin your introductory paragraph with the thesis statement itself, or you may begin with a general remark leading into the thesis statement. The important rule for beginning writers to remember is to include the thesis statement somewhere in the first paragraph.

Model: Introductory Paragraph

The following introductory paragraph begins with interesting information and ends with the thesis statement.

Long after the American West had been comparatively citified, a large part of western Canada, known as the North Peace Country, remained a wilderness. The Peace River, which gives the region its name, flows from the Canadian Rockies to the Arctic Sea, through

some of the wildest canyons and most fertile farmland in North America. In both its history and its terrain, the North Peace is a microcosm of the Canadian West.[1]

From the thesis statement the reader can tell that the essay will deal with the history and terrain of the North Peace as it relates to the Canadian West. In the sample expository composition on page 115, you will find one more example of an introductory paragraph.

Writing the Body

The *body* of the essay is the main part of the paper.

The purpose of the body is to develop the topic stated in the introduction by presenting information and illustrations about it. The body paragraphs should follow a logical organization, should include a sufficient number of illustrations, and should be unified.

Logical organization is an ordering of thoughts and ideas that makes sense. If the paper explains the steps in a process, the arrangement of ideas should follow the order in which the steps are done. For a paper explaining reasons, the reasons should be arranged in the order of their importance. There are also other ways to organize information in an expository essay, but the important point is that readers can easily follow the progression of ideas.

Sufficient illustrations are necessary to develop the topic of your paper. Illustrations include details, examples, facts and figures, and reasons that support and explain the thesis. Specific illustrations make your paper interesting as well as informative.

A *unified composition* is one in which each idea presented relates to the thesis statement. Each paragraph develops a different aspect of the thesis statement, but all of the paragraphs deal with the same basic idea.

[1]From "History at Peace" by Carol Easton in *Westways,* June 1976. Copyright © 1976 by the Automobile Club of Southern California. Reprinted by permission of *Westways.*

Writing the Conclusion

The purpose of the *conclusion* is to bring the reader back to the main idea of the paper by restating it in a new way.

A good conclusion also gives the reader a sense of completion, of having come to the end of a discussion or argument. Writers use different techniques in writing conclusions. Some refer to the thesis statement and briefly summarize the main points of the paper. Some conclude with an interesting quotation or statistic about the topic, and some end on a personal note or statement of opinion. You may use any of these methods of writing a conclusion, but remember that the conclusion is not the place to add new ideas; all the significant ideas about your subject belong in the body.

Model: A Concluding Paragraph

The following conclusion is taken from Kent Dannen's essay about the life and work of the famous conservationist Enos Mills. Notice that the paragraph makes a general statement about Enos Mills' accomplishment and that it ends with a personal statement about ecological preservation.

> Enos Mills was proud of the work that he had done to preserve the wild beauty of the Rockies for later generations of Americans. He believed when he died that protection in national parks assured the immortality of wild beauty, that wild gardens forever would be sources of inspiration. But we know now that our gardens will inspire us forever only if those who love them continue to defend the wilderness with the single-minded devotion shown by Enos Mills, father of Rocky Mountain National Park.[1]

[1]From "Rocky Mountain Man" by Kent Dannen in *Westways*, August 1976. Copyright © 1976 by the Automobile Club of Southern California. Reprinted by permission of *Westways*.

Writing Assignment I: *An Expository Essay*

A. Prewriting

Gather the notes, thesis statement, and informal outline that you wrote for Writing Practices 3 through 7. Reread them before you begin to write, adding information or illustrations where needed, and deleting parts that do not apply to your thesis.

B. Writing

The Introduction: Write an introductory paragraph incorporating the thesis statement you have already written. You may begin the paragraph with the thesis statement or lead into it using other information.

The Body of the Essay: Write the body of the essay, developing the thesis statement you presented in the introductory paragraph. Strive for a logical organization of ideas and information. As you write, consider whether each idea relates to your thesis statement.

The Conclusion: In writing the concluding paragraph, use any of the techniques you have read about to achieve a sense of completion. You may refer to your thesis statement by summarizing the main points of your essay. Or you might want to end on a personal note by stating your opinion about the topic.

The Title: The *title* of an expository essay should clearly tell the reader what the essay is about. When titles are too general, the reader does not know what to expect. For example, on page 115 is an essay titled "How to Tame a Hawk." From the title you can tell that the essay is about taming hawks. If a more general title such as "Hawks" were used, readers might expect to read about the habits of hawks or the development of hawks.

Thinking about your thesis statement may help you decide on a title for your essay. Many writers wait to compose their title until they have finished their essays; others like to have working titles from the beginning.

C. Postwriting

Revising: If possible, set your paper aside for a few days so that you will approach your revision with a fresh and more critical eye. Then use the checklist on the following page as a guide to revising your essay.

> ## *Checklist for Revising an Expository Essay*
>
> 1. The topic is suitably focused.
>
> 2. The introduction helps interest the reader and contains a thesis statement that clearly states the topic of the essay.
>
> 3. Each paragraph in the body presents new information about the topic.
>
> 4. The essay includes sufficient illustrations about the topic.
>
> 5. The information in the essay logically organized.
>
> 6. The essay is unified; each idea relates to the thesis statement.
>
> 7. The conclusion returns to the main idea of the essay, which is restated in some way.
>
> 8. The title clearly tells what the essay is about.

When you have completed your revision, rewrite your paper. Then check it for errors in grammar and mechanics by using the Proofreader's Checklist at the back of the book.

The Process Analysis Essay

A *process analysis essay* explains the steps in a process: how to cook a meal, throw a curve ball, or solve a math problem.

An expository composition that explains a process tells the reader clearly and completely how to do or understand something. It presents information in an orderly way, taking the reader step by step through the process itself. For clarity, a process essay usually is organized according to the steps in the process, telling the first step first, then the second step, then the third step, and so on.

Model: A Process Analysis Essay

The following expository composition explains a specialized process: how to tame a hawk. As you read through the essay, adapted from Jack Samson's *Falconry Today*, follow the notes in the left-hand margin. These notes explain how each paragraph presents information about the process of taming a hawk.

How to Tame a Hawk

The introduction defines *falconry* and gives background information. The last sentence is the thesis statement.

Falconry—hunting with hawks—is one of the few surviving sports that date to the earliest days of recorded human history. Today the popularity of falconry in the United States is growing, especially among young people who are drawn by the nostalgic value as well as by the simple thrill of the sport. Falconry, however, is a sport that requires much preparation and patience. In fact, one of the most difficult and important lessons a beginner has to learn is how to tame the hawk.

This paragraph tells what equipment is needed and where the hawk is kept.

The first equipment a novice falconer needs is a set of jesses. (*Jesses* are strips of light but very tough leather that always remain on the hawk's legs.) Leather jesses should be fastened to the legs as soon as possible after capture. A leash or length of leather should then be fastened to the jesses, and finally the end of the leash is fastened to a perch in a dark room. The hawk is kept in a darkened room until it has calmed down and realized that it is not being attacked or hurt.

The second paragraph of the body gives ways to calm the hawk and get it used to a human.

Whatever the kind of hawk—an eyas hawk (raised from the nest), passager (immature hawk), or haggard (adult)—the beginner will have the same basic problem at first: to calm down the hawk and get it used to its new owner and environment. The initial weeks of captivity are the most important. Falconers in olden days slept beside the cages, keeping a candle or a lantern lit most of the time, and stroking and quietly talking to the birds. A gentle voice, slow movement, and constant encouragement from the falconer are vital in these early stages if the hawk is to accept and tolerate its new partner.

This paragraph explains the significance of the hawk's eating and tells how the hawk should be fed.

The newly acquired hawk must be induced to take food. It may not do this for several days, but even the hawk that has undergone severe trauma during capture will eventually succumb to the temptation of fresh meat. The hawk's first food in captivity is the beginning of its accepting a human, although each hawk has its own timetable in arriving at this compromise. The hawk should eat all its meals from the hand of the falconer at this stage, since it must come to associate food with the human. The falconer should try to get the hawk to eat voluntarily. Force-feeding a hawk may provide the nourishment to keep it alive but does nothing to establish a compatible relationship between bird and owner.

This paragraph gives information about how long it takes to tame a hawk.

There is no rule about how long it will take for a captured hawk to gentle down and stop frantically resisting the owner's attempts to approach it slowly or to hold it on a gloved fist. Some hawks can be gentled in days, but others may take months. Also, there is no hard-and-fast formula for the number of hours a day or night a falconer must spend with a hawk to gentle it. The time in the "mew"—the darkened room to which a falconer brings a new hawk—varies with the wildness of each bird and with the degree of trauma experienced in its capture.

The conclusion explains the purpose behind the process of taming a hawk and tells what qualities experienced falconers think most important for taming a hawk properly.

The gentling of hunting hawks is simply aimed at setting up some form of communication between human and bird. Until the hawk stops fearing the falconer, no training to hunt can begin. It is a long time from the moment of capture—when the hawk, screaming in rage and defiance, falls on its back with wings spread, beak open, and talons straining to sink into a hand—to when a hawk will perch on a gloved hand within inches of a falconer's face, accept food from the human's hand, and allow its feathers to be stroked. Experienced falconers know that eventually the moment will come, but it takes patience and persistence. Learn how to wait, they tell the young falconers. That is one of the most valuable secrets to the ancient art of falconry.[1]

For Your Writer's Notebook

After reading "How to Tame a Hawk," recall an experience you have had with an animal, perhaps training a dog or horse, learning how to milk a cow, or encountering an animal in its natural surroundings. As a notebook entry, write your memory of that experience. Include sensory details of the creature's appearance—perhaps the texture of its coat or its color, as well as sounds the animal made and smells you associate with it. Also, write of your own thoughts and feelings about the experience.

Writing Assignment II: *A Process Analysis Essay*

A. Prewriting

An expository essay that explains a process is basically a "how to" paper. Your purpose is to give information about how to do or understand something. As you consider potential subjects, be certain they fit into this "how to" category.

---

[1]Adapted from *Falconry Today* by Jack Samson. (Walck, 1976). Reprinted by permission of the author.

Deciding on a Subject: A "how to" essay is best written from experience. Even if you read a great deal about a subject, you will find it difficult to explain a process you have never gone through yourself. One way to begin finding a subject is to allow time to think about your own areas of interest and experience. You may have a talent or hobby, such as painting, roller-skating, swimming, or playing a musical instrument. Perhaps you are fascinated by science fiction, jazz, comic books, poetry, or organic gardening. All these areas are potential subjects for a "how to" paper.

Narrowing the Subject: As you think of your own areas of interest and experience, write them down on a piece of scratch paper. Then look at each subject and try to decide how you would narrow it down to a "how to" topic. For example, if the area you enjoy most is painting, you could think of the processes that are a part of painting. Perhaps you could write a composition about how to paint a still life or how to work with watercolors. If you cannot find a simple process to explain in your first area of interest, go to the next area on your list.

Do not be discouraged if you cannot think of a topic right away. Remember that your area of interest does not have to be unusual. How you approach the topic and what you say about it are more important.

Planning the Essay: Next, follow the steps you have learned for planning an essay.

1. Narrow the subject to a topic that can be covered in detail.

2. Gather information about the topic.

3. Write a thesis statement.

4. Make an informal outline.

B. Writing

Write a first draft, using your outline and notes to guide you. As you write, be sure to follow chronological order, making each step clear to the reader. Define any terms your readers may not know.

C. Postwriting

Before writing your final draft, revise your essay with a classmate, parent, friend, teacher, or writing group. As your teacher directs, ask someone to read your essay to see if he or she can follow the steps you have explained. Use the person's responses as a basis for revising. Read the sections that follow on improving coherence and revising an essay before completing your revision.

Improving Coherence in the Expository Essay

Coherent writing is writing in which the logical relationships between ideas are apparent.

Writers can improve the coherence of their expository essays in several ways. The simplest approach is to use *transitional devices*—words and phrases such as *first, second, then, now,* and *also.* Other methods are the *use of pronouns* to refer to nouns or other pronouns; *paraphrase,* the restating of words and phrases; and *repetition,* the repeating of key words and phrases.

Model: Coherence

In the following paragraphs from "How to Tame a Hawk" the transitions are underlined. Their purpose in the paragraphs are explained in the left-hand margin.

Repetition: *falconry* **is repeated three times in the introduction. Paraphrase:** *the sport* **means "falconry."**

Falconry—hunting with hawks—is one of the few surviving sports that date to the earliest days of recorded human history. Today the popularity of falconry in the United States is growing, especially among young people who are drawn by the nostalgic value as well as by the simple thrill of the sport. Falconry, however, is a sport that requires much preparation and patience. In fact, one of the most difficult and important lessons a beginner has to learn is how to tame the hawk.

Transitional device: *first* **tells order of process. Paraphrase:** *novice falconer* **means "the beginner." Use of pronoun:** *it* **refers to the hawk.**

The first equipment a novice falconer needs is a set of jesses. (*Jesses* are strips of light but very tough leather that always remain on the hawk's legs.) Leather jesses should be fastened to the legs as soon as possible after capture. A leash or length of leather should then be fastened to the jesses, and finally the end of the leash is fastened to a perch in a dark room. The hawk is kept in a darkened room until it has calmed down and realized that it is not being attacked or hurt.[1]

Writing Practice 8: *Improving Coherence*

Divide a sheet of paper into four columns with the following headings: *Transitional Words, Pronouns, Paraphrases,* and *Repetition.* Then read over your process analysis paper to find examples of each kind of transition and copy these words and phrases into the proper columns on your paper. When you have finished, look over your list to determine whether you have given your reader enough help with coherence. If not, concentrate on increasing the emphasis on coherence as you revise your paper.

---

[1]Adapted from *Falconry Today* by Jack Samson. (Walck, 1976.) Reprinted by permission of the author.

Revising a Process Analysis Essay

The best way to revise a rough draft is to wait at least a day after finishing it. This gives you a new perspective on your composition, and you are more likely to find the places that are unclear. Reading your composition as if you knew nothing about the subject will also help you improve the clarity of your writing.

As you read over your essay, check each sentence and paragraph to be certain that your ideas follow in a sensible order and that you are saying exactly what you mean. When you revise, you smooth out passages and then rewrite your paper as a final draft.

Writing Practice 9: *Revising a Process Analysis Essay*

Use the following checklist to revise your process analysis paper, checking it carefully against each of the points. (Your teacher may wish to read your paper first or may give you additional instructions about revision.) Make changes on your rough draft and then recopy your paper before turning it in. As a final step, proofread your paper using the Proofreader's Checklist at the back of the book.

Checklist for Revising a Process Analysis Essay

1. The topic is sufficiently limited for the length of the paper.

2. The introductory paragraph includes the thesis statement and presents interesting background information about the topic.

3. Each paragraph develops the thesis statement.

4. Each step in the process is clearly and fully explained, using a logical organization.

5. The composition includes sufficient illustrations.

6. The composition makes use of transitions to improve coherence.

7. The conclusion refers to the main idea of the composition by restating it in a new way.

8. The composition has a title that previews the content of the paper.

Writing Examination Essays

Much of what you have already learned about writing expository essays will help you to write good examination essays. Both types of essays require working with a limited topic, developing a thesis statement, and supporting your main idea with illustrations such as examples, quotations, facts, and figures. Successful essay examination writing, however, also depends on your ability to understand each direction exactly, to write directly and thoroughly, and to budget your time properly.

Types of Essay Examinations

Items on essay examinations generally fall into three categories: comparison, trace, and explain. Determining each item's type will help you to organize your ideas.

The purpose of *comparison items* is to test your understanding of the relationship between two aspects of a subject: how they are alike and how they are different from one another.

Comparison items often are given when you are studying two or more historical periods, works of literature, systems, processes, or people. For example, suppose your class has been studying systems of government around the world. A possible question for an essay exam might be "What are the similarities and differences between the U.S. Congress and the British Parliament?" The words *similarities and*

differences are cue words to help you recognize this type of essay. In the following examples, other common cue words are *italicized*.

Tell how the wet tropics and the dry tropics are *alike and different*.

What are the *similarities and differences* between Shakespeare's lovers in the two plays you have read?

What characteristics do animal communication and human language have *in common?*

The purpose of *trace items* is to test your understanding of the interrelating parts of your subject or to test your understanding of how your subject works as a process.

Trace items often follow study of the steps in a process, or a series of events and their outcome. Some trace items are identified by the word *trace*, as in "*Trace* the events leading to the French Revolution." In the following examples cue words for trace items are *italicized*.

List and discuss the steps in the human digestive process.

Review the major steps in assembling a car engine.

Outline what happens during photosynthesis.

Enumerate and discuss the accomplishments made during the reign of Julius Caesar.

The purpose of *explain items* is to test your ability to analyze a subject.

Explain items often are given when you have been studying causes, results, definitions, or interpretations. In an explain item you are instructed to give information to explain the reason or cause of your subject, the results of your subject, the definition of a relevant word or phrase, or interpretations of the meaning of your subject.

The most frequently used words in explain items are *explain* and *discuss*. Other similar words that you can look for are *describe, tell, analyze, interpret, criticize,* and *define*. In the following examples of explain items, the cue words are *italicized*.

Describe the effects of PCB on water in the United States.

Discuss the major dangers to human health caused by smoking.

Analyze the importance of the blockades during the Civil War.

Define the word <u>metaphor</u> and give an *interpretation* of the central metaphor in the following poem.

121

Writing Practice 10: *Categorizing Essay Questions*

The following sample essay directions fall into the categories of comparison, trace, or explain items. Number a sheet of paper and write the correct category after each direction or question number. First study the following example.

> a. Compare the major scientific predictions of Leonardo da Vinci with those of H. G. Wells.
>
> comparison

1. Outline the process involved in the formation of a volcano.
2. In what ways are bee and ant colonies like human social structures? In what ways are they different?
3. What is hyperventilation and how does it affect the body?
4. Discuss the importance of the "Underground Railroad" during the Civil War.
5. Trace the development and formation of the State of Israel.
6. Tell what characteristics the writing styles of William Faulkner and Ken Kesey have in common.
7. Discuss three groups that tried to form utopian societies.
8. List and discuss the steps by which members of the electoral college are elected in this state.

Planning Your Writing Time

One of the biggest problems students face in taking exams is budgeting time. Three steps will help you avoid this problem.

First, allow time to preview the entire examination. Read through all the directions and items before you begin writing, so that you know the kinds of items on the exam and which ones you can answer readily. Write the answers to items you are sure of first, to get full credit for what you know; leave the more difficult questions until later. For a one-hour exam you should allow five minutes for previewing the items.

Second, budget time for each question. To ensure enough time to finish the exam, make a rough estimate of the amount of time you can spend on each item. If your examination is an hour long and you need to answer three items, budget five minutes for previewing, five minutes at the end for reviewing your answers, and a little over fifteen minutes for each item. If your teacher assigns point values for each item, take the points into consideration when budgeting your time. For example, if the first two items are worth twenty-five points and the final item is worth fifty points, you know that you should budget twice as much time for writing the final item as you did for the first two.

Write the exact time you should begin answering each item. If you find yourself falling behind schedule, you may want to leave an item and go on to the next one in order to finish. If you do not finish an item, leave sufficient blank space between it and the next one, so that you can go back during the reviewing period to complete it.

Third, allow time to review and check your answers. Always leave a short amount of time at the end of the exam to reread your answers, checking to be certain that you have answered each item thoroughly and that you have made no errors in grammar, punctuation, or spelling. Often you will be writing quickly, and it is easy to leave out words or make other careless mistakes. For a one-hour exam allow about five minutes for this checking procedure.

Reading Directions

Be sure to read all directions carefully and completely before you begin writing an essay.

Directions for each item often contain important cue words that tell you how to organize your answer. In the following sample examination directions, the notes in the left-hand margin explain the specific items of the exam.

1. Fact about playwrights	1 Unlike the novelist, the writer of a play seldom uses a narrator's voice to talk directly to the audience and guide their
2. Cue word	2 responses to characters and actions. *Select* a play you have read
3. Direction and cue	3 this year and *write an essay* explaining how the playwright guides the audience's emotions to the central characters and
4. Content and organization	4 action. You might consider such techniques by the playwright as using similar or contrasting characters, the effect of setting on the audience, and the characters' responses to each other.
5. Direction **6. Direction**	5 6 *Give examples* from the play you select. *Do not give* a plot summary.

The preceding examination has four separate instructions: (1) select a play you have read this year, (2) write an essay of explanation, (3) give examples from the play, and (4) do not give a plot summary of the play. You must understand each of these instructions in order to write a good essay in response.

Examination items also indicate the range of information you can cover in your essay. Careful reading will tell you how to limit each answer. For example, the preceding examination limits the scope of your essay to one play that you have read during the year. You may not discuss more than one play, and you may not discuss a play you read two years ago. Because careful reading of directions is so important, never skim over them to save time. Read all directions thoroughly. If your teacher permits, underline the cue words and the specific instructions for easy reference.

Writing Practice 11: *Identifying Instructions*

Each of the following examinations contains several instructions. On a separate sheet of paper, list the separate directions in each. Also, identify any cue words you find. First, study the example.

> a. From your readings on Mayan civilization, choose one aspect of Mayan culture that interests you and write an essay telling why you feel it was important. Write at least three paragraphs on this subject. Do not make a list of accomplishments of the civilization.
>
> Choose one aspect of Mayan culture. (direction)
> Write an essay of explanation. (direction)
> Telling why (cue words)
> Write at least three paragraphs. (direction)
> Do not make a list of accomplishments. (direction)

1. In many countries farmers have successfully used crop rotation to help the quality of the land. From your readings select two examples of successful crop rotation and write an essay analyzing why they were successful. Include information explaining why each particular crop was chosen to rotate with the other.

2. Democracy, government by the people, originated in ancient Greece and flourished in the city-state of Athens. There are many differences, however, between Athenian democracy and today's Western democracy. Write an essay comparing Athenian democracy and Western democracy. Include the making of laws and the voting system in your points of comparison.

Organizing Your Essay Examination

Organizing your thoughts before you begin to write is essential for essay examinations.

First, jot down key words or phrases that occur to you as you read each examination item during the previewing period. You can write your ideas in the margins of the examination sheet or on a piece of scratch paper, if one is allowed. These ideas will serve as an idea bank to help you get started on the answer.

Second, write a very brief outline for each question if time allows. You do not want to waste valuable writing time making a complete outline, but a rough idea of what point to begin with, what examples to use, and what sequence to write in will help make your answer complete and coherent.

Third, write the most important information in the opening sentences or opening paragraph, if it is a longer essay. An essay exam answer is different from an essay you write over an extended period of time. Essay answers should get directly to the point, answer the item in clear and concise language, and be brief but complete.

Unless your directions instruct otherwise, you do not need to write an introduction to your essay. You may focus attention on the topic by repeating a word or phrase from the exam directions in your opening statement or by referring directly to the topic by name. For example, read the following sample essay item.

> List three important changes in the game of baseball since 1950. Explain the effects of each change.

Notice how in the first sentence of the following response, the writer repeats a key phrase in the item and introduces the information sought.

> Since 1950 baseball has doubled the number of its teams, gone to a more lively ball to increase distance, and admitted the unionization of baseball players.

125

Getting directly to the point in an exam essay serves two purposes. First, if for some reason you are unable to finish the essay, you have at least indicated that you know part of the answer. Second, giving the three changes makes a kind of outline for the essay: you can discuss the changes in the order that you have first given them.

After you have made your main point in the opening sentence, continue by developing your ideas and supporting them with illustrations, such as details, examples, quotations, facts, and figures.

Model: *An Essay Exam*

The following sample essay answer shows how to focus on the most important information first and then discuss it in detail. As you read, follow the notes in the margin.

Instructions: Identify and explain the social structure of Europe during the Middle Ages.

First sentence makes main point; second sentence explains feudal system.

Example of king's rights and duties

Definition of *fiefdom*
Definition of *vassal*
Example of vassals' rights and duties

Definition of *bound*

Example of peasants' rights and duties

Concluding statement

The feudal system was the social structure of Europe during the Middle Ages. The system has been described as a pyramid, with a broad base of peasants at the bottom, several levels of nobility in the middle, and the king at the top. In a feudal society all members had certain rights and duties connected with those rights. The king, to begin with, was lord of the entire realm and owned all the land. His duties included protecting all of those who served his kingdom. Since he couldn't rule everywhere at once, the king divided his realm into parcels of land called fiefdoms, each controlled by a vassal in chief. Vassals were nobles who were tenants of the king. In return for their land, they owed the king a share of their crops, taxes, military service, and above all, their loyalty. The chiefs of the fiefdoms in turn divided their lands and responsibilities among lesser noblemen, down to the lowest knights in the hierarchy. The knights parceled out the actual farming to the peasants who were bound to the land. Being bound meant that the peasants could not leave the land to find a better place; their duty was to their lord. It was their right, though, to have the protection of their lord, who was responsible for them. Because of the duties and privileges of each group, the feudal system was a strong, interlaced social structure.

Writing Practice 12: *Writing Opening Sentences*

On a separate sheet of paper, write two opening sentences for one or more of the following essay examinations. Include the main information you would use for the essay in the opening sentence and try to repeat some of the phrases from the item. Save your sentences for the next assignment.

1. Many of the changes in the sport of football over the last thirty years have been highly controversial. Select three of these changes and write an essay explaining their effects on the game.

2. Television's effect on reading and studying habits among young people is a much-debated subject. Using your personal experience or the experiences of your friends, write an essay analyzing television's impact. Make clear whether you believe the effect has been positive or negative.

3. A stereotyped view of men is that they are always supposed to be strong, silent types who do not express much emotion and who are more concerned with action than thought. Draw on your knowledge of characters in fiction, movies, on television, or in history and write an essay about one man who does not fall into this stereotype. Use examples to tell why this person does not fit the stereotyped model.

4. "Honesty is the best policy" is a saying people like to repeat. Is the saying always true? Write an essay giving your opinion about the value of being completely honest in every situation.

5. Mark Twain once said, "Everyone complains about the weather, but no one does anything about it." The same is often true of the future. Many people are concerned about what the future will bring but are uncertain of what to do about it. Write an essay comparing how you feel about the future with how your parents (or one of your friends/siblings/teachers) feel about the future. Write not only about your personal future but also about the future in general of this country and of this planet.

Writing the Comparison-and-Contrast Essay

In a comparison-and-contrast examination you will find at least two items to liken and contrast: two people, events, attitudes, and so on. To write an effective response you should define or identify both items in your essay. For example, if you are comparing common law with Napoleonic law, you should define both of your terms at the beginning of the essay. If the terms cannot be defined in a simple sentence, give examples and details to describe them.

Next, it is important to decide on the points of comparison. Ask yourself how the items are alike and how they are different. Decide before you begin writing whether you will use a point-by-point comparison or a block comparison in your essay.

Writing the Trace Essay

In responding to a trace item, you should first be sure of its scope. For example, if the directions cover only the time period of the Boxer

Rebellion in China, do not write about the years before or after this period. To go outside the boundaries set by the exam detracts from your concentration on your response and in some cases can result in a wrong answer.

Next, be certain to define any terms that are important to your essay. Sometimes the instructions specify a definition; however, if you are using a key term or an unusual term, you should define it even if you are not instructed to do so. Do not waste your time defining commonly accepted terms unless the definition is in some way relevant to your essay. For example, in writing about the electoral college, you would not need to make a complete definition of the word *democracy*. You would need to define it, however, if you were writing about the origin of the Democratic party.

Finally, trace examinations usually ask you to follow a sequence of some kind. As you think through your response or write your brief outline, be certain that you keep the steps or the chain of events in their proper order.

Writing the Explain Essay

Since there is a wide range of explain instructions, first be certain that you spot the cue word in the exam so that you follow the instructions exactly. If you are asked to define a term and give an example, do just that. Do not compare it with another term or explain its history. Staying focused on the exact directions is essential to writing a good essay answer.

Some explain items may be long and complex, requiring careful reading and interpretation on your part. The instructions may direct you to do several things in your response. Allow yourself enough time to organize your thoughts so that you cover all parts of the directions. The following is an example of a complex explain item.

> Several kinds of ''escape'' literature have become extremely popular in the twentieth century. Discuss one type of escape literature that is currently popular, name at least one writer who does that kind of writing, and describe briefly his or her work. Finally, account briefly for the popularity of escape literature in the twentieth century.

The item directs you to do four things:

1. *Discuss one type of escape literature that is currently popular.*
   Name one type of escape literature, describe it, and explain what it is like.

2. *Name at least one writer who does that kind of writing.*
   When *at least* appears in a question, you know that you are not required to give more than one example. If there is time to write about more than one, you can do so, or you can add another example at the end of the examination during the review time.

3. *Describe briefly his or her work.*
The cue word *describe* tells you to give characteristic details and examples of the writer's work. *Briefly* tells you to summarize the most important points and not try to write everything you know about the subject.

4. *Account briefly for the popularity of escape literature in the twentieth century.*
This statement asks you to make a judgment and to give reasons why the literature is popular. Base your response not only on your personal opinion but also on reasons discussed in class and on reasons from the reading you have done on the subject.

In beginning the explain essay, you should define or identify any key terms. For the preceding exam you should include a brief definition of escape literature in your opening statement.

Writing Assignment III: *An Essay Examination*

Using the essay items listed in Writing Practice 12 or a question your teacher assigns, write an essay response.

A. Prewriting

Preview the exam, noting questions, cue words, and directions. Allow time for each question plus five minutes for review at the end. Write a brief, informal outline of notes for each question.

B. Writing

As you write each answer, keep to your schedule. Include the most important information in the first sentences of each answer. Then use transitions, pronouns, and careful repetition to clarify relationships between sentences and between ideas.

C. Postwriting

Use one of the checklists that follow to review your work. Make legible changes in your first draft. Finally, read your revised draft for correct grammar, mechanics, and spelling using the Proofreader's Checklist at the back of the book.

The Comparison-and-Contrast Essay

1. The terms are defined clearly and completely and adequately described with examples and details. Similarities and differences are noted and compared.

2. Illustrations (such as details, examples, facts, and figures) are used to support the essay.

3. The essay stays within the limits of the directions.

The Trace Essay

1. The response stays within the scope of the instructions; the directions are followed exactly.

2. The terms are defined clearly and completely.

3. The ideas are presented in a chronological order.

4. Illustrations (such as examples, details, facts, and figures) are used to support the essay.

The Explain Essay

1. The instructions are thoroughly followed in the order given.

2. All the key terms are defined or identified.

3. The response is supported with sufficient illustrations to make the point clear.

Sentence Combining:
Inserting Modifiers

Inserting Modifiers

For information on adjectives and adverbs, see pages 396-435.

When one word describes another word, it *modifies* that word and is called a *modifier.*

Inserting *modifiers* from one sentence into another sentence allows a writer to produce interesting, economical writing. The modifer *interesting* in the following example has been inserted into the first sentence, called the *base sentence.*

Base Sentence: The lecture included a slide presentation and music.

Insert: The lecture was interesting.

Combined: The *interesting* lecture included a slide presentation and music.

Since the word *interesting* modifies (or describes) the same lecture mentioned in the base sentence, the modifier can be inserted without altering the writer's meaning. The new sentence, consequently, is a more interesting and more economical version of the original sentences.

Any number of modifiers can be inserted into the base sentence, as the following example shows.

Base Sentence: The person has an attitude.

Insert: The person is successful.
The attitude is positive. (,)
The attitude is calm.

Combined: The *successful* person has a *calm, positive* attitude.
or
The *successful* person has a *positive, calm* attitude.

Successful modifies *person; positive* and *calm* both describe *attitude.* (Notice that the modifiers *positive* and *calm* can be interchanged.)

The signals you will use in this lesson indicate the correct punctuation for sentences that have modifiers. The signal (,) means a comma should be placed *before* the modifier when it is inserted into the base sentence. The signal (*and*) means that this word should be included *before* the modifier. Use a comma plus *and* before the modifier when you see the signal (*,and*).

Exercise 1: *Inserting Modifiers*

Combine the following sets of sentences by inserting modifiers. Consider the first sentence the base sentence and use the signals in parentheses. Where there are no signals, decide whether you need to use both commas and *and*. Study the examples carefully.

Examples

a. The boy ran into the house to escape the rain.
   The boy was sneezing.
   The boy was sniffling. (,)
   The house was warm.
   The rain was cold.
   The rain was wet. (,)
   The sneezing, sniffling boy ran into the warm house to escape the cold, wet rain.

b. The police lieutenant awoke refreshed from her nap.
   The lieutenant was overworked.
   The nap was short.
   The nap was well-deserved.
   The overworked police lieutenant awoke refreshed from her short, well-deserved nap.

1. The child gazed out the window, watching the people in the street.
   She was bored.
   She was restless. (*and*)
   The window was open.
   The people were busy.
   The street was crowded.
   The street was noisy. (,)

2. Mrs. Cohen searched in all the drawers of her desk to find the lost bill.
   The drawers were messy.
   The drawers were disorganized. (,)
   Her desk was a roll-top.
   The bill was for the telephone.

3. The coyote howled with a cry in the distance.
   The coyote was solitary.
   The coyote was young. (,)
   The cry was strange.
   The cry was mournful. (*and*)
   The distance was dark.

4. The guitar was ready for the concert at the park.
   The guitar was tuned.
   The guitar was repaired. (*and*)
   The guitar was electric.
   It was an outdoor concert.
   It was a municipal park.

5. Sitting in the car, Sergio watched the rain fall against the windows and shook his head, wondering why he hadn't replaced the battery.
   The car was stranded.
   The rain was heavy.
   The rain was beating. (,)
   The battery was old.
   The battery was run-down. (,)

6. When the Bengal tiger disappeared from the cage, the audience applauded the magician's trick.
   The tiger was frightening.
   The cage was locked.
   The cage was iron.
   The audience was amazed.
   The magician was young.
   The trick was incredible.

7. Their money was hidden in the garage above a beam.
   The garage was detached.
   The beam was wooden.

8. Celia installed a stereo and a radio in her car.
   The radio was am-fm.
   Her car was sporty.
   Her car was new.

9. The surfer caught the wave, her body riding with the force of the ocean.
   The surfer was alert.
   The surfer was eager.
   The wave was thrilling.
   Her body was graceful.
   The force was tremendous.

10. The man made a wish on the object, aware of the danger but hoping for the best.
The man was anxious.
The man was greedy.
The object was mysterious.
The object was small.
The danger was possible.

Inserting Phrases as Modifiers

For more information on phrases, see pages 512-531.

A *phrase modifier*, a string of words (with no subject and no verb) that acts as an adjective or adverb, provides more specific information and can also be inserted into a base sentence.

As the following examples show, the phrases are attached as closely as possible to the word or words they modify in the base sentence. In these examples, underlining acts as a new signal to show you which words to insert into the base sentence.

Base Sentence: The crowd enjoyed the refreshments that were served.

Insert: The refreshments were in the lobby.

The refreshments were enjoyed during intermission.

Combined: The crowd enjoyed the refreshments that were served *in the lobby during intermission.*

Base Sentence: Mrs. Ortega jogged and then left.

Insert: She jogged early in the morning.

She jogged on the quiet streets.

She left quite punctually.

She left at 8:00.

She left for work.

Combined: Mrs. Ortega jogged *early in the morning on the quiet streets* and then left *quite punctually at 8:00 for work.*
or
Early in the morning on the quiet streets, Mrs. Ortega jogged and then left *quite punctually at 8:00 for work.*
but not
Quite punctually, Mrs. Ortega jogged *early in the morning on the quiet streets* and then left *for work at 8:00.*

As the preceding example illustrates, phrase modifiers can be inserted at different places in the base sentence as long as they are still clearly attached to the words they modify. *Quite punctually* cannot be moved to the beginning of the sentence because this phrase tells when Mrs. Ortega left for work, not when she jogged.

Phrase modifiers often begin with prepositions—words such as those listed here:

above	at	between	near	to
across	before	beyond	on	toward
after	behind	by	over	under
against	below	down	past	underneath
along	beneath	during	through	until
among	beside	in	throughout	up

Exercise 2: Inserting Phrases as Modifiers

In the first five sentences on the next page insert the underlined phrases into the base sentence (the first sentence in each set). The last five sentences have no underlining clues. For these sentences decide what phrases can be added to the base sentence, using all the information that is given. Study the following examples; then write each combined sentence on a sheet of paper. Remember that some phrases may be inserted at different places for variety.

Examples

a. The athlete ran swiftly.

He ran at the sound of the gun.

He ran toward the finish line.

He was in the Number 10 jersey.

The athlete in the Number 10 jersey ran swiftly toward the finish line at the sound of the gun.

or

At the sound of the gun, the athlete in the Number 10 jersey ran swiftly toward the finish line.

Long introductory phrases are often followed by a comma when they precede the subject of the sentence.

b. You could clearly see a figure jogging.

The figure was on the top of the distant bluff.

The jogging was alongside a dog.

It was a dog with pointed ears.

You could clearly see a figure on top of the distant bluff, jogging alongside a dog with pointed ears.

1. He posted the announcement.
   The announcement was of the high school play.

   He posted it on the bulletin board.

   He posted it above the testing schedule.

2. Jesse agreed to run.
   His agreement was against his better judgment.

   The running was for student council.

   The running would be against the most popular girl.

   The girl was in the class.

3. He stood, singing.
   He was singing very noisily.

   He was in the shower.

   He was under the beating water.

4. The teen dashed after the little girl who was unaware.
   The teen dashed without regard for his own welfare.

   The teen dashed into the street.

   She was unaware of the approaching truck.

   The truck was behind her.

5. Juan and Rosa were opposites, but they admired each other for
   many traits.
   They were opposites in tastes.

   They were opposites in upbringing. (,)

   They were opposites in values. (,and)

   They admired in secret.

   They admired from a distance.

6. She sat watching the players kicking the ball and wondered.
   She was without the slightest desire to participate.
   The players were in their striped shirts and solid shorts.
   They were kicking the ball down the muddy field.
   She wondered at their serious obsession.
   The obsession was with the game.

7. He grew tired of waiting.
   He grew tired toward the end of the day.
   He was waiting for her call.
   He was like a lonely mutt.
   The mutt was without a master.

8. Eric and Coleen practice their skating routines.
   They practice for weeks.
   They practice before every competition.
   They practice with great care.
   They practice in the rink.
   The rink is near their hometowns.

9. Chichén Itzá is the site.
   The site is of ancient pyramids, an observatory, and a ballpark that were built.
   They were built by the Mayans.
   They were built over 2,000 years ago.
   They were built in the Yucatán Peninsula of Mexico.

10. Mr. Jones counted his money while his eyes feasted.
    He counted it after each workday.
    He counted it into stacks.
    The stacks were of coins.
    The stacks were across the table.
    The feast was on the gold and silver.
    The gold and silver were before him.

Writing Practice: *Revising an Expository Essay*

Reread one of the expository essays you have completed and re-examine the sentence patterns you used. Select several sentences that could be improved by using any of the sentence combining methods you have learned. Join sentences that are too short; divide sentences that are too long; insert phrases and modifiers where appropriate.

137

5 Research Writing

Writing a Research Paper

The *research*, or *term*, *paper* is a long, formal essay presenting specific information drawn from several sources.

Writing a research paper involves the same skills used in writing an expository essay but also requires using library resources and identifying those sources in parenthetical documentation and a bibliography. Some research papers simply bring together the existing information on the topic in an organized way. Others answer a specific question or draw conclusions.

Preparing a research paper requires thorough planning and careful work. In this chapter you will learn to follow each step in the research process: choosing and limiting a topic, finding and evaluating sources of information, taking notes, making an outline, writing a rough draft with parenthetical documentation, and preparing the final draft with a bibliography. Your research paper will be easier to write and more effective if you follow the procedure outlined in this chapter.

Choosing and Limiting a Topic

Once you have decided on an interesting subject, limit it to a topic that is neither too general nor too specific. Your topic should be broad enough to include interesting information and narrow enough so that you can discuss it in depth. If your teacher suggests a certain length for the assignment, that suggestion will also influence how you narrow the topic.

One way to decide whether your topic is adequately limited is to check your library's resources. If you find whole books written on your topic, it is probably too general; on the other hand, if you find very little information on the topic, it may be too limited. If your topic covers many years (the history of American film, for example) or many categories or groups (religions of the world), it is probably too general for a research paper.

Suppose you are interested in almost everything connected with motion pictures. You probably already realize that the history of

motion pictures or even a history of motion pictures before World War II is too broad a topic, so you decide to focus on the silent film period. However, an hour in the library convinces you that this topic is still too general. After looking at the books and articles that most interest you, you decide to focus on a particular event—the change from silent movies to sound.

Writing Practice 1: *From Subject to Limited Topic*

Divide a sheet of paper into two columns with the headings *Subjects* and *Limited Topics*. Use brainstorming to discover general subjects that interest you and list them in the first column. In the second column write five limited topics, developed from the subjects in the first column, for a short research paper.

Getting an Overview

When you have decided on your topic, the next step is to get an overview, or general idea, of what is involved in that topic. If you have decided to discuss the transition from silent movies to sound, for example, you could check the entries under *sound* and *motion pictures* in several encyclopedias for an overview. You could also look through books with general information about movie history. Subject cards in the card catalogue, the *Readers' Guide*, and encyclopedias are also good places to find background information on your topic.

Writing Practice 2: *Getting an Overview*

For information on reference books, see pages 636-647.

Choose the topic from Writing Practice 1 that you would most like to research. Using the card catalogue in your library and the *Readers' Guide to Periodical Literature*, find two or more books and two or more articles with information about the topic you have selected. Write the titles of the books and articles, the name and dates of the magazines where the articles appear, and the names of the authors. If you cannot locate enough sources, think about how the topic can be broadened.

Developing Basic Questions

After you read enough background information to have a general understanding of your topic, you can then list the basic questions you will try to answer in your paper. This list will help later as you decide what information to put on your note cards. (Using the *Who? What? Where? When? Why?* and *How?* system is one way to gather ideas for questions.) Once you have listed the questions your paper will answer, you may discover new areas that your questions do not cover, or you may find that your topic involves too many questions and must be limited even further.

A preliminary list of basic questions for a research paper on the advent of sound movies might look like the following one:

Why were the earliest movies silent?

Why did it take so long for the first sound motion pictures to appear?

What problems did inventors face in adding sound to moving pictures?

How and when were these problems solved?

Who solved them?

When did the first sound motion picture appear?

Where was the first sound motion picture produced?

How did the silent film industry react to the sound motion picture?

How did sound affect the film industry?

Writing Practice 3: *Developing Basic Questions*

After reading to gain background information, prepare a list of basic questions about your research paper topic or a topic you select for this assignment. The *Who? What? Where? When? Why?* and *How?* system or the Pentad (see Chapter 1) will help you develop ideas for questions. Finally, organize your list of questions as in the preceding example.

Gathering Information

The next step in the research process is to gather information for your paper from books and magazines, personal interviews, pamphlets, and other resources. Chapter 24 will tell you how to locate and use library resources.

The Bibliography Card

Because readers often want to know what books, articles, and pamphlets were used in a writer's research, the writer attaches a list of these sources, called a *bibliography,* at the end of the research paper. As you gather information, note the title, author, place and date of publication, and other necessary information on a *bibliography card.* Having such cards will make it much easier for you to prepare the final bibliography.

Bibliography entries follow a standard form. The form used by most writers and researchers is found in the *MLA Handbook,* published by the Modern Language Association. Although the MLA form is used in this chapter, your teacher may ask you to use one of the many other acceptable forms.

The following bibliography card shows the form for a book; magazines, newspapers, pamphlets, and personal interviews have a slightly different form.

> ①
>
> *Slide, Anthony. Aspects of American Film History Prior to 1920.*
>
> *Metuchen, New Jersey: The Scarecrow Press, Inc., 1978*

The circled number in the upper-left corner of the sample bibliography card identifies Anthony Slide's book as source Number 1. Numbering each source will save time later when you take notes from that source.

Model: Bibliographic Form

The following list, composed of fictitious authors and titles, shows the format for other kinds of bibliography entries. Note that you would use underlining to indicate italics when you write or type a bibliography.

Book by One Author

Fleece, Jason. *Searching for Gold in Aegean Backwaters*. Rome: Myth

Press, 1978.

Book by More Than One Author

Bow, Mary, and John Arrow. *Straight Shooting*. Lansing: University of

Michigan Press, 1983.

Essay Within a Collection of Pieces by Different Authors

Windward, Lee. "Sailing the Open Seas." In *Sailor Beware*. Ed. Travis

Seek and Lindsay Find. New York: Mainsail and Tallship Books,

1984. 6–20.

Edition of a Work of Literature

Austere, Jane. *Gone with the Times*. Ed. Pamela Perfect. London:

Lowe Classics, 1933.

Article in an Encyclopedia or Other Reference Work

Line, Sally. "Eels." *Encyclopedia Animalia*. 1982 ed.

Article from a Monthly Magazine

Manly, Strouther. "Fowl Flight." *Wings, Beaks, and Talons* May 1980:

43-50.

Article from a Newspaper (No Author Given)

"Ninety Percent Voter Turnout." *Athens Gazetteer and Daily Phillipic* 5

Nov. 1980: 37.

Review of a Film, Book, or Play

Knight, Daly. Rev. of *Afternoon of a Morning Person,* by Woolsey

Wakely. *Search.* 12 Jan. 1982: 53.

Interview

Midas, David. Interview. *Worldwide Investment Analysis* 9 March

1980: 6-9.

Radio or Television Program

"Moving Monsters." *Movietime Matinee,* CBS, 23 Jan. 1979.

Pamphlet

United States Cong. House. *Report on Air Disasters.* By J. R.

Daedalus. Washington, D.C.: GPO, 1979.

Writing Practice 4: *Preparing Bibliography Cards*

Using your library's card catalogue and *Readers' Guide*, locate the sources you will use in your research. Prepare a bibliography card for each source. If you are not writing a research paper, select a topic for this assignment and prepare five bibliography cards.

Taking Notes

The next step in the research process is to take notes from the sources you have located. Keep your list of basic questions in mind. When a piece of specific information relates to your questions, record that information on a note card. Avoid taking notes on unrelated information. For example, you may discover intriguing facts about the first movies produced in color, but if your topic is limited to the advent of sound movies, you will not need this information. Skim a book's table of contents and use the index at the back of the book to locate sections or pages related to your topic.

Putting your notes on note cards will make the task of organizing them later much easier. Limit each card to information about one item or idea, so you can arrange these cards later to fit the organization of your outline.

Before you begin to take notes on a card, place the circled bibliography card number for that source in the upper-right corner of the card. For example, if *Birth of the Talkies* is source Number 2, every note card with information from this source should have the circled number 2 in the upper-right corner. Putting this source number on the card saves work; you will not have to list the title of the source on each note card. Under the source number place the page number(s) from which your note is taken. You may also want to put a topic heading in the upper-right corner of the card.

It is important to take notes very carefully. Usually, you will summarize or record information in your own words. You may want to write your notes in phrases or use abbreviations and symbols (& for *and*, for example), but be certain that your notes are complete enough to be understood later. Sometimes, you will want to record an author's exact words because they are important or especially well-chosen. Do this sparingly, however, remembering to quote exactly and to put quotation marks around the author's words. *Plagiarism*, using another's words as your own, is an unfair and illegal practice. If you take notes in your own words and mark quotations, you can avoid plagiarism.

Notice the location of the source number, the page number, the topic heading, and the writer's information presented in the sample note card on the following page.

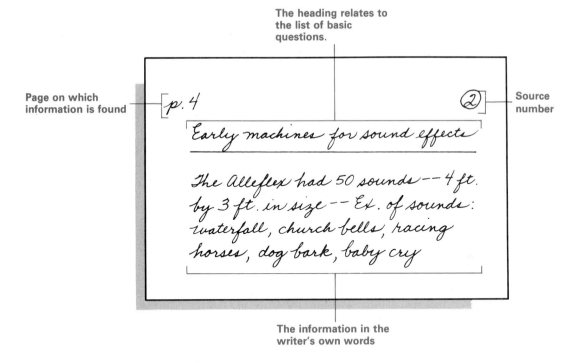

The heading relates to the list of basic questions.

Page on which information is found

p. 4

② Source number

Early machines for sound effects

The Alleflex had 50 sounds -- 4 ft. by 3 ft. in size -- Ex. of sounds: waterfall, church bells, racing horses, dog bark, baby cry

The information in the writer's own words

After taking notes on all your sources, sort the cards into stacks that correspond to your list of questions. Do you have enough information to answer each question adequately? Have you located new information that will require changing some of your basic questions, or have you discovered new questions? This is the time to look up any further information you need.

Writing Practice 5: *Taking Notes*

Using your research paper topic (or another topic you select for this assignment), write note cards on the information you find in at least four sources.

The Thesis Statement

After you have reviewed your basic questions and your research notes, you are ready to formulate the thesis statement of your research paper. The thesis statement is one sentence that clarifies exactly what your paper will cover. For instance, for a paper recounting the transition from silent to sound movies, the thesis statement might be: *Although attempts to link film and sound had begun as early as 1895, the changeover from silent to sound movies took place during the five eventful years between 1925 and 1930.*

This thesis statement presents the limited topic—*the changeover from silent to sound movies*. It also indicates the direction the paper will take—it will trace the history of the changeover.

If your research paper brings together and organizes existing information on your topic, your thesis statement, like the one above, can be a one-sentence summary of that information. If your paper answers a question or draws a conclusion, your thesis statement can be expressed as a one-sentence answer to the question or as a statement of the main point of your research.

Your thesis statement may not always be expressed in the final draft of your research paper. However, it guides you as you organize your formal outline and compose the first draft of your paper.

Writing Practice 6: *Expressing a Thesis Statement*

Review your list of research questions, as well as the note cards you wrote for Writing Practice 5. On the basis of the information you have gathered, decide the main direction your paper will take. Will it trace a history? Explain causes and/or effects? Discuss the parts of a process? Write the thesis statement that identifies your limited topic and clarifies how you will deal with that topic.

The Formal Outline

Once you have reviewed your note cards and sorted them into stacks that correspond to your basic questions, you can prepare a *formal outline.* Because a research paper involves organizing information clearly and logically, an outline that lists the order of the points to be discussed is essential. The formal outline uses Roman numerals (I, II, III), capital letters (A, B, C), and Arabic numerals (1, 2, 3) to show the order, relationship, and relative importance of ideas as the paper is being organized. If additional subcategories are required, lowercase letters (a, b, c) may be used.

An outline in which all the headings are stated as complete sentences is a *sentence outline;* one in which only words and phrases are used as headings is called a *topic outline.* These two forms should not be mixed in the same outline.

The following topic outline is for a research paper on the transition from silent to sound movies:

   I. Sound with early silents
       A. Background music
       B. Special sound effects
       C. Singers and actors

  II. Attempts to link film and sound
       A. Edison's Kinetophone
           1. Problem with synchronization
           2. Problem with amplification
       B. The sound-on-film process
       C. De Forest's work

 III. The reaction of Hollywood
       A. Resistance of most film companies
       B. Warner Brothers
           1. Partnership with Western Electric
           2. Production of *Don Juan*
       C. William Fox
           1. Purchase of Case-Spondable system
           2. Movietone News Service

  IV. Arrival of the "talkies"
       A. Success of *The Jazz Singer*
       B. Problems to surmount
           1. Technicians and equipment
           2. Stationary microphones
           3. Voices of silent film stars

   V. Importance of silent films today

Notice that there are always two or more divisions under a heading (see Roman numerals I–III) or none at all (see Roman numeral V). The divisions (or subheadings) show how a broad point is subdivided into smaller parts; when a point cannot be divided into two or more parts, there is no reason for a subheading.

Compare the first part of the following outline in sentence form to the preceding topic outline.

I. The early silent films were accompanied with sound.
   A. Organs and pianos were used in the background.
   B. Stagehands created special effects.
   C. Singers performed songs, and actors spoke dialogue.

Writing Practice 7: *Making a Formal Outline*

Using the information you have gathered on note cards, write either a formal sentence outline or a topic outline for a research paper on the topic you have selected. Let the thesis statement you developed for Writing Practice 6 guide you in organizing your outline.

The Rough Draft

The next step is to write a rough, or first, draft of the research paper, using your formal outline and note cards. The term *rough* indicates that this draft will not be a perfect, final product; most writers focus on putting their ideas into clear, well-organized sentences and paragraphs at this stage. Later, in the final draft, they concentrate more closely on spelling, punctuation, and grammar.

Begin by organizing your note cards to correspond with your outline. A research paper is a longer essay; so remember or review the paragraph—and essay—writing skills you have studied. You may find that some of your notes do not fit the final organization of your paper or that you need more details to develop your topic. Do not be afraid to omit or add information to improve the quality of your paper.

Two important parts of writing a rough draft are incorporating quoted material and adding parenthetical documentation.

Using Quotations

If you plan to use an author's exact words in your research paper, you will need to know the procedures for placing quotations. Long quotations, which consist of more than three lines of poetry or four lines of prose, are separated from the body of the paper. A short statement followed by a colon usually introduces the long quotation, and the quotation is then indented ten spaces from the left-hand margin. Because this special form indicates that the passage is a quotation, the quotation marks at the beginning and end of the passage are omitted.

Model: *Using Long Quotations*

The following example, part of the paper "Sound Comes to the Movies," shows how to introduce and indent a long quotation.

> Meanwhile, other scientists were experimenting with a different method of linking sound with film: the sound-on-film process, in which electrical currents are used to capture the sound directly on photographic film. Frederic Thrasher, author of *Okay for Sound,* provides the following explanation of the process:
>
>> When the sound is reproduced, a photoelectric cell is used to convert the variations in the light beam as it passes through the "sound track" of the moving film, into electrical currents which in turn are changed into sound at the loudspeakers. (7)

Short quotations of fewer than five lines are not indented; quotation marks at the beginning and end of such passages indicate that the words are a quotation. A short quotation should fit smoothly into the sentence or paragraph to which it is added, as the following examples show.

> Millions identified with such silent stars as Charlie Chaplin, "the bum who wanted above all else to attain human dignity" (Manchel, When Pictures 39), and Mary Pickford, "America's sweetheart."

Adding Parenthetical Documentation

Documentation is a reference to your source. *Parenthetical documentation* tells readers where they can locate the sources of important information or exact quotations used in the paper. Any material you have quoted exactly must be documented to give the author credit. Unusual facts or ideas developed by a particular author are also documented, since these are the products of that author's research or original thinking. However, when several sources mention the same facts or ideas, the information is considered general knowledge and does not require a parenthetical reference.

As you write your rough draft, include each parenthetical reference immediately after material to which it applies.

The model shows how parenthetical documentation appears in a finished research paper. Notice the following features of parenthetical documentation as you examine the model form below and the model research report on pages 152-159.

1. Parenthetical references are brief, usually containing only the author's last name and the specific page number or numbers from which a quotation or information was taken. Documentation gives only as much information as is necessary for the reader to locate the source in your bibliography. Keep in mind, then, that any source you document in the text of your report must be included in your bibliography.

2. Each reference is enclosed in parentheses.

3. No comma follows the author's last name, and the page number is not identified by the word *page* or an abbreviation (*p.* or *pp.*). Where the title is needed to specify a work by a particular author, a comma separates the name and the title; again, no comma precedes the page number. If a title only (no author's name) is used, no comma separates the title and page number.

4. A title in parenthetical documentation may be shortened, using the main or key word or words, with articles (*the, a, an*) left out. Include the word under which the source is alphabetized in your bibliography.

5. Parenthetical documentation appears in the text of your report, either at the end of a sentence or where a pause occurs in the sentence, and is *followed* by sentence punctuation (comma, period, etc.). If your parenthetical reference follows a quotation, it comes after the end quotation mark but before the sentence punctuation. When a reference is made at the end of an indented quotation, it comes after the last period or other end punctuation.

Model: *Parenthetical Documentation*

These sample parenthetical references show the MLA form for various sources; your teacher may ask you to use this form or another accepted form of documentation.

The word *source* below refers to any text listed in your bibliography: a book, magazine article, or the like. Notice that quotation marks enclose the titles of magazine or newspaper articles or any shorter work that is part of a longer work (an essay that appears in an anthology, for example). Titles of books are underlined.

Source by One Author—only one source by this author listed in bibliography

(Fleece 2)

Source by More Than One Author—only one source by these authors listed in bibliography

(Kagan and Jones 16-22)

Source When More Than One Title by the Same Author or Authors Appears in Bibliography

(Fleece, Searching for Gold 2)

(Kagan and Jones, "Traveling by Jet" 16-22)

Article from a Daily Newspaper When Author Is Given (Note that the letter of the newspaper section precedes the page number.)

(Smith A12)

Magazine or Newspaper Article for Which No Author Is Given

("Lifesavers" 28)

("Ninety Percent Voter Turnout" C7)

When the Author's Name is Used in the Text of the Report (*According to Fleece* . . . or *Smith says,* . . . etc.)

(2)

(12)

When Referring to an Entire Source Rather Than a Specific Page

(Windward)

Interview (Use the last name of the person interviewed under which the interview is listed in your bibliography.)

(Midas)

Radio or Television Program (Use the title under which the program is listed in your bibliography.)

("Moving Monsters")

Model: A Research Report

As you read the following research report, notice the form as well as the content.

Sound Comes to the Movies

"Silent" movies, popular from the early 1900s to about 1930, were never really silent. Audiences usually enjoyed background music, often provided by a theater organ or ragtime piano, as they watched the action on the screen. At appropriate times the sounds of thunder, waterfalls, or stampeding horses were created from the orchestra pit by hidden stagehands, who rattled, scraped, and banged all sorts of objects together. Sometimes, singers performed a song written especially for the movie, or actors toured with the film to speak portions of the dialogue. None of these sounds, however, came from the film itself; for this reason, the films were called "silents."

The idea of talking movies was an old one. In 1877, Thomas Edison showed his new talking machine, the phonograph, to a group of reporters. One was so impressed that he made the following predictions in the <u>Scientific American</u>:

Indent long quotations
ten spaces from
left-hand margin.

> It is already possible by ingenious optical contrivances to throw stereoscopic photographs of people on the screen in full view of the audience. Add the talking phonograph to counterfeit their voices, and it would be difficult to carry the illusion of real presence much further. (Geldud 9)

This "illusion of real presence" was to be the goal of scientists and inventors for the next fifty years. Before actors on the screen would actually speak to the audience, however, a way to link film and sound had to be found. In 1895, Thomas Edison made one of the first attempts to do so with a machine called a "Kinetophone." The Kinetophone connected Edison's phonograph with another machine that projected film for one person—a kind of peep show. However, this experiment did not result in sound's coming to the movies for two reasons. In the first place, Edison was unable to synchronize, or match, the film with the sound. Also, he failed to develop a means to amplify, or increase, the sound, so that it could be heard by a larger audience. Discouraged, Edison abandoned his Kinetophone project in 1913 (Manchel, When Movies 2–3).

Meanwhile, other scientists were experimenting with a different method of linking sound with film: the sound-on-film process, in which electrical currents are used to capture the sound directly on photographic film. Frederick Thrasher, author of Okay

153

for Sound, provides an explanation of the process:

> When the sound is reproduced, a
> photoelectric cell is used to convert the
> variations in the light beam as it passes
> through the "sound track" of the moving
> film, into electrical currents which in
> turn are changed into sound at the
> loudspeakers (7).

Although inventors would continue to experiment with separate sound and film devices, the sound-on-film process proved more successful. Because the sound was captured directly on the film, the process eliminated one major obstacle to talking motion pictures—that of synchronization.

The other great obstacle—that of amplifying sound—was surmounted by an inventor named Lee De Forest in 1907. Often called "the father of radio," De Forest invented an amplifier tube that allowed sound to be made sufficiently loud for a large audience. De Forest also worked from 1912 to 1922 to perfect the sound-on-film process and in 1921

exhibited a movie of himself talking. Although he
went on to film stage musicals and even introduced
the first sound newsreel in 1924, he was unable to
gain the attention of the major film companies.
(Geldud 98–99)

By 1924, silent films were enjoying wide success
as millions of movie-goers the world over enjoyed
films with such popular silent stars as Charlie
Chaplin, "the bum who wanted above all else to attain
human dignity" (Manchel, When Pictures 39), and
Mary Pickford, "America's Sweetheart." The major film
companies, riding the wave of success, had invested
heavily in stockpiles of new equipment and large
inventories for production of silent films. These men,
many of whom had made huge fortunes in the silent
film industry, were unwilling to risk it all on an
experiment that had not even developed a completely
reliable technology. Thus, most of the major film
producers remained unimpressed with the technological
marvel of the sound-on-film process.

Incorporate short
quotations into text.

One film company, however, was far from successful. In 1925, Warner Brothers, on the verge of bankruptcy, formed a partnership with Western Electric, which now owned the rights to De Forest's amplifier tube. This partnership gave Warner Brothers the right to use a sound-on-film process called "Vitaphone" and thus to produce sound movies (Manchel, When Movies 5–7). Using this system, the company produced their first sound film, Don Juan, which was first shown at Broadway's Warner Theater on August 6, 1926. In the history of film, however, Don Juan is not considered the first "talkie" because its sound consisted only of music, nor did it attract much interest or much of an audience. The era of the "talkie" had not yet arrived (Walker 26).

Meanwhile, another important technological

advance had been made that was to help bring sound to films. Working from an idea of De Forest's, Theodore W. Case and Earl I. Spondable developed an attachment that allowed sound films to be shown on silent projectors, thus eliminating the need for heavy investment in new equipment. The movie mogul William Fox purchased the Case-Spondable sound-on-film process and used it in the development of Movietone News Service. From their beginning in January of 1927, the Movietone Newsreels were enormously popular. Audiences were amazed to see and hear celebrities such as Charles Lindbergh, who was filmed taking off on his famous trans-Atlantic flight. Sound had come to newsreels, but not yet to the movies (Manchel, When Movies 7).

Undeterred by the mild reception of Don Juan, Sam Warner had gone on in 1926 to make a sound film called The Jazz Singer, based on the popular Broadway musical about a son who wanted to become a jazz singer against his father's wishes. The film was a huge success for three reasons: the appeal of the show's star, Al Jolson; the three songs sung by Jolson; and nine words of dialogue spoken by Jolson. These nine words—"You ain't heard nothin' yet, folks. Listen to this!"—marked the end of the silent film era (Manchel, When Movies 10).

The success of The Jazz Singer saved Warner Brothers and convinced other major movie producers to investigate and invest in sound movie systems, but many problems remained. Finding capable technicians and installing sound equipment in studios were the

157

least of them. Noisy cameras had to be placed in special soundproof booths called "ice boxes," from which more than one cameraman was pulled just in time to prevent suffocation (Manchel, <u>When Movies</u> 13). For a while, the concept of the moving camera disappeared. Movement on the screen became slow and artificial; actors were weighted down with concealed microphones or forced to stand awkwardly in front of microphones hidden in flowerpots or behind large objects. Many silent film stars had to be trained to use their voices, and despite the voice coaches rushed to Hollywood, more than one film star failed to make the transition.

New technological developments gradually improved both the sound quality of films and the mobility of cameras, and by 1931, film companies had moved to the sound-on-film process used in the industry today (Fredricks). Although the great era of silent films ended over fifty years ago, the artistry of the first silent stars, the directors, and camera operators continues to influence each new generation of filmmakers. And for the millions of fans all over the world who continue to watch their favorite "silents" at movie revival houses and on late-night television, the Golden Age of the silent film has never really ended.

Bibliography

Fielding, Raymond, ed. <u>A Technological History of Motion Pictures and Television.</u> Berkeley: U of California P, 1967.

Double space between heading and first entry.

Begin at left margin. Indent five spaces.

An abbreviated form of the publisher's name is used.

Fredericks, Bernard. "Sound Recording." <u>Hollywood Speaks! An Oral History</u>. Ed. Mike Steen. New York: Putnam's, 1974. 319-25.

Galliazzo, Tony. "Sound in the Movies: A Capsule History from Edison's Cylinder to Multiple-Track 70mm Stereo." <u>Modern Photography</u> Jan. 1971: 48+.

Geldud, Harry M. <u>The Birth of the Talkies</u>. Bloomington: Indiana UP, 1975.

MacGowan, Kenneth. <u>Behind the Screen</u>. New York: Dell, 1965.

Manchel, Frank. <u>When Movies Began to Speak</u>. Englewood Cliffs, N.J.: Prentice, 1969.

Use three hyphens to indicate same author as previous entry.

---. <u>When Pictures Began to Move</u>. Englewood Cliffs, N.J.: Prentice, 1969.

Stanley, Robert H. <u>The Celluloid Empire: A History of the American Movie Industry</u>. New York: Hastings, 1978.

Thrasher, Frederic, ed. <u>Okay for Sound</u>. New York: Duell, 1946.

Walker, Alexander. <u>The Shattered Silents: How the Talkies Came to Stay</u>. New York: Morrow, 1979.

Wright, Basil. <u>The Long View</u>. New York: Knopf, 1974.

Think and Discuss

1. The first line of this research report catches the reader's attention by stating a contradiction: "Silent movies . . . were never really silent." What descriptive details does the paragraph include to illustrate this statement?

2. Is the thesis statement part of the paper? If so, where do you find it?

3. What milestone in the development of sound films occurred in 1926? What words explain the importance of that milestone?

4. The concluding paragraph of "Sound Comes to the Movies" mentions the continuing effect of silent movies on modern filmmakers and modern fans. What words state that effect? How does the last sentence of the research paper echo the first sentence?

Writing Assignment I: *Writing the Rough Draft*

Using your note cards and formal outline, write the rough draft of your research paper. Follow the steps for prewriting, writing, and postwriting.

A. Prewriting

Gather the note cards, thesis statement, and formal outline that you wrote in Writing Practices 5–7. Review your material for completeness and relevance before you begin writing.

B. Writing

You may want to begin your draft, as the author of "Sound Comes to the Movies" did, with an interesting or unusual sentence. If you have decided to include your thesis statement in your research paper, consider putting it at the end of your introductory paragraph.

As you write, follow your formal outline and prewriting notes. Use transitions to link sentences and paragraphs and to show how ideas are related. Add parenthetical documentation where needed, and be sure to insert quotations correctly.

Many research papers end with a paragraph that summarizes the ideas presented and discusses their significance. By referring in the conclusion to a detail mentioned in the introduction, you can give your paper a feeling of completeness.

C. Postwriting

As directed by your teacher, form groups of three or four and trade rough drafts with your classmates. Read one another's papers carefully. Then write the answers to the following questions for each paper.

1. What part of the paper do you like best?

2. What is the thesis statement of the paper? Where is it?

3. Do any parts of the paper seem unrelated to the thesis statement? If so, which parts?

4. Do any parts of the paper need more explanation? If so, which parts?

The Bibliography

After you have completed a rough draft of the research paper, write the final bibliography, using the bibliography cards you prepared earlier. The final bibliography includes only those sources you actually used. Before beginning, be certain that the information on your bibliography cards is accurate, complete, and in the correct order. Then arrange your cards alphabetically by the author's last name. If no author is listed for a source, alphabetize it by the first major word in the title. Taking the information directly from your cards, write the bibliography on a separate sheet of paper. If an entry requires more than one line, indent the second and all other lines five spaces. If you use two sources written by the same author, do not rewrite the author's name in the second listing; instead, use three hyphens in place of the name for all other sources by that author. Both the following books are by Frank Manchel:

Manchel, Frank. *When Movies Began to Speak.*

Englewood Cliffs, N.J.: Prentice, 1969.

---. *When Pictures Began to Move.* Englewood Cliffs,

N.J.: Prentice, 1969.

An abbreviated form of
the publisher's name is
used.

Before beginning your bibliography, look closely at the sample bibliography on p. 159. Notice that the listings for magazine and newspaper articles and anthology selections indicate page numbers but no page numbers are listed for books.

The bibliography form in this section conforms to the MLA style. Your teacher may have you use another style.

The Final Draft

Before you begin the final draft of your research paper, revise your rough draft carefully. Check to see that you have covered all the important points about your topic and have arranged information in the best possible order. Read the rough draft thoroughly and take out any details that do not relate to your topic or contribute to your paper as a whole.

The following is a rough draft of a paragraph in the research paper "Sound Comes to the Movies." As you read, notice the deletions and corrections the writer has made. The notes in the left-hand margin explain the changes.

The success of The Jazz Singer saved Warner

Brothers and convinced the other major movie

producers to investigate and invest in sound movie

systems. However, there were still many problems to

remained

surmount. Since Warner Brothers owned the rights to

Vitaphone, the other companies had to choose from a

variety of sound-on-disc or sound-on-film systems.

Finding capable technicians and installing sound

them

equipment in studios were the least of these problems.

Too wordy

Unnecessary
information

Unnecessary repetition

162

In revising the preceding paragraph, the writer decided to take out one piece of information. Even though this information relates to the topic, it detracts from the paragraph as a whole by breaking up the flow of ideas. While it is difficult to take out details you have carefully researched, in revision it is important to think of the general organization of ideas and delete any information that does not contribute to the paper as a whole.

Writing Practice 8: *Writing the Final Draft*

If you have completed the steps in Writing Assignment I, gather and read your classmates' responses to your rough draft. Consider ways to highlight sections of the paper that your classmates especially liked. If your classmates did not understand how a section of your paper related to the thesis statement, you will need to clarify the connection or perhaps delete that section. Reread your rough draft, making notes about changes and adding necessary explanations.

Use the following checklist to go over your research paper one last time. Then write your final draft.

After you finish the final draft, write a final bibliography, following the directions in this chapter. Then proofread your paper, using the checklist at the back of the book.

Checklist for Revising the Research Report

1. The subject is limited to a topic that can be developed in a research paper.

2. The topic is adequately developed with factual information from outside sources.

3. Each item of information in the final paper explains or develops the topic in some way.

4. The paper has an introductory paragraph introducing the topic and a concluding paragraph that summarizes or comments on the topic.

5. Important theories, unusual or specific facts, and quotations have parenthetical documentation.

6. The parenthetical documentation is ordered correctly and follows a standard form, such as MLA.

7. Information in the bibliography is ordered correctly according to a standard form.

8. Quotations are placed correctly in the paper.

Sentence Combining: *Inserting Phrases and Clauses*

Inserting Participial Phrases

For more information on participles, see pages 470-473.

For more information on phrases, see pages 512-531.

I n the last section on Sentence Combining, you learned how to insert modifiers into sentences. You can also add information to a sentence by inserting phrases that begin with a present or past participle verb form. (For a more detailed discussion of participial phrases, see Chapter 19.)

Base Sentence: Ann Johnson gradually devoted more and more of her time to creative writing.

Insert: Ann Johnson was <u>trained as a pharmacist</u>.

Combined: *Trained as a pharmacist*, Ann Johnson gradually devoted more and more of her time to creative writing.

Some verbs must be changed to the *-ing* form when they are inserted as descriptive phrases. In the following example the signal (*-ing*) indicates that a change in the verb is necessary.

Base Sentence: The elderly man contributed his time and money to the local clean-up campaign.

Insert: He <u>remembered</u> how lovely the neighborhood had been. (*-ing*)

Combined: *Remembering how lovely the neighborhood had been*, the elderly man contributed his time and money to the local clean-up campaign.

As the next few examples show, participial phrases may be inserted at the beginning, middle, or end of the base sentence. However, to avoid confusing or illogical statements, the phrase must always be clearly attached to the word or words it describes.

Base Sentence: The small puppy crouched by its owner.

Insert: The puppy was frightened by the thunder.

Combined: The small puppy, *frightened by the thunder,* crouched by its owner.
or
Frightened by the thunder, the small puppy crouched by its owner.
but not
The small puppy crouched by its owner, *frightened by the thunder.*

A comma usually follows these phrases when they are inserted at the beginning of a sentence. A phrase appearing in the middle or at the end of the sentence is set off with a comma or paired commas only if it provides additional information that *is not essential* to the sentence's meaning. A phrase that provides information *essential* to the sentence's meaning is not set off with commas when it appears in the middle or at the end of the sentence.

Notice how commas are used in the following examples:

Base Sentence: Dogs are often struck by cars.

Insert: Dogs are allowed to run loose in the street.

Combined: Dogs *allowed to run loose in the street* are often struck by cars.
[No commas are used because the phrase provides essential information about which dogs are struck by cars.]

Base Sentence: My grandfather and I enjoyed cooking the elaborate dinner.

Insert: We swapped recipes. (*-ing*)
We corrected one another constantly. (*and* + *-ing*)

Combined: My grandfather and I, *swapping recipes and correcting one another constantly,* enjoyed cooking the elaborate dinner.
[Commas set off the phrase because it is not essential.]

In the preceding example notice that two participial phrases connected by *and* are inserted into the base sentence.

Exercise 1: Inserting Participial Phrases

After studying the examples, combine the following sets of sentences by inserting the underlined participial phrases into the base sentences (the first sentence in each set). Be sure to insert the phrases in the places that make the most sense, using commas and conjunctions where necessary. Many phrases can be attached to the beginning of sentences for variety. Write the combined sentences on a sheet of paper.

Examples

a. Mrs. Garcia has built a small greenhouse beside her garage. Mrs. Garcia has used her retirement productively. (*-ing*)

Using her retirement productively, Mrs. Garcia has built a small greenhouse beside her garage.

b. Locusts swarmed in the fields. They were creating chaos. They were causing fear among the peasants.

Creating chaos, locusts swarmed in the fields, causing fear among the peasants.

1. Su Ling continued to work out every day. She was encouraged by her coach. (keep *-ed* form)

2. Ms. Garrison gave us all a warm hug. She was delighted by the surprise going-away party.

   She was saddened at the thought of leaving. (*but*)

3. George gave Harry the signal. He turned out the lights. (*-ing*)

4. Annie stood at the edge of the diving board. She positioned herself carefully. (*-ing*)

   She waited for the sound of the gun. (*-ing*)

5. Quickly, he threw the blanket on the fire. He stamped his feet. (*-ing*)

   All the flames were out. (*until*)

6. The freeway continued for miles. It wound through the mountains. It ended by a picturesque lake.

7. Anita has no manners. She always chews with her mouth open. She never cares about her appearance.

8. The lion leapt with all of its strength.
   It spotted the zebra.

9. George Washington Carver discovered nearly 300 uses for the peanut.
   He experimented almost daily.

10. Carver left his owner after the Civil War in order to gain an education.
    He was once kidnaped by slave catchers.
    He was recovered by his owner.

Exercise 2: Combining Sentences into a Paragraph

Combine each of the sets of sentences on the next two pages; the first five sets have signals. On a separate sheet of paper, write the combined sentences in the order they appear so that they form a paragraph. Study the examples before you begin.

Examples

a. The director sewed together pieces of fabric.
   The director was <u>finishing costumes</u>.

   They were <u>for the school play</u>.

   The director is <u>talented</u>.

   The director is <u>young</u>. (,)

   The fabric is <u>dark</u>.

   The fabric is <u>gaudy</u>. (,)

   Finishing costumes for the school play, the talented, young director sewed together pieces of dark, gaudy fabric.

b. He hummed quietly.
   He was <u>turning the seams</u>.

   The seams were <u>on the colorful garments</u>.

   He did this <u>with expertise</u>.

   He hummed quietly, turning the seams on the colorful garments with expertise.

c. Actors tried on their costumes.
   They were <u>all around him</u>.

   They were <u>enthusiastic</u>.

   They were <u>amateur</u> actors.

   They were <u>laughing</u>.

   They laughed <u>with excitement</u>.

   All around him, enthusiastic amateur actors tried on their costumes, laughing with excitement.

d. The director ignored the clamor.
   He was <u>totally absorbed</u>.

   The absorption was <u>with his work</u>.

   The work was <u>last minute</u>.

It was the clamor of the students.

It was excited clamor.

The director, totally absorbed with his last-minute work, ignored the excited clamor of the students.

Finishing costumes for the school play, the talented, young director sewed together pieces of dark, gaudy fabric. He hummed quietly, turning the seams on the colorful garments with expertise. All around him, enthusiastic amateur actors tried on their costumes, laughing with excitement. The director, totally absorbed with his last-minute work, ignored the excited clamor of the students.

1. The woman rests her knitting.
    The woman is in the photograph.

    She rests it on a table.

    The table is beside her.

    The table is small.

    The table is round. (,)

2. She looks dignified.
    She is wearing a dress and a shawl.

    The dress is simple.

    It is dark. (,)

    The shawl is white.

    The shawl is fringed. (,)

3. Her head is erect and her eyes peer ahead.
    Her head is covered by a white turban.

    Her eyes are behind wire spectacles.

    The eyes are dark.

    They are penetrating. (,)

    They peer into space.

4. Nothing in the photo suggests that this woman is the hero.
    The photo is ordinary-looking.

    The hero is famous.

    The hero is American.

    The hero was called Sojourner Truth.

5. The woman inherited a mysticism.
    The woman was born about 1797.

169

The birth was in upstate New York.

The woman called herself Sojourner Truth. (-*ing*)

The mysticism was deep.

The mysticism was from her mother.

6. She left New York City.
It was one day in 1843.

She carried only a small bag, twenty-five cents, and her new name: Sojourner Truth.

It was a bag of clothes.

7. The woman lectured everywhere.
She walked from one town to another.

The woman was six foot tall.

She lectured on women's rights.

She lectured on emancipation.

8. She used her eloquence and mind to debate some of the nation's leaders.
She was standing tall and erect.

She was on the speaker's platform.

Her eloquence was forceful.

Her eloquence was spellbinding.

Her mind was quick.

Her mind was incisive.

The leaders were most powerful.

Many of the leaders were politicians who did not always agree with her.

9. She had a meeting.
It was during the Civil War.

It was with President Lincoln.

It was at the White House.

10. She proved that even one woman alone can affect the course of American history.
She integrated the streetcars.

The streetcars were in Washington.

She demanded the right to vote.

The vote was in a Presidential election.

She was speaking forcefully everywhere.

Inserting Adjective Clauses

For more information on adjective clauses, see pages 538-540.

Inserting an *adjective clause* that modifies (or describes) a noun or pronoun in the base sentence is another way to add specific information to a sentence. An *adjective clause* is a group of words that has a subject and verb and that acts as an adjective. The clause contains a relative pronoun that sometimes acts as the subject of the clause. (Adjective clauses are discussed in Chapter 20.)

Base Sentence: Mrs. Jefferson was elected to the city council last week.

Insert: Mrs. Jefferson lost her sight a year ago. (*who*)

Combined: Mrs. Jefferson, *who lost her sight a year ago,* was elected to the city council last week.

The combined sentence was formed by inserting the information about Mrs. Jefferson's loss of sight into the base sentence. Notice that the words *Mrs. Jefferson* are removed from the sentence to be inserted and replaced by the relative pronoun *who*. In the combined sentence the word *who* attaches the adjective clause to the words *Mrs. Jefferson.*

Adjective clauses often begin with one of the following words.

who, whom, that	relate to people
whose	relates to possessives (*its, her, his, their*)
when	relates to a time
where	relates to a place
which, that	relate to things
why	relates to a reason

When a sentence is combined with an adjective clause, the signal tells which word takes the place of a noun or pronoun in the insert sentence and helps to relate the inserted information (the clause) to the base sentence. In each of the following examples notice that the relative pronoun is clearly attached to the word or words it modifies.

Base Sentence: A young boy went on to become an Olympic swimmer.

Insert: Lifeguards once rescued him from a riptide. (*whom*)

171

Combined: A young boy *whom lifeguards once rescued from a riptide* went on to become an Olympic swimmer.

Base Sentence: Mrs. Greenstein donated a motorcycle from her shop to the boosters' raffle.

Insert: Her son is on our football team. (*whose*)

Combined: Mrs. Greenstein, *whose son is on our football team,* donated a motorcycle from her shop to the boosters' raffle.

Base Sentence: She gave us directions to the French restaurant.

Insert: We are to meet for lunch at the French restaurant tomorrow. (*where*)

Combined: She gave us directions to the French restaurant *where we are to meet for lunch tomorrow.*

Clauses that are essential to a sentence's meaning are not set off by commas. In the following examples the clauses are necessary to understand the entire sentence.

Base Sentence: Those drivers are a menace.

Insert: The drivers change lanes without signaling. (*who*)

Combined: Those drivers *who change lanes without signaling* are a menace.

Base Sentence: She called him at the precise moment.

Insert: He needed cheering up the most at the precise moment. (*when*)

Combined: She called him at the precise moment *when he needed cheering up the most.*

When an adjective clause can be omitted from a sentence without changing the meaning, set off the clause with a comma or paired commas. The commas indicate that the clause *is not essential.*

Base Sentence: Mount St. Helens erupted in May of 1980.

Insert: Mount St. Helens is located in Washington. (*which*)

Combined: Mount St. Helens, *which is located in Washington,* erupted in May of 1980.

Exercise 3: Inserting Adjective Clauses

Combine the following sets of sentences by inserting adjective clauses into the base sentences (the first sentence in each set). Be certain to use commas when the inserted clauses contain *nonessential* information. Signals for the clauses to use are provided for you in the first five sets. Study the examples before you write your sentences on a sheet of paper.

Examples

a. The committee chose club members to investigate the disappearance of the files.

The committee chose club members who were extremely trustworthy to investigate the disappearance of the files.

b. "Get-rich-quick" schemes are common in times of economic recession.
They rarely pay off. (*which*)
"Get-rich-quick" schemes, which rarely pay off, are common in times of economic recession.

1. I admire creative people.
They are able to amuse themselves with crafts and other hobbies. (*who*)

2. Whenever we drive to the mountains, we play word games to pass the time.
The mountains are over eighty miles north of here. (*which*)

3. The youth had either left town or carefully hidden himself somewhere.
The police wanted him for questioning. (*whom*)

4. Doctors are called pediatricians.
Their patients are babies and children. (*whose*)

5. Erika bought the new convertible.
She had wanted it for a long time. (*that*)

6. Jesse reads a great deal and has an excellent vocabulary.
He is my next-door neighbor.

7. When I arrived home from vacation, I was unable to find the place.
I had hidden my car keys in the place.

8. It is incredible that people still drive large luxury cars in this age.
In this age we are concerned with excessive fuel consumption.

9. The speaker presented several reasons.
   For those reasons we should oppose the proposition.

10. The photographs don't do the city justice.
    I took them on my trip to Paris last summer.

Writing Practice: *A Short Biography*

If you look in the reference section of your high school or public library, you may find a volume titled *The Dictionary of American Biography*. This volume contains short biographies of noted Americans, giving details about an individual's birth, residence, and accomplishments. It explains why the individual is considered an outstanding American. Suppose that seventy years from now you are listed as a noted American in this reference book. What would your outstanding accomplishments be? Would you be listed for setting several world records in diving or skiing, or for winning an Olympic gold medal? Would your achievements be in medicine or astronomy? Perhaps you will be remembered as an outstanding parent or as the writer of a best-selling book on friendship. Write a notebook entry about yourself, seeing yourself as you would like the writers of this reference book to see you seventy years from now. You may make your entry a humorous one if you like; perhaps you set a world record for spitting watermelon seeds or for winning an Academy Award in a horror film. If possible, look at a short biography in one of your library reference books before you begin.

As you write your entry, use some of the sentence-combining skills you have studied in this unit.

6 Persuasive Writing

Writing to Persuade

Persuasive writing is writing that attempts to convince readers to think or act in a certain way.

When you write persuasively, your goal is to convince readers to accept your ideas or opinions. Your purpose may also be to urge readers to adopt a specific course of action. In this chapter you will learn to recognize facts and opinions; you will study how words work to affect a reader's emotions and reasoning. You will also read about the importance of knowing your audience. Finally, you will learn methods of arguing from emotion and from logical reasoning, both to improve your own persuasive writing and to help you evaluate the many kinds of persuasive writing you encounter daily.

Recognizing Facts and Opinions

An *opinion* is an idea or belief that is based on personal judgment. A *fact* is a piece of information that can be objectively verified.

Facts may be verified by observing, by reading, by researching, or by talking to people. When a fact is verified, it cannot be challenged. Unlike facts, however, opinions are subject to dispute. Opinions, because they represent someone's personal judgment, are always open to disagreement. For this reason, opinions are the best topics for persuasive writing. Facts, however, when used appropriately, can support an opinion. They provide the evidence to defend the writer's viewpoint.

The following examples illustrate the differences between facts and opinions:

Fact: President John F. Kennedy was our country's youngest President.

Opinion: President John F. Kennedy was one of our country's finest public speakers.

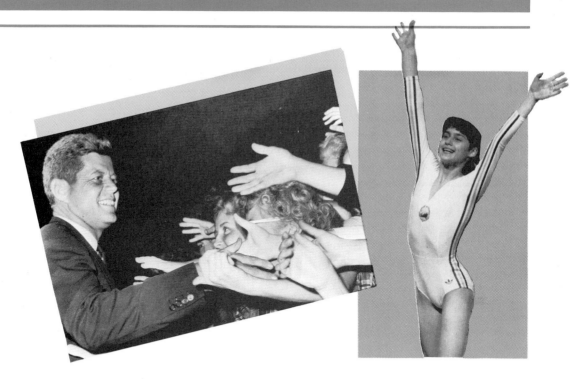

Fact: Nadia Comaneci was the first gymnast to achieve a perfect score of ten in an Olympic competition.

Opinion: Nadia Comaneci is the world's greatest gymnast.

Writing Practice 1: *Recognizing Facts and Opinions*

The following sentences contain both facts and opinions. Number a sheet of paper from one to eight. As you read each sentence, decide whether it is a fact or an opinion. Write *fact* or *opinion* beside the corresponding number on your paper.

1.   Nadia Comaneci brought worldwide recognition to the sport of gymnastics.

2.   At the age of fourteen, she competed in the 1976 Olympic Games, held in Montreal, Canada.

3.   At the time, she stood four feet tall and weighed eighty-six pounds.

4.   Her small stature along with her overwhelming drive to win the gold medal enhanced her opportunity.

5.   Prior to the 1976 Olympics, no gymnast had ever scored a perfect ten in an Olympic competition.

6. By the end of the competition, Nadia had not only won seven gold medals but also received as many perfect scores of ten.

7. Before the 1976 Olympics, most gymnastics fans had heard about Nadia.

8. After the Olympics, all sports fans knew Nadia as the best gymnast in the world.

The Appeal to Emotion

Some persuasive writing appeals to your emotions. People who have a product to sell or a cause to advance often appeal to your emotions to persuade you to buy, believe, or act. For example; the advertisement on this page makes such an appeal: the advertisers want you to have a warm feeling for the people on the bicycles so that you will trust the company that makes them. In addition, the ad attempts to sell you on the idea that the riders are having fun and that if you buy one of their bicycles you will have fun, too. Do you think the ad would convince you to buy one of the company's bicycles? What features are most convincing?

Descriptive words are often used to appeal to your emotions. Soft drink commercials, for example, use words such as *refreshing taste* or *tart and tingling*.

An appeal to your emotions is not necessarily dishonest. Ads for sending money to help needy children may appeal to your sense of decency, and public service ads that ask you to lower your thermostat may appeal to your sense of duty. What is important is to recognize when appeals are based on emotion, so that you can decide whether or not you want to be influenced.

Writing Practice 2: *A Magazine Advertisement*

Imagine that you are an ad writer for a nationwide magazine. You have a new account, Fly-Way Vacation Airlines, and you want to impress them with your first ad. You have written the following basic format, but now you must complete a final draft. On a separate sheet of paper, write the ad, filling in the words you would choose from the group in parentheses. You may substitute words of your own if you can think of improvements. Be prepared to discuss your choices in class.

For more information on adjectives and adverbs, see pages 396-437.

(Fly, Jet, Slip) away to (sunny, warm, torrid) Jamaica! (Sandy, Shining, Beautiful) beaches, jungle waterfalls, (sweet, friendly, welcoming) smiles, sailing in the (inviting, brilliant, glowing) sunshine, dancing in the (romantic, fantastic, wonderful) moonlight—all this (awaits, is in store for, we promise) you in (friendly, beautiful, exciting) Jamaica. The new (inexpensive, low-cost, cheap) air fares put a Jamaican holiday within your (reach, budget, financial range). We have vacations for singles, (newlyweds, honeymooners, just-marrieds), families, (sportsmen, sports lovers, sports nuts), everyone—at the (top, most elegant, finest) resort in Jamaica. Contact your travel agent, or send in this (handy, convenient, easy-to-mail) coupon. (Act Now! Do It Today! Don't Delay!)

Writing Practice 3: *Judging an Advertisement*

Look through several magazines or newspapers and select an advertisement for a particular product, perhaps for your favorite food. Underline the words in the ad that describe the product and appeal to your emotions. Then write a brief statement of opinion explaining why you think the ad is or is not convincing.

Advertising Techniques

Some of the techniques used in advertising are also used in other types of persuasive writing and can be identified by name.

Card Stacking

This approach involves using only the evidence that will prove one side of an argument. The arguer "stacks the cards" heavily on one side and ignores the other, making it seem that there is only one possible conclusion. For example, if you were to write an editorial attacking student apathy about local politics but neglect to say that the student political volunteer rate had increased dramatically during the previous year, you could be accused of "card stacking."

Name Calling

People respond emotionally to labels, or names, a writer gives to individuals, groups, ideologies, or ideas. For example, if you write, "He's just a dropout," some people will have a strong negative reaction to the term *dropout* without waiting for specific information about the individual. In politics the label *radical* provokes extreme reactions. Labeling is usually a deceptive technique because it puts attention on a generality and avoids the particular person or issue.

Glittering Generalities

Statements using words and phrases that sound impressive—*freedom, honor, peace, duty,* and so on—in a general way are called *glittering generalities.* They have appeal, a glittering surface, but little or no substance. For example, a campaign statement such as, "We all enjoy the highest standard of living of any nation in the world," is designed to give the voter a good feeling rather than to convey truthful information. That good feeling will help readers accept the idea behind the statement, which may be that they should vote for this particular candidate, who is patriotic because he or she has faith in the economy.

Transfer

Transfer is a common approach used by persuasive writers when they want the positive quality of a famous person to transfer to a product or cause. When you see an advertisement that shows a film star or sports figure using a product, the advertisers want your good feelings about the famous person to transfer to the product and to a good feeling about yourself if you buy the product.

The reverse of this approach is called *guilt by association.* If a product is associated with someone who produces a negative impression, you will not want to identify with him or her. For example, you may have noticed ads against smoking that feature very unattractive people. The message is that if you smoke, you will be identified in a negative way with the people in the ad.

Testimonial

A *testimonial* is a direct endorsement of a product, person, or cause. A famous person may lend his or her name for the advertisement and may also speak directly in the ad. A well-known politician may endorse a young politician for office, through a testimonial praising the young politician. When a sports star appears in an ad telling you to eat the brand of cereal he or she eats, this is another kind of testimonial. This approach is very similar to the transfer technique.

Plain Folks

The *plain folks* approach attempts to make you feel comfortable with the people in the advertisement because they are "plain folks" just like you. Television ads showing housewives doing the laundry,

husbands helping to clean out sinks, or an office worker talking about a headache remedy use the plain folks approach. The potential buyer is supposed to think, "Those people are just like me and my family, and if they use that product I should, too."

Bandwagon

"Everybody's doing it" is the motto of the *bandwagon* approach. It suggests that a product is good or a cause is right because it has wide support, and the appeal is for you to *jump on the bandwagon,* an expression meaning "to join the crowd." This approach tries to make you feel that if you buy the "right" brand of tennis shoes or vote for the right candidate, you will be accepted as an insider, not set apart from the crowd.

Writing Assignment I: *An Advertisement*

A. Prewriting

Think of a product you would like to sell—a bicycle, car, video game, snow skis, computer software, or food product. Or instead you might invent a product, such as a robot who mows lawns or takes out the garbage. Make a list of descriptive words to use in selling the product. Include some words that appeal to the emotions.

B. Writing

Consider which kind of advertising technique would work best in selling your product. Then write a convincing advertisement using this technique along with some of the words you listed in the prewriting exercise. Remember that your purpose is to make your readers want to buy the product. Direct your ad to your classmates and peers.

C. Postwriting

Share your advertisement with your classmates in one of the following ways.

1. Use your written advertisement as the basis for presenting an oral sales pitch to your classmates.

2. Design a poster ad by writing your advertisement on a large sheet of construction paper. Then use your own illustrations or pictures from magazines or newspapers to create an eye-catching ad.

The Appeal to Reason

Persuasion through logical reasoning is called *argumentation*. In the next sections you will learn the techniques of sound reasoning, both to use in your own writing and to recognize in the arguments you hear and read.

When you use sound reasoning, you do not resort to any of the persuasive techniques such as card stacking or glittering generalities. Instead, your argument is both *truthful* and *valid*.

The word *truthful* you already know. The word *valid* has a special definition when it refers to reasoning: in a valid argument one idea proceeds logically from another. To understand the difference between truthful and valid, consider a statement that is obviously not truthful: "Pigs can fly." The following three statements are an attempt to prove that pigs can fly.

First Statement: *All winged things can fly.*

In formal argumentation the first statement is a general statement, called the *first*, or *major, premise*.

Second Statement: *All pigs have wings.*

The second statement talks about a subset of the first statement (in this case "pigs" are a subset of "all winged things") and is called the *second*, or *minor, premise*.

Third Statement: *Therefore, pigs can fly.*

The third statement is a conclusion that proceeds logically from the first two statements. In a logical argument when the first two statements are accepted, then the conclusion must be accepted as well. This is what is meant by a *valid argument.*

Even though the argument about pigs is valid, it is obviously not true. The first premise, that all winged things can fly, can easily be disproved; many winged things such as ostriches, for example, cannot fly. The second premise, that all pigs have wings, is contradicted by experience.

A good argument is both valid and truthful, as the following example demonstrates.

First Premise: *All U.S. senators are United States citizens.*

By definition a United States senator must be a citizen to hold office; you can check on this information in an encyclopedia or a history book.

Second Premise: *Margaret Chase Smith was a U.S. senator.*

Notice that the preceding premise relates to the first: "Margaret Chase Smith" is a subset of the larger class of senators in general. You can check on the truthfulness of this statement in a reference book.

Conclusion: *Therefore, Margaret Chase Smith was a United States citizen.*

Since both the first and second statements are true, you can draw the *valid* and *truthful* conclusion that Margaret Chase Smith was a United States citizen.

In everyday talking and writing, arguments are usually not formally stated with a major and minor premise. However, these premises are often included in the arguments without being stated. When you pay attention to the premises of an argument—what the speaker or writer *assumes* to be true—you can better judge the reasoning of the argument.

Often you will find that arguments are not logical for two reasons: first, the arguer jumps to a quick conclusion without giving enough evidence to support the conclusion; and second, the arguer does not give the right kind of evidence to justify the conclusion of the argument. The writing practice that follows will help you to examine the importance of providing the right kind of evidence for your arguments.

Writing Practice 4: *Developing Valid Arguments*

Write two arguments similar to the preceding examples, each containing a first and second premise and a conclusion. Base the first argument on an untruthful statement, such as "All winged things can fly." Base the second argument on a truthful statement, such as "All senators are United States citizens." Then develop both arguments using logical reasoning. Select one of your arguments to read to your classmates, and have them state whether it is true and whether it is valid.

Recognizing False Reasoning

F alse reasoning consists of *logical fallacies*, errors in reasoning. As a reader, you need to be aware of these logical fallacies so that you will not be fooled into drawing a wrong conclusion. As a writer, you should be aware of these common errors in order to avoid them yourself.

Begging the Question

In logic the question is the issue being argued. When someone makes a statement that assumes the truth without proving it, that person's argument *begs the question*. This fallacy is also called *arguing in a circle*. For example, consider the following statement.

> Sheila is a terrible student. I know that because she never studies.

The writer claims that the conclusion is true simply by stating that it is: Sheila is a terrible student because she never studies. Unless the person making the statement is with Sheila all of the time, the statement could be untrue due to either exaggeration or lack of knowledge. Begging the question avoids the real issue of an argument by assuming the conclusion to be true without offering proof.

Ignoring the Question

Ignoring the question means "losing sight of the main issue," as in the following example.

> Jim should have been given the Most Valuable Player Award after the baseball season. He worked hard all season to improve his batting average, was well-liked by the team, and was often praised by the coach. Yes, Jim was cheated out of a well-deserved award.

Jim's friend is ignoring the main issue: What did Jim do as a baseball player to merit the award? The preceding argument offers evidence of Jim's popularity and hard work but no proof that he was the best player on the team.

Ad Hominem Argument

Ad hominem is a Latin phrase meaning, literally, "to the man." An ad hominem argument diverts the audience's attention from the question by making a personal attack on an individual. It is often an appeal to prejudice. You may find the ad hominem argument in political writing, as in the example on the following page.

What can you expect from candidate Russell? Her political cronies are from the ultraliberal wing of the party that wants to lead us into a welfare state. She has been self-employed all her life and doesn't know how to work within an organization. Furthermore, how can you trust a mother who doesn't want to stay at home and be a good parent to her ten-year-old child?

Nothing in this argument speaks to the issue of candidate Russell's qualifications for the job. Instead, it makes an emotional appeal based on loaded words (*welfare state*) and prejudicial assumptions about self-employed workers and mothers.

Oversimplification

Sometimes, an arguer will make a conclusion about a problem without fully taking into consideration the causes behind it. By hurrying to solve the problem, the speaker or writer assumes that it has a single cause or preceding event, as in the following example:

Ever since Mr. Janos became high school principal, student test scores have improved. Mr. Janos must be responsible for the improvement.

Any cause-and-effect argument such as the preceding one must be able to stand up under close examination. The following questions reveal that the argument oversimplifies the issue:

a.   Is the single event assumed to be sufficient cause, or are there other causes that have not been considered?

In the preceding argument the single assumed cause is Mr. Janos' becoming principal. What other causes could be at work? For example, were the test scores of incoming freshmen improving anyway? Were test scores nationally improving? Were there any other staff or curriculum changes at the high school?

b.   Do the other causes more adequately explain the effect?

It seems unlikely that one person could affect the test scores of an entire school. It is more likely that one or more of the other suggested causes influenced the scores.

c.   Is the conclusion based on the right cause or causes, and is the conclusion truthful and valid?

In the argument about Mr. Janos, the conclusion is based on an oversimplified cause, so it is neither truthful nor valid.

Either-Or Argument

Another kind of oversimplification is the *either-or argument*, which draws extreme conclusions and ignores the possibility of several variations in between. For example, "Either you deliberately forgot to bring your homework to class as a gesture of defiance, or you think you can get everyone's sympathy by acting absent-mindedly." This kind of oversimplification allows only two conclusions, and both are probably wrong. Many issues are unsuitable to either-or conclusions. With issues of behavior, ethics, morality, and religion, absolute statements of right or wrong are usually impossible.

False Comparison

Comparing one thing to another is an effective way of making a subject clear to an audience. A false comparison, however, can lead to a false conclusion. Sometimes persuasive writers will intentionally insert a false conclusion to mislead their audience. Occasionally the false comparison is an unintentional oversimplification, as in the following example.

A common saying in Presidential election years is, "Don't switch horses in midstream." This saying suggests that conventional wisdom advises against bringing in a new President after four years.

The comparison is obviously false. A President after four years in office is not "midstream" at all but is at the end of a period of time designated by the Constitution.

Writing Practice 5: *Identifying False Reasoning*

Look through ads or articles for examples of false reasoning or listen for arguments that use false reasoning. Magazine articles, newspaper editorials, talk shows, and conversations are all good sources to explore. On a separate sheet of paper, write a paragraph explaining one example of false reasoning that you find. State the argument and show why it is badly reasoned. Be prepared to discuss what sort of evidence or what other changes would be needed to improve the argument.

Writing Practice 6: *Supporting an Argument with Reasons*

The following sentences are conclusions to be supported by reasons in an argument. Select a conclusion you support or write a conclusion of your own. On a sheet of paper, write three or more valid and truthful reasons to support the conclusion. If necessary, use reference books or other material to find evidence to support your argument.

Before you write, think carefully about whether or not your reasons could be supported with sufficient evidence.

1. My school's system of elections does (or does not) ensure that the most popular and qualified candidates for student offices will win.

2. The grading system in this school is (or is not) fair to the majority of students.

3. Today's movies do (or do not) provide teenagers with good models of human behavior.

4. The legal age limit for all drivers should (or should not) be lowered to age fourteen.

5. Security is (or is not) more important than happiness.

Model: A Persuasive Essay

Writers of persuasive essays, articles, and editorials want to convince their readers to believe as they do and perhaps to act in a certain way.

In the essay that follows, Marya Mannes wants to convince her readers that cheating, lying, bribing, and other forms of corruption are partly due to society's unwillingness to draw a definite line between right and wrong. As you read this essay, try to determine the kinds of arguments the writer uses to persuade readers to accept her point of view. Does she appeal mostly to emotion, or to reason? What evidence does she present to support her ideas?

The Thin Grey Line

Introduction

[1] "Aw, they all do it," growled the cabdriver. He was talking about cops who took payoffs for winking at double parking, but his cynicism could as well have been directed at any of a dozen other instances of corruption, big-time and small-time. Moreover, the disgust in his voice was overlaid by an unspoken "So what?": the implication that since this was the way things were, there was nothing anybody could do.

Body

[2] Like millions of his fellow Americans, the cabdriver was probably a decent human being who had never stolen anything, broken any law or willfully injured another; somewhere, a knowledge of what was probably right had kept him from committing what was clearly wrong. But that knowledge had not kept a thin grey line that separates the two conditions from being daily greyer and thinner—to the point that it was hardly noticeable.

[3] On one side of this line are They: the bribers, the cheaters, the chiselers, the swindlers, the extortioners. On the other side are We—both partners and victims. They and We are now so perilously close that the only mark distinguishing us is that They get caught and We don't.

[4] The same citizen who voices his outrage at police corruption will slip the traffic cop on his block a handsome Christmas present in the belief that his car, nestled under a "No Parking" sign, will not be ticketed. The son of that nice woman next door has a habit of stealing

cash from her purse because his allowance is smaller than his buddies'. Your son's friend admitted cheating at exams because "everybody does it."

Thesis Statement

[5] Bit by bit, the resistance to and immunity against wrong that a healthy social body builds up by law and ethics and the dictation of conscience have broken down. And instead of the fighting indignation of a people outraged by those who prey on them, we have the admission of impotence: "They all do it."

[6] Now, failure to uphold the law is no less corrupt than violation of the law. And the continuing shame of this country now is the growing number of Americans who fail to uphold and assist enforcement of the law, simply—and ignominiously—out of fear. Fear of "involvement," fear of reprisal, fear of "trouble." A man is beaten by hoodlums in plain daylight and in view of bystanders. These people not only fail to help the victim, but, like the hoodlums, flee before the police can question them. A city official knows of a colleague's bribe but does not report it. A pedestrian watches a car hit a woman but leaves the scene, to avoid giving testimony. It happens every day. And if the police get cynical at this irresponsibility, they are hardly to blame. Morale is a matter of giving support and having faith in one another; where both are lacking, "law" has become a worthless word.

[7] How did we get this way? What started this blurring of what was once a thick black line between the lawful and the lawless? What makes a "regular guy," a decent fellow, accept a bribe? What makes a nice kid from a middle-class family take money for doing something he must know is not only illegal but wrong?

[8] When you look into the background of an erring "kid" you will often find a comfortable home and a mother who will tell you, with tears in her eyes, that she "gave him everything." She probably did, to his everlasting damage. Fearing her son's disapproval, the indulgent mother denies him nothing except responsibility. Instead of growing up, he grows to believe that the world owes him everything.

[9] The nice kid's father crosses the thin grey line himself in a dozen ways, day in and day out. He pads his expenses on his income-tax returns as a matter of course. As a landlord, he pays the local inspectors of the city housing authority to overlook violations in the houses he rents. When his son flunked his driving test, he gave him ten dollars to slip the inspector on his second test. "They all do it," he said.

[10] The nice kid is brought up with boys and girls who have no heroes except people not much older than themselves who have made the Big Time, usually in show business or in sports. Publicity and money are the halos of their stars, who range from pop singers who can't sing to ballplayers who can't read: from teen-age starlets who can't act to television performers who can't think. They may be excited by the exploits of spacemen, but the work's too tough and dangerous.

[11] The nice kids have no heroes because they don't believe in heroes. Heroes are suckers and squares. To be a hero you have to stand out, to excel, to take risks, and above all, not only choose

between right and wrong, but defend the right and fight the wrong. This means responsibility—and who needs it?

[12] Today, no one has to take any responsibility. The psychiatrists, the sociologists, the novelists, the playwrights have gone a long way to help promote irresponsibility. Nobody really is to blame for what he does. It's Society. It's Environment. It's a Broken Home. It's an Underprivileged Area. But it's hardly ever You.

[13] Now we find a truckload of excuses to absolve the individual from responsibility for his actions. A fellow commits a crime because he's basically insecure, because he hated his stepmother at nine, or because his sister needs an operation. A policeman loots a store because his salary is too low. A city official accepts a payoff because it's offered to him. Members of minority groups, racial or otherwise, commit crimes because they can't get a job, or are unacceptable to the people living around them. The words "right" and "wrong" are foreign to these people.

[14] But honesty is the best policy. Says who? Anyone willing to get laughed at. But the laugh is no laughing matter. It concerns the health and future of a nation. It involves the two-dollar illegal bettor as well as the corporation price-fixer, the college-examination cheater and the payroll padding Congressman, the expense-account chiseler, the seller of pornography and his schoolboy reader, the bribed judge and the stealing delinquent. All these people may represent a minority. But when, as it appears now, the majority excuse themselves from responsibility by accepting corruption as natural to society ("They all do it"), this society is bordering on total confusion. If the line between right and wrong is finally erased, there is no defense against the power of evil.

Conclusion
Call to Action

[15] Before this happens—and it is by no means far away—it might be well for the schools of the nation to [teach] . . . a daily lesson in ethics, law, and responsibility to society that would strengthen the conscience as exercise strengthens muscles. . . . For corruption is not something you read about in the papers and leave to courts. We are all involved.[1]

Think and Discuss

1. In "The Thin Grey Line" Marya Mannes writes for a general audience. Do you think the argument she presents relates to the experience of most people? How?

2. What is the main point the writer makes in this essay? Does she support her argument with sufficient evidence or reasons? What are they?

---

[1]"The Thin Grey Line" by Marya Mannes. Copyright © 1963 by Marya Mannes. Reprinted by permission of Harold Ober Associates, Inc.

3. Does this essay make any emotional appeals to the reader? If so, cite examples of emotional language used.

4. Does the author use any of the persuasive techniques you have studied? If so, where does she use them?

5. Does this essay commit any logical fallacies that you have studied? If so, what are they?

6. In paragraphs 12–14, Marya Mannes argues that "Today, no one has to take any responsibility." Is this a valid argument? Why or why not?

7. Do you agree with the solution the author suggests for the problem? Be prepared to discuss why you do or do not feel that her solution is convincing.

Planning a Persuasive Essay

The *persuasive essay* is an essay that makes an argument. It can argue for or against an issue; it can make an appeal to emotion, to reason, or to both; it can use the persuasive and logical approaches you read about earlier in this chapter. Before beginning a persuasive essay, you want to know three things: (1) the point of view you will take, (2) the nature of your audience, and (3) the method of your argument and the evidence you will use.

Knowing Your Point of View

In persuasive writing, *point of view* refers to your opinion on an issue. For example, if you were writing about the effect of TV commercials on viewers, your point of view might be either that the commercials have little or no effect or that they have considerable effect on what products people buy.

To be persuasive you must first know your subject thoroughly. You must be able to cite reasons and give evidence in support of your argument. When you already have definite opinions about a subject, review them carefully to be certain they can be supported by logical argument. When you need to write about a subject you do not know well, explore the issues thoroughly before deciding on a point of view.

You may want to begin your research by talking with friends and family about the subject. Seeing different sides to the issue can help clarify your own point of view. Next, research your subject to find as much reliable information about it as possible. You will want to see

193

resources and perhaps consult an authority on the subject. Another way to gather information is to interview people or take an informal poll to get a perspective or a general opinion about your subject.

Finally, it always helps to be generally informed about current local, national, and global events. Being aware of important issues will give you a background of information that will help when you form your own opinions. Newspapers, books, magazines, and news programs are sources you can consult daily.

Knowing Your Audience

Advertisers know that in order to write successful advertisements, they must understand the nature of their audience: its age range, interests, and buying power. Television ads, for example, are scheduled to appeal to a particular viewing audience. Products such as golf balls or running shoes that would interest sports fans appear during weekend sports programs; new toys are advertised during the morning children's programs. The better that writers know the audience they write for in a persuasive essay, the better they are able to make arguments geared to convince that audience.

Model: A Persuasive Letter

The writer of the following letter is a high school senior involved in community efforts to develop a forest area as a public park. He addresses this letter to an adult friend, but similar letters will be sent to members of community clubs, service organizations, churches, and synagogues. As you read the letter, decide how effectively it will appeal to an adult audience.

2330 Glenmary Drive
Harristown, KY 42501
April 29, 1984

Dear Ms. Wong,

Would you like to enjoy a pine-scented, shady picnic area, a tree-lined nature trail, and a scenic view overlooking forests and fishing streams? These benefits, and more, can be yours when Harristown's Forest Park is developed and opened for everyone to enjoy.

At present the park is reserved for use by a limited number of clubs. However, an additional 1,500 acres, developed for recreational use, would give the park two public picnic areas, a nature trail for hikers, a horseback-riding trail, and a scenic drive. In the future an outdoor theater and a lakeside campsite will put summertime entertainment and relaxation just a short drive from town.

The Harristown Forest Park Action Committee invites you to a benefit carnival next Saturday, May 5, at the county fairgrounds, from 9 A.M. to 11 P.M. There will be rides, a giant barbecue, games, and amusements for everyone. Proceeds from the carnival will go toward the development of Forest Park.

We hope you agree that planned development of our nearby natural resources is a good way to provide recreation for all ages. Join us at the carnival and visit the Forest Park Action Committee booth to find out more about our plans. We need your help to make Forest Park a place all of us can enjoy.

Sincerely,

Jim Stuvic

Jim Stuvic

Think and Discuss

1. Does Jim's letter use language that will make his readers sympathetic toward the committee's efforts to develop Forest Park? What sentences do you think are most effective?

2. What does Jim's letter ask the reader to do specifically?

3. Do you think Jim's opening question is an effective way to begin an appeal? Why or why not?

4. Jim's letter does not directly state that the reader should contribute to the development of Forest Park, but it does suggest reasons that Ms. Wong and others might want to do so. What are those reasons?

5. If you were a member of Jim's committee and could rewrite his letter to make it more effective, what changes would you make?

Writing Practice 7: *Writing for a Specific Audience*

Jim's audience for the Forest Park letter consists of adults who could be expected to take an interest in the project and to contribute time and money toward making it a success. If Jim were to write to a different audience (perhaps his friends and other high school students, for example), he would rephrase parts of the letter in order to appeal to that special audience.

Rewrite Jim's letter for one of the following specific audiences. Keep the main idea of the letter and use the same information but change the language to suit the audience you select. Feel free to add any facts or ideas that would increase the persuasiveness of the letter.

1. High school students

2. Retired people

3. Friends interested in hiking and camping

4. City officials, such as the mayor

5. Residents of the community

Writing Practice 8: *A Call to Action*

Write an announcement that could be read over your school's public address system or published in the school paper. Your purpose is to persuade your listeners to adopt a course of action. Choose one of the following situations or make up one of your own as the basis for your announcement. Remember to support your argument with reasons why your audience should do as you ask.

1. A controversial speaker is coming to lecture students about a proposed local law that would place a 9 P.M. curfew on everyone under eighteen years of age. You want as many students as possible to attend in order to show their response.

2. School officials have canceled a midwinter music festival be-
    cause the last two festivals were poorly attended. You announce
    a weekend rally to show that students want a festival this year
    and will plan ways to make it a success. You want a big turnout
    at the rally.

3. Vandalism has destroyed parts of your campus. You feel that
    your classmates can do more to keep the campus clean and safe.
    Suggest ways students can prevent vandalism and give them
    reasons for caring about their campus.

4. Select a controversial issue from a book, a newspaper, or
    magazine. It can be a local, state, national, or even global
    problem. State your views on the issue and convince your
    audience to write letters to their (local or national) elected
    representatives in support of your position.

5. A schoolwide election will be held to decide whether or not
    friendly visitors from another galaxy should be allowed to
    observe a typical day in your school. State your views on the
    subject and convince your audience to vote the way you suggest.

Organizing Your Ideas: The Thesis Statement

In a persuasive essay the thesis statement tells the subject of the argument and the writer's point of view on the subject. The following thesis statements make the writer's opinion clear.

High school students should have complete freedom in making decisions about which courses to take.

The United States should keep its commitment to develop alternate sources of energy by putting more money into researching solar power.

More courses on marriage and families should be offered in high school so that every graduate will understand the responsibilities of married life.

A good thesis statement gives an opinion that can be supported with sound reasoning and evidence. Value judgments—statements putting a higher value on one thing over another—are not suitable as thesis statements because they are not arguable. For example, the opinion "Table tennis is more fun than bumper pool" is a value judgment, not a statement that can be argued logically. Any opinion based solely on taste is also unsuitable for a thesis statement. For example, "Art history is my favorite subject" may be a true statement, but it is not one that can be changed by an appeal to logic. When you write a thesis statement, remember to express an opinion that you can support with logical argument and evidence.

One way to develop a thesis statement is to ask yourself questions about the subject, as the following examples demonstrate.

Subjects	*Questions*
School vandalism	What can students do to prevent vandalism on campus? What are the principal causes of vandalism at this school? Who is responsible?
Junk food ads on radio and television	Should junk food advertising be banned on radio and television? Does the government have an obligation to prevent the advertising of unhealthy foods?
Teenage unemployment	What are the causes of teenage unemployment in the community? What can be done to remedy it?

Asking questions can help you focus your interest in the subject. If, for example, you have chosen to write about school vandalism, think about why vandalism is a problem. You may decide that the problem is student apathy and, therefore, you want to concentrate on reasons and ways for students to become involved in the prevention of vandalism. If, on the other hand, you decide that the real problem is the motives of the vandals themselves, you might focus on what can be done to help them.

Once you have defined the problem and asked questions to help establish your point of view you are ready to formulate your thesis statement. Since the thesis statement in a persuasive essay tells your point of view and often your conclusion about an issue, it is a good idea to research your subject thoroughly before formulating the thesis statement. You want to be certain of your ideas and opinions before planning an essay around them.

After investigating the subject and assembling information about it, you are ready to compose your thesis statement. The following thesis statements based on the subject of vandalism give two examples of different conclusions:

1. Vandalism has grown into a major problem because of student apathy. Students should know that damage to valuable equipment affects all school activities and should volunteer to help in the new School Watch program and the Speakers' Bureau.

2. The real cause of vandalism is the lack of work opportunities for teenagers locally. Students should join the Committee on Youth Employment to help seek solutions to the problem.

Each thesis statement does the following: (a) it sets forth the main subject of the essay "Vandalism"; (b) it expresses the writer's point of view on the major cause of the problem, which is student apathy in the first statement and lack of employment opportunities in the second; and (c) it asks its audience to act, by helping with a School Watch program and a Speakers' Bureau in the first and by joining the Committee on Youth Employment in the second.

Writing Assignment II: *A Persuasive Essay*

A. Prewriting

Deciding on an Issue: Make a list of six issues that are important to you and that are good topics for persuasive essays. Write each one in the form of a question, as in the following examples:

1. Should physical education be a required subject in high school?

2. Should local and federal laws on the buying and selling of firearms be stricter?

3. Should the penalty for drunk driving be more severe on teenagers or adults?

4. Should a class in computers be a high school graduation requirement?

5. Should the nationwide legal drinking age be twenty-one?

6. Should the United States send funds to help victims of floods, earthquakes, and other natural disasters in countries with anti-American policies?

7. Should a junior college education be free to all high school graduates?

8. Should the government devote more of its budget to space exploration?

Using Questioning Skills: From your list, select an issue that you feel strongly about. Using the *Who? What? When? Where? Why?* and *How?* questioning system, write a series of questions about the issue. Study the following examples first. (For a review of this technique, reread the section on questioning in Chapter 1.)

1. What is the issue? What is my point of view on it?

2. Who does the issue concern? Who is affected by it?

3. When did the issue arise?

4. Where did it arise?

5. Why has it become a problem?

6. How can it be solved?

Investigating the Topic: Even though you may have decided on your point of view, gather information about all sides of the issue. Use a variety of resources for information, including magazine and newspaper articles, interviews with people, and radio and television reports. Keep notes on your research.

B. Writing

After gathering all the necessary information about the issue, write a thesis statement to use as the basis for a persuasive essay. Remember that the thesis statement in a persuasive essay appeals to the audience *to do* or *to believe* something. For this assignment assume that your audience consists of your teacher and classmates.

C. Postwriting

Read your thesis statement to another person—a classmate, parent, teacher, or friend. Then ask your partner to restate the issue and your point of view in his or her own words. If your partner is unsure what your thesis statement is, you will need to rewrite it in clearer language. In the next few Writing Practices, you will use this thesis statement in developing a persuasive essay.

Organizing Your Ideas: The Topic Outline

The persuasive essay, like other essays, follows a general pattern of organization. The *introductory paragraph*, sometimes called the *thesis paragraph*, introduces the main idea and usually contains the thesis statement. The *body*, usually several paragraphs long, explains the main idea and presents reasons and evidence in support of the writer's opinion. The *conclusion* summarizes the points of the paper or restates the thesis for emphasis in a new way.

Preparing an informal outline, such as the following one, will help you to organize your ideas and plan your arguments. (Informal outlines are discussed on page 104.)

Vandalism
"Don't care" attitude of students
Ways of cutting it down
School Watch program
Speakers

Damage caused by vandalism
Broken office machines and typewriters
Business classes canceled
School work not completed
Damage to sports equipment
Fewer sports activities
Gym closed weekends

Solutions to vandalism
School Watch program
Student volunteers for campus patrol
Hall guards for coordinators
Speakers' Bureau
School referendum on problem
Volunteers for visiting parent and civic groups

Student Involvement
Students as source of problem
Students as solution

Writing the Persuasive Essay

Writing the Introductory Paragraph

In a good persuasive essay the opening paragraph establishes the topic in a way that will immediately interest the reader. Although the introductory paragraph often includes a thesis statement that clearly and directly sets forth the main point of the essay, the practice is not mandatory.

In "The Thin Grey Line" by Marya Mannes, the writer does not include a thesis statement in the opening paragraph. Experienced writers often vary the standard practice of including the thesis statement in the introduction by leading up to the statement with examples or evidence. Such a technique builds the readers' interest and desire to identify the writer's viewpoint and formulate their own conclusions. In "The Thin Grey Line" the thesis statement does not appear fully expressed until paragraph 5: "Bit by bit, the resistance to and immunity against wrong that a healthy social body builds up by law and ethics and the dictation of conscience have broken down."

Less-experienced writers usually take the direct approach of including the thesis statement in the introductory paragraph, where it presents the main idea of the essay and establishes the writer's opinion about it. The following example demonstrates how to include the thesis statement in the introductory paragraph:

> "Class canceled due to lack of equipment." "Sorry, no open gym this weekend." Are these the kinds of signs you expect to see at Jefferson High? If you think it cannot happen here, then you should know about the recent wave of vandalism on campus. If you do not know about the problem, you are part of the problem: student apathy and indifference is allowing the vandalism to go unchecked. Perhaps it has not affected you personally. Your locker has not been smashed, or your gym class equipment has not been stolen, but it is just a matter of time. The administration is doing what it can to improve the condition, but students can take steps to help, too. Join the new School Watch system designed to keep the entire campus safe, or join the Speakers' Bureau to discuss the issue and increase everyone's awareness of the problem.

Writing Practice 9: *An Introductory Paragraph*

Using the thesis statement you developed in Writing Assignment II, write an introductory paragraph for a persuasive essay. In your paragraph include a thesis statement that clearly and directly sets forth the main idea of the essay.

Writing the Body of the Essay

When you write a persuasive essay, it is important to keep in mind both the audience for which you are writing and also the purpose of your essay.

Knowing your audience helps determine what points you will make and how you will make them. For example, the essay on vandalism would be written differently for each of the following audiences: high-school students, readers of the local newspaper, readers of a nationally distributed literary magazine, members of a parent-teacher association.

The purpose in writing a persuasive essay is to convince your audience to accept your point of view. Decide before you begin writing whether your purpose is to change your audience's mind or to call them to action. You can achieve your purpose with appeals to emotion or appeals to reason, but most persuasive writers use a combination of the two. Persuasion by emotional appeal only is very difficult to maintain throughout an essay. The most effective persuasion usually results by combining an appeal to reason with an appeal to emotion.

For example, in "The Thin Grey Line" Marya Mannes argues logically about the effect of public indifference on public morality. She supports her argument with examples of dishonest behavior from real-life situations and includes a wide range of experiences to support her claim that the problem is a dangerous one for all members of society. She makes her essay more persuasive by combining logical argument with an appeal to her readers' emotions. In the following line, she uses emotional language to make readers feel the extreme nature of the problem: "And instead of the fighting indignation of a people outraged by those who prey on them, we have the admission of impotence: 'They all do it.'" Words like *indignation* and *outraged* invite the audience to feel indignant and outraged as well.

In a persuasive essay the appeals to logic and emotion are directed toward the same purpose: to persuade the audience. As you write a persuasive essay, keep your purpose in mind; this will prevent you from straying from the main point of the paper. For example, the whole purpose of "The Thin Grey Line" is to convince the reader that he or she has a moral responsibility to draw a line between right and wrong for the good of the society. Marya Mannes does not stray from this specific subject by going into an explanation of laws affecting moral behavior or even by examining the causes of the present problem in depth. She concentrates on the problem itself. One way to keep your purpose in mind is to have your thesis statement in front of you as you write; this will help focus your attention and pinpoint your ideas.

Writing Practice 10: *Developing the Body of a Persuasive Essay*

Using the thesis paragraph you have already written, write the body of a persuasive essay. Begin by writing down three major points you will cover. Then develop these points into three separate paragraphs supported with examples and details. Try to include both an appeal to emotion and an appeal to reason in your paragraphs.

Writing the Conclusion

The *conclusion* of a persuasive essay often summarizes the arguments of the essay and, for emphasis, restates the thesis in a slightly different way. A summary of arguments helps the reader see how each point adds up to a valid conclusion. Restating the thesis helps to bring the argument full circle by demonstrating that the ideas expressed in the introduction have been treated fully.

Persuasive essays can also end by making a call to action. For example, the essay on vandalism could end by urging students to join the School Watch and Speakers' Bureau. Persuasive essays can also conclude with a prediction about what will happen if the audience does not support the writer's point of view; the vandalism essay could end with a bleak description of a school closed down because of damages. Still another way to conclude a persuasive paper is to offer solutions to the problem. Any of these types of endings can be combined with an appeal to action, as it could in the vandalism paper calling for student participation in preventing the problem. Finally, persuasive papers often conclude with an emotional statement about the subject. For example, the vandalism essay could end with an emotional appeal about the need for students to band together, emphasizing school loyalty and pride. Reread the conclusion to "The Thin Grey Line" and note what method Marya Mannes uses to end her persuasive essay.

Writing Practice 11: *Concluding a Persuasive Essay*

Write a conclusion for your persuasive essay. Restate your thesis statement, and try to convince readers to accept your point of view. If appropriate, encourage them to carry out a specific action.

Writing Practice 12: *Responding and Revising*

After you have completed the first draft of your persuasive essay, exchange papers with classmates as your teacher directs. Read each other's drafts, noting the following checklist items. For each paper list two positive features, such as a clear thesis statement or good use of evidence. Also list two areas for improvement, such as correcting a sentence fragment, or adding reasons to support your viewpoint.

Using the suggestions from your partner or group and the checklist items below, revise your essay and rewrite it, incorporating any necessary changes.

Checklist for Revising a Persuasive Essay

1. The thesis statement is an arguable one, not a value judgment or a matter of personal taste.

2. The thesis statement is clear and direct. It gives the topic of the essay and expresses a point of view.

3. The argument of the essay is developed with at least three important points supported with examples and details.

4. The essay is directed to a specific audience and uses language suitable for that audience.

5. The essay uses sound reasoning and includes an appeal to emotion.

6. The essay presents sufficient evidence to support the conclusion.

7. The essay is unified. Each paragraph helps develop the thesis statement.

8. The essay is coherent. The reader can move easily from one idea to the next.

Sentence Combining:
Appositives and Absolute Phrases

Inserting Appositives

For more information on appositive phrases, see pages 520-522.

In the last section on sentence combining, you inserted adjective clauses into sentences. Sometimes, as the following example shows, a sentence containing several adjective clauses may sound awkward or wordy.

> Monopoly, *which is a notoriously long-lasting game,* was once played in a bathtub for thirty-one hours, *which is a record noted in the* Modern-Day Almanac, *which is a reputable source.*

The preceding sentence can be improved by using *appositives* instead of adjective clauses.

> Monopoly, *a notoriously long-lasting game,* was once played in a bathtub for thirty-one hours, *a record noted in the* Modern-Day Almanac, *a reputable source.*

An *appositive* is a word or group of words that means the same as a noun or pronoun in the sentence. (Appositives are discussed in Chapter 19.) In the following examples the words *the smallest planet in our solar system* have the same meaning as the word *Mercury.*

Base Sentence: Mercury is the planet closest to the sun.

Insert: It is the smallest planet in our solar system.

Combined: Mercury, *the smallest planet in our solar system,* is the planet closest to the sun.

For greater variety the appositive can often be shifted to the beginning of the sentence, preceding the noun it modifies.

Base Sentence: Croquet is rapidly experiencing a revival.

Insert: It was a lawn game.

It was popular in the early 1900s.

Combined: Croquet, *a lawn game popular in the early 1900s,* is rapidly experiencing a revival.

> or

A *lawn game popular in the early 1900s,* croquet is rapidly experiencing a revival.

Appositives are usually set off by commas because they provide additional information that is not essential for an understanding of the sentence's meaning.

Exercise 1: *Inserting Appositives*

After studying the examples, combine each of the sets of sentences by inserting an appositive. As you write the combined sentence on a sheet of paper, try shifting some appositives to the beginnings of the sentences for variety. In the first five sets, the words that become appositives are underlined.

Examples

a. Samuel Mudd died without clearing his name.

He was <u>the doctor who treated John Wilkes Booth.</u>

He was <u>President Lincoln's assassin.</u>

Samuel Mudd, the doctor who treated John Wilkes Booth, President Lincoln's assassin, died without clearing his name.

b. Dr. Schmidt teaches us how to keep our bodies alive and healthy.

She is an expert in social ecology.

An expert in social ecology, Dr. Schmidt teaches us how to keep our bodies alive and healthy.

207

1. The document is stored in the Library of Congress.
   The document is a landmark in judicial history.

2. Our drama department is producing *Ten Little Indians*.
   It is a mystery by Agatha Christie.

3. Miguel sold his first book to a publisher.
   Miguel is a free-lance writer of children's stories.

4. The main course was prepared in a microwave oven.
   The main course was turkey tetrazzini.

5. Applause filled the theater as she read the name of the winner.
   The winner was a newcomer in the motion picture industry.

6. The music was a perfect accompaniment to the Renaissance wedding.
   The music was a harp and a mandolin.

7. Portuguese is the language of Brazil and Portugal.
   It is a Romance language.

8. Our vacation was the perfect ending to a wonderful summer.
   Our vacation was a week at my aunt's farm.

9. Vancouver is surrounded by waterways and spectacular mountains.
   It is a city closely tied both culturally and economically to the United States.

10. Reading and writing are taught to students throughout the world today.
    They were once skills belonging only to the clergy.

Exercise 2: *Inserting Appositives*

The following sets of sentences can be combined by inserting appositives. After you study the examples, write a combined sentence on a sheet of paper for each of the sets. Remember that some appositives can be shifted to the beginning of the sentence. In the first five sets, the words that become appositives are underlined.

Examples

a. "Mr. Ed" was patterned after "Francis."
"Mr. Ed" was a talking horse in a popular television show.
"Francis" was a talking mule in several old movies.
"Mr. Ed," a talking horse in a popular television show, was patterned after "Francis," a talking mule in several old movies.

b. Ida B. Wells helped organize the NAACP in 1909.
She was a lifetime crusader against racial discrimination.
A lifetime crusader against racial discrimination, Ida B. Wells helped organize the NAACP in 1909.

1. The gift was thoroughly appreciated by the happy newlyweds.
It was a brightly wrapped set of monogrammed towels.
They were a young couple who had met in college.

2. Tornadoes have been known to circulate 500 mph winds.
They are violently whirling columns of air.
500 mph winds are a force capable of cutting a mile-wide path of destruction through cities and towns.

3. Dr. Daniel Hale Williams performed the first successful heart operation in 1893.
He was the founder of the first hospital for black Americans.

4. Coretta King has made important contributions to the cause of civil rights.
Coretta King is the widow of Martin Luther King, Jr.

5. Filled with hydrogen, the *Hindenburg* tragically exploded one hundred feet above its landing site.
Hydrogen is a highly flammable gas.
The *Hindenburg* was a German dirigible that had safely crossed the Atlantic.
The landing site was a crowded New Jersey airfield in 1937.

6. The Bee Gees popularized disco-rock in the late seventies.
The Bee Gees were a soft-rock group who first rose to fame in the early sixties.

7. Beverly Rivera is attending the university to obtain a degree in psychology.
   She is a retired postal clerk.
   Psychology is a field she always wanted to study.

8. Ms. Gianattia is well known for her support of our athletic programs.
   She is our assistant principal in charge of curriculum.

9. Vivien Leigh won a second Oscar for her performance as Blanche in *A Streetcar Named Desire*.
   She was the Academy Award winning actress who played Scarlett in *Gone with the Wind*.
   A Streetcar Named Desire was a 1952 movie that also starred Marlon Brando.

10. Charlie McCarthy was willed to the Smithsonian Institution by Edgar Bergen.
    Charlie McCarthy was a loquacious wooden dummy.
    Edgar Bergen was a famous ventriloquist.
    The Smithsonian Institution is a national museum located in Washington, D.C.

Inserting Absolute Phrases

You can also enrich your sentences by inserting *absolute phrases*. An *absolute phrase* is related in meaning to the sentence in which it is inserted but does not modify a specific word in the sentence. The following examples show how absolute phrases are inserted into a base sentence.

Notice that the helping verbs (*was, were, is*) are omitted in the combined sentence.

Base Sentence: The woman stood wearily in the doorway.

Insert: *The children* were *asleep in their beds*.

Insert: *The task of moving* was *finished*.

Combined: *The children asleep in their beds, the task of moving finished*, the woman stood wearily in the doorway.

For variety, absolute phrases can also be inserted at the end of the sentence:

Base Sentence: The nurse pushed the last stretcher down the corridor.

Insert: *The crisis* was *past*.

Insert: *The halls* were *now dark and silent*. (*and*)

Combined: The nurse pushed the last stretcher down the corridor, *the crisis past and the halls now dark and silent.*

Absolute phrases are always separated from the rest of the sentence by a comma or commas.

Exercise 3: *Inserting Absolute Phrases*

Study the example carefully and then combine each set of sentences on the next page by inserting absolute phrases. For the first five sets, the underlining signal indicates which words will be inserted into each base sentence. When you write your sentences on a sheet of paper, put the absolute phrase at the beginnings of some sentences for variety. Remember that commas separate an absolute phrase from the rest of the sentence.

Example

a. Cilla enjoyed the colorful performance.
The dancers were twirling rapidly.

The sound of guitars was filling the air.

The dancers twirling rapidly, the sound of guitars filling the air, Cilla enjoyed the colorful performance.

211

1. The carnival was a loud, colorful sight.
    <u>Balloons</u> were <u>flying overhead</u>.

    <u>Firecrackers</u> were <u>exploding sharply</u>.

    <u>Crowds of people in wild costumes</u> were <u>romping in the streets</u>.

    (*and*)

2. The hurricane unleashed its power on the coastline.
    <u>Winds</u> were <u>overturning cars</u>.

    <u>Waves</u> were <u>crushing boats against their docks</u>.

3. The scientist continued his experiments late into the night.
    <u>The research deadline</u> was <u>approaching quickly</u>.

4. The old mule trudged wearily up the dirt road.
    <u>The cart</u> was <u>sagging from the weight of the gold</u>.

5. The harsh ocean waves roared furiously behind.
    <u>Gusts of wind</u> were <u>carrying papers into the air</u>.

    <u>Their force</u> was <u>blowing sand into our eyes</u>. (*and*)

6. Ray's hands were clutching the newspaper tightly.
    His eyes were glued to the article in the upper right-hand corner.

7. They shopped carefully for a new car.
    The money was already in the bank.

8. She put her hands on his shoulders with the tenderness of a mother's touch.
    His face was contorted with pain.
    Memories of the loss were still fresh in his mind.

9. Paula turned her attention to caring for the garden.
    The effects of the heavy rain were past.
    The day was sunny and clear.

10. She greeted us in her familiar, cheerful voice.
    The previous day's disagreement was forgotten.

Exercise 4: Combining Sentences to Form a Paragraph

Some of the following sets of sentences do not contain signals but all can be combined using adjective clauses, appositives, and absolute phrases. (For a review of adjective clauses, turn to pages 534–555.) Decide which sentence in each set will be the base and then insert the other sentences to form a single sentence. On a separate sheet of paper, write the combined sentences in paragraph form.

1.   The world's first Ferris wheel was created especially for the Columbian Exposition of 1893.
      It was also the largest one ever built.
      The exposition was a celebration honoring the 400th anniversary of Columbus' discovery of America.

2.   George Ferris designed the unique ride.
      He was a bridge builder.
      He lived in Pittsburgh. (*who*)
      The ride would carry over 1200 people in thirty-six cars. (*which*)

3.   Ferris persisted and raised the money.
      Fair officials were scoffing at his idea.
      He needed the money to start his own company.

4.   The pieces were shipped to the Chicago lake front.
      Several companies were building the huge parts at different locations.
      The lake front was where the wheel was to be assembled.

5.   In March 1893 the axle arrived in Chicago from Pittsburgh.
      The axle was a forty-five-foot-long piece of steel.
      The piece of steel would turn the Ferris wheel.
      Pittsburgh was where it had been built.

Writing Practice: *A Letter to the Editor*

At the end of every year, the portrait of an individual who has had a great effect on the world appears on the cover of *Time* magazine, and that person is designated Man or Woman of the Year. This honor is kept a secret, and readers enjoy wondering who will be chosen each year. In December many readers even send letters to the magazine nominating someone for this honor. Review the past year, thinking about the important events and the personalities who shaped them. What person do you feel had the greatest impact on the world or perhaps just on your own life?

In note form, list your reasons for believing this person should be Man or Woman of the Year. Support your ideas with specific details and use the library if you need further information. Then write a well-organized letter to the editor explaining whom you would nominate, developing your opinion with supporting details.

Use some of the sentence-combining techniques you have learned to make the sentences in your letter interesting and varied.

Imaginative Writing

Imagination is your inner camera to the world; it helps you perceive the world and the people in it in a unique way. Imagination is the source of new ideas, inventions, and solutions. Although it is important in all kinds of writing, it is most essential in imaginative writing: short stories, novels, plays, and poems. In imaginative writing, you have the opportunity to create settings, characters, plots, and experiences and to express your ideas through the richness and beauty of language. In this chapter you will use your imagination and language skills to write poetry, a short story, and a dramatic scene.

Elements of Poetry

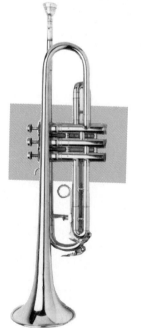

From its beginnings poetry has been closely associated with music. The earliest known poems were meant to be sung or chanted rather than spoken. In the nineteenth century the word *song* could mean either "a poem" or "words set to music." The lyrics of many popular songs today use the elements traditionally associated with poetry: rhyme, meter, and verse patterns.

Formal poetry is poetry that follows a standard form.

Formal poetry uses a pattern of repeating sounds called *rhyme* and *alliteration*, a pattern of repeating rhythm called *meter*, and a pattern of repeating lines called *stanzas*. Just as, in a song, a beautiful tune increases your enjoyment of the words to the lyrics, so in poetry the musical effects of repeating sounds and rhythms increase your enjoyment of the poem.

Rhyme in Poetry

Words that rhyme share the same end sounds. In rhyming poems the rhyming words come at the end of each line. In most formal poetry the rhyming words rhyme exactly.

Model: A Formal Poem Using Rhyme

Read the poem on the following page by Wendell Berry and notice the use of rhyme and repetition.

To Know the Dark[1]
To go in the dark with a light is to know the light.
To know the dark, go dark. Go without sight,
and find that the dark, too, blooms and sings,
and is traveled by dark feet and dark wings.

—*Wendell Berry*

Think and Discuss

1. What words in the poem rhyme exactly? Where do they appear?

2. What specific words are repeated several times? What effect does this repetition have on the meaning of the poem?

3. In what way does the poet use two contrasting ideas to make a statement?

Exact rhyme (also called *full,* or *perfect, rhyme*) means the repetition of almost identical sounds. Sometimes, only the first letter in the words differs, as in Wendell Berry's rhyming words *light/sight* and *sings/wings.* When words sound similar but not identical, the effect is

---

[1]"To Know the Dark" from *Farming: A Hand Book* by Wendell Berry. Copyright © 1970 by Wendell Berry. Reprinted by permission of Harcourt Brace Jovanovich, Inc.

called *near rhyme*. (This is also known as *half*, or *slant*, *rhyme*.) In near rhyme, words may share repeating vowel sounds (such as *moon/ bloom, June*) or repeating consonant sounds (*song/clang/ring*).

Repetition of Sound in Poetry

Another kind of sound effect in poetry is the *repetition* of exact words. How many times does the poet repeat the word *dark* in "To Know the Dark"?

Assonance is the repetition of vowel sounds to create a rhyme: *show/stone, us/sun, field/knees. Consonance* is the repetition of consonant sounds to create a rhyme: *tongue/sang, book/thick, waste/mast.*

Another musical effect poets use is called *alliteration*. Words alliterate when they *begin* with the same sound. Alliteration can be used to emphasize the meaning of the words.

Models: Poems Using Alliteration

Notice how the poet uses alliteration to emphasize word meanings in the following stanza from "The Waking."

I **w**ake to **s**leep, and take my **w**aking **s**low.
I **f**eel my **f**ate in what I cannot **f**ear.
I learn by **g**oing where I have to **g**o.[1]

—Theodore Roethke [boldface added]

The following poem by Lucille Clifton uses alliteration and repetition to create a musical effect. Identify each pair of alliterating words as you read the poem and be prepared to discuss how the use of alliteration and repetition enhances the meaning of the poem.

let there be new flowering[2]
let there be new flowering
in the fields   let the fields
turn mellow for the men
let the men keep tender
through the time   let the time
be wrested from the war
let the war be won
let love be
at the end

—Lucille Clifton

From "The Waking" by Theodore Roethke from *The Collected Poems of Theodore Roethke* Copyright © 1953 by Theodore Roethke. Reprinted by permission of Doubleday & Company, Inc. and Faber and Faber Ltd.

[2]"let there be new flowering" from *An Ordinary Woman* by Lucille Clifton. Copyright © 1974 by Lucille Clifton. Reprinted by permission of Random House, Inc.

Writing Practice 1: *Creating a Rhymed Poem*

Write a poem of at least four lines using the musical effects of rhyming words and alliteration. You may want to use Wendell Berry's poem "To Know the Dark" as a model for writing your own. You might write a poem about something you know well, as Wendell Berry wrote about the dark. Use one of the following rhyming patterns in your poem: either rhyme the first two lines and the last two lines, or rhyme the first and third lines and the second and fourth lines.

Meter in Poetry

Meter **means "rhythmic pattern of sound."**

The meter of a poem is like the rhythm of a piece of music. You can determine the meter of a poem by listening to the pattern of stressed and unstressed syllables. *Stressed* means "accented," or "spoken more loudly." In most words over one syllable, you can easily hear which syllable is stressed, or accented:

POetry   oHIo   caNOE

When you say these words aloud, you pronounce the syllable in capital letters louder than the other syllables. Another way of writing stress marks is to use an accent (').

The speech that people use in their everyday lives is rhythmic. For example, if you say, "I just got home from school," you are using a rhythmic speech pattern:

I just got home from school.

The difference between your everyday speech rhythms and the rhythms of poetry is consistency. In your usual speech you do not intentionally speak in regular rhythms, but when poets choose to write using regular meter, each line of the poem follows that meter with only minor variations. As with rhyme, poets try to choose a meter that helps enhance the meaning of the poem.

Models: Rhythm in Poetry

In the following poem by Naomi Replansky, the rhythm is that of a child's jumping rope song. In this meter there are four stresses to each line. (The first two stanzas are marked.) Read the poem aloud and listen to the stresses in each line until you hear four.

An Inheritance[1]

Five dollars, four dollars, three dollars, two,
One, and none, and what do we do?

This is the worry that never got said,
But ran so often in my mother's head

And showed so plain in my father's frown
That to us kids it drifted down.

It drifted down like soot, like snow,
In the dream-tossed Bronx, in the long ago.

I shook it off with a shake of my head,
I bounced my ball, I ate warm bread,

I skated down the steepest hill.
But I must have listened, against my will:

When the wind blows wrong, I can hear it today.
Then my mother's worry stops all play

And, as if in its rightful place,
My father's frown divides my face.

—*Naomi Replansky* [stress marks added]

---

[1]"An Inheritance" by Naomi Replansky. First printed in *A Geography of Poets*, Edward Field, Bantam, 1979. Reprinted by permission of Naomi Replansky.

This regular, singsong meter is appropriate to the poem. Naomi Replansky is writing about a childhood experience of realizing how much her parents were worried about money. Even though this is a serious subject, the poet is thinking about how this worry was passed on to her from childhood; she uses the jumping rope rhythm of her childhood to fit the subject of her poem.

Regular meter can produce many different effects, depending on the kind of rhythm used in the poem. In the following poem by Robert Frost, the mood is very different from "An Inheritance." Read the poem aloud and listen for five stresses in each line. (The first stanza is marked for you.) Also, listen for the mood of the poem. What feeling is the poet telling you about?

Acquainted with the Night[1]

I have been one acquainted with the night.
I have walked out in rain—and back in rain.
I have outwalked the furthest city light.

I have looked down the saddest city lane.
I have passed by the watchman on his beat
And dropped my eyes, unwilling to explain.

I have stood still and stopped the sound of feet
When far away an interrupted cry
Came over houses from another street,

But not to call me back or say good-bye;
And further still at an unearthly height,
One luminary clock against the sky

Proclaimed the time was neither wrong nor right
I have been one acquainted with the night.

—*Robert Frost* [stress marks added]

---

[1]"Acquainted with the Night" from *The Poetry of Robert Frost* edited by Edward Connery Lathem. Copyright 1928, © 1969 by Holt, Rinehart and Winston. Copyright © 1956 by Robert Frost. Reprinted by permission of Holt, Rinehart and Winston, Publishers, the Estate of Robert Frost, and Jonathan Cape Ltd.

The meter in this poem is regular, but it does not produce a singsong effect. Rather it is a steady rhythm, like the rhythm of someone walking. The speaker in this poem is telling you what it means to be "one acquainted with the night." It is a lonely experience, and the meter of the poem helps you feel it, through a steady, walking rhythm. What lines in the poem most help you understand the experience?

Writing Practice 2: *Using Meter in Poetry*

Write a short poem using a regular meter in each line. It will probably be helpful to reread Naomi Replansky's poem on page 318, which uses four stresses to the line, and Robert Frost's poem, which uses five stresses to the line. The following ideas can be used as suggestions for your poem.

1. In "An Inheritance" Naomi Replansky writes about inheriting her parents' worry and her father's frown that went with the worry. Write a poem about a quality (not an object or anything material) that you have inherited from your parents or grandparents. For example, think of some way in which you are like one of your parents or grandparents. Are you independent, shy, stubborn, curious, or carefree? Like Naomi Replansky you may want to begin your poem by saying how this quality was passed down to you and how you feel about it.

2. "Acquainted with the Night" tells about someone who feels isolated, apart from others. Robert Frost associates this feeling with walking by himself at night. Write a poem about feeling isolated or alone. Before you begin, think about what you do when you feel alone. Do you go to a special place? Do you go out walking? What do you notice around you when you are feeling alone? Is the aloneness a sad feeling, a frightening feeling, or a satisfying feeling? In your poem tell the reader your feelings and observations.

Free Verse Poetry

For information on the structure of English, see pages 648-661.

Over the last century poets writing in English have been exploring ways of making poems without using the formal elements of rhyme, regular meter, and stanzas. This experimentation has spread so that most poets today are writing what is called *free verse, or nonformal poetry.*

Free verse poetry does not follow a standard form; the poet structures the language in a way that best expresses the meaning of the poem.

Poets today, like poets of all centuries, are fascinated with connecting word sounds and patterns to express meaning through the flow of language. Rather than using words according to formal patterns, however, many contemporary poets are writing poems that try to convey insights and experiences in new ways. Poets working with free verse often make up their own kinds of structure; they may use rhythms close to those of jazz, for instance, or they may arrange line breaks so that the poem forms a picture on the page.

Model: Using Ordinary Speech Rhythms in Poetry

One way poets create new effects is by using everyday language and speech rhythms in their poems. Listen to the ordinary speech rhythms in the following poem by Robert Hayden.

Those Winter Sundays[1]
Sundays too my father got up early
and put his clothes on in the blueblack cold,
then with cracked hands that ached
from labor in the weekday weather made
banked fires blaze. No one ever thanked him.

I'd wake and hear the cold splintering, breaking.
When the rooms were warm, he'd call,
and slowly I would rise and dress,
fearing the chronic angers of that house,
Speaking indifferently to him,
who had driven out the cold
and polished my good shoes as well.
What did I know, what did I know
of love's austere and lonely offices?

Chronic means "constant."

Offices here means "acts performed for someone."

—*Robert Hayden*

Think and Discuss

1. This poem has its own music and rhythm, even though it does not use formal rhyme or meter. For example, the first line in the poem sounds like someone talking; it has an everyday speech rhythm. What other lines sound like ordinary speech?

2. Mixed in with the casual speech rhythms are lines that give the poem a musical effect. To create this effect the poet uses assonance, consonance and alliteration, as in the following lines:

. . . cracked hands that	Assonance:	*cracked/hands*
ached/from labor in the	Consonance:	*cracked/ached*
weekday weather made/	Assonance:	*ached/labor/made*
banked fires blaze.	Alliteration:	*weekday/weather*

What other examples of assonance, consonance, and alliteration do you find in the preceding poem?

3. Robert Hayden's poem also presents its experience through imagery. An *image* is a vivid sensory detail, a description that helps you see, hear, feel, taste, or smell. The images that

[1]"Those Winter Sundays" from *Angle of Ascent: New and Selected Poems* by Robert Hayden. Copyright © 1975, 1972, 1970, 1966 by Robert Hayden. Reprinted by permission of Liveright Publishing Corporation.

Hayden uses make his father come alive. For example, the poet begins by telling you that his father got up early, in the "blueblack cold." The word *blueblack* helps you to imagine the scene: cold enough to turn a person's fingers blue, so dark and early that it was still black outside. What other images in the poem help you picture the scene and the situation?

Writing Assignment I: *Composing a Free Verse Poem*

A. Prewriting

Making a Word Cluster: Many poems, such as Robert Hayden's "Those Winter Sundays," are based on a strong memory of a person, a place, or an experience. Try to recall a memory that you feel deeply about and use that memory as the subject of your poem.

Make a word cluster for your memory by writing down words you associate with it. Use words that bring back the sights, sounds, tastes, and smells of the experience. For example, suppose that you remember being with your grandfather at his house when you were a child. You might write some of the following ideas in your word cluster.

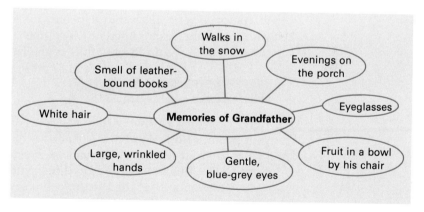

Focusing on an Image: Next, try to recall what is most important about your memory. What is the first sight or image that comes into your mind as you remember? Try to recall the feelings you had about your memory. Perhaps the memory about your grandfather is special to you because it is one of the last memories you have of him. As you think, write down the words as they come to you.

Suppose you recall your grandfather standing by a window, staring at you as you played in the snow. You remember this clearly because it was the last time you saw your grandfather, and so you write the words on the following page.

The Winter of His Last Year

Grandfather's warm, wrinkled hands
Clutch the cold window sill
In the winter of his last year
I play in the snow drifts
Stopping to smile and wave
At grandfather's loving gaze
Behind the glowing window pane
Feeling the circle of his love
And stricken, for one brief moment,
By the sunlit halo of his white hair.

B. Writing

Using some of the details from your word cluster, write a free verse poem about a special memory. Include sensory details of sight, sound, smell, touch, or taste to make your memory come alive for the reader. Write at least five lines. To begin your poem, write your thoughts in lines or phrases as they come to you. If you find it easier to write sentences or a paragraph, do so. After your ideas are on paper, circle the words, phrases, or lines that you want to include in your poem. Use what you have learned about rhythm and alliteration to compose your ideas into a poem. Experiment by manipulating words and phrases in different ways. Read your poem aloud to hear the rhythm of words and the flow of the language.

C. Postwriting

Revising with a Partner: After you have completed the first draft of your poem, read it aloud to a partner—either a friend, a classmate, a parent, or your teacher. With your partner, work on improving the word choice, line breaks, and rhythmic patterns.

After you are satisfied with your poem, write your final draft. Use the Proofreader's Checklist at the back of the book to make final corrections.

Sharing with a Group: As your teacher directs, read your poem aloud to a small group of classmates. Ask each member to comment on one feature of your poem that he or she particularly liked, such as an image, the use of alliteration, sensory detail, or the rhythm.

Line Breaks in Free Verse Poetry

When poets do not count out stresses for each line or end each line with a rhyming word, how do they decide where to break off a line of poetry? The answer is that each poet has his or her own rules about line breaks. The length of the line depends on the subject of the poem and how the poet is writing about it.

Models: Line Breaks in Free Verse Poetry

If you were writing a poem about sights you glimpsed from a moving car, you might write in very short lines:

> Proud mother duck
> parades with ducklings attached.
> Two women patiently
> flick reed poles
> into brown water—waiting.
> Lean, long-legged,
> the running man
> wearing earphones
> tunes out the world.

In general, short lines give poems a compressed, staccato effect, like rapid phrases of music. What other subjects can you think of that would be appropriate for short lines of poetry?

Long lines of poetry tend to give a flowing, melodic effect. The following section of a poem by Diane Wakoski uses long lines to create the effect of someone so enthusiastic about the subject that she goes on and on, flooding the reader with images.

An *ode* is a poem of praise.

[from] Ode to a Lebanese Crock of Olives[1]

for Walter's Aunt Libby's diligence
in making olives

As some women love jewels
and drape themselves with ropes of pearls, stud their ears
with diamonds, band themselves with heavy gold,
have emeralds on their fingers or
opals on white bosoms,
I live with the still life
of grapes whose skins frost over with the sugar forming inside,
hard apples, and delicate pears;
cheeses,
from the sharp fontina, to icy bleu,
the aromatic chevres, boursault, boursin, a litany of
thick bread, dark wines,
pasta with garlic,
soups full of potato and onion;
and butter and cream,
like the skins of beautiful women, are on my sideboard.

—*Diane Wakoski*

The preceding poem uses long lines to convey an overflow of praise for its subject. What other subjects would fit into long lines of poetry?

The following poem by Carl Rákosi uses a different effect. Instead of varying the length of the lines, the poet separates some words from the others. As you read this poem aloud, pause before you read the words that have been set off.

[from] The Experiment with a Rat[2]

Every time I nudge that spring
                              a bell rings
and a man walks out of a cage
assiduous and sharp like one of us
and brings me cheese.
                    How did he fall
                              into my power?

—*Carl Rákosi*

Assiduous means "diligent."

---

[1]From "Ode to a Lebanese Crock of Olives" in *Waiting for the King of Spain* by Diane Wakoski, Black Sparrow Press, 1976. Reprinted by permission of the author.

[2]"The Experiment with a Rat" by Carl Rákosi from ERE-Voice, New Directions, 1971. Reprinted by permission of Carl Rákosi.

Setting words apart focuses attention on them, making them stand out on the page. It also helps create a sense of rhythm. For example, suppose the last thought of the preceding poem had been written in the following manner.

How did he fall into my power?

You would read the preceding line all together, in one breath. However, the question is written on two lines in the original poem.

How did he fall
    into my power?

You read the question with a brief pause after the word *fall*. Line breaks are one important way the poet has of showing how a poem should be read.

Writing Practice 3: *Line Breaks in Free Verse Poetry*

Write a free verse poem, paying close attention to line length and line breaks. Use one of the following suggestions to get started or write the poem on a subject of your choice. As you write, remember to use specific sensory details to help the reader experience your poem.

1. Think of a subject appropriate to short lines: an action such as a race, an event such as an eclipse, or an experience such as watching lightning. Write a poem on the subject, using short lines.

227

2. Think of a subject appropriate to long lines: an action such as waves hitting a beach, an event such as a snowfall, or an experience such as drifting off to sleep or dreaming. Write a poem on the subject, using long lines to convey your meaning.

3. You may decide to write a poem that has both long lines and short lines. An action that involves a series of continuous motions and stops, such as riding a bicycle, swimming, mowing a lawn, or washing a car, might be appropriate to a mixture of long and short lines. Try writing your poem first, and then read the poem aloud as you look for the best places to break the lines. You may try several different versions until you find the one that best conveys your meaning.

Figurative Language

An important way poems communicate is through figurative language—language that imaginatively represents one thing in terms of another. Figurative language can also have a striking effect in both imaginative and expository prose.

The two most widely used types of figurative language are *simile* **and** *metaphor.*

Simile and metaphor are special types of comparisons. When people make comparisons in everyday life, they usually compare things that are similar: "This house looks just like the one I grew up in." When poets use simile and metaphor, however, they make comparisons between things that are not apparently similar but may have a particular quality or feature in common.

Model: A Poem Using Comparisons

Find the comparisons in the following lines from the poem "My Teeth."

[from] My Teeth[1]

The up-front ones are marvelous,
tiny dancers braving the wind,
shapely and disciplined.

—*Ed Ochester*

---

[1]From "My Teeth" in *Dancing on the Edges of Knives* by Ed Ochester. Copyright 1973 by Ed Ochester. Reprinted by permission of the author and the University of Missouri Press.

Think and Discuss

While there is no apparent similarity between teeth and dancers, the poet makes you think of ways in which they are alike. He calls them both "shapely and disciplined." In what other ways are your teeth like dancers?

Similes

A *simile* is a comparison stated with *like, as,* or *than* and sometimes with verbs such as *seems* or *appears.*

The comparison must be between two different types of items. For example, the comparison "Central High seems just like my old school" is not a simile for the reason that two *similar* types are being compared.

Model: *A Poem Using Similes*

The following simile is from "Tulips" by Sylvia Plath, a poem about being in the hospital.

> They have propped my head between the pillow and the sheet-cuff
> Like an eye between two white lids that will not shut.

—Sylvia Plath

The poet uses a simile to make two connections. The pillow and sheet-cuff seem to her like eyelids, and her head seems like the eye between the eyelids.

As you read the final two stanzas from "Tulips," identify as many similes as you can. The poet is speaking about the bright red tulips in her hospital room.[1]

Before they came the air was calm enough,
Coming and going, breath by breath, without any fuss.
Then the tulips filled it up like a loud noise.
Now the air snags and eddies round them the way a river
Snags and eddies round a sunken rust-red engine.
They concentrate my attention, that was happy
Playing and resting without committing itself.

The walls, also, seem to be warming themselves.
The tulips should be behind bars like dangerous animals;
They are opening like the mouth of some great African cat,
And I am aware of my heart: it opens and closes
Its bowl of red blooms out of sheer love of me.
The water I taste is warm and salt, like the sea,
And comes from a country far away as health.

—Sylvia Plath

The kind of simile a poet chooses depends on the whole poem. For example, in "Tulips" Sylvia Plath writes that the tulips fill up the air in her room "like a loud noise." Since she is in a hospital, where everything should be quiet, the effect of a loud noise is shocking. The simile says that the tulips are not beautiful to her, but are something shocking.

Writing Practice 4: *A Poem with Similes*

Write a short poem in which you use similes to make a comparison between two different types of items. You might like to write a poem that is a list of similes about one subject. For example, a humorous poem could begin: "You are as beautiful as . . ." and then continue with a list of similes. Things can be beautiful in different ways, so you might write:

You are as beautiful as a new pair
    of patent leather boots,
as beautiful as a field of wet hay,
as beautiful as French toast,
as beautiful as algebra . . .

---

[1]From "Tulips" in *Ariel* by Sylvia Plath. Copyright © 1962 by Ted Hughes. Published in Great Britain by Faber & Faber Limited, London. Reprinted by permission of Harper & Row, Publishers, Inc. and Olwyn Hughes, Literary Agent.

If you prefer, you may write about another quality instead of beauty:

> You're as funny as . . .
> The evening is as sad as . . .
> The icicle is as delicate as . . .

You may, instead, write about any other quality that interests you. Decide before you begin writing whether you want a humorous effect, a beautiful effect, a melancholy effect, or some other effect.

Metaphors

Like a simile, a *metaphor* makes a connection between two different types of items. Unlike a simile, a metaphor does not use any linking words, such as *like, as, seems,* or *appears*.

A metaphor tells you, in effect, that two unlike items are the same in some special way. Poets use metaphor to help their readers discover connections between things. Metaphor shows the reader how to see the world in a new way by making connections that are unusual and interesting.

Model: *A Poem Using Metaphors*

In the following poem, Robert Bly uses metaphor to express two important connections that he notices. Try to identify them as you read.

Taking the Hands[1]

Taking the hands of someone you love,
You see they are delicate cages . . .
Tiny birds are singing
In the secluded prairies
And in the deep valleys of the hand.

—*Robert Bly*

The poet compares the hands "of someone you love" with "delicate cages," such as those that hold singing birds. If this were a simile, it would read, "You see they are *like* delicate cages." Since it is a metaphor, there is no connecting word. In this way metaphors are more concise than similes and sometimes have a more intense effect on the reader.

---

[1]"Taking the Hands" from *Silence in the Snowy Fields* by Robert Bly, Wesleyan University Press, 1962. Copyright © 1962 by Robert Bly. Reprinted by permission of the author.

Robert Bly also compares the hand to a landscape of prairies and deep valleys. The first metaphor in the poem is stated directly: "You see they are delicate cages." The second metaphor is called an *implied metaphor* because the connection between the two items is implied rather than stated directly. The phrase "the deep valleys of the hand" tells you that the poet is likening the hand to a landscape with deep valleys.

Models: Poems Combining Simile and Metaphor

Many poems commonly use a combination of simile and metaphor to convey their ideas, feelings, and impressions. The following poem by J. P. White describes a river flooding a town. As you read, notice how the poet uses figurative language to help share the experience of the flood.

Flood[1]

Our town slept as the river rose.

The black belly of sky
under which it dreamed
was swollen with tons of rain.

All night it rained,
a troop of men driven back to the roof's edge.
Lightning tangled over the water.

Wind snapped off the arms of our one oak.
Dogs shrunk into doorways weeping with cold.
I remember watching my sisters crouch beneath a candle
inside the crammed darkness of our swimming house.

Fed by such a fierce thickening of rain,
our red sleek river jammed in the night,
spilling its banks, lashing every house
with its matted tail of mud & water.

There are those that will tell you
it sounded like the rumbling echo
of a train lost in a tunnel.

But I will ask you to imagine
a thin black horse
standing in a field
grinding its oats.

—*J. P. White*

---

[1]"Flood" from *In Pursuit of Wings* by J. P. White. Reprinted by permission of Panache Books.

The images in "Flood" are all realistic. The poem describes a natural disaster, using words that help the reader see, hear, and feel the experience. Many poets use figurative language for an effect that is the opposite of realistic. They want the reader to react to a thought or an image that is in some way strange or mysterious. The following poem by Bill Knott uses first a metaphor and then a simile to express the poet's feelings about the nature of poetry. Can you identify the metaphor and the simile?

Poem to Poetry[1]
for Jennifer Kidney

Poetry,
you are an electric,
a magic, field—like the space
between a sleepwalker's outheld arms . . .

—Bill Knott

Think and Discuss

1. What is the first example of figurative language in the preceding poem? Is it a simile or a metaphor?

2. What metaphor does J. P. White use to describe the rain in his poem?

3. The poet also uses an implied metaphor in the lines, "lashing every house/with its matted tail of mud & water," which compare the river to an animal lashing its tail. Where in the poem do you learn what animal the poet is referring to? Can you identify the simile and the last metaphor of the poem? Do you think his use of simile and metaphor is effective?

4. How are the images in "Flood" unlike the images in "Poem to Poetry"? What does "Poem to Poetry" tell you about Bill Knott's idea of poetry?

Personification

When a poet uses metaphor to compare an object, an animal, or a concept to a human being, that metaphor is called *personification*. Personification gives human qualities, thoughts, or actions to non-human subjects.

Models: Poems Using Personification

Some poets personify objects by letting them speak as if they were human, as in the following lines from the poem "Mirror" by Sylvia Plath.[1]

I am silver and exact. I have no preconceptions.
Whatever I see I swallow immediately
Just as it is, unmisted by love or dislike.

Sylvia Plath

In the preceding lines the mirror speaks and describes itself with human qualities. Poets also use personification as an extended metaphor, carrying the comparison throughout the poem. The following poem by Emily Dickinson continues the comparison of a mountain with a human through both Stanzas.

The Mountain
The mountain sat upon the plain
In his eternal chair,
His observation omnifold,
His inquest everywhere.

The seasons prayed around his knees,
Like children round a sire:
Grandfather of the days is he,
Of dawn the ancestor.

—*Emily Dickinson*

Omnifold means
"all-encompassing."

Think and Discuss

In showing the mountain as a person, Emily Dickinson describes it as sitting in an "eternal chair," observing its surroundings. What other phrases indicate personification in the poem? How are the seasons personified?

Writing Practice 5: *A Poem Using Metaphor*

Write a poem based on a metaphor using additional images and similes if you wish. Some of the following suggestions may be helpful in writing your poem.

---

[1]From "Mirror" in *Crossing the Water* by Sylvia Plath. Copyright © 1963 by Ted Hughes. Originally appeared in *The New Yorker*. Published in Great Britain by Faber & Faber Limited, London. Reprinted by permission of Harper & Row, Publishers, Inc. and Olwyn Hughes, Literary Agent.

1. Reread the Robert Bly poem on page 231 for an example of a simple love poem. You might base your own poem on hands as well, or on the eyes or the voice of someone you love. Think of what the person's eyes, voice, or hands remind you of most. Perhaps the hands remind you of birds; perhaps they remind you of a sound, like a whisper. Use the comparison you think of as the metaphor for your poem.

2. Reread "Flood" on page 232. Perhaps you also have been through a frightening experience. Using your experience as the main idea of your poem, describe your experience using similes or metaphors. Include vivid sense images.

3. Reread the poem "Poem to Poetry" on page 233. This poem has a mysterious feel to it. You can write your own mysterious "Poem to Poetry" or a mysterious poem to anything else: "Poem to Outer Space," "Poem to the Law of Gravity," "Poem to Spaghetti," or "Poem to Sleep." Use the form of Bill Knott's poem as an example of how to structure your own poem. For example, you can begin as he does, using your own subject: "Car engines/you are . . . ," "Geometry/you are . . . ," or whatever subject you choose. Then continue the poem with a metaphor and a simile as your descriptions.

4. Reread the poem "The Mountain" on page 234. To create a poem using personification, think of an animal or object (such as a crocodile, a butterfly, a window, a streetlight, the rain, or the night). Then imagine what it might be like as a human being. Is it a young or an old person? Try to think of it in a human action of some kind, speaking or thinking, dreaming or feeling a strong emotion. Think of how it would be clothed or how it would act. Use some of your comparisons as the basis of your poem.

Elements of Fiction

Short stories and novels are constructed from three basic elements: *characters, setting,* and *plot.* When you read stories, you want to know who is involved (characters), when and where the story takes place (setting), and what happens to the characters (plot). Most story writers use a combination of experience and imagination to create stories. Even if a story is primarily fictional (not based on truth), the characters, setting, or plot may be based on the writer's own experiences. In this section, you will learn how to use the three elements of fiction along with your imagination and experiences to create a short story.

Creating Setting

The setting of a story includes details that tell where and when the story takes place.

The setting may be realistic, resembling places that actually exist or might exist, or the setting may be highly unrealistic, as it might appear in the mind of one or more characters.

Model: A Story Setting

In the following passage from Katherine Anne Porter's *Pale Horse, Pale Rider*, a hospital corridor is exaggerated in its dimensions and hospital attendants appear dreamlike to a girl who is desperately ill.

> "There is no bed yet," said Miss Tanner, as if she said, We are short of oranges. Dr. Hildesheim said, "Well, we'll manage something," and Miss Tanner drew the narrow trestle with bright crossed metal supports and small rubbery wheels into a deep jut of the corridor, out of the way of the swift white figures darting about, whirling and skimming like water flies all in silence. The white walls rose sheer as cliffs, a dozen frosted moons followed each other in perfect self-possession down a white lane and dropped mutely one by one into a snowy abyss.
>
> What is this whiteness and silence but the absence of pain? Miranda lay lifting the nap of her white blanket softly between eased fingers, watching a dance of tall deliberate shadows moving behind a wide screen of sheets spread upon a frame. It was there, near her, on her side of the wall where she could see it clearly and enjoy it, and it was so beautiful she had no curiosity as to its meaning. Two dark figures nodded, bent, curtsied to each other, retreated and bowed again, lifted long arms and spread great hands against the white shadow of the screen; then with a single round movement, the sheets were folded back, disclosing two speechless men in white, standing, and another speechless man in white, lying on the bare springs of a white iron bed. The man on the springs was swathed smoothly from head to foot in white, with folded bands across the face, and a large stiff bow like merry rabbit ears dangled at the crown of his head.[1]

Think and Discuss

What details from the preceding selection establish the *real* place of the action? What details show that the time and place seem fantastic and unreal to the sick patient, Miranda?

[1]From *Pale Horse, Pale Rider* by Katherine Anne Porter. Copyright 1937, 1965 by Katherine Anne Porter. Reprinted by permission of Harcourt Brace Jovanovich, Inc. and Jonathan Cape Ltd.

Writing Practice 6: *Listing Details of Setting*

Consider writing the first part of a short story about an incident in your life or in the life of someone you know. Or you may want to use your imagination to invent the characters, setting, and plot. You could also base your story on a combination of real and imaginary experiences.

To begin your story, make a list or a word cluster of the sights, sounds, tastes, textures, and smells that are part of the setting. Consider the following questions as you recall or imagine the details of the setting.

1.   What is the season, the time of day, and the time of year when your scene begins?

2.   What is the first thing you notice about the scene? For example, is it deserted or full of people? Is the area beautiful, ordinary, or ugly? What makes it that way?

3.   What sounds do you associate with the scene? If it is peaceful, do you hear the sounds of people? Animals? If it is noisy, do you hear the grinding of machines or the shouts of children playing in the street?

4.   What tastes or smells would a person notice in this scene?

5.   Imagine that you are in the middle of the scene and then look straight ahead and ask yourself what you see. Look to the right and left and notice what you see there. Turn around and notice how the scene changes. Now focus on something small in your scene, perhaps something small enough to fit in your hand. What does it look like?

Use some of the details from your list or word cluster to write a paragraph describing the setting of your story. Save your story setting for a future writing assignment.

Creating Plot

Plot refers to the sequence, or order, of events in a story.

Plots may be very simple or very complicated; in fact, there may be more than one plot in a story. Whether the story line is simple or complicated, the reader must be able to identify events, their order, and their importance. *Time clues,* such as the words *meanwhile, before, after, until, next, during, finally,* and *as,* help readers follow the action of the story. In some instances, the reader must not only identify events and actions that are directly stated, but also interpret an event that is only suggested.

In most stories conflict is an important part of plot. Conflict may take place inside a character. For example, a character may experience an inner battle, guilt, or indecision. More frequently, however, conflict takes place between two or more characters. The conflict in a story, and what the characters decide to do about it, is often the central point of the story.

In many stories and dramas, the conflict builds to a *climax*, the high point. Some stories end at the climax or shortly thereafter. The climax for most stories, however, forms the *turning point*, after which the events lead to a *resolution*, or ending, of the conflict.

Model: Conflict in a Story

Conflict may also involve the circumstances in which characters find themselves. In the novel *Walkabout* by James Vance Marshall, two American children survive a plane crash in the Australian Outback, a desolate desert region far from any towns or settlements. They attempt to walk to Adelaide, the city in which their uncle lives, but grow hungry and tired from lack of food and water and from walking in the hot sun. Suddenly a native boy appears. Although they cannot understand each other's language, the American children and the bush boy, as he is called, make friends. The native boy knows they need to be led to safety, but he also believes that the American girl has seen the image of death in his eyes and that he will certainly die. In the following chapter the story reaches its climax: the bush boy has started to leave Mary and Peter, the stranded children who need him in order to survive. As you read, notice how their dependence on the native boy and his near desertion intensify the problem of survival.

The children watched him. The girl was pale and breathing quickly. The boy was whimpering; shocked, frightened, caught up in a cross fire of emotions he couldn't begin to understand. But one fact did penetrate the haze of his bewilderment. The bush boy, for the second time since their meeting him, was deserting them. Their lifeline, once again, was drifting away.

Suddenly and violently, he flung off his sister's hand and rushed stumbling into the desert.

"Come back!" His voice was frightened. "Come back. Come back."

The bush boy walked on, unheeding, apparently unhearing, like a sleep-walker. But Peter wouldn't be denied. Blindly he launched himself at the bush boy's legs, clutching him round the knees.

"You're not to go," he panted.

And he hung on, like a leech.

The bush boy was jerked to a halt, was shaken out of his trance. He put his hands on the white boy's shoulders, pushing him gently away. But Peter wouldn't release his grip.

"You're not going." He repeated it over and over again. "Not going. Not going. Not going."

The bush boy squatted down, so that his face was close to the little one's, so that the little one could look into his eyes and see the terrible thing that was there. With their faces less than eighteen inches apart the two boys stared into each other's eyes.

But to the bush boy's astonishment, the little one didn't draw back; gave no exclamation of terror; seemed to see nothing wrong. He got to his feet. Puzzled. For a moment hope came surging back.

A *lubra* is a female adolescent.

Perhaps the lubra had been mistaken; perhaps the Spirit of Death had been only passing through him, resting awhile as he passed from one tribe to another; perhaps he had left him now.

He retraced his steps, back toward the girl.

But as soon as he neared her, hope drained away. For at his approach the lubra again shrank back; in her eyes all the former terror came welling up.

The bush boy knew then that he was going to die. Not perhaps today, nor tomorrow, nor even the next day. But soon. Before the coming of the rains and the smoking of spirits out of the tribal caves. This knowledge numbed his mind, but didn't paralyze it. He was still able to think of other things. Of the queer strangers, for example—the lubra and the little one—of what would happen to them. When he died, they would die too. That was certain, for they were such helpless creatures. So there'd be not one victim for the Spirit of Death but three. Unless he could somehow save them?

A *yacca* is a kind of evergreen tree.

It seemed, on the face of it, an impossible undertaking. With a stem of yacca he traced a pattern in the sand: circle after circle, symbolic rings of protection against Wulgaru, the Spirit of Death. And at last, in a moment of sudden inspiration, he saw what had to be done. He must lead the strangers to safety, to the final goal of his walkabout, the valley-of-waters-under-the-earth. And they must waste no time. For who knew how much time they would have.

He gathered up the *worwora* and smoothed out the ash of the fire.

"*Kurura*," he said, and struck out across the desert.

A *billabong* is a blind channel leading out from a river.

The little one followed him at once. But the lubra didn't move. He thought for a long time that she had decided to stay by the billabongs, but in the end she too started to follow, keeping a long way behind.[1]

Think and Discuss

1. In the first paragraph, what descriptive details help the reader realize what the children are feeling?

---

[1]From *Walkabout* by James Vance Marshall. Copyright © 1959 by James Vance Marshall. Revised edition copyright © 1971 by William Morrow and Company, Inc. Reprinted by permission of Sundance–Publishers and Distributors, Littleton, Massachusetts.

2. What clues in the passage reveal that the bush boy is experiencing an inner conflict?

3. At what point in the passage does the bush boy change his mind? How does this affect the chain of events that follow?

4. The resolution of the story is only suggested near the end of the passage. How do you think the story will end based on the details that are given?

Writing Practice 7: *Plotting the Action*

Using the incident you chose in Writing Practice 6, make an outline of events that will make up the action of your story. List the events in chronological order—that is, as they occur in time. Later, as you write the story, you may wish to alter the sequence of events or start your story at a different point in time.

The action in your story should involve some kind of conflict that leads to a climax. Underline the event that represents the climax or high point of your story. Then show in your list how the conflict will be resolved near the end of the story.

Creating Characters

Characters **are the actors in a literary work. Usually thought of as people, they can also be animals, creatures from another planet, or even robots.**

Details that help readers learn about characters include statements the narrator makes directly, the characters' dialogue and manner of speech, the characters' actions, and the reactions of characters to one another.

Model: Using Details to Describe Character

In the following passage from Jack London's story "War," the author uses many details to give information about the character. As you read the passage note the many descriptive details the author uses to describe the character.

> He was a young man, not more than twenty-four or -five, and he might have sat his horse with the careless grace of his youth had he not been so catlike and tense. His black eyes roved everywhere, catching the movements of twigs and branches where small birds hopped, questing ever onward through the changing vistas of trees and brush, and returning always to the clumps of undergrowth on either side. And as he watched, so did he listen, though he rode on in

silence, save for the boom of heavy guns from far to the west. This had been sounding monotonously in his ears for hours, and only its cessation would have aroused his notice. For he had business closer to hand. Across his saddlebow was balanced a carbine.

So tensely was he strung that a bunch of quail, exploding into flight from under his horse's nose, startled him to such an extent that automatically, instantly, he had reined in and fetched the carbine halfway to his shoulder. He grinned sheepishly, recovered himself, and rode on. So tense was he, so bent upon the work he had to do, that the sweat stung his eyes unwiped, and unheeded rolled down his nose and spattered his saddle pommel. The band of his cavalryman's hat was fresh-stained with sweat. The roan horse under him was likewise wet. It was high noon of a breathless day of heat. Even the birds and squirrels did not dare the sun, but sheltered in shady hiding places among the trees.[1]

Writing Practice 8: *Creating a Short Story Character*

Create a character description of the main character in the short story you outlined in Writing Practice 7. Before you begin, clearly picture your character. Describe the person's physical appearance, as well as his or her personality, and character. Consider the following questions in writing your character description.

1.   What does your character look like? If you met this person on the street, what would you notice first? For example, does he or she have curly red hair, an awkward stance, or unusual height?

2.   What is the person's background? From what type of environment does he or she come? What kind of education or job does the person have?

3.   How do the character's actions, speech patterns, or habits reflect the kind of person he or she is?

4.   What is your character's main dream or goal? Is he or she an ambitious person? Is the character someone who lets others lead? Does your character know what he or she wants in life?

Creating Dialogue

A *dialogue* is a conversation between two or more characters.

Short stories, novels, and plays all make use of dialogue between and among characters as a means of telling the story.

---

[1]From "War" in *The Night Born* by Jack London. Reprinted by permission of I. Milo Shepard.

Writers can describe characters directly, as well as indirectly, through dialogue. Dialogue lets the reader or audience hear what the characters have to say about themselves and others. As a reader or viewer, you notice not only what they say but also how they say it, what kind of mood they are in, and how they react to other characters.

Model: *Dialogue*

As you read the following paragraphs from Doris Lessing's "Through the Tunnel," note how the author combines narration, details of setting, and dialogue.

Going to the shore on the first morning of the holiday, the young English boy stopped at a turning of the path and looked down at a wild and rocky bay, and then over to the crowded beach he knew so well from other years. His mother walked on in front of him, carrying a bright striped bag in one hand. Her other arm, swinging loose, was very white in the sun.

The boy watched that white, naked arm, and turned his eyes, which had a frown behind them, toward the bay and back again to his mother. When she felt he was not with her, she swung around.

"Oh, there you are, Jerry!" she said. She looked impatient, then smiled. "Why, darling, would you rather not come with me? Would you rather—" she frowned, conscientiously worrying over what amusements he might secretly be longing for which she had been too busy to imagine.

He was very familiar with that anxious, apologetic smile. Contrition sent him running after her. And yet, as he ran, he looked back over his shoulder at the wild bay; and all morning, as he played on the safe beach, he was thinking of it.

Next morning, when it was time for the routine of swimming and sunbathing, his mother said, "Are you tired of the usual beach, Jerry? Would you like to go somewhere else?"

"Oh, no!" he said quickly, smiling at her out of that unfailing impulse of contrition—a sort of chivalry. Yet, walking down the path with her, he blurted out, "I'd like to go and have a look at those rocks down there."[1]

Think and Discuss

1. What details about the setting in the first paragraph help you visualize the scene? How are the two characters introduced?

2. How does the writer let readers know that the mother is anxious about her son?

3. What does the dialogue reveal about the relationship between the mother and her son?

Writing Practice 9: *Creating Characters Through Dialogue*

Based on the character description you wrote in Writing Practice 8, write a brief dialogue between the main character and another character in your story. Strive for natural language that reveals certain traits about your characters. For example, if one of your characters is impatient, you may want him or her to speak in short, abrupt phrases. In your dialogue, show what the main character is like by the reactions and responses of the second character.

Point of View

Point of view is the position from which the events of the story are observed.

Sometimes, the author uses an *omniscient point of view*, meaning that the narrator can share with the reader everything about characters and events. Other times, however, the narrator uses a *limited point of view*, restricted to the position of telling about events as one character sees, does, and thinks about them.

---

[1]From *The Habit of Loving* by Doris Lessing (T. Y. Crowell). Copyright © 1957 by Doris Lessing. Reprinted by permission of Harper & Row, Publishers, Inc., and Curtis Brown Ltd., London, on behalf of Doris Lessing.

Another point of view is *first-person narration*, in which readers learn about other characters and events from the point of view of a character who is also the storyteller. Sometimes, this character is trustworthy; other times, he or she is not. The reader has to use the information presented by the narrator, compare it with other characters' actions and statements, and then judge the reliability of the narrator.

Model: First-Person Point of View

In the following passage from Jesse Stuart's story "Split Cherry Tree," the narrator is a character in the story, so the point of view is first-person narration. As you read the narrator's description of his father's visit to school, think about how you would describe the father. Then complete the activities that follow the selection.

"We have a big black snake over here we caught yesterday," says Professor Herbert. "We'll chloroform him and dissect him and show you he has germs in his body, too."

"Don't do it," says Pa. "I believe you. I jist don't want to see you kill the black snake. I never kill one. They are good mousers and a lot o' help to us on the farm. I like black snakes. I jist hate to see people kill 'em. I don't allow 'em killed on my place."

The students look at Pa. They seem to like him better after he said that. Pa with a gun in his pocket but a tender heart beneath his ribs for snakes, but not for man! Pa won't whip a mule at home. He won't whip his cattle.

"Man can defend hisself," says Pa, "but cattle and mules can't. We have the drop on 'em. Ain't nothin' to a man that'll beat a good pullin' mule. He ain't got th' right kind o' a heart!"

Professor Herbert took Pa through the laboratory. He showed him the different kinds of work we were doing. He showed him our equipment. They stood and talked while we worked. Then they walked out together. They talked louder when they got out in the hall.

When our biology class was over I walked out of the room. It was our last class for the day. I would have to take my broom and sweep two hours to finish paying for the split cherry tree. I just wondered if Pa would want me to stay. He was standing in the hallway watching the students march out. He looked lost among us. He looked like a leaf turned brown on the tree among the treetop filled with growing leaves.

I got my broom and started to sweep. Professor Herbert walked up and says, "I'm going to let you do that some other time. You can go home with your father. He is waiting out there."

I laid my broom down, got my books, and went down the steps.

Pa says, "Ain't you got two hours o' sweepin' yet to do?"

I says, "Professor Herbert said I could do it some other time. He said for me to go home with you."

"No," says Pa. "You are goin' to do as he says. He's a good man. School has changed from my day and time. I'm a dead leaf, Dave. I'm behind. I don't belong here. If he'll let me I'll get a broom and we'll both sweep one hour. That pays your debt. I'll hep you pay it. I'll ast 'im and see if he won't let me hep you."

"I'm going to cancel the debt," says Professor Herbert. "I just wanted you to understand, Luster."

"I understand," says Pa, "and since I understand, he must pay his debt fer th' tree and I'm goin' to hep 'im."[1]

Think and Discuss

1. After reading the passage, what words would you use to describe the father?

2. What specific clues guided you in reaching your conclusion concerning the character of the father?

3. Who is the narrator of the story? How would the passage be different if it were written from the father's point of view?

Writing Assignment II: *Creating a Short Story*

A. Prewriting

Gather the various story parts you have written in Writing Practices 6—9. Reread your list of events, making additions or deletions before you begin your story. Then reread your story parts and underline the parts that you want to include.

B. Writing

Use your plot outline as a guide for writing the first draft of your story. Include descriptive details and dialogue from previous Writing Practices where appropriate. Consider the first draft of your story as a "discovery draft." Often the process of writing inspires new ideas or details. Do not hesitate to make changes as you write or to explore new directions that will make your story more appealing. A good story may require many changes. Experiment with different ways to begin or end your story; add sensory details to make the setting believable; insert dialogue where appropriate; incorporate action that is exciting, unusual, or surprising.

---

[1]From "Split Cherry Tree" by Jesse Stuart. Originally published in *Esquire* Magazine. Reprinted by permission of the Jesse Stuart Foundation, Inc., Judy B. Dailey, Chair, P.O. Box 391, Ashland, KY 41114.

C. Postwriting

For information on punctuating dialogue, see pages 604-605.

Revising by Yourself: As you read over your discovery draft, think about your readers. Keep only the most essential and interesting parts of the story. Fill in any gaps by adding necessary details. Use the following checklist to revise your story.

Checklist for Revising a Short Story

1. Does the story begin in an interesting or unusual way?

2. Are the characters and setting described in detail? Does the description of setting include the use of sensory details? Are the major characters described through their words, actions, thoughts, and physical appearances?

3. Do the main events in the plot unfold in a logical sequence? Is there a relationship between the events and the characters? Does the plot build to a climax? Is there a conflict that is resolved in the end?

4. Is the story narrated using the same point of view throughout?

5. Is the language clear and correct? Are sentences complete? Is there a variety of sentence patterns? Is the wording exact?

Use the Proofreader's Checklist at the back of this book to check your story for correct sentence structure, grammar, mechanics, and spelling.

Revising with a Partner: Share your story with a partner before you write your final draft. Ask your partner to read your story and to complete the following steps.

1. Read the story draft the first time for content, clarity, and interest.

2. Identify the climax of the story.

3. Point out the part you found to be most interesting or exciting.

4. Suggest parts that need to be clarified or details that need to be added or deleted.

5. Read over the final draft after it has been revised. Check for correct sentence structure, grammar, mechanics, and spelling.

Sharing in Small Groups: When the final story draft is completed, gather with four or five classmates and share your stories by reading them aloud for enjoyment. Members of the group may comment on the features that they particularly liked in each story and may suggest details that need to be added or deleted.

Elements of Drama

Although drama includes the basic story elements of setting, characters, and plot, *dialogue* is more essential to a play than it is to a short story. It is largely through the dialogue that the audience learns the characters and the plot in a play. Plays are written in *acts* or *scenes* instead of paragraphs or chapters, and the scripts include descriptive details about the setting and action in the form of *stage directions*. In this section, you will read about the elements of drama and compose a dramatic scene.

Creating the Setting for a Play

In a play the setting is created partly by the author's *stage directions*, partly by the action, and partly by the dialogue. On stage the setting is made clear by the furniture, costumes, painted backgrounds, music, and lighting. A printed program may also establish the setting by telling you that Act I takes place in the Forest of Arden or that Scene 2 takes place the next afternoon.

Model: The Setting of a Play

You can see how a writer creates setting through stage directions in the following excerpt from George Bernard Shaw's *Pygmalion*. What details describe the time and place? What characters are a part of the setting?

Act One

London at 11:15 P.M. Torrents of heavy summer rain. Cab whistles blowing frantically in all directions. Pedestrians running for shelter into the portico of St. Paul's church (not Wren's cathedral but Inigo Jones's church in Covent Garden vegetable market), among them a lady and her daughter in evening dress. All are peering out gloomily at the rain, except one man with his back turned to the rest, wholly preoccupied with a notebook in which he is writing.

The church clock strikes the first quarter.

Creating Dramatic Characters Through Dialogue

Playwrights do not provide audiences with descriptive details and explanations about the characters seen on stage. Instead, the dialogue —the words the characters speak—must reveal motivations for their actions and their reactions to each other.

Model: The Dialogue of a Play

In the following selection from *An Enemy of the People* by Henrik Ibsen, Dr. Stockmann, Medical Officer of the Municipal Baths, reveals his discovery that the town's public baths, known for their beneficial effects, are contaminated. As you read, imagine what Dr. Stockmann (Dr. S) is like, based on his dialogue and the way he talks.

HOVSTAD. What are you driving at, Doctor?

DR. S [*Standing still by the table*]. Isn't it the universal opinion that our town is a healthy spot?

HOVSTAD. Certainly.

DR. S. Quite an unusually healthy spot, in fact—a place that deserves to be recommended in the warmest possible manner either for invalids or for people who are well—

MRS. S. Yes, but my dear Thomas—

DR. S. And we have been recommending it and praising it—I have written and written, both in the "Messenger" and in pamphlets—

HOVSTAD. Well, what then?

DR. S. And the Baths—we have called them the "main artery of the town's life-blood," the "nerve-centre of our town," and the devil knows what else—

BILLING. "The town's pulsating heart" was the expression I once used on an important occasion—

DR. S. Quite so. Well, do you know what they really are, these great, splendid, much praised Baths, that have cost so much money—do you know what they are?

HOVSTAD. No, what are they?

MRS. S. Yes, what are they?

DR. S. The whole place is a pesthouse!

PETRA. The Baths, father?

MRS. S.[*at the same time*]. Our Baths!

HOVSTAD. But, Doctor—

BILLING. Absolutely incredible!

DR. S. The whole Bath establishment is a whited, poisoned sepulchre, I tell you—the gravest possible danger to the public health! All the nastiness up at Mölledal, all that stinking filth, is infecting the water in the conduit-pipes leading to the reservoir; and the same cursed, filthy poison oozes out on the shore too—

HORSTER. Where the bathing-place is?

DR. S. Just there.

HOVSTAD. How do you come to be so certain of all this, Doctor?

DR. S. I have investigated the matter most conscientiously. For a long time past I have suspected something of the kind. Last year we had some very strange cases of illness among the visitors—typhoid cases, and cases of gastric fever—

MRS. S. Yes, that is quite true.

DR. S. At the time, we supposed the visitors had been infected before they came; but later on, in the winter, I began to have a different opinion; and so I set myself to examine the water, as well as I could.

MRS. S. Then that is what you have been so busy with?

DR. S. Indeed I have been busy, Katherine. But here I had none of the necessary scientific apparatus; so I sent samples, both of the drinking-water and of the sea-water, up to the University, to have an accurate analysis made by a chemist.

HOVSTAD. And have you got that?

DR. S [*showing him the letter*]. Here it is! It proves the presence of decomposing organic matter in the water—it is full of infusoria. The water is absolutely dangerous to use, either internally or externally.

MRS. S. What a mercy you discovered it in time.

DR. S. You may well say so.

HOVSTAD. And what do you propose to do now, Doctor?

DR. S. To see the matter put right—naturally.

HOVSTAD. Can that be done?

DR. S. It must be done. Otherwise the Baths will be absolutely useless and wasted. But we need not anticipate that; I have a very clear idea what we shall have to do.

MRS. S. But why have you kept this all so secret, dear?

DR. S. Do you suppose I was going to run about the town gossiping about it, before I had absolute proof? No, thank you. I am not such a fool.

PETRA. Still, you might have told us—

DR. S. Not a living soul. But to-morrow you may run round to the old Badger—

MRS. S. Oh, Thomas! Thomas!

DR. S. Well, to your grandfather, then. The old boy will have something to be astonished at! I know he thinks I am cracked—and there are lots of other people think so, too, I have noticed. But now these good folks shall see—they shall just see—! [*Walks about, rubbing his hands.*] There will be a nice upset in the town, Katherine; you can't imagine what it will be. All the conduit-pipes will have to be relaid.

HOVSTAD [*getting up*]. All the conduit-pipes—?

DR. S. Yes, of course. The intake is too low down; it will have to be lifted to a position much higher up.

PETRA. Then you were right after all.

DR.S. Ah, you remember, Petra— I wrote opposing the plans before the work was begun. But at that time no one would listen to me. Well, I am going to let them have it, now! Of course I have prepared a report for the Baths Committee; I have had it ready for a week, and was only waiting for this to come. [*Shows the letter.*] Now it shall go off at once. [*Goes into his room and comes back with some papers.*] Look at that! Four closely written sheets!—and the letter shall go with them. Give me a bit of paper, Katherine—something to wrap them up in. That will do! Now give it to—to—[*stamps his foot*]—what the deuce is her name?—give it to the maid, and tell her to take it at once to the Mayor.[1]

Think and Discuss

It is clear from his dialogue that Dr. Stockmann is disturbed by his discovery: "The whole Bath establishment is a whited, poisoned sepulchre, I tell you—the gravest possible danger to the public health!" It is also apparent from the following dialogue that he plans to take action:

> HOVSTAD. And what do you propose to do now, Doctor?
> DR. S. To see the matter put right—naturally.
> HOVSTAD. Can that be done?
> DR. S. It must be done. Otherwise the Baths will be absolutely useless and wasted. . . .

Based on the excerpt from the play, how do Billing, Petra, Hovstad, and Mrs. Stockmann react to Dr. Stockmann's announcement? Do you think they will be sympathetic to his plans to clean up the public baths? Is there any indication in the dialogue that Dr. Stockmann may be opposed in his efforts?

Writing Assignment III: *Creating a Dramatic Dialogue*

A. Prewriting

As your teacher directs, divide into groups of three or four. One person in the group should record the dialogue that the members create. Brainstorm together to generate some basic ideas for a brief dialogue based on one of the following situations or, if you prefer, a situation of your own.

1. Two (or three) men or women argue about who was the most popular forty years ago when they were in high school together.

---

[1]From *An Enemy of the People* by Henrik Ibsen (Dryden Press Edition, 1947). Courtesy of Holt, Rinehart and Winston, Publishers.

2.   Three people are standing at a bus stop. The bus is late, and each person has a different response to the delay.

3.   Two men or women are planning an important party. They are quite snobbish and want to invite only the "right" people. As they plan, they realize that their ideas of which people are "right" are very different.

4.   The year is A.D. 3000. The scene is a classroom. The teacher announces to the class that he or she is an alien and that the entire school is about to be transported to another planet for observation.

Before you begin working on the dialogue, ask yourself three questions:

Where is the scene taking place?

What is your character like (what sort of person are you)?

What do you feel about the other characters in the scene?

For example, in the first suggested situation you could build a scene around two men who have been friends for life but who realize that each has a completely different version of what they were like in high school. Another possibility is to build a scene around two people meeting at a high school reunion after many years who remember that they never really liked each other in school. At first they are friendly and warm, then cool, then angry.

B. Writing

As you work together to create your drama, strive to develop natural and believable dialogue between characters. *Show* what the characters are like through their words, mannerisms, gestures, impressions, and responses to one another.

The recorder should indicate who speaks the lines by writing the speaker's name, a colon (:), and then the dialogue. You may include notes in parentheses () to describe actions and manners of speaking, as in the following example:

KAREN: (Looks at Mary, sighs, moves back toward the desk and stands there for a moment.) Well, there doesn't seem to be any other way with you; you'll have to be punished.

C. Postwriting

After the dialogue has been completed, each member of the group will need to make a copy and read the dialogue several times to become familiar with it. Then practice reading the dialogue as a group. Strive for a natural tone of voice but read with expression and use gestures for emphasis.

After your group has practiced reading the dialogue, present it to your class.

Sentence Combining: Using Nouns

Inserting Noun Clauses

For more information on clauses, see pages 534-553.

Changing a sentence to a *noun clause* and inserting it into a base sentence is also an effective way to add sentence variety. A *noun clause* is a group of words that contains a subject and verb and that functions as a noun in the base sentence. (Noun clauses are discussed in Chapter 20.) The (*who*), (*what*), (*when*), (*where*), (*why*), and (*how*) signals in this lesson are used to insert noun clauses into sentences.

In the following examples the signal *something* in the base sentence is *replaced* by all or part of the sentence following it. (The signals *someone*, *somehow*, and *somewhere* work in the same way as the signal *something*.)

Base: Dan Whitewater assumed *something*.

Insert: His house was insured against natural disasters.

Combined: Dan Whitewater assumed *his house was insured against natural disasters*.

Base: We discussed *something*.

Insert: We could build our float for the parade. (*where*)

Combined: We discussed *where we could build our float for the parade*.

Base: My brother still doesn't understand *something*.

Insert: Mom beat him in the bowling tournament. (*how*)

Combined: My brother still doesn't understand *how Mom beat him in the bowling tournament*.

Base: The Ortiz family never discovered *someone*.

Insert: Someone left a plant on their doorstep. (*who*)

Combined: The Ortiz family never discovered *who left a plant on their doorstep*.

Base: *Something* and *something* were two problems that still perplexed the girls on the cross-country team.

Insert: They could purchase new uniforms. (*how*)
They could practice. (*where*)

Combined: *How they could purchase new uniforms* and *where they could practice* were two problems that still perplexed the girls on the cross-country team.

Signals such as (*it . . . that*), (*it . . . how*), or (*the fact that*) are also often used to join the inserted clause with the base. In the following examples notice how these signals are used.

Base: The scientists excitedly announced *something*.

Insert: A cure for the strange disease had been discovered. (*the fact that*)

Combined: The scientists excitedly announced *the fact that a cure for the strange disease had been discovered.*

Base: *Something* has come to our attention.

Insert: Ann has accepted a scholarship to the Wisconsin Technical Institute. (*it . . . that*)

Combined: *It* has come to our attention *that Ann has accepted a scholarship to the Wisconsin Technical Institute.*

Exercise 1: Inserting Noun Clauses

On a separate sheet of paper, combine each of the following sets of sentences into a single sentence by inserting noun clauses into the base sentence (the first one in each set). The first five sentences contain signals; the last ten sentences are unsignaled, and you must decide how to insert noun clauses. Study the examples before you begin.

Examples

a. *Something* is beyond my comprehension.
These problems can be solved in so short a time. (*how*)
How these problems can be solved in so short a time is beyond my comprehension.

b. Mr. Herrera told him *something*.
The tulip bulbs should be planted.
Mr. Herrera told him when the tulip bulbs should be planted.

Eliminate (of) in the combined sentence. It is included only to help understand the meaning of the base sentence.

1. In her first address to the student body as principal, Ms. Thomas assured the students (of) *something*.
    She would be as visible and accessible as possible. (*that*)

2. *Something* is the reason we must acquit him.
    We have a reasonable doubt as to his guilt. (*the fact that*)

3. *Something* made me suspect *something*.
    Rosa hadn't written to me in many months. (*the fact that*)
    Her health was failing. (*that*)

4. *Something* never occurred to Othello.
    Iago could be a lying villain. (*it . . . that*)

5. The whole city is talking about *someone*.
    Someone will replace Mrs. Johnson as mayor. (*who*)

6. *Something* is an important part of the research.
    You concluded something from your experiment.

7. *Something* amazes me.
    So many people are ignorant of their rights and responsibilities as citizens.

8. *Something* isn't necessary.
    You enclose a cover letter with your application.

9. I've always wanted to live *somewhere*.
    The weather is mild all year long.

10. Would you please show me *something*?
    This camera differs from the one I've been using.

11. Can you be so sure (of) *something?*
    Gold will drop in value soon.

12. All the entrants in the fifty-kilometer race were told *something.*
    They must complete seven laps of the course.

13. *Something* doesn't necessarily mean *something.*
    The applicant is older.
    He or she will be better or worse at the job.

14. *Something* did not affect Flora's success as a real estate agent.
    She was confined to a wheelchair.

15. The experiment Mrs. Espinoza ran for our class showed *something.*
    Magnets attract metal.

Inserting Possessives and Gerunds

For more information on possessives, see pages 311-313.

For more information on gerunds, see pages 472-474.

The signal (*pos*) in this section indicates that two sentences can be combined by changing a noun to the *possessive* (the form of the noun that indicates ownership or relationship). The following sentences are combined by changing the nouns *Marie, children,* and *trees* to their possessive forms: *Marie's, children's, trees'.* Notice that the possessive is formed with an apostrophe (') or an *apostrophe* and the letter *s* ('*s*). (For more information about forming possessives, see Chapter 9.)

Base: The dog is a collie.

Insert: Marie owns the dog. (*pos*)

Combined: *Marie's* dog is a collie.

Base: The museum in Indianapolis has a display of antique toys.

Insert: The toys belonged to children. (*pos*)

Combined: The museum in Indianapolis has a display of antique *children's* toys.

Base: The leaves were turning gold and brown.

Insert: The leaves were on the trees. (*pos*)

Combined: The *trees'* leaves were turning gold and brown.

Pronouns used in these combinations have the following possessive forms.

Pronoun	Possessive Pronoun
I, me	my
we, us	our
you	your
he, him	his
she	her
they, them	their
it	its

Notice how possessive pronouns are used in the following examples:

Base: The wet jackets lay on the floor in a heap.

Insert: We owned the jackets. (*pos*)

Combined: *Our* wet jackets lay on the floor in a heap.

Base: After they washed and waxed it, the old car looked like a new model.

Insert: The car belonged to them. (*pos*)

Combined: After they washed and waxed it, *their* old car looked like a new model.

Possessives are often combined with the (-*ing*) signal to convert a verb into a noun called a *gerund*. For example, in the sentence "The shouting in the hall interrupted our studying," the subject of the sentence is the gerund *shouting,* a noun formed by adding -*ing* to the verb *shout*. The direct object is the gerund *studying,* a noun formed by adding -*ing* to the verb *study*. (Gerunds are discussed in Chapter 17.) In the following examples the (*pos*) signal and the (-*ing*) signal are used together to replace *something* in the base sentence.

Base: *Something* frightened me.

Insert: Sean yelled. (*pos* +-*ing*)

Combined: *Sean's yelling* frightened me.

Base: Elaine can listen to *something* every day without getting bored.

Insert: Barbra Streisand sings. (*pos* + -*ing*)

Combined: Elaine can listen to *Barbra Streisand's singing* every day without getting bored.

Base: According to the coach *something* is uncertain.

Insert: We will receive the award. (*pos + -ing*)

Combined: According to the coach *our receiving the award* is uncertain.

Exercise 2: *Inserting Possessives and Gerunds*

On a separate sheet of paper, combine each of the following sets of sentences into one sentence. The signals for inserting possessives and gerunds are given in the first five sentences; the last five sentences lack signals but can also be combined with possessives and gerunds. Study the examples before you begin.

Examples

a. *Something* made Sheila aware that he was choking.
Kevin gasped for breath. (*pos + -ing*)

Kevin's gasping for breath made Sheila aware that he was choking.

b. *Something* disturbed the baby-sitter.
The child played with paint.

The child's playing with paint disturbed the baby-sitter.

1. *Something* surprised Mr. Alvarez.
The plants bloomed early in the spring. (*pos + -ing*)

2. The coach encouraged *something*.
They practiced good sportsmanship during scrimmages and league games. (*pos + -ing*)

3. The audience applauded *something*.
The students danced and sang in the production. (*pos + -ing*)

4. It's inconceivable that *something* would cause him to lose his job.
The man refused to work in the condemned building. (*pos + -ing*)

5. *Something* will prevent *something*.
I limp. (*pos + -ing*)
I will ride in the race Sunday. (*pos + -ing*)

6. *Something* shows how they appreciate *something*.
The class laughs.
Russ jokes around.

7. *Something* makes *something* believable.
The book cites numerous examples.
It predicts earthquakes.

8. *Something* interrupted *something*.
   The telephone rang.
   I typed.

9. *Something* helped him to lose twenty pounds.
   Carlos dieted and exercised all summer.

10. Your parents will understand *something*.
    You do not want to become a doctor.

Writing Practice: *Describing the Action*

Look through old magazines or newspapers and cut out an action photograph of someone you would like to write about—a skier, a diver, a dancer, a horseback rider, a football player, or a cheerleader. Imagine what this person is like and the kinds of feelings he or she might be experiencing.

Make a list of details describing the action in the photograph and the person's physical appearance, personality, and unique qualities. Also list details describing the setting of the picture. For example, if you chose a photograph of a diver poised at the edge of a diving board, you could describe not only the diver's physical appearance and feelings but also the height of the diving board, the depth of water, and the number of people watching.

Use the details from your list to write a paragraph describing the person and the action in the photograph. In your description, use some noun clauses to tell the *who? what? when? where? why?* and *how?* of the situation.

Attach your photograph and descriptive paragraph to a sheet of paper and share it with your classmates.

8 Business Writing

Form for a Business Letter

Social letters vary a good deal in appearance, but when you write a business letter, you should follow a definite form.

Begin by choosing standard-sized white paper of good quality. Typewritten letters are preferable because they are easier to read, but if you do not have access to a typewriter or do not type well, write in ink in your most legible handwriting. To keep your handwriting in even lines, try putting a sheet of heavily lined paper under your page so that you can see the lines as you write.

The appearance of your letter is important because it tells the receiver something about you. A good business letter should be neat. It should contain no mistakes in spelling, grammar, or punctuation, and it should follow the business letter form exactly.

The first page of a business letter should be framed in white by the margins around the letter. In order to decide where to begin writing, you will have to judge the length of your letter. The top and bottom margins should be equal; the left- and right-hand margins should also be about equal. Whether you are typing or writing, the left-hand margin should be kept straight.

Do not write or type on the back of the first sheet of a business letter. If your letter takes up more than a single sheet, begin a second page with the name of the person to whom you are writing, the page number, and the date as the heading. Leave about an inch from the top of the second sheet to the one-line heading and four lines of space below the heading. If your letter does require a second page, it should contain at least three lines of the body of the letter.

The correct form for a business letter is shown in the example on page 262.

Heading

The three-line heading goes in the upper right-hand part of the first page. The first line contains your street address or rural route and apartment number, if there is one. The second line contains your city, state, and ZIP code number. The date on which the letter is written goes on the third line. Notice that the only commas in the heading

occur between the city and the state on the second line and between the day of the month and the year on the third line. There is no comma between the state and the ZIP code or at the end of the lines of the heading. If your street address contains an apartment number, an additional comma goes between the name of the street and the apartment number.

12712 Speedway Overlook Road, Apartment 5

Inside Address

The inside address gives the name of the person or company to whom you are writing, the street address, city, state, and ZIP code. If you are writing to a particular person, you can include a short title to go on the first line along with the name.

Ms. Glenda Ferris, Manager

However, if the title is a long one, it should be written on a separate line.

Mr. Wayne Chong
Manager of Customer Service Relations

The inside address begins four lines below the heading and is even with the left-hand margin.

If you do not know the name of the person who will be handling your letter, you may address it to a title (such as *Director of Advertising* or *Personnel Director*) or to a department (such as *Admissions Office* or *Complaint Department*). It is always a good idea to specify the department in the company to which you are writing.

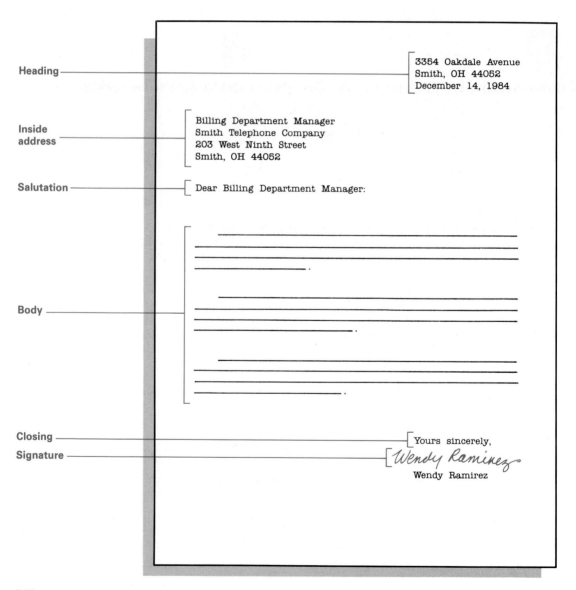

Heading — 3354 Oakdale Avenue
Smith, OH 44052
December 14, 1984

Inside address — Billing Department Manager
Smith Telephone Company
203 West Ninth Street
Smith, OH 44052

Salutation — Dear Billing Department Manager:

Body —

Closing — Yours sincerely,
Signature — Wendy Ramirez
Wendy Ramirez

Salutation

Skip two lines of space below the inside address and then write the salutation, the word *Dear* followed by the name of the receiver. In a business letter the salutation is always followed by a colon.

      Dear Ms. Olofski: Dear Mr. Williamson:

When you do not know the name of the person to whom you are writing, you may use "Dear Sir or Madam" as your salutation, or you may use the title of the person or department.

      Dear Black Magic Soil Sales Department:

      Dear Box Office Manager:

      Dear Credit Department Manager:

Body

Skip two lines of space after the salutation and begin the body of your letter. A business letter should be single-spaced with a line of space between paragraphs. If you use the semiblock style, as in the example on page 265, each paragraph will be indented a few spaces. In the block style, however, each paragraph begins at the left-hand margin. (See pages 264–266 for more information about block and semiblock styles.)

As in any kind of writing, you should begin a new paragraph when you change the subject of your writing. Many business letters, such as an order letter, contain only a single paragraph; others may contain several paragraphs or even more than one page.

Closing

Skip two lines of space after the body and write your closing. The left-hand margin of the closing should be aligned with the left-hand margin of the heading. The following examples show appropriate closings for a business letter.

Yours truly,	Very truly yours,
Sincerely yours,	Sincerely,

For more information on proper capitalization, see pages 608-622.

Notice that the closing is always followed by a comma. When you write a closing of more than one word, only the first word is capitalized.

Signature

Your signature should always be written in ink, neatly and legibly, below the closing. If you type your letter, skip four lines of space and type your name. Then sign your name in ink in the space between the closing and your typewritten name.

Semiblock, Block, and Full Block Style

Any of the three business letter forms is acceptable for handwritten or typed business letters.

Semiblock Form

The model letter on page 271 and all of the sample letters in this chapter are written in the semiblock form. Each paragraph of the letter's body is indented either five or ten spaces. The heading, closing, and signature are aligned somewhat to the right of the center of the paper. All the other parts of the business letter (the inside address, the salutation, and the body) begin at the left-hand margin.

Block Form

The block form differs from the semiblock form in only one respect: paragraphs in the body of the letter are not indented. Every paragraph begins at the left-hand margin. The only difference between block and semiblock forms is that paragraphs are indented in the semiblock form.

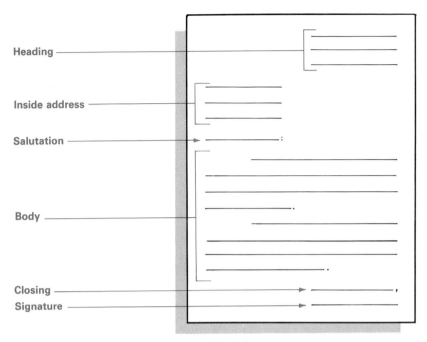

Heading

Inside address

Salutation

Body

Closing
Signature

Semiblock form

Block form

Full block form

Full Block Form

In the full block style every part of the business letter begins at the left-hand margin. The paragraphs in the body of the letter are not indented. Many people think that the full block form looks unbalanced because everything begins at the left, but this form does save some time for the typist because there are no indentions.

A diagram of business letter forms is shown on page 265.

Writing Practice 1: *Using Business Letter Forms*

On a sheet of paper, set up forms for two of the following business letters. Draw lines to indicate the body of the letter and write all the other parts according to the information provided. Use today's date in the heading of your letter.

1. Seymour Marzulli, who lives at 556 Bloomfield Avenue, Apartment 2, in Camden, New Jersey 08109, is writing to the Service Manager of Eastern Auto Car Parts, 101 South Essex Avenue in Orange, New Jersey 07050.

2. Mrs. Gail P. Bunch, who lives at 1240 Filmore Street, San Francisco, California 94115, is writing to the subscription department of *Sports Illustrated Magazine,* 541 N. Fairbanks Court, Chicago, Illinois 60611.

3. David B. Saltzman lives at 272 Noviembre Drive in El Paso, Texas 79935. He is writing Jim McNeil, Order Department Manager, at McNeil Brothers Nurseries, Inc., 603 Bowman Drive, Dansville, New York 14437.

4. Ms. Noreen Clematis lives at 4700 North Prospect Road in Peoria, Illinois 61614. She is writing to the Admissions Department at the University of Colorado, Boulder, Colorado 80309.

5. Roger Carpathia, who lives at 14968 S.E. Caruthers Court in Portland, Oregon 97233, is writing to the librarian at the Multnomah County Medical Society, 2188 S.W. Park Avenue, Portland, Oregon 97201.

Folding the Letter

There are two acceptable ways to fold a business letter, depending on the size of the stationery and the size of the envelope.

1. If you are using a long envelope for a letter on 8½ × 11 inch paper or a short envelope for a letter on 5½ × 8½ inch stationery, fold your letter into thirds as follows:
   a. Fold the bottom third of the paper one third of the way to the top and make a crease.
   b. Fold the top third of the paper down and make a second crease. Your letter will now be folded in thirds.
   c. Insert the letter into the envelope with the open end at the top of the envelope.

2. If your envelope is too small for the letter to fit when folded in thirds, fold your letter as follows:
   a. Fold the letter in half, bringing the bottom half up. Make a crease.
   b. Fold the right third of the letter toward the left side and make a crease.
   c. Fold the left third of the letter over the right third and make a crease.
   d. Insert the letter into the envelope with the open end at the top of the envelope.

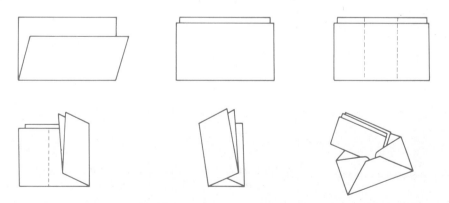

Addressing the Envelope

Like your stationery, the envelope in which you mail a business letter should be plain white and standard-sized. The name and address of the person or company you are writing to should be typed or written exactly as it appears on the inside address of the letter. Begin writing the address slightly below and to the left of the envelope's center. Your name and address belong in the upper left-hand corner as the return address.

See page 269 for a list of state abbreviations accepted by the post office. Always be certain to include a ZIP code in your return address and in the address of the receiver, since letters without ZIP codes may be delayed. If you do not know the ZIP code of the person to whom you are writing, look it up in the ZIP code directory found in every post office and most libraries.

Kathie Bartholomew
3068 South Linden Road, Apt. 608
Flint, MI 48507

Greenway Distributors
Card Services Division
5832 Dangerfield Road
Hillside, IL 60162

Abbreviations

The United States Post Office has approved the following two-letter abbreviations for states, possessions of the United States, and Canadian provinces to be used with ZIP codes.

Alabama **AL**	Montana **MT**	Wyoming **WY**
Alaska **AK**	Nebraska **NE**	Canal Zone **CZ**
Arizona **AZ**	Nevada **NV**	District of
Arkansas **AR**	New	Columbia **DC**
California **CA**	Hampshire **NH**	Guam **GU**
Colorado **CO**	New Jersey **NJ**	Puerto Rico **PR**
Connecticut **CT**	New Mexico **NM**	Virgin Islands **VI**
Delaware **DE**	New York **NY**	Alberta **AB**
Florida **FL**	North Carolina **NC**	British
Georgia **GA**	North Dakota **ND**	Columbia **BC**
Hawaii **HI**	Ohio **OH**	Manitoba **MB**
Idaho **ID**	Oklahoma **OK**	New
Illinois **IL**	Oregon **OR**	Brunswick **NB**
Indiana **IN**	Pennsylvania **PA**	Newfoundland **NF**
Iowa **IA**	Rhode Island **RI**	Northwest
Kansas **KS**	South Carolina **SC**	Territories **NT**
Kentucky **KY**	South Dakota **SD**	Nova Scotia **NS**
Louisiana **LA**	Tennessee **TN**	Ontario **ON**
Maine **ME**	Texas **TX**	Prince Edward
Maryland **MD**	Utah **UT**	Island **PE**
Massachusetts **MA**	Vermont **VT**	Quebec **PQ**
Michigan **MI**	Virginia **VA**	Saskatchewan **SK**
Minnesota **MN**	Washington **WA**	Yukon
Mississippi **MS**	West Virginia **WV**	Territory **YT**
Missouri **MO**	Wisconsin **WI**	Labrador **LB**

Writing Practice 2: *Addressing Business Letter Envelopes*

On a sheet of paper, draw outlines for four envelopes. Address all the following envelopes, using your name and home address for the return address.

1. You are writing to Mr. Perry Milefski, president of Interstate Motor Freight Lines, 500 Trade Center, Montgomery, Alabama 36108.

2. You are writing to the order department of Magic Mountain Photo Supply Company, 728 Warm Springs Road, Ketchum, Idaho 83340.

3. You are writing to the Personnel Department, Ben Franklin Bank, North Main Office, 1068 Westminster Street, Providence, Rhode Island 02909.

4. You are writing to Dr. Chu Ming, Director, Community Health Services, Inc., 2590 N. Germantown Road, Memphis, Tennessee 38134.

Content of a Business Letter

A letter may be written in exactly the right form yet may be an absolute failure. What you say and how you say it are even more important than the form of the letter.

Before you begin to write, it is a good idea to think about what you want to say. Ask yourself the following three questions:

1. What do you want the reader to do? (What is the purpose of your letter?)

2. What must the reader know in order to do this? (What information must be included in your letter?)

3. How can you get the reader to do this? (What is the most effective way of wording what you want to say?)

If you spend a few minutes thinking about the answers to these questions, the content of your business letter is practically guaranteed to be effective.

People who read business letters usually process many letters a day. They must be able to read and react to a letter quickly. Business letters should never leave the reader with unanswered questions. They should include all the information the reader needs to know. If essential information is left out of the letter, the reader will have to take the time to write a letter asking for that information, and long delays will result.

Consider what is wrong with the following business letter:

164 E. 82nd Street, Apt. 8C
New York, NY 10028
April 10, 1984

Credit Collections, Inc.
169 W. 34th Street
New York, NY 10001

Dear Credit Department Manager:

You have been billing me for a record I returned to Silverdust Record and Tape Club. It was defective, and I have no intention of paying for a defective record that I no longer have. Please stop sending me bills and credit my account.

Yours truly,

Loren McAffee

Loren McAffee

The person who tries to process this letter will have the following unanswered questions:

1. What is the writer's account number?

2. What is the name of the record the writer is being billed for?

3. What is the price of the record?

4. When and how was the record returned to the company?

5. Was the record insured when it was mailed? Does the writer have a receipt for it?

When writing a business letter, be clear and concise. Include all the necessary information, and write as briefly as you can.

Use vocabulary and language that is suitable for the intended audience. Avoid being overly chatty. A good way to develop a clear, concise writing style is to write as if you were speaking to the person—including only the essential details. The tone of the letter should be courteous and pleasant, even if you are angry because of a mistake the company has made. The person who reads and processes your letter is almost certainly not the person who caused the error.

As you read the following business letter, think about how you would change it.

9 Tricorne Road
Lexington, MA 02173
July 30, 1984

Order Department
Plainview Chronograph, Inc.
708 Fischer Avenue
Chicago, IL 60648

Dear Order Department:

On May 15, 1984, I ordered a calculator chronograph wristwatch and enclosed a check for $69.95. You have cashed the check, but the wristwatch has never arrived. What happened?

The watch was supposed to be a graduation present for my older brother Jim. My two sisters and I saved our money for months and washed cars to earn the $69.95 for the watch.

Whenever the mail comes, all of us rush to the mailbox to see if the watch has arrived, but so far we've been disappointed every time.

If for some reason my order cannot be filled, then I think I want my money back or else maybe I want to order another watch. Which do you think would be quicker? Awaiting your reply, I am

Yours truly,

Lee Ann Zambie

Lee Ann Zambie

Think and Discuss

1. What information in the letter could have been omitted? Why?

2. What specific details concerning the wristwatch need to be added in order for the company to make adjustments?

3. In the last paragraph, the writer is unclear about what she wants the company to do. How could she be more specific?

4. The last sentence sounds inappropriate for a business letter. How would you change it?

Writing Practice 3: *Writing an Effective Business Letter*

Rewrite either the letter to Credit Collections, Inc., on page 271, or the preceding letter to Plainview Chronograph, Inc. Before you begin, answer the three questions on page 270 about the content of a business letter. This will help your letter to be clear, concise, and complete. Use the correct form for a business letter as shown on page 275, and express yourself in a courteous tone. Then use the Checklist for Proofreading Business Letters on page 286 to make final corrections.

Letters of Request

B y following the guidelines for form and content already given in this chapter, you can write an effective business letter to cover any information that needs conveying in a work environment. You will probably benefit, however, from additional practice with the five common types of business letters discussed in this and the following sections.

In a *letter of request,* you are asking for something—information, a completed job, a catalogue, maps, or an appointment. Occasionally, you will write a letter asking someone in the business world to do a special favor. For example, you might write to ask a psychologist to visit your psychology class to discuss the kinds of help available in your community to students with emotional problems, or you might write to the director of a local film company, asking to arrange for a class visit.

A letter of request should be especially courteous so that the person responding will want to do what you request. If you are asking for information, it is always a good idea to include a stamped, self-addressed envelope with your request, to enable them to respond efficiently and quickly.

Model: A Letter of Request

If you are thinking about going to college, you will be writing several letters of request for college catalogues and for interview appointments. Look on the following page at the sample letter of request written to the Director of Admissions at a college. What specific features does this letter have that make it a particularly effective letter of request? If you were a college administrator, would you be willing to comply with this person's requests?

```
                                            4608 Alpine Avenue
                                            Cincinnati, OH 45242
                                            November 18, 1984


        Director of Admissions
        University of Chicago
        5801 S. Ellis Avenue
        Chicago, IL 60637


        Dear Director of Admissions:


            I am a senior in high school and will graduate next June.  I
        am interested in pursuing a career in physics, and my science
        teacher has told me that the University of Chicago has an
        exceptional physics department.

            Will you please send me your current catalogue for the College
        as well as any additional information you may have about courses
        of study in the physical sciences and in mathematics?

            Thank you very much.


                                            Yours sincerely,


                                            Emma Jane Catlip

                                            Emma Jane Catlip
```

Writing Practice 4: *A Letter of Request*

Write one of the following four letters of request or one of your own choosing. Include all the essential information.

1. Write a letter to the Sierra Club, 530 Bush Avenue, San Francisco, California 94108. Ask for information about student membership rates and about local activities in your area. Ask also for a list of current environmental legislation that the club is endorsing.

2. Write a letter to the Metropolitan Museum of Art, Box 255, Gracie Station, New York, New York 10028. Ask for their current catalogue of books, stationery, reproductions, and gifts sold at the museum's gift shop.

3. Write a letter to the Personnel Director at Highspeed Airlines Employment Office, Hartsfield Atlanta International Airport, Atlanta, Georgia 30366. Ask for information about requirements for becoming a flight attendant.

4. Write a letter to the Consumer Information Center, Department 38, Pueblo, Colorado 81009. Ask for the catalogue of free and low-cost pamphlets published by the Government Printing Office.

Use the Checklist for Proofreading Business Letters on page 286 to correct your letter.

Order Letters

In an *order letter*, you are requesting that a company send you merchandise. You should describe the merchandise completely and exactly. Write the size, model number, color, and any special features of the merchandise you are ordering. You might also mention when and where you saw the merchandise advertised.

Be sure to state in the letter how you are paying for the order. Usually either a check or a money order is enclosed with an order letter. Never send cash through the mail; it may be lost, and you have no proof that you sent it.

Model: An Order Letter

A sample order letter is shown below. What essential information has the writer included?

6798 Beaumont Woods Place
Honolulu, HI 96822
April 8, 1984

Save the Seals
A Nonprofit Corporation
P.O. Box 10987
Los Angeles, CA 90048

Dear Save the Seals Order Department:

Please send me one small-sized adult T-shirt with a blue seal hand-screened on white 100 per cent cotton. The lettering on the T-shirt says, "Save the Seals." I saw the T-shirt advertised in the spring issue of the National Audubon Society's magazine.

I am enclosing a check for $7.50 for the T-shirt and for postage and handling.

Thank you very much.

Yours truly,

Lin Tang

Lin Tang

Writing Practice 5: *An Order Letter*

Write one of the following order letters or one of your own choosing.

1. Order twenty-four color wallet photos to be made from a photograph or negative that you are enclosing with your letter. Write to the Order Department, Terra Cotta Studios, P.O. Box 987, Long Island City, New York 11101. You are enclosing $1.95 for the photos plus $.75 to cover postage for a total of $2.70.

2. Enclose $12.50 for resoling your Long-Wear running shoes, which you are mailing separately via parcel post. Describe the shoes exactly so that when they arrive, they will be easily identified as yours. Write to Pat and Mike's Olympic Resoling, Inc., 5800 Lacy Road, Madison, Wisconsin 53711.

3. Send $4.95 for a copy of *Wilderness Log Cabins*, a book of instructions on how to build twenty-five different designs of log cabins. Write to Walden Wilderness Homes, Rural Route 90, Lake of the Forest, Kansas 66012.

4. Write to Native American Crafts Company at 1069 West Via Del Condito, Phoenix, Arizona 85039. Enclose $14.95 for a pair of soft glove-tanned natural color leather moccasins, size 7, fringed style with a hard sole.

Use the Checklist for Proofreading Business Letters on page 286.

Letters of Adjustment

The purpose of a *letter of adjustment* is to convince a company or an individual to replace damaged merchandise, refund money, or correct an error in billing. You must present all the information that is needed in order to correct the mistake. State the problem and then present the evidence clearly and logically. It may help to describe the problem step by step, in chronological order. Remember, however, not to include unnecessary details, only necessary details.

After you have described the problem, tell the company or individual what it is you want done. Do you want new merchandise, or do you want a refund? Do you want your account credited? If you are not sure of the best method of making the adjustment, let them know.

A letter of adjustment should always be courteous in tone. Assume that the company is reliable and that you are going to receive the adjustment you are asking for. If you do not hear from the company within several weeks, you should send a follow-up letter, citing the date of your first letter and restating the problem.

Model: *A Letter of Adjustment*

A sample letter of adjustment follows. Notice how the writer clearly and courteously described the problem and included all the information the company needed to reply.

5908 S. Crestwood Avenue
Richmond, VA 23226
February 10, 1984

Customer Service Department
Bellview Stationery Supplies, Inc.
1090 Eastwood Avenue
Franklinton, NC 27525

Dear Customer Service Department:

On December 18 I ordered 500 white gummed labels with my name and address. I mailed you a check for $4.25 to pay for the labels ($3.50) and the postage and handling charge ($.75).

I am attaching a sample of the labels, which arrived yesterday. Please note that the address is incorrect. It should be 5908, not 6908.

Please send me a new order of address labels with the correct name and address as shown below:

Kathleen Hovland
5908 S. Crestwood Avenue
Richmond, VA 23226

If you wish me to return the incorrect labels, please let me know and I will be glad to do so. Thank you for your help.

Very truly yours,

Kathleen Hovland

Kathleen Hovland

Writing Practice 6: *A Letter of Adjustment*

Write one of the following letters of adjustment, using your name and address and the current date. Make up any details that you need in order to write an effective letter.

1.   You bought a pair of terrycloth shorts for $8.95 from Sportswear, Inc., 2086 Tupello Road, Baton Rouge, Louisiana 70808. The first time that you washed the shorts, they shrank so badly that they no longer fit. Tell how you are returning the shorts and what you want the company to do.

2.   Your local telephone company has charged you for a long-distance call to Mexico City, Mexico, that you did not make. Enclose a copy of the bill and state the amount of the call and when it was made. You wish the company to credit your account.

3.   You tried a new brand of dry cat food for your cat. The package says that satisfaction is guaranteed or your money will be refunded. Your cat refuses to taste the cat food, let alone eat it. Write to YumYums, Inc., 1008 Twinlakes Boulevard, Kankakee, Illinois 60901. Enclose the box top of YumYums and ask for a refund.

Use the Checklist for Proofreading Business Letters on page 286.

Letters of Appreciation

There will be occasions when you want to write a letter thanking someone for special efforts on your behalf or for his or her work in

general. A *letter of appreciation* is the business letter counterpart of a thank-you note. Since people in business and public life often receive critical letters and complaints, a letter of praise or thanks for work well done is always appreciated.

When writing a letter of appreciation, be sure to identify yourself, usually at the beginning of the letter. Then explain why you are writing the letter, expressing your thanks briefly and courteously.

Model: *A Letter of Appreciation*

A sample letter of appreciation is shown. How well do you think the writer has carried out the guidelines for a letter of appreciation?

289 Tanglewood Drive
Biloxi, MS 39531
March 19, 1984

The Honorable Jean D'Angelo
House Office Building
Washington, D.C. 20013

Dear Ms. D'Angelo:

I am an eleventh grader at Norland High School in Biloxi, Mississippi. My government class has been studying legislation that is currently in the House of Representatives and the Senate that directly affects funding for special high school science programs. I am assigned to study and discuss the bill (HR-108) that you introduced into the House in February.

Everyone in my class agrees that this is a very good bill and one that will help school systems provide additional resources for students who are interested in the sciences. We have asked our parents to write letters expressing their support of the bill to their representatives in Congress.

We hope that your legislation passes. Thank you for your good work.

Yours truly,

Jason Rothstein

Jason Rothstein

Writing Practice 7: *A Letter of Appreciation*

Write a letter of appreciation to someone you think is doing a good job. Some writing suggestions are listed below.

1.   A teacher or an official in your school

2.   An elected official in your city or county

3.   Your senator or representative in Congress

4.   A community leader

5.   A business group that has sponsored an athletic team

Use the Checklist for Proofreading Business Letters on page 286.

Letter of Application

An effective *letter of application* can impress an employer enough so that he or she will want to interview you. The letter should give the impression that the writer is neat and responsible, as well as qualified for the job. When many letters are received for a single job, those that are messy or contain errors in spelling and grammar are quickly discarded.

A letter of application should contain all of the following information as shown in the example letter on page 283:

a.   *When and how you heard about the job.* Identify the job for which you are applying and tell when and how you heard about it.

b.   *Personal data.* Include your age, year in school, grade average, and any other information that might be relevant to the job.

c.   *Your qualifications.* List previous experience, special training, interest in the field, and long-range career plans. You may not have had any direct experience in the kind of job for which you are applying. If so, try to think of experiences you have had that are in some way related to the job. (See the sample letter that follows.) Also, be sure to include personal characteristics such as reliability and a willingness to work hard.

d.   *Your references.* Give the names and addresses of two or three adults who can attest to your character and ability. References cannot be relatives. Any adult who knows you well, such as a teacher, neighbor, member of the clergy, or former employer

1204 Churchill Road
Lyndhurst, Ohio 44124
March 30, 1984

Ms. Jane Ferrara
Director, Department of Parks and Recreation
Lyndhurst City Hall
17908 Mayfield Boulevard
Lyndhurst, Ohio 44124

Dear Ms. Ferrara:

I am writing to apply for the position of assistant recreation instructor at one of the city parks during the summer months. I have learned from an article in today's Herald that the city will be hiring six high school students to work as assistant recreation instructors this summer. Please consider me as an applicant.

I am a junior at East Hills High School. During the past three years my grade point average has been 3.3, or B+. I am preparing for college and am interested in majoring in physical education. For the past six years I have been a member of various track-and-field teams. I have been the assistant manager of a Little League team sponsored by the Optimists' Club for the past two years.

Last summer I worked as an assistant counselor at Park Day Camp with a boys' group of nine- and ten-year-olds. Mrs. Katie Oppenheim, director of the camp, can tell you about my reliability and ability to work with young people.

Ever since I can remember, I have been interested in athletics. I consider myself proficient in track-and-field events, soccer, baseball, football, and tennis. I also hold an American Red Cross Lifesaving Certificate.

The following persons can tell you more about my character and qualifications for the job.

Mrs. Katie Oppenheim, Director of Park Day Camp
2610 Fenwick Road, University Heights, Ohio

Mr. Philip Wenszlaw, Physical Education Instructor and Coach, East Hills High School, 1411 Eastwood Road, Mayfield Heights, Ohio
Mrs. Annemarie Cantwell, Principal of East Hills High School, 1411 Eastwood Road, Mayfield Heights, Ohio

At your convenience, I would be glad to come to City Hall for an interview. You can reach me at home after school and in the evenings. My telephone number is 394-1689.

Yours sincerely,

Louis Novallo

Louis Novallo

may serve as a reference. Before giving a person's name as a reference, however, ask that person for permission to do so.

e. *Request for an interview.* Ask for an interview, at the employer's convenience, and be sure to tell when and where you can be reached by telephone to make an appointment.

Think and Discuss

Answer the following questions about the model letter of application.

1. How did the writer hear about the job?

2. What important personal data did he include?

3. What special qualifications or experience does the writer describe that might make the employer grant an interview?

4. What essential information did the writer include for the two references?

Writing Practice 8: *Writing a Letter of Application*

Look through the local newspaper for a job advertisement that interests you. It can be either a summer job or the type of job you may want in the future as a career. Write a letter of application for this job, and include all the information listed in the section on writing a letter of application. Follow the correct form for business letters and proofread your letter carefully, using the checklist on page 286.

Personal Résumé

An alternative to writing a lengthy letter of application is to outline your background and experience in a personal résumé and attach a short *cover letter*.

The purpose of the résumé is to interest an employer in you. In a résumé you include only the information that would have a direct bearing on whether or not you are qualified for the job. You can often use the same résumé to apply for several jobs.

The cover letter that accompanies your résumé will be a brief letter of introduction. Do not repeat information given in the résumé; instead, begin your letter by identifying the job for which you are applying and by telling how you heard about the job. Then state that you are enclosing a résumé of your qualifications and references. Close your cover letter with a request for an interview.

Model: A Personal Résumé

A personal résumé usually includes the following kinds of information. Notice how the résumé incorporates this information in an acceptable format.

Theresa A. Nardoia

Address:	14410 Peerless Place Newark, New Jersey 07114
Telephone:	498-6220
Personal:	Born September 19, 1969 in Newark, New Jersey Marital status: Single Health: Excellent Height: 5'4" Weight: 110 Social Security Number: 073-92-2068
Education:	Junior, Salazzaro High School, college preparatory course 3.0 grade point average (B)
Extracurricular activities:	Vice president, Key Club, a service organization Captain, girls' basketball team
Skills:	Can type 65 words per minute Can operate microfilm and duplicating machines
Work experience:	Central Newark Community Center, Newark, N.J — Volunteer office work and help interview Spanish-speaking clients on Saturdays from 1983 to date Ryan Community School, Newark, NJ — Assisted instructor in summer programs for teaching English skills to Spanish-speaking students, summer 1983
References:	Dr. Orin Lorenzo, Pastor, Newark United Methodist Church, Newark, New Jersey Dr. Natalie Crohn, Director, Central Newark Community Center, Newark, New Jersey Ms. Julia Wolk, Instructor, Ryan Community School, Newark, New Jersey

Writing Practice 9: *A Personal Résumé*

Write a personal résumé following the preceding model. Adapt the résumé to the job for which you wrote a letter of application in Writing Practice 8. Then write a short cover letter to accompany the résumé. Use the Checklist for Proofreading Business Letters on the next page to proofread your résumé and cover letter.

Proofreading a Business Letter

Before you mail a business letter, proofread it carefully for completeness, form and errors. Use the following checklist as a guide in proofreading your business letters.

Checklist for Proofreading Business Letters

Form and Appearance

1. The letter is neatly written in ink or typed with no smudges or obvious corrections.

2. The letter is centered on the page with each part having the correct amount of spacing above and below.

3. The left-hand margins are even. Left-hand margins of the heading and closing align. Left-hand margins of the inside address and the salutation align.

4. The right-hand margin of the letter body is fairly even.

5. Your signature is legible and written in ink.

Punctuation

1. A comma comes between the city and state. No comma is between the state and ZIP code.

2. A comma comes between the day of the month and the year in the heading.

3. A colon follows the salutation.

4. A comma follows the closing.

Capitalization

1. The names of streets, cities, and states in the heading and inside address are capitalized.

2. The name of the month in the heading is capitalized.

3. The title of the person to whom you are writing and the names of the department and company listed in the inside address are capitalized.

4. The salutation *Dear* and all nouns are capitalized.

5. Only the first word of the closing is capitalized.

Filling Out Forms

Businesses and government offices use forms to obtain and store information. Since you will be filling out such forms for the rest of your life, the following guidelines will give you some instruction and practice on how to do so accurately and efficiently.

1. Read the directions carefully and completely before beginning to fill out the form.

2. Always use blue or black ink or a typewriter. Never use a pencil.

3. Print—do not write—the information requested in the form. Make sure your responses are clear and legible.

4. Read the fine print carefully.

5. Most forms require a signature at the end of the form. Sign your name as you usually write it.

Driver's License Application Form

To get your driver's license you will have to take and pass a written examination and a driving test. Before you can apply for a license in most areas, you will have to pass an approved driver education course if you are under eighteen years of age. In addition, you will need the signature of your parent or legal guardian on your application. Before you begin the application procedure, get a copy of your state driver's information booklet and study the rules and procedures you will need to know in order to pass the tests. In the booklet you will find directions on how to apply for a license, what identification you will need, information about the kind of questions you will be asked, and special instructions if you want a license to drive a vehicle other than an automobile.

Before you fill out the application form, look at how it is organized. Then read the instructions completely and carefully. On the sample form on page 288, you will notice that the right-hand areas are reserved for the department issuing your license to record information about your test results, restrictions on your license and identification. Do not write in any space except where instructed. As in filling out all forms, print legibly in ink or type in the information. Where you are to sign your name (*Signature of Applicant*), write your name as you normally do. It should be the same name you use on other legal forms, such as bank checks and contracts.

On the following Applicant's Declaration Sheet, the top line is for a current driver's license number. If you are applying for a license for the first time, you will not have any number to put in that space. In the next item you will check *Operator* because you want a license to operate a motor vehicle. However, you might also want to operate a moped, so you would also check that box. People who need a chauffeur's license for business purposes or who need a license for legal identification will check one of the other boxes. If you want a license to operate a motorcycle, check to see if there is a special application form for that examination.

APPLICANT'S DECLARATION SHEET

DE-36 (3/80)

MICHIGAN DRIVER LICENSE NUMBER	APPLICATION DESIRED ☐ OPERATOR ☐ CHAUFFEUR ☐ MOPED ☐ PERSONAL I.D.	(FOR DEPARTMENT USE ONLY)		
		LICENSE EXP. YEAR:	LICENSE TYPE:	DATE ISSUED:
(FIRST NAME) (MIDDLE NAME) (LAST NAME)		COUNTY CODE:	APPLICATION NUMBER:	
		ENDORSEMENTS:	PREVIOUS LIC. (STATE-NO. EXP. YEAR)	
(CURRENT RESIDENCE ADDRESS) (APT. OR LOT NO.) (COUNTY)		CORRECTIVE LENSES REQUIRED?	YES ☐	NO ☐
(CITY OR TOWN) Michigan (ZIP CODE)		(check one) OTHER RESTRICTIONS:		
EYE COLOR ___ ft. ___ in. HEIGHT WEIGHT SEX	MONTH DAY YEAR DATE OF BIRTH	DRIVER ED. CERTIFICATE AND T.I.P. INFORMATION		

PLEASE ANSWER THE FOLLOWING QUESTIONS BY CHECKING YES OR NO

DRIVER ED. CERTIFICATE NUMBER:		ISSUING SCHOOL CODE.	
1. Do you have a physical disability or handicap? (Do not include glasses)	Yes ☐ No ☐	BIRTH CERTIFICATE NUMBER:	STATE & ___ COUNTY
2. Have you ever been subject to a recurrent or uncontrolled loss of consciousness?	Yes ☐ No ☐	VALIDATE DRIVER ED. CERTIFICATE?	☐
3. Is your driving privilege currently suspended, revoked or denied?	Yes ☐ No ☐	ISSUED T.I.P.	☐
4. Will you need a classified endorsement?	Yes ☐ No ☐	HOME PHONE:	

4. Will you need a classified endorsement?	Yes ☐ No ☐	ROAD SIGN TEST	DATE ___/___ DATE ___/___	PASS ☐ FAIL ☐ PASS ☐ FAIL ☐
5. Will you be operating a motorcycle on public streets and highways?	Yes ☐ No ☐	WRITTEN TEST	# DATE ___/___ # DATE ___/___ # DATE ___/___	PASS ☐ FAIL ☐ PASS ☐ FAIL ☐ PASS ☐ FAIL ☐
(SIGNATURE OF APPLICANT) (DATE)				

REMARKS:	FEE DUE:
THE PERSON DESCRIBED IS AUTHORIZED TO OPERATE A MOTOR VEHICLE WHEN ACCOMPANIED BY AN EXAMINER CERTIFIED BY THE MICHIGAN DEPARTMENT OF STATE	INITIAL OF EXAMINER

Writing Practice 10: *Filling Out a Form for a Driver's License*

Since you may not live in the state where the sample form is used, try to get the form used in your state and fill it in accurately. If you cannot get your state's form, make a copy of the preceding application for a driver's license examination. Follow the directions for filling in information exactly, and give all the information requested. Be sure to sign your legal name where it is indicated. Also, put the date of your signature in the appropriate place.

Sentence Combining: Using Infinitives and Punctuation

Inserting Infinitives and Objects

For more information on infinitives, see pages 474-475.

An *infinitive phrase*, a phrase composed of the word *to* plus a verb, can also be used to insert one sentence into a base sentence. The (*to* + *verb*) combination may appear at the beginning, middle, or end of a sentence, as the following examples show:

Base: Kuni needs *something*.

Insert: Kuni studies her German lessons more thoroughly than I do.
(*to* + *verb*)

Combined: Kuni needs *to study her German lessons more thoroughly* than I do.

Base: *Something* is what our grandfather taught us.

Insert: We treat older people with respect. (*to* + *verb*)

Combined: *To treat older people with respect* is what our grandfather taught us.

Base: Are you willing (to do) *something*?

Insert: You work overtime. (*to* + *verb*)

Combined: Are you willing *to work overtime*?

Base: *Something* is what Bob does during his leisure time.

Insert: He goes down to the pier (to do) *something*.

Insert: He watches the people fishing and water skiing from boats.

Combined: *To go down to the pier to watch the people fishing and water skiing from boats* is what Bob does during his leisure time.

Notice that in some cases the verb changes form when it is combined with the base sentence in an infinitive phrase: *goes/to go*, *improved/to improve*. Remember that *is*, *are*, *was*, and *were* are formed from the infinitive *to be*.

Exercise 1: *Inserting Infinitives and Objects*

After studying the examples, combine each of the following sets of sentences into a single sentence by following the (*to* + *verb*) signal. In the first five sentences the signals are given; in the last five sentences no signals are given, and you must decide how to combine the sentences by inserting infinitives.

Examples

a. The posters warned us *something*.
We are aware of the importance of fire prevention in the home. (*to* + *verb*)
The posters warned us to be aware of the importance of fire prevention in the home.

b. *Something* is her ambition in life.
She becomes an astronaut for NASA. (*to* + *verb*)
To become an astronaut for NASA is her ambition in life.

1. The brochure encouraged employers (*to do*) *something*.
They hire the disabled. (*to* + *verb*)

2. Kit considered his boss *something*.
His boss was the most honest and most intelligent person he had ever met. (*to* + *verb*)

3. The instructions told us (*to do*) *something* and *something*.
We read the advertisement. (*to* + *verb*)
We find the hidden persuasive devices. (*to* + *verb*)

4. *Something* and *something* are the goals of Zen.
One attains enlightenment by intuition. (*to* + *verb*)
One achieves discipline through meditation. (*to* + *verb*)

5. *Something* requires that the partners have the ability (*to do*) *something*.
The partners win at bridge. (*to* + *verb*)
The partners communicate successfully during the bidding about the cards in their hands. (*to* + *verb*)

6. *Something* and *something* would be a harrowing experience.
One loses one's bearings in a crowded, foreign city.
One is unable to speak the language.

7. My parents gave me the self-assurance (*to do*) *something*.
I try new experiences.

8. Do you prefer *something* or *something* during the summer?
You vacation out in the woods.
You relax at home.

9.   *Something* is *something*.
     One neglects one's pet.
     One is completely insensitive to the needs of animals.

10. Our coach is thrilled (to do) *something* and then (to do) *something*.
     She gives us all the training and technique she can offer.
     She sees it pay off in our winning first place.

Using the Colon, the Dash, and Parentheses

For more information on colons, dashes, and parentheses, see pages 590-594.

The *colon*, the *dash*, and *parentheses* can also be used to insert one or more sentences into a base sentence. However, each of these punctuation marks has a special, limited function. Writers must avoid using these marks incorrectly or relying on them too heavily. The new signals for these combinations are (*colon*), (*dash*), (*paired dashes*), and (*parens*).

In the following examples notice that the *colon* follows the base sentence and introduces a specific listing of something already mentioned. Notice that words repeated in the insert sentence can be dropped in the combined sentences.

Base: We had to look for the following objects on the treasure hunt.

Insert: The objects were an apple core, a hairpin, a stick of sugarless gum, and a ball of yellow yarn. (*colon*)

Combined: We had to look for the following objects on the treasure hunt: *an apple core, a hairpin, a stick of sugarless gum, and a ball of yellow yarn.*

Base: His suitcase was stuffed with small gifts for the children.

Insert: The gifts were a harmonica for Eric, a card game for Amy, and a box of watercolors for Beth. (*colon*)

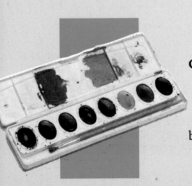

Combined: His suitcase was stuffed with small gifts for the children: *a harmonica for Eric, a card game for Amy, and a box of watercolors for Beth.*

The *dash* can be used to insert a specific listing of items *before* the base sentence that refers to them.

Base: These were the things she enjoyed while living on the farm.

Insert: She enjoyed caring for the livestock and working in the open fields. (*dash*)

291

Combined:	*Caring for the livestock, working in the open fields*—these were the things she enjoyed while living on the farm.

A *dash or paired dashes* can also be used to insert a sudden change of thought into a base sentence. The punctuation separates the interruption from the rest of the sentence.

Base:	Last week we raked together all the leaves in our yard.
Insert:	No, it was three weeks ago. (*paired dashes*)
Combined:	Last week—*no, it was three weeks ago*—we raked together all the leaves in our yard.

Writers use parentheses to insert added information when they do not want to draw attention away from the base sentence.

Base:	Mrs. Beaker helped us start the stalled car.
Insert:	Wouldn't you know she had jumper cables? (*parens*)
Combined:	Mrs. Beaker (*wouldn't you know she had jumper cables?*) helped us start the stalled car.

Base:	We visited Mrs. Hernandez and watched her work on a large metal sculpture.
Insert:	She is my neighbor. (*parens*)
Combined:	We visited Mrs. Hernandez (*my neighbor*) and watched her work on a large metal sculpture.

> A sentence within a sentence should not begin with a capital letter.

Exercise 2: Using the Colon, Dash, and Parentheses

On a sheet of paper, combine each of the following sentence sets into a single sentence. In the first five sets, follow the signal. Study the example before you begin.

Example

a. Marshall sent the gift to his aunt while she was in the hospital.
The gift was a thrilling mystery novel. (*parens*)
Marshall sent the gift (a thrilling mystery novel) to his aunt while she was in the hospital.

1. Each of these days was stormy last week.
The days were Monday, Tuesday, Thursday, and Saturday. (*dash*)

2. Luisa played the role of Dr. Watson in the grade school play.
   Luisa is my little sister. (*parens*)

3. There were two reasons I couldn't do my homework.
   I lost my notebook and I had the flu. (*colon*)

4. Our research papers are due on November 25.
   They are due during class, not after. (*paired dashes*)

5. Geometry involves solving problems step by step.
   Geometry is a course I love. (*parens*)

6. These are what I like best about school.
   Geometry, music, and sports are what I like best.

7. I especially enjoyed some of the acts put on by the students.
   The acts were Lou's African dance, Marty's knife-throwing act, and Bart's talking dog.

8. Your book report must include the following things.
   The things are the title of the book, a description of the setting, and your opinion of the main character.

9. Two teenage boys stopped when the accident occurred and helped direct traffic.
   Maybe they were older.

10. You will need all the following equipment for this experiment.
    The equipment is two pieces of copper wire, a Bunsen burner, a magnet, and a large beaker.

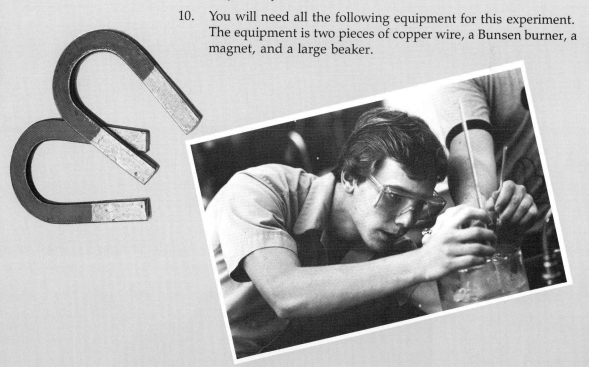

Exercise 3: Combining Sentences

This paragraph exercise is a review of many of the sentence-combining skills you have studied. Combine each of the following sets into a single sentence. On a sheet of paper, write the combined sentences to form a paragraph. For the first five sets, use the signals.

1. The Renaissance was marked by outstanding achievements and discoveries in many areas.
    The areas included art, music, science, and literature. (*colon*)

2. These were the accomplishments of one man, Michelangelo Buonarroti.
    The accomplishments were the designs for the Laurentian Library, the painting of the Sistine Chapel ceiling, and the sculpture *David*. (*dash*)

3. Michelangelo's frescoes in the Sistine Chapel are based on religious themes.
    The frescoes were completed in four years. (*parens*)
    The themes were the creation of the world, Adam and Eve, and the Last Judgment. (*colon*)

4. Leonardo da Vinci was an artist of the Renaissance.
    He was also Italian. (*parens*)

5. This important concept referred to *something*.
    The concept was chiaroscuro. (*parens*)
    Leonardo opposed light against dark in his paintings. (*pos + ing*)

6. These familiar masterpieces by Leonardo show his use of chiaroscuro.
   The masterpieces are *The Mona Lisa, The Last Supper*, and *St. John, the Baptist*.

7. All these were areas in which Leonardo excelled.
   The areas were painting, sculpture, music, and engineering.

8. *Something* proves Leonardo da Vinci was equally talented as an engineer and inventor.
   He designed such items as a machine gun and an adjustable monkey wrench.

9. The accomplishments of other Italian scientists also explain *something*.
   Italy was considered the center of the Renaissance period in history.

10. In 1543 Nicolaus Copernicus found *something* and published this knowledge.
    The sun, rather than the earth, is the center of our solar system.

11. Later, Galileo Galilei became the first man (to do) *something*.
    He studied the heavens with a telescope.

12. *Something* was also an important Renaissance achievement.
    Explorers sailed into unknown areas (to do) *something*.
    They discovered new continents and trade routes.

13. These voyages were all accomplished during the Renaissance.
    The voyages were Columbus' trip to America, Vasco da Gama's exploration of the West African coast, and Magellan's trips to South America and the East Indies.

14. *Something* also marks the Renaissance as a great literary period.
    Shakespeare wrote all his famous tragedies and comedies then.

15. *Something* makes one realize *something*.
    Someone studies the Renaissance closely.
    This was a time period in which much was accomplished.

Writing Practice: *Applying Sentence-Combining Skills to Writing*

The following list contains specific details for a paragraph on the subject of blue whales. After reading the details, restrict the subject to a topic, organize the details, and write a paragraph on the restricted topic. As you do, use some of the sentence-combining skills you have learned to make your writing interesting and varied. It is not necessary to use all the details in your paragraph.

Largest animal in the world
Not a fish
A mammal
Length can be up to ninety feet
Weight can be 125 tons
Moves to warmer waters to breed
Usually found in polar seas
Rarely seen in tropical waters
Feeds on krill—animals that are like shrimp
Strains the krill from water
Uses plates of baleen to do this
Baleen plates fringe each side of whale's mouth
The plates are made of horny material
Plates are triangular
The blue whale has baleen plates but no teeth.
When enough krill are caught in mouth, whale dives and swallows
Stomach holds two tons of food
Whale is insulated by thick layers of fat or blubber
Can't smell
Can't see well
Relies on sense of hearing and touch
Research suggests that whales communicate by sound
A solitary animal
Not found in schools
Schools are groups of whales
Blue whale may become extinct
Too many were killed by whalers

2
Grammar and Usage

9 Nouns

Understanding Nouns

Nouns name things. They name the objects you see around you—perhaps a chair, a window, or a tree. Your own name is a noun. Nouns also name some things that you cannot see, such as thoughts or ideas. You can learn to recognize nouns in three ways: by learning the definition of a noun, by studying the classes of nouns, and by learning the features that distinguish a noun from other parts of speech. In the following sections you will study and practice each of these ways to identify nouns.

Defining Nouns

A *noun* is usually defined as a word that names a person, a place, a thing, or an idea.

Lisa reads constantly.	[name of a person]
Death Valley is extremely hot and dry.	[name of a place]
The old *car* stalled again.	[name of a thing]
Honesty is important.	[name of an idea]

Exercise 1: Identifying and Defining Nouns

Write the following sentences, underlining each noun. Above each noun write whether it names a person, a place, a thing, or an idea.

Examples

a. Miss Lo grew up in China.

     person   place
     Miss Lo grew up in China.

b. Martin Luther King, Jr., made many fine speeches about freedom.

person   thing
Martin Luther King, Jr., made many fine speeches about
idea
freedom.

1. Luis can play trumpet and trombone.

2. Babylon was famous for its fabulous hanging gardens.

3. Ann saw several young cobras at the zoo in Oklahoma City.

4. Too much power may corrupt a person.

5. France gave the United States a statue symbolizing liberty.

6. Chief Joseph wanted freedom and peace for his people.

7. Anne Bradstreet was an important poet in America.

8. Some scientists believe a huge serpent lives in Loch Ness, a lake in Scotland.

9. The law should provide justice and safety for all citizens.

10. Jimmy Carter grew up in Georgia on a farm where peanuts were the main crop.

Classifying Nouns

Two classes of nouns are *proper nouns* and *common nouns*.

Proper nouns name specific persons, places, things, or ideas. All other nouns are called *common nouns*.

Genuine Risk won that race.

The noun *Genuine Risk* is proper because it names a specific horse. In the following sentence the noun *horse* is common because it is not a specific name.
Proper nouns are capitalized; common nouns are not.

Old Baldy loomed ahead of us.	[proper noun]
The *mountain* loomed ahead of us.	[common noun]
Marie Curie was from *Poland*.	[proper nouns]
The *scientist* was from another *country*.	[common nouns]

Many proper nouns, and some common nouns, are *compound nouns* because they are made up of more than one word.

Compound proper nouns have two or more capitalized words:

San Diego Freeway	[one thing]
Dodge City	[one place]
Mary McLeod Bethune	[one person]

Compound common nouns may be spelled as one word, as two or more separate words, or as a hyphenated word.

One word: baseball, silverware, classroom

Two words: tennis court, health club, police station

Hyphenated word: jack-in-the-box, son-in-law, self-confidence

Note: Consult your dictionary for the correct spelling of compound nouns.

Nouns may also be classified as *concrete* or *abstract.*

A *concrete noun* names something that can be perceived through the senses (an object such as a house or the Lincoln Memorial). An *abstract noun* names a quality, a thought, or an idea (such as freedom or talent). The noun *house,* for example, is both common and concrete; *Julian Bond* is a proper noun and a concrete noun. The noun *friendship* is a common noun and an abstract noun.

Nouns that stand for a group are called *collective nouns.*

Some collective nouns are *jury, group,* and *class.*

Exercise 2: Identifying Noun Classes

Write the following sentences, underlining common nouns once and proper nouns twice. Write *A* above each abstract noun.

Example

a. Robin Williams, who played Mork from Ork, also starred in the role of Popeye.

Robin Williams, who played Mork from Ork, also starred in

A

the role of Popeye.

1. Daisy Bates of Little Rock, Arkansas, courageously saved her daughter-in-law.

2. The beautiful Ponca State Park is located in Nebraska on the Missouri River.

3. The *Titanic* met a tragic fate in the Atlantic Ocean.

4. In cartoons Mickey Mouse, created by Walt Disney, gave many children pleasure.

5. A famous member of the Harlem Globetrotters was the player named Meadowlark Lemon.

6. Casey Jones, engineer of the Cannonball Express, worked for the Illinois Central Railroad.

7. Jim Henson, a puppeteer, created many popular characters, including Kermit the Frog, Miss Piggy, and Fozzie Bear.

8. A successful modern dancer, José Limon was best known for his role as Othello in the ballet *The Moor's Pavane*.

9. The American spacecraft *Apollo 11* lifted off for the moon in the late sixties, with the astronauts Michael Collins, Neil Armstrong, and Edwin Aldrin aboard.

10. The name *America* was first used in 1507 when Martin Waldseemüller prepared a map showing the new continent.

Finding a Noun by Its Features

Four features set off nouns from other parts of speech. Most nouns have at least one of these features; many have all four.

1. Nouns often follow determiners.

The most common determiners are the words *a, an,* and *the,* which are also called *articles.* Some other common determiners are *any, each, many, one (two, three . . .), some, that, these, this,* and *those.*

a girl	*four* cats
an automobile	*many* friends
the bird	*some* cities

2. Nouns may be either singular or plural.

Many nouns have both a *singular* and a *plural* form. The plural form names more than one person, place, thing, or idea. Some nouns have the same form for both the singular and plural.

Singular	Plural
one baby	two babies
one deer	five deer
one finger	two fingers
one fox	several foxes
one house	many houses

3. Nouns may show ownership or relationship.

Both singular and plural nouns have *possessive forms* that show ownership or relationship. The possessive forms are made by the addition of an apostrophe (') and -*s* or just an apostrophe.

The horse that Felicia owns is a palomino. *Felicia*'s horse is a palomino.	[ownership]
The leg of the horse was broken. The *horse*'s leg was broken.	[relationship]

4. Nouns may be formed with a suffix such as -*ation*, -*ism*, -*ment*, -*ness*, or -*ance*.

A *noun suffix* is an ending that makes a word a noun. *Strange* becomes the noun *strangeness* when the suffix -*ness* is added. These suffixes are clues that the words are nouns.

attend + ance	=	attendance
capital + ism	=	capitalism
consider + ation	=	consideration
fond + ness	=	fondness
retire + ment	=	retirement

Proper nouns do not exhibit as many noun features as common nouns do. Proper nouns, for instance, seldom take a plural form—there are few reasons to speak of *seven Albert Einsteins* or *two Australias*. Often proper nouns do not take a determiner—you seldom hear of *the Italy* or *the Jackie Robinson*. In only a few cases do proper nouns follow determiners: *the United States, the Rocky Mountains,* and *the Virgin Mary.* Nevertheless, proper nouns exhibit one important characteristic of nouns; they can be made possessive: *United States'* resources, the *Rocky Mountains'* beauty, the *Virgin Mary's* statue.

Exercise 3: Identifying Nouns

Using what you have learned about the features of a noun, identify the nouns in the following sentences. Write the sentences, underlining each noun. (Your teacher may ask you to explain how you identified the nouns.)

Example

a. The students were disturbed by the sound of the car's stuck horn.
The <u>students</u> were disturbed by the <u>sound</u> of the <u>car's</u> stuck <u>horn</u>.

1. Many farmers and ranchers consider the coyote a pest and a danger.

2. There are several mistaken beliefs about this animal, which native Americans called "the smartest creature on earth."

3. The most widespread misconception about coyotes is that they prey on cattle and sheep.

4. The truth is that scientists have never documented a single case of coyotes killing either cattle or sheep.

5. Coyotes may feed on an animal that has died from other causes.

6. Experiments show that the coyote prefers meat that has not been freshly killed and would rather feast on an old carcass.

7. Despite these facts many people believe that coyotes are responsible for the killing of many lambs each year.

8. The lamb is one of the most helpless animals in existence and catches many diseases and ailments.

9. Sheep and lambs have a high mortality rate, and most coyotes apparently feed on animals killed by nature.

10. Nevertheless, traps and poisoned baits are set, killing thousands of coyotes each year (as well as destroying other wild animals—including many members of endangered species).

Review: Understanding Nouns

The following paragraph about Niagara Falls contains twenty-three nouns, and the first three of them are already underlined for you. Using what you have learned in the previous sections of this chapter, list the remaining twenty nouns on a separate sheet of paper. If the noun is concrete, write *C* beside it; and if the noun is abstract, write *A* beside it. Be prepared to explain how you were able to identify each noun you listed. Consider each of the four features of a noun, and tell which feature applies to a given noun from this paragraph.

> Both the Canadians and Americans experimented with discovering the violent power of the great Niagara Falls. Three large British ships, used in the War of 1812 and stationed at Lake Erie, were condemned, and it was decided to send them over the falls to see the amount of destruction that would result. The first boat was torn apart by the rapids even before going over the falls, and the second filled with water before it reached the falls, but the third "took the leap gallantly and retained her form till lost in the cloud of mist below." Only a fragment of this boat was later found.

Applying What You Know

From a newspaper, magazine, or book select a passage that is about one or two paragraphs long. Using what you have learned earlier in this chapter, identify the nouns in your excerpt and list them on a sheet of paper. Beside each noun write the different classes to which it belongs: *concrete* or *abstract, compound, common* or *proper,* or *collective.* Remember that a noun may belong to more than one class at the same time.

Using Nouns

Forming the Regular Plurals of Nouns

The plural of most nouns is formed by adding the suffix *-s* or *-es* to the singular form. Plurals formed in this way are called *regular plurals.*

Form the regular plural of most nouns by adding the suffix -s.

Singular	Plural
one dog	two dogs
one school	many schools
one tournament	several tournaments

Form the regular plural of nouns ending in s, sh, ch, x, or z by adding the suffix -es.

Singular	Plural
one bus	several buses
one wish	two wishes
one match	many matches
one box	ten boxes
one buzz	a few buzzes

Form the plural of nouns ending in o preceded by a vowel by adding the suffix -s. Form the plural of most nouns ending in o preceded by a consonant by adding the suffix -es.

Singular	Plural
one radio	three radios
one hero	several heroes

Exception: The plurals of most nouns that end in o and that have to do with music take only the suffix -s: banjos, solos, pianos, concertos, duos.

Note: The preceding rules apply also to proper names: the Coles, the Joneses, the Moraleses.

Exercise 4: Forming Regular Noun Plurals

All the nouns in the sentences on the following page are regular nouns and appear in *italics*. Write the sentences and change each singular noun to its plural form by adding either -s or -es. Underline each noun you make plural.

Examples

a. The *church* and *synagogue* offered to help the *victim* of the *flood*.

The *churches* and *synagogues* offered to help the *victims* of the *floods*.

b. The *boy* trimmed the *bush* and the *shrub* and then swept the *sidewalk* and *porch*.

The *boys* trimmed the *bushes* and the *shrubs* and then swept the *sidewalks* and *porches*.

---

1. Only the *echo* from the *canyon* answered the barking *fox*.

2. The *bunch* of wild *grass* tied with the violet *ribbon* decorated the *table*.

3. The strange, drooping *moss* and the *screech* of the *owl* made the *camper* nervous.

4. The *ax* and *torch* were found near the *arch* of the *fortress*.

5. The *clash* and *crash* of the *thunderbolt* shook the large *birch* and *pine*.

6. The *buzz* from the power *line* ruined the *transmission* of the *radio*.

7. He had to pay *tax* on the antique *glass*, the gold *box*, and the jeweled *brooch*.

8. We had to fill in the *scratch* on the *piano* with *wax* and *polish*.

9. The *guard* inspected the *catch* on the door and the *latch* on the *window* during the *recess*.

10. The *fizz* and *hiss* of the *chemical* seem sinister to the *student* in the *class*.

Forming the Irregular Plurals of Nouns

Many *irregular plurals* are formed by changing the spelling and adding the suffix *-s* or *-es* to the singular form.

Form the plural of most nouns that end in *y* preceded by a consonant by changing the *y* to *i* and adding the suffix *-es*.

Singular	Plural
one battery	four batteries
one celebrity	a dozen celebrities

Form the plural of nouns that end in *y* preceded by a vowel by adding the suffix *-s*.

Singular	Plural
one buoy	two buoys
one day	seven days

Exceptions: Proper nouns ending in y are made plural simply by adding the suffix *-s: Kennedy, Kennedys; July, Julys; Langtry, Langtrys; Foy, Foys.*

Form the plural of some nouns ending in *f* or *fe* by changing the *f* or *fe* to *v* and adding the suffix *-es*.

Singular	Plural	Singular	Plural
calf	calves	self	selves
elf	elves	sheaf	sheaves
half	halves	shelf	shelves
knife	knives	thief	thieves
life	lives	wife	wives
loaf	loaves	wolf	wolves

Note: Not all words ending in *f* or *fe* form their plurals as the preceding words do. Some form their plurals with the addition of the suffix *-s* only:

Singular	Plural
roof	roofs
dwarf	dwarfs
chief	chiefs
belief	beliefs
safe	safes

If you are not certain how to form the plural of any noun, check your dictionary.

Exercise 5: *Forming Irregular Noun Plurals*

Write the following sentences, changing each of the nouns in *italics* to its plural form. Underline each noun you make plural.

Example

---

    a. On *Friday* the *company* will give higher *salary* to their *staff*.
       On *Fridays* the *companies* will give higher *salaries* to their *staffs*.

---

1. The family *crest* must have belonged to *McHaney* or *Kelly*.
2. The *cry* of the *monkey* startled the *calf* at the zoo.
3. The *sky* looked overcast, so the *thief* stole the *donkey* for the *journey*.
4. The *library* will be closed for the *party* and then for the *holiday*.
5. Our *family* climbed up on the *roof* to survey the *country* where the great *victory* took place.
6. In what *key* should the *melody* in the *rhapsody* be played?
7. *Kennedy* became important in making government *policy* and establishing *priority*.
8. The *life* of the *fly* puzzled the *authority* in the *laboratory*.
9. Put the *knife* on the *shelf* away from the *baby*.
10. The *belief* about the *galaxy* presented *mystery* for the *university* to solve.

Form some irregular plurals by changing a vowel sound.

Singular	*Plural*
mouse	mice
foot	feet
goose	geese
louse	lice
man	men
tooth	teeth
woman	women

Some words have the same form for both the singular and the plural. Many nouns naming animals belong to this group, as well as some nouns naming nationalities.

Rosa caught a nice *trout.*

Rosa caught eight nice *trout.*

The following words have the same form for singular and plural:

antelope	deer	moose	series
bream	elk	pike	species
carp	grouse	Portuguese	swine
Chinese	Japanese	salmon	trousers
cod	means	scissors	Vietnamese

Another group of irregular plurals fits no pattern. This group includes nouns that have been adopted from foreign languages and have retained their foreign plural endings. Some of the most common of these follow. Check other such plurals in your dictionary.

Singular	*Plural*	*Singular*	*Plural*
analysis	analyses	datum	data
axis	axes	hypothesis	hypotheses
basis	bases	larva	larvae
crisis	crises	medium	media
criterion	criteria	phenomenon	phenomena

Plural nouns that end in *-en* also are irregular. The most common of these are *child, children; ox, oxen;* and *brother, brethren. Brethren* is now rarely used except in religious matters. In most cases the regular plural *brothers* is used.

Exercise 6: *Forming Irregular Noun Plurals*

Write the following sentences, putting each noun appearing in *italics* into its correct plural form. Underline each noun you make plural.

Example

a. The *foot* of the *goose* will be webbed like the *foot* of the *duck.*
   The *feet* of the *geese* will be webbed like the *feet* of the *ducks.*

1. The *woman* wondered how the *man* would face the *crisis.*

2. The *child* saw the *trout, catfish,* and *carp* swimming in the *pool.*

3. The *analysis* indicated the *louse* on the *swine* carried the *germ*.

4. Don't put your *foot* down wrong, or you may squash the tiny *mouse* or step on the *larva*.

5. The *woman* raised the *moose* and the *goose* to show at the exhibit.

6. The *phenomenon* of the habits of the *salmon* fascinated the *Japanese*.

7. The *tooth* of the *mouse* will be damaged by chewing on the *roof*.

8. The *child* decided not to buy any *coat* made from the skin of *deer*.

9. The stampeding *antelope* ran into our *clothes* and got tangled up in John's *trousers*.

10. The *datum* on the *larva* of the *grasshopper* became the *basis* of the new *hypothesis*.

Forming the Plurals of Compound Nouns

If a compound noun is written as one word, form the plural by adding -s or -es.

Singular	Plural
one racehorse	some racehorses
one spoonful	seven spoonfuls
one wristwatch	three wristwatches

Exception: The plural of *passerby* is *passersby*.

When a compound noun is written as two or more separate words or is hyphenated, use the most important word in the compound to form the plural.

Singular	Plural
sister-in-law	sisters-in-law
Congressional Medal of Honor	Congressional Medals of Honor
vice president	vice presidents
self-image	self-images

Sometimes, it is difficult to tell which is the most important word in a compound noun (*fourteen-year-old, fourteen-year-olds*). When in doubt, check your dictionary to find the plural form.

Exercise 7: *Forming Compound Noun Plurals*

Write the following sentences, making each of the *italicized* nouns plural. Underline each of the plural nouns that you form.

Examples

a. Coretta's *brother-in-law* are both *police officer*.
   Coretta's *brothers-in-law* are both *police officers*.

b. Julia Child put four *cupful* of stuffing in the duck.
   Julia Child put four *cupfuls* of stuffing in the duck.

1. We put away our *hockey stick* and poured several *cupful* of cocoa.

2. Judy has two *sister-in-law* and three *stepbrother*.

3. The *ex-President* spoke to the radical *left-winger*.

4. I put several *handful* of *mothball* in the trunk.

5. Where are the *baseball,* the *tennis ball,* and the *scoreboard?*

6. The *attorney-general* from three states have collected *boxful* of complaints about that scheme.

7. My *daughter-in-law* supervised three *playground*.

8. The *seven-year-old* ran for the *merry-go-round* in the front of the *campground*.

9. The two *girlfriend* had *snapshot* taken for their *yearbook*.

10. The earthquake caused waves in the *swimming pool,* but no *skyscraper* shook.

The Possessive Form of Nouns

Nouns can be made *possessive,* to show ownership or relationship, as the following examples show.

Emilio's car is in better condition than *Fred's* car.

The *women's* club discussed the Equal Rights Amendment.

My *parents'* eyes are brown.

311

Possessive forms are indicated by an apostrophe (') and the letter -s or by an apostrophe only.

If a noun is singular, add an apostrophe and the letter -s to form the possessive.

Singular Noun	*Possessive Form*
The *bus* annoyed us.	The *bus's* fumes annoyed us.
The *berry* fell.	The *berry's* juice stained the rug.

If a noun is plural and does not end in -s, add an apostrophe and the letter -s to form the possessive.

Plural Noun	*Possessive Form*
The *children* were loud.	The *children's* party was loud.
The *geese* awoke us.	The *geese's* honking awoke us.

If a noun is a plural and ends in -s, add only an apostrophe to form the possessive.

Plural Noun	*Possessive Form*
We have two *dogs*.	The *dogs'* flea collars need to be changed.
There are six old *cups*.	The *cups'* handles were missing.

For more about possessives, see the section in Chapter 22 on the use of the apostrophe.

Exercise 8: *Forming Possessive Nouns*

Write the following sentences, using the correct possessive form for each *italicized* noun. Underline the possessives you form.

Examples

---

a. *Mort* old football injury sometimes bothers him.
   Mort's old football injury sometimes bothers him.

b. The *men* locker room was flooded.
The *men's* locker room was flooded.

1. The *pharaohs* tombs were pyramids filled with treasures.

2. The *oxen* endurance compensated for the slowness of their pace.

3. Two of *China* contributions to our culture are gunpowder and macaroni.

4. Many *poets* graves are located in Westminster Abbey.

5. The *Peasants* Revolt in the fourteenth century helped end serfdom in England.

6. Billie Jean King proved that *women* tennis is as exciting as *men*.

7. The *knives* rusted blades were another indication of the *climate* dampness.

8. *King Solomon* mines were reputed to be fabulously rich.

9. *Hannibal* elephants, used for war, were the ancient equivalent of *today* tanks.

10. The best-selling mystery novels in the world are *Agatha Christie*.

Capitalizing Proper Nouns

A *proper noun* names a *specific* person, place, or thing and is always capitalized.

Capitalize the names and titles of specific people, places, and things.

Common Noun	Proper Noun
my friend	Lavinia Paters
our town	Detroit
a doll	Miss Muffett

Note: Capitalize words showing family relationships or titles only when they are part of a name or when they are used instead of a name.

Common Noun	Proper Noun
my aunt	Aunt Iris
my grandfather	Did you call, Grandfather?
the professor	Professor Jane Washington
the doctor	Dr. J. Cohen, M.D.

Capitalize the main words in the name of a specific building, landmark, or institution.

Do not capitalize words such as the articles *a*, *an*, and *the*, as well as prepositions and conjunctions with fewer than five letters.

Common Noun	Proper Noun
this building	the Museum of Modern Art
the monument	the Statue of Liberty
your school	the University of Wisconsin

Capitalize nouns that name specific regions of the country but not nouns that merely indicate direction.

Marin County is *north* of San Francisco.	[direction]
Cotton is not generally grown in the *North*.	[region]

Capitalize the first and last words and all important words in the title of a book, poem, story, song, movie, television series, newspaper, magazine, or work of art.

Common Noun	Proper Noun
book	*The Daughter of Time*
poem	''Taught Me Purple''
story	''The Interlopers''
song	''When I'm Sixty-Four''
movie	*Death on the Nile*

television show	"Coal: Solution or Pollution?" [episode] *All in the Family* [series]
newspaper	*The New York Times* the *Los Angeles Times*
magazine	*New West* magazine
art	"The Bathers"

Note: The titles of longer works, such as novels, magazines, newspapers, movies, and television series, are *italicized* in print and underlined in handwriting. The titles of shorter works are enclosed in quotation marks. *The* is not capitalized unless it is part of a name, as in *The New York Times*.

Capitalize the names of nationalities, races, and religions.

Common Noun	Proper Noun
a religion	Buddhism
a people	Hopi
the ancient ruler	the Egyptian pharaoh

Capitalize the name of a team, an organization, a government agency, or a business.

Common Noun	Proper Noun
a team	the Los Angeles Dodgers
an organization	the Elks
an agency	the Central Intelligence Agency
a business	Peter Pan Cleaners

Capitalize nouns that name school courses when they are followed by a numeral or name a specific course.

The names of language courses are capitalized. (Nouns followed by a letter or number are generally capitalized.)

Gretchen does well in science and especially enjoyed *Science 300*.

Ricardo signed up for algebra, band, geography, and *Spanish*.

Exercise 9: Capitalizing Proper Nouns

The following sentences contain both proper and common nouns. Write each sentence, capitalizing the proper nouns. Underline the nouns you capitalize.

Example

---

a. The man sitting next to my uncle is dr. ling, who teaches biology at a college in the west.

The man sitting next to my uncle is Dr. Ling, who teaches biology at a college in the West.

1. My father's two favorite comedians were uncle miltie and moms mabley.

2. After the long winter, mother said she wished we could move to the southwest.

3. "You can tell that to the judge," said sergeant pearson firmly.

4. Carlotta signed up for tennis, french, and history 400 for the summer session.

5. After church, reverend murphy told my father that he'd known grandfather lopez.

6. Mr. agung comes from indonesia, which is south of asia.

7. The south's most respected general was general robert e. lee.

8. The native americans of the midwest were more nomadic than those of the southwest.

9. Kim can't take latin because she has physics 100 at that hour.

10. One of my aunt's law teachers was judge crater.

Review: Using Nouns

The following sentences contain singular nouns that need to be made plural and possessive nouns that need an apostrophe and in some cases a final -s. Write the sentences correctly, underlining the nouns you change.

Example

---

a. My sister Lisa has all of Stevie Wonder record.

My sister Lisa has all of Stevie Wonder's records.

1. Sixteen mouse came running out of the woodwork and attacked my cat Morris.

2. One of the first woman to get a major political partys nomination for governor was Congresswoman Ella Grasso.

3. The scientists were puzzled by conflicting datum on the computers printout.

4. The two half of the nation were united by the Union Pacific Railroads tracks.

5. Jacks chili has two spoonful of vinegar.

6. Many industry need to cut back on the factories pollution of the air and water.

7. Bessie Colemans ability as a stunt pilot attracted the worlds attention.

8. Both composers concertos called for two piano.

9. Two of the mens hero are Ralph Nader and Julian Bond.

10. Abigail Adams urged President John Adams expansion of females political power.

11. Charles Eastman book, *Indian Boyhood,* is most interesting.

12. Both of Sherry Smiths brother-in-law live near Rick Montezs family.

13. The two spy smuggled out the messages by placing them in loaf of bread.

14. Fred and Luis were furious because their boss at Tudburys Department Store said they had to dress up as elf during the stores Christmas party.

15. Harris book discusses all the famous mummy, werewolf, and zombie, as well as Frankensteins monster.

Write the sentences on the following page, capitalizing and underlining the proper nouns. Be certain to capitalize all the important words in a proper noun made up of more than one word.

Example

a. Singer gladys knight attended archer high school, which is in the south, and studied music, english, and journalism.

Singer <u>Gladys Knight</u> attended <u>Archer High School</u>, which is in the <u>South</u>, and studied music, <u>English</u>, and journalism.

16. An italian, marco polo, was one of the first europeans to visit the east.

17. Have you ever been to cripple creek, colorado, dad?

18. This morning jessica court dissected a frog in biology, and this afternoon she dissected a sonnet in english.

19. My uncle, dr. p. parks, called the san francisco fire department to get his cat, maggie, out of a tree.

20. Wasn't a dramatization of dorothy sayers's book *the unpleasantness at the bellona club* shown on *masterpiece theater*?

Writing Focus: *Using Specific Nouns in Writing*

Good writers use specific nouns to print a clear and exact picture for readers. For example, the noun *tennis* is more specific than the noun *sport*. Whenever possible, use specific nouns to make your writing more precise, informative, and clear.

Assignment: *Inventor at Work*

Imagine that you are an inventor who has just come up with a wonderful invention designed especially for high school students. Your invention is easy to use yet challenging and fun, and is reasonably priced. What have you invented? What does it look like? How does it work? What does it do?

In order to market your new invention, you must write a sales brochure for it. In your brochure, you will need to describe the invention and explain what it does. Direct the language of the brochure to students who might purchase your invention. As you write, include specific nouns that will make your writing clear and concrete.

Use the steps on the following page to complete your brochure.

A. Prewriting

Brainstorm ideas about your invention. Imagine what it might look like, how it could work, and what it can do. As you brainstorm, write down words, phrases, or sentences, that come to mind. When you have run out of ideas, read over what you wrote. Underline the ideas that best describe and explain your invention.

B. Writing

Use the best ideas from your brainstorming session to write one or more paragraphs about your invention for a sales brochure. Include specific details that describe how it looks and explain what it does. Strive to make the invention sound practical and appealing so that your fellow classmates will want to buy it. Remember to use specific nouns to make your writing precise.

C. Postwriting

Use the following checklist to revise your work.

1. Have I adequately described and explained my invention?

2. Are specific nouns used effectively to make the writing precise?

Edit your work using the Proofreader's Checklist at the back of the book. If appropriate, share your writing with your classmates. You may want to draw an illustration of your invention and include both your illustration and writing in a student magazine entitled *Inventions of the 1980s*.

10 Pronouns

Understanding Pronouns

Because they take the place of nouns, pronouns save a speaker or writer from having to use a sentence such as the following one.

> The teacher told the students that the students could leave early if the students' work was finished.

In the following sections you will learn to identify pronouns through their definitions, their classifications, and the features that distinguish them from other parts of speech.

Defining Pronouns

> A *pronoun* is usually defined as a word that takes the place of one or more nouns or other pronouns.

Marcia heard the news, but *she* didn't believe *it*.

> The word (or words) to which a pronoun refers is called the *antecedent.* An antecedent usually comes before the pronoun.

Jenny thought the room was dull, and *she* decided to paint *it*.

A pronoun may refer to more than one antecedent:

Professional players Ron Breuer, Marvin Delph, and Sidney Moncrief played on the same college team. *They* were called "The Three Basketeers."

In the preceding sentence the pronoun *they* has three antecedents: *Ron Breuer, Marvin Delph,* and *Sidney Moncrief.*

Sometimes an antecedent follows its pronoun.

When *she* found *her* ring, Eileen cried with happiness.

Before *their* final exam Connie and Duane studied every night.

Since *they* had grown up in Ecuador, the children had never seen snow.

The antecedent of a pronoun may also appear in a preceding sentence.

The Garners couldn't open the suitcase. *They* had locked *it* and forgotten the key!

Sometimes a pronoun replaces a word group that functions as a noun.

Tanaka's first novel, *which* has just won an award, will be made into a movie.

A single pronoun can be used in place of an entire sentence.

The ladder will not collapse. I'm sure of *that!*

Exercise 1: *Identifying Pronouns and Antecedents*

Write the following sentences, underlining each pronoun. Then draw an arrow from the pronoun to its antecedent.

Example

a. The statue was so badly broken that it couldn't be repaired.

The statue was so badly broken that it couldn't be repaired.

1. The car can't be driven. It has a dead battery.

2. Foxes and coyotes are very intelligent, but they are difficult to tame.

3. Jim didn't do his homework because he didn't understand it.

4. Lunch from the cafeteria looked very strange today. It smelled even stranger.

5. Cheeses and meats are important foods because they are high in protein.

6. Käthe Kollwitz was a German artist who was famous for her printmaking.

7. Juanita likes chemistry because it is easy for her to complete the experiments.

8. Because the Sioux and Cheyenne were great horse riders, they have been called "the best cavalry the world has ever seen."

9. Here today, gone tomorrow. That certainly is true!

10. Kim and Maury began writing a movie script, but they lost their patience and never finished it.

Grouping Pronouns by Classes

The following sections cover five classifications, or kinds, of pronouns: *personal, demonstrative, interrogative, relative,* and *indefinite.* Learning the distinctions between these classes will help you to identify pronouns and, in turn, to use them correctly in speaking and writing.

Personal Pronouns

Personal pronouns have different forms to show whether the speaker or writer is referring to himself or herself, to the person or people being addressed, or to a third person or persons. Personal pronouns may be either singular or plural.

	Singular	*Plural*
First Person:	I, me	we, us
Second Person:	you	you
Third Person:	he, she, him, her, it	they, them

When speakers and writers refer to themselves, they use *first-person pronouns.*

Singular	Plural
I drive carefully.	*We* drive carefully.
The movie bored *me*.	The movie bored *us*.

Speakers and writers use *second person* to refer to the person or persons being addressed. Notice that the pronoun *you* is both singular and plural.

You drive carefully.	*You* are all careful drivers.
The movie bored *you*.	The movie bored both of *you*.

When speakers and writers refer to a third party, they use *third-person pronouns*.

Singular	Plural
He *She* } drives carefully. *It*	*They* drive carefully.
The movie bored } *him.* *her.* *it.*	The movie bored *them*.

Sometimes personal pronouns are combined with *-self* or *-selves* to make the *reflexive* forms of personal pronouns.

I woke *myself* up.

Give *yourself* a present!

He *himself* wrote that play.

	Singular	Plural
First Person:	myself	ourselves
Second Person:	yourself	yourselves
Third Person:	himself herself } itself	themselves

Note: The forms *hisself* and *theirselves* are not a part of Edited Standard English.

Reflexive pronouns have two uses. One use is to refer to the subject of the sentence and to repeat its meaning.

I woke *myself* up.

You can see for *yourself*.

Jim didn't hurt *himself* when he fell.

Evita made *herself* a purse.

This cellophane tape keeps sticking to *itself*.

The American colonies wanted to govern *themselves*.

A second use of reflexive pronouns is to add emphasis to a statement. When they do so, they are often called *intensive pronouns*. Intensive pronouns may immediately follow the noun or pronoun they intensify, or they may be moved to the end of the sentence.

The governor *himself* presented the award.

The governor presented this award *himself*.

I made this *myself*.

Exercise 2: *Identifying Personal Pronouns*

Write the following sentences and underline the personal pronouns. Write *1* above pronouns in the first person, *2* above pronouns in the second person, and *3* above pronouns in the third person.

Examples

a. Marcia taught her little brother how to fish.

              3

Marcia taught her little brother how to fish.

b. The buzzer warned us of the end of the hour.

                        1

The buzzer warned us of the end of the hour.

1. We do not know much about the mysterious ruins at Stonehenge, England.

2. Have you seen Stonehenge? It is constructed of huge stone blocks and was probably built in 2200 B.C.

3. Stonehenge must have been built by primitive people, yet how did they move such great stones?

4. We visited the great pillars, and I wandered about the strange monument.

5. That man is an expert. Ask him to explain the mystery of the site to us.

6. The circles of crude pillars with large slabs on top of them amazed me!

7. The Romans were in early Britain; perhaps they built Stonehenge by themselves.

8. Ms. Sybil Leek told us that she thinks ancient magicians were the builders. Should we believe her?

9. Professor G. S. Hawkins announced a startling fact. He discovered the stones were arranged so that certain stars appeared above them.

10. The unknown builders created a giant calendar of stone at Stonehenge. They may have used it for an observatory as well.

The Possessive Form of Personal Pronouns

Personal pronouns, like nouns, have possessive forms to show ownership or relationship.

	Singular	*Plural*
First Person:	my, mine	our, ours
Second Person:	your, yours	your, yours
Third Person:	his her, hers its	their, theirs

Several possessive pronouns—*my, our, your, her,* and *their*—are always followed by a noun.

My sister and *your* sister wear *their* hair in the same style.

Our daughter must make up *her* own mind.

Some possessive pronouns can be used alone: *mine, ours, yours, hers,* and *theirs.*

That car is *mine;* the blue car is *yours;* and the green car is *theirs.*

Hers is the white house; *ours* is the red.

The possessive pronouns *his* and *its* can be used before a noun or alone.

Carlos enjoys using *his* camera. He likes *its* gadgets.

That camera is *his*. This case is *its*.

Note: Possessive pronouns do *not* have an apostrophe and an *s*.

Exercise 3: Identifying Possessive Pronouns

Write the following sentences on a separate sheet of paper and underline each possessive pronoun.

Example

a. It's no wonder the cat is complaining; its bowl is empty.
   It's no wonder the cat is complaining; its bowl is empty.

1. Marie Rothschild did not graduate from college because her family did not believe in higher education for women.

2. Her father was a scientist, and his specialty was insects— particularly the flea.

3. Marie, too, decided to study the flea and its habits.

4. Hers was important research. Two universities bestowed their highest honors on Marie.

5. By making movies of fleas, she analyzed their jumping power.

6. Theirs is great. If our jumping ability were compared with a flea's, ours would be much less.

7. My legs couldn't lift me over the horse 100 times. Could yours?

8. Your wildest guess would probably fall short of a flea's takeoff speed.

9. Its acceleration is twenty times greater than that of a moon rocket reentering earth's atmosphere. That beats mine!

10. Marie Rothschild also was an early protester of poison insecticides and their dangerous side effects. She certainly has my admiration.

Demonstrative Pronouns

The small group of *demonstrative pronouns* consists of four words: *this, that, these,* and *those.* Demonstrative pronouns point out specific persons, places, things, or ideas.

This is my sister.

That costs too much.

Like the personal pronouns, the demonstrative pronouns have singular and plural forms. The words *this* and *that* point out singular nouns; the words *these* and *those* point out plural nouns.

This is my favorite song.   Jules bought *that*.
I'm taking *those*.

Sometimes, a demonstrative pronoun has no antecedent, that is, no noun to which it refers. Its antecedent is understood.

This (girl) is my sister.

That (coat) costs too much for me to buy.

These (wrenches) are the new tools for shop class.

Note: When *this, that, these,* and *those* are used in front of nouns, they are modifiers, not pronouns.

This book is a good one.   [adjective]

These animals are ocelots.   [adjective]

Exercise 4: Identifying Demonstrative Pronouns and Noun Modifiers

Write each of the following sentences, underlining all demonstrative pronouns. (Be sure that you underline demonstrative pronouns rather than noun modifiers.) If the words *this, that, these,* or *those* are each used to modify a noun, circle both the word and the noun it modifies.

Examples

a. That was the biggest upset of our football season.
   That was the biggest upset of our football season.

b. What is that watermelon doing in your locker?
   What is (that watermelon) doing in your locker?

1.   These are the arrowheads my sister found last summer.

2.   Would you put this in your glove compartment, please?

3. I've never understood these forms.

4. I usually hate fish, but this is delicious.

5. Look, that is something crawling up your sleeve.

6. Watch out for that thing crawling up your sleeve.

7. That was the most embarrassing moment of my life.

8. We took those pictures at canoe camp last summer.

9. I'll take three of these, two of those, and this.

10. After seeing those amazing films, I made up my mind about that.

Interrogative Pronouns

Interrogative pronouns are used in asking questions. The interrogative pronouns, *who, whom, whose, which,* and *what,* appear in place of unnamed people, places, or things.

Who was the "Man in the Iron Mask"?

Whom have you decided to nominate?

Whose is the orange car?

Which of these do you want?

What will we do this Friday night?

Sometimes a word such as *by, to, with, from, on,* or *for* may come before the interrogative pronoun.

To *whom* should I give this note?

For *which* of them is it?

On *what* do you base your opinion?

Notice that in the preceding examples each interrogative pronoun stands for an unnamed person, place, or thing. None of the pronouns modifies a noun; rather, each takes the place of a noun in the question. If the word *which, what,* or *whose* is used in front of a noun, it is used as an adjective, not as an interrogative pronoun.

Which do you like best?	[interrogative pronoun]
Which jeans do you like best?	[modifier]

Exercise 5: Identifying Interrogative Pronouns and Noun Modifiers

Write each of the following sentences, underlining all interrogative pronouns. When the word *which, what,* or *whose* is used to modify a noun, circle both the word and the noun modified.

Examples

    a. Who won the 1979 World Series?
       Who won the 1979 World Series?

    b. Which woman is Dr. Ling?
       (Which woman) is Dr. Ling?

1. To whom do you refer?

2. Which is the article we're supposed to read?

3. Which hound chased what?

4. What made that terrible noise?

5. On what floor is Mr. Ortega's office?

6. Of whom does that girl remind you?

7. Who is the speaker at the assembly?

8. What right do they have to ask that?

9. Whose is the house on the hill?

10. What plane will they be taking?

Relative Pronouns

The *relative pronoun* introduces a group of words that modifies a noun or pronoun in the sentence. The relative pronoun is *related* to that noun or pronoun, which is its *antecedent.*

These are the slides *that* we made in biology lab.

In the preceding sentence the word *that* is a relative pronoun and refers to the antecedent *slides.* The relative pronoun connects *slides* to another group of words: *we made in biology lab.* This group of words has a subject, *we,* and a verb that tells what the subject did, *made.* A group of words that has a subject and a verb that tells what the subject is or does is called a *clause*. A clause introduced by a relative pronoun is called a *subordinate clause*. A more accurate definition of a relative pronoun is a pronoun that refers to an antecedent and connects or relates it to a subordinate clause.

The following words are called *relative pronouns* when they are used to introduce a group of words that modify a noun or pronoun.

which	who	whose
that	whom	what

This book is by Ann Beattie, *who* wrote *Chilly Scenes of Winter*.

There is a film version of *Chilly Scenes of Winter*, *which* Ann Beattie wrote.

The book *that* Ann Beattie wrote was made into a movie.

We met Ann Beattie, *whose* second novel was well received.

Ann Beattie, *whom* you met last week, lives in Connecticut.

Note: Many of these words can act as modifiers, interrogative pronouns, or demonstrative pronouns, depending on their use in a sentence.

Which do you like?	[interrogative pronoun]
Which tractor do you like?	[modifier]
I'll buy the blue shirt, *which* is on sale.	[relative pronoun]
That is Max's cat.	[demonstrative pronoun]
That cat is Max's.	[modifier]
The cat *that* has black stripes is Max's.	[relative pronoun]

Exercise 6: Identifying Relative Pronouns and Antecedents

The sentences on the following page contain relative pronouns, each with a clear antecedent. Write the sentences and circle the relative pronoun in each sentence. Underline the antecedent.

Example

a. The tire that blew out was the right front one.

The tire (that) blew out was the right front one.

1. Americans did well at the 1964 Olympics, which were held in Tokyo.

2. Billy Mills, who is part Sioux, won the 10,000-meter run.

3. Six black Americans who competed in track events won gold medals.

4. The sport that the Japanese excelled in was judo.

5. American Al Oerter, whose discus throw won the gold medal, was a three-time winner of that title.

6. Luck wasn't with the Russian basketball players, whom the Americans defeated in a close contest.

7. Russian skater Lidia Skoblikova, however, won four gold medals for speed-skating, which is a demanding event.

8. The Olympic Games that the modern world knows are different from the ancient Greek games.

9. The early games, which are a part of recorded history, included chariot racing.

10. According to legend, Hercules, who is a mythical Greek hero, established the stadium at Olympia in 1222 B.C.

Indefinite Pronouns

Indefinite pronouns do not refer to specific persons or things. Often they do not have antecedents.

Each has its advantages.

Doesn't *something* look suspicious here?

Somebody wants to see you.

Some indefinite pronouns are always singular in meaning.

anybody	everybody	nobody
anyone	everyone	no one
anything	everything	one
each	much	somebody
either	neither	someone

Some indefinite pronouns are always plural in meaning.

both	few	many	others	several

A few indefinite pronouns may be either singular or plural, depending on how they are used in a sentence.

all   any   most   none   some

Some was spilled.	[singular]
Some were oak trees.	[plural]
All the money is lost.	[singular]
All the seats are taken.	[plural]

If a word is used in front of a noun, it is a modifier, not a pronoun.

Each of the apples is ripe.	[indefinite pronoun]
Each apple is ripe.	[modifier]

Exercise 7: *Identifying Singular and Plural Indefinite Pronouns*

Write the following sentences, underlining the indefinite pronouns in each. Write *S* above the pronoun if it is singular or *P* if it is plural. (Some sentences have more than one indefinite pronoun, and some have indefinite pronouns used as modifiers.)

Examples

a. Each of the players is given a number.

   S
   Each of the players is given a number.

b. Some of the players were disqualified.

   P
   Some of the players were disqualified.

1. Someone in the class is going to the speech contest.

2. One of my hobbies is stamp collecting.

3. Something in the engine or the transmission is broken.

4. Both of the sheep were in the pasture.

5. Both twins promised to come, but neither is here.

6. Everybody says that nothing works.

7.   Each of us was glad that some food was left.

8.   The hats in the hall are mine; either is all right for you to use.

9.   Each marigold seed has sprouted, so others are going to be planted.

10.   Neither pair of jeans fits, so each pair will be returned.

Finding a Pronoun by Its Features

Three features distinguish pronouns from other parts of speech.

1. A pronoun may be singular or plural.

Personal (including reflexive and possessive), demonstrative, and indefinite pronouns have singular or plural meanings.

	Singular	*Plural*
Personal:	I, you, he, she, it, me, him, her	we, you, they, us, them
(Reflexive):	myself, yourself, himself, herself, itself	ourselves, yourselves, themselves
(Possessive):	my, mine, your, yours, his, her, hers, its	our, ours, your, yours, their, theirs
Demonstrative:	this, that	these, those
Indefinite:	anybody, everybody, each, nobody, one, someone, either	others, few, both, several, many

Singular pronouns take the singular form of the verb; plural pronouns take the plural form of the verb.

She sings in the choir.   *They* sing in the choir.

Notice that interrogative and relative pronouns do not have different forms for the singular and plural.

Which is yours?

Which are yours?

I want the dog *that* has brown spots.

I want the dogs *that* have brown spots.

2. The form of a pronoun depends on its function in a sentence.

Personal pronouns have both subject forms and object forms.

Subject Forms	Object Forms
I, we	me, us
you	you
he, she, it, they	him, her, it, them

3. Pronouns may show gender.

Some singular personal (including reflexive and possessive) pronouns are masculine, feminine, or neuter.

Masculine: he, him, his, himself

Feminine: she, her, hers, herself

Neuter: it, its, itself

Other singular pronouns are neither masculine nor feminine.

I, me, myself, you, yourself

None of the plural pronouns shows gender.

we, us, they, them, you, ourselves, themselves, yourselves

Exercise 8: Identifying Pronouns by Their Features

Write the following sentences, underlining each pronoun. Be prepared to explain the features by which you identified each one.

Examples

a. My grandfather knew a man who wrote one poem every day for one year.
My grandfather knew a man who wrote one poem every day for one year.

b. Don't you want that for your birthday?
Don't you want that for your birthday?

1. Our friend sent us her graduation picture.

2. If she gives me her address, I'll send her a card.

3. My sister told him a funny story about that.

4. That chair needs one of its legs mended.

5. Loretta's brother made that guitar himself.

6. His dog doesn't know its head from its tail.

7. Wrap this package and give it to me, please.

8. Which is the essay that you wrote, Rosa?

9. During a vacation Lindsay saw her aunt and uncle at their farm.

10. They left our tour group and wandered off by themselves to watch the fire burn itself out.

Review: Understanding Pronouns

Write each of the following sentences, underlining the personal pronouns and their reflexive and possessive forms. Then draw an arrow from each pronoun to its antecedent.

Examples

a. Wherever she goes, Laura carries her compass with her.

Wherever she goes, Laura carries her compass with her.

b. Pedro, if you want to be sure of your answers, you should solve the problems yourself.

Pedro, if you want to be sure of your answers, you should

solve the problems yourself.

1. Marcia, have you seen the giant cow towering above its surroundings in Janesville, Wisconsin?

2. Because they dig in the city, Kim and his friends call themselves "urban archeologists."

3. A city has much history hidden beneath its surface; often old buildings have been demolished and their contents buried.

4. Sally said, "Remember that John and his brother are my cousins."

5. Eleanor, Steve, and Karen said they grabbed their belongings and ran from the house as soon as it started to burn.

6. Because it stings when applied to a cut, iodine is not Kiyo's first choice for an antiseptic; she wants a soothing salve on her cut!

7. Raoul, don't feed them if you want those kittens to stop hanging around your door.

8. Jennifer's dog hides its toys under her bed, so she hears it all night gnawing on a rubber bone.

9. Anita promised herself that she would earn enough money to buy a car, and she reached her goal. Now a new car is hers.

10. Hernando, Michael, and Rachel spent their vacations rafting on the Colorado River. They had trouble negotiating its rapids, but theirs was an exciting trip.

Each of the following quotations contains one or more pronouns. List each pronoun and write the classification to which it belongs.

Example

a. Photographs, which cannot themselves explain anything, are inexhaustible invitations to deductions, speculation, and fantasy. —*Susan Sontag*

which—relative
themselves—personal (reflexive)
anything—indefinite

11. The Vice Presidency is sort of like the last cooky on the plate. Everybody insists he won't take it, but somebody always does. —*Bill Vaughan*

12. Slang is a language that rolls up its sleeves, spits on its hands and goes to work. —*Carl Sandburg*

13. I know only two tunes: one of them is "Yankee Doodle," and the other isn't. —*Ulysses S. Grant*

14. The man who has no inner life is the slave of his surroundings. —*Henri Frédéric Amiel*

15. Everybody is a genius at least once a year; a real genius has his original ideas closer together. —*G. C. Lichtenberg*

16. I don't know who my grandfather was; I am much more concerned to know what his grandson will be. —*Abraham Lincoln*

17. Nothing is terrible except fear itself. —*Francis Bacon*

18. To speak ill of others is a dishonest way of praising our-selves. —*Will and Ariel Durant*

19. Where I was born and where and how I have lived is unimportant. It is what I have done with where I have been that should be of interest. —*Georgia O'Keeffe*

20. And I, to whom so great a vision was given in my youth,—you see me now a pitiful old man who has done nothing, for the nation's hoop is broken and scattered. —*Black Elk*

Applying What You Know

On a sheet of paper, list the pronouns in the following paragraphs. Next to each pronoun write the classification to which it belongs. (Your teacher may ask you to explain how you identified each one.)

The bicycle had what is called the "wabbles," and had them very badly. In order to keep my position, a good many things were required of me, and in every instance the thing required was against nature. Against nature, but not against the *laws* of nature . . . whatever the needed thing might be, my nature, habit, and breeding moved me to attempt it in one way, while some immutable and unsuspected law of physics required that it be done in just the other way. I perceived by this how radically and grotesquely wrong had been the lifelong education of my body and members. They were steeped in ignorance; they knew nothing—nothing which it could profit them to know. For instance, if I found myself falling to the right, I put the tiller hard down the other way, by a quite natural impulse, and so violated a law, and kept on going down. The law required the opposite thing—the big wheel must be turned in the direction in which you are falling. It is hard to believe this, when you are told it.

—From *"Taming the Bicycle"* by *Mark Twain*

None of them knew the color of the sky. Their eyes glanced level, and were fastened upon the waves that swept toward them. These waves were of the hue of slate, save for the tops, which were of foaming white, and all of the men knew the colors of the sea. The horizon narrowed and widened, and dipped and rose, and at all times its edge was jagged with waves that seemed thrust up in points like rocks.
Many a man ought to have a bathtub larger than the boat which here rode upon the sea. . . .

—From *"The Open Boat"* by *Stephen Crane*

The study of words is not merely something that has to do with literature. Words are your tools of thought. You can't even think at all without them. Try it. If you are planning to go downtown this afternoon you will find that you are saying to yourself: "I think I will go downtown this afternoon." You can't make such a simple decision as this without using words. . . .

Your words are all that we, your friends, have to know and judge you by. You have no other medium for telling us your thoughts—for convincing us, persuading us, giving us orders.[1]

—From *Thirty Days to a More Powerful Vocabulary*
by *Wilfred Funk and Norman Lewis*

Using Pronouns

Many problems in the use of pronouns arise in making pronouns agree with their antecedents and in using the various forms of personal pronouns. In the following sections you will practice using pronouns in Edited Standard English.

Agreement of Pronouns and Antecedents

A pronoun must agree with its antecedent in number.

When an antecedent is singular, use a singular pronoun to refer to it.

The *dog* wagged *its* tail.

Ms. Yamoto read *her* summation to the jury.

When an antecedent is plural, use a plural pronoun to refer to it.

Six *dogs* threw back *their* heads and howled at the moon.

We called *our* parents yesterday.

---

[1]From *Thirty Days to a More Powerful Vocabulary* by Wilfred Funk and Norman Lewis. Reprinted by permission of Harper & Row, Publishers, Inc.

When an antecedent is followed by a prepositional phrase, be certain the pronoun agrees with the antecedent and not the object of the preposition.

The *winner* of both trophies read *his* speech.

The *contestants* on the game show changed *their* answers.

Exercise 9: Making Possessive Pronouns and Antecedents Agree in Number

Write the sentences on this page and the next, choosing the correct pronouns from those in parentheses. Underline the pronoun you select.

Example

a. The dogs in the pack threw (itself, themselves) across the ice, pulling the sled behind.

The dogs in the pack threw themselves across the ice, pulling the sled behind.

1. The gallery with the beautiful painting was destroyed when (its, their) roof collapsed.

2. Drivers who fail to study for the driver's examination only harm (itself, themselves).

3. Dr. Sanchez, who worked long hours in the emergency wards of both city hospitals, knew (her, their) patient would receive good care at Central Community.

4. The boughs of the old, gnarled apple tree on the Hudson farm sagged, pulling down (its, their) heavy load of fruit.

5. The small kittens sitting by the warm stove in our neighbors' kitchen purred and licked (itself, themselves) contentedly.

6. The senator outlined the state legislature's plans for a new conservation program in (his, its) interview with the press.

7. Pulling (their, his) cloak tight for warmth, Benjamin Banneker spent long nights outside studying the stars.

8. The wind howled at the crowds huddled on the street corners and stretched (its, their) icy tentacles toward (them, it).

9. Do all the countries that belong to the United Nations guarantee (its, their) citizens freedom of speech?

10. We cousins, who thought Grandmother to be very serious and strict, laughed (herself, ourselves) sick at (her, their) stories about our parents' antics as children.

Indefinite Pronouns and Antecedents

Some indefinite pronouns are always singular, and some are always plural. Others, such as *all, any, some, most,* and *none,* may be either singular or plural, depending on their use in a sentence.

When an indefinite pronoun is the antecedent of another pronoun, the second pronoun should agree in number with its antecedent.

Each of the boys likes *his* hamburgers rare and juicy.

Several of the girls finished *their* projects ahead of time.

All of the cherries were ripe, so we picked *them.*	[plural meaning]
All of the milk was sour, so we threw *it* out.	[singular meaning]

Three situations regarding antecedents and pronouns demand special care on the writer's part.

---

1. **Use a plural pronoun when two or more antecedents are joined by *and*.**

A sister and brother may sometimes have *their* differences.

My friends and I caught *our* limit of catfish.

---

2. **Always use a singular pronoun when two or more singular antecedents are joined by *or* or *nor*. Use a plural pronoun when two or more plural antecedents are joined by *or* or *nor*.**

Deanna *or* Stacey must have forgotten *her* books when *she* left.

Neither Don *nor* Malcolm likes *his* part-time job.

Either skunks *or* chipmunks let *their* presence be strongly known.

Neither oaks *nor* maples keep *their* leaves in winter.

---

3. When singular and plural antecedents are joined by *or* or *nor*, the pronoun agrees with the nearer antecedent.

Neither Cassie *nor* her cousins could eat the pizza *they* made.

Either the twins *or* Steven will lend you *his* equipment.

Exercise 10: *Making Indefinite Pronouns and Antecedents Agree in Number*

Write the following sentences, inserting the correct pronouns from the choices in parentheses. Underline the pronoun you select.

Example

a. Some of the girls in the musical have already learned all (their, her) lines, and one of the girls has mastered (her, their) dance routine.
Some of the girls in the musical have already learned all their lines, and one of the girls has mastered her dance routine.

1. Some of his shirts were in bad condition, so Manuel carefully washed and mended (them, it).

2. Either Mrs. Ortego or her sons will be happy to show you (her, their) backyard and garden.

3. Several of the rosebushes had been sorely neglected, so we pruned (them, it) and put on fertilizer.

4. I left a dish of apricots here last night; did you find (them, it)?

5. The man and woman who run the veterinary clinic in Sandwich have (their, her) own ambulance for emergency pet care.

6. Several of the children in the class had finished (its, their) finger paintings, but others hadn't begun (it, theirs).

7. After the game neither the coaches nor the players could locate (his, their) bus.

8. Either one of the neighbors' boys or my little brother left (his, their) jacket on the porch.

9. Since all the old furniture was still in good condition, we decided to use (it, them) in the family room.

10. In all the commotion neither my aunt nor my parents could find (their, her) coats and other belongings after the family reunion.

Agreement in Gender of Pronouns and Antecedents

A pronoun must agree in gender with its antecedent.

Singular antecedents create few problems. When a singular antecedent is masculine, use the masculine pronouns *he, his,* or *him* to refer to it. When a singular antecedent is feminine, use the pronouns *she, her,* or *hers.* When the antecedent is neuter, use *it* or *its* to refer to the antecedent.

Hernando took *his* children to *his* office yesterday.

Did you hear Eileen read *her* report to the committee?

Johnine said the book was *hers.*

One of the dogs has ticks in *its* fur.

Sometimes, however, an antecedent is a singular indefinite pronoun that can refer to either a male, a female, or a mixed group. Traditionally, the masculine pronoun has been used when the gender of the antecedent is unclear.

Each of the students will have *his* picture taken.

More recently, however, many speakers and writers have begun to use *his or her* in this situation or to recast the sentence so that the antecedent is plural.

Each of the students will have *his or her* picture taken.

The students will have *their* pictures taken.

Exercise 11: Making Pronouns and Antecedents Agree in Gender

Write each of the following sentences, choosing the correct pronoun from those given in parentheses. Underline the pronoun that you select.

Examples

    a. Either Cecily Tyson or Leslie Uggams started (her, their) career as a singer, not as an actress.

      Either Cecily Tyson or Leslie Uggams started <u>her</u> career as a singer, not as an actress.

    b. Anyone who has frequent headaches should have (his or her, their) eyes checked.

      Anyone who has frequent headaches should have <u>his or her</u> eyes checked.

1. Neither of the others gave any reason for (his or her, their) lateness.

2. All the speakers must have gotten (his or her, their) jokes from the world's oldest joke book.

3. Jennifer or her sisters must decide for (themselves, herself) how much (they, she) will spend.

4. Either the members of the finance committee or the president will give (his or her, their) views first.

5. Lois or her brothers might hurt (himself, herself, themselves) if (he, she, they) trip over that wire.

6. One of the women wanted (her, their) money back, but the others were very satisfied with the quality of (her, their) purchases.

7. Both Lana and Kathy wanted (her, their) own way about the choice of restaurant.

8. One of the members of the boys' choir lost (their, his) place, and suddenly everyone was off key.

9. Either the Washington sisters or Dominique will bring (her, their) projector.

10. Some of the club members wanted to plan (his, their) picnic (himself, themselves).

Using Subject Pronouns

The *subject forms* of the personal pronouns (sometimes called the *nominative case*) are as follows:

Singular	Plural
I	we
you	you
he, she, it	they

Use the subject form whenever the pronoun is the subject of a verb.

I hope the party starts soon.

We know that *she* will arrive shortly.

Ken and *she* knew the answer.

When a pronoun is part of a compound subject, use the subject form.

Nicole and *I* went to the movies.

Linda and *he* are bringing records to the party.

If you are uncertain which form of the pronoun to use in a compound construction, use the form you would use if the pronoun were by itself.

Note: When using a personal pronoun to refer to yourself, always place the pronoun that refers to you last.

Bob and *I* completed the project.

Use the subject form whenever the pronoun follows a form of the verb *be* and identifies or renames the subject of the sentence.

The winner of the art contest was *she*.

The speaker will be *he*.

It is *I*.

Note: The expression *It's me* is acceptable in informal spoken English. In formal situations and in Edited Standard English, however, use the subject form when the pronoun is a subject complement.

It's *I*.

It is *we* who complained.

Julio answered the phone, "This is *he*."

When a pronoun is used before a noun subject or before a noun that follows a form of *be* and identifies or renames the subject, use the subject form of the pronoun.

We tenants complained to the landlord.

It was *we* women whom you saw.

Exercise 12: *Using Subject Pronouns*

Write each of the following sentences, choosing the correct form of the pronoun from the choices given in parentheses. Underline the pronoun you select.

Example

---

a. It was (they, them) who played that trick.
   It was they who played that trick.

1. (We, Us) students collected cans for the recycling drive.

2. Kathy and (she, her) bought identical dresses for the party.

3. I thought I saw Michael, but it wasn't (he, him).

4. Freddy and (she, her) made all the furniture in their house.

5. The photo contest judges are Luis, (she, her), and (I, me).

6. It was (we, us) sophomores who won the tournament.

7. (He and I, I and he) joined the museum.

8. The president of the committee will be either (she or I, her or I).

9. (Them and us, Them and we, They and we) are concerned about the energy crisis.

10. (You and me, You and I) saw Marcia, or at least, I think it was (she, her).

Using Object Pronouns

The *object form* of the personal pronoun is called the *objective case*.

Singular	Plural
me	us
you	you
him, her, it	them

Use the object form of the personal pronoun when the pronoun is the direct object of the verb.

The class elected *her*.

Don't call *me*! I'll call *you*.

Use an object form of the personal pronoun when the pronoun is the indirect object of the verb.

The salesperson gave *them* a free sample.

Are you going to give *me* an excuse for not calling?

Use an object form of a personal pronoun when the pronoun is the object of a preposition.

The tiny dog was barking at *us*.

There are few secrets between *him* and *me*.

Use an object form of the personal pronoun when the pronoun is the subject, object, or predicate pronoun of an infinitive. The infinitive form of the verb begins with the word *to: to pray, to call*. Infinitive phrases have subjects, objects, or complements.

The lifeguard told *us* to stop splashing.	[subject of the infinitive]
Does she want Irene to wake *her?*	[object of the infinitive]
Ken wants the star to be *him*.	[predicate pronoun]

When a pronoun is part of a compound object, use the *object form.*

Nobody told my *parents* and *me* the news.
I saw *you* and *him.*

When a pronoun is joined with a noun that is the object, use the object form of the pronoun.

Few people understand *us* geniuses.
Several of *us* sophomores recounted the votes.

Exercise 13: Using Object Pronouns

Write each of the following sentences, choosing the correct pronouns from those given in parentheses. Underline the pronouns you select.

Example
---

    a. Are you going with Pat and (he, him)?
       Are you going with Pat and him?

1. The Joneses asked (she, her) to baby-sit.

2. That book was a present from (they, them) to (us, we).

3. Don't scare (he and I, him and me, he and me) with your stories!

4. The teacher gave too much work to (we, us) overworked students.

5. Nobody likes (him and her, he and she) to sing.

6. Between (you and I, you and me) I think this movie is a waste of money.

7. Both of her sisters want to be (she, her).

8. The party won't be the same without Theresa and (him, he).

9. If you want (we, us) to be there, call (he or I, him or me).

10. Did anyone give (we, us) drivers a reason to take (they, them)?

Using Who *and* Whom

T he relative and interrogative pronouns *who* and *whom* are sometimes a source of confusion. Although the word *whom* is being used less and less in recent years, in formal writing the distinction between *who* and *whom* should be recognized.

Who is the subject form and should be used when the pronoun serves a subject function. *Whom* is the object form of the pronoun and should be used for direct and indirect objects and objects of the preposition. *Who* and *whom* are interrogative pronouns when they are used to ask a question.

Who goes there?	[subject of sentence]
The winner is *who?*	[predicate nominative]
Whom did they elect?	[direct object]
Whom did they tell that story?	[indirect object]
To *whom* shall I give this check?	[object of the preposition]

Who and *whom* are relative pronouns when they introduce a subordinate clause. To choose the proper form decide how the pronoun functions within the clause.

I need to know *who* wrote *My Ántonia.*	[subject of clause]
I saw the teacher *who* is replacing Miss Hughes.	[subject of clause]
She was the one *whom* I asked.	[direct object of the verb *asked* in the clause]

The object form *whom* is also used as the subject of the infinitive.

We wondered *whom* to see about the problem.

Nobody knew *whom* to blame.

Exercise 14: *Using* Who *and* Whom

Write the following sentences, filling in the blanks with either *who* or *whom.* Underline the pronoun that you supply.

Example

a. _____ shall I say is calling?
Who shall I say is calling?

1. For _____ did she buy that funny valentine?

2. _____ is going to the game by bus?

3. _____ at the party danced the most?

4. The winner was _____?

5. The man on the corner is the one _____ has the used car for sale.

6. You will take the place of _____ in the contest?

7. Mr. Jones told us with _____ to talk about our problem.

8. I want to have the teacher _____ gives the least homework.

9. He is the friend _____ I most admire.

10. _____ did the judges select as the winner?

Incomplete Constructions

In an incomplete construction, use the same form of the pronoun that you would use if the sentence were complete.

An *incomplete construction* is a sentence with part left for the reader to complete.

Penny received more votes than I.	[*than I did*]
Did James run faster than she?	[*than she did*]

In the preceding sentences the pronouns are in the subject form. If the pronoun functions as the subject of a missing verb, use the subject form of the pronoun. When the pronoun functions as an object, use the object form.

Did she call you more often than me?	[*than she called me*—object]

Choose your pronouns carefully when you write incomplete constructions because the meaning of an incomplete construction sometimes can be ambiguous. If you use a subject form of the pronoun, the sentence will have one meaning. If you use the object form, the sentence will mean something entirely different.

Subject:	Did she call you more often than I?	[*than I called you*]
Object:	Did she call you more often than me?	[*than she called me*]

349

Using Possessive Pronouns

Personal pronouns have a completely different form to show possession (see the section on possessive pronouns earlier in this chapter). Interrogative and relative pronouns show possession with the form *whose*.

> *Whose* car is that blue one?

> I saw a woman *whose* hair was green.

The indefinite pronouns that can be made possessive form their possessives as nouns do, by adding an apostrophe and an *-s: everyone's, everybody's, somebody's, anybody's, anyone's, one's.*

The main problem presented by the possessive pronouns is that of spelling. Notice that the indefinite possessive pronoun is the *only one* that uses an apostrophe.

The following words are contractions rather than possessive pronouns.

> it's [*it is*], you're [*you are*], they're [*they are*], who's [*who is*]

Do not use an apostrophe with a possessive pronoun other than the indefinite pronoun.

everyone's idea	its power
somebody's dream	your house
anybody's guess	their hometown
one's hopes	whose hat

Exercise 15: Using Pronouns in Incomplete Constructions and as Possessives

Write each of the following sentences and choose the correct word from the pair given in parentheses. Underline the words that you select.

Example

a. Our cat caught (its, it's) tail in the door.
   Our cat caught its tail in the door.

1. The other team scored more points than (we, us).

2. My sister asked if you would bring (your, you're) guitar.

3. (Who's, Whose) to find out (who's, whose) books these are?

4. No one in this class has studied longer than (she, her).

5. I don't know whether (their, they're) ready or not.

6. (Everyones, Everyone's) idea of a good time is not the same as (yours, you'res).

7. (Their, They're) car has a flat tire on (its, it's) left side.

8. For whom was (your, you're) letter of complaint intended?

9. The hamster has chewed (its, it's) way out of (its, it's) cage.

10. Who would dare insult (your, you're) cousin, (whose, who's) seven feet tall!

Avoiding Unnecessary Pronouns

Do not use a pronoun following a noun to form a double subject. When you write and speak, you should avoid these unnecessary pronouns.

An asterisk (*) indicates a sentence with a feature that is not a part of ESE.

*My friend she just bought a new car.
My friend just bought a new car.

*Jeff he won a Merit Scholarship.
Jeff won a Merit Scholarship.

Avoiding Shifts in Pronouns

When writing, do not shift needlessly from one person to another, for such shifting can cause confusion, as the following examples show.

*I hate eating in a restaurant where you sit in the dark, struggling to find your spaghetti by the dim light of one small candle. [Needless shift from first person to second person]

I hate eating in a restaurant where *I* sit in the dark, struggling to find *my* spaghetti by the dim light of one small candle.

An asterisk (*) indicates a sentence with a feature that is not a part of ESE.

*One's grades usually correspond to your study habits. [Needless shift from third person to second person]

One's grades usually correspond to *one's* study habits.
    or
Your grades usually correspond to *your* study habits.

351

Now look at the following paragraph:

> It seems as if students are always being criticized. If *you* are quiet and mind *your* own business, commentators say *you* are apathetic and uninvolved. If the students do become involved and politically active, then *they* are called rebels and troublemakers. *We* simply can't win.

The previous paragraph uses person inconsistently; the students are referred to as *you, they,* and *we.* The following paragraph is rewritten in third person. Notice how easy it is to understand.

> It seems as if students are always being criticized. If they are quiet and mind their own business, commentators say they are apathetic and uninvolved. If the students do become involved and politically active, then they are called rebels and troublemakers. They are called names if they don't take a stand on every issue and if they do. They simply can't win.

Exercise 16: *Avoiding Shifts in Pronouns*

Each of the following sentences contains an unnecessary change in pronoun usage. Rewrite each sentence, correcting the use of pronouns. Underline the pronoun you have substituted for the incorrectly used pronoun. (In some cases you may need to change a verb as well as the pronoun.)

Example

a. A person doesn't know how much he or she can accomplish until you try.

A person doesn't know how much he or she can accomplish until he or she tries.

1. If those people went to Gordon's surprise party, I'm sure you enjoyed yourselves.

2. Whenever a person buys a used car, you may be buying trouble.

3. If you snore in class, a student can expect an angry teacher.

4. Somebody thinks it's easy to find a parking place, until you look for one.

5. I hate movies where you have to wait in line.

6. Dog owners can make their pets obey if you follow a few rules.

7. When one hasn't had enough sleep, you can expect your brain and body to react sluggishly.

8. Any person who dares to sample Jo Ann's chili will get the surprise of your life.

9. When you start a diet, a person learns what suffering is.

10. When people are in love, you may do silly things sometimes.

Using Antecedents Clearly

When you write or speak, be sure to clarify all antecedents of your pronouns so that readers and listeners understand to whom or to what each pronoun refers. You should avoid ambiguous, general, and indefinite pronoun references.

Reword sentences in which the antecedent of the pronoun is ambiguous. An antecedent is ambiguous if it has two or more meanings.

Ambiguous:	Maria and Sally rode in her car. [Whose car?]
Clear:	Maria and Sally rode in Sally's car.
Ambiguous:	Don called Phil after he had taken his final exam. [Who took the exam?]
Clear:	Don called Phil after Phil had taken his final exam.

Reword sentences in which the pronouns *which, this, that,* or *it* refer to vague ideas.

General:	The extreme heat put a strain on the city's power. People ran their air conditioners and fans to maximum capacity. Overuse caused shorts. *This* led to fires. [What, exactly, caused the fires?]
Clear:	The extreme heat strained the city's power supply because people used air conditioners and fans to maximum capacity. This overuse of electrical equipment led to shorts and subsequently to fires.
General:	Our band won first place in the state contest and was selected to march at the Orange Bowl, *which* makes us very proud. [*Which* refers to no particular word or idea but is used to sum up several ideas.]
Clear:	Our band won first place in the state contest and was selected to march at the Orange Bowl, honors that make us very proud.

Do not use *you* or *they* without clear antecedents. Avoid using *you* or *they* with unknown antecedents; instead, try to name clear and specific antecedents.

Indefinite: *You* sometimes feel lost in a large high school. *They* have so many students that *they* don't learn *your* name until the semester is half over.

Clear: A *student* sometimes feels lost in a large high school, where *teachers* have many *students*. A teacher may not learn a *pupil's* name until the semester is half over.

Exercise 17: Making Clear References to Pronoun Antecedents

Each of the following sentences or passages contains a pronoun that does not clearly refer to an antecedent. Make revisions that will remedy the faulty references.

Example

    a. Larry reminded Mick that he needed to call home.
       Larry reminded Mick to call home.

1.   The Lees asked the Coles if they could drive them to the park.

2.   The lab smelled of gas and alcohol, which gave me a headache.

3.   When you go to college, they make you work hard.

4.   My mother dislikes that company because they are so pushy about selling you their product.

5.   This morning I got a shock from the toaster, fell on the cat, and brushed my teeth with shaving cream. It made me want to go to bed.

6.   Linda told Marcia that her brother was waiting for her.

7.   When you swim at the city pool, they don't put up with any nonsense in the water.

8.   The Blazers and the Bucks were tied in the third quarter, but they finally won by two points.

9.   The silverware was dirty, the food was overcooked, and the waitress was rude. That made me angry.

10.   When Dawkins and the other player both leaped for the ball, a foul was called on him.

Review: Using Pronouns

Write each of the following sentences, correcting any problems in pronoun usage. Underline the corrected pronouns. (Some sentences contain more than one error.)

Examples

a. Ms. Washington gave the best report topic to Cloris and I.
Ms. Washington gave the best report topic to Cloris and <u>me</u>.

b. Some members of the audience shouted its disapproval of the villain of the play.
Some members of the audience shouted <u>their</u> disapproval of the villain of the play.

1. Each of the writers explained their philosophy to the audience.

2. To whom should Tanya and me speak about the problem?

3. Either Dan or Pete has forgotten it is their turn to feed the dogs.

4. Not one of the radio stations had the story on their news.

5. Neither the cat nor the dogs liked wearing its new flea collars.

6. Since the captains are Alexandra and he, alternates will be you and me.

7. One of the radios you lent my brother and I has something wrong with their volume control.

8. Neither an orange nor those grapes are enough in itself to be a good lunch.

9. Please ask that woman if it is she whose dog had their picture in *Time* magazine.

10. Reporters for the newspaper staff this semester will be Coretta, him, and me.

Rewrite each of the sentences on the following page so that the pronoun clearly refers to its antecedent, and correct any other pronoun problems. (There may be more than one way to correct any one sentence.)

Example

a. Carla informed Marcie that she would receive the science prize.
Carla informed Marcie that Marcie would receive the science prize.

11. Jack reminded Malcolm that he needed to get gas.

12. My sister she went through my drawers, took my best pen, and spilled milk on my homework, which made me mad.

13. When a customer enters that jewelry store, he or she will notice how snobbish they seem.

14. Lydia told Carmen she could ride with her cousin.

15. You should never stare fixedly at a baboon or grin at one; it seems like an act of aggression and may trigger an attack.

16. When a person joins the army, they put you through they're rigorous physical training.

17. I ate too much popcorn at the fair and then rode the roller coaster; it made me feel queasy.

18. Lisa asked Karen if she knew who's party was Saturday.

19. Campers should check for ticks because they can give you several nasty diseases.

20. I dislike sales because they push you to get at the bargains.

Writing Focus: *Using Pronouns*

You can strengthen your writing by using pronouns to avoid unnecessary repetition and to vary the structure of your sentences. Be sure that the pronouns you use are in the correct form and agree with their antecedents in number and gender.

Assignment: *A Lesson Well Learned*

Both in and out of the classroom, there are lessons to be learned. We learn to appreciate people—parents, special friends, and good teachers. We learn to avoid things—driving too fast, overeating, fighting. We also learn how to do things—play tennis, make speeches, operate a computer. Recall some of the lessons you have learned in your life and the people who have helped you learn them.

Use the steps on the next page to complete this assignment.

A. Prewriting

Make a list of eight to ten important lessons you have learned. Select one to write about that is significant or memorable. Use the Six Basic Questions method described in Chapter 1 to generate ideas about this particular experience. Jot down questions that need to be answered like the following: *Who* was involved in the experience? *What* took place? *Where* did it take place? *When* did it take place? *Why* was it important to me? *How* did I learn the lesson? Answer your questions specifically in words, phrases, or sentences. Review your answers and group them into an organizational pattern that will help you write about your experience.

B. Writing

Using your answers, write one or more paragraphs explaining how you learned the lesson. Tell about who or what was involved, what happened in the order it happened, and the lesson you were taught. Be sure to include specific details in your account. As you write, pay particular attention to the pronouns you use and their antecedents.

C. Postwriting

Revise your first draft using the following checklist.

1. Have I answered the questions *who? what? when? where? why?* and *how?* in explaining the lesson I learned?

2. Have I used each pronoun in its correct form?

3. Does each pronoun agree with its antecedent in number and gender?

Edit your work using the Proofreader's Checklist at the back of the book.

11 Verbs

Understanding Verbs

Every complete sentence must have at least one verb. When used effectively, verbs can communicate the emotion, thought, or action that is the essence of a good sentence. In the following sections you will begin your study of verbs by learning to recognize them through their definition, the classes into which they can be grouped, and the features that distinguish them from other parts of speech.

Defining Verbs

A *verb* is usually defined as a word that expresses action or a state of being.

Superman *leaps* over the building. Jennifer Gaston *worked* for the Peace Corps.	[action]
A caterpillar *becomes* a butterfly or moth. Tina *is* intelligent.	[being]

Exercise 1: Identifying Verbs

Write the following sentences, underlining the verb in each.

Examples

a. Jackie won the school's science prize.
   Jackie <u>won</u> the school's science prize.

b. The city is famous for its antipollution laws.
   The city <u>is</u> famous for its antipollution laws.

c. Workers carefully examined the new communications satellite before its launching.
   Workers carefully <u>examined</u> the new communications satellite before its launching.

1. KoKo the gorilla is one of the most unusual animals of her species in the primate world.

2. She talks in sign language.

3. KoKo's trainer is animal researcher Francine Patterson.

4. Ms. Patterson patiently trained KoKo for six years in a controlled environment.

5. During those years the inquisitive gorilla mastered about 375 words.

6. She communicates with her trainer by American Sign Language.

7. Although her IQ is slightly below that of a human child, Koko learns complex ideas.

8. She identifies pictures in books by name.

9. She answers Ms. Patterson's questions with obvious intelligence.

10. Oddly enough, KoKo discovered two unfortunate by-products of language on her own—the lie and the insult.

Grouping Verbs by Classes

Verbs function either as *action verbs* or *linking verbs*. In addition, if a verb is part of a verb phrase, it is either a *main verb* or a *helping verb*.

Action verbs show either physical or mental action.

The hungry baby *shrieked* relentlessly. Cars *screeched* to a halt at the light.	[physical action]
Romma *thought* of a plan. The skiers *hoped* for snow.	[mental action]

Linking verbs link the subject of a sentence to a noun, a pronoun, or an adjective in the predicate.

Boris *is* a dancer.
[*Is* links the subject *Boris* with *dancer*.]

Lemons *taste* sour!
[*Taste* links the subject *lemons* with *sour*.]

The most commonly used linking verbs include forms of the verb *be: am, are, is, was, were, been,* and *being.* The following list gives some other commonly used linking verbs.

appear	grow	seem	stay
become	look	smell	taste
feel	remain	sound	turn

Notice that many verbs in the preceding list may be either action or linking verbs. Look at the way a verb is used in a sentence to decide whether the verb shows action or is linking.

Action: Jan *tasted* the sour milk.
Linking: The milk *tasted* sour.

Action: Please *turn* the page, Lisa.
Linking: Lisa *turned* gray with horror.

In general, if you can substitute *became* or *was* for the verb, it is a linking verb.

The milk *tasted* sour.
[*The milk* was *sour.*]

Lisa *turned* gray with horror.
[*Lisa* became *gray with horror.*]

A verb may be either a single verb or part of a verb phrase. (A *verb phrase* contains two or more verbs that act as a single verb.)

Action verbs are further classified as transitive and intransitive verbs. Transitive verbs take objects (He spends money.). Intransitive verbs are complete in themselves (She sleeps.). See pages 499–500 for this discussion.

The last verb of a verb phrase is the *main verb.* The other verbs in the phrase are *helping verbs* because they *help* the main verb express action.

In the following sentences the helping verbs are underlined once and the main verbs are underlined twice.

Mark <u>will</u> <u>stay</u> until Saturday.

Jack <u>has</u> <u>seen</u> many movies.

Helping verbs include forms of *be* as well as some other frequently used verbs.

is	are	does	will	have	might
am	be	did	shall	has	must
was	been	can	should	had	
were	do	could	would	may	

Sometimes the main verb is separated from helping verbs by words such as *always, usually, never, not,* and so on. These words are not part of the verb phrase.

I will always remember Mama.

Jack has never been afraid of heights.

You should not have driven so long.

Did you ever see this play?

Exercise 2: *Identifying Verbs and Verb Phrases by Class*

Write each of the following sentences, underlining each verb. If a sentence contains a verb phrase, underline the phrase once and the main verb twice. Write *A* over every main verb that is an action verb. Put a *T* next to the sentence if the action verb is transitive; put an *I* if it is intransitive. Write *L* over every main verb that is a linking verb.

Examples

    a. Has anyone seen *The Empire Strikes Back?*

                  A

    Has anyone seen *The Empire Strikes Back?* T

    b. I have never been so proud!

             L

    I have never been so proud!

1. The fire has been raging all night.
2. Elaine has been a singer for years.
3. The television has never broken before.
4. Who will bring the potato salad to our Fourth of July picnic?
5. Do you feel faint?
6. You must feel this velvet fabric.
7. The dog was growling ferociously at the burglar climbing in through the window.
8. Have you been skiing this winter?
9. I will think of you every day!
10. We must not forget the key.

Finding a Verb by Its Features

Verbs have one or more of the following three features.

1. A verb has *tense*. It shows events happening in time.

I *study* today.
I *studied* yesterday.
I *will study* tomorrow.

There are six verb tenses—three *simple* and three *perfect tenses:* *simple present, simple past, simple future, present perfect, past perfect,* and *future perfect.*

I *jog* every day.	[present]	
I *jogged* yesterday.	[past]	simple tenses
I *will jog* tomorrow.	[future]	

I *have jogged* many miles.	[present perfect]	
I *had jogged* ten miles by yesterday.	[past perfect]	perfect tenses
By Sunday I *will have jogged* fifteen miles.	[future perfect]	

The *principal parts* of a verb are used with helping verbs to form the different tenses. Every verb has three principal parts: the *present,* the *past,* and the *past participle.*

Present	Past	Past Participle
sing	sang	(has) sung
try	tried	(has) tried
laugh	laughed	(has) laughed
see	saw	(has) seen

2. Verbs have a form that ends in *-ing*.

The *-ing* form of the verb, used with a form of the helping verb *be,* forms the *progressive form* of various tenses.

She *is reading.*	[present progressive]
She *was reading.*	[past progressive]
She *will be reading.*	[future progressive]

3. A verb agrees with its subject in number.

I *jog*.	He *jogs*.
You *study*.	She *studies*.

A final *-s* is added to almost all verbs in the present tense, when the subject is in the third-person singular.

Exercise 3: *Identifying Verbs and Verb Phrases*

Write the following sentences, underlining each verb or verb phrase. Your teacher may ask you to explain whether you used the traditional definition or the description of verb features to identify the verbs.

Examples

 a. Juanita Hall won many acting awards.
 Juanita Hall won many acting awards.

 b. Their new car will be an economy model.
 Their new car will be an economy model.

1. The famous rock group recorded its first demonstration tape in a garage.

2. Terry will pursue a career in veterinary science.

3. The Phoenician alphabet is the ancestor of our own.

4. The strange hills in northeastern Nebraska were formed by glaciers in the last ice age.

5. The famous Hope Diamond supposedly carries a curse.

6. Our class was seriously discussing the possibility of life on other planets.

7. Detroit produced many popular singers.

8. My sister will buy an electric typewriter with her birthday money.

9. According to a popular legend Romulus was the first king of Rome.

10. Dracula was created by the writer Bram Stoker.

Review: Understanding Verbs

Write the following sentences, underlining each verb or verb phrase. Write *A* over each action verb, *L* over each linking verb, and *H* over each helping verb.

Examples

a. Susan has not tasted the soup, which smells delicious.

$$\overset{H}{\underline{\text{Susan has}}} \text{ not } \overset{A}{\underline{\text{tasted}}} \text{ the soup, which } \overset{L}{\underline{\text{smells}}} \text{ delicious.}$$

b. Joanne will be studying for her exams all next week.

$$\overset{H}{\underline{\text{Joanne will}}} \overset{H}{\underline{\text{be}}} \overset{A}{\underline{\text{studying}}} \text{ for her exams all next week.}$$

1. The little boy laughs whenever he sees a clown.

2. Roberta may never sing again.

3. By the end of the summer, we will have traveled through fourteen states.

4. Hasn't Ann seemed sad lately?

5. Juan, please taste this sauce and add some salt if necessary.

6. The cat has been sleeping in the same spot all day.

7. You must not speak loudly because the baby is sleeping.

8. The icy water felt wonderful.

9. Wendy feels certain that we should not leave so late.

10. The phone has been ringing all evening.

11. That water looks calm, but it is really quite treacherous.

12. I have never been so embarrassed in my life!

13. Next week we will look at a new apartment.

14. John was a lawyer before he changed careers.

15. The Clarksons have traded their old car for a newer one.

16. That door has always locked by itself.

17. That bright light on the horizon could possibly be a ship.

18. The electric company is constantly raising its prices.

19. Does Eleanora ever sing professionally?

20. Why did the alarm ring so early?

Applying What You Know

In a newspaper or magazine, locate a recent account of a news or sports event. Using what you have learned in the preceding sections, identify the verbs and verb phrases in the selection and list them on a sheet of paper.

Using Verbs

The following sections will emphasize *using* verbs: using verb tenses correctly, solving problems in verb agreement, choosing between easily confused verbs, using active and passive voice, and maintaining consistency of tenses. As you work through the sections, use the preceding Understanding Verbs sections if you need help in recognizing verbs.

Using Verb Tenses

The *tense* of a verb indicates the time of the action or state of being. The three simple tenses are *present*, *past*, and *future*.

Present Tense

Use the present form of the verb to express *present tense*. In the present tense add *-s* or *-es* to the verb that is used with singular nouns or with *he, she,* or *it*. No ending is added when the verb is used with plural nouns or with the pronouns *I, you, we,* or *they*.

He			I		
She	} *leaves* tomorrow.		You		
It			We	} *leave* tomorrow.	
Clair			They		
			Clair's sisters		

Verbs in the present tense can describe two different kinds of action: an action happening right now (in the present) or an action that is habitual (happens repeatedly).

A fly *crawls* up the window.	[happening now]
A fly *spreads* germs.	[habitual action]

Past Tense

Actions that happened in the past are described by verbs in the *past tense*. Whether the verb's subject is singular or plural, form the past tense of most verbs by adding the ending *-d* or *-ed*.

> Rosa Bonheur *painted* in a style different from that of Renaissance artists.

> A wagon train *carried* the settlers out west.

> Thousands of wagon trains *carried* settlers out west.

Note: Some verbs—such as *carry*—undergo spelling changes when the *-ed* ending is added.

Many verbs, however, use forms other than *-d* or *-ed* to mark the past tense. Such verbs are called *irregular*, and their endings must be memorized, though you know many of them already.

> Lena Horne *sang* on Broadway and in the movies.

> A great white shark *swam* beneath our boat.

The following commonly used verbs have irregular past tense forms.

Present	Past	Past Participle
become	became	become
begin	began	begun
blow	blew	blown
break	broke	broken
bring	brought	brought
build	built	built
burst	burst	burst
buy	bought	bought
choose	chose	chosen
come	came	come
dive	dived or dove	dived
do	did	done
draw	drew	drawn
drink	drank	drunk
drive	drove	driven
eat	ate	eaten
fall	fell	fallen

Present	Past	Past Participle
fly	flew	flown
give	gave	given
go	went	gone
grow	grew	grown
keep	kept	kept
know	knew	known
lay	laid	laid
lead	led	led
leave	left	left
lie	lay	lain
meet	met	met
ride	rode	ridden
ring	rang	rung
rise	rose	risen
run	ran	run
say	said	said
see	saw	seen
set	set	set
shake	shook	shaken
shrink	shrank	shrunk
sing	sang	sung
sink	sank	sunk
sit	sat	sat
sleep	slept	slept
speak	spoke	spoken
spend	spent	spent
spring	sprang	sprung
stand	stood	stood
steal	stole	stolen
swear	swore	sworn
swim	swam	swum
take	took	taken
teach	taught	taught

Present	Past	Past Participle
think	thought	thought
throw	threw	thrown
wake	woke or waked	waked
wear	wore	worn
write	wrote	written

Exercise 4: Changing Verb Tenses from Present to Past

Write the following sentences, changing the present tense verbs to verbs in the simple past tense. Underline the verbs you change.

Examples

a. When the rain falls, my shirt and socks shrink.
   When the rain fell, my shirt and socks shrank.

b. My little sister blows up a balloon until it breaks.
   My little sister blew up a balloon until it broke.

1. We freeze our peaches so they keep well.

2. Television series from the new fall season come and go.

3. The smart golfer frequently takes his club and cleans it.

4. Students choose the project that they do.

5. Robin Hood, the English outlaw, steals from the rich and gives to the poor.

6. None of us ride with him because of the way he drives.

7. The lifeguard throws off her sunglasses and swims to the rescue.

8. My father says his government job brings him money, but the government taxes take it right back.

9. Bob throws his money away, but Caroline spends hers carefully.

10. He thinks before he speaks, and he always chooses his words carefully.

Future Tense

The *future tense* is composed of the helping verb *will* or *shall* and a main verb.

The main verb does not change its ending in any way.

The Science Fiction Convention *will meet* in London.

Your restaurant *will* never *succeed*.

The future tense expresses an action that will take place in the future.

The comet *will reappear* in forty years.

The future tense is sometimes used to make predictions.

Arkansas *will defeat* Texas by a wide margin.

The difference between *shall* and *will* is growing less distinct all the time, and few speakers now differentiate between the two. One use of *shall,* however, is to imply that the future action *must* be performed because of specific circumstances.

This criminal *shall* be confined for ten to fifteen years.

You *shall* be very sorry for that.

In formal English the words *I* and *we* take *shall* instead of *will* for a helping verb.

General MacArthur said, "I *shall* return."

We *shall* work out this problem.

Exercise 5: *Using Future Tense Verbs*

Write the following sentences, supplying the future tense form of each verb that is shown in parentheses. Use *shall* with the words *I* and *we;* elsewhere use *will.* Underline the verb phrases you form.

Examples

a. Many scientists hope that solar power _____ our energy needs. (answer)

Many scientists hope that solar power will answer our energy needs.

b. We _____ a better mousetrap. (build)
We shall build a better mousetrap.

1. The weather forecaster on the evening news predicts it _____ cool and sunny. (be)

2. Inflation probably _____ to grow worse. (continue)

3. Perhaps someday scientists _____ a cure for cancer. (discover)

369

4. Maya Angelou _____ at the convention. (speak)

5. Before the end of the century, it is possible that Americans _____ on Mars. (walk)

6. I _____ 10,000 erasers for misbehaving in class. (clean)

7. Ecologists hope that the whooping crane and other endangered species _____. (survive)

8. We always _____ for a cure for the common cold. (hope)

9. The school _____ some hearty turkey hash just before Thanksgiving vacation. (serve)

10. "We _____ again," chuckled the villain, curling his mustache. (meet)

Verbs in the Perfect Tenses

The three perfect tenses are the *present perfect*, the *past perfect*, and the *future perfect*. The perfect tenses are composed of a main verb preceded by a helping verb that is a form of *have (have, has, had)*.

The *present perfect tense* is composed of the helping verb *have* or *has* and the past participle of a verb. The present perfect tense usually describes an action begun in the past that may continue to the present. It is frequently used to describe an ongoing action.

Mike *has worked* at the drive-in for six months.

My sisters *have taken* up golf.

In the preceding examples the working at the drive-in and the playing of golf started in the past and continue in the present.

Another use of the perfect tense is to describe an action that is already completed.

He *has taken* the test already.

The stores *have announced* when the sales will begin.

The *past perfect tense* is formed with the helping verb *had* and the past participle of a verb. The past perfect tense usually describes an action that took place in the past before another action.

I *had been* sixteen for a month before I took my driver's exam.

Maria wanted the library book, but someone *had checked* it out.

The *future perfect tense* is composed of the helping verbs *will have* or *shall have* with the past participle of the verb. The future perfect tense describes a future action that will be completed before another future action.

By September *I shall have lost* fourteen pounds.

After this graduation Joanne *will have earned* two degrees.

Exercise 6: *Using the Perfect Tenses of Verbs*

For each of the following sentences, decide whether the verb in parentheses should be in the present perfect, past perfect, or future perfect tense. Write the sentences, supplying the correct forms of the verbs. Underline the verb phrases you form.

Examples

a. The radio station _____ the story before it checked the facts. (broadcast)

The radio station had broadcast the story before it checked the facts.

b. My grandmother _____ New York every year for the last eighteen years. (visit)

My grandmother has visited New York every year for the last eighteen years.

c. When I finish Huck Finn, I _____ four books in one month. (read)

When I finish Huck Finn, I shall have read four books in one month.

1. Julius Caesar went to the Forum, although the soothsayer _____ against going. (warned)

2. The United States _____ a member of the United Nations from the beginning. (be)

3. Maria ran back to the bus immediately, but her purse _____. (disappear)

4. Because this bus is so late, my family _____ dinner when I arrive home. (finish)

5. I _____ this movie five times already! (see)

6. Fortunately, just before the accident, the hospital staff _____ its emergency procedures. (rehearsed)

7. By the time this letter arrives, you _____ already _____ the sweater. (receive)

8. Lisa _____ in every basketball game this season. (play)

9. The fire _____ because of an overloaded circuit. (start)

10. The weather _____ much colder by Thanksgiving, so we will need warm clothes for hiking. (turn)

Using the Progressive Forms of Verbs

The *progressive forms* of verbs express ongoing action. These verb phrases are composed of a form of the helping verb *be* and a main verb ending in *-ing*. Each of the six tenses has a progressive form.

Present Tense, Progressive Form

Singular	Plural
I am learning.	We
You are learning.	You } are learning.
He }	They
She } is learning.	
It }	

Past Tense, Progressive Form

Singular	Plural
I was learning.	We
You were learning.	You } were learning.
He }	They
She } was learning.	
It }	

Future Tense, Progressive Form

Singular	Plural
I shall be learning.	We shall be learning.
You }	You } will be learning.
He }	They
She } will be learning.	
It }	

Present Perfect Tense, Progressive Form

Singular

I
You } have been learning.
He
She } has been learning.
It

Plural

We
You } have been learning.
They

Past Perfect Tense, Progressive Form

I
You
He } had been learning.
She
It

We
You } had been learning.
They

Future Perfect Tense, Progressive Form

I shall have been learning.
You
He
She } will have been learning.
It

We shall have been learning.
You
They } will have been learning.

Exercise 7: Using the Progressive Forms of Verbs

Rewrite the sentences on the following page, changing the *italicized* verbs to their progressive forms. Do not change the tense of the verb. Underline the verb phrases you form.

Examples

a. Odetta *sings* at the Newport Folk Festival.
   Odetta is singing at the Newport Folk Festival.

b. The Blazers *have played* the Milwaukee Bucks for several years.
   The Blazers have been playing the Milwaukee Bucks for several years.

1. Our team seemed full of spirit as they *played* the last few minutes.

2. As Luis and Laura finished cultivating the garden, it *began* to rain.

3. At the time of the accident the authorities *should have taken* drastic measures.

4. The principal *will ask* to see you in her office tomorrow if you come in.

5. When they finally found the answer, scientists *had tried* for years to unlock the secret.

6. Some scientists *predict* a new ice age.

7. The Cornhuskers *led* Alabama by seven to six.

8. Leslie Uggams and Ben Vereen *played* title roles in the television series *Roots.*

9. The electronics store *will have* a sale on speakers.

10. By next month the class *will have prepared* for the dance for six months.

Solving Problems in Verb Agreement

One hallmark of verbs is that they have tense; another is that a verb *agrees* with its subject.

A verb must agree with its subject in number. If a subject is singular, use the singular form of the verb; if the subject is plural, use the plural form of the verb.

Except for the verb *be*, the only tense forms of a verb that change to show agreement are those in the present tense. In the present tense, verbs take the ending *-s* or *-es* if their subjects are either singular nouns or the pronouns *he, she,* and *it*. Plural nouns and the pronouns *I, you, we,* and *they* take the verb form without the *-s* or *-es* ending.

The car *races.*

He ⎫
She ⎬ *races.*　　[Singular nouns and these pronouns take
It ⎭　　　　　　the *-s* or *-es* ending in the present tense.]

The eight cars *race*.

I
You
They   } *race*.
We

[Plural nouns and these pronouns do not take the *-s* or *-es* ending in the present tense.]

Unlike other verbs, the verb *be* has three forms for the present tense. The extra form is for the pronoun *I,* and it is the verb *am.* The verb *am* is used only with *I,* whether it is used as a main verb or as a helping verb.

I *am* tired.

I *am dissecting* a frog in biology.

She *is* Korean.

She *is getting* a driver's license.

They *are* vegetarians.

They *are filming* the news story.

Other verbs have only one form in the past tense. The verb *be,* used by itself or as a helping verb, has two forms in the past tense: *was* and *were.* The form *was* is used with singular nouns and the pronouns *I, he, she,* and *it.* The form *were* is used with plural nouns and with the pronouns *we, you,* and *they.*

I *was* sick.

It *was* cold outside.

You *were* healthy.

They *were* termites.

I *was sneezing* violently.

It *was snowing* hard.

You *were doing* push-ups.

They *were destroying* our garage.

Exercise 8: *Making Different Forms of* Be *Agree with Subjects*

Write the following sentences, supplying the correct form of *be* from the forms given in parentheses. Underline the form of *be* you select.

Example

    a. We (was, were) studying grammar.
       We were studying grammar.

1. I (am, is) taking the bus downtown.

2. They (was, were) playing ball in the empty lot.

3. It looks like the Tigers (are, is) going to lose this game.

4. We have been too busy; we (is, are) exhausted.

5. These pumpkins that we (was, were) going to make into jack-o'-lanterns (are, is) rotten.

6. Summer has ended now that the trees (is, are) turning colors.

7. Hardly any vegetable (are, is) blue, except for ripe eggplants, which almost (is, are).

8. You (wasn't, weren't) at home when they (were, was).

9. We (was, were) wondering if you (was, were) coming.

10. If you (are, is) late, I (am, is) going to leave without you.

Finding the True Subject to Determine Agreement

Sometimes the true subject of a sentence and the verb may be separated by other words. If a phrase comes between the subject and the verb, do not be tempted to make the verb agree with the noun closest to the verb. Find the true subject. An asterisk (*) denotes a sentence with a feature that is not part of Edited Standard English.

*A bowl of apples were on the table.   [incorrect agreement]
A bowl of apples <u>was</u> on the table.   [correct agreement]

In the preceding sentences the agreement error is easy to make because the plural noun *apples* comes between the verb and its singular true subject, *bowl*. In the following example several nouns separate the true subject (S) and its verb (V):

       S   V

The <u>goal</u> of the other first *explorers, fur trappers,* and *traders* <u>was</u>

different from the missionaries' goals.

Another problem in agreement arises when the true subject of the sentence comes *after* the verb. The usual order of subject and verb is often reversed in questions.

    V   S

There <u>is</u> no <u>reason</u> to stop the experiments.

    V   S

Why <u>are</u> <u>lemons</u> sour?

Exercise 9: Making Verbs Agree with Their True Subjects

In the following sentences the verbs or verb phrases do not agree with their true subjects. Write each sentence, changing each verb to its correct form. Underline the true subject once and the verb or verb phrase twice.

Examples

a. One of the joys of vacations are sleeping late.
   One of the joys of vacations is sleeping late.

b. What is the history assignments I missed?
   What are the history assignments I missed?

---

1. One of the members were sick.

2. Why has the armadillos become so numerous when other animals grow scarcer?

3. Every single member of all the choirs have food poisoning.

4. There is early morning speed-reading classes every day.

5. The problem that faced the settlers, the miners, the traders, and the merchants were overwhelming.

6. Why is the power company's workers in the building today?

7. The salaries of the coach and the English teacher is not equal.

8. The line for both movie theaters are around the corner.

9. Where are the set of golf clubs that you want to sell?

10. The magazine for enlisted people and veterans print true-life adventure stories.

Agreement with Indefinite Pronouns

When an indefinite pronoun is the subject of a sentence, its verb must agree with it in number.

Some indefinite pronouns are singular in meaning; others are always plural; and a few can be either singular or plural, depending on their meaning in the sentence.

The following indefinite pronouns are always singular and take a singular verb.

anybody	everybody	no one
anyone	everyone	one
each	neither	somebody
either	nobody	someone

Everybody is invited to the grand opening of the new museum.

Each of the insects works for the good of the colony.

Neither of the twins likes to dress like the other.

One of those records is good for dancing.

The indefinite pronouns *both, many, several, few,* and *others* are always plural and take the plural form of the verb.

Both of the children are geniuses.

Many of those restaurants require ties.

Are several of those paintings original oils?

The pronouns *all, any, most, some,* and *none* may be either singular or plural. If the pronoun refers to one person or thing, it is singular and takes a singular verb. If it refers to more than one, it is plural.

None of the house has been painted yet.	[singular meaning]
None of the chairs have been painted yet.	[plural meaning]
Most of the guests have left.	[plural meaning]
Most of the dress is stained.	[singular meaning]

Notice that the noun that comes between the indefinite pronoun (the subject) and the verb gives a clue as to whether the indefinite pronoun is singular or plural in meaning.

Exercise 10: *Making Verbs Agree with Indefinite Pronoun Subjects*

Write each of the sentences on the next page, choosing the correct verb from those in parentheses. Underline the subject once and the verb or verb phrase that agrees with it twice.

Examples

 a. Each of the girls on the drill team (furnish, furnishes) her own uniform.

  Each of the girls on the drill team furnishes her own uniform.

 b. Neither of those shows (interest, interests) him very much.

  Neither of those shows interests him very much.

1. Each of us (pay, pays) for some part of the trip.

2. We checked the windows thoroughly, and none (was, were) damaged.

3. Obviously, one of these dogs (has, have) tangled with a skunk recently.

4. Either Vicki Carr or Stevie Wonder (is, are) appearing on that show tonight.

5. We asked Mary and Sam to the party, but neither (is, are) able to come.

6. Not one of the students in the sophomore class (has, have) type AB blood.

7. Both of those objects (is, are) hovering over the lake!

8. I've tried on every gym suit from this box, and each (is, are) too big for me.

9. Nobody ever (remember, remembers) how to spell Ms. Yrkoeufski's name.

10. None of these books (is, are) overdue at the library.

Subject-Verb Agreement with Compound Subjects

Two or more subjects joined by the word *and* always take the plural form of the verb.

Jack and Jill are waiting.

The students and the professor have spoken at the conference.

Red, yellow, and blue are the primary colors.

Note: Some subjects that seem to be plural are actually singular. For instance, *chicken and dumplings* is considered as *one* dish, not *two;* you use a singular form of the verb.

Chicken and dumplings is our family's favorite meal for special occasions.

The names of businesses and brands usually take the singular form of the verb.

Washington, Gomez, and Ling is the best law firm in the downtown business area.

Bright and Early is a new alarm clock that plays "the Star-Spangled Banner" and shakes your bed.

When a compound noun names something considered as a single unit, use a singular verb.

Two or more singular subjects joined by *or* or *nor* take the singular form of the verb.

Mark or Kevin has drawn this cartoon.

Either biology lab or algebra class is canceled today.

Unfortunately, neither rain, sleet, nor snow stops the post office from delivering bills.

Two or more plural subjects joined by *or* or *nor* take the plural form of the verb.

Either frogs *or* toads live by that pond.

Neither roses *nor* peonies bloom in winter.

When a singular subject and a plural subject are joined by *or* or *nor*, the verb agrees with the subject nearer to it.

Either Lisa *or* the Ortega sisters are going to the basketball game.

Neither chives *nor* garlic is needed in this recipe.

Either the dog *or* the cats are going to have to stay outside at night.

Exercise 11: Making Verbs Agree with Compound Subjects

Write the following sentences, choosing the correct verb from the pair of verbs in parentheses. Underline the subject once and the verb or verb phrase twice.

Examples

a. Rags and Riches (is, are) the most unusual clothing store in town.
   Rags and Riches is the most unusual clothing store in town.

b. Maurice and Kim (was, were) excused from school early today.
   Maurice and Kim were excused from school early today.

1. Rings and Things (is, are) the name of the new jewelry store.

2. First National Savings and Loan (is, are) where I keep my money.

3. Neither cereal nor eggs (appeal, appeals) to me.

4. The main bank and the corner bakery (buy, buys) ads in the student newspaper.

5. Atchison, Topeka, and Santa Fe (was, were) stops along a famous western railroad.

6. Either Abbott or Costello (ask, asks), "Who's on First?"

7. Both station wagons and the newest pickup truck (has, have) flat tires.

8. Kelly or her sisters (is, are) baby-sitting for us.

9. The teacher and the students (send, sends) their letters of complaint to the "Growls and Howls" department of the school paper.

10. Records or a song book (is, are) the best gift for Raoul.

Collective Nouns and Agreement Problems

Words like *team, group, committee,* and *audience* are called *collective nouns* because they name a collection of individuals acting together as a unit.

> If a collective noun refers to a group working as a unit, it takes the singular form of the verb. If the noun refers to the individual members of the group, it takes the plural form.

The audience is leaving.

[The audience is regarded as a unit.]

The audience were cheering as if their lives depended on it.

[meaning the people in the audience]

The committee is announcing its decision today.

[The committee is regarded as a unit.]

The committee are having disagreements on that subject.

[meaning the members of the committee]

Note: Most collective nouns form their plurals as other nouns do—with the suffix -s.

The team is practicing.

Both teams are practicing.

Plural collective nouns, of course, always take the plural form of the verb.

Exercise 12: Making Verbs Agree with Collective Nouns

Each of the following sentences contains a collective noun used as a subject. Decide which of the verbs in parentheses is most appropriate to the meaning of each sentence and then rewrite the sentence with the verb you have selected. Underline the main verb or verb phrase in the sentence.

Examples

a. The band (is, are) marching in the town's centennial parade.
   The band is marching in the town's centennial parade.

b. The band (buy, buys) all of their own uniforms.
   The band buy all of their own uniforms.

1. A crowd (was, were) gathered around the display of electric trains.

2. The crowd (was, were) waving their signs and placards angrily.

3. The flock (graze, grazes) peacefully on the green hillside.

4. The flock (run, runs) off in twenty different directions.

5. The orchestra (was, were) taking out their instruments and tuning up.

6. The orchestra (give, gives) its first concert tomorrow night.

7. The public (demand, demands) honesty from all of its elected officials.

8. The public (has, have) argued about many concerns.

9. The swarm (was, were) buzzing around the hollow tree trunk.

10. The swarm (was, were) buzzing wildly as they tried to protect their queen and their honey stores.

More Agreement Situations

Don't *and* Doesn't

Some speakers and writers have difficulty handling the words *don't* and *doesn't* in Edited Standard English. Both *don't* and *doesn't* are *contractions*; that is, they are shortened forms for the phrases *do not* and *does not*.

Don't is the contraction of *do not*. Use *don't* with plural subjects and the pronouns *I, you, we,* and *they.*

Many people don't like anchovies.	[plural subject]
You don't like anchovies.	[pronoun]

Doesn't is the contraction of *does not*. Use *doesn't* with singular nouns and the pronouns *he, she,* and *it.*

The cat doesn't like riding in the car.	[singular noun]
He doesn't exercise enough. It really doesn't matter anymore.	[pronoun]

Nouns That Are Plural in Form

Use the singular form of the verb for nouns that are plural in form but have a singular meaning.

athletics	genetics	news
civics	mathematics	physics
economics	mumps	politics

Politics is one subject I never discuss!

Mumps is a painful disease.

Nouns That Have No Singular Form

Use a plural form of the verb with nouns that have no singular form.

pliers	shears	trousers	pants
scissors	jeans	slacks	suspenders

Western jeans are expensive in Europe.

Are those scissors sharp?

Note: If the word *pair* precedes the noun, use a singular form of the verb.

That pair of scissors is not sharp.

Titles and Names of Countries

Use the singular form of the verb for titles of works of art or for the names of countries.

The Netherlands is known for its tulips.

Ahmal and the Night Visitors is a popular opera at Christmas.

Short Stories has fifty tales by contemporary writers.

Amounts

Use a singular form of the verb for words and phrases that express time and amounts (money, fractions, weight, and volume).

Two miles is more than two kilometers.

Three quarters of my garden has been eaten by animals.

Five dollars isn't enough for both of us to see that movie.

When these amounts are thought of individually and not as a unit, the plural form of the verb may be used.

These last miles are taking forever to drive.

Years go by quickly as you get older.

Predicate Nominative

When the subject and the predicate nominative (a noun or pronoun in the predicate that means the same as the subject) are different in number, use a verb that agrees in number with the subject.

My job includes typing and mailing the bills.

The woods and the meadow are part of my property.

Every *and* Many a

When the words *every* or *many a* precede the subject, use the singular form of the verb.

Many a farmer bemoans this drought.

Every dog, cat, and hamster in the house is hungry.

Exercise 13: *Making Verbs Agree with Subjects*

Write the sentences on the following page, choosing the form of the verb in parentheses that agrees with the subject. Underline the form you choose.

Examples

a. She (don't, doesn't) play tennis.
   She doesn't play tennis.

b. Every leaf and flower (is, are) in bloom.
   Every leaf and flower is in bloom.

1. The United States (have, has) great variety in its terrain.

2. More money and shorter hours (is, are) the union's demands.

3. Dinner and the movies (cost, costs) ten dollars.

4. Twenty dollars (is, are) the necessary deposit to reserve a room.

5. Either political science or civics (is, are) John's favorite course.

6. Two thirds of the seats (is, are) empty every night.

7. *Anna and the King of Siam* (is, are) the story on which the play *The King and I* was based.

8. Many a sailor (has, have) dreamed of sailing around the world.

9. The years (doesn't, don't) go quickly when you're young.

10. Those pants (is, are) too short!

Verbs Often Confused

Three pairs of verbs—*lie/lay*, *sit/set*, and *rise/raise*—are frequently confused because they sound alike and have similar meanings.

Lie/Lay

Lie and lay are easy to use correctly if you remember their principal parts.

Present	Past	Past Participle
lie	lay	(has, have, had) lain
lay	laid	(has, have, had) laid

Lie means "to rest in, or to get into, a horizontal position." *Lie* is intransitive.

I *lie* on the beach.

I *lay* on the beach.

I *have lain* on the beach.

Lay means "to place or put something." *Lay* is transitive. When using the verb *lay*, state the object that is being put or placed.

I *lay* the mail on the counter.

I *laid* the mail on the counter.

I *have laid* the mail on the counter.

Rise/Raise

Rise means "to go up" or "to get up." *Rise* is intransitive. *Raise* means "to move something upward." *Raise* is transitive. When using the verb *raise,* tell the object that is being moved upward.

Raise is a regular verb, but *rise* is an irregular verb. Notice the principal parts:

Present	Past	Past Participle
rise	rose	(has, have, had) risen
raise	raised	(has, have, had) raised

The temperature *rises* every afternoon.
The temperature *rose* ten degrees yesterday afternoon.
The temperature *has risen* twenty degrees since this morning.

Julio *raises* the flag on holidays.
Julio *raised* the flag yesterday.
Julio *has raised* the flag again.

Sit/Set

Sit means "to be seated." *Sit* is intransitive. *Set* means "to place something" or "to put it somewhere." *Set* is transitive. When you use the verb *set,* tell what object is being placed.

The cat *sits* on the porch. [The cat *is seated.*]

I *set* the dishes on the table. [I *placed* the *dishes.*]

Present	Past	Past Participle
sit	sat	(has, have, had) sat
set	set	(has, have, had) set

Miriam *sits* at the first desk.
Miriam *sat* at the first desk.
Miriam *has sat* at the first desk.

He *sets* the radio on the nightstand.
He *set* the radio on the nightstand.
He *has set* the radio on the nightstand.

Exercise 14: Choosing the Correct Form of Often-Confused Verbs

Write each of the following sentences and supply the correct form of the verb from the pair of words given in parentheses.

1. My brother has dirty socks _____ all over his room. (lying, laying)

2. I had just _____ down the groceries when I heard the phone ring. (sat, set)

3. Yesterday I _____ new tiles in the kitchen. (lay, laid)

4. The camper had _____ down on an anthill. (lain, laid)

5. The market has _____ the price of meat. (raised, risen)

6. Yesterday Wanda _____ under the apple tree, reading all afternoon. (lay, laid)

7. _____ down your books and _____ down and have some cocoa. (Sit, Set) (sit, set)

8. Ralph _____ serious questions about the state of the economy. (rose, raised)

9. Marcia _____ at the counter and _____ her packages beside her. (set, sat) (set, sat)

10. The price of gold _____ and then dropped again. (raised, rose)

Write an original sentence for each principal part of each of the following verbs: lie, lay, sit, set, rise, raise.

Example

raise: The lion raises its head to look at me. (present)
      Our family raised delicious corn last summer. (past)
      Divers have not yet raised the *Titanic*. (past participle)

Using the Active and Passive Voices

Verbs may be in either the *active* or the *passive voice*.

When the subject performs the action expressed by the verb, the verb is in the *active voice*.

The object of the verb receives the action.

> Carolyn washed and waxed the car.
> [The subject, *Carolyn*, performs the action of washing and waxing; the object, *car*, receives that action.]

> The dog buried the bone.
> [The subject, *dog*, performs the action of burying; the object that receives that action is *bone*.]

In the following examples the subject receives the action expressed by the verb.

> The car was washed and waxed by Carolyn.

> The bone was buried by the dog.

When the verb expresses action received by the subject, the verb is in the *passive voice*.

A verb in the passive voice is composed of a form of the helping verb *be* plus a past participle (*washed, buried*). Only transitive verbs can be used in the passive voice. The object of an active-voice verb becomes the subject of a passive-voice verb (*car, bone*). The one who performs the action is the object of a preposition (*by Caroline, by the dog*).

Passive: Michael *is adored* by his children.
  Active: His children *adore* Michael.

Passive: Those cabins *were built* by people.
  Active: People *built* those cabins.

One use of the passive voice in writing is for variety. Also, if the performer of an action is unknown or unimportant, the passive voice may express the idea better than the active voice can. You must be careful, however, because overusing the passive voice can make your writing static. Sentences written in the passive voice also sound awkward sometimes.

Exercise 15: Using Active and Passive Voice

Write each of the sentences on the following page. If a sentence is in the active voice, rewrite it in the passive; if it is in the passive voice, rewrite the sentence in the active voice.

Example

---

a. Marilyn was stung by a bee.
  A bee stung Marilyn.

389

1. The huge elm tree was struck by lightning.

2. Rick slammed the baseball out of the park.

3. Joel and Marge planned a party for Luiz.

4. The idea was first thought of by Diane.

5. The fire was started by two careless campers.

6. Flames consumed the forest.

7. The camera was invented by a Frenchman in 1839.

8. Carrie raised some questions about the new budget.

9. The eclipse will be observed by both amateur and professional astronomers.

10. The judge found the defendant guilty of the crime.

Consistency of Tenses

One common flaw in writing occurs when the writer, for no apparent reason, changes verb tenses. The following passage illustrates the difficulty of following writing that shifts from tense to tense. An asterisk (*) indicates writing with a feature that is not part of Edited Standard English.

> *The Divine Comedy* by Dante begins when the narrator is lost in a dark wood. The time was just before Easter. As he tried to find his way through the forest, his path was barred by a leopard, a lion, and a wolf. He gives himself up for lost, when suddenly a white figure appeared. It is the spirit of the Roman poet Virgil, who was sent by the Blessed Virgin and by Beatrice to help the narrator. (Beatrice, the woman the narrator loved, was in heaven.) Virgil takes the narrator on a tour of Purgatory and the nine circles of Hell. Then Virgil led him to Heaven.

Reading such a passage is like being caught in a time machine that has short-circuited. The reader is thrown from the present to the past and then is jolted back to the present, only to be transported to the past again.

Notice how much more smoothly the passage reads when the tense does not shift:

> *The Divine Comedy* by Dante begins when the narrator is lost in a dark wood. The time is just before Easter. As he tries to find his way through the forest, his path is barred by a leopard, a lion, and a wolf. He gives himself up for lost, when suddenly a

white figure appears. It is the spirit of the Roman poet Virgil. He has been sent by the Blessed Virgin and by Beatrice to help the narrator. (Beatrice, the woman the narrator loves, is in Heaven.) Virgil takes the narrator on a tour of Purgatory and the nine circles of Hell. Then Virgil leads him to Heaven.

The preceding passage has been rewritten in the present tense. When the present tense is used, as it is above, to describe events that actually took place in the past, it is called the *narrative present*. The narrative present has several uses: to summarize the events of a story, play, or novel; or to describe the events in a process, as in the following examples.

1. Moss *grows* on the northern sides of trees because this side of a tree *is* generally moister. The southern side of a tree *is* that which usually *gets* the most sunshine and *is* therefore drier and warmer. Mosses *prefer* the cooler, damper side.

2. When we *inhale*, the air sacs in the lungs *fill* with air. Oxygen molecules from the air pass through the capillary walls and into the blood, where they *combine* with hemoglobin of the red blood cells. At the same time, the blood stream *sends* molecules of carbon dioxide back into the air sacs, and these molecules *leave* the system when we *exhale*.

Sometimes the narrative present is used to tell entire short stories or novels, and it is often used in telling jokes or anecdotes.

Exercise 16: Making Verb Tenses Consistent

The passages on the next page are written in a mixture of present and past tense. Rewrite each passage according to the tense indicated in parentheses. Underline each verb whose tense you change.

Example

a. Two turtles go into a restaurant and order sodas. It suddenly begins to rain. One turtle said to the other, "You better go home and get our umbrella." "Okay," replied the second turtle, "but don't drink my soda while I'm gone."

Three months passed. The first turtle muttered, "I guess he isn't coming back. I'll drink his soda." From outside came the voice of the second turtle: "If you drink my soda, I won't go home and get the umbrella." (Change to present tense.)

Two turtles go into a restaurant and order sodas. It suddenly begins to rain. One turtle <u>says</u> to the other, "You better go home and get our umbrella." "Okay," <u>replies</u> the second turtle, "but don't drink my soda while I'm gone."

Three months <u>pass</u>. The first turtle mutters, "I guess he isn't coming back. I'll drink his soda." From outside <u>comes</u> the voice of the second turtle: "If you drink my soda, I won't go home and get the umbrella."

1. *Don Quixote* is the story of an old Spanish gentleman who reads so many romances that they affect his mind. He decided to become a famous knight, although knights no longer existed except in the books he read. He mounts a bony old horse he called his steed, placed a basin on his head for a helmet, and courageously rode out to right the wrongs of the world. (Change to present tense.)

2. Raindrops form from the tiny droplets in clouds. Water vapor condensed on these droplets and made them larger, or else several droplets stuck together. If the temperature of the air through which the raindrops fell is freezing, the drops turn into sleet. In summer strong air currents sometimes blew the drops upward into freezing air. As the frozen droplets fall, a thin layer of water droplets collects in the cloud, and freezes. When the droplets finally became too heavy for the air currents to hold up, they fell to earth as hail. (Change to present tense.)

3. In the 1890s Carry Nation became famous for her all-out war against liquor. She knew the suffering alcohol could cause and decided to put all saloons out of business. In a typical protest she boldly enters a saloon carrying a hatchet. She is accompanied by her loyal followers, who undauntedly sing hymns. She swings her hatchet and splinters bars, tables, and bottles. Although she is frequently arrested for disturbing the peace, she does not end her courageous crusade. Neither jails nor jeers can stop her. She carries on her crusade for years, until age and failing health force her to retire. She died in 1911. (Change to past tense.)

Review: Using Verbs

Write each of the following paragraphs, supplying the proper form of each verb in parentheses. Underline the verbs you supply.

Example

a. The common house mouse is a social animal who likes to live in groups. Its breeding season (be) from spring to fall, and each pair of mice possibly (raise) up to ten litters a year. In cold climates or cold seasons, mice (seek) shelter in buildings. A house rarely (have) just one mouse; a building usually (have) several. Mice (be) destructive. Once in the house, they (eat) food, cloth, and other goods. They are (know) to carry parasites and germs. The pest originally (come) from Asia, but it now (be) found all over North and South America.

The common house mouse is a social animal who likes to live in groups. Its breeding season is from spring to fall, and each pair of mice possibly raises up to ten litters a year. In cold climates or cold seasons, mice seek shelter in buildings. A house rarely has just one mouse; a building usually has several. Mice are destructive. Once in the house, they eat food, cloth, and other goods. They are known to carry parasites and germs. The pest originally came from Asia, but it now is found all over North and South America.

1. During the Civil War many women (be) spies and scouts. The greatest of these heroes (be) Harriet Tubman, a former slave. By the time her career ended, she (make) nineteen trips into the South and (lead) many runaway slaves to freedom. Tubman (work) unpaid as a nurse during the early years of the war and (treat) both black and white soldiers. She also (spy), since she could travel easily through the South. Having (see) how slaves might escape, she (gather) information and (show) the fugitives an escape route. Tubman (take) part in army raids, sometimes serving as a military leader, sometimes as a guide. For these brave acts and others, she (earn) the title "General Tubman."

2. I was taking an evening stroll by the edge of the golf course with my dog Mo. It (be) a warm and pleasant evening, but strangely quiet and misty. I (see) that Mo and I (be) alone this evening. No neighbors (be) out stretching their legs after dinner. As the sky (grow) darker, we (begin) to start back home. Suddenly, as we passed a small pond, I heard a strange noise and stopped. Mo perked up his ears and (growl). Bubbles (rise) swiftly to the surface of the pond. I (think) it (be) a muskrat or

large snapping turtle, but then the bubbles (become) huge and boiling, and I realized something enormous must be under the water—but what? Suddenly something long and black (burst) upward from the water! Sleek, wet, and striped with yellow, it (stand) almost six feet tall. For a moment I (think) a sea serpent was surfacing, but then I realized the truth—it was only a thrifty skin diver in a wetsuit, who was collecting golf balls from the bottom of the pond.

3.   The body uses copper to form red blood cells and hair pigment. Copper (be) found in muscle fibers, nerve coverings, and enzymes that help build tissues. Humans (require) only a small amount of copper, so deficiencies in copper (be) rare. Similarly, an overdose of copper (be) equally rare, since the body (tend) to discard unneeded quantities. Liver and shellfish (be) foods rich in copper; nuts, raisins, brewer's yeast, and cereals also (be) good sources of copper.

Writing Focus: *Using Vivid Verbs*

You can greatly improve your writing by including vivid verbs to *show* action precisely and clearly. Let the subject of your sentence *wiggle, fidget, jerk, start* or *sway* rather than *move.* Avoid overusing such general verbs as *make, has, have, does, do, are, is,* and *were.*

Assignment: *That's Incredible!*

Imagine that you were one of the spectators at the event in the photograph on page 395. The photo froze a moment in time, but you were present during the entire sequence of events. What you witnessed was truly amazing! What action might have occurred both before and after the picture was snapped?

For this assignment, write one or more paragraphs describing the action in the photograph. Use words to paint a picture of the action you saw. Your writing will be evaluated for correct and effective use of verbs.

Use the following steps to complete this assignment.

A. Prewriting

Study the photograph carefully. List everything you see. Let your imagination take you into the picture. Free write about what you

"see." (Review Chapter 1 for an explanation of free writing if necessary.) Concentrate on the details that made the action amazing. Let your imagination go until nothing else occurs to you. Reread your free writing and underline the words, phrases, and sentences that best describe the incredible action.

B. Writing

Using your free writing, write one or more paragraphs describing the amazing action you saw as if you were one of the spectators in the photograph. Start your account by setting the scene. Then create a moving picture of what happened before, during, and after the photo was snapped. Help your readers "see" and "experience" the action. Use vivid, specific verbs to depict the action that you saw.

C. Postwriting

Revise your first draft using the following checklist.

1. Are there specific details that give a clear picture of the scene?

2. Are there vivid, active verbs that convey the action?

3. Is each verb in the proper tense, and does it agree in number with the subject?

    Edit your work using the Proofreader's Checklist at the back of the book. If appropriate, share your writing with your classmates.

12 Adjectives

Understanding Adjectives

Adjectives, which describe or modify nouns, add detail to writing and make it more descriptive and more interesting. Notice, for example, how much more vivid the following sentence is with adjectives.

Cows rested near the barn in the meadow.

Large, brown-and-white spotted cows rested near the old, weathered barn in the lush, green meadow.

In the following sections you will learn to identify adjectives in three ways: by their definition, by their division into classes, and by the features that distinguish them from the other parts of speech.

Defining Adjectives

An *adjective* is usually defined as a word that modifies a noun or pronoun.

Adjectives answer certain questions about nouns or pronouns.

What Kind?	*new* car, *old* car, *speedy* car, *inexpensive* car
Which One?	*this* car, *that* car, *those* cars
What Quantity?	*three* cars, *few* cars, *all* cars, *several* cars
How Much or How Many?	*limited* quantity

Adjectives are often placed near the words they modify, but sometimes other words separate an adjective from the word it modifies.

The book was *funny*.

The bus is usually *late* during the rush hour.

Exercise 1: *Identifying Adjectives*

Write each of the following sentences, underlining all adjectives. Draw an arrow from each adjective to the word it modifies. (Do not include the words *a, an,* or *the.*)

Examples

  a. This book is a new collection of ghost stories by famous writers.

  This book is a new collection of ghost stories by famous writers.

  b. Every customer who ate a cheese sandwich at that restaurant got a terrible stomachache.

  Every customer who ate a cheese sandwich at that restaurant got a terrible stomachache.

1   Several cardinals come each morning to the bird feeder in our back yard.

2.   Our three dogs made a large hole under the wire fence and then had a digging contest in the tulip garden.

3.   A large bolt of lightning struck the oak tree in the backyard last night.

4.   Many people are nervous about several reports of unidentified flying objects in the night sky.

5.   Many people believe that goats eat tin cans, but the goats really nibble only the can labels.

6.   In Greek mythology the golden apple was really the common apricot.

7.   Hungry porcupines do much damage to young trees in American forests.

8.   The largest bell in the world is a Russian one that weighs 180 tons.

9.   The fuzz on a tennis ball gives the ball a slower flight and a trickier bounce.

10.   Both of our neighbors were in car accidents, but neither one was hurt, since both drivers wore safety belts.

Grouping Adjectives by Classes

Some adjectives, such as *pretty, hungry, old,* and *new,* do not belong to a special class. Other adjectives, however, fall into one of five categories: (1) articles, (2) proper adjectives, (3) pronouns used as adjectives, (4) nouns used as adjectives, and (5) predicate adjectives.

The most frequently used group of adjectives is
articles—the, a, **and** *an.*

The is called a *definite article* because it refers to a definite person or object. *A* and *an* are called *indefinite articles* because they do not indicate a specific person or object.

We saw *the* movie last night.	[specific movie]
Should we go out and get *a* sandwich?	[no particular sandwich]
This recipe calls for *an* orange.	[no particular orange]

The word *a* is used before words that begin with consonant sounds; *an* is used before words that begin with vowel sounds.

an apple	*a* grape
an hour	*a* minute
an Airedale	*a* beagle
an empty glass	*a* full glass

Proper adjectives **are formed from proper nouns.**

Proper Noun	Proper Adjective
America	*American* wheat
East	*Eastern* climate
Boston	*Bostonian* accent
Africa	*African* continent
Japan	*Japanese* pottery

Some pronouns can act as adjectives in a sentence.

Pronoun	Adjective
That is right.	*That* answer is right.
We need *more*.	We need *more* lumber.
Please hold *these*.	Please hold *these* eggs.

The word is used as a pronoun if it stands alone and replaces a noun or other pronoun within the sentence. The word is an adjective if it modifies a noun or pronoun but does not replace one.

The following words may be used as both pronouns and adjectives.

all	either	much	some	those
another	few	neither	such	what
any	many	one	that	which
both	more	other	these	
each	most	several	this	

Nouns are frequently used as adjectives to describe or clarify another noun or a pronoun.

Where is the *gasoline* pump?

A *winter* coat must be warm.

Have a *cheese* sandwich for lunch.

That *cement* mixer is huge!

When a word that is normally a noun does the work of an adjective in a sentence or phrase, it is considered an adjective.

Note: A possessive noun is considered a noun, not an adjective. The sentence "John's book has been lost" contains no adjectives.

An adjective that follows a linking verb and modifies the subject of the sentence is a *predicate adjective.*

Alaska is *cold* in the winter.

Janine seems *worried* about her sister.

Carla felt *proud* after winning her tennis match.

Exercise 2: Identifying Adjectives and Adjective Classes

Write the following sentences, underlining the adjectives. Where appropriate, label the adjectives *A* for *article*, *P* for *proper adjective*, *PA* for *predicate adjective*, *N* for *noun used as adjective*, and *PR* for *pronoun used as adjective*. (Remember that some adjectives do not fall into any of these categories.)

Examples

a. Two early leaders in the suffrage movement were sisters.

               A   N

Two early leaders in the suffrage movement were sisters.

b. They believed all American women should have the right to vote.

           PR   P   A

They believed all American women should have the right to vote.

1. These two women, Victoria Woodhull and Tennessee Claflin, were extraordinary.

2. When they were young, the girls traveled with a family medicine show.

3. In their teens they met an American financier, who offered them some excellent advice about the stock market.

4. These women became the first female brokers on Wall Street and also started a controversial newspaper.

5. In 1871 the two sisters appeared before a congressional committee to ask for equal rights for all women.

6. Victoria's stirring speech made her a popular figure in the suffrage movement.

7. She even organized her own political party and ran as a Presidential candidate.

8. On election day, however, both sisters were in jail because of an unfortunate incident.

9. They had published an angry article about a famous preacher, and shocked officials imprisoned them.

10. This setback did not stop the spunky sisters; they emerged from jail and continued to be strong, influential women.

Finding an Adjective by Its Features

Three features—degrees of comparison, intensifiers, and suffixes—may distinguish adjectives from other parts of speech.

Adjectives may change forms to show differences in comparison.

The three degrees of comparison are *positive, comparative,* and *superlative.* The "regular" form of an adjective, which simply describes a quality, is the *positive degree.* The *comparative degree* compares two persons or things; the *superlative degree* compares three or more persons or things.

Positive: This music is *loud.*

Comparative: This band's music is *louder* than that band's.

Superlative: This music is the *loudest* I have ever heard.

Most one-syllable adjectives and some two-syllable adjectives add *-er* to form the comparative degree. Adjectives of more than two syllables and some two-syllable adjectives form the comparative with the word *more.*

Positive	Comparative	Positive	Comparative
happy	*happier*	difficult	*more* difficult
light	*lighter*	even	*more* even
loose	*looser*	expensive	*more* expensive
tan	*tanner*	harmful	*more* harmful

Similarly, most one-syllable adjectives and some two-syllable adjectives form the superlative by adding *-est.* Some two-syllable adjectives and all adjectives of more than two syllables form the superlative with *most.*

Positive	Superlative		Positive	Superlative
happy	*happiest*		difficult	*most* difficult
light	*lightest*		even	*most* even
loose	*loosest*		expensive	*most* expensive
tan	*tannest*		harmful	*most* harmful

The words *less* and *least* are used before all adjectives to show less of a quality.

Positive	Comparative	Superlative
dangerous	*less* dangerous	*least* dangerous
interesting	*less* interesting	*least* interesting
silly	*less* silly	*least* silly

Some adjectives form the comparative and superlative forms in an irregular way. See page 408 for more on irregular adjectives.

Exercise 3: Identifying Comparative and Superlative Forms of Adjectives

The following passage contains ten adjectives that are *italicized*. Number your paper 1-10 and write down each adjective. State whether it is in its comparative or superlative form.

Example

a. My love for you, my sugarplum, is *higher* than the *highest* mountain, *deeper* than the *deepest* ocean, *more enduring* than stone or steel.

1. higher—comparative
2. highest—superlative
3. deeper—comparative
4. deepest—superlative
5. more enduring—comparative

Perhaps the *largest* natural explosion in recent times was the eruption of Krakatoa, an island off Indonesia, in 1883. When Krakatoa exploded with a force twenty-six times *greater* than an H-bomb, smoke and clouds turned a huge area *darker* than the *most starless* night. The fiery explosion created an even *more terrible* disaster: one of the *largest* tidal waves in memory. The *biggest* waves sank boats and destroyed villages. The *most conservative* estimate of deaths was 36,417. The explosion has been called "the *loudest* noise in history." In comparison with Krakatoa, other volcanic eruptions have been *less devastating*.

Adjectives may follow *intensifiers*.

Intensifiers include such words as *very, quite, rather, really, too,* and *fairly*. Intensifiers are words that modify other modifiers, including adjectives, by telling "to what extent."

I was *very* hungry.

I was *quite* hungry.

I was *rather* hungry.

A *fairly* large dog guarded the house.

A *really* large dog guarded the house.

A *somewhat* large dog guarded the house.

Adjectives may have *suffixes*.

Some adjectives have suffixes that distinguish them from other kinds of words. Recognizing these suffixes as a feature of adjectives can help you identify them. The following list shows the most common adjective suffixes.

Noun	+	*Suffix*	=	*Adjective*
rain		-y		*rainy*
friend		-less		*friendless*
fear		-ful		*fearful*
danger		-ous		*dangerous*
honor		-able		*honorable*
child		-ish		*childish*
child		-like		*childlike*
nation		-al		*national*
awe		-some		*awesome*

Verb	+	*Suffix*	=	*Adjective*
help		-ful		*helpful*
consider		-ate		*considerate*
manage		-able		*manageable*
thank		-less		*thankless*
act		-ive		*active*

Adding a suffix to some words may require a slight spelling change. Check a dictionary for help with spelling.

Exercise 4: Identifying Adjectives by Intensifiers and Suffixes

Write the following sentences, underlining all adjectives. Label intensifiers *I* and circle the suffixes of adjectives formed with suffixes.

Example

a. Mike thinks skydiving is quite glorious, but I think it's dangerous and somewhat crazy.

Mike thinks skydiving is quite glori(ous), but I think it's
danger(ous) and somewhat crazy.

---

1. The speedy service at that restaurant makes it a very dependable place for a quick lunch.

2. We saw a really funny play about a forgetful professor who invented a comical vegetable called a grunion.

3. A somewhat rusty car with a mysterious license plate was found along the coastal road.

4. Scrooge was quite selfish until a frightful experience made him generous and cheerful.

5. My Irish setter was pretty, courageous, intelligent, and very destructive with shoes and other chewable items.

6. A really sleepy driver should pull off the road and take a brief rest.

7. I am returning this product because it is defective and too expensive and because it has an awful odor when the box is left open.

8. The extremely cool mountain air smelled tangy and wonderful.

9. In this terrifying novel a virtuous young girl is held prisoner by a devilish sorcerer who, by using a magical potion, plans to turn her into a vampire.

10. My very talented brother has a rather large collection of extremely lifelike sculptures.

Review: Understanding Adjectives

Write the following paragraphs and underline at least sixty adjectives, including articles. (The first two are shown in *italic* for you.) When you have finished, be prepared to explain how you identified each adjective. Does it fit the definition of an adjective? Does it fit into one of the large classes of adjectives? Does it have any distinguishing features of an adjective?

One night we turned on *the* evening news and learned that some teenagers had just taken a record-breaking ride on a Ferris wheel—for no apparent reason. Well, these dauntless riders did, in fact, have a logical motive. They were seeking a place for themselves in the *Guinness Book of World Records* by completing the longest ride on a Ferris wheel! The drive to break an established record has spurred many people on to superhuman feats. The big question, it seems to me, is this: who thinks of these outlandish stunts?

A quick flip through the amazing *Book of Records* is always a humorous experience. If, for instance, we thought we could spin more plates at the same time than other people, we, too, might see our names on the printed page. But we would have to beat the masterful spinning of Holley Gray who, while he appeared on British television, spun the greatest number of plates at one time and won the championship title.

The strange records that people have attained are endless. One man walked fifteen miles while he balanced a milk bottle on his head! Another secured a world record by simply balancing on one leg for thirteen hours. Perhaps other acrobats could maintain a longer balance—well, good luck to them.

Applying What You Know

In the following description of a bookstore from Ernest Hemingway's novel *A Moveable Feast,* there are more than forty adjectives, with the first three underlined for you. Read the selection carefully, using what you have learned to identify the adjectives. Then list at least forty of them on a sheet of paper. (Do not include articles.)

In those days there was no money to buy books. I borrowed books from the rental library of Shakespeare and Company, which was the library and bookstore of Sylvia Beach at 12 rue de l'Odéon. On a cold windswept street, this was a warm, cheerful place with a big stove in winter, tables and shelves of books, new books in the window, and photographs on the wall of famous writers both dead and living. The photographs all looked like snapshots and even the dead writers looked as though they had really been alive. Sylvia had a lively, sharply sculptured face, brown eyes that were as alive as a small animal's and as gay as a young girl's, and wavy brown hair that was brushed back from her fine forehead and cut thick below her ears and at the line of the collar of the brown velvet jacket she wore. She had pretty legs and she was kind, cheerful and interested, and loved to make jokes and gossip. No one that I ever knew was nicer to me.

I was very shy when I first went into the bookshop and I did not have enough money on me to join the rental library. She told me I could pay the deposit any time I had the money and made me out a card and said I could take as many books as I wished.

There was no reason for her to trust me. She did not know me and the address I had given her, 74 rue Cardinal Lemoine, could not have been a poorer one. But she was delightful and charming and welcoming and behind her, as high as the wall and stretching out into the back room which gave onto the inner court of the building, were shelves and shelves of the wealth of the library.[1]

Using Adjectives

Throughout the following sections you will be asked to put your knowledge of adjectives to use in these ways: selecting the proper comparative and superlative forms of adjectives, using clear and logical comparisons, and choosing specific adjectives. For any help you may need in recognizing adjectives and their different forms, refer to the preceding Understanding Adjectives sections.

Using the Comparative and Superlative Forms

Studying the following points about the comparative and superlative forms of adjectives will help you use these forms correctly.

The comparative form compares two persons or things.

This watch is *better* than my old one.

Their team is *more experienced* than ours.

A cheetah is *faster* than a greyhound.

---

[1]From "Shakespeare & Company" in *A Moveable Feast* by Ernest Hemingway. Copyright © 1964 by Ernest Hemingway, Ltd. (New York: Charles Scribner's Sons, 1964). Reprinted by permission of Charles Scribner's Sons, the Executors of the Ernest Hemingway Estate, and Jonathan Cape Ltd.

The superlative form compares more than two persons or things.

> This watch is the *best* one manufactured in the United States.
>
> Their team is the *most experienced* in the Big Ten.
>
> The cheetah is the *fastest* of all mammals.

Most short adjectives, those of one or two syllables, form their comparatives and superlatives with -*er* and -*est*.

low—*lower—lowest*	high—*higher—highest*
sleepy—*sleepier—sleepiest*	happy—*happier—happiest*

The spelling of some adjectives must be changed before the -*er* and -*est* suffixes are added.

If the positive degree ends in the letter *y*, change the *y* to *i* before adding -*er* or -*est*.

Positive	Comparative	Superlative
silly	*sillier*	*silliest*
lively	*livelier*	*liveliest*
spicy	*spicier*	*spiciest*

If the positive degree ends in the letter *e*, drop the *e* before adding -*er* or -*est*.

Positive	Comparative	Superlative
fine	*finer*	*finest*
pale	*paler*	*palest*
true	*truer*	*truest*

If the positive degree ends in a single consonant preceded by a single vowel, double the final consonant before adding -*er* or -*est*.

Positive	Comparative	Superlative
thin	*thinner*	*thinnest*
hot	*hotter*	*hottest*
fat	*fatter*	*fattest*

Some adjectives change forms completely for the comparative and superlative degrees.

A few irregular adjectives do not form their degrees of comparison with -er and -est or more and most and less and least. Here are some examples.

Positive	Comparative	Superlative
good	better	best
bad, ill	worse	worst
far	farther	farthest
many, much	more	most
little	less or lesser	least

Your cold is *worse* than mine, but Sam's is *worst* of all.

This location is *better* than that one.

This job requires *more* time than the other one.

Exercise 5: Using Comparative and Superlative Forms of Adjectives

Write the following sentences, supplying the correct form of the adjective in parentheses. Underline the adjective you supply.

Examples

    a. Today is _____ than yesterday. (sunny)
      Today is sunnier than yesterday.

1. Mario is the _____ person I have ever known. (brave)

2. The record store has many classical albums but _____ popular records. (many)

3. I thought the movie *Horse Feathers* was _____ than *Duck Soup*. (funny)

4. I have only a little money, but Denise has even _____ than I do. (little)

5. That is the _____ orange I have ever eaten! (juicy)

6. The water in the Caribbean seems _____ than the water in the north Atlantic. (blue)

7. The distance between my house and the market is far, but the ride to the movies is even _____. (far)

8. Copper pots are more efficient because copper is a _____ conductor of heat than iron is. (good)

9. Was last summer's hurricane _____ than the storm of '62? People say that the one in 1962 was the _____ of all. (bad)

10. That was the _____ movie I have ever seen—even _____ than the one I saw last night. (dull)

Avoid double comparisons when using the comparative or superlative forms of adjectives.

An asterisk (*) denotes a feature that is not part of Edited Standard English.

Do not add *-er* or *-est* to irregular forms.

*This snowstorm was worser than the last one.

This snowstorm was *worse* than the last one.

*That was the bestest movie I've ever seen.

That was the *best* movie I've ever seen.

Similarly, do not add *more* or *most* to irregular forms or to adjectives that use *-er* or *-est* to form the comparative and superlative.

*This pen is more better than the old one.

This pen is *better* than the old one.

*It seems more colder than it is.

It seems *colder* than it is.

Using Comparative and Superlative Forms Clearly

Comparisons should be stated clearly and logically. The following guidelines will help you make better use of comparisons.

The reader must understand clearly what things are being compared.

---

*The blossoms of the lilac are more colorful than many other bushes.

In the preceding statement blossoms are being compared with bushes, not with other blossoms. The sentence should be revised:

The blossoms of the lilac are more colorful than the blossoms of many other bushes.

Similarly, the following sentence does not clearly state what two things are being compared.

*The President's job is far more demanding than most people.

The sentence should be revised for greater clarity and precision.

The President's job is far more demanding than most people's jobs.

Use the word *other* or *else* when comparing a person or thing with the rest of the group to which it belongs.

---

*Oklahoma City covers a larger area than any city in the United States.

The preceding sentence is not logical because Oklahoma City is a city in the United States; the sentence implies that Oklahoma City covers an area larger than it itself covers. Such illogical comparisons can usually be corrected by the addition of the word *other* or *else*.

Oklahoma City covers a larger area than any *other* city in the United States.

Exercise 6: Correcting Double and Unclear or Illogical Comparisons

The following sentences have double comparisons and comparisons that are not clearly or logically stated. Rewrite the sentences, revising them to correct the double comparisons and the unclear or illogical comparisons.

Examples

a. A bulldog's disposition is actually much more agreeable than a terrier.
   A bulldog's disposition is actually much more agreeable than a terrier's disposition.

b. Jupiter is larger than any planet in our solar system.
   Jupiter is larger than any other planet in our solar system.

1. The hazards of skiing are greater than mountain climbing.

2. Lincoln was taller than any American President.

3. The pitcher was more fatigued than anyone on the team.

4. Mixing this sauce by hand is more better than mixing it with a blender.

5. The hamster was more fonder of bananas than it was of any food.

6. Oregon is more concerned about ecology than any state.

7. This dog is smarter than any dog we've ever had.

8. Audie Murphy received more decorations than any soldier in World War II.

9. Queen Victoria had a longer reign than any British monarch.

10. The durability of steel is greater than aluminum.

Using Specific Adjectives

The following sentence makes a statement that is certainly not very striking.

A house stood on the hill.

Adjectives can add details and interest to an otherwise bare and lifeless sentence.

A *sinister, old* house stood on the *barren* hill.

A *small, white* house stood on the *grassy* hill.

A *tumbledown, little* house stood on the *rocky* hill.

To be effective, adjectives should add clear and exact detail to the nouns they modify. Some adjectives, however, are used so often and so automatically that they have lost their force.

Overworked adjectives fall into three main groups—vague, all-purpose adjectives; too-popular adjectives; and clichés.

Vague, all-purpose adjectives are so general that they offer readers and listeners little that is specific or truly descriptive.

This book is *good*.

The weather was *nice*.

The homework assignment was *bad*.

411

The preceding statements on page 411 would be clearer and more meaningful if they did not rely on such tired, all-purpose adjectives. The sentences are improved by rewriting them in the following way.

This book is *fast-moving, suspenseful,* and *well plotted.*

The weather was *brisk, sunny,* and *cold.*

The homework assignment was *long, tedious,* and *confusing.*

Too-popular adjectives are so overused they have lost their effectiveness. The field of advertising has helped overwork a large group of words, such as *fabulous, fantastic, spectacular, sensational, terrific, incredible,* and *spellbinding.* Overuse has drawn these words away from their original meanings, and many are now merely fancy, overused synonyms for words like *good* or *bad* or *interesting.* Something *fabulous,* for instance, is something from myth or fable, or something astounding. A fire-breathing dragon may be fabulous; the Taj Mahal may be fabulous; but hamburgers and T-shirts are not fabulous, no matter how desirable they may be.

Similarly, there are adjectives that become so popular they dominate many speakers' conversations for a few months or years and then disappear. A few years later these adjectives, usually favorite slang terms, sound dated and silly. The following adjectives from past decades are such terms.

1920s:	He's a *bully* fellow.	She's a *grand* girl.
1930s:	He's a *square* fellow.	She's an *all-right* girl.
1940s:	He's a *reet* fellow.	She's a *zooly* girl.
1950s:	He's a *cool* fellow.	She's a *neat* girl.
1960s:	He's an *outa-sight* fellow.	She's a *tough* girl.
1970s:	He's a *bad* fellow.	She's a *mean* girl.

Phrases such as these are used repeatedly and eventually become trite, hackneyed phrases, or *clichés.* Many clichés involve adjectives linked with nouns in a combination you have heard or read many times. If such a tired and expected adjective should creep into your writing, replace it with one that is not overused. The following are examples of clichés:

The *majestic* mountains rose to *dizzying* heights.

This soap will give you a *dazzling* wash with *lightning* speed.

The *fiery* redness of the setting sun was a *breathtaking* sight.

Sometimes an adjective that has become a cliché in a phrase can be replaced by another adjective. Other times, however, it is better to recast the sentence and use different parts of speech to express the descriptive details.

Cliché: The *kingly* lion snored in its cage.

Improved: The lion slept in its cage like an old monarch, lost in his dreams and snores.

Improved: Even as the lion snored in its cage, it seemed regal.

Exercise 7: Using Specific, Vivid Adjectives

Each of the following sentences relies on a vague and overused adjective. Rewrite the sentences, replacing each *italicized* adjective with two or three specific, vivid ones. You may need to make other slight changes in the sentences.

Examples

a. The soup was *awful*.
   The soup was cold, lumpy, and greasy.

b. Our coach is *nice*.
   Our coach is fair and patient.

1. The movie was *good*.

2. The storm was *bad*.

3. Those shoes are *nice*.

4. My dog is *great*.

5. My car is *awful*.

6. You look *fine*.

7. The sandwiches were *delicious*.

8. The night was *beautiful*.

9. The hike was *unpleasant*.

10. The play was *terrible*.

Review: Using Adjectives

Some of the sentences on the next page contain incorrect adjectives that are part of an unclear or illogical statement. Revise and improve these sentences. If a sentence is correct, write *C* beside its number.

Examples

    a. The day was more hotter than we had expected.
       The day was hotter than we had expected.

    b. The intelligence of the dolphin is greater than that of the shark.
       C

1. Our chances in this game now look gooder than they did at the half.

2. Clarence is the tallest of the two boys.

3. Clarence is the tallest of the three boys.

4. I never felt more embarrasseder in my life.

5. The taste of sugar is far sweeter than honey.

6. Shelly is a higher scorer than anyone on her Monday-night bowling team.

7. Emily Brontë may have been the more talented of the three gifted Brontë sisters.

8. That movie has to be absolutely the most worst movie ever made.

9. Which of the two moons of Mars is more larger?

10. After two hours of horseback riding, I didn't know which part of my body was sorer.

11. Writing a short story is harder than a poem.

12. The last skit in the show was the funniest of them all.

13. Which of those three cities has the lesser air pollution?

14. Not only did he not apologize, but also he didn't seem the leastest bit sorry.

15. This small, battered coin is valuabler than that large, gleaming gold one.

16. Many people have one foot that is slightly larger than the other.

17. The salary of the supervisor is higher than the cook.

18. Our tire went flat, but what was more bad, our trusty spare was flat too.

19. Chuck has the deeper voice of anyone in choir.

20. Chuck has the deeper voice of the two soloists.

Writing Focus: *Using Specific Adjectives in Writing*

Specific adjectives can give your writing life, color, and feeling by adding sensory details of sight, smell, sound, taste, and touch. Too many adjectives as well as overused ones such as *pretty, great,* or *nice,* can overwhelm or deaden your writing, however. Strive to use precise adjectives that will make your writing more effective.

Assignment: *Time Passes*

Notice the two photographs on pages 416 and 417, each showing the same scene but taken many years apart. How do the scenes compare? What things have stayed the same? What things are different? How might someone living in the area feel about the changes?

Think about the preceding questions, and write one or more paragraphs comparing the two scenes in the photographs. Describe both scenes by comparing and contrasting details that show their similarities and differences. Write as though you are telling a person who moved away about the changes in the area. Your writing will be evaluated for correct and effective use of adjectives. Use the steps on the following pages to complete this assignment.

A. Prewriting

Divide a piece of paper into two columns: *old view* and *new view*. In the old view column, list what you see in the photograph in as much detail as you can. You might start in one corner of the picture and move around it in an orderly fashion. Adjacent to each point in the first column, write comments in the *new view* column about the similarities and differences you observe. Go back over your lists, underlining the key points or ideas that best compare the two scenes. Decide on an effective order for your information. You might discuss points about one scene first, then discuss the same points about the other scene. Or you might discuss both scenes together under main ideas like houses, roads, or landscape.

B. Writing

Write one or more paragraphs comparing the two scenes in the photographs. Use your prewriting lists to help you. Remember that if

you discuss a point about the scene in the older photograph, you must discuss the same point about the scene in the newer one. Compare and contrast both the similarities and differences of the two scenes, using specific adjectives to provide details.

C. Postwriting

Revise your first draft using the following checklist.

1. Have I compared and contrasted the two scenes using details that show their similarities and differences?

2. Have I used fresh, specific adjectives?

Edit your work using the Proofreader's Checklist at the back of the book. If appropriate, share your writing with your classmates and teacher and discuss specific areas in your community that have undergone similar changes.

13 Adverbs

Understanding Adverbs

Adverbs, like adjectives, are words that modify. They add details to your writing, thus making it more specific and interesting. You can recognize adverbs through their definition, their division into classes, and the features that separate them from other parts of speech.

Defining Adverbs

An *adverb* is usually defined as a word that modifies a verb, an adjective, or another adverb.

Modifying a verb:	Marissa left *early* so she could practice *longer*.
	The doves cooed *mournfully*.
Modifying an adjective:	The fog was *unusually* thick.
	Duane is an *exceptionally* talented singer.
Modifying an adverb:	He behaved *very* cleverly.
	Almost miraculously, the accident was avoided.

Adverbs supply details of time, place, and manner by answering the questions *how? how often? when? where?* and *to what extent?*

How:	The sun glared *mercilessly*.
How often:	Do tulips bloom *annually?*
When:	Sherry will arrive *tomorrow*.
Where:	The cat strolled *outside*.
To what extent:	The fan ran *too* noisily.

Exercise 1: *Identifying Adverbs*

Write the following sentences, underlining each adverb. Then draw an arrow from each adverb to the word it modifies. (Be prepared to tell if the adverb modifies a verb, an adjective, or another adverb. You should also be able to tell what question the adverb answers.)

Examples

a. The documents were completely destroyed in the fire.

The documents were <u>completely</u> destroyed in the fire.

b. The landlord is here now.

The landlord is <u>here</u> <u>now</u>.

1. The mothers very proudly discussed their children.

2. The sweater that Calvin bought yesterday is dark blue.

3. The scientists excitedly discussed a completely new transportation system.

4. The two sisters seldom see each other, but they write often and frequently talk on the phone.

5. The very active baby completely destroyed her new toy.

6. The politician earnestly promised an improved tax structure.

7. Was the sun terribly strong yesterday?

8. Denise decisively returned her opponent's serve.

9. I nearly forgot to pack my light beige shoes.

10. The irate customer quickly turned and walked out of the store.

Grouping Adverbs by Classes

Not all adverbs easily fall into classes or groups. Adverbs such as *sometimes, suddenly, eagerly, quickly,* and *happily* conform to the definition of an adverb but cannot be grouped into a special class. There are, however, four classes of adverbs: (1) interrogative adverbs, (2) affirmative and negative adverbs, (3) intensifiers, and (4) nouns used as adverbs. Recognizing these four classes will help you identify the words as adverbs.

Adverbs used to ask questions are called *interrogative adverbs.*

Where is the ball game being played?

When will you call?

How do you winterize a car?

Why don't planets twinkle as stars do?

The interrogative adverbs are *where, when, how, why,* and the less common *whence* and *whither.* These adverbs may be used in asking direct questions: *Where are the pliers?* They may also be used to introduce indirect questions within a sentence: *I don't know where the pliers are.* They are also used alone from time to time: *Jerry wanted to fix his radio, but he didn't know how.*

A small group of adverbs is called the *affirmative and negative adverbs.* The only affirmative adverb, the word *yes,* frequently occurs as an independent element in a sentence.

Yes, I saw that movie.

The most common negative adverbs are the words *no* and *not.*

No, we will *not* go.

That plant is *not* ragweed.

The word *not* often appears as the contraction *n't (will not = won't).* Sometimes you must add the helping verb *do* when using the word *not.*

Truman wants a puppy.

Truman does *not* want a puppy.

Note: *No* is used more often as an adjective than as an adverb. To distinguish the adverb *no* from the adjective *no,* look at the word that it modifies. Adverbs modify verbs, adjectives, and other adverbs. Adjectives modify nouns and pronouns.

No, I did not hear that.   [adverb]

I will wait *no* longer.   [adverb]

That is *no* reason to cry.   [adjective]

No citizen should neglect the duty of voting.   [adjective]

Intensifiers (adverbs that answer the question *to what extent?*) can modify both adjectives and adverbs. Intensifiers always come directly in front of the words they modify. Some common intensifiers are *very, too, complete, quite, rather, somewhat, unusually, extremely, totally,* and *so.*

I am *totally* confused!

Our house is *rather* small.   [modifying adjectives]

Ivan drove *extremely* carefully.

Marlene amazed everyone by singing   [modifying adverbs]

so beautifully.

An asterisk (*) denotes a feature that is not a part of Edited Standard English.

Note: Unlike other adverbs, intensifiers can modify adverbs and adjectives but not always verbs. The following statement, for instance, is incomplete.

   *We fought very!

Sometimes, nouns—especially those naming a time or a place—are used as adverbs. Some pronouns may also act as adverbs.

We went *home.*

We can't go *either.*

Exercise 2: *Identifying Adverbs and Adverb Classes*

Each of the quotations on the next page contains one or more adverbs. Write the quotations, underlining all adverbs. If an adverb belongs to a special class (interrogative adverbs, affirmative and negative adverbs, intensifiers, nouns used as adverbs), indicate the class beneath the quotation.

Example

a. You can always tell a real friend: when you've made a fool of yourself, he does not make you feel that you've done a permanent job.

You can always tell a real friend: when you've made a fool of yourself, he does not make you feel that you've done a permanent job.

not = negative

1. When I want to understand what is happening today or try to decide what will happen tomorrow, I look back.

—Oliver Wendell Holmes, Jr.

2. A little credulity helps one on through life very smoothly.

—Elizabeth Cleghorn Gaskell

3. I won't think about it today. I'll think about it tomorrow when I can stand it.

—Margaret Mitchell

4. Tomorrow we again embark upon the boundless sea.

—Horace

5. No great man is ever born too soon or too late.

—Norman Douglas

6. Then they will realize that we Indians know the One true God, and that we pray to Him continually.

—Black Elk

7. How do I love thee? Let me count the ways.

—Elizabeth Barrett Browning

8. Old soldiers never die;
They only fade away!

—British Army song

9. People often grudge others what they cannot enjoy themselves.

—Aesop

10. We often despise what is most useful to us.

—Aesop

Finding an Adverb by Its Features

Two features—degrees of comparison and suffixes—help to distinguish adverbs from other parts of speech.

Adverbs may change forms to show degrees of comparison.

Most one-syllable adverbs add -er for the comparative form and -est for the superlative form.

Positive	Comparative	Superlative
early	earlier	earliest
fast	faster	fastest
hard	harder	hardest
late	later	latest
long	longer	longest
near	nearer	nearest
quick	quicker	quickest
slow	slower	slowest
soon	sooner	soonest

Most other adverbs, however, show degrees of comparison by adding *more* and *most* or *less* and *least*.

Positive	Comparative	Superlative
rudely	*more* rudely	*most* rudely
proudly	*more* proudly	*most* proudly
desperately	*more* desperately	*most* desperately
economically	*less* economically	*least* economically
likely	*less* likely	*least* likely
popularly	*less* popularly	*least* popularly

Adverbs may be formed with suffixes.

Many adverbs end in the suffix -ly. Such adverbs are frequently formed by adding -ly to an adjective, as illustrated in the examples on the following page.

neat—*neatly*   impatient—*impatiently*
happy—*happily*   courageous—*courageously*

Other adverb suffixes are *-ward*, *-ways*, and *-wise*.

Exercise 3: *Identifying Adverbs and the Words They Modify*

Write the following sentences, underlining the adverbs. Then draw an arrow from each adverb to the word it modifies. (Be prepared to explain how you identified each adverb.)

Example

a. Is it fairly common that storms arise so quickly?

Is it fairly common that storms arise so quickly?

1. Why do some people recall their dreams more easily than others?

2. Yesterday I worked so hard that last night I fell asleep instantly on the couch.

3. That bus leaves earlier than the train, but the train arrives sooner.

4. I frequently transfer my day's worries into my dreams, so I toss constantly all night.

5. Our air conditioner works best when the humidity is low; when the humidity is high, the air conditioner works only moderately well.

6. Janice plays tennis better than I do, but she doesn't mind playing with me.

7. Clarissa, who has a fairly even disposition, became extremely angry when the salesperson treated her so rudely.

8. Kevin studied more diligently than anyone else in our class, so he confidently entered the exam room and finished the test more quickly than I did.

9. Moose are rarely seen in New York State, but yesterday a very large brown moose marched assuredly across the New York Thruway.

10. Yes, that remark is certainly true. Ian absolutely travels the most often of anyone in the family.

Review: Understanding Adverbs

Write the sentences on this page and the next, underlining all adverbs. Then draw an arrow from each adverb to the word or words it modifies.

Examples

a. Recently astronomers have discovered some extremely puzzling phenomena.

Recently astronomers have discovered some extremely puzzling phenomena.

b. Even today, we are not certain about the nature of these discoveries.

Even today, we are not certain about the nature of these discoveries.

1. Neutron stars are large stars that have apparently collapsed.

2. These collapsed stars are incredibly dense and quite small.

3. Neutron stars, sometimes called *white dwarf stars,* can rotate very rapidly.

4. A swiftly spinning neutron star regularly emits radiation.

5. Such stars, constantly sending out radioactive signals, are now called *pulsars.*

6. Only very small stars could rotate so rapidly and not fly apart.

7. More mysterious than the pulsars are the newly discovered ''black holes.''

8. A black hole is still smaller and even denser than a neutron star.

9. Scientists presently believe black holes are the result of the collapse of really large stars.

10. Einstein predicted black holes years ago, but they have only recently been detected.

11. Most simply, the large star is so compressed that its gravity becomes exceptionally strong.

12. So great is the pull of gravity that light cannot escape it.

13. The star simply seems to disappear forever.

14. Still, scientists believe it exists, although it is permanently invisible.

425

15. Its gravity may be one of the most powerfully strong forces in the universe.

16. Absolutely invisible, but unbelievably powerful, the black hole is a scientific puzzle.

17. What would happen to an object drawn directly inside a black hole's force?

18. Scientists certainly won't learn the answer quickly.

19. We will never be able actually to see inside a black hole.

20. When will we ever know what happens to something once it is caught in the force of a black hole?

Applying What You Know

In the following paragraphs from Richard Connell's story "The Most Dangerous Game," there are more than twenty adverbs. (The first two are underlined for you.) Using what you have learned in the previous sections, identify at least twenty adverbs and list them on a sheet of paper in the order in which they appear.

He lifted the knocker, and it creaked up stiffly, as if it had never before been used. He let it fall, and it startled him with its booming loudness. He thought he heard steps within; the door remained closed. Again Rainsford lifted the heavy knocker, and let it fall. The door opened then, opened as suddenly as if it were on a spring, and Rainsford stood blinking in the river of glaring gold light that poured out. The first thing Rainsford's eyes discerned was the largest man Rainsford had ever seen—a gigantic creature, solidly made and black-bearded to the waist. In his hand the man held a long-barreled revolver, and he was pointing it straight at Rainsford's heart.

Out of the snarl of beard two small eyes regarded Rainsford.

"Don't be alarmed," said Rainsford, with a smile which he hoped was disarming. "I'm no robber. I fell off a yacht. My name is Sanger Rainsford of New York City."

The menacing look in his eyes did not change. The revolver pointed as rigidly as if the giant were a statue. He gave no sign that he understood Rainsford's words, or that he had even heard them. He was dressed in uniform, a black uniform trimmed with gray astrakhan.

"I'm Sanger Rainsford of New York," Rainsford began again. "I fell off a yacht. I am hungry."

The man's only answer was to raise with his thumb the hammer of his revolver. Then Rainsford saw the man's free hand go to his forehead in a military salute, and he saw him click his heels together and stand at attention. Another man was coming down the broad marble steps, an erect, slender man in evening clothes. He advanced to Rainsford and held out his hand.

In a cultivated voice marked by a slight accent that gave it added precision and deliberateness, he said: "It is a very great pleasure and honor to welcome Mr. Sanger Rainsford, the celebrated hunter, to my home."

Automatically Rainsford shook the man's hand.

"I've read your book about hunting snow leopards in Tibet, you see," explained the man. "I am General Zaroff."

Rainsford's first impression was that the man was singularly handsome; his second was that there was an original, almost bizarre quality about the general's face. He was a tall man past middle age, for his hair was a vivid white; but his thick eyebrows and pointed military mustache were as black as the night from which Rainsford had come.[1]

Using Adverbs

In the following sections you will practice using the different forms of adverbs, learn to distinguish between easily confused adjectives and adverbs, and learn to avoid double negatives. As you work through the sections, refer back to Understanding Adverbs for any help you may need in identifying adverbs.

Using the Comparative and Superlative Forms

Form the comparative and superlative degrees of some one-syllable adverbs by adding *-er* and *-est*.

Positive	Comparative	Superlative
soon	*sooner*	*soonest*
late	*later*	*latest*

Form the comparative and superlative degrees of adverbs ending in *-ly* by adding *more* and *most* or *less* and *least*.

[1]From "The Most Dangerous Game" by Richard Connell. Copyright 1924 by Richard Connell; copyright renewed 1952 by Louise Fox Connell. Reprinted by permission of Brandt & Brandt Literary Agents, Inc.

Positive	Comparative	Superlative
swiftly	*more* swiftly	*most* swiftly
fortunately	*less* fortunately	*least* fortunately

Form the comparatives and superlatives of some adverbs in an irregular fashion.

Positive	Comparative	Superlative
badly/ill	*worse*	*worst*
far	*farther/further*	*farthest/furthest*
little	*less*	*least*
much	*more*	*most*
well	*better*	*best*

The comparative degree of the adverb is used when comparing two things.

> A hawk can see *better* than an owl.

> Sara swims *less often* this year than last year.

The superlative degree is used when comparing more than two.

> The batter who hits *most consistently* of anyone else on the team is Gomez.

> The one who sings *best* in the choir will be given the solo.

When using the comparative and superlative forms of adverbs, you should avoid the following errors:

Do not add *-er* or *-est* to irregular forms.

> *This engine acts worser than it did yesterday.

> This engine acts *worse* than it did yesterday.

> *He ran lastest in the race.

> He ran *last* in the race.

Similarly, do not add *more* or *most* to adverbs that use *-er* or *-est* in their comparative and superlative forms. Avoid this double comparison.

*They arrived more sooner than we had expected.

They arrived *sooner* than we had expected.

*Roberto scored most earliest in the game.

Roberto scored *earliest* in the game.

Exercise 4: *Using the Comparative and Superlative Forms of Adverbs*

Write the following sentences, supplying the correct forms of the adverbs indicated in parentheses. Underline the adverbs you supply.

Example

a. I don't exercise much; I should try to do so _____. (often)

I don't exercise much; I should try to do so more often.

1. The team wasn't playing well at the start of the new season, but they're doing _____ now. (well)

2. I came late, and Morrey came later still, but Gina came _____ of all. (late)

3. The horse behaved somewhat badly this morning, and unfortunately it is acting even _____ now. (badly)

4. This band sounded terrible last week, but surprisingly it's playing a bit _____ this time. (well)

5. Of all the sports, Leia enjoys basketball _____. (little)

6. The rabbit jumped _____ than the cat did. (high)

7. The snow was high everywhere but drifted _____ of all against the garage door. (deeply)

8. The fans cheered _____ when Sugar Ray Leonard stepped into the ring than they had cheered earlier. (loudly)

9. The information that arrives _____ of all is the information we will have to use. (soon)

10. Malcolm can run the mile race _____ than Scott. (fast)

Choosing Between Adjectives and Adverbs

Most adjectives and adverbs offer little difficulty to speakers and writers. Three pairs of words, however, create some confusion: *bad* and *badly*, *good* and *well*, and *slow* and *slowly*.

The following rule will help you distinguish in general whether an adjective or an adverb should be used.

Use an adverb to modify a verb, an adjective, or another adverb; use an adjective to modify a noun or pronoun. (Remember that a word following a linking verb and modifying the subject of a sentence must be an adjective.)

The man looked *slyly* at the money.
[adverb following an action verb, telling in what manner]

The man looked *sly*.
[adjective following a linking verb, describing the subject *man*]

Bad/Badly

Bad, an adjective, is often used after linking verbs (such as *be, become, seem, feel,* and *taste*). *Badly*, in Edited Standard English, is always an adverb that is used to modify action verbs, adjectives, and other adverbs.

I had a *bad* headache.	[adjective]
My head was aching *badly*.	[adverb]
This apple is *bad*.	[adjective]
The apples had rotted *badly*.	[adverb]

Good/Well

Good, an adjective, is used to modify a noun or pronoun, not a verb.

He makes *good* soup.

These tacos taste *good!*

Well can be used as either an adjective or an adverb. *Well* can follow a linking verb and can be used as an adjective to express different meanings.

Well can be used as an adjective meaning "in good health."

The sick chicken is now *well*.

Linda feels *well* again.

Well can be used as an adjective meaning "in a good or satisfactory state."

It is *well* that we've had such good weather.

Well can be used as an adjective meaning "nicely dressed or groomed."

You look *well* in that color.

Joe looks *well* with his mustache.

The adverb *well* means "satisfactorily" or "in a pleasing or capable manner." When it modifies an action verb, *well* tells how an action was performed.

The team played *well* in the tournament.

Tina does *well* in math.

Slow/Slowly

Slow is an adjective used to modify nouns or pronouns.

The train is *slow* tonight.

A *slow* walk is relaxing.

Slowly, **an adverb, is used to modify an action verb, an adjective, or another adverb.**

Judd speaks *slowly* when he wants to make his point.

The *slowly* rising tide became rough.

Note the comparative forms of *slow* and *slowly:*

Positive	Comparative	Superlative
slow	*slower*	*slowest*
slowly	*more* slowly	*most* slowly

Note: The word *slow* is sometimes used as an adverb following the verbs *drive* or *go,* as on traffic signs.

Exercise 5: Choosing Between Adjectives and Adverbs

Write the following sentences, selecting the correct word from the words in parentheses. Underline the words you choose.

Example

a. The team played (good, well).
The team played well.

1. The car was working (good, well) when we left, but after about an hour the engine began to knock (bad, badly).

2. Jennie is (good, well) at science, and her sister does (good, well) in art.

3. Larry didn't go to varsity swimming practice because his knee hurt (bad, badly).

4. I thought I knew how to take pictures (good, well), but all my snapshots were (bad, badly).

5. The time went so (slow, slowly) that I couldn't concentrate very (good, well).

6. Although this work season is (slow, slowly), we all are feeling (good, well).

7. The milk still tasted (good, well), but the homemade ice cream didn't freeze (good, well) enough.

8. Soon the patient was (good, well) enough to walk (slow, slowly) through the halls.

9. The bloodhounds were able to smell (good, well), and they immediately knew that the air didn't smell (good, well).

10. The acting in the play was rather (bad, badly), but the musical numbers were done (good, well).

Avoiding Double Negatives

When two negative words are used where only one is necessary, the construction is called a *double negative*. Double negatives are not a feature of Edited Standard English, as indicated by the asterisk (*).

*I didn't do nothing.

I *didn't* do anything. [or] I did *nothing*.

*I don't have none.

I *don't* have any. [or] I have *none*.

Do not use the adverb *not* with *hardly, scarcely, no, nothing, none*, and in some cases *but* and *only* to make a single negative statement.

---

*I don't hardly ever go to the movies.

I *hardly ever* go to the movies.

I *don't usually* go to the movies.

Avoid double negatives when using the words *only* and *but* in a negative way, meaning "no more than."

---

*I don't have but three dollars.

I have *but* three dollars.

*I don't have only three dollars.

I have *only* three dollars.

Using Adverbs Clearly and Logically

Comparisons involving adverbs, like those involving adjectives, should be stated clearly and logically. It should be clear to the reader exactly what things are being compared.

I like lizards better than my brother. [unclear]

The statement above should be revised since it could mean two things:

I like lizards better than my brother does.
or
I like lizards better than I like my brother.

Consider another example:

I've known Laura longer than Carl.	[unclear]
I've known Laura longer than Carl has.	[clear]
I've known Laura longer than I've known Carl.	[clear]

Include the word *else* or *other* when comparing one member of a group to the other members of the group.

Sarah Bernhardt acted more brilliantly than any actress of her time. [illogical]

The preceding statement is not logical. Since Sarah Bernhardt was an actress of her time, the statement asserts that she acted better than herself—which is illogical. Such statements can usually be revised by adding the word *other* or *else*.

Sarah Bernhardt acted more brilliantly than any other actress of her time.

Exercise 6: Correcting Unclear or Illogical Adverbs and Double Negatives

The sentences on the following page use adverbs in unclear or illogical ways or contain double negatives. Write the sentences, revising them so that they conform to Edited Standard English.

Example

a. I hate fried liver more than my sister.
   I hate fried liver more than my sister does.

1. I take care of my sister more often than my brother.

2. Forty-nine-year-old "George" the gander lived longer than any goose in history.

3. I don't have no need to study English.

4. She doesn't have hardly any of her allowance left.

5. I talked to Jerry longer than Luis.

6. Elaine studies harder than anybody in her class.

7. I don't have only enough money to see one movie.

8. Birds eat more insects than frogs.

9. It was a beautiful Saturday night, but they didn't have nothing to do.

10. I like spinach better than you.

Review: Using Adverbs

Some of the sentences below and on the next page contain adverbs used inappropriately. Rewrite these sentences to eliminate the errors. If a sentence is correct, write *C*.

Example

a. We had to hike more farther than we thought.
   We had to hike farther than we thought.

1. Which of the two stores is more nearer?

2. Of all the buses, that one is the slower.

3. I played more badly today than I did yesterday.

4. I never thought no cookout could be as bad as our first one.

5. The dog eats more slow than the cat.

6. Which of the two skaters practices most often?

7. The new school bells ring more loud than the old ones.

8. I think that of all recording stars, Ray Charles sings most well.

9. Which of the twins studies most?

10. The cat moved slow to the fireplace, curled up, and fell asleep.

11. Jan's essay was the best written of the two.

12. It seemed that Max didn't never feel good.

13. Gretchen never pitched more well in no game before.

14. Can't you speak slower?

15. One of the twin cities is slightly larger than the other.

Writing Focus: *Using Exact Adverbs in Writing*

Effective use of adverbs in writing produces clarity and order. Adverbs such as *early, outside,* and *wisely* show details relating to time, place, and manner. Exact adverbs also help clarify and connect ideas.

Assignment: *Consequences*

As you read the following passage, notice how the adverbs (printed in **boldface**) emphasize the connections between statements.

> **Supposedly,** threatened species of whales were protected by regulations of the International Whaling Commission. What **actually** happened was that the regulations were **not** strict **enough. Consequently,** almost 40,000 whales were hunted and killed in 1971. Laws are **now** tighter, but violation of them is still frequent. **Indeed,** several countries have **not** complied with the regulations. Threatened whales will **obviously** become extinct if the regulations continue to be ignored.

For this assignment, think of a school regulation or rule you believe students should comply with. Write one or more paragraphs explaining why you think the rule is important and telling what consequences result when it is ignored. Use the passage above as a model, and include specific details to support your reasons. Write for your classmates. Your work will be evaluated for correct use of adverbs.

Use the following steps to complete this assignment.

A. Prewriting

Make a list of five school regulations you think are important. Choose one to write about that seems most important. At the top of a sheet of

paper, write down the rule clearly and precisely. Under the rule, make a list of at least three reasons why you think students should comply with the rule. Then add any consequences resulting if the rule is ignored. Read over your list and number your reasons and consequences from least to most important.

B. Writing

Using your list, write one or more paragraphs explaining why you think a particular school regulation is necessary. Clearly state in a topic sentence the rule and your position concerning it. Then support your statement with reasons and consequences. Use adverbs like *accordingly, also, besides, first, second, mainly, previously,* and *primarily* to help you connect and show relationships between your ideas and statements.

C. Postwriting

Use the following checklist to revise your first draft.

1. Have I clearly stated the rule and my opinion concerning it in a topic sentence?

2. Have I supported my opinion with convincing reasons and consequences?

3. Have I used exact adverbs to describe, organize, and clarify ideas?

Use the Proofreader's Checklist at the back of the book to edit your work. If appropriate, share your writing with your classmates.

14 Prepositions
Understanding Prepositions

Prepositions help words work together in sentences by showing relationships among words. Learning the definition of prepositions and recognizing their role in a sentence are two ways to begin your study of this part of speech.

Defining Prepositions

A *preposition* is usually defined as a word that shows a relationship between a noun or pronoun and another word or words in the sentence.

Notice, in the following examples, how the prepositions show different relationships.

The bird flew *into* the tree. The bird flew *over* the tree.
The bird flew *near* the tree. The bird flew *under* the tree.

In each of the preceding sentences, the preposition shows the relationship between the noun *tree* and the verb *flew* by indicating where the bird flew in relation to the tree: *into* it, *near* it, *over* it, or *under* it.

Since a preposition connects words, it never appears alone; instead, it is always part of a prepositional phrase.

A *prepositional phrase* consists of the preposition (*P*), its object (*O*), and any modifiers (*M*) the object may have.

In the following examples the prepositional phrases are *italicized* and the parts labeled.

        P   O
The story was *beyond belief.*

    P   M   M   O
We ran *out the back door.*

        P   M   M   O
The monster's mouth was filled *with long, gleaming fangs.*

Sometimes a preposition has a compound object, as in the following prepositional phrases.

$$\text{The library will remain closed } \underset{\text{P}}{during} \text{ the } \underset{\text{O}}{winter} \text{ and } \underset{\text{O}}{spring}.$$

The library will remain closed *during the winter and spring*.

We wrote a letter *to Joel, Barry, and Corinne*.

Sometimes the object of a preposition is a group of words.

I will vote *for whichever candidate has the best tax proposal*.

The following list is of the most common one-word prepositions.

about	beside	inside	throughout
above	besides	into	till
across	between	like	to
after	beyond	near	toward
against	but [*meaning*	of	under
along	except]	off	underneath
amid	by	on	until
among	concerning	onto	unto
around	down	out	up
at	during	outside	upon
before	except	over	with
behind	for	past	within
below	from	since	without
beneath	in	through	

Compound prepositions are those consisting of more than one word.

according to	by way of	on account of
along with	in addition to	out of
aside from	in front of	prior to
because of	in spite of	together with
by means of	instead of	with respect to

Exercise 1: *Identifying Prepositional Phrases*

Write the sentences from the following page, underlining all prepositional phrases. Write *P* above the prepositions and *O* above the objects. Remember that a preposition can have more than one object.

Example

---

a. The view from the mountaintop was awesome.

$$\text{The view } \underset{\text{P}}{from} \text{ the } \underset{\text{O}}{mountaintop} \text{ was awesome.}$$

1. A popular tune by a famous country-and-western singer boomed over the loudspeakers in the Nashville bus station.

2. A large knapsack of green khaki lay on the floor beside a weary youth.

3. Dressed in blue jeans and a plaid shirt, the youth sat on an orange plastic chair in the waiting room.

4. Across from him a patient father amused his small daughter with whimsical stories about the advertisements in a magazine.

5. Crowds gathered in neat lines by the ticket counter, where a smiling young man in a blue uniform worked steadily.

6. The loudspeaker crackled with static as the delay of the bus from Atlanta was announced.

7. Amid the confusion caused by the heavy holiday traffic, an angry woman argued with the ticket agent about her missing luggage.

8. Tired of the magazine and her father's stories, the young child climbed onto his lap and closed her eyes.

9. An attractive woman burdened with a briefcase and several packages wrapped in bright paper looked around the waiting room.

10. Spying the man with the sleeping child in his arms, the woman raised her arms in greeting and moved toward them.

Distinguishing Prepositions from Other Parts of Speech

Some prepositions can be used as other parts of speech.

The cat is *outside*.	[adverb]
The player ran *outside* the foul line.	[preposition]

If a word is used as a preposition, it must have an object. To determine if a word is an adverb or part of a prepositional phrase, determine its use in the sentence. An adverb modifies a verb, an adjective, or another adverb. The preposition in a prepositional phrase links its object to another word or words in the sentence.

Note: When *to* is followed by the plain form of a verb, it is considered part of an infinitive and is not considered a preposition: *to* dance, *to* play, *to* sing.

Exercise 2: *Identifying Prepositional Phrases*

Write the following passage, underlining the prepositional phrases. Then label the prepositions *P* and the objects *O*. (Be certain that a word is actually being used as a preposition and not as an adverb or as some other part of speech.)

Example

a. Muhammad Ali was sent to Africa on a mission by President Carter.

                                     P   O   P   O   P

Muhammad Ali was sent to Africa on a mission by

     O

President Carter.

(The following passage by Tom Brown, Jr., is a true story of a younger man trained in woodlore by an old Apache. The narrator has just met Rick, the old man's grandson, and the boys immediately have become friends.)

> After we had talked through half the afternoon, Rick took me home to meet his grandfather, a man who would be my teacher and guide for the next nine years. Stalking Wolf had come to New Jersey to be near his son, who lived there. I was in awe of him from the beginning. He was of medium height and lean, the grandson of a medicine man, and a tracker and hunter for his Apache band. To Rick and me he was the Spirit of the Woods.[1]

Review: *Understanding Prepositions*

In the following paragraphs from Dorothy Johnson's "Scars of Honor," there are more than twenty-five prepositional phrases, with the first one underlined. Use what you have learned in the preceding sections to identify at least twenty-five prepositional phrases, and list them on a sheet of paper.

> Charles Lockjaw died last summer on the reservation. He was very old—a hundred years, he had claimed. He still wore his hair in

---

[1]From *The Tracker: The Story of Tom Brown, Jr.,* as told to William Jon Watkins, as it appears in the *Reader's Digest*, November 1978. Copyright © 1978 by Tom Brown, Jr., and William Jon Watkins. Reprinted by permission of Prentice-Hall, Inc., and *Reader's Digest*.

braids, as only the older men do in his tribe, and the braids were thin and white. His fierce old face was like a withered apple. He was bent and frail and trembling, and his voice was like a wailing of the wind across the prairie grass.

Old Charley died in his sleep in the canvas-covered tepee where he lived in warm weather. In the winter he was crowded with the younger ones among his descendants in a two-room log cabin, but in summer they pitched the tepee. Sometimes they left him alone there, and sometimes his great-grandchildren scrambled in with him like a bunch of puppies.

His death was no surprise to anyone. What startled the Indian agent and some of Charley's own people, and the white ranchers when they heard about it, was the fact that some of the young men of the tribe sacrificed a horse on his grave. Charley wasn't buried on holy ground; he never went near the mission. He was buried in a grove of cottonwoods down by the creek that is named for a dead chief. His lame great-grandson, Joe Walking Wolf, and three other young Indians took this horse out there and shot it. It was a fine sorrel gelding, only seven years old, broke fairly gentle and nothing wrong with it. Young Joe had been offered eighty dollars for that horse.[1][underscore added]

Applying What You Know

From a science textbook or library book, select a passage containing at least ten prepositional phrases. Copy the passage and underline the prepositional phrases. If a single-word adverb or adjective could convey the same information, write the prepositional phrase and the substitute word at the bottom of your paper.

Using Prepositions

In the following sections you will practice using prepositions in a way that conforms to Edited Standard English. You will also learn about the correct placement of prepositional phrases.

Commonly Confused Prepositions

The following guidelines will help you use commonly confused prepositions in a way that conforms to Edited Standard English.

---

[1]From "Scars of Honor" by Dorothy M. Johnson. Copyright 1950; renewed © 1977 by Dorothy M. Johnson. First published in Argosy. Reprinted by permission of McIntosh and Otis, Inc.

Accept/Except

Accept **is a verb meaning "to receive or take possession of something."**

I *accept* this award with my usual great humility.

Except **is a preposition meaning "with the exception of" or "not including."**

Everyone voted on the issue *except* Mr. Jefferson.

Among/Between

Use *between* when referring to two people or things.

There are profound differences *between* the United States and the Soviet Union.

We need to keep this a secret *between* you and me.

Use *among* when referring to more than two people or things.

Competition *among* the players grew intense.

Keep this a secret *among* the three of us.

Use *between* when referring to the individual relationships between two items, even if the items are part of a larger group.

Weeds grew *between* the rows of corn.

The distance *between* the stars is great.

Beside/Besides

Beside **means "being next to."**

I was walking down the street with my dog *beside* me.

Erica sits *beside* me in chemistry class.

Besides means "in addition to" or "moreover."

> *Besides* turkey, there were also ham and chicken on the table.

In/Into

In means "already inside."

> The pearls are *in* the safe.

Into is used to indicate the act of entering or being put inside.

> We went *into* the kitchen to investigate the strange noise.

Past/Passed

Past can be used as an adjective, an adverb, or a preposition.

We talked over *past* times.	[adjective modifying *times*]
Did you see Harold when he drove *past*?	[adverb modifying *drove*]
The truck roared *past* us, honking loudly.	[preposition]

The word *past,* however, should not be used as a verb. The verb that it sounds like is correctly written *passed.*

> One of the linemen *passed* the ball to Mean Joe Green.

Exercise 3: Using Commonly Confused Prepositions

Write the sentences on the next page, choosing the correct word from the choices in parentheses. Underline the words you select.

Example

> a. The skiing competition will be most fierce (between, among) Germany and the USSR.

The skiing competition will be most fierce between Germany and the USSR.

1. I like all winter sports (accept, except) ice-skating.

2. We ran (in, into) the kitchen to check the stove.

3. No one liked the movie (accept, except) Darby.

4. Carrie continued studying for her final exams well (past, passed) midnight.

5. No one (beside, besides) Dana was late.

6. Please put the small folding table (beside, besides) the yellow sofa.

7. Those moles seem to live (in, into) our garden.

8. Are there any similarities (between, among) the Spanish and Portuguese languages?

9. Have you lived anywhere else (beside, besides) California?

10. There were constant arguments (between, among) the six convention delegates.

Problems in Preposition Usage

The following rules will help you avoid some common problems in using prepositions. Sometimes people use unnecessary prepositions or use one preposition when another is correct according to Edited Standard English.

Use either *about* or *at* with expressions of time, but not both.

An asterisk (*) denotes a sentence with a feature that is not part of Edited Standard English.

*We will arrive at about 9 o'clock.

We will arrive *at* 9 o'clock.

We will arrive *about* 9 o'clock.

Do not use *at* with *where*.

---

*Do you know where the movie is at?

Do you know *where* the movie is?

Do not use *by* to mean "with."

*That movie is all right by us.

That movie is all right *with* us.

Do not use *of* instead of the helping verb *have.*

*We could of won if we'd played better.

We could *have* won if we'd played better.

Use just the preposition *off,* not *off of.*

*The cat fell off of the bed.

The cat fell *off* the bed.

Do not use the word *on* with the verb *blame.* Use *blame* by itself.

*Who blamed it on me?

Who *blamed* me for it?

Do not use *to* as a replacement for *at.*

*I'll call when I arrive to the bus station.

I'll call when I arrive *at* the bus station.

Do not use *to* when it is unnecessary.

*Where are you going to?

Where are you going?

Do not use the preposition *than* with the word *different.* Use *from* instead.

*Your essay is different than mine.

Your essay is *different from* mine.

Do not use *with* when it is unnecessary.

*We visited with Ms. Sanders.

 We visited Ms. Sanders.

*We continued with our journey.

 We continued our journey.

*The students were issued with library passes.

 The students were issued library passes.

Exercise 4: Using Prepositions Correctly

Write each of the following sentences, changing prepositions to conform to Edited Standard English. (It might be necessary to reword a sentence slightly.) Underline any changes you make.

Example

>   a. If you want to live in Boston, it's all right by me.
>   If you want to live in Boston, it's all right <u>with</u> me.

1. Does anyone know where the fireworks are at?

2. I was so hungry I could of eaten a whole box of crackers.

3. All of the employees were issued with discount coupons.

4. If the flowerpots fell off of the balcony, don't blame it on me.

5. Downhill skiing is quite different than cross-country skiing.

6. The play should begin at about 8:30.

7. Please save us a seat when you arrive to the concert.

8. In what way is rayon different than nylon?

9. I can't remember where I put the keys at.

10. If I had a watch, I would of known what time it was.

Placement of Prepositional Phrases

Prepositional phrases can be used as adjectives to modify nouns or pronouns.

The spy *in the trenchcoat* approached.   [adjective]

447

Prepositional phrases also can be used as adverbs to modify verbs, adjectives, or other adverbs.

The spy approached *with caution*.   [modifying verb]

His heart was full *of apprehension*.   [modifying adjective]

He walked down *through the long alley*.   [modifying adverb]

Prepositional phrases should be placed so they clearly modify the appropriate words. The following newspaper advertisement shows the result of a poorly placed prepositional phrase.

Lost—Wristwatch by a lady with a cracked face.

The placement of a prepositional phrase can affect the meaning of a sentence.

The professor spoke to the students from Sweden.

The professor from Sweden spoke to the students.

If a prepositional phrase is used as an adjective, it is usually placed next to the noun or pronoun it modifies.

The woman *from France* took a boat *from Australia*.

With few errors, the paper was judged the best in class.

If a prepositional phrase is used as an adverb, it can sometimes be moved within a sentence without changing the meaning.

We will leave *in the morning*.

In the morning we will leave.

If a sentence contains more than one verb, be certain the prepositional phrase modifies the correct verb.

The car that we rented broke down *during the afternoon*.
[*During the afternoon* tells when the car broke down.]

The car that we rented *during the afternoon* broke down.
[*During the afternoon* modifies *rented*, telling when the car was rented.]

Exercise 5: Placing Prepositional Phrases

Some of the following sentences are unclear because the prepositional phrases are not well placed. Revise these sentences so that their meaning is clear. If a sentence is clear, write *C* after that number on your paper.

Example

a. The lion growled ferociously at the children in the cage.
   The lion in the cage growled ferociously at the children.

1. I bought a dress after parking the car in the new boutique.
2. We walked over the ocean for several miles to watch the sun set.
3. The dog loves to sleep on the blanket with a bushy tail.
4. The cat hid after chasing the visitor under the couch.
5. Have you ever noticed the bird in the tree with red wings?
6. The high winds during the hurricane damaged the house.
7. My friend with automatic transmission just bought a new car.
8. After an injury, Noelle couldn't play tennis on her wrist.
9. The children with spots enjoyed watching the cows.
10. After school Elyse and Clark worked on their science project.

Review: Using Prepositions

Each of the following sentences contains one or more prepositions that are not used according to Edited Standard English. Revise the sentences to correspond with standard usage.

Example

a. We should of followed the directions more closely.
   We should have followed the directions more closely.

1. I would of enjoyed my skiing trip more if I hadn't had to travel so far among the mountain and my cabin.
2. I'd be happier if someone else won the award beside me.
3. Our reporter visited with the woman just named mayor.

4. Between you, Steve, and me, we can come up with the money.

5. When the principal sent for us, we knew we were into trouble.

6. Igor, we shall continue with the experiment and create a monster different than the last one.

7. We past the accident at about 7 o'clock.

8. All the science students accept Ann were issued with new microscopes, which were quite different than the old ones.

9. I should of eaten something beside toast for breakfast.

10. If you had decided first where you were going to, you could of planned your trip better.

11. When you got besides their guard, you could have past the ball.

12. I shouldn't of excepted the invitation.

13. I ran in the kitchen and found the cat into the bowl of tuna salad.

14. The three delegates argued hotly between themselves.

15. After the storm past over, we continued our hike.

Writing Focus: *Using*

Prepositional Phrases in Writing

As a writer, you can use prepositional phrases to add details and information and to show relationships among words in sentences. Use prepositional phrases to make your writing clear and precise.

Assignment: *The Good Samaritan*

Imagine that you have just won $500 on a television game show. The money, however, must be donated to your favorite club, charity, or organization.

After you have decided who will receive the money, write one or more paragraphs explaining your choice to the television audience. Your writing will be evaluated for correct and effective use of prepositional phrases.

Use the steps on the next page to complete this assignment.

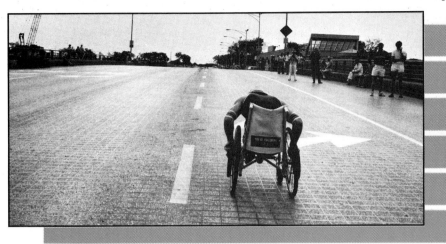

A. Prewriting

To help you decide who should receive the $500, first make a list of five or six possible recipients. Choose two that you most favor. List their names at the top of a sheet of paper. Under each name, list the many ways the organization could use the money. For example, an orphanage might buy needed supplies for children, or the Special Olympics might be able to send more people to participate in the games. To the list add your reasons for giving them the $500. Based on your list, decide which organization will receive the money.

B. Writing

Using your list, write one or more paragraphs explaining your decision to donate the $500 to a particular organization. Include at least three reasons for your choice. Also suggest possible ways the group can use the money. As you write, use prepositional phrases to add details.

C. Postwriting

Use the following checklist to revise your draft.

1. Does my writing clearly state my decision?

2. Have I provided at least three reasons for my choice?

3. Have I used prepositional phrases correctly to provide details and to show relationships?

Edit your work using the Proofreader's Checklist at the back of the book. If appropriate, share your writing with your classmates. Discuss with them the process you used in making your decision.

451

15 Conjunctions
Understanding Conjunctions

Like prepositions, conjunctions help to show the relationship between words or groups of words in a sentence. You can identify conjunctions by learning their definition and the classes into which they can be grouped.

Defining Conjunctions

A *conjunction* is usually defined as a word that connects other words or groups of words.

Conjunctions can connect words.

> Do you prefer apples *or* pears?

> The apples were old *but* good.

> Julio picked *and* ate some apples.

> That sheep dog is large *yet* gentle.

Conjunctions can connect phrases.

> The car backed out the driveway *and* into the street with rush hour traffic.

> Conjunctions can also connect sentences and clauses to make a complete thought.

> I like cats, *but* they make me sneeze.

> We can't go to the movies *until* the dishes are done *and* the table is cleared.

Exercise 1: Identifying Conjunctions

Write the following sentences, underlining all conjunctions. (Your teacher may ask you to explain what words or groups of words each conjunction connects.)

a. Is it quicker to walk on the path through the woods or around the lake?

Is it quicker to walk on the path through the woods or around the lake?

b. I like mangoes very much, but I have never tasted a papaya fruit.

I like mangoes very much, but I have never tasted a papaya fruit.

1. The plot of the story was confusing yet exciting.

2. Juanita walks to work every day, for she enjoys the exercise.

3. Neither Pluto nor Jupiter is visible without a telescope.

4. Sam and I would like to visit Japan and China next year.

5. King Tut's tomb was an exceptional find, for few Egyptian tombs have survived without being plundered for treasure.

6. Avocados are tasty but fattening!

7. The architect I. M. Lum has worked on buildings in both America and China.

8. Kim will not swim in the ocean, nor will she swim in my swimming pool.

9. I have searched the house and the car, but I still can't find my keys and my glasses.

10. Lake Tahoe is on the border of two states, so a visitor there can stay either in California or in Nevada.

Classifying Conjunctions

There are three kinds of conjunctions: *coordinating conjunctions, subordinating conjunctions,* and *correlative conjunctions.*

Coordinating conjunctions join elements of equal rank, such as two nouns (or a noun and a pronoun), two verbs, two phrases, or two independent clauses. The most common coordinating conjunctions are *and, but, or, nor, for,* and *yet.*

Coordinate elements should have *parallel structure*.

Ken bought a bicycle *and* roller skates.

Does the baby walk *or* talk yet?

The scissors are in the drawer *or* on the desk.

Karen visited Madrid, *but* she didn't go to Barcelona.

Exercise 2: Identifying Coordinating Conjunctions

On a sheet of paper, copy the following passage about Manhattan, underlining the ten coordinating conjunctions. The first one is done for you.

Images of confinement certainly haunt me in Manhattan but the first thing that always strikes me, when I land once more on the island, is its fearful and mysterious beauty. Other cities have built higher now, or sprawl more boisterously over their landscapes, but there is still nothing like the looming thicket of the Manhattan skyscrapers, jumbled and overbearing. Le Corbusier hated this ill-disciplined spectacle, and conceived his own Radiant City, an antiseptic hybrid of art and ideology, in direct antithesis to it. His ideas, though, mostly bounced off this vast mass of vanity. Tempered though it has been from time to time by zoning law and social trend, Manhattan remains a mammoth mess, a stupendous clashing of light and dark and illusory perspective, splotched here and there by wastelands of slum or demolition, wanly patterned by the grid of its street system, but essentially, whatever the improvers do to it, whatever economy decrees or architectural fashion advises, the supreme monument to that elemental human instinct, Free-For-All.[1]

Le Corbusier was a famous and influential French architect who helped design the United Nations headquarters in New York.

Subordinating conjunctions join unequal elements in a sentence.

---

after	before	till
although	if	unless
as if	in order that	whatever
as long as	provided	when
as much as	since	whenever
as soon as	so that	where
as though	than	wherever
because	though	while

---

[1]From *Destinations: Essays from Rolling Stone* by Jan Morris. © 1980 by Rolling Stone Press and Jan Morris. Reprinted by permission of Oxford University Press, Inc.

The subordinating conjunction may link a word or phrase to a main clause. (A *clause* is a group of words with a subject and a verb.)

> *When* angry, count ten before you speak, *if* very angry, a hundred.
>
> —Thomas Jefferson

The most common use of the subordinating conjunction, however, is to join two clauses.

We got our allowance *after* we swept and washed the floor.

I always listen to the radio *while* I am driving.

Because he likes to cook, Len opened a restaurant.

A clause beginning with a subordinating conjunction is always a dependent clause and must be joined to an independent clause.

Exercise 3: *Identifying Subordinating Conjunctions*

Write the following sentences, underlining the subordinating conjunctions you find.

Example

    a. Carlos didn't show his anger although he felt it boiling inside.

    Carlos didn't show his anger although he felt it boiling inside.

1. We wanted to go camping somewhere where there wouldn't be a lot of other people.

2. On our last camping trip it seemed as if half the city had come out to camp with us.

3. Wherever we stepped, there was litter or another camper.

4. When night came, we discovered that the people next to us had brought their portable television set.

5. It's hard to enjoy the wilderness while a rerun of *Gilligan's Island* is blaring in the background.

6. As soon as I got to sleep, I was awakened by someone screaming about a bear.

7. A neighboring camper was in a pine tree yelling because a bear had tried to get in his sleeping bag.

8. After we investigated the situation, we discovered the "bear" was only another camper's large poodle.

9. We then had to call the fire department, since the man wouldn't come down from the tree.

10. Next time we won't set up camp unless we are really in the wilderness.

Correlative conjunctions are used only in pairs.

---

both . . . and	not only . . . but also	as . . . as
either . . . or	whether . . . or	as . . . so
neither . . . nor		so . . . as

Neither Katy *nor* Kim knew which bus to take.

We don't know *whether* we should sell the car *or* get the motor repaired.

As the plane rolled over, *so* did my stomach.

Exercise 4: *Identifying Correlative Conjunctions*

Write the following sentences, underlining the correlative conjunctions that you find.

Example

---

a. Fred broke not only his collarbone but also his wrist and thumb.

Fred broke not only his collarbone but also his wrist and thumb.

---

1. Send either a check or money order to confirm your furniture purchase.

2. The streets were not only icy but also winding and full of high snow drifts.

3. John can play both flute and saxophone professionally as accompanist or soloist.

4. Do you know whether Stan's Inn or Harry's Hotel has any vacancies?

5. We don't know whether our dog was lost or stolen.

6. As a magnet draws iron filings, so a picnic lunch seems to draw ants.

7. Helen has not only a parrot but also two cockatiels and a toucan in her house.

8. We need either a new television set or a better antenna to get clearer reception.

9. Either Linda or Karen will call us when Sheila and Pam arrive at the museum.

10. People should visit the dentist regularly, whether they want to or not.

Review: *Understanding Conjunctions*

Write the following sayings, underlining all the conjunctions. Beneath each sentence write each conjunction and the class to which it belongs: coordinating, subordinating, or correlative. (Some sentences have more than one conjunction.)

Example

a. When the cat's away, the mice will play.
When the cat's away, the mice will play.

when—subordinating

1. I cannot be your friend and your flatterer, too.

2. When two play, one must lose.

3. There is nothing either good or bad but thinking makes it so.

4. As the twig is bent, so is the tree inclined.

5. While there's life, there's hope.

6. Don't count your chickens before they're hatched.

7. None are so blind as those who refuse to see.

8. If you have a bad name, you are half-hanged.

9. The thread will break where it is weakest.

10. Lock the stable door before the horse is stolen.

11. Nobody does as much work today as he is going to do tomorrow.

12.   As the worker is good or bad, so the work is.

13.   When we are out of sympathy with the young, our work in the world is over.

14.   People who eat until they are sick must fast until they are completely well.

15.   As a moth gnaws at a garment, so does envy consume those who are envious.

16.   If you fear to suffer, you will suffer from fear.

17.   People without hope need no enemies because they have defeated themselves.

18.   Sheep flock together, but eagles fly alone.

19.   A lie can go around the world while the truth is getting its britches on.

20.   Though malice may dim truth, it cannot put it out.

Applying What You Know

From a magazine, newspaper, or book, select a passage several paragraphs in length. Using what you have already learned in the previous sections, identify the conjunctions and list them on a separate sheet of paper. Beside each conjunction write the class to which it belongs.

Using Conjunctions

In the following sections you will learn how to use conjunctions in a way that conforms to Edited Standard English. As you work through the additional sections on conjunctions, use the preceding Understanding Conjunctions sections for any help you may need in identifying conjunctions.

Choosing the Right Conjunction

Conjunctions not only combine elements such as words, phrases, and clauses, but they also show relationships, as you can see in the following examples.

Marcia will go, *and* Anne will go, too.

Marcia will go, *but* Anne cannot.

Either Anne will go *or* Marcia will.

Neither Anne *nor* Marcia will go.

Anne went *because* Marcia could not.

Anne went *although* Marcia could not.

To use conjunctions effectively, you must be conscious of the differences among their meanings. Some writers tend to use *and* as an all-purpose conjunction.

I really wanted to go to the game, *and* there were no tickets left, *and* I stayed home.

Such a stringy sentence does not give the reader clear signals about the relationships among the statements. A good revision incorporates conjunctions that express the relationships more precisely.

I really wanted to go to the game, *but* there were no tickets left; *so* I stayed home.

Sometimes changing a weak conjunction means you have to change other parts of the sentence as well, perhaps even the order of clauses.

I wanted to see better, *and* I stood up.

I stood up *because* I wanted to see better.

Because I wanted to see better, I stood up.

Exercise 5: *Using Conjunctions Precisely*

Revise the sentences on the following page by replacing the vague conjunctions with ones that state the intended meanings more precisely. In some sentences you may have to change more than just the conjunction to make the sentence clear and tight. Remember to use commas where necessary.

Examples

a. One of Dinah's sisters is quite tall, and the other is shorter than average.
   One of Dinah's sisters is quite tall, but the other is shorter than average.

b. The dog was lonely, and it began to howl mournfully.
The dog was lonely, so it began to howl mournfully.
or
Because the dog was lonely, it began to howl mournfully.

1. The other team was favored to win, and we beat them.

2. We are putting a new floor in our attic, and we will have more storage space.

3. I would jingle the car keys, and the dog would always know that we were going for a ride.

4. Margo doesn't like physical exercise, and she signed up for tennis anyway.

5. Arlo wants to strengthen his shoulder muscles, and he is working with weights.

6. Most packaged food products contain sugar, and people get more sugar than they realize.

7. I spilled pepper on my sleeve, and I began sneezing.

8. I finished my homework, and David was just beginning.

9. We shop at that grocery store, and it has excellent bargains on Mondays.

10. This brand is cheaper, and it's a better product than many higher-priced items.

Conjunction Difficulties

The following information will help you avoid common problems in using conjunctions.

Faulty Parallelism

Sentence parts joined by coordinating or correlative conjunctions must be *parallel*: they must be similar in type, form, or structure. A sentence containing faulty parallels will be awkward.

An asterisk (*) denotes a sentence with a feature that is not part of Edited Standard English.

*The trip was *short* but an exciting *experience*. (adjective and noun—not parallel)

The trip was *short* but *exciting*. (two adjectives—parallel)

Learn to recognize faulty parallelisms by identifying the type, form, and structure of the sentence parts joined by a conjunction.

> *Many sports figures agree that *determination, desire* to win, and *to work* hard are necessary for success. (two nouns and an infinitive—not parallel)

> Many sports figures agree that *determination, desire* to win, and hard *work* are necessary for success. (three nouns—parallel)

> *They get together often *to swim* or *watching* a movie. (infinitive and gerund—not parallel)

> They get together often *to swim* or *to watch* a movie. (two infinitives—parallel)

Troublesome Conjunctions

As is not used to mean "that" or "whether."

> *I don't know as I should tell you what she said.

> I don't know *that* I should tell you what she said.
> I don't know *whether* I should tell you what she said.

The following construction uses more words than necessary to express its meaning. The word *whether* alone will suffice.

> *The President did not say as to whether he would veto the bill.

> The President did not say *whether* he would veto the bill.

The construction *but what* is frequently heard in conversations but is not a feature of Edited Standard English.

> *I don't know but what the store overcharged us.

> I think *perhaps* the store overcharged us.
> I think *that* the store overcharged us.

The word *either* used as part of a correlative construction needs to be followed by the word *or*. The word *neither* is followed by the word *nor*.

> *Either snow nor rain will make us cancel the trip.

> *Either* snow *or* rain will make us cancel the trip.
> *Neither* snow *nor* rain will make us cancel the trip.

Except should not be used as a conjunction. The conjunction *unless* should be substituted for it.

> *I can't go except I get an advance on my allowance.
>
> I can't go *unless* I get an advance on my allowance.

Like should not be used as a conjunction. The subordinating conjunction *as* or *as if* should be used when a subordinate clause makes a comparison.

> *The movie monster looked like it was made of clay.
>
> The movie monster looked *as if* it were made of clay.

Avoid using *try and*. The more accurate expression is *try to*.

> *I will try and study harder.
>
> I will *try to* study harder.

Where should not be substituted for the conjunction *that*.

> *I see where gasoline prices are going up again.
>
> I see *that* gasoline prices are going up again.

The conjunction *while* means "at the same time as"; it should not be substituted for *although* or *though*.

> *While Shirley MacLaine began her career as a dancer, her greatest success was as an actress.
>
> *Although* [or *Though*] Shirley MacLaine began her career as a dancer, her greatest success was as an actress.

Review: Using Conjunctions

Each of the following sentences contains a conjunction (or a word used as a conjunction) that is not a feature of Edited Standard English. Revise the sentence so that the inexact or wordy conjunction is eliminated.

Examples

a. While Bill Cosby was a dropout in his youth, he later received a doctor's degree in education.

Although Bill Cosby was a dropout in his youth, he later received a doctor's degree in education.

b. Your health will benefit if you consume neither large amounts of sugar or excessive quantities of starch.

Your health will benefit if you consume neither large amounts of sugar nor excessive quantities of starch.

1. I don't know as I'd be brave enough to ride that wild horse.

2. Kelly read where scientists may soon find a cure for the common cold.

3. My room always looks like a tornado has just passed through it.

4. I can't yet say as to whether we can go with you to the movie Friday night.

5. I see where the movie we have wanted to see is now playing.

Rewrite each of the following sets of sentences as one sentence, using conjunctions that will help the reader understand the relationships between ideas. Underline the conjunctions you add.

Examples

a. Sarah and Cara Washington are twins. Lisa and Luisa Perez are not.

Sarah and Cara Washington are twins, but Lisa and Luisa Perez are not.

b. I go for walks. My cat always follows me.

Whenever I go for walks, my cat always follows me.

6. The dog looked like an English setter. It was really only a handsome mutt.

7. I practiced playing my bagpipes. The neighbors complained I was giving them headaches.

8. Pedro made the honor roll. Lisa made the honor roll. Kim made the honor roll.

9. I need a car. I could get a job at Delivery Service Company.

10. I cooked the potatoes. My brother set the table.

Writing Focus: *Using Conjunctions in Writing*

Writers often use conjunctions to glue their thoughts together and to make their writing flow more smoothly. Conjunctions tell readers how one idea or event relates to another. Using the appropriate conjunctions can help make your writing clear and precise.

Assignment: *Lunch Break*

The bell rings. Class is over. It is time for lunch. You gather your books and eagerly move toward the door. How does your school change as students begin their lunch break? What do you hear? Smell? Taste?

Write one or more paragraphs describing your lunch break at school. Write for a new student who is soon to attend your school. Give concrete details of movements, sounds, smells, people, and objects so that the person will know exactly what to expect. Your writing will be evaluated for effective use of conjunctions.

Use the steps on the next page to complete this assignment.

A. Prewriting

Use the clustering technique, described in Chapter 1, to generate details about lunch at your school. Jot down words and phrases that occur to you as you recall the sights, sounds, and smells of lunchtime. Include specific details about where students eat and what they eat.

B. Writing

Using some of the ideas in your word cluster, write one or more paragraphs describing what it is like to eat lunch at your school. Begin your description with the sound of the bell ending one class. Then move to the actual lunch period. Include details that paint a moving picture of what you see, taste, and smell. Remember that the new student doesn't know what to expect, so be specific and clear. As you write, use conjunctions to combine ideas and to make relationships between ideas clear.

C. Postwriting

Use the following checklist to revise your first draft.

1. Have I included specific details relating to the sights, sounds, smells, and tastes during lunch period at school?

2. Are there sentences that can be combined with conjunctions?

3. Have I used appropriate conjunctions to show the relationships between ideas? Are my ideas coordinated or subordinated?

Edit your paragraphs using the Proofreader's Checklist at the back of the book. If appropriate, exchange your writing with a partner who should check for the effective use of coordinating and subordinating conjunctions.

16 Interjections
Understanding Interjections

An *interjection* is usually defined as a word that expresses strong or sudden emotion. The interjection can also show milder emotion, such as surprise.

Interjections are not grammatically related to the rest of the sentence; they serve as independent elements to show feeling or to summon attention.

Various parts of speech may be used as interjections.

Rats!	[noun]
Help!	[verb]
Great!	[adjective]
Never!	[adverb]
In a pig's eye!	[prepositional phrase]

Other words are never used as anything other than interjections: *Oh! Gee! Gosh! Ah! Alas! Hark! Oops! Eek! Wow! Jumping Jiminy!*

Exercise 1: *Identifying Interjections*

Write the following sentences, underlining each interjection.

Example

a. Alas! We've ruined another meal.
   Alas! We've ruined another meal.

1. Stop! You're about to sit on a scorpion!

2. When one United States general was asked to surrender, he sent back a one-word reply: "Nuts!"

3. This boa constrictor could not possibly hurt me—help!

4. Good grief, the dog has eaten my sandwich.

5. Hark! The herald angels sing!

6. Ouch! That switch gave me a shock!

7. Come on! You know you can win.

8. Aha! I've caught you in the act, Mr. Snodberry!

9. Now I will juggle five of these eggs at once—oops!

10. Warning! These grounds are patrolled by attack dogs.

Using Interjections

An interjection expressing strong emotion is usually set off by an exclamation point.

Ugh! There's a fly in my soup!

The weather forecaster predicted enough snow to close the schools. Hooray!

An interjection that expresses a relatively mild emotion is usually set off by a comma.

Oh, I don't know about that.

Uh-oh, I forgot to mail that letter.

The punctuation that you use with an interjection indicates the amount of emotion you want to convey. Notice that if an interjection is followed by an exclamation point, the next word is capitalized because it really begins a new sentence. If the interjection is followed by a comma, the next word merely continues the sentence and is not capitalized.

Ugh! *That* food looks disgusting.

Oh, *that* food doesn't look very appetizing.

Exercise 2: Punctuating Interjections

Write the sentences on the following page, underlining the interjections. Place an exclamation point after interjections that you think show strong emotion and a comma after milder interjections.

Circle the punctuation you insert. Capitalize words where necessary, and underline them.

Example

a. Help get me out of here.

Help (!) Get me out of here.

1. Well we could go to the movies tomorrow.
2. Watch out that highway is a dangerous road to drive.
3. Oops I forgot Megan's address as well as her phone number.
4. Oh no Derek has locked the keys in the car.
5. Great I'd love to hike through that national park.
6. Never no one else besides me can ever drive my car.
7. Oh the cat will get itself down from that tree.
8. Whew I thought this heat wave would never break.
9. Hey you're not supposed to be on that property.
10. Thank goodness this long, tiring day is over.

Writing Focus: *Interjections*

Interjections are used to express strong emotions or sudden feelings, usually in dialogue. When you write dialogue, use interjections that are appropriate for the speaker.

Assignment: *A Dog's Life*

Imagine that when you come home from school one day, your dog meets you as usual—barking, jumping, licking. Then the dog sits at your feet and says, "So, how was your day?" You stare at him in disbelief. "Good grief, you can talk!"

Write the conversation that you and your dog might have. Let your dialogue reveal your personalities through language, especially appropriate interjections. Give your classmates and teacher a glimpse of your dog's life from *his* point of view.

Use the following steps to complete this assignment.

A. Prewriting

Imagine what you and your dog might talk about if he really could talk. Make a list of topics of conversation that you might discuss. Select one topic and free write about it from your dog's point of view. For example, one topic may be the kind of meals you feed your dog. Imagine what he might say so you can speak and write from his point of view.

B. Writing

Use your free writing as a basis for writing a short dialogue. Begin with a few sentences describing the scene in which you discover your dog can talk. Then write the dialogue, using the conversation from your free writing. Let the dialogue develop naturally as you and your dog discuss a particular topic. Include appropriate interjections.

C. Postwriting

Revise your first draft using the following checklist.

1. Does my dialogue sound "realistic" for the situation? Have I written my dog's responses from his point of view?

2. Have I used interjections accurately and correctly to express emotion?

3. Have I punctuated and capitalized the interjections and other elements of dialogue correctly?

    Edit your dialogue using the Proofreader's Checklist at the back of the book. If appropriate, ask a classmate to take your dog's part and read the dialogue with you to your class.

17 Verbals

Understanding Verbals

Although not classified as a part of speech, verbals function almost like a ninth part of speech. In the next sections you will begin a study of verbals by learning to recognize them and their functions in a sentence.

Defining Verbals

A *verbal* is usually defined as a word that is formed from a verb but used in a sentence as an adjective, an adverb, or a noun. There are three kinds of verbals: the *participle*, the *gerund*, and the *infinitive*.

A *participle* is usually defined as an adjective formed from a verb.

We heard the *howling* wind.

We listened to the *screaming* gulls and *pounding* waves.

The *fluttering* leaves warned us of an *approaching* storm.

Each *italicized* word functions as an adjective, but each is formed from a verb. These words, formed by adding *-ing* to the present form of the verb, are called *present participles*.

Remember that the *-ing* form of the verb can also be used with one or more helping verbs to form a verb phrase. Only when the *-ing* verb form modifies a noun or pronoun in the sentence is it a participle.

| The wind *was howling*. | [verb phrase] |

| The *howling* wind rattled the windows. | [participle] |

Howling mightily, the wind rattled the windows.

[participle]

Past participles, which are the past participle form of the verb, describe the results of completed actions.

Shattered glass covered the floor.

The *rusted* lock was useless.

We can never replace the *destroyed* documents.

The *broken* limb lay in the backyard.

Like the present participle, the past participle has a double nature. If it has a helping verb, it is part of the verb phrase of the sentence. If it modifies a noun or pronoun, it serves as an adjective. Since participles have this double nature, it is important to see exactly how they are used in a sentence: as part of a verb phrase or as a participle that functions as an adjective.

Our basement *had been flooded* by the storm.	[verb phrase]
Our *flooded* basement was full of carp.	[participle]
Natalie *had broken* the swimming record.	[verb phrase]
The *broken* jar leaked honey.	[participle]

When a participle performs as an adjective, it may appear before the word it modifies or after it.

The *galloping* horse raced across the canyon floor.

The horse, *galloping* across the canyon floor, left its pursuers far behind.

The *forgotten* treasure of jewels and gold lay in the cave for years.

The treasure of jewels and gold, *forgotten,* lay in the cave for years.

Exercise 1: *Identifying Participles*

Write the following sentences, underlining the participles used as adjectives. Then draw an arrow from each participle to the word it modifies.

Example

a. The cheering crowd gave the players new courage.

The cheering crowd gave the players new courage.

---

1. The cackling hens were scratching in the barnyard dust for their food.

2. Tired and distracted, the truck driver was jolted by the flashing lights.

3. Kirstin, excited about her vacation, was going downtown to buy some new skiing equipment.

4. The freshly fallen snow twinkled in the rays of the setting sun.

5. The traveling musicians had hoped to leave on the early bus, but they played an encore for the cheering audience.

6. The glowing campfire embers and the rustling pines were making Pat feel drowsy.

7. The smoke rising from the outdated chimneys was clouding the early morning air.

8. The trained accountants balanced the confusing books quickly.

9. Wandering aimlessly, Mack was unnerved by the milling crowds and rushing traffic.

10. The creeping tortoise was gaining ground slowly with its plodding pace.

A *gerund* is usually defined as a word ending in *-ing* that is formed from a verb and that functions as a noun.

You need sturdy, well-fitting shoes for *hiking*.

Dreaming is a mysterious process.

Many people dread *dieting*.

Boiling will purify that water.

Gerunds can be used in all the ways that nouns are used.

Yodeling isn't hard to learn.	[gerund as subject]
Are we born with the fear of *falling?*	[gerund as object of a preposition]
Gary's hobby is *cooking*.	[gerund as predicate nominative]
Mary hates *ironing*.	[gerund as direct object]
She gives *spelling* a lot of attention.	[gerund as indirect object]

Gerunds always do the work of nouns. Be careful not to confuse gerunds with participles performing a different function: working as adjectives or as parts of a verb phrase.

Writing is one of humanity's greatest inventions.	[gerund]
Susannah is *writing* a report on dolphins.	[part of verb phrase]
I need some extra *writing* paper.	[participle as adjective]

Exercise 2: Identifying Gerunds

Write the following sentences, underlining all gerunds.

Example

    a. Jogging is good for circulation.
     Jogging is good for circulation.

1. Exercising is necessary for physical fitness.

2. Running is becoming popular for overall exercise.

3. Another good activity is swimming.

4. I'm noticing that many people enjoy backpacking.

5. Sailing and snorkeling are two popular water sports.

6. Landlubbers may prefer biking or horseback riding to air or water sports.

7. The daring may like spelunking, or cave exploring.

8. Handball offers lots of running and lunging and is an exhausting sport.

9. The Lunts are opening a gym with equipment for exercising.

10. Sweating and panting are good for you—within reasonable limits.

An *infinitive* is a verb form preceded by the word *to: to have, to look, to lower*.

Working in a sentence, an *infinitive* is defined as a form of the verb, usually preceded by the word *to*, that is used as a noun, an adjective, or an adverb.

We like *to bowl*.	[infinitive used as a noun—direct object]
We need a place *to stay*.	[infinitive used as an adjective, modifying the noun *place*]
It's too late *to register*.	[infinitive used as an adverb, modifying the adjective *late*]

Infinitives functioning as nouns are commonly used in positions where nouns occur: they are used as subjects, direct objects, and predicate nominatives, as well as other kinds of verb complements.

To succeed will be very hard.	[subject]
We need *to win*.	[direct object]
Our plan is *to cooperate*.	[predicate nominative]

Do not confuse the *to* in an infinitive with the preposition *to*, which is always followed by a noun or pronoun.

Infinitives	**Prepositional Phrases**
(*to* followed by verb)	(*to* followed by noun or pronoun)
I love *to dream*.	We walked *to church*.
I like *to feel* warm.	Please give these books *to them*.
Are you able *to see* clearly?	Can we wear jeans *to school*?

Exercise 3: Identifying Infinitives

The following sentences all contain infinitives. Write the sentences and underline each infinitive. Beneath the sentence tell whether the infinitive is used as a noun, an adjective, or an adverb.

Example

a. Carrie has always liked to swim.

   Carrie has always liked to swim.

   to swim—noun

1. Luisa hopes to finish.
2. Beverly left to phone.
3. That target is hard to hit.
4. The best person to see for career planning is the guidance counselor.
5. My only goal is to pass.
6. To leave would seem impolite.
7. I still have all these raffle tickets to sell.
8. We came too late to apply.
9. The algebra problems were easy to solve.
10. The perfect Saturday morning project is to sleep as late as possible without interruptions.

Review: Understanding Verbals

Write the sentences from the following page, underlining the verbals in each. Beneath each sentence identify the verbals as *present participle, past participle, gerund,* or *infinitive*. Also, tell how the verbal is used in the sentence: as a *noun,* an *adjective,* or an *adverb*.

Examples

a. The first great Central American culture to arise was the Olmec civilization.

   The first great Central American culture to arise was the Olmec civilization.

   to arise—infinitive—adjective

    b. The blazing lights and scattered confetti helped to create the carnival's frantic atmosphere.

    The <u>blazing</u> lights and <u>scattered</u> confetti helped <u>to create</u> the carnival's frantic atmosphere.

    blazing—present participle—adjective
    scattered—past participle—adjective
    to create—infinitive—noun

1. Chinese is an interesting language, but it is difficult to learn.

2. Damaged roofs and fallen trees indicated a tornado's path.

3. The dogs, growling and barking, frightened the prowler away.

4. Skiing is an enjoyable sport, but the equipment is too expensive.

5. The lock, rusted and crumbling, broke easily.

6. The siren was only a warning, not a signal of immediate danger.

7. Through the frosted glass, snow is sparkling in the moonlight.

8. Hiking, camping, and canoeing are Pete's favorite activities.

9. The sleeping student suddenly awoke, yawning and blushing.

10. The barn, weathered and sagging, was painted by many artists.

11. The boys jog and perform demanding workouts at the gym.

12. The books, stacked and numbered, are ready for shelving.

13. Using the clay pot, David learned to cook casseroles.

14. Working together, Juan's family plans to remodel the house.

15. Checking your home once each year for fire hazards is a good way to avoid a needless disaster.

Using Verbals

Verbals help make writing concise by providing a realm of words that have the vitality of verbs but that can do more than verbs alone, as you can see from the following pairs of examples. In the second example in each pair, a verbal has been used to combine and condense ideas into a compact and vivid sentence.

The horse neighed. The horse stood at the gate.
The *neighing* horse stood at the gate.   [participle]

| My brother bowls. This is his favorite sport. | |
| My brother's favorite sport is *bowling*. | [gerund] |

| Many people diet. They find it difficult. | |
| Many people find it difficult *to diet*. | [infinitive] |

Participles used as modifiers may precede or follow the word they modify.

The *leaping* frog eluded the heron.

[present participles]

The frog, *leaping*, eluded the heron.

The *polished* table looked like new.

[past participles]

The table, *polished*, looked like new.

Notice how a participle following the word it modifies is set off by punctuation.

The fans, screaming, jumped to their feet.

Note: A participle that precedes the word it modifies may sometimes be set off with punctuation.

More than one participle may be used to modify a word.

The dog, *running* and *panting*, couldn't catch the rabbit.

A *freezing, blasting* wind drove us back inside the cabin.

Notice that when two participles precede the word they modify, they can be separated by commas. Two participles following a modifier are usually joined by *and*.

Exercise 4: Using Verbals

Combine each set of sentences on the next page into one sentence by making the *italicized* word into a verbal. (The words in parentheses tell you what kind of verbal to form.) Underline the verbals you form.

Example

a. George *stares*. His sister said it was impolite. (infinitive)

George's sister said it was impolite to stare.

1. The flower *wilts*. It drooped in a vase. (present participle)

2. Treasure can be *discovered*. It is difficult. (infinitive)

3. The glass *shattered*. The glass flew into the air. (past participle)

4. Maria Tallchief *danced*. It was her profession. (gerund)

5. Everyone *errs*. It is easy. (infinitive)

6. The wolf sat on the ridge. It *howled*. (present participle)

7. The jeans *tore*. The jeans could not be mended. (past participle)

8. You must *plan* a good trip. A good trip demands this. (gerund)

9. The cat *slept*. The mice left the cat alone. (present participle)

10. The water pipes *froze*. They burst from the pressure. (past participle)

Writing Focus: *Using Verbals in Writing*

Verbals function almost like a part of speech. They have the vitality of verbs but can do more than verbs alone. By using the three kinds of verbals—participles, gerunds, and infinitives, you can make your writing more lively, varied, and concise.

Assignment: *All Aboard!*

Imagine that you are a tour guide in a newly discovered galaxy. You are responsible for informing a group of excited tourists about special sights of interest. Your group is taking a tour through the galaxy aboard a brand new double-deck spaceship.

Write one or more paragraphs explaining what the passengers are seeing as they move through this new galaxy. Call their attention to particular sights. Be specific in your commentary as you both inform and entertain your group. Your writing will be evaluated for correct and effective use of verbals.

Use the following steps to complete this assignment.

A. Prewriting

Use your imagination to draw a mental map of the new galaxy; include planets, stars, suns, moons, and any new strange forms.

Generate information about your galaxy by using the six basic questions method described in Chapter 1. Jot down questions like the following that need answers: *Who* lives in the galaxy? *What* does the galaxy contain? *Where* did that particular sun come from? *When* was the galaxy formed? *Why* did giant raccoons evolve on that moon? *How* do the inhabitants of that star grow food? Answer all your questions specifically in words, phrases, and sentences. Review your answers and group them into an organizational pattern that reflects movement through space and time.

B. Writing

Using your answers, write one or more paragraphs explaining what your passengers are seeing on their tour of the galaxy. Include specific details so that people not on the tour could also visualize the galaxy. You might begin sentences with phrases like "Coming up on your right . . ." to help your passengers orient themselves in space and time. As you write, use verbals to make your writing clear and varied.

C. Postwriting

Use the following checklist to revise your work.

1. Have I included enough information about particular sights in the galaxy?

2. Are there specific details that help my audience visualize the galaxy?

3. Have I used verbals correctly and effectively?

Edit your work using the Proofreader's Checklist at the back of the book. If appropriate, share your writing with classmates. You may want to create and illustrate a student pamphlet entitled *Strange New Worlds*.

18 Sentence Patterns

Understanding Sentences

Defining Sentences

A *sentence* is usually defined as a group of words that expresses a complete thought.

A group of words that does not express a complete thought is called a *sentence fragment*.

Sentence Fragment: on the weekend or on Monday
the striped cat on the chair
Maria and her aunt

Complete Sentence: We will leave either on the weekend or on Monday.
The striped cat on the chair hasn't moved for hours!
When will Maria and her aunt arrive?

Exercise 1: Identifying Sentence Fragments and Sentences

Number your paper 1–10. If one of the following groups of words does not express a complete thought, write *SF* next to its number. If a group of words is a sentence, write the sentence. Begin each sentence with a capital letter and place the appropriate punctuation at its end.

Examples

---

a. beyond any chance of recovery
    SF

b. movie production has stopped because the actors are on strike
    Movie production has stopped because the actors are on strike.

1. with a song in my heart

2. an earsplitting concert Saturday night

3. julio's new car gets very good mileage

4. she wrote the book in nine months, and it's a best seller

5. the plot is exciting, and the characters fairly interesting

6. never in a million years

7. because the library and the school

8. which of the two records would you rather have

9. a double-record set of new songs

10. a large glacier is moving south into some shipping lanes

Types of Sentences

Sentences may be divided into four main types, each type serving a different purpose: *declarative, interrogative, imperative,* and *exclamatory.*

The *declarative sentence* makes a statement and ends with a period.

> The only poisonous lizard in the United States is the Gila monster.

An *interrogative sentence* asks a question and ends with a question mark.

> Are there any poisonous lizards in the United States?

An *imperative sentence* gives an order or makes a request. Mildly imperative sentences end with a period; strongly imperative sentences end with an exclamation point.

> Name a poisonous lizard native to the United States.
>
> Remove that lizard now!

An *exclamatory sentence* expresses surprise or strong feeling and ends with an exclamation point.

> A Gila monster is chasing me!

Exercise 2: Identifying and Punctuating Types of Sentences

Write each of the following sentences, adding the appropriate end mark. Beside each sentence identify it as *declarative, interrogative, imperative,* or *exclamatory.*

Examples

    a. Do not fold, spindle, or mutilate
       Do not fold, spindle, or mutilate. (imperative)

    b. Rosita is the best singer in the choir
       Rosita is the best singer in the choir. (declarative)

1. Can you explain what a quasar is

2. Never put bananas in the refrigerator

3. A number of large medical centers are in Chicago, Illinois

4. Waiter, there's a fly in my soup

5. Does everyone always dream in color

6. The Faversham Oyster Fish Company has been in existence for over 800 years

7. Don't leave your keys in your car

8. Good grief, all the rats are loose in the biology room

9. Please tell me what time the movie is over

10. Shangri-La is a mythical kingdom where no one grows old

The Parts of a Sentence

To express a complete thought, a sentence must have two parts: a *subject* and a *predicate.* The *subject* of the sentence is the person, place, thing, or idea that the sentence is about. The *predicate* says something about the subject.

Subject	Predicate
My dog	has fleas.
Odetta	is a famous folk singer.
The letter on the desk	came this afternoon.

The Subject

Complete Subjects and Simple Subjects

A *subject* may be only one word, or it may be several. All the words composing the subject are called the *complete subject*. The main word or words in the complete subject are called the *simple subject*.

The only person for this job is Susette.

Complete Subject: *The only person for this job*

Simple Subject: *person*

Mrs. Yuan's daughters run the China Flower Restaurant.

Complete Subject: *Mrs. Yuan's daughters*

Simple Subject: *daughters*

Joslyn Art Museum in Omaha has a fine collection.

Complete Subject: *Joslyn Art Museum in Omaha*

Simple Subject: *Joslyn Art Museum*

Exercise 3: Identifying Complete and Simple Subjects

Write the following sentences. Underline each complete subject once and each simple subject twice.

Example

a. The program after the news will be a special on nuclear plants.
   The program after the news will be a special on nuclear plants.

1. The tallest animal in the world is the giraffe.

2. The world's heaviest creature is probably the blue whale.

3. A length of up to 140 feet makes the sea-dwelling ribbon worm the longest animal.

4. The sperm whale has the largest brain in the animal kingdom.

5. The world's largest eggs are laid by the whale shark.

6. The eyes of the giant squid are larger than long-playing records.

7. The record for long-distance land speed belongs to the antelope.

8. The fastest of all swimming birds is the genoo penguin.

9. The living reptile of greatest size is the saltwater crocodile.

10. The longest-living mammal in the world is the human.

Compound Subjects

A *compound subject* consists of two or more simple subjects that are joined by a coordinating conjunction and that have the same verb.

Compound subjects are *italicized* in the following sentences.

Books and *magazines* are available in the library.

Compound Subject:	Books and magazines
Simple Subjects:	Books
	magazines

Marian Anderson, Beverly Sills, and *Leontyne Price* are great singers.

Compound Subject:	Marian Anderson, Beverly Sills, and Leontyne Price
Simple Subjects:	Marian Anderson
	Beverly Sills
	Leontyne Price

Compound subjects, like one-word simple subjects, may take modifiers.

The *ambassador* from Ghana and the British *manufacturer* agreed.

Compound Subjects:	ambassador
	manufacturer

An old, dilapidated *barn* and a *shed* with no roof were on the property.

Compound Subjects:	barn
	shed

Understood Subjects

The imperative sentence, which gives an order or makes a request, is different from other sentences: it does not name the subject. The subject is always *you*, meaning the person being addressed. Subjects of this kind are called *understood subjects.*

Lend me five dollars, please.

Understood Subject: *You* [*You* lend me five dollars, please.]

Call me about the assignment.

Understood Subject: *You* [*You* call me about the assignment.]

Look at that strange storm cloud.

Understood Subject: *You* [*You* look at that strange storm cloud.]

Even if the sentence names the person who is addressed, the true subject is still the understood *you*.

Hand me that wrench, Nicky.

Subject: *You* [understood]

Officer, please give me some directions.

Subject: *You* [understood]

Exercise 4: Identifying Complete, Compound, and Understood Subjects

Write the sentences on the next page, underlining the complete subject of each. If the sentence has a compound subject, circle each of the simple subjects. If the sentence has an understood subject, write *You* (*understood*) beneath it.

Examples

a. Maria and Kim have the leads in the one-act play.

(Maria) and (Kim) have the leads in the one-act play.

b. Dad, lend me the car keys, please.
   Dad, lend me the car keys, please.
   Subject: You (understood)

1. Report this to the authorities at once.

2. Shirley Chisholm and Gloria Steinem appeared on the talk show.

3. The checkered shirt and the jeans with the patch are mine.

4. Wait for the dial tone.

5. *Liberty, Fraternity,* and *Equality* were the watchwords of the French Revolution.

6. The priest from St. Anne's and the new rabbi play golf together.

7. Mankowitz or Washington will substitute for the injured player.

8. Dr. Frankenstein, show us your experiment.

9. Our metal fence and our television antenna were struck by lightning.

10. Don't forget to take your tickets.

Subjects in Inverted Order

The subject usually appears in the first part of the sentence, before the predicate. Sometimes, however, this order is reversed: the predicate precedes the subject.

When the predicate comes before its subject, the sentence is in *inverted order*.

Questions are frequently in inverted order.

> Which candidate do you like best?

To find the simple subject of a question, rephrase the question to make it a statement.

> You do like which candidate best.

Simple Subject: you

Verb: do like

Questions are not the only sentences that use inverted order. Sentences that begin with prepositional phrases often use inverted order, also. To find the simple subject of such a sentence, find the word whose action or state of being is described by the verb.

> Deep in the marsh grows the rare blue mushroom.

Verb: grows

Who or what grows? the mushroom

Note: A simple subject is never part of a prepositional phrase. Sometimes, a simple subject is modified by a prepositional phrase, but do not mistake part of the phrase for the subject.

One of the players was disqualified.

One of our calves wins ribbons at the fair.

Expletives

When the words *here* **and** *there* **introduce verbs that precede their subjects, they are called** *expletives*.

       V   S
There *is* no *homework* in Spanish today.

     V   S
Here *comes* the news *bulletin*.

The words *here* and *there* are never used as subjects of sentences. When either of them begins a sentence, it is usually a sign that the verb will come before the subject.

     V   S
There *go* our *chances* for the championship.

     V   S
Here *stands* a famous *landmark*.

Exercise 5: Identifying Simple Subjects

Write the following sentences, underlining each simple subject.

Examples

   a. Across the desert crept the tiny caravan.
      Across the desert crept the tiny caravan.

   b. Are any tickets available yet?
      Are any tickets available yet?

1. Out of the Old West comes the Lone Ranger.

2. Here is the bus to Prairie Grove.

3. Where is my library book about heart transplants?

4. There are many stories about that old house.

5. Will you give me some change for a phone call?

6. Under the fence and across the courtyard slithered the cobra.

7. What will we have for breakfast tomorrow?

8. There are several methods for putting out fires.

9. In the Kingdom of Camelot lived a magician.

10. Do you have some good hiking boots?

The Predicate

The *predicate* of the sentence says something about the subject. Every predicate must contain a *verb* or a *verb phrase*. (A *verb phrase* is two or more verbs working as a unit.) Sometimes, a predicate consists of the verb only.

Subject	Predicate
The traffic	slowed.
The dogs	had barked.
The papers	must have been lost.

All the words that compose the predicate are called the *complete predicate*. The verb or verb phrase is called the *simple predicate*.

Mike practices on his tuba every day.

Complete Predicate: practices on his tuba every day

Simple Predicate: practices

Sometimes the words in a verb phrase are separated by modifiers.

His sister has always played in marching bands.

Strange lights are often seen down in the swamp.

The adverbs *always* and *often* are not parts of simple predicates.

Exercise 6: Identifying Predicates

Write the following sentences. Then underline each complete predicate once and each simple predicate twice.

Examples

a. The rain fell in torrents.
The rain <u>fell</u> in torrents.

b. Phillis Wheatley was an early American poet.
Phillis Wheatley <u>was</u> an early American poet.

1. More people speak Chinese than any other language.

2. Chinese is also the oldest spoken language.

3. English ranks as the second most dominant language in the entire world.

4. Hindustani is spoken by the third-largest group of people.

5. Written language originated first in Mesopotamia.

6. The Cherokees invented the first written native American language in North America.

7. The most recent new language has developed in the last hundred years.

8. This language is called New Guinea Pidgin English.

9. Over 3,000 different languages now exist in the world.

10. Of these languages English contains the largest number of words.

A *compound verb* **has two or more verbs or verb phrases that share the same subject.**

      S   V   V
The buffalo *snorted* and *charged.*

S   V   V
We *have worked* very hard and *deserve* a reward.

      S   V   V
The backpacker *took* the wrong trail, *forgot* the camping equip-
                           V
ment, and then *stepped* on a snake.

Exercise 7: Identifying Compound Verbs

Each of the sentences on the next page contains a compound verb. Write each sentence, underlining the simple subject once and the verb phrase or verbs that make up the compound verb twice.

Examples

    a. The broadcast begins at 9 o'clock and ends at noon.
       The <u>broadcast</u> <u>begins</u> at 9 o'clock and <u>ends</u> at noon.

    b. This wonderful invention slices and mashes vegetables.
       This wonderful <u>invention</u> <u>slices</u> and <u>mashes</u> vegetables.

1. The mystery of the ship *Mary Celeste* has puzzled and intrigued people for years.

2. In 1872 the crew of the ship *Dei Gratia* saw the *Mary Celeste* and noticed its strange movements.

3. A sailor rowed over and boarded the small ship.

4. He searched the ship and discovered no crew or passengers.

5. The ship showed little damage and offered few clues.

6. Food still was on the table and seemed fresh.

7. An unfinished letter was found but offered no explanation.

8. The ship's windows were covered and battened with boards.

9. Perhaps pirates had boarded and kidnaped the crew.

10. Many people have studied but never solved this strange case.

Review: *Understanding Sentences*

Write each of the following sentences, underlining each complete subject once and each complete predicate twice. Then beneath each sentence write the simple subject and the simple predicate.

Example

    a. Only one of the fields was damaged by the hail.
       <u>Only one of the fields</u> <u>was damaged by the hail</u>.

       Simple subject—one
       Simple predicate—was damaged

1. The packet of letters had suddenly disappeared.

2. Both of the girls are here now.

3. Under the cushion of the couch was my class ring.

4. A few of the cattle were lost in the last blizzard.

5. Half a quart of milk is needed for this recipe.

6. Six of the houses were damaged in the earthquake.

7. Can you show me how to solve this problem?

8. Much of our time was wasted there.

9. Both the new movies have had good reviews.

10. Are two of those mine?

11. Have you seen my shoes and socks?

12. The dog has eaten the plant and the newspaper.

13. At the beginning of the school year, everyone has new notebooks to fill.

14. Maggie will write and perform those songs.

15. There are not enough towels for the beach.

16. Has anyone fed the cats?

17. All the laundry is clean and folded.

18. Do you have any good radio stations in this town?

19. During the night a storm knocked over that tree.

20. Where should I park the car?

Using Sentence Patterns

Billions of English sentences have been written and spoken, but most sentences follow six patterns:

1. *S–V* (Subject-Verb)

2. *S–LV–PA* (Subject-Linking Verb-Predicate Adjective)

3. *S–LV–PN* (Subject-Linking Verb-Predicate Nominative)

4. *S–V–DO* (Subject-Verb-Direct Object)

5. *S–V–IO–DO* (Subject-Verb-Indirect Object-Direct Object)

6. *S–V–DO–OC* (Subject-Verb-Direct Object-Object Complement)

In the following sections you will learn to recognize the different sentence patterns and the components that make up each of them.

S-V *Sentence Pattern*

The simplest sentence pattern in English consists of a subject (*S*) and a verb (*V*).

Subject	*Verb*
Joe	slept.
She	finished.
This	works.

Few sentences are as brief as the preceding ones, but many are still basically this simple pattern. The subject may have some kind of modification, and the verb may be a verb phrase, but the pattern remains the same. When a pattern has modifiers added to it, it has been *expanded.* Just as the subject may have modifiers, so may the verb, as the following examples show.

Joe	is sleeping	*very soundly.*	[adverbs added]
This	will work	*in an emergency.*	[prepositional phrase added]
I	*often* wrote	*to my cousin.*	[adverb and prepositional phrase added]

In addition to modification, a sentence may have compound subjects or predicates while retaining the basic sentence pattern.

    S   V   V
Joe woke and yawned.

    S   S   V
Laura and she finished.

    S   S V   V
Laura and she paint and write.

Both modifiers and compounds may be used to expand the basic *S–V* pattern.

    S   V   V
Joe woke slowly and yawned with pleasure.

    S   S   V
Laura and she quickly finished.

    S   S   V   V
Laura and she always paint in the evening and sometimes write.

Exercise 8: *Identifying Subjects and Verbs*

Write the following sentences, underlining the simple subjects once and the verbs or verb phrases twice. Then label your answers *S* for subject, and *V* for verb.

Examples

a. The bells were ringing loudly.

     S   V
The <u>bells</u> <u>were ringing</u> loudly.

b. He and his friend left here in a big hurry.

 S   S V
<u>He</u> and his <u>friend</u> <u>left</u> here in a big hurry.

1. Janice surfs in the summer.
2. Somewhere the sun is shining brightly.
3. The man and the boys with the cameras stood aside.
4. The alarm will flash and beep in case of emergency.
5. Mr. Scoggins golfs and fishes for recreation.
6. The hounds were baying excitedly at the raccoon.
7. Our climb to the top was stopped by the snowstorm.
8. The choir and the soloist will be performing in both programs.
9. A yellow-bellied sapsucker was singing by my window.
10. The two horror movies will be showing at the drive-in until Saturday.

Complements

In sentences that follow the *S–V* pattern, the subject and verb are able to express a complete thought. Sentences that follow the other patterns, however, need yet another element to express a complete thought: a *complement*.

A *complement* is a word or a group of words that completes the statement begun by the subject and verb.

The shot was nearly *foul*.

The bruise felt *painful*.

That woman will be *mayor*.

There are three different kinds of complements: *subject complements, objects,* and *object complements*.

Subject Complements

A *subject complement* is a noun, a pronoun, or an adjective that gives information about the subject.

Rats are extremely *destructive*.

Rats are *rodents*.

The adjective *destructive* above describes the subject *rats*. In the second sentence the noun *rodents* identifies *rats* as a specific sort of animal.

A subject complement must follow a linking verb.

The most common linking verb is *be*. Other common linking verbs are *become, feel, look, remain, seem, smell, sound, stay, taste,* and *turn*.

The bread is *stale*.
The subject *bread* is linked to its complement *stale*.

These paintings were *masterpieces*.
The subject *paintings* is linked to its complement *masterpieces*.

Predicate Adjectives

There are two kinds of subject complements. The first is the *predicate adjective*, which describes or modifies the subject.

The knight was *loyal*.

The lemonade was *sour*.

The two hall monitors were *angry* about getting caught sleeping on duty.

Predicate adjectives modify the subject, and they can be further modified themselves.

Helen of Troy was very *beautiful*.	[adverb modifying predicate adjective]
She was *famous* for her beauty.	[prepositional phrase modifying predicate adjective]

Predicate adjectives, in addition to taking modifiers, can also be *compound*. That is, two or more predicate adjectives can describe the subject.

The band uniforms are *green* and *white*.

The popcorn tasted *burnt* and *stale*.

The new coach was *tall, bearded,* and *bald*.

Exercise 9: Identifying Predicate Adjectives

Write the following sentences and underline the predicate adjectives. Then draw an arrow from each predicate adjective to the simple subject it modifies.

Examples

a. The house seemed strangely quiet.

The house seemed strangely quiet.

b. The air was full of angry hornets.

The air was full of angry hornets.

1. The hike was exhilarating.
2. The air smelled fresh and clean in the mountains.
3. The chipmunks looked fat and sassy.
4. The trail became steeper in the afternoon.
5. Our packs seemed much heavier then.
6. The weather turned hot and clear.

7.   Our lunch tasted good in the open air.

8.   Before sunset the sky grew cloudy again.

9.   The evening breeze was gentle but crisp.

10.   Our legs were heavy with fatigue.

Predicate Nominatives

The second kind of subject complement is the *predicate nominative,* **which is a noun or pronoun joined to the subject by a linking verb. Rather than describing the subject as the predicate adjective does, the predicate nominative** *identifies* **or** *renames* **the subject.**

The new vice president is *Sheila.*

You are the lucky *winner.*

The winners were *Ken* and *she.*

Note: If the predicate nominative is a pronoun, remember to use the subject form.

The winner is *she.*

Like predicate adjectives, predicate nominatives can be compound. Two or more of them may be used to identify the subject.

Ethel Waters was a *singer* and fine *actress.*

Exercise 10: *Identifying Predicate Nominatives*

Write the following sentences and underline each predicate nominative you find.

Example

---

a. The mysterious stranger in black was I.
   The mysterious stranger in black was I.

1.   The Phoenicians were great traders and sailors of the ancient world.

2.   Their greatest cities were Tyre, Sidon, and Byblos.

3.   People influenced by the Phoenicians are you, most other Americans, and I.

4. Our heritage from them is their written alphabet.

5. Two more of their inventions left to us are purple dye and false teeth.

6. Great inventors, merchants, and navigators of their times were they.

7. The Phoenicians were also expert workers with glass.

8. The Phoenicians may have been the first navigators around Africa and the early discoverers of America.

9. The first planners of a Suez Canal may have been the Egyptians or they.

10. Lucky heirs of their inventive foresight are we of the modern world.

Sentence Patterns with Subject Complements: S-LV-PA, S-LV-PN

Abbreviations for sentence patterns with subject complements are *S–LV–PA* (Subject–Linking Verb–Predicate Adjective) and *S–LV–PN* (Subject–Linking Verb–Predicate Nominative).

Modifiers can be added to this pattern without changing the basic sentence pattern.

Subject	Linking Verb	Predicate Adjective
The *roses*	*are*	deep *red* with long stems.
The *ducklings*	*look*	comically *fuzzy* with their yellow down feather coats.

Subject	Linking Verb	Predicate Nominative
Wild *roses*	*are* not	very large *flowers*.
Good old *Mickey*	*is*	the new *captain* of the team.

Sentences that follow these two patterns can be expanded by compounds.

    S   LV   PN   PN
Kevin is an Explorer *scout* and a *member* of the band.

               S   LV PA   PA   PA
The accident *victims were pale, shaken,* but *unhurt.*

                 S   LV   PN   PN
Two famous Western *women were Calamity Jane* and *Belle Starr.*

     S   LV PA   PA
The *solution* to the problem *is plain* and *simple.*

Exercise 11: *Identifying Sentence Patterns with Subject Complements*

Write the following sentences. Underline the subjects, the verbs or verb phrases, and the predicate adjectives or predicate nominatives. Above each basic sentence part, write the appropriate abbreviation.

Examples

a. Diana Ross is an outstanding rock singer and a fine actress in the movies.

    S   LV   PN   PN
Diana Ross is an outstanding rock singer and a fine actress in the movies.

b. The litmus paper turned pink in the solution.

          S   LV   PA
The litmus paper turned pink in the solution.

1. Two widely known columnists are Abigail Van Buren and Ann Landers.

2. Their advice columns are extremely popular throughout the United States.

3. Their answers to letters are thought by many people to be witty and wise.

4. Actually the two women are identical twin sisters who live in different cities.

5. Esther Lederer is Ann Landers' real name.

6. "Dear Abby" is really Pauline Phillips.

7. The birthplace of the twins is Sioux City, Iowa.

8. In 1955 Esther became "Ann Landers" of newspaper fame in Illinois.

9. Pauline Phillips became "Dear Abby" in California just six months later.

10. One hundred million readers are their devoted audience.

Direct Objects

The *direct object*, another kind of complement, completes the statement begun by the subject and verb.

A *direct object* is a word or a group of words that appears in the predicate and receives the action expressed by the verb.

Direct objects are used only after *action verbs*.

```
      S    V    DO
```
My dog chases *wasps*.

The direct object *wasps* completes the statement begun by the subject and verb. Because the verb describes an action that is performed upon something, *chases* is an action verb. The noun or pronoun upon which the action is performed is the direct object of the verb.

The direct object is a noun or pronoun answering the question *what?* or *whom?* about the subject and verb.

William G. Sill composed *symphonies*.
[William G. Sill composed *what? Symphonies* is the direct object.]

Like other complements, direct objects can be expanded and modified.

Joanne chased the *dog* with the red collar.
[prepositional phrase modifying the direct object *dog*]

Have you read the new *book* about the four astronauts landing on Mars?
[prepositional phrase modifying the direct object *book*]

When the direct object is a pronoun, be certain that the pronoun is in the object form.

I called *him* last night.

We never saw *them* again.

Not all action verbs take direct objects. Those that do are called *transitive verbs* because they transmit the actions to the direct objects. Certain action verbs, such as *sleep* and *go,* seldom take direct objects. Action verbs that do not take direct objects are called *intransitive verbs. Intransitive* means "not transitive, not transmitting action to an object."

We *bought* a car.	[transitive]
The snow *fell.*	[intransitive]

Many verbs can be used in different ways. The following sentences show the same verb as a linking verb, a transitive verb, and an intransitive verb.

The chili *smelled* spicy.	[linking verb]
We *smelled* the different perfumes.	[transitive verb]
Those rotten eggs certainly *smelled.*	[intransitive verb]

Since verbs have this versatility, they require special attention when you are analyzing or writing sentences. You must determine exactly how the verb is being used to understand if it is linking, transitive, or intransitive.

Sentence Patterns with Direct Objects: S-V-DO

The pattern of a sentence containing a direct object is Subject–Verb–Direct Object *(S–V–DO).*

Subject	*Verb*	*Direct Object*
Elephants	like	peanuts.
We	rode	mopeds.
Pam	plays	tennis.

Like other patterns, this one may be expanded by adding modifiers.

Subject	Verb	Direct Object
Hungry *elephants*	always *like*	*peanuts* in the shell.
After supper *we*	sometimes *ride*	our twin *mopeds*.
The athletic *Pam*	faithfully *plays*	*tennis* every day.

Direct objects, like other elements in a sentence pattern, can be made compound. A verb may take two or more direct objects.

Subject	Verb	Direct Object		Direct Object
Elephants	like	peanuts	and	carrots.
Elephants	dislike	mice	and	nose colds.

Exercise 12: *Identifying Sentence Patterns with Direct Objects*

Write the following sentences and underline each simple subject, verb or verb phrase, and direct object. Then write the appropriate label over each of these parts of the *S–V–DO* sentence pattern.

Examples

a. The doctor wrote a prescription for the cough medicine.

        S   V   DO
The doctor wrote a prescription for the cough medicine.

b. Marcia uses no chemicals or sprays on her flower and vegetable garden.

     S   V   DO   DO
Marcia uses no chemicals or sprays on her flower and vegetable garden.

1. Native Americans gave many words to the English vocabulary.

2. They also provided names for many places.

3. Nebraska and the Dakotas take their names from Native American words.

4. Similarly, Black English introduced many words and phrases into the English language.

5. It originated *jazz, yam,* and *galoot.*

6. The Portuguese donated *savvy* and *palaver* to English.

7. Chinese immigrants invented *look-see* and *Johnny-come-lately* for American usage.

8. Spanish speakers added *cafeteria, adobe,* and *chili* to the American vocabulary.

9. After Jewish immigrants arrived, Americans began using the words *schmaltzy* and *schlep.*

10. All these contributions add vitality and diversity to American English.

Sentence Patterns with Indirect Objects: S-V-IO-DO

An *indirect object* is a noun or pronoun in the predicate that comes before the direct object and tells *to whom* or *for whom.*

Subject	Verb	Indirect Object	Direct Object
The *plumber*	*sent*	*us*	the *bill.*
My *sister*	*mailed*	*me*	a *postcard.*
Marcia	*presented*	*him*	the *award.*
My *aunt*	*will give*	*you*	a *cat.*
Herb	*baked*	*us*	some *bread.*
Charlotte	*sang*	the *children*	a *ballad.*

The abbreviation for this type of sentence pattern is *S–V–IO–DO.* For a sentence to have an indirect object, there must also be a direct object.

Indirect objects can be changed into prepositional phrases by moving them to the ends of sentences and adding *to* or *for* in front of them.

That nice old man sold *me* the Brooklyn Bridge.	[indirect object]
That nice old man sold the Brooklyn Bridge *to me.*	[prepositional phrase]

If the preposition *to* or *for* appears before the noun or pronoun, the group of words is a prepositional phrase. An indirect object is never part of a prepositional phrase. An indirect object is a noun or pronoun following the verb and occupying the appropriate position in the sentence pattern *S–V–IO–DO*.

Subject	Verb	Indirect Object	Direct Object
Spiders	*give*	*me*	the *shivers*.

Indirect objects, like nouns and pronouns in other sentence positions, can be modified. Two common modifiers are the adjective and the prepositional phrase.

       S   V   IO   DO
The *ad offered people* with computer experience good *jobs*.

       S   V   IO   DO
Juan gave the new *student* in school a *smile*.

Like other complements, indirect objects can be compound. A verb may take two or more indirect objects.

       S   V   IO   IO   DO
I showed *Marcia* and *Freddie* the assignment.

When a pronoun functions as an indirect object, it must be in its object form, just as it must when it is a direct object.

Sherry told *Terry* and *me* to ride.	[not *Terry and I*]
We gave *him* and *her* matching T-shirts.	[not *he and she*]

Exercise 13: Identifying Sentence Patterns with Indirect Objects

Write each of the sentences on the following page, underlining the key words in its sentence pattern. Above these words write the appropriate abbreviations.

Examples

a. The old explorer gave the man with a map a puzzled stare.

              S   V   IO   DO
    The old <u>explorer</u> <u>gave</u> the <u>man</u> with a map a puzzled <u>stare</u>.

b. The saleswoman showed Pat and me the selection of records.

```
              S         V     IO        IO      DO
The saleswoman showed Pat and me the selection of records.
```

1. Carrie mailed her cousin from Tennessee an extraordinary bar mitzvah present.

2. The zoo attendant showed Pam and me the baby cobras in the cage.

3. The manager told the woman with the complaint the store policy.

4. The rescuers cooked Jan and me some soup to help us warm our bodies.

5. Mr. Diaz presented the child a savings bank.

6. That problem gave the others and me a hard time.

7. Lisa made the orphaned lamb a bed by the stove.

8. George sent his two sisters in the navy funny postcards.

9. The detective told the butler and her the strange story of how the jewels disappeared.

10. The government gave every soldier with a good record a pay increase.

Sentence Patterns with Object Complements: S–V–DO–OC

An *object complement* is a noun or an adjective in the predicate that identifies or explains the direct object.

The sentence pattern that uses an object complement is abbreviated *S–V–DO–OC*. This sixth sentence pattern closely resembles the pattern *S–V–IO–DO*. The similarity, as well as the difference, is shown in the following examples.

```
S   V    IO      DO
I showed Ralph a turkey.
```

```
S   V    DO      OC
I called Ralph a turkey.
```

The nouns in the predicate of the first sentence above are the indirect object and the direct object. They refer to two different things, *Ralph* and the *turkey*. The nouns in the predicate of the second sentence are the direct object and the object complement. They both refer to the same person, *Ralph*.

Just as a limited number of verbs take indirect objects, so only a few take object complements. The following examples show some of these verbs at work.

Subject	Verb	Direct Object	Object Complement
We	elected	Luisa	vice president.
They	named	the horse	Shadow.
The judge	pronounced	him	a free man.
They	considered	you	a hero.
The Queen	made	him	a knight.
We	thought	the play	a mistake.

Occasionally an adjective serves as an object complement.

Subject	Verb	Direct Object	Object Complement
We	thought	the meal	terrible.
The judge	pronounced	them	guilty.
We	believed	the answer	right.
She	found	the play	boring.
They	considered	the incident	forgotten.
The umpire	called	the ball	foul.

Like other sentence elements, object complements can be compounded and modified.

    S   V   DO   OC   OC
We found her *pleasant* and most *cooperative*.

    S   V   DO   OC
They elected you *leader* of the club.

    S   V   DO   OC
We found the room very *messy*.

          S   V   DO   OC   OC
The veterinarian pronounced my dog *pregnant* and *healthy*.

Exercise 14: *Identifying Sentence Patterns with Object Complements*

Write each of the following sentences, underlining each of the key parts in its sentence pattern. Then write the appropriate abbreviation above each of these parts.

Examples

    a. Cassy believes jogging healthful.

       S   V   DO   OC
      Cassy believes jogging healthful.

    b. Scientists declare smoking a waste of money and a threat to health.

       S   V   DO   OC   OC
      Scientists declare smoking a waste of money and a threat to health.

1. The referee declared the play illegal.

2. The doctor pronounced the patient completely cured.

3. We named the puppy with the spots Patch.

4. Marcus considered flying saucers a complete hoax until he saw that strange light in the sky.

5. A man in the crowd called the astronaut a hero.

6. Rita found Mexican food exceptionally delicious.

7. Aunt Petunia named me heir of her entire fortune.

8. Irv Robbins considers houseflies the lowest form of life in the universe.

9. The President appointed Mrs. Figueroa an ambassador to Africa shortly after assuming office.

10. The Master of Ceremonies crowned her the new Miss Tangerine at the convention.

Summary of Sentence Patterns

A sentence needs a subject and a predicate to state a complete thought. One sentence pattern consists of a subject and a verb or verb phrase: *S–V*.

```
 S    V
```
Snow melts.

```
 S    V
```
Babies cry.

```
  S       V
```
Elephants remember.

Modifiers and compounds can be used to expand a sentence pattern.

```
        S         S     V
```
Several *students* and *teachers attended.*

```
            S  V
```
The quick brown *fox ran* away.

```
     S              V
```
The *heap* of leaves *burned* quickly.

```
 S      V
```
She replied with a smile.

Some predicates require more than a verb or verb phrase to state a complete thought. Such a predicate must also have a *complement,* a word or group of words that completes the meaning of the sentence. Subject complements may be either *predicate adjectives* or *predicate nominatives.* These patterns are *S–LV–PA* and *S–LV–PN.*

```
  S    LV     PA
```
That smells delicious.

```
    S    LV    PA
```
The *dogs looked strange* in their sweaters.

```
 S   LV     PN
```
Toads are amphibians.

```
    S   LV          PN
```
A *sonnet is* a lyrical *poem* with fourteen lines.

The fourth sentence pattern has a different kind of complement, the direct object: *S–V–DO.*

```
     S  V        DO
```
The *mice ate* the *crackers.*

```
    S     V              DO
```
Shirley wanted some new *boots* with low tops.

The fifth sentence pattern consists of both a direct object and an indirect object: *S–V–IO–DO.*

```
      S   V          IO        DO
```
The *store sent* the wrong *person* the *bill.*

```
     S      V            IO          DO
```
The *school presented* the top *student* a large *prize.*

507

The sixth sentence pattern consists of both a direct object and an object complement: *S–V–DO–OC*.

S   V   DO   OC
They elected her secretary.

S   V   DO OC
The *neighbors consider* the *man snobbish.*

S   V   DO OC
The *mechanic pronounced* my old *car dead.*

Review: Sentence Patterns

Write each of the following sentences, underlining the key parts of its sentence structure. Then write the appropriate labels above these parts. Finally, beneath each sentence write the sequence of abbreviations that shows its sentence pattern.

Examples

a. The old tree fell down with a thunderous crash during the storm.

S V

The old <u>tree</u> <u>fell</u> down with a thunderous crash during the storm.

Sentence pattern: S–V

b. The horse looked strong and full of spirit.

S   LV   PA   PA

The <u>horse</u> <u>looked</u> <u>strong</u> and <u>full</u> of spirit.

Sentence pattern: S–LV–PA

1. Many superstitions exist.

2. Owls are tremendously wise.

3. A vampire must sleep in a coffin.

4. Midnight is a haunted hour.

5. A horse chestnut brings you good luck.

6. Redheads are usually quick to lose their tempers and sharp with their tongues.

7. Opals cause you terrible misfortune of some kind.

8. The sound of thunder will sour fresh milk.

9. Dragons consider all gold their personal property and defend their right to it.

10. Leprechauns and ghostly horses live in Ireland.

Write each of the following sentences, underlining and labeling each basic sentence part. After each sentence write its sentence pattern.

Examples

a. The typewriter is a useful invention.

>   S   LV   PN
> The typewriter is a useful invention. S–LV–PN

b. The first typewriter could be typed at only five words in a minute even after much practice.

>   S   V
> The first typewriter could be typed at only five words in a minute even after much practice. S–V

11. The earliest typewriters had one big disadvantage for typists proofreading their work.

12. Typists could not see the typewritten words on the paper in the typewriter.

13. Without a doubt these typewriters gave typists some problems when trying to produce quality work.

14. In 1874 Christopher Sholes invented a better typewriter.

15. His typewriter might seem strange to those of us who use computer keyboards today.

16. The Sholes typewriter could type only capital letters without lowercase letters.

17. During the next few years various inventors gave the typewriter improvements.

18. In the 1880s typists could see typewritten words without removing the paper from the typewriter.

19. Typists declared the typewriter a tremendous improvement over past machines and a great success!

20. There began a new era for typists.

Writing Focus: *Varying Sentence Patterns in Writing*

Good writers use a variety of sentence patterns in their writing in order to keep readers interested in what they have to say and to present their ideas in the best possible way. Choose appropriate sentence patterns and write them correctly to make your writing clear and interesting.

Assignment: *Good Advice?*

The following list contains proverbs, or familiar sayings, you have probably heard many times.

> If at first you don't succeed, try, try again.
>
> Absence makes the heart grow fonder.
>
> Out of sight, out of mind.

For this assignment, choose one of the proverbs listed on page 569 or another one you may know. Write one or more paragraphs with a variety of sentence patterns explaining how the saying has or has not been true in your life. Provide personal examples. Write for your classmates.

Use the following steps to complete this assignment.

A. Prewriting

Carefully read the proverb you have chosen and make sure you understand its meaning. List some of your life experiences that either prove or disprove the truth of the saying. Review your list, and underline the details and ideas that seem to be the most important to your explanation. Number your examples in an order to clearly make your point.

B. Writing

Write one or more paragraphs explaining how the proverb has or has not been true in your life. Include examples from your personal experience to support your opinion. Consider using the proverb near the beginning of your paper in a topic sentence. As you write, use a variety of sentence patterns and avoid sentence fragments.

C. Postwriting

Use the following checklist to revise your first draft.

1. Have I supported my opinion about the truth of the proverb with convincing examples from my personal experience?

2. Are all my sentences complete?

3. Have I varied my sentence patterns?

Edit your paragraphs using the Proofreader's Checklist at the back of the book.

19 Phrases

Understanding Phrases

A *phrase* is a group of words that does not contain both a subject and a predicate and that performs a single function in a sentence.

In the following sections you will learn about four types of phrases: *verb phrases, prepositional phrases, verbal phrases,* and *appositive phrases.*

Verb Phrases

A *verb phrase* is a group of words composed of a main verb and one or more helping verbs that together act as the main verb in a sentence.

Kelly *must have been wondering* about us.

Kelly *will wonder* about us.

Kelly *is* always *wondering* about us.

Each of the groups of *italicized* words in the preceding sentences is a verb phrase. Standing by themselves, they contain no word that could be a subject. They work as a single verb might work, acting as the main verb of a sentence: Kelly *wondered* about us.

Prepositional Phrases

Just as verb phrases do the work of a single verb, so prepositional phrases do the work of an adjective or adverb. A prepositional phrase that modifies a noun or pronoun is called an *adjective phrase.*

The people *from Japan* toured our city.

Some *of us* couldn't see the stage well.

The words *from Japan* and *of us* are prepositional phrases modifying the noun *people* and the pronoun *some*.

A prepositional phrase that modifies a verb, an adverb, or an adjective is called an *adverbial phrase*.

The package should arrive *before this weekend.*

The prepositional phrase *before this weekend* modifies the verb phrase *should arrive*, telling when the package will arrive.

Prepositional phrases are almost always used as adjective or adverb phrases.

We read the article *about the arctic expedition.*
[adjective phrase modifying the noun *article*]

The alligator slithered *into the swamp.*
[adverb phrase modifying the verb *slithered*]

Those *with passes* may go to the library.
[adjective phrase modifying the pronoun *Those*]

My fingers were numb *with cold.*
[adverb phrase modifying the adjective *numb*]

Exercise 1: Identifying Verb Phrases and Prepositional Phrases

Write the sentences on the following page, underlining each verb phrase and prepositional phrase. Then label each verb phrase *VP*, each prepositional phrase that acts as an adjective *ADJ*, and each prepositional phrase that acts as an adverb *ADV*.

Example

---

a. The submarine has disappeared beneath the sea's surface.

                VP   ADV
The submarine has disappeared beneath the sea's surface.

1. They had survived the worst hurricane in history.

2. Jane might be practicing in the band room.

3. The Mississippi River is called "The Father of Waters."

4. Joan of Arc certainly must be one of history's most remarkable women.

5. Our quarterback must have been hurt by the tackle.

6. My homework is finished on time.

7. The ruler of the Norse gods was called Odin.

8. Crows and ravens are considered very intelligent by scientists.

9. The new students at school were taking a tour of the library before class started.

10. The bottom of the boat was thick with barnacles.

Verbal Phrases

Verbals are words formed from verbs that function as nouns, adjectives, or adverbs. Verbals can take modifiers, just as nouns, adjectives, and adverbs can. Verbals also take complements, since they are formed from verbs.

A verbal with its modifiers and complements is called a *verbal phrase* and can be used as a single noun, adjective, or adverb is used. You will study three kinds of verbal phrases: *participial phrases, gerund phrases,* and *infinitive phrases.*

Participial Phrases

A *participle* is a verb form used as an adjective.

We watched the *smoldering* pile of leaves.   [present participle]

The young woman, *sobbing,* withdrew.   [present participle]

The *reduced* price caught our attention.   [past participle]

The house, *gutted* by fire, was torn down.   [past participle]

A *present participle* is formed by adding *-ing* to the present verb form. A *past participle* is formed from the past form of the verb. (Past participles usually end in *-ed*, *-d*, *-t*, *-en*, or *-n*.)

Like regular adjectives, participles can be modified by single-word adverbs and by prepositional phrases that function as adverbs.

A *participial phrase* is a participle plus its modifiers and complements.

Juanita, *arriving early*, noticed something strange.
[present participle modified by an adverb]

Juanita, *arriving with the keys*, noticed something strange.
[present participle modified by a prepositional phrase]

The lawn mower, *ruined completely*, was sold for scrap.
[past participle modified by an adverb]

The lawn mower, *ruined by misuse*, was sold for scrap.
[past participle modified by a prepositional phrase]

Juanita, *arriving early with the keys*, noticed something strange.
[present participle modified by both an adverb and a prepositional phrase]

The lawn mower, *completely ruined by misuse*, was sold for scrap.
[past participle modified by both an adverb and a prepositional phrase]

Since participles are formed from verbs, they can also take complements. The complement may be any of several kinds, but most commonly it is a direct object.

DO
The man *teaching the class* is Fred Washington.

DO
The kangaroo, *taking the carrot*, accidentally bit me.

DO
Into the office came a tall woman *carrying a briefcase*.

In each of the preceding sentences, the participle takes a direct object as its complement.

Notice, too, that participial phrases may come before or after the noun or pronoun they modify.

Excited about the award, Ms. Bard gave a short speech.

Ms. Bard, *excited about the award*, gave a short speech.

Busily writing a letter, Ken didn't hear the telephone.

Ken, *busily writing a letter*, didn't hear the telephone.

Exercise 2: *Identifying Participial Phrases*

Write the following sentences, underlining the participial phrases. Then draw an arrow from each participle to the noun or pronoun that it modifies.

Examples

a. The lawyer winning that case was Mrs. Zabinski.

The lawyer <u>winning that case</u> was Mrs. Zabinski.

b. Floating lazily in the shallows, the huge bass ignored my bait.

<u>Floating lazily in the shallows</u>, the huge bass ignored my bait.

1. The window broken by my baseball was an expensive one.
2. The teacher giving the fewest homework assignments gets a prize.
3. Wounded by the porcupine, the dog had to be taken to the vet.
4. A special safety film will be shown to the students taking drivers education.
5. Feeling embarrassed by the attention, Elena nodded shyly to the audience.
6. The canal-like constructions seen on the surface of Mars are really natural formations.
7. My sister has read every book written by James Baldwin.
8. Scanning the sky for a sign of clouds, the hikers plodded on.
9. Miss Redwing, hearing the results of the election, smiled broadly.
10. The principal, presenting our class the trophy, looked a bit dubious.

Gerund Phrases

A *gerund* is a verb form ending in *-ing* that acts as a noun.

You need sturdy, well-fitting shoes for *hiking.*

Dreaming is a mysterious process.

Many people dread *dieting.*

Boiling will purify that water.

A *gerund phrase* consists of a gerund and its modifiers and complements.

Gerunds can be modified by adjectives, adverbs, and preposi-tional phrases.

Whistling loudly is the parrot's only trick.
[gerund modified by adverb]

Whistling in the dark helps keep up your courage.
[gerund modified by prepositional phrase]

Loud whistling at strangers is rude, crude, and vulgar.
[gerund modified by adjective and prepositional phrase]

Gerunds can also take complements.

Whistling the national anthem is difficult.
[gerund taking a complement—the direct object *national anthem*]

Like a single gerund, gerund phrases may be used in all the ways that nouns can.

The constant dripping of the faucet is most distracting.
[gerund phrase as subject]

My most unusual experience was *falling into a vat of mayonnaise.*
[gerund phrase as predicate nominative]

We heard *the low grumbling of the thunder.*
[gerund phrase as direct object]

They saved themselves by *keeping active during the blizzard in the Colorado mountains.*
[gerund phrase as object of a preposition]

Exercise 3: Identifying Gerund Phrases

Write the following sentences, underlining each gerund phrase. Then beneath each sentence identify the function of the gerund phrase. (Be prepared to identify the parts of the phrase.)

Examples

a. Doing difficult crossword puzzles is Ann's favorite pastime.

Doing difficult crossword puzzles is Ann's favorite pastime.

Doing difficult crossword puzzles—subject

b. We were kept awake by the yowling of cats in the alley.

We were kept awake by the yowling of cats in the alley.

the yowling of cats in the alley—object of preposition

1. Western civilization has a history of disliking certain animals.

2. Hating all snakes seems natural to some people.

3. These people dislike the snake's crawling and sinister hissing.

4. Chinese thinking on snakes is altogether different.

5. The snake is revered for having great intelligence and beauty.

6. Calling a woman a snake is a compliment in China.

7. Another Western tradition is hating wolves intensely.

8. Killing livestock, children, and travelers are supposedly the wolf's favorite activities.

9. Actually wolves are renowned for their quick thinking and remarkably deep feeling for one another.

10. Being wolfish can also mean being intelligent, loyal, and generous to your fellows.

Infinitive Phrases

An *infinitive* is a verb form preceded by the word *to.*

In sentences, infinitives are verb forms, usually preceded by the word *to,* that function as nouns, adjectives, or adverbs.

An *infinitive phrase* is an infinitive plus its modifiers and complements.

Jan likes *to walk slowly.*
[infinitive phrase = infinitive + adverb]

Jan likes *to walk slowly along the beach.*
[infinitive phrase = infinitive + adverb + prepositional phrase]

Jan likes *to walk her horse slowly along the beach.*
[infinitive phrase = infinitive + direct object + adverb + prepositional phrase]

When used as nouns, infinitive phrases can perform most of the functions that a noun can perform: subject, direct object, predicate nominative, and object of a preposition.

To lie to the voters is wrong.
[infinitive phrase used as subject]

We need *to buy a present for our cousin.*
[infinitive phrase used as direct object]

Sharon's greatest ambition is *to climb Mount Everest.*
[infinitive phrase used as predicate nominative]

Infinitive phrases are often used as adjectives and adverbs. When infinitive phrases are used as adjectives, they act like single-word modifiers to modify nouns or pronouns.

We need a place *to stay right now.*

That father-daughter dinner will be something *to remember for a long while.*

Infinitive phrases used as adverbs act like single-word modifiers to modify verbs, adjectives, and other adverbs.

Todd has registered for the first time *to vote in the next Presidential election.*
[infinitive phrase modifying a verb]

It's too late *to register for this class.*
[infinitive phrase modifying an adjective]

The bus driver was driving too slowly *to arrive on time at the regional basketball tournament.*
[infinitive phrase modifying an adverb]

Exercise 4: Identifying Infinitive Phrases

Write the following sentences and underline each infinitive phrase. Beneath each sentence write how the infinitive phrase is used: as a noun, an adjective, or an adverb. If it is used as a noun, tell how it is used: subject, direct object, predicate nominative, or object of a preposition.

Examples

a. Several foolish people have attempted to go over Niagara Falls in a barrel.

Several foolish people have attempted to go over Niagara Falls in a barrel.

infinitive phrase used as a noun (direct object)

b. The mechanic left to get a new part.

The mechanic left to get a new part.

infinitive phrase used as an adverb to modify left

1. To eat crackers in bed is a crumby experience.
2. Lori exercised to build up her endurance for the hike.
3. Here is a magazine to read until your appointment.
4. I have always wanted to own an antique convertible.
5. To dream of missing a final exam is supposedly very common.
6. We were pleased to see our relatives from El Paso.
7. It is hard to peel onions without shedding some tears.
8. J.B. is expected to make the all-American team.
9. LeRoy decided to ask for a raise in his allowance.
10. This is the soap to make your dingy wash dazzling once again.

Appositive Phrases

An *appositive* is a noun or pronoun that follows or precedes another noun or pronoun to identify or clarify it.

Ms. Jefferson, the *lawyer*, appealed the case.

The winner, *Secretariat,* was a great horse.

A *scavenger,* the buzzard serves as one of nature's sanitation workers.

Like other nouns and pronouns, appositives can be modified by adjectives and prepositional phrases to form *appositive phrases.*

My aunt, *a lieutenant in the United States Air Force,* is stationed in Puerto Rico.
[The prepositional phrase *in the United States Air Force* modifies the appositive *lieutenant.*]

Cheops's pyramid, *the largest Egyptian pyramid,* is 147 meters high.
[The adjectives *the, largest,* and *Egyptian* modify the appositive *pyramid.*]

Exercise 5: Identifying Appositive Phrases

Write the following sentences, underlining each appositive phrase. Then draw an arrow from it to the noun or pronoun it modifies. (Be prepared to identify the modifiers and complements in the phrases.)

Example

a. I ordered a healthburger, a sandwich of peanut butter and bean sprouts.

I ordered a healthburger, a sandwich of peanut butter and bean sprouts.

1. Language, humanity's greatest invention, exists in many forms.

2. Eyak, an Alaskan Indian language, is spoken only by two elderly sisters.

3. There are several equally rare languages, tongues with only a handful of surviving speakers.

4. The Chippewas, native Americans of Minnesota, had one of the most complex languages in the world.

5. English has the most irregular verbs, at least 194 of the trouble-some critters.

6. The simplest verb system belongs to Esperanto, an invention of modern times.

7. An idea that never developed, Esperanto is artificial.

8. It was designed as a universal language, simple and easy.

9. Swahili, an African language, has no irregular verbs.

10. Dr. Harold Williams, a language whiz, could communicate in fifty-two different languages, a modern record.

Review: Understanding Phrases

In the following selection from Stephen Crane's *The Red Badge of Courage,* there are many phrases of the types you have studied in the previous sections: verb, prepositional, participial, gerund, and infinitive. On a sheet of paper, list at least thirty phrases in the order in which they appear. Beside each phrase identify its type. (When prepositional phrases appear as modifiers in other phrases, do not count them as separate phrases. For example, in the sentence, *Walking down the long corridor, we saw tangled cobwebs*, list *walking down the long corridor* as a participial phrase.) The first two phrases in the selection are underlined for you; do not include them in your list.

The lieutenant sprang forward bawling. The youth saw his features wrathfully red, and saw him make a dab <u>with his sword</u>. His one thought <u>of the incident</u> was that the lieutenant was a peculiar creature to feel interested in such matters upon this occasion.

He ran like a blind man. Two or three times he fell down. Once he knocked his shoulder so heavily against a tree that he went headlong.

Since he had turned his back upon the fight, his fears had been wondrously magnified. Death about to thrust him between the shoulder blades was far more dreadful than death about to smite him between the eyes. When he thought of it later, he conceived the impression that it is better to view the appalling than to be merely within hearing. The noises of the battle were like stone; he believed himself liable to be crushed.

As he ran on he mingled with others. He dimly saw men on his right and on his left, and he heard footsteps behind him. He thought that all the regiment was fleeing, pursued by these ominous crashes.

In his flight the sound of these following footsteps gave him his one meager relief. He felt vaguely that death must make a first choice of the men who were nearest; the initial morsels for the dragons would be then those who were following him. So he displayed the zeal of an insane sprinter in his purpose to keep them in the rear. There was a race.

Applying What You Know

From a magazine, book, or newspaper you have read, select a passage about five or six paragraphs long. Then, on a sheet of paper, write the first twenty phrases in the selection, including verb, prepositional, participial, gerund, infinitive, and appositive phrases. Next to each phrase identify its type and function in the sentence. Finally, rewrite the passage, replacing each phrase with a single-word verb or modifier. How do these changes affect the piece of writing?

Using Phrases

In the following sections you will study and practice using phrases. You will learn how to use commas with phrases, how to place phrases in sentences to avoid ambiguity, and how to use nouns and pronouns as modifiers of gerunds. In addition, you will learn some special uses of infinitive phrases. As you work on using phrases in your writing, refer to the sections in Understanding Phrases for any help you may need in identifying the different kinds of phrases.

Using Commas with Participial Phrases

A participial phrase used at the beginning of a sentence is called an *introductory participial phrase* and is always set off by a comma.

> *Driving through the pouring rain,* we could barely see the road ahead.
>
> *Signed and witnessed,* the document was official.
>
> *Tired and aching from practice,* the players limped away.

Sometimes a participial phrase appears within a sentence. If the phrase is necessary to the meaning of the sentence, it is called an *essential phrase* and is *not* set off by commas.

> All students *having passes* are excused from school.
> [If the participial phrase *having passes* is removed, the meaning changes to *All students are excused from school*.]

The person *sitting by Cindy* is the new exchange student.
[The phrase *sitting by Cindy* is essential because it identifies the person.]

Essential participial phrases usually identify someone or something; they point out *which one* is being discussed.

A phrase that merely adds description or extra information but does not identify anything or anyone is *nonessential*. Set off nonessential participial phrases from the rest of the sentence with commas.

The center, *dribbling down the court,* suddenly tripped.
[nonessential phrase, set off by commas]

The player *dribbling down the court* is our center.
[essential phrase, not set off]

The towels, *soaked by the sea,* were wadded into our beach bags.
[nonessential phrase, set off by commas]

The towels *hanging on the line* were pulled down by the dog.
[essential phrase, not set off]

One way to determine whether a phrase is essential or nonessential is to ask yourself if the participial phrase identifies the word it modifies, or if it only adds extra description. Another way is to say the sentence aloud. If the phrase is essential, it should flow, without pause, into the rest of the sentence. A speaker usually pauses slightly before and after a nonessential phrase.

Exercise 6: *Identifying and Punctuating Participial Phrases*

Write each of the following sentences, underlining each participial phrase. If the phrase is nonessential, add the appropriate commas. If the phrase is essential and needs no punctuation, write *essential phrase, no punctuation needed* beneath the sentence. Circle the commas you insert.

Examples

a. The crowd cheering and stamping drowned out the announcer.

The crowd ⊙ cheering and stamping ⊙ drowned out the announcer.

b. The contestant selected as most talented was the juggler.

The contestant selected as most talented was the juggler.

essential phrase, no punctuation needed

1. The person elected secretary will be in charge of publicity, too.

2. Hearing the new evidence the lawyer shook her head in disbelief.

3. A lone windmill creaking mournfully overlooked the deserted farm.

4. The band members exhausted by marching practice were all ready for a break.

5. The shorts given to me for gym class are five sizes too big.

6. First published in 1936 the novel is still a best seller.

7. The woman wearing the silk dress is Miss Ling.

8. The four books picked by Kevin were detective novels.

9. The bacon burned to a crisp filled the air with smoke.

10. The player breaking Babe Ruth's record for home runs is Hank Aaron.

Placing Participial Phrases

Participial phrases must be carefully placed in a sentence, or they will seem to modify a different word than the writer intended, with confusing or unintentionally humorous results. Introductory participial phrases demand particular attention: they must always modify the noun or pronoun following them. If they do not, their effect may be misleading or ridiculous:

Scratching fleas and hanging by its tail, the photographer watched the monkey.

Covered with butter, I served the pancakes.

As you can see, the preceding sentences have misplaced participial phrases. The sentences must be revised so that the participial phrases clearly modify the correct words:

Scratching fleas and hanging by its tail, the monkey amused the photographer.

The pancakes, covered with butter, were served.

Another common problem in placing participial phrases occurs when the writer forgets to put *any* word within the sentence that the phrase modifies. A participial phrase *must* modify some word within the sentence.

Waving and shouting, the rescue plane came near.

Tired from the long hike, even a meal of beans sounded tempting.

Participial phrases such as those in the preceding examples are called *dangling participles,* since they dangle from the sentence and are not attached to any word or words they can modify. To eliminate a dangling participle, rewrite the sentence so that the participle has a word it logically modifies.

Waving and shouting, the stranded sailors saw the rescue plane come near.

Tired from the long hike, Patty thought even a meal of beans sounded tempting.

Exercise 7: *Using and Punctuating Participial Phrases*

Write the following sentences and provide the proper punctuation. If the participial phrase does not clearly modify a proper word, revise and rewrite the sentence so that it does. Underline the participial phrases and circle any commas you insert.

Example

a. Spurring her horse Carla raced after the other riders.

Spurring her horse ⊙ Carla raced after the other riders.

1. Freshly washed and folded the sheets were stacked in the hospital linen closet.

2. Possessing great agility the extremely flexible animal outwitted its enemy.

3. Jody watched a comet sitting in his backyard.

4. Waiting for concert ticket sales to begin the night grew colder.

5. The junior honor roll students will meet in that room selling yearbooks.

6. The teakettle whistling shrilly filled the room with steam.

7. Jack puzzled by the metric measurements in the cookbook put too much salt in the casserole.

8. Suspended over the rooftops we saw the full moon.

9. Not knowing any of the answers the test was graded zero.

10. I drowsily watched the countryside riding in the bus.

Using the Possessive Form Before a Gerund

A noun or pronoun preceding a gerund is in the possessive form.

The boat's tossing made us a bit seasick.

The gerund phrase *The boat's tossing* is the subject of the sentence. The possessive form *boat's* is used because it modifies the gerund *tossing,* telling which tossing: *the tossing of the boat.*

His saying that was not very wise.

The gerund phrase *His saying that* is the subject of the sentence. The possessive form *His* is used because the pronoun *His* modifies the gerund *saying.*

Exercise 8: Using the Possessive Form with Gerunds

Write each of the sentences on the following page, supplying the correct form of the noun or pronoun in parentheses. Underline the word you supply.

Examples

a. For many years scientists puzzled over the _____ twinkling. (firefly)

For many years scientists puzzled over the firefly's twinkling.

b. The _____ starting and dying indicated a problem with the gas line. (engine)

The engine's starting and dying indicated a problem with the gas line.

1. _____ pitching was legendary to anyone who knows about baseball. (Satchel Paige)

2. _____ hurling for the National Negro League set records and won countless awards. (He)

3. An _____ best playing is usually over in a few short years. (athlete)

4. Part of Paige's legend is _____ enduring so long as a major athlete. (he)

5. Athletes are, unfortunately, noted for _____ early fading. (they)

6. _____ playing professionally past the age of forty or so is unusual. (They)

7. This phenomenal _____ playing was still good when he was fifty-nine. (man)

8. Paige was equally famous for _____ quick and funny sayings. (he)

9. Of course, _____ achieving 300 shutouts had already made him a baseball immortal. (he)

10. He advised against a _____ carrying on in society, eating fried foods, and running at all. (person)

The Infinitive Without To

The infinitive is usually the word *to* plus the present form of a verb, such as *to love, to praise,* or *to go.* Occasionally, however, the word *to* is dropped from the infinitive or infinitive phrase.

We didn't hear the bell *ring.*

The word *ring* is a shortened form of the infinitive *to ring.* The infinitive often drops the word *to* when it is used with certain verbs, such as *dare, feel, hear, help, know, let, make, need, please, see,* and *watch.* In these situations the word *to* is understood.

We felt the line (*to*) *jerk.*

The fire fighters made the unruly crowd (*to*) *move* back across the street.

We helped Luisa (*to*) *pack* her suitcase.

The Infinitive as an Independent Element

Sometimes phrases are *independent elements* in a sentence. An independent element is not a basic part of a sentence; it is not subject, object, verb, or modifier. It is connected to the sentence by idea but not by structure; that is, it has no grammatical connection with any part of the sentence but rather adds an extra thought, a tacked-on comment. Infinitive phrases are frequently used as independent elements. Independent elements, like modifying nonessential phrases, should be set off by commas.

> *To put it bluntly,* this meat loaf tastes like burnt rubber.

> The test, *to tell the truth,* was not altogether fair.

> I failed, *to be perfectly frank.*

Each of the preceding *italicized* phrases is an infinitive phrase used as an independent element, and each is set off by punctuation. Notice the importance of the comma in the third sentence. Without the comma, *to be perfectly frank* becomes the direct object, and the sentence has an altogether different meaning.

Exercise 9: Identifying and Punctuating Infinitive Phrases

Write each of the following sentences, underlining the infinitive phrase. Beneath the sentence identify the infinitive phrase as an independent element or as an infinitive with the *to* omitted. If the infinitive phrase is an independent element, supply the comma that it needs. Circle the commas you insert.

Examples

a. To be honest I can't tell you that.

To be honest ⊙ I can't tell you that.

independent element

b. No one dared go out in the blizzard.

No one dared go out in the blizzard.

infinitive with to omitted

1. Someone let the boat drift away from the shore.

2. To be perfectly clear on this point I am not a crook.

3. We heard the motor sputter its death gasp.

4. Jana saw the coach signal from the sidelines.

5. To make a long story short I got the job.

6. We helped index the new books in the library.

7. To get to the main point I need a raise.

8. The mayor to put it as briefly as possible was simply wrong about the whole issue.

9. We watched the girls' tennis teams practice.

10. Mr. Whitewater makes all his dogs behave very well whenever they go out.

Review: Using Phrases

Write each of the following sentences, correcting any errors that have been made in using phrases. Underline the corrected phrases. Circle any commas you insert and then underline any words you make possessive.

Examples

a. Quivering with pain the dog allowed the vet to remove the porcupine needles from its nose.

Quivering with pain ⊙ the dog allowed the vet to remove the porcupine needles from its nose.

b. I saw a rattlesnake riding my motorcycle across the barren desert.

Riding my motorcycle across the barren desert ⊙ I saw a rattlesnake.

c. The teacher was irritated by the students whispering through her lecture.

The teacher was irritated by the students' whispering through her lecture.

1. My socks covered with cockleburs were itching and cutting me without even walking.

2. Him barging into the special planning meeting like that was extremely rude.

3. Anne gave her Saint Bernard a bath in the corroded tub no easy task.

4. Walking to school in the rain the bus passed a crowd of people without stopping.

5. To make a long story short we caught the thief with his hands in the cash register.

6. The blue jays shrieking and dive-bombing attacked the blood-thirsty weasel.

7. Roberto getting the scholarship for his college education didn't surprise anyone.

8. Infested with fleas our garage had to be sprayed by the exterminator.

9. To get back to the main point I need help to complete my physics project.

10. The principal commended Miss Teeters student teaching after she saw the class play.

11. The dog a Doberman pinscher helps guard the warehouse from intruders.

12. *Gulliver's Travels* a satire makes fun of human failings.

13. The fire crew dug long, wide trenches to stop the blaze spreading farther.

14. We saw several fish standing on the dock waiting for people to feed them.

15. Whirling its propeller furiously the takeoff was completed during the rainstorm.

16. We were all surprised by him saying that he refused to go along with the idea.

17. A speech was given by Richard Kim the exchange student from Korea.

18. Finished with dinner we cleared the table to get ready to play the new game.

19. The rocks worn by centuries of rain and wind had peculiar shapes.

20. The California condor an endangered species may soon become extinct.

Writing Focus: *Using Phrases in Writing*

Many different types of phrases are available to you as a writer—verb, adjective, adverbial, appositive, gerund, participial, and infinitive. To strengthen your writing style, choose appropriate phrases to add details, to combine sentences, and to vary sentences.

Assignment: *A Night to Remember*

Imagine that you are accidentally locked in an amusement park overnight. You are all alone. You do not even have any money to make a phone call. What do you do? How do you feel?

For this assignment, write one or more paragraphs describing your overnight experience in the deserted amusement park. Include details that appeal to your senses as well as accounts of any strange happenings that occurred. Your writing will be evaluated for the correct and effective use of phrases.

Use the steps on the following page to complete this assignment.

A. Prewriting

Picture the deserted amusement park at twilight. Imagine how the park begins to change as night falls. Make a word cluster, as described in Chapter 1, that describes what you might see, hear, smell, or feel during the night. Choose details from your cluster that most accurately and vividly describe your experience. Consider their order of presentation. You might use a chronological approach, telling what happened in the order of occurrence. Or you might write about the experience by relating a dominant impression such as fear and foreboding.

B. Writing

Using your word cluster, write one or more paragraphs describing your experience. Use specific details so that the readers can sense what it is like to be in a deserted amusement park at night. As you write, use various kinds of phrases to add specific sensory details, to combine sentences, and to vary sentences.

C. Postwriting

Revise your first draft using the following checklist.

1. Have I included specific details to describe my experience?

2. Have I used and punctuated phrases correctly and effectively?

Use the Proofreader's Checklist at the back of the book to edit your work. If appropriate, share your writing with your classmates and compare descriptions.

20 Clauses

Understanding Clauses

The clause, a group of words that has its own subject and verb, is a basic structure in the English language. In the following sections you will begin your study of clauses by learning to identify two kinds: independent and subordinate. You will also study three types of subordinate clauses: adjective, adverbial, and noun.

Defining Clauses

A *clause* is usually defined as a group of related words having both a subject and a verb.

To determine whether a group of words is a clause or a phrase, ask if the group of words contains *both* a subject and a verb. If both a subject and verb are present, the group of words is a clause.

Clause:	I left *as soon as the movie was over.* [The subject is *movie*; the verb is *was over*.]
Phrase:	I left *after the movie.* [*After the movie* is a prepositional phrase.]
Clause:	Ms. Washington stayed home *because she had the flu.* [*She* is the subject; *had the flu* is the predicate.]
Phrase:	Ms. Washington stayed home *because of illness.* [*Because of illness* is a prepositional phrase.]

Independent and Subordinate Clauses

There are two kinds of clauses: those that can stand alone and those that cannot.

A clause that can stand alone is called an *independent clause* because it can express a complete thought by itself. Every sentence must contain an independent clause.

The team ran out onto the court for the game.

The fans cheered wildly.

Each of the preceding sentences is really an independent clause, standing by itself. Independent clauses can be joined together by the coordinating conjunctions *and, but, or, nor, for, so,* and *yet*. When two independent clauses are joined into one sentence, the result is called a *compound sentence*.

The team ran out onto the court for the game, and the fans cheered wildly.

The team ran out onto the court for the game, so the fans cheered wildly.

The team left the court after the game, but the fans still cheered wildly.

Now look at the following example:

Marcia is a good athlete although she is small.

The independent clause in the preceding sentence is *Marcia is a good athlete.* This clause can stand alone. The second clause, however, could not be a sentence, since it does not express a complete thought and it cannot stand alone.

*Although she is small.

The sentence is marked with an asterisk (*) because it does not conform to Edited Standard English.

A clause that does not express a complete thought is called a *subordinate clause.* It must be joined to an independent clause to form a part of a sentence.

A subordinate clause may come either before or after an independent clause.

Independent Clause	Subordinate Clause
I liked the book	because it was exciting.
I vacuumed the rug	while my sister raked the leaves.

Subordinate Clause	Independent Clause
When the package didn't arrive,	we were puzzled.
After the pearls were recovered,	the detective claimed a large reward.
If you want to be on time,	you need to hurry.

A subordinate clause may also appear in the middle of an independent clause. In the following sentences the subordinate clauses are *italicized*.

The dog *that bit me* was a poodle.

The person *who sells the most* wins a prize.

The place *where we shop* is Smith's Emporium.

Exercise 1: Identifying Independent and Subordinate Clauses

Write the following sentences, underlining each independent clause once and each subordinate clause twice. Above the subject of each clause write *S;* above the verb or verb phrase write *V.* (Some sentences contain two independent clauses; some contain an independent clause and a subordinate clause.)

Examples

    a. We saw the house where Laura Ingalls Wilder lived.

        S   V   S   V
        We saw the house where Laura Ingalls Wilder lived.

    b. We have a car, but it is being repaired.

        S   V   S   V
        We have a car, but it is being repaired.

1. Pat likes being a camp counselor although the pay is low.

2. Whenever Terry is near a rose, she sneezes violently.

3. Muhammad Ali's victory looked doubtful, but he won the fight.

4. Rita will drive if we help pay for the gas.

5. Owls look wise, yet they are not exceptionally intelligent.

6. I had better get to the library because I have a report due on Monday.

7. I want to visit Loch Ness, where the fabulous monster is supposed to be.

8. My sister saw the King Tut exhibit when it was on tour.

9. We couldn't leave for the party until Fred found his shoes.

10. Delores won the acting award, and everyone applauded.

The subject of a subordinate clause may be either a noun or a pronoun. In addition to such pronouns as *he, she,* and *it,* many subordinate clauses use another kind of pronoun for a subject (*S*): words such as *who, whose, whoever, what, which,* and *that.*

We saw the movie *that was filmed in Antarctica.*

The lawyer examined the evidence *which seemed most crucial* to her client's defense.

A "Trekkie" is a fan *who is devoted to Star Trek.*

Mark mistakenly threw away the pumpkin *that was to become the jack-o'-lantern.*

One peculiarity of the subordinate clause is that it may sometimes begin with a pronoun that is not the subject (*S*), but the direct object (*DO*), as the following sentences illustrate.

We listened to the new records *that Liz got.*

Mother Teresa is a person *whom many people admire* for her courage and compassion.

These must be the keys *that Nickie lost.*

Exercise 2: *Identifying Subordinate Clauses*

Write the sentences on the following page, underlining each subordinate clause. Then label the subject of the subordinate clause *S*, the verb or verb phrase *V*, and the direct object (if there is one) *DO*.

Examples

a. When people diet, they should still eat balanced meals.

When people diet, they should still eat balanced meals.

537

b. This is the model of the medieval castle that we made for history class.

$$\begin{array}{ccc} & \text{DO} & \text{S} & \text{V} \end{array}$$

This is the model of the medieval castle that we made for history class.

1. There are few people who are more versatile than Pearl Bailey.

2. When she began her career, she was a dancer in New York.

3. Later, she became known as a jazz singer who also had a way with comedy.

4. She added acting to her list of accomplishments when she appeared on Broadway in 1946.

5. After she scored a huge success on Broadway, she appeared in a number of films.

6. She appeared on television, which she added to her list of successes.

7. When the all-black performance of *Hello, Dolly* was produced, she received excellent reviews for her starring role.

8. In 1975 she received an honor that she has treasured.

9. She was one of the people who were appointed as U.S. delegates to the United Nations.

10. In 1977 she was given an honorary degree by Georgetown University because she has made so many contributions to society.

Three Types of Subordinate Clauses

A subordinate clause can act as an adjective, an adverb, or a noun. Although the clause is longer than a single-word part of speech and frequently longer than a phrase, it functions exactly as a single-word adjective, adverb, or noun would.

Adjective Clauses

A subordinate clause that modifies a noun or pronoun is called an *adjective clause.*

This is the watch *that I got for my birthday.*

The subordinate clause *that I got for my birthday* modifies the noun *watch*. It answers the question *Which?*

The *italicized* part of each of the following sentences is an adjective clause. An arrow has been drawn from the first word of the adjective clause to the noun or pronoun that is modified.

The people at the party *who saw the UFO* were interviewed by the Air Force.
[Notice that the adjective clause does not always come directly after the word it modifies.]

At the party John wore a tie *that lit up.*

The state *where the largest scout camp is located* is New Mexico.

Brown recluse spiders, *which are highly poisonous,* like secluded, quiet places.

Many adjective clauses begin with a relative pronoun. *Relative pronouns* are the words *who, whom, whose, which,* and *that.* These pronouns are closely related to the word they modify because they restate that word.

I caught the mouse *that got into our pantry.*

We met an astronaut *who had walked on the moon.*

A *pronoun* is a word that takes the place of a noun or another pronoun. The noun or the pronoun that the pronoun stands in place of is called the pronoun's *antecedent*. In the preceding sentences the antecedents are *mouse* and *astronaut*.

Within the adjective clause itself, the relative pronoun may serve as a subject or an object.

S　　　V
There are a few fish *that can travel on land.*

DO　　　　　S　　V
We read an article *that a famous scientist wrote.*

Exercise 3: Identifying Adjective Clauses and Relative Pronouns

Write the sentences on the following page, underlining each adjective clause and circling each relative pronoun. Then draw an arrow from the relative pronoun to its antecedent. Below each sentence designate whether the relative pronoun is the subject of the adjective clause or the direct object of the adjective clause.

Examples

a. My favorite sweat shirt is the one that is always several sizes too large.

My favorite sweat shirt is the one (that) is always several sizes too large.

that = subject of the adjective clause

b. Ms. Washington announced the members whom she had picked for the stage crew.

Ms. Washington announced the members (whom) she had picked for the stage crew.

whom = direct object of the adjective clause

1. Empress Maria Theresa of Austria was a remarkable woman who saved her country from bankruptcy and revolution.

2. Abigail Adams sent the American forces coded information on the British in the letters that she wrote to her husband.

3. Cleopatra was the famous queen whom both Julius Caesar and Mark Antony loved.

4. The Sahara Desert, which is nearly as large as the United States, has less than an inch of rainfall each year.

5. There may be thousands of planets in our galaxy that could support life.

6. The states that are most often struck by tornadoes are in the South and Midwest.

7. The term *boulder* means "a stone that is larger than ten inches in diameter."

8. People who want to see falling stars should watch the sky between midnight and dawn.

9. The state that has the most frequent windstorms is Oklahoma.

10. The highest peak that is found in North America is the great Mount McKinley.

Adverbial Clauses

A subordinate clause that modifies a verb, an adjective, or an adverb is an *adverbial clause.*

The hogs ate *as if they wanted to set a record for greediness.*

The subordinate clause in the preceding sentence functions as an adverbial clause, modifying the word *ate,* and answers the question *How?*

The *italicized* part in each of the following sentences is an adverbial clause, modifying the verb of the main clause.

Before the tornado struck, the air grew still and oppressive.
[*When* did the air grow still and oppressive?]

We went skin diving *where there were no sharks.*
[*Where* did the skin diving take place?]

We didn't take that apartment *because the manager didn't allow pets.*
[*Why* wasn't the apartment taken?]

Akira went to the party *although he had to leave early.*
[*Under what conditions* did Akira go to the party?]

Adverbial clauses can also modify adjectives or adverbs.

This pizza is spicier *than you like.*
[modifies the adjective *spicier*]

The team played harder *than they ever had before.*
[modifies the adverb *harder*]

The first word in an adverbial clause is usually a *subordinating conjunction,* which joins the adverbial clause to a word or words in the main clause. Subordinating conjunctions perform two functions: they *link* the adverbial clause to the main clause of the sentence, and they show the *relationship* between the two clauses.

Penny went to Howard University *because her brother went there.*

The adverbial clause *because her brother went there* modifies the verb *went.* The subordinating conjunction *because* joins the adverbial clause

541

to the main clause and also shows the relationship between the two clauses. In this instance the adverbial clause states the cause of something; it tells why.

The following words are commonly used as subordinating conjunctions. Some consist of more than one word. These compound subordinating conjunctions function as a unit, working in exactly the same way as one-word subordinating conjunctions.

after	even though	though
although	if	until
as far as	in order that	when
as if	provided that	whenever
as long as	since	where
as though	so that	wherever
because	than	whether
before	that	while

Exercise 4: *Identifying Adverbial Clauses and Subordinating Conjunctions*

Write the following sentences, underlining the adverbial clauses and circling the subordinating conjunctions. Below each sentence identify the word that is modified by the clause and tell its part of speech.

Examples

a. After my brother saw the Harlem Globetrotters, he became their biggest fan.

After my brother saw the Harlem Globetrotters, he became their biggest fan.
The adverbial clause modifies the verb *became*.

b. The wallaby is smaller than its relative, the kangaroo, is.

The wallaby is smaller than its relative, the kangaroo, is.

The adverbial clause modifies the adjective *smaller*.

1. Biologist Rachel Carson wrote about environmental problems before most other people were aware of them.

2. When people read her books, they became concerned about ecology.

3. Pollution was more widespread than they had suspected.

4. Some of this pollution has been found so dangerous that people are frightened to drink the water, eat untreated food, and breathe the air.

5. Ms. Carson was certain that the pollution must be stopped to preserve the environment.

6. She fought against many chemical pesticides, since their poisons can pass through the whole food chain.

7. Although the poisons are meant for insects, they can contaminate plants and other animals.

8. Poultry and animals could eat contaminated grains, so that the poisons could end up on our dinner tables.

9. The disadvantages of these pesticides might be greater than any advantages they might have.

10. Because Ms. Carson campaigned long and hard, legislation against dangerous chemical pesticides was passed.

Sometimes an adverbial clause appears incomplete; it may lack a subject, a predicate, or both. These ''incomplete'' structures are still considered adverbial clauses, however, because the missing parts are understood.

You have a better chance *than I.*
[You have a better chance *than I do:* verb understood]

When riding in a car, you should always wear a seat belt for the greatest safety.
[*When you are riding in a car,* you should always wear a seat belt: subject and helping verb understood]

Clauses whose missing parts are filled in by the reader are called *elliptical adverbial clauses. Elliptical* means ''a part has been omitted.''

Younger people require larger quantities of food *than elderly people.*
[elliptical adverbial clause: *than elderly people require*]

I never saw a wild deer *before moving here.*
[elliptical adverbial clause: *before I moved here*]

Some elliptical clauses, such as *before moving here,* resemble participial phrases. An elliptical adverbial clause is *always* introduced by a subordinating conjunction; a participial phrase is not, as illustrated by the examples on the next page.

| I never saw a deer before moving here. | [elliptical adverbial clause] |
| Moving here, I finally saw a deer. | [participial phrase] |

Exercise 5: Identifying Parts and Types of Adverbial Clauses

The following sentences contain adverbial clauses, some of which are elliptical. Write each sentence, underlining each adverbial clause. Below the sentence identify the subject and verb of the adverbial clause. If the clause is elliptical, supply the understood parts beneath the sentence.

Examples

a. When visiting the South Pole, people are often startled by the beautiful auroras.

When visiting the South Pole, people are often startled by the beautiful auroras.

subject: people
verb: are visiting

b. My sister wanted to work a year before she went to college.

My sister wanted to work a year before she went to college.

subject: she
verb: went

1. If the Platte River were any more shallow, it wouldn't be visible at all.

2. When early explorers named it, they named it aptly.

3. The word *Platte* is appropriate because it means "flat."

4. When first seen, the Platte looks "a mile wide and an inch deep."

5. In some places it seems no deeper than a puddle.

6. When hot weather rolls around, much of the Platte goes dry.

7. It will be full of sandbars as far as you can see.

8. When the pioneers moved westward, many followed the Platte River.

9. This was not surprising because one of the world's great natural roads ran beside the river.

10. It was a natural highway better than many constructed roads.

Noun Clauses

When a subordinate clause functions as a noun in a sentence, it is called a *noun clause*.

A noun clause can perform any function that an ordinary noun can; it can serve as subject, direct object, indirect object, predicate noun, appositive, or object of a preposition.

Whoever donates to the fund gets an inscribed plaque.
[noun clause as subject]

The mechanic didn't know *what the problem was*.
[noun clause as direct object]

Grandfather will give *whatever is robbing the henhouse* a load of buckshot.
[noun clause as indirect object]

I wouldn't want to guess about *what will happen*.
[noun clause as object of the preposition *about*]

The executive's problem was *that she hated to fire anyone*.
[noun clause as predicate noun]

The biggest trophy goes to the champion team, *whoever wins the conference title*.
[noun clause as appositive]

Noun clauses usually begin with one of the following words: *who, whoever, whom, whomsoever, whomever, what, whatever, that, which, when, how, where, wherever,* or *whether*. Sometimes, the introductory word serves merely as a conjunction to join the noun clause to the main clause of the sentence. Other times, however, the introductory word may function as the subject, direct object, or modifier within the noun clause itself.

I knew *that she called*.
[*She* is the subject of the noun clause; *that* serves only to join the clause to the rest of the sentence.]

I know *how we can accomplish the task*.
[*We* is the subject of the noun clause; *how* is an adverb modifying *can accomplish*.]

When the conjunction serves only to join the noun clause to the remainder of the sentence, it can usually be dropped without changing the sentence's meaning.

We knew *that we should leave early.*

We knew *we should leave early.*

Exercise 6: Identifying Noun Clauses and Their Introductory Words

Write the following sentences, underlining each noun clause and circling the word that introduces the clause. If the introductory word can be dropped without changing the meaning of the sentence, draw an X through it. Beneath each sentence tell how the noun clause functions within the sentence.

Examples

    a. We could order whatever we wanted at the restaurant.

      We could order (whatever) we wanted at the restaurant.

      direct object

    b. I believe that the guilty person is Colonel Mustard.

      I believe (that) the guilty person is Colonel Mustard.

      direct object

1. The director thought that the play was moving too slowly.
2. How the squirrels got into our attic is a mystery.
3. The old prospector claimed that there were large uranium deposits in the mountains.
4. The customers demanded that the store return their money.
5. I know who put the salt in the sugar bowl.
6. What I want for my birthday is a pair of chinchillas.
7. Miss Shimura doesn't know who can help you.
8. Give these old magazines to whoever wants them.
9. I think that I have eaten too much guacamole.
10. California is where most American movies are made.

Review: Understanding Clauses

Write the following sentences, underlining the subordinate clauses. Beneath each sentence write whether the subordinate clause is an adjective, an adverbial, or a noun clause. If it is an adjective or an adverbial clause, draw an arrow from the clause to the word or words it modifies. If it is a noun clause, write its function beneath the sentence.

Examples

a. Early arctic explorers quickly discovered that their scientifically designed equipment was inadequate.

Early arctic explorers quickly discovered that their scientifically designed equipment was inadequate.

noun clause, direct object

b. The clothing and tools that the Eskimos had designed were superior in many cases.

The clothing and tools that the Eskimos had designed were superior in many cases.
adjective clause

1. One of the most gifted writers who ever lived was William Shakespeare.

2. Although his works are famous throughout the world, we know relatively little about his life.

3. We know that he was born in April 1564 in England.

4. Although we have much information on other writers of the time, we know little about Shakespeare's youth, habits, personality, or education.

5. We do not even know what his religion was.

6. What we do know is that he created some of the greatest characters in literature.

7. He presents these characters in situations that are dramatic and revealing.

8. The character Othello, for instance, shows how jealousy can destroy a noble mind.

9. Hamlet is an appealing, bright, young man who is trapped in an impossible situation.

10. Romeo and Juliet dramatize the sort of passionate love that can be destructive.

11. The play *King Lear* presents characters who are representatives of the best and worst of humanity.

12. Shakespeare is often praised because he portrayed realistic and spirited women.

13. His best heroines are women who speak their minds and are not passive.

14. His Cleopatra is a woman who is unforgettable.

15. There is Cordelia, who is honest, loving, and brave.

16. Portia, who is a character in *The Merchant of Venice*, is quick-witted and spunky.

17. Few writers could invent villains that are nastier than William Shakespeare's.

18. Iago is one of the most despicable characters that ever trod a stage.

19. What he wants to do is destroy the brave Othello.

20. He employs a plan that is a masterpiece of creativity and cold-blooded cunning.

Using Clauses

In the following sections you will practice punctuating clauses. As you work through the exercises in the next sections, refer to Understanding Clauses for any help you might need in recognizing the different kinds of clauses and their functions in explaining the message of a sentence.

Punctuating Adjective Clauses

An *essential adjective clause* adds information that is necessary to the meaning of a sentence.

The physics teacher will give an *A* to every student *who gets an* A *on the final.*

The adjective clause in the preceding example is *who gets an* A *on the final.* It is an essential clause since the meaning of the sentence would change radically if the clause were dropped:

The physics teacher will give an *A* to every student.

Do not use commas with an essential adjective clause.

Sometimes, however, the adjective clause only adds extra information, information that does not change the basic meaning of the sentence.

Riko, *who is a good student,* received an *A* in physics.

The adjective clause in the preceding sentence, *who is a good student,* is *nonessential* because the basic meaning of the sentence would remain the same if the clause were dropped:

Riko received an *A* in physics.

A speaker generally pauses before and after a nonessential clause. Read the following sentences aloud, and you will see how the pauses set the nonessential clauses off a bit from the rest of the sentence.

My car, *which is eleven years old,* probably won't last much longer the way I drive.

In Hawaii we saw Mrs. Diaz, *who was visiting her daughter.*

We visited the city of St. Joseph, Missouri, *where the pony express started.*

Exercise 7: Punctuating Adjective Clauses

Write the sentences on the following page, using commas to set off any nonessential clause from the rest of its sentence. Underline the adjective clauses and circle the commas you insert.

Examples

a. Dianne Feinstein who is a Democrat was elected mayor of San Francisco.

Dianne Feinstein , who is a Democrat , was elected mayor of San Francisco.

549

b. The first person who developed a pure white marigold received an enormous cash prize.

The first person who developed a pure white marigold received an enormous cash prize.

1. The Wright brothers were not the first persons who flew by mechanical means.

2. In 1380 J. B. Dante who was an Italian mathematician built a set of artificial wings.

3. He made several flights over a local lake that were quite successful.

4. Later, he had an accident that caused the left wing to break.

5. His subsequent fall which broke his leg ended his flying career.

6. In 1678 Besnier who was a French locksmith perfected a glider.

7. He did not take many chances on his first test flight which was off a chair.

8. He later made a flight that took him over a neighbor's roof.

9. Besnier who was not a daredevil sold his glider to a traveling acrobat.

10. The acrobat used the glider in demonstrations that made him the hit of county fairs.

Punctuating Adverbial Clauses

An introductory adverbial clause is *always* followed by a comma.

When I ate, my dog kept looking at me soulfully.

If the introductory clause were not set off, the reader might run the two clauses together and get a jolt:

When I ate my dog / kept looking at me soulfully.

The comma prevents momentary confusion.

Usually an adverbial clause is not set off by a comma when the clause appears at the end of a sentence. However, a comma is often used before an adverbial clause that begins with *though* and *although* and before *as* and *since* when they mean "because."

Jenny didn't do well on the test, *although* she had studied very hard.

We didn't remove the storm windows, *as* we thought the cold weather would continue.

Raoul withdrew from the contest, *since* he found he was ineligible.

Exercise 8: *Punctuating Adverbial Clauses*

Write the following sentences, adding commas wherever they are necessary. Underline the adverbial clauses and circle the commas you insert.

Examples

a. When the school band gave its holiday concert the band director put a large bow on her baton.

  When the school band gave its holiday concert ⊙ the band director put a large bow on her baton.

b. We shouldn't swim there if there isn't a lifeguard.

  We shouldn't swim there if there isn't a lifeguard.

1. When Europeans first came to South America the Incas had a great civilization.

2. They had developed an irrigation system better than any developed in Europe.

3. Their engineering was also better than the Europeans' was.

4. When the Inca empire was at its height it had highly skilled surgeons and dentists.

5. We owe much of our modern diet to the Incas since they were the first to cultivate the potato and several other vegetables.

6. Although Native Americans supposedly never discovered the wheel there are indications that the Incas may have used wheels.

7. The Incas built towers so that they could observe the sun's movements.

8. They may have had a calendar though this is not certain.

9. Certain statues and structures look as though they might have been decorated with symbols for days and months.

10. Many of the Incas' fine statues and beautiful goldwork remain although much was looted or destroyed by the Europeans.

Review: Using Clauses

Write each of the following sentences, underlining each adjective clause and circling the noun or pronoun that it modifies. Add commas where necessary to set off a nonessential clause from the rest of the sentence. Circle the commas you insert.

Examples

a. The Supremes who were three high school girls from Detroit became one of America's top singing groups.

The (Supremes) ⊙ who were three high school girls from

Detroit ⊙ became one of America's top singing groups.

b. The American animal that is most dangerous is the buffalo.

The American (animal) that is most dangerous is the buffalo.

1. The nineteenth-century American who went west by covered wagon was a hardy soul.

2. These westward treks which were arduous were often made by groups of people.

3. A large group of pioneers that traveled together formed a "wagon train."

4. Roads that were rugged or nonexistent often made the trip uncomfortable.

5. Oxen which were slow but extremely hardy made the best work animals.

6. The jolting ride was one that shook the pioneer's teeth and bones.

7. Enterprising pioneer women learned to use the jolting which marked every mile of the journey.

8. Those who owned cows would milk them in the morning.

9. They hung buckets of cream on the wagons which jiggled and jolted all day long.

10. By evening the cream that had been in the bucket had turned to fresh butter.

Write the following sentences and add all necessary punctuation. Underline each adverbial clause and circle the commas you insert. (Remember that adverbial clauses may be elliptical clauses.)

Examples

a. It takes more facial muscles to frown than it does to smile.

It takes more facial muscles to frown than it does to smile.

b. When the mail carrier arrives my dog barks wildly.

When the mail carrier arrives, my dog barks wildly.

11. Winds are caused when air temperatures differ.

12. The sun heats some portions of the earth more than it heats others.

13. When the earth's surface is warmed the heat is conducted into the air.

14. Warm air is lighter than cool air.

15. It is warmer because its molecules are moving more rapidly.

16. The rapidly moving molecules spread farther apart than cold air molecules.

17. Because the molecules are less dense the warm air exerts lower pressure.

18. Wherever one of these low pressure centers exists colder, heavier air flows toward it.

19. The winds blow because differences in temperature and pressure cause the air to move.

20. You can predict coming weather by observing the wind though you must know what to look for.

Writing Focus: *Using Clauses in Writing*

You can improve your writing by using clauses to add details, to combine sentences, to show relationships, and to vary sentence structure. To decide whether a clause should be set off by punctuation, determine its position and function in the sentence.

Assignment: *A Restaurant in the Future*

Imagine that you are on a time machine that projects you several hundred years into the future. The time machine bumps you to a futuristic restaurant. As you enter the restaurant, what might you see, hear, smell, touch, taste, or feel? Once you are inside, a couple invites you to join them for dinner. What kind of meal might you eat? How is it served?

For this assignment, write a description of your experience in this futuristic restaurant. Describe what the restaurant and the people in it look like. Describe the meal you eat. Include sensory details in your description that will help your readers feel as though they have been there. Consider that your description will be evaluated for effective use of clauses.

Use the following steps to complete the assignment.

A. Prewriting

Before writing the description, make a word cluster for the futuristic restaurant you visit. (See Chapter 1 for an explanation of clustering.) Give your restaurant a name. Then imagine the setting of the restaurant. Will it be somewhere on earth, in outer space, or on a distant planet? In your word cluster, write details about what you might see, hear, smell, touch, taste, or feel. Let your imagination go as you try to visualize your experience. Include specific details about how people look and act, the kind of meal you eat, and how it is served.

B. Writing

Write a description of a restaurant of the future, using some of the ideas in your word cluster. Include sensory details that will give readers a clear picture of your experience. Describe the restaurant, the

people, and the meal you eat. As you write, vary your sentences by using clauses in different ways.

C. Postwriting

Using the following checklist, revise your first draft.

1.   In my description, have I included enough specific details about every sight, sound, smell, texture, and taste that I imagined?

2.   Are clauses used effectively to vary the structure of sentences?

3.   Are there sentence fragments or short sentences that can be combined by using clauses?

4.   Have I punctuated each clause correctly?

Edit your revision, using the Proofreader's Checklist at the back of the book. If appropriate, share your writing with the members of your class and discuss how eating out in the future could be different from having a meal in a restaurant today.

21 Sentence Structure

Understanding Sentences

In this section you will learn the four basic sentence types. This knowledge will help you to vary your sentence structure, an important part of effective writing.

Four Sentence Structures

Every sentence must contain at least one independent clause. Some sentences contain more than one independent clause and may contain subordinate clauses as well. Sentences can be classified according to the types of clauses they contain. Every sentence has one of four basic structures: *simple, compound, complex,* or *compound-complex.*

A *simple sentence* contains only one independent clause and no subordinate clauses.

        S   V
Fish swim.

The subject and verb in a simple sentence may have complements and modifying words and phrases.

                            S   V   DO
The brightly colored fish at the aquarium fill the tanks.

A simple sentence may contain a compound subject, a compound verb, or a subject and verb that are both compound. It remains a simple sentence, however; the compound elements are part of only one independent clause.

          S   S   S   V   V
Kathy, Julio, and Kim made the posters and distributed them.

A *compound sentence* contains more than one independent clause but no subordinate clause.

Independent Clause		Independent Clause
The sky was cloudy,	and	a chilly drizzle was falling.

The independent clauses may have compound subjects and verbs, but there must be two (or more) independent clauses.

$$\text{Cows and zebras are herbivorous; they eat vegetable matter.}$$

Cows and zebras <u>are</u> herbivorous; they <u>eat</u> vegetable matter.

A *complex sentence* contains only one independent clause, but it can have several subordinate clauses.

Subordinate	Independent	Subordinate
After Troy fell,	Aeneas fled with his father,	who had to be carried.
While we were shopping,	we noticed a man	who had an unusual hairstyle.

A *compound-complex sentence* contains more than one independent clause and at least one subordinate clause.

Subordinate	Independent	Independent
After they both ate lunch,	Carol went to her house,	and Anne went to work.
Although it was late,	Joey was still studying,	and his mother was sorting her files.

Exercise 1: *Identifying Sentence Structures*

Write the sentences on the following page, underlining each independent clause once and each subordinate clause twice. Below each sentence identify whether that sentence is *simple, compound, complex,* or *compound-complex.*

Examples

a. When water freezes, it expands.

When water freezes, it expands.

complex sentence

557

b. The Rocky Mountains were called "The Shining Mountains" by native Americans.

The Rocky Mountains were called "The Shining Mountains"

by native Americans.

simple sentence

1. The roller skate was invented in Belgium in the eighteenth century.

2. The four-wheeled roller skate, as we know it, did not appear until almost a century later.

3. The first roller rink opened in Rhode Island in 1866, and rinks appeared in Europe soon afterward.

4. When the Grand Hall Olympia Rink opened in London, it was the world's largest rink, but it operated for only four years.

5. The largest modern rink, which is located in Illinois, is the Fireside Roll-Arena.

6. Roller hockey was invented in 1870, and now there is an international Roller Hockey Association that sponsors world championship competitions.

7. Britain took the first world championship, but Portugal, which has won eleven championships, is the most frequent victor.

8. Skates can be speedy; the world's official record is almost twenty-six miles an hour.

9. This record was set in Italy, where a number of speeding records have been made.

10. A Canadian who was a glutton for punishment skated from New York to California, which is a trip of 3,100 miles.

Review: Understanding Sentences

Write the sentences on the following page, and beneath each one list and label the independent clauses and the subordinate clauses. Then underline the simple subject or subjects in each clause once and the verb or verbs twice. Finally, identify the sentence structure as *simple, compound, complex,* or *compound-complex.*

Example

a. My brother is now playing the bagpipes, which doesn't make our neighbors too happy.

My <u>brother</u> <u>is</u> now <u>playing</u> the bagpipes
—independent clause
<u>which</u> <u>doesn't</u> <u>make</u> our neighbors too happy
—dependent clause
complex sentence

1. The world's largest geyser is Waimangu, which is in New Zealand.

2. This geyser resembles a volcano erupting.

3. Waimangu is a relatively young geyser; it first appeared during the summer of 1886.

4. The geyser was created when a great volcanic eruption altered much of the island.

5. The American geyser Old Faithful erupts regularly and with the same force each time.

6. The eruptions of Waimangu, however, are both irregular and dangerous.

7. The geyser sometimes explodes unexpectedly; when this happens, steam and boiling mud are flung into the air.

8. Although the eruptions are always spectacular, the geyser is more active at certain times than it is at others.

9. At its peak performance, it flings stones, mud, and water to a height of 1,500 feet.

10. An unexpected eruption that killed three people resulted in the geyser's basin being railed as a safety precaution.

11. Visitors traveling through the region will see a mysterious and alien landscape.

12. Ponds boil and craters seethe like witches' cooking pots.

13. One dangerous area is named The Inferno, meaning "hell."

14. The rocks are stained yellow with sulfur, and the earth is too hot to touch.

15. Poking a stick into the ground causes a spurt of steam or boiling water to rise.

16. Since the lakes are often steaming and sulfurous, a foul smell hangs in the air, and large mudholes burble while puffs of steam rise and drift.

17. Although there are ghastly and unearthly sights, there is beauty in the area as well; strangely colored lakes make the spectator feel as if he or she is in some sort of wonderland.

18. Although you can take scores of snapshots, you can never capture the strange magnificence of this exotic world.

19. Naturally heated pools of clear water are good for swimming.

20. The major lake, Rotomahana, seems to be a slab of turquoise; in addition, it has green islands full of ferns and vines.

Using Sentences

In the following sections you will learn to recognize and avoid run-on sentences and sentence fragments in your writing. You will also use your understanding of the four basic sentence structures to vary the sentence structure in your writing.

Avoiding Run-On Sentences

When two or more sentences are joined with a comma or with no punctuation at all, the resulting group of words is called a *run-on sentence.*

Run-On:	Go down to the end of this block, then look to the left.
Correct:	Go down to the end of this block. Then look to the left.
Run-On:	Davey is a good pitcher his sister is a good fielder.
Correct:	Davey is a good pitcher; his sister is a good fielder.

Run-on sentences may be corrected by separating the sentences completely or by joining them with appropriate punctuation or wording.

You may separate the sentences with end punctuation.

Run-On:	Today is Julian Bond's birthday, mine is tomorrow.
Correct:	Today is Julian Bond's birthday. Mine is tomorrow.

You may use a semicolon to separate closely related sentences.

Run-On: Robin can't go on the canoe trip he has a broken arm.

Correct: Robin can't go on the canoe trip; he has a broken arm.

You may also use a semicolon and a conjunctive adverb to join the two sentences. The adverb, which is always followed by a comma, shows the relationship of one of the sentences to the other.

Run-On: I can no longer work full time, maintain the household, and still serve on four committees, I resign.

Correct: I can no longer work full time, maintain the household, and still serve on four committees; *therefore*, I resign.

You may use a comma followed by a coordinating conjunction to combine the two sentences.

Run-On: Art is building a burglar alarm system his sister is helping him.

Correct: Art is building a burglar alarm system, *and* his sister is helping him.

You may change one of the sentences into a subordinate clause.

Run-On: Sophia Sanchez has been appointed to the mayor's special task force, she is director of the Community Health Agency.

Correct: Sophia Sanchez, *who is director of the Community Health Agency*, has been appointed to the mayor's special task force.

Exercise 2: Correcting Run-On Sentences

Using the methods mentioned in the previous section, correct each of the run-on sentences here and on the following page. Write the corrected sentences on a separate sheet of paper.

Example

a. Nancy Lieberman is first-round draft pick of the Dallas Diamonds, she played a game with the Celtics.
   Nancy Lieberman, who is first-round draft pick of the Dallas Diamonds, played a game with the Celtics.

1. On his sixty-fifth birthday, Jack LaLanne towed sixty-five row-boats for almost a mile, they were loaded with 6,500 pounds of wood pulp.

2. A strep throat outbreak has spread among 900 inmates at the county jail, the jail has been quarantined since last weekend.

3. Jerome Robbins is a well-known choreographer, he has choreographed Broadway musicals, such as *Fiddler on the Roof.*

4. The trucking industry has been deregulated one bus company has lowered its fares by 10 percent.

5. Strokes are caused by blockages or breaks in blood vessels supplying the brain, during a stroke a part of the brain is destroyed because of a lack of blood.

6. Fleer Corporation of Philadelphia claims that it invented bubble gum, it is suing Topps Chewing Gum Company for monopolizing the rights to photos of major league baseball players for bubble gum cards.

7. Cities in the North report that they are losing industries, more and more industries are moving to the Sunbelt states.

8. The administration has endorsed a settlement between the federal government and the Passamaquoddy and Malecites more than 12.5 million acres of land in Maine are in dispute.

9. Volcanic ash has covered the Boeing training field in Moses Lake, Washington, Boeing is temporarily moving its training operation to Montana.

10. In a journal called *Signs of Spring,* Laurel Lee writes about her life-and-death battle with Hodgkin's disease, she is a divorced mother of three young children.

Avoiding Sentence Fragments

Fragments are not complete sentences. Remember the three requirements for a complete sentence:

1. A sentence expresses a complete thought.

2. A sentence has a subject.

3. A sentence has a verb.

In a sentence fragment, one or more of these requirements is missing.

Sentences that do not conform to Edited Standard English are marked with an asterisk (*).

| **Incomplete Thought:** | *Because it is so hot. |
| **Sentence:** | Because it is so hot, few people entered the marathon. |

No Subject:	*Hurried into the river.
Sentence:	A mother duck and thirteen ducklings hurried into the river.
No Verb:	*The Beaux Arts Trio appearing in a Beethoven concert.
Sentence:	The Beaux Arts Trio is appearing in a Beethoven concert.

Phrases, clauses, and appositives are sentence fragments when they are written independently, because they do not express complete thoughts.

A *phrase* does not have both a subject and a predicate. When a prepositional phrase, infinitive phrase, participial phrase, or gerund phrase is written as a sentence, it is a sentence fragment.

Fragment:	*In the stacks of the university library.
Sentence:	Teresa spent three days working in the stacks of the university library.
Fragment:	*Hank waiting for the Staten Island ferry.
Sentence:	Hank, waiting for the Staten Island ferry, met an old neighbor from Decatur, Georgia.
Fragment:	*Singing in the rain.
Sentence:	Singing in the rain can lead to pneumonia.

A *subordinate clause* contains both a subject and a verb but does not express a complete thought. A subordinate clause must be attached to an independent clause; it cannot stand alone.

Fragment:	*Before the bus leaves for Sea World.
Sentence:	Before the bus leaves for Sea World, be sure to check the return schedule.
Fragment:	*Because he gives her too much work.
Sentence:	Alice is angry with Frank because he gives her too much work.

An *appositive* is a word or group of words that identifies a noun or pronoun. An appositive cannot be punctuated as a sentence because it does not express a complete thought.

Fragment:	*A delicious dish of cheese-stuffed pasta in tomato sauce.
Sentence:	Al's mother made manicotti, a delicious dish of cheese-stuffed pasta in tomato sauce.

Exercise 3: Correcting Sentence Fragments

Revise the following sentences, correcting all sentence fragments. (There may be several ways to correct any one fragment.)

Examples

a. Marika had to throw the lobster back into the water. Because it was too little.
Marika had to throw the lobster back into the water because it was too little.

b. Ira Gershwin wrote the lyrics to "They Can't Take That Away from Me." Which is from the movie *Shall We Dance?* with Fred Astaire and Ginger Rogers.
Ira Gershwin wrote the lyrics to "They Can't Take That Away from Me," which is from the movie *Shall We Dance?* with Fred Astaire and Ginger Rogers.

1. To finish before the deadline. We will have to work late every night.

2. Jeremy is working at a used car lot on South Street. Washing and waxing the cars.

3. Because two of the students are still missing. We cannot leave the beach yet.

4. We bought a nylon tent. With twenty-six books of stamps saved from the supermarket.

5. She brewed a fragrant pot of tea when we arrived at the resort after a night of moonlight skiing. A blend of mountain teas, oranges, and spices.

6. The Ammers found many changes in their life-style. After moving to Boston, Massachusetts, from San Francisco, California, to start a new profession.

7. Tracy sketched the sleeping male mandrill. A baboon with blue and scarlet markings on its face.

8. Although it is well past midnight. None of the children shows any signs of being sleepy, even though they had a tiring day at the beach.

9. Have you read *The Invisible Man?* Ralph Ellison's only published novel.

10. More than 150 people applied for the job. Creating unbelievable chaos in the normally quiet office.

Improving Sentence Style

By now you have probably discovered that it is not always easy to say clearly and smoothly what you mean. A sentence may be grammatically correct and still be ineffective. This section will give you some suggestions on improving your sentence style.

Diction

When students are serious about trying to improve their writing, they sometimes try to use difficult words and write in long, involved sentences. Such writing, they think, sounds "more educated." However, the aim of all your writing should be to express your ideas as clearly and simply as possible. Look at the following sentences, for example.

Poor: By elevating the window, she was able to observe that the atmospheric conditions had undergone a change and that there was precipitation of a rather heavy nature.

Better: By raising the window, she saw that the weather had changed and that it was raining heavily.

Diction means "word choice." Whenever you write, you must think about your audience and purpose, for these considerations affect your choice of words. You can see why a letter to a friend, for example, would have more informal language than a term paper in English. Even when you write a formal paper, however, keep in mind that your goal is always to say what you mean in the clearest—which usually means the simplest—way possible. In this sense, *simple* does not mean writing a series of short, choppy sentences that sound like the writing of a third-grader. *Simple* does mean using a vocabulary that accomplishes your purpose without forcing the reader to resort to an unabridged dictionary or to a technical book. *Simple* also means that your sentences sound smooth and are reasonable in length.

Poor: During our sojourn at your celebration, our level of pleasure rose to extremely high degrees.

Better: We enjoyed ourselves immensely at your party.

Poor: The bovine creature catapulted over the lunar body.

Better: The cow jumped over the moon.

Conciseness

A mark of good writing is conciseness: get to the point, and do not waste words. Being concise does not mean that your writing needs to sound like a telegram. It does mean, however, that you should always proofread your first draft to eliminate wordiness, stalling, and unnecessary repetition. Do not be afraid to come right out and say what you mean.

Poor: It has come to my attention that certain correspondences pertaining to the romantic relationship between my parents in the days before their marriage are located in a cardboard receptacle on the topmost storage shelf in the closet near the front door of the apartment.

Better: I found my parents' old love letters in a box on the top shelf of the front closet.

Poor: In the event that nobody would communicate with her about an excursion for the Fourth of July, Suzanne had several alternate plans in mind for ways in which she might occupy herself on that day.

Better: In case no one called her with plans for the Fourth of July, Suzanne had several things in mind that she could do.

Poor: I tiptoed quietly toward the car, thinking in my mind that I was probably unobtrusively hidden from view.

Better: I tiptoed toward the car, thinking I was hidden.

Weak Constructions

Action verbs may be written in either the active voice or the passive voice.

Active: The right fielder *caught* the line drive.

Passive: The line drive *was caught* by the right fielder.

Whenever possible, use the active voice instead of the passive voice. The active voice is stronger and more effective.

Weaker: At the graduation ceremony, tickets were taken and programs were handed out by eleventh-graders.

Stronger: At the graduation ceremony, eleventh-graders took the tickets and handed out the programs.

Sentences that begin with "There is . . ." and "There are . . ." should also be rephrased whenever possible.

Weaker:	There are three reasons why everyone objected to the new rule.
Stronger:	Everyone objected to the new rule for three reasons.
Weaker:	There is not enough time for the performers to attend the party before the play.
Stronger:	The performers do not have enough time to attend the party before the play.

Exercise 4: Improving Sentence Style

Revise the following sentences to improve diction, conciseness, and weak constructions. Write the revised sentences.

Example

a. The consensus of opinion among the delegates by a show of hands was to adjourn the proceedings until the next week.
   The delegates voted to adjourn the meeting until the next week.

1. There are few people who realize how lucky they are to enjoy good health until disease strikes them.

2. The variegated hues of the hibiscus graced the foliage adjacent to the fence.

3. There was something that needed to be discussed, but neither of them wanted to be the first to bring it up.

4. Invitations to the young artists' preview were sent by the gallery owner to members of the press.

5. In the event that you do not find me or any of the members of my family in our abode, please attempt to reach me by mail.

6. Three reasons for requesting zoning variances were given by the young lawyer representing the developer.

7. The books were packed by Gwen and taken to the Veterans Hospital.

8. There is a certain kind of tool, which must be sharp, that is necessary for anyone who is trying to cut a linoleum block.

9. The names of the three winners are announced by the disc jockey at noon every Saturday.

10. It is the job of one full-time county employee to give water and to give fertilizer to every potted plant in the offices of the county government.

Review: Using Sentences

Revise each of the following, correcting sentence fragments and run-ons.

1. Albacore is an important game fish in the Atlantic and Pacific Oceans, it is found in waters of 60 to 66 degrees Fahrenheit.

2. Child-resistant containers have significantly reduced accidental poisoning deaths, for example, deaths from lye products for children under five have decreased 50 percent.

3. The highest navigable lake is 2½-mile-high Lake Titicaca. Known as the Lake of the Clouds.

4. The element selenium was discovered by the Swedish scientist Jöns Berzelius, it is used in photocopy machines and TV cameras.

5. Benjamin Hooks urges every black citizen to register and vote, by becoming a political force, he believes, blacks can influence national and local elected leaders.

6. A new kind of nuclear weapon has been developed. Which is deadly to humans but does much less damage to buildings and property than H-bombs.

7. You can nod and say "Howdy" to a stranger on the trail according to *The Cowboy Catalogue* don't wave because raising a hand can cause a horse to bolt.

8. Graphologists say that a far-forward slant indicates an outgoing, warm personality, a very large capital *I* shows a writer with a high opinion of himself or herself.

9. *Walden Two* is a novel about a utopian community. Written by B. F. Skinner, a behavioral psychologist.

10. It is a good idea to throw a jacket or other object in its path. When being chased by a bull.

11. Americans suffering from acne spend almost $200 million a year for doctors, they spend at least $125 million for medicine.

12. The state with the greatest percentage of shoreline as its boundary is Hawaii. Which is made up of eight islands.

13. Pope John Paul II visited Brazil. Where he urged enthusiastic audiences to embrace traditional values and secure the family.

14. An important index to the nation's economy is the Gross National Product (GNP), it is the total output of goods and services.

15. In 1886 in Haymarket Square in Chicago. A crowd of labor unionists and police clashed in the Haymarket Riot.

16. The word *bachelor* comes originally from two Latin words that mean "dairy farm." *Bacca,* cow, and *-arium*, place.

17. In geometry a decahedron is a solid figure having ten surfaces, a hendecahedron has eleven surfaces.

18. Several years ago a syndicated 'columnist asked her readers if they would have children if they had to do it all over again more than 70 percent said no.

19. Bees build honeycomb, rows of hexagonal cells, from wax, it is used for storing honey, pollen, and eggs.

20. The most famous of the mythical gorgons is Medusa. Whose glance could turn a human to stone.

Writing Focus: *Improving*

Sentence Structure in Writing

You can strengthen your writing style and make your writing more lively by using a variety of sentence structures. As you write, strive to use a combination of simple, compound, complex, and compound-complex sentences. Make sure you use complete sentences and avoid sentence fragments or run-ons.

Assignment: *Survival*

Imagine that you were marooned on a deserted island in the Pacific for six months. After being rescued, you are asked to write an article for a magazine about how you survived. The editor asks you to concentrate on explaining exactly what you did during the first three days, which were the most crucial.

As you write, consider that your article will be evaluated for correct and varied sentences.

569

Use the following steps to complete this assignment.

A. Prewriting

Picture the physical surroundings, food and water sources, and any useful items you might find on the island. List the essential items you will need to survive. Then list the steps you would follow in order to survive. Don't worry about the order of the steps. For now, jot down everything you can think of that will help explain how you would survive on an island, using specific details. Then group and number the steps in the order you would perform them.

B. Writing

Using your list, write an article explaining how you survived on a deserted island. Concentrate on the events during the first three days. Then go through the steps of what you actually did to survive. Use words like *first, next, then,* and *while* to connect ideas. As you write, pay attention to using a variety of complete sentences.

C. Postwriting

Revise your first draft using the following checklist.

1. Have I included specific details that explain how I survived?

2. Is my explanation organized so that each step follows the one before?

3. Have I varied the structure of my sentences?

Edit your draft using the Proofreader's Checklist at the back of the book. If appropriate, share your writing with your classmates to compare methods of survival.

3
Mechanics

22 Punctuation

The Uses of Punctuation

In general, punctuation works in four ways: to separate, to link, to enclose, and to show omission.

Use a mark of punctuation *to separate* certain ideas or elements in your writing so they do not run together. For example, a period (.) separates one sentence from another. A comma (,) separates items within a sentence.

> Tom campaigned vigorously, stirred enthusiasm, and won. In fact, he won by a landslide.

Use a mark of punctuation *to link* ideas or words. For example, a hyphen (-) joins parts of compound words.

> Mary is my sister-in-law.

Quotation marks ('') are an example of punctuation used *to enclose*. These marks are usually used in pairs to set off a speaker's exact words.

> "I'll cook some chili," Sam announced.

Note that quotation marks have a dual role. They enclose a direct quotation and, at the same time, separate the speaker's words from the rest of the sentence.

An apostrophe (') is used *to omit* a letter or letters from a word, as in the contraction *didn't*.

> Jackie didn't call. [Jackie did not call.]

Exercise 1: Identifying Uses of Punctuation

Write the following sentences. Beneath each one indicate whether the punctuation separates, links, encloses, or shows omission.

Example

a. Let's go to the antique show. It opens tomorrow.
   apostrophe—shows omission; period—separates

1. Early American patchwork quilts followed certain patterns. One pattern is called "courthouse steps."

2. "That quilt is in flawless condition," the man argued.

3. We bought a couch, a rug, and two lamps.

4. I hope my grandmother hasn't thrown out her oak rocking chair.

5. Where's my coat? I left it here, but now I can't find it.

6. The Shakers were very inventive. Did you know they invented the clothespin?

7. "I can't imagine that old table is valuable," Louise laughed.

8. Linda bought some fabric, quickly cut out panels, and made curtains for her kitchen.

9. Wouldn't you love a big, soft, comfortable sofa?

10. My sister-in-law keeps her books in an old library cabinet. Those cabinets aren't made anymore.

The Period

The *period* is used as an end mark to separate sentences or as a mark that shows the omission of letters in abbreviations.

Use a period after a *declarative sentence*. A declarative sentence makes a statement.

It has started to rain.

We wondered when the rain would stop.

Use a period after a mildly *imperative sentence*. An imperative sentence makes a command.

Please wait in line.

Call me tomorrow.

Generally, use a period to show the omission of letters from some *abbreviations*.

Dr.	doctor
A.M.	ante meridiem [before noon]
P.M.	post meridiem [after noon]
Sr.	senior
Mr.	mister
Sgt.	sergeant
Chas.	Charles

Use a period with some abbreviations (such as *Ms.* and *Mrs.*) that cannot be spelled out.

Note: Do not use a period following the abbreviations for metric units (*5 cc, 20 kg, 100 ml*), two-letter postal abbreviations for states in addresses (*NJ—New Jersey, CA—California, TX—Texas*), and for most governmental agencies (*NATO, NASA, TVA*). In addition, some large corporations have abbreviated their names without using periods, and some other common abbreviations are also written without periods: *CBS, TWA, YWCA, AM, FM, mph, TV.*

Exercise 2: Using the Period

Write the following sentences, using periods where necessary. Remember to capitalize the first word in each sentence. Circle the periods you insert.

Examples

a. Stu is a disc jockey on radio he never plays disco music.

Stu is a disc jockey on radio⊙ He never plays disco music.

b. Call Jack Wallace, Jr, to see if his party starts at 7 PM.

Call Jack Wallace, Jr ⊙ , to see if his party starts at 7 P ⊙ M.

1. Dr Walters has a TV in her office in town you can watch it while awaiting your appointment.

2. Mrs Lytton has a job interview tomorrow at Computerage, Inc in Dayton she's applying for a job as a division supervisor.

3. Pour 100 ml of liquid onto the piece of stone according to our professor, Dr A Morton, the stone will turn blue.

4. Joseph's Uncle Armstrong works for the FBI he is stationed in St Louis.

5. While in Egypt, Sgt B Lyons visited the Pyramid of Cheops it was built earlier than 2000 BC and is still standing!

6. That toaster is guaranteed for two years send the warranty card to the following address:
Electrik Ease, Inc
Product Div
1500 Gen Robt E Lee Pl
Atlanta, GA 30336

7. All the recipes in Ms Greene's cookbook have been converted to the metric system instead of saying, "Add 1 oz," the recipe now reads, "Add 28 gr of chocolate."

8. At 10 AM tomorrow "The Humor Hour" will feature the works of S J Perelman and Mark Twain the program's station is 1050 on the AM dial.

9. John Jordan, Jr, used to be an agent in the CIA now he works for IBM.

10. Prof Wm Marks invited us to a lunch and lecture at St Joseph's College his lecture is titled "Life in the American Home in AD 2000," but he may change his topic if his audience is not interested in the subject matter.

The Question Mark

A question, or an *interrogative sentence,* ends with a question mark that separates it from the sentence that follows.

Who brought the coleslaw? It's delicious.

Why didn't you wear a raincoat? It's pouring!

Note: When a question is part of a declarative sentence, it is an *indirect question* and is followed by a period.

Who broke the statue?	[question]
Eddie wondered who had broken the statue.	[indirect question]

The Exclamation Point

An exclamation point indicates strong feeling.

Place an exclamation point after a strongly imperative sentence.

Close the windows! There are bees outside.

Stop chasing that dog immediately! It's only a puppy.

Remember that a mild imperative can end with a period. An exclamation point shows stronger feeling.

Please wait for the bell.

Run quickly!

Place an exclamation point after an exclamation.

Help! I'm falling!

How happy we are that you'll stay! We love company.

Watch out! The sidewalk is slippery.

Exercise 3: *Using End Punctuation*

Write the following sentences, placing a question mark, an exclamation point, or a period where necessary. Circle the punctuation marks you insert.

Examples

---

a. Where are the scissors You used them yesterday

Where are the scissors (?) You used them yesterday ⊙

b. Watch out That dog bites

Watch out (!) That dog bites ⊙

1. Hurry Bring some water

2. Why hasn't the package arrived yet When did you mail it

3. Hush There are deer right outside the door

4. Please be seated The show is about to begin

5. Congratulations When was the baby born

6. Mike asked if he had to wear a tie

7. Drive carefully, please Do you know the quickest route

8. Would you like dessert now, or would you rather wait until later

9. Ouch Who left pins on the floor

10. Diane wondered who had ordered the flowers Was it Allen

The Comma

The comma separates words, phrases, or clauses within sentences.

Use a comma to separate words or word groups in a series.

We have a dog, three cats, and a parrot.

Our family has lived at the beach, on a farm, and in Boston.

The producers knew they had a hit when the play went smoothly, when the audience cheered, and when the reviewers gave rave notices.

Note: When the last two items in a series are joined by a coordinating conjunction (such as *and* or *or*), a comma precedes the conjunction. When *all* the items in a series are joined by coordinating conjunctions, do not use commas.

For breakfast we had orange juice, bacon and eggs, and toast. [Notice that when items commonly go together—such as *bacon and eggs*—they can be paired as one item.]

After breakfast we took a walk and visited friends and then shopped.
After breakfast we took a walk, visited friends, and then shopped.

When two or more adjectives precede a noun, use a comma to separate the adjectives.

A narrow, winding, overgrown path twisted up to the house.

Two small, furry puppies barked incessantly.

Note: Do not use a comma between the last adjective and the noun that follows it. In some instances you should not use a comma between adjectives. Do not use a comma unless the conjunction *and* makes sense in its place.

> Ann cherished her gold wedding ring.
> [You would not say "gold *and* wedding ring."]

> Larry couldn't part with his faded, worn-out dungarees.
> Larry couldn't part with his faded *and* worn-out dungarees.
> [The *and* makes sense; therefore, use a comma.]

Exercise 4: *Using the Serial Comma*

Write each of the following sentences, inserting commas where necessary. Circle the commas you insert.

Examples

a. Sara is allergic to milk eggs and butter.

Sara is allergic to milk ⊘ eggs ⊘ and butter.

b. Dark threatening clouds rolled by.

Dark ⊘ threatening clouds rolled by.

1. The antique wooden box was filled with old coins rare stamps and valuable jewelry.

2. Eager energetic tourists climbed the staircase in the castle's tower walked to the narrow window and peered out.

3. Mix together the flour water eggs and sugar.

4. The room was filled with lilacs and roses and daffodils; flowers were in pitchers in vases and in baskets.

5. The play's director the star and the producer waited anxiously paced the floor and rushed for the reviews in the morning paper.

6. Every morning Wendy does sit-ups jumps rope and walks on her hands; she has an effective efficient exercise program.

7. My three biggest fears are being trapped in an elevator being chased by a bear and being caught in a fire.

8. Would you rather drive across the country camp in Canada or sail on a freighter on your long summer vacation?

9. Five restaurants two boutiques a pharmacy a hardware store a card shop and a supermarket have rented space at the new mall and expect a busy successful year.

10. Having lived in his house for forty years, the tired lonely man packed his possessions swept the floor and left.

Use a comma to separate independent clauses that are joined by the coordinating conjunctions *and, but, or, nor, for, so,* or *yet*.

I locked the car, *but* I foolishly left the windows open.

The car thief had an easy job, *for* the windows were open.

My car was robbed, *and* it was my own fault.

Now I always check my car doors and windows, *so* I don't make the same mistake twice.

Note: In placing commas, watch out for compound verbs. Be certain that the sentence actually has two independent clauses.

Exercise 5: *Commas with Coordinating Conjunctions*

Write the following sentences, placing commas where necessary. Circle the commas you insert.

Example

---

a. We were exhausted for we had been driving all day.

   We were exhausted ⊘ for we had been driving all day.

1. Herman told a story that was hard to believe but he promised it was true.

2. One day Herman's friend Bert left his office and he absent-mindedly got into the wrong car.

3. Bert started the car and drove off for his key fit in the ignition.

4. The car's rightful owner (Paul) realized his car was missing so he called the police and reported it stolen.

5. Bert soon returned to his office and calmly went back to work for he had no idea that he had driven the wrong car.

579

6. Paul left work and expected to walk home yet he saw his car parked where he had left it.

7. Paul thought, "Either I've gone crazy and lost my mind or someone has played a trick on me!"

8. Paul was glad to have his new sports car back so he got in and drove off.

9. Paul was immediately arrested for driving a stolen car for he had reported the "theft" to the police.

10. Now Paul never parks his sports car on the street near his office nor does Bert ever enter a car without first checking the license plate!

Use a comma to separate introductory adverbial clauses, introductory participial phrases, and long or successive introductory prepositional phrases from the rest of the sentence.

Introductory Adverbial Clauses

Before the featured movie began, the audience saw three short films.

When the movie ended, half the audience was asleep.

Introductory Participial Phrases

Exercising every day, Marge lost five pounds easily.

Filled with a sense of adventure, Juan traveled all over the world.

Long or Successive Introductory Prepositional Phrases

Late in the afternoon on a beautiful spring day, we packed a picnic basket and drove into the country.

In the shop on the corner of Madison Avenue and Sixty-Fifth Street, beautiful winter clothes are on sale.

Note: Short introductory prepositional phrases usually are not followed by a comma unless the comma is needed to make the meaning clear.

After the movie we went to dinner.
[no comma]

In the room above, the baby cried for hours.
[Use a comma so the sentence is not misread "above the baby."]

Use a comma to separate some short introductory elements from the rest of the sentence.

Use a comma following mild interjections and the words *yes, no, well, why, still,* and *now* when they introduce a sentence.

No, I'm not leaving.

Heavens, it's cold outside.

Yes, I do want some dessert.

Note: When these words are used as adverbs, they should not be followed by a comma.

Now it's getting dark.   [no comma]

Use a comma after the noun of direct address when it appears at the beginning of a sentence.

Julio, when is the soccer match?

Ms. Lauder, I'll finish the assignment by Friday.

Note: A noun of direct address at the end of a sentence is preceded by a comma.

When would you like an appointment, Mr. Clarke?

Introductory transitional expressions such as *yet, however, accordingly, thus, consequently, hence, therefore,* and *besides* are followed by a comma.

Consequently, all shops will be open late on Fridays.

However, the restaurant will close at six o'clock.

Note: A transitional expression at the end of a sentence is preceded by a comma.

I prefer to shop early in the day, however.

In general, use a comma after any introductory expression that would be followed by a pause if you were speaking.

Use a comma to separate contrasting words, phrases, and clauses introduced by the word *not.*

The fund needs money, not good intentions.

That magazine is published weekly, not monthly.

Exercise 6: Commas with Introductory Elements and Interrupters

Write the following sentences, placing commas where necessary. Circle the commas you insert.

Example

a. After eating a huge meal Carla stretched out on the sofa and took a nap.

   After eating a huge meal ⊙ Carla stretched out on the sofa and took a nap.

1. When America held its Bicentennial celebration cities and towns featured many anniversary events.

2. On the Fourth of July in 1976 thousands of ships sailed around Manhattan.

3. Having set sail from Newport, Rhode Island many old sailing vessels made their way down the East Coast.

4. Yes the Bicentennial generated much patriotic spirit.

5. In Lexington and Concord near Boston people enacted colonial events.

6. Excited by the boats and fireworks huge crowds of people flocked to the water.

7. That boat is really an old ship not a modern replica.

8. Well I think many people made money selling Bicentennial souvenirs.

9. Frances I saw you dressed as Betsy Ross in the parade.

10. Still many children had live history lessons during the anniversary celebration.

When words, phrases, and clauses appear within—or interrupt —the sentence, place a comma both before and after the expression. Paired commas enclose these words, phrases, or clauses and separate them from the rest of the sentence.

Use paired commas with nouns of direct address when they interrupt the flow of a sentence.

When, Karen, will the job be finished?

Use paired commas with transitional expressions that interrupt the flow of the sentence.

People left, however, when it began to rain.

Note: Be certain that a phrase is really used as an interrupter.

We'll leave, I hope, before sunrise.	[interrupter]
I hope that we'll leave before sunrise.	[no commas]

Use paired commas with contrasting expressions when they interrupt the sentence.

I like to watch ice hockey, not field hockey, on TV.

Exercise 7: Using Paired Commas

Write the following sentences, using paired commas where necessary. Circle the commas you insert.

Examples

---

a. Did you know that Tallahassee not Miami is the capital of Florida?

Did you know that Tallahassee ⊘ not Miami ⊘ is the capital of Florida?

b. The market carries plums only in the summer; strawberries on the other hand are usually available all year.

The market carries plums only in the summer; strawberries ⊘ on the other hand ⊘ are usually available all year.

1. How do you know Ms. Farmer that the store will be open Monday night?

2. A steady diet of balanced meals not a crash diet is the best way to stay thin and healthy.

3. The university's work-study program is based on the theory that on-the-job experience not just classroom training is important.

4. It's unpleasant I imagine to have cats if you're allergic to them.

5. Cantonese food is not spicy; Szechwan food on the other hand is very hot.

6. Will the strike be over Mayor by the beginning of next term?

7. Riding a bicycle in fact is good exercise.

8. I have heard Luis that you play tennis well; the tennis camp I think is looking for an instructor.

9. Vacations in my opinion are important for people who work hard.

10. An almanac not an encyclopedia is the best place to find weather predictions.

Use paired commas to enclose nonessential phrases and nonessential clauses and to separate them from the rest of the sentence.

Nonessential phrases and *clauses* are those that could be omitted without changing the meaning of a sentence. They are not essential to the main thought conveyed by a sentence.

The Tyler house, *which is on the corner of Market Street,* is a historical landmark. [nonessential adjective clause]

Barbara Ling, *running the fund-raising campaign,* raised money for the flood victims. [nonessential participial phrase]

In the preceding sentences the phrase and the clause set off by commas are not necessary to the meaning of the sentences. Essential phrases and clauses, on the other hand, are necessary to the meaning of a sentence and are not set off by commas.

The house *that is on the corner of Market Street* is a historical landmark. [The adjective clause *that is on the corner of Market Street* identifies the house and is essential to the meaning of the sentence.]

The woman *running the fund-raising campaign* raised money for the flood victims. [essential participial phrase]

Note: When a nonessential phrase or clause appears at the end of a sentence, use only one comma preceding it.

My first cat was Tabby, who was gray with black stripes.

Use paired commas to enclose nonessential appositives and nonessential appositive phrases that interrupt a sentence.

When an appositive merely explains the meaning of the noun or pronoun to which it refers—and the appositive could be removed without changing the meaning of the sentence—it is nonessential and should be set off by paired commas.

Dr Marcus, my dentist, opened a new office in the fashionable business area of Manhattan.

Georgia O'Keeffe, an American painter, has lived in New Mexico for many years.

When an appositive distinguishes the noun or pronoun it explains from other people or things, it is essential and is not set off by commas.

My cousin Frank and I are good friends.	[*Frank* identifies the cousin.]
The movie *Hair* was an adaptation of a Broadway play.	[*Hair* identifies the movie.]

Note: When a nonessential appositive appears at the beginning or end of a sentence, one of the paired commas is omitted.

A dedicated teacher, Lynn Evans teaches night courses and summer sessions.

Our family spent every summer at "Hillside Acres," *our farm in Pennsylvania.*

Exercise 8: Commas with Nonessential Phrases and Clauses

Write the sentences from the next page, placing commas where necessary. Circle the commas you insert.

Examples

a. Frank Townsend my closest friend lives in Burbank.

Frank Townsend ⊙ my closest friend ⊙ lives in Burbank.

b. The British Museum which is in London houses the original Magna Carta.

The British Museum ⊙ which is in London ⊙ houses the original Magna Carta.

585

1. Reruns of *The Mary Tyler Moore Show* which ran on Saturday nights for many years are still shown on daytime TV.

2. Chicago which is located on the shores of Lake Michigan is exceptionally windy in winter.

3. A student who has studied in Paris said that the courses at the Sorbonne which is in Paris are challenging.

4. My friend Lola was in *A Chorus Line* a successful Broadway play.

5. Dr. Alonzo Cruz head of the veterinary hospital complained that his dog won't eat any food that comes from a dog-food can!

6. An avid skier Tommy Ling heads for the slopes every weekend that is cold and snowy.

7. Burnett Sullivan living in Mexico sends a letter every week to his friend who lives in Tucson.

8. Marcella King who has a newborn baby works on her novel when her child naps.

9. My oldest sister Denise has invited me to spend my vacation at her ranch which is in New Mexico.

10. Before we sign the final papers for the house that we want to buy, we must consult our lawyer who will make certain everything is in order.

Commas are also used to separate a variety of items that may occur within a sentence. These conventional uses of the comma do not follow the rule of placing a comma where a pause would occur in speech. Custom and tradition dictate the placement of these commas.

Use a comma to separate parts of geographical names and parts of dates. When dates and geographical names occur within a sentence, use a comma to separate the entire name or date from the rest of the sentence.

We lived in Tucson, Arizona, when I was a child.

Mail your entry card by January 15, 1984, to Big Bargain Sweepstakes, 1375 Los Altimiros Drive, Los Angeles, California 91603.

The Carters were married on Monday, April 12, 1975, in London, England.

Note: In addresses a comma is not used between the street number and the street name or between a state name and the ZIP code. In dates a comma is not used between the name of the month and the date. A comma is not necessary when only a month and year are given in a date (*October 14, 1947*, but *October 1947*).

Use a comma to separate a person's name from a degree, title, or affiliation that follows it.

Louisa Maya, Ph.D.

Jack Jackson, Sr.

Joel Walters, RAF

Note: When used in a sentence, the degree or title is also followed by a comma.

Professor Julia Lewis, Ph.D., was named head of the history department.

Exercise 9: *Commas in Dates and Place Names*

Write the following sentences, placing commas where they belong. Circle the commas you insert.

Example

a. The movie was filmed on location in Paris France and in Venice Italy.

The movie was filmed on location in Paris ⊘ France ⊘ and in Venice ⊘ Italy.

1. Although Columbus Day really fell on Wednesday October 12 people celebrated it on Monday October 10.

2. Amy Weng Ph.D. announced the opening of her office on Monday September 22 1984 at 1033 Park Avenue Erie New Jersey.

3. I was born on August 20 1950; it was a Tuesday that year.

4. Joel Parks Sr. and Wendy Miller were married in October 1980; in fact, they were married on October 29 1980.

5. Kendra Slywyn M.D. went to college in San Diego California and to medical school in Chicago Illinois.

6. Last month's snowstorm was the worst to hit Philadelphia Pennsylvania since the blizzard of February 1948.

7. Please send your cards to Emma Peel M.D. 121 Carpenter Street South Orange New Jersey 07079.

8. On January 31 1978 we were in Paris France and about to leave for Vienna Austria.

9. Although Martha was born in Atlanta Georgia, she grew up in Seattle Washington.

10. Did you send the letter to 101 West 78th Street New York New York 10024 or to 101 East 78th Street New York New York 10021?

The Semicolon

The *semicolon,* a stronger mark of punctuation than the comma, signals a more definite break in thought—a longer pause. In fact, you might think of the semicolon as a "weak period."

Use a semicolon to separate closely related independent clauses that are not joined by a coordinating conjunction.

One of the twins has traveled all over the world; the other rarely leaves home.

August is the busiest month at the beach; it's easier to find a place to stay in July.

Use a semicolon between independent clauses when the second clause begins with a transitional expression such as *therefore, however, besides, in fact,* or *for example.*

This was Sue's first trip to Wyoming; *in fact,* it was her first trip west of the Mississippi.

Everyone had already seen the local movie; *therefore,* we decided to go bowling.

Use a semicolon to separate items in a series when one or more of the items contains commas.

The judges for the dog show were Dr. Mel Hall, a veterinarian; Mary Stewart, a trainer; and Dr. Alma Lopez, a researcher.

Driver's examinations will be given on Monday, June 12; Monday, June 19; and Wednesday, June 21.

Use a semicolon between independent clauses when commas appear within the clauses.

We had wanted to drive from Colorado to Arizona; but since a blizzard made driving hazardous, we decided to fly.

Having studied all week, Linda entered the exam confidently; she still found the test challenging, however.

Exercise 10: *Using the Semicolon*

Write the following sentences, using semicolons where necessary. Circle the semicolons you insert.

Example

---

a. Jogging is good exercise however, runners should be careful about overexertion.

Jogging is good exercise⟨;⟩ however, runners should be careful about overexertion.

1. José loved to cook in fact, he planned to open a restaurant.

2. Local artists contributed work to the benefit the show was a great success.

3. The international menu included couscous, a dish from North Africa, Peking duck, a Chinese delicacy, and borsch, a Russian beet soup.

4. The actors' contracts will be up in June nevertheless, they will star in the show next year.

5. Large dogs effectively scare most intruders however, big dogs need a lot of space.

6. Before Jack entered the Boston Marathon, he ran every day as a result, he was able to run the distance in good time.

7. After receiving her Ph.D., Joanne hoped to teach but she had trouble finding a job.

8. Alan Alda starred in last week's episode of *M*A*S*H* he also wrote and directed it.

9. The collection of French paintings will travel to museums in Philadelphia, Pennsylvania Atlanta, Georgia Dallas, Texas and Phoenix, Arizona.

10. National parks are crowded with tourists in the summer visitors must therefore make reservations in advance.

The Colon

When a *colon* separates elements within a sentence, it calls attention to the word, phrase, or list that follows it.

Be sure to pack *the following* items: a toothbrush, a pair of slippers, a robe, and a towel.

These are the main ingredients in the salad: cabbage, bean sprouts, water chestnuts, and snow peas.

The hotel offers *four* types of accommodations: room with bath, suite, private villa, and cabin.

Note: The introductory statement preceding a colon should be a complete sentence. Do not use a colon between a verb and its direct object or after a preposition. (An asterisk [*] denotes a sentence with a feature that is not part of Edited Standard English.)

*For the hike you should pack: walking shoes, insect repellent, and a hat.
For the hike you should pack the following items: walking shoes, insect repellent, and a hat.

Use a colon to separate an introductory statement from an explanation, an appositive, or a quotation.

His adventures had earned him an apt nickname: "Fearless Herman."

Heed these words of advice: "Look before you leap."

The colon should also be used in three conventional situations. These uses have grown from custom and tradition.

Use a colon to separate a salutation from the body of a business letter.

Dear Lois Nathan: Dear Dr. Navarro:

Use a colon to separate hour and minutes in expressions of time.

12:15 P.M.   7:30 this evening

Use a colon to separate chapter numbers from verse numbers in references from the Bible.

Job 4:9   John 5:15

Exercise 11: *Using the Colon*

Write the following sentences, placing colons where necessary. Circle the colons you insert.

Examples

a. The concert begins at 8 30 P.M.

   The concert begins at 8 (:) 30 P.M.

b. When I saw the Missouri, I understood its nickname "Big Muddy."

   When I saw the Missouri, I understood its nickname (:) "Big Muddy."

1. Sitting at the typewriter, John wrote these words "Now is the time for all good men to come to the aid of their party."

2. The YWCA offers three courses in physical fitness yoga, calisthenics, and dance exercise.

3. Have you ever read any of these classic mysteries *The Moonstone, The Murder of Roger Ackroyd*, or *Five Red Herrings?*

4. Everyone knows Louis Armstrong's nickname "Satchmo."

5. Rev. Thomas referred us to these readings John 13 1, Job 12 3, and Proverbs 12 5.

6. Which of these proverbs makes more sense "Out of sight, out of mind" or "Absence makes the heart grow fonder"?

7. Both of these old movies start at 6 15 tonight *The Lady Vanishes* and *Laura*.

8. Bob always gives the same unusual advice "Look wise and seem mysterious."

9. There's only one word to describe a Midwestern winter freezing.

10. Which of the following presents would you prefer a book, some records, a wallet, or a calculator?

The Dash

The *dash* is similar in use to the colon. However, you might think of the dash as pointing backward, since it calls attention to the word or word group that precedes it.

Use a dash to separate an introductory series or thought from the explanation that follows.

Making the swimming team—that was my main goal.

Decorations in red and black—these colors gave the party a Chinese flavor.

Use a dash to separate a sudden change in thought.

I could daydream all day about the beach—oh, the phone is ringing.

First we'll have dinner and then go out—I wonder what I'll cook.

Use a dash to show omission of words in dialogue. The dash shows a break in a person's speech.

"What is—?" Susan began.

When the elements separated by a dash occur within a sentence, use dashes in pairs to enclose the word or group of words and to separate them from the rest of the sentence.

Use paired dashes to enclose a phrase or clause that shows a sudden break in thought or a sharp change in tone.

Timothy finished the difficult history exam—can you believe it?—in two hours.

We have all dreamed at one time or another—now admit it—of being famous stars.

Use paired dashes to enclose appositive phrases that require a stronger pause than that for commas. Use paired dashes for parenthetical phrases containing commas.

People hurried indoors when the northeaster—a severe storm with heavy wind and rain—swept over the island.

Tim's dogs—a spaniel and a terrier—barked loudly.

Some science courses—biology, for example—require laboratory as well as classroom time.

Two companies—Langor, Inc., and Smith, Jones, and Wells—have merged.

Exercise 12: Using the Dash

Write the following sentences, using dashes where necessary. Circle the dashes you insert.

Example

a. Roast beef sandwiches yes, they're my favorite.

Roast beef sandwiches⬭yes, they're my favorite.

1. Just run the distance that was the thought in my mind during the marathon.

2. Grandma Moses you won't believe this first began to paint when she was over seventy years old!

3. "You never let me" Jackie began.

4. The Colorado ski slope a steep, bumpy hill was not meant for beginners.

5. "Devil's Face" they didn't give the mountain that name without good reason.

6. Patience that's the main requisite for birdwatching.

7. Joanie said that Bob wherever he is would bring some new blank cassettes.

8. Has anyone ever heard Sarah she just cut a record sing blues?

9. Visitors to Notre Dame a beautiful cathedral in Paris, France are always overwhelmed by its stained-glass windows.

10. I love the beach so much that I could spend a month make that two months just living by the ocean.

Parentheses

Used to enclose elements that interrupt a sentence, *parentheses* show a stronger break than do commas or dashes. In fact, words in parentheses are set off from the rest of the sentence. Parentheses enclose items that provide additional information.

A few foods (oranges and apricots) are rich in potassium.

Mrs. King's plant shop (exotic plants) opens next week.

Does aspirin help relieve sciatica (back pain)?

Note: The punctuation mark appears outside the parentheses at the end of a sentence.

Exercise 13: Using Parentheses

Write the following sentences, using parentheses where necessary. Circle the parentheses you insert.

Examples

a. French and Spanish both Romance languages have words that are similar.

French and Spanish (both Romance languages) have words that are similar.

b. Would you like a glass of H_2O water?

Would you like a glass of H_2O (water)?

1. Mercury the planet nearest to the sun is too hot to sustain life as we know it.

2. The school is on Summer Street the street near the library and is convenient to public transportation.

3. To learn calligraphy the art of beautiful handwriting, you must have patience.

4. Dorothea Lange 1895–1965 was a well-known American photographer who documented the difficult life of migrant farmers during the Depression.

5. The members of NATO North Atlantic Treaty Organization signed a new trade agreement last week.

6. Add two cups of brown sauce see directions for brown sauce on page 234 to the vegetables.

7. Famous Wall Street the home of the New York Stock Exchange took its name from a defense wall that had been erected there in 1653.

8. According to statistics, Tokyo the capital of Japan has a very low crime rate.

9. The bazaar was filled with decorative items made of brass an alloy of copper and zinc.

10. Having decided that her wardrobe was dull, Janice paid an extravagant price for purple shoes and a magenta a reddish-purplish hue skirt.

The Hyphen

The *hyphen* is used to link the parts of some compound words. It also links the part of a word begun on one line with the part finished on the next. Although some general rules govern the use of the hyphen, make it a habit to consult a dictionary if you are unsure about how to hyphenate any given word.

Use a hyphen to link the parts of compound nouns that begin with the prefixes *ex-*, *self-*, *all-*, and *great-* or that end with the suffix *-elect*.

ex-president   great-grandfather
self-image   president-elect
all-star

Use a hyphen to link the parts of compound nouns that include a prepositional phrase.

man-of-war   son-in-law

Many compound nouns are not hyphenated. Some are written as two separate words (*tennis court*); others are written as a single word (*baseball*).

Use a hyphen to link prefixes with proper nouns or adjectives.

mid-January   pre-Columbian
anti-American   un-American

In general, use a hyphen to link the parts of a compound adjective when it precedes the noun.

short-term lease   thought-provoking idea
two-ton truck   300-page book

Note: Do not use a hyphen if the adjective follows the noun. (*The idea was thought provoking.*)

Use a hyphen to link parts of a fraction used as an adjective.

one-half fare   two-thirds full

Note: You may omit the hyphen when the fraction is used as a noun. (*One fifth of the seats were taken.*)

Use a hyphen to link the parts of a compound number between twenty-one and ninety-nine.

twenty-five dollars   thirty-nine steps

Use a hyphen when a word is divided at the end of a line.

After a long search we found the missing con-
tainer of coins.

Judy had cleaned the room and must have misplaced the box.

Note: Place a hyphen only between syllables; one-syllable words cannot be hyphenated. A word should not be hyphenated if doing so would leave just one letter on either line. A word that already contains a hyphen should be divided only at the hyphen. (An asterisk [*] denotes a sentence with a feature that is not part of Edited Standard English.)

*I beg you not to le- ave.	[The word *leave* should not be hyphenated.]
*I am sad whenever you go a- way.	[The word *away* should not be hyphenated.]
*The audience was a pro-Ran- ger group.	[The term *pro-Ranger* should be divided only at its hyphen.]

Do not hyphenate abbreviations at the end of a line.

*The movie begins at 8 P.- M.	[Do not hyphenate P.M.]

Exercise 14: Using the Hyphen

Write each of the following sentences, using hyphens where necessary. Circle the hyphens you insert.

Example

    a. The baby always takes a mid afternoon nap.

       The baby always takes a mid (-)afternoon nap.

    b. Cross country skiing is a favorite sport of mine.

       Cross (-) country skiing is a favorite sport of mine.

1. My brother in law doesn't like to swim in the ocean; he is afraid of being stung by a man of war.

2. We always heard the same words of advice from our great grandmother: "Self respect, self knowledge, and self love are the most important possessions you can acquire."

3. Jim's grandmother is a self reliant woman; she lives in the Midwest for one half of the year and travels south in mid December for the winter.

4. An ear splitting explosion tore through the finished building and leveled it.

5. The ex President's speech stirred a lot of pro American feeling; heart warming applause filled the room and cheers of support rose to an exciting pitch.

6. Since two thirds of the class had previously taken a course in pre Columbian art, the professor skipped some of the basic material and proceeded to the next part of his lecture.

7. Melissa's down to earth attitude calmed everyone during the crisis.

8. The artists of the post Impressionist era are now much admired; in the 1890s, however, the members of that just formed group were not well respected artists.

9. Charles raced off on his ten speed bike and finished his paper route in record breaking time.

10. Gloria's well worn jeans were paint stained and patched, so she discarded them with a halfhearted toss.

The Apostrophe

The *apostrophe* is used to show the omission of letters or numbers, to form the plural of letters or numbers, and to form possessive nouns.

Use an apostrophe to show that a letter or letters have been omitted from contractions.

---

can't	cannot
isn't	is not
I'll	I will
o'clock	of the clock

Use an apostrophe to show that the first two numbers have been omitted from a year.

'80   '76

Use an apostrophe to form the plural of letters, numbers, and words.

He's in his late 20's.

There are four *i*'s in *Mississippi.*

Do not use so many *and*'s and *but*'s when you speak.

Note: No apostrophe is needed when making centuries and decades plural.

What will the 1980s be like?

Photography was invented during the 1800s.

Add an apostrophe and an *s* to make a singular noun possessive.

| Bill | Bill's car |
| house | house's yard |

To show possession add an apostrophe and an *s* to a plural noun that does not end in *s*.

| women | women's |
| children | children's |

When a plural noun ends in *s*, add only an apostrophe to show possession.

| dogs | dogs' |
| windows | windows' |

Note: The possessive forms of personal pronouns do not have apostrophes. By using an apostrophe with a personal pronoun, you are showing omission, not possession.

its	[possession]
it's	[contraction of *it is*]
whose	[possession]
who's	[contraction for *who is*]

Exercise 15: Using the Apostrophe

Write the sentences from the next page, using apostrophes where needed. Circle the apostrophes you insert.

Examples

a. I cant believe hes in his 40s.

I can ' t believe he ' s in his 40 ' s.

b. Weve been invited to ride on the Ortegas sailboat this summer.

We ' ve been invited to ride on the Ortega ' s sailboat this summer.

1. I can always recognize Mrs. Martins handwriting by the way in which she dots her *i*s.

2. People dont believe were nearing the end of the 1900s; the 90s will be quite a decade!

3. Marshas car is fast, but it cant be as fast as Mikes.

4. Its amazing that the Smiths Irish Setter can wag its tail so quickly.

5. How many *n*s are in Jennifers name?

6. Carlos grandfather—whos in his 90s—cant walk quickly, yet his mind is as quick as yours or mine.

7. Havent you heard the expression "Mind your *p*s and *q*s"? Whats its meaning?

8. When Juanita was in her 20s, she thought people in their 40s were old; now shes older and has very good reason to change her mind.

9. Theyve promised to be home by the childrens curfew, which is 12 oclock.

10. The Winklers fashionable car is from the 1950s; its in great condition.

Quotation Marks

Quotation marks, which usually occur in pairs, enclose a word or group of words and separate them from the rest of the sentence.

Use quotation marks to enclose a speaker's or writer's exact words.

"I'll be a Yankee fan forever," Julie asserted.

The hitchhiker's sign read, "Denver or Dubuque."

"Why does it always rain," Nicole asked, "on my birthday?"

Notice that in the last example sentence the direct quotation is interrupted by the words *Nicole asked*. The second part of the quotation does not begin with a capital letter because it is not a new sentence. Use a capital letter to begin each new quotation and each new sentence within a quotation.

Note: Use quotation marks only to enclose a speaker's exact words. Do not use quotation marks in an indirect quotation.

"Where's the party?" Jim asked.	[direct quotation]
Jim asked where the party was.	[indirect quotation]

A direct quotation is often separated from the rest of the sentence by commas. In some instances a question mark or an exclamation point is used with quotation marks. The following rules will tell you how to place marks of punctuation used with quotation marks.

Place commas and periods inside closing quotation marks.

"I hope the movie ends soon," whispered Jake.

Julio replied, "It will be over in five minutes."

Place colons and semicolons outside closing quotation marks.

Lewis calls his cat "The Craziest Feline in Georgia"; however, he's never seen my cat.

Two reasons explain why the class voted Janice "Most Likely to Succeed": she's smart and she works hard.

Place question marks and exclamation points inside the closing quotation marks if just the quotation is a question or an exclamation. If the whole sentence is a question or an exclamation, place the marks outside.

Jean asked, "Where's my coat?"

Do you want to read a story called "A Year in the Rain"?

Jack could only utter, "Watch out!"

"Sit down!" Judy yelled.

Use quotation marks to enclose the titles of short stories, essays, short poems, songs, television programs, magazine articles, and parts of a book.

In high school, did you ever read Hawthorne's story "The Ambitious Guest"?

Joan Didion's essay "The White Album" is an interesting piece on the 1960s.

The ever-popular Bee Gees' hit song "Saturday Night Fever" has sold millions of copies both in the United States and in the rest of the world.

An article entitled "Early American Weather Vanes" (from *Antiques* magazine) supplied much of the information for Chapter 12, "Folk Art," in our book on American art.

Use quotation marks to enclose nicknames and slang expressions.

Benny Goodman was called "The King of Swing."

In the 1950s "pad" and "groovy" were popular expressions among the "beat generation."

Exercise 16: Using Quotation Marks

Write the following sentences, using quotation marks where needed. Circle the quotation marks you insert.

Examples

a. Linda Ronstadt's hit songs, such as Heat Wave and Blue Bayou, have earned her this title: Superstar.

Linda Ronstadt's hit songs, such as ⁽⁾ Heat Wave ⁽⁾ and ⁽⁾ Blue Bayou, ⁽⁾ have earned her this title: ⁽⁾ Superstar ⁽⁾ .

    b. How old were you, John asked, when you first read *Alice in Wonderland*?

        ❝ How old were you, ❞ John asked, ❝ when you first read *Alice in Wonderland*? ❞

1. Many people were horrified when Elvis Presley first appeared on television and sang Jailhouse Rock.

2. Who will win the New Hampshire primary? Neil asked. I think it will be a close race.

3. Pedro said that the weirdest movie he had ever seen was based on Shirley Jackson's *The Haunting of Hill House*; he shivered just remembering when Julie Harris whispered, Whose hand was I holding?

4. Did you know that dogs and cats cannot see colors? Mitzi asked. Then she added, Even so, I know without a doubt that my dog's favorite color is red!

5. The following two department stores have been listed as Best Bets: Benjamin Buzz Burn's Discount Center and The Bargain Hunter.

6. Denise wrote the article Household Hints, which appeared in *Living* magazine; the first hint reads, Use club soda to remove stains from clothes or carpeting.

7. I have a friend, Lena said, who is a fabulous tennis player. She has won every state tournament this year.

8. Three famous monarchs of Russia were Peter I, known as The Great; Catherine II, also known as The Great; and Nicholas II, who was the last Russian czar.

9. Did you ever see the painting by Monet, Penny asked, that hangs in the Metropolitan Museum of Art?

10. Was Lon Chaney called The Man of a Thousand Faces? I just read about him in the essay Horror Greats.

Single Quotation Marks

Use single quotation marks to enclose a direct quotation that occurs inside another quotation. Use single quotation marks to enclose titles normally enclosed in double quotation marks when these titles occur within a direct quotation.

Meg queried, "Who said, 'To be or not to be'?"

Ivan complained, "I just listened to Bob Dylan's song 'Positively Fourth Street' and didn't understand the words."

Writing Dialogue

When you write the words said by two or more people having a conversation, you write *dialogue*. The exact words of the speakers are enclosed in quotation marks. Usually the speakers are identified by "words of saying"—*Janet said, cried Tom, Lisbeth wondered, asked Janet.* These "words of saying" are not enclosed in quotation marks and are often separated from the quoted material by commas.

"I am studying medicine," Lisa stated proudly.

Lee cheered, "We're going to win!"

"Please bring my sweater," José said, "and my scarf."

If a question mark or an exclamation point occurs where one of these separating commas should be used, omit the comma and use the question mark or exclamation point to separate the quoted material.

"Don't be late!" Bill warned.

When writing dialogue, begin a new paragraph whenever the speaker changes.

"I think the city's budget for snow removal is too large," Jessica argued. "The money could be better used in other ways."

"You're mistaken," John countered. "If the city is unprepared for a big storm, a heavy snow would cripple it. Look what happened during the winter of '79!"

Victoria was unconvinced. "Well, I disagree. I think the city should use that money to build neighborhood parks and playgrounds."

Sometimes, a direct quotation runs for more than one paragraph. When this happens, use quotation marks at the beginning of the quotation, at the beginning of each subsequent paragraph, and at the end of the entire quotation. (Notice that this is one situation in which quotation marks are not used in pairs.)

Kim began, "People just use too much energy. Fuel has now become an expensive and increasingly less available item, and we must adjust our life styles.

"At one time the fuel supply seemed endless. All of us surrounded ourselves with more and more energy-intensive devices: big cars, electric gadgets for the home, electric heaters, and so on. Now electricity is too expensive, and the supply is dwindling.

"The problem is not insurmountable. Americans will simply have to slow down their life styles. Soon we might all be bicycling to work, wearing thermal clothes in winter, and eating by candlelight."

Review: Using Punctuation

Write the following dialogue, using punctuation where necessary. Circle the punctuation marks you insert.

Movies seem so simple John said when you watch them on the screen. I bet however that things dont always go smoothly behind the scenes!

Im sure youre right Paulette agreed. There must be Im sure problems among the cast who surely disagree now and then problems with the budget which I imagine is always too small and pressures about the deadline. Although the audience only sees the results I know problems must start with the casting. Werent there some well known problems with filming *Gone with the Wind* the film classic of the 30s

Yes I believe there were said John When they were choosing the stars the producer wanted Bette Davis I think Im right about this to play Scarlett O'Hara. She was under contract with another studio however so the producer had to find someone else.

Luis added Heres another example of a movie that had casting problems *Casablanca.* Did you know that the leading roles which were played by Ingrid Bergman and Humphrey Bogart were originally intended for other stars He continued Only Bogey not anyone else could have said these famous words Heres looking at you kid.

Were taking Mrs Ortegas film course which meets at 400 PM on Monday Wednesday and Friday Paulette offered. We thought wed film a short story for our final project and we were considering Willa Cathers The Sculptors Funeral however I hope we dont have too many problems! Because we have such a tight schedule the problems wont go on forever she continued. The film has to be finished for the final project which is due on Friday June 19 1984.

Good luck! Luis shouted and waved goodbye. Youll be busy!

Writing Focus: *Improving Punctuation in Writing*

Punctuation marks are like road signs that writers use to guide readers through their writing. The marks show readers when to pause or stop. They also connect ideas and clarify items of interest. Like drivers who must learn to read and follow road signs, writers use punctuation to avoid confusion and to make their writing flow more smoothly.

Assignment: *A Show of My Own*

Imagine that you have just been selected as the host of a new television talk show. The producer has asked for your ideas and suggestions about the kind of show you want. Think about the talk shows you may have seen on TV. How will your show be different? Who will appear on your first show? How will you appeal to the interests of your television audience?

For this assignment, write a preview of your first television talk show for a television guide. The purpose of the preview is to inform viewers about your new talk show by giving details about time and date, guest appearances, and special features. As you write, consider that your preview will be evaluated for correct punctuation.

Use the following steps to complete this assignment.

A. Prewriting

Divide a sheet of paper into the following categories: *names for the show, guests, special features, topics for discussion*. Brainstorm ideas for each of these categories. Generate as many ideas as possible by writing for five or ten minutes. Write words, phrases, or sentences under each category without judging the merit of your ideas. When you have run out of ideas, reread what you wrote and underline the details that you want to include in your show.

B. Writing

Using the details from your brainstorming list, write a preview of your first talk show. Include the time, date, and name of the show, guest appearances, special features, and topics of discussion. Appeal to your television audience by giving as many details as possible to interest them in watching your show. Remember to include the specific date and time your show will be aired. As you write, pay particular attention to providing correct punctuation.

C. Postwriting

Use the following checklist to revise your first draft.

1.   Have I provided sufficient details to inform my audience about my show?

2.   Is my punctuation correct in each sentence?

Use the Proofreader's Checklist at the back of the book to edit your work. Share the preview of your talk show with your classmates. If appropriate, include your preview in a classroom book entitled *TV Guide of Talkshows*.

23 Capitalization

Learning to Capitalize

The rules of capitalization that follow indicate the uses of capitals in Edited Standard English. By following these rules when you write, you increase the likelihood that your meaning will be readily understood. For example, consider the following sentences.

Let's meet at the store on Elm Street at 6:30.

Let's meet at The Store at 6:30.

In the first sentence above, *the store* means a shop on Elm Street; when capitalized, *The Store* refers to a specific shop, which is named "The Store." The meaning of the sentence changes when the words *the store* are capitalized.

Capitalization That Sets Off Groups of Words

An important use of capitalization is to set off groups of words.

Always capitalize the first word of a sentence.

By capitalizing the first word of each sentence, you separate that sentence from the preceding one. (An asterisk [*] denotes a sentence with a feature that is not a part of Edited Standard English.)

*The freeways are convenient. during rush hours, however, traffic creeps along these crowded highways.

The freeways are convenient. During rush hours, however, traffic creeps along these crowded highways.

Capitalize the first word of a direct quotation.

Capitalize the first word of a direct quotation, even if the quotation is a fragment.

"You're a fabulous swimmer," Jana exclaimed.

"It takes a lot of practice," Shelley said. Then she laughed and admitted, "And strong arms!"

Note: When a direct quotation is interrupted, capitalize the word that begins the quotation but not the one that begins the second part of the quotation.

"It takes a lot of practice," admitted Shelley, "and strong arms!"

Exercise 1: Capitalizing Sentences

Write each of the following sentences, inserting capital letters where necessary. Underline the words you capitalize.

Examples

a. many animals are now endangered species. their habitats have been destroyed.

Many animals are now endangered species. Their habitats have been destroyed.

b. "zoos are helping to preserve some species," Len explained. he added, "the zoos try to duplicate the animals' natural environment."

"Zoos are helping to preserve some species," Len explained. He added, "The zoos try to duplicate the animals' natural environment."

1. "have you ever played backgammon?" Luke asked.

2. "no, I haven't," Alicia replied, "but I'd like to learn."

3. backgammon is easier than chess. you can learn the basics much more quickly.

4. "i prefer backgammon because the games are quicker," Joan offered.

5. most checkerboards have a backgammon board on the back. have you noticed that?

6. "so that's what that board is," Paul remarked. "can you use the checkers to play?"

7. because it involves throwing dice, backgammon is half skill and half luck.

8. "you move pieces quickly around the board," Sheila explained, "and at the same time try to block your opponent's pieces."

9. "a good throw of the dice can help you out," Jill explained. "that," she added, "is where the luck comes in."

10. "watch out!" Amanda warned. "once you begin playing you can go on for hours."

Usually capitalize the first word in a complete line of poetry.

(Capitalization in poetry sometimes varies with the poet's style.)

Two ears and but a single tongue
By nature's laws to us belong.
The lesson she would teach is clear:
Repeat but half of what you hear.

Capitalize the first word, the last word, and all other important words in the title of a work of art.

This rule applies to the titles of books, chapters, stories, magazines, poems, plays, movies, newspapers, musical works, paintings, sculptures, and television shows and series. Unimportant words are prepositions and conjunctions with fewer than five letters.

Breaking Away is a delightful movie about teenagers.

Anne of a Thousand Days is a movie about Anne Boleyn.

"The Destructors" is a short story by Graham Greene.

Exercise 2: Capitalizing Titles

Write the following sentences, capitalizing the titles according to the rules you have learned. Underline the words you capitalize. (Titles of books and other works of art that are *italicized* in print should be underlined in handwriting. Underline these titles twice.)

Example

---

a. *star wars* and *the invasion of the body snatchers* are both science fiction movies.

Star Wars and The Invasion of the Body Snatchers are both science fiction movies.

1. The song "as time goes by" from the movie *casablanca* has become a classic.

2. The Broadway musical *west side story* is based on Shakespeare's play *romeo and juliet*.

3. Ms. Harris would rather listen to any opera, like *the magic flute*, than listen to popular music, like the Beatles' song *"hard day's night."*

4. Did you ever hear Judy Garland sing "somewhere over the rainbow" from *the wizard of oz?*

5. I love the "march of the tin soldiers" from *the nutcracker suite.*

6. The book *summertime,* which tells the history of many American resorts, talks about Atlantic City in Chapter 2, "by the sea."

7. The rights of apartment tenants are well explained in an article titled "how to get the most from your lease," which appeared in *new york* magazine.

8. Two of my favorite essays in Joan Didion's book *the white album* are "quiet days in malibu" and "in the islands."

9. Did you ever see the "chuckles the clown" episode on *the mary tyler moore show?*

10. The scenic Hudson Valley is captured in paintings such as Weir's *view of the highlands from west point* and Johnson's *off constitution island.*

Capitalization That Sets Off Single Words

Capital letters are used for proper nouns and proper adjectives. A *proper noun* is the name of a specific person, place, animal, or thing; a *proper adjective* is an adjective formed from a proper noun. The following rules are for capitalizing proper nouns.

Capitalize the names of specific people.

Jackie, Anita, and Raoul won prizes.

Pauline Cohen is my best friend.

Capitalize a title that precedes, or takes the place of, a person's name, as in direct address.

Judge Marks spoke to the witness.

When, Judge, will you speak to the witness?

Marcia wrote an interesting paper on General Patton.

Note: Capitalize the words *President* and *Vice President* only when they precede a person's name or when they refer to our highest government offices.

President Kennedy was a charismatic figure.

The President will address the nation on Tuesday.

The vice president of the student council announced the job.

Capitalize words that show family relationships when they precede a person's name or when they are used in place of someone's name.

Aunt Edith just opened an antique shop in Philadelphia.

Where did you put the scissors, Grandfather?

Note: Do not capitalize words that show family relationships when they are preceded by a personal pronoun.

I would like you to meet my mother.

Capitalize the abbreviation for a person's name or title.

Dr. Jaffee is a good dentist.

Ms. Helbrun's brother is John Helbrun, Jr., who runs the biggest department store in town.

Exercise 3: Capitalizing Proper Nouns

Write the following sentences, using capital letters where necessary. Underline the words you capitalize.

Examples

---

a. Yesterday joanne collier invited my brother to a party.
   Yesterday Joanne Collier invited my brother to a party.

b. When, doctor, do you expect the nurse to return?
   When, Doctor, do you expect the nurse to return?

1. Students enjoyed professor yen's course even though he was the strictest professor at the university.

2. The senator, juan cortes, lived near my aunt, mrs. nickels.

3. Martin mandez, jr., looks just like his father.

4. Would it be all right, mother, if joanna and I spent the weekend at aunt grace's?

5. My sister is doing research with dr. adams, who is a well-known heart specialist.

6. My grandfather wrote a letter to the president to complain about inflation; the vice president answered.

7. Irene's father, paul dodge, sr., said that judge wainscott is an extremely fair judge.

8. Did you hear, mother, that the president has asked our senator to join his cabinet? senator jakes has accepted.

9. My friend barbara has invited aunt alice to dinner.

10. The members chose miss peng and rev. johnson to represent them on the panel; the first meeting is at governor gray's office.

Capitalize the names of specific places.

We flew over the Grand Canyon in Arizona during our flight to San Diego.

Is Lake Mead in Nevada?

The corner of Hollywood and Vine is a famous Hollywood intersection.

Note: Capitalize the names of compass directions only if they refer to a specific region or are part of an address.

Three blocks north on Broadway is West Forty-sixth Street.

Carmen is from the South and isn't used to cold Northern winters.

Ellen lives in a small town in the northwest corner of South Dakota.

Capitalize the names of buildings, institutions, monuments, businesses, and organizations and the abbreviations of organizations.

New York University is one of several colleges located in New York City.

The Ballet Folklorico from Mexico will appear next weekend in Philadelphia at the Academy of Music.

Carlos works for IBM in a new building near the campus of Cornell University.

Capitalize the names of nationalities, religions, races, and languages. The proper adjectives formed from these nouns are also capitalized.

Two French students visited our school.

Our Moroccan guide spoke English, French, and Arabic.

Many Americans love Chinese food, especially when it's spicy!

Capitalize the abbreviations A.D., B.C., A.M., and P.M. Note that abbreviations for measurements (*kg, cm, oz., lb.*) are not capitalized.

The party starts at 9 P.M.

The Parthenon in Athens was built in 432 B.C.

Capitalize the names of stars, planets, and other heavenly bodies.

Did the Mariner spacecraft visit Mars or Jupiter?

You can usually locate the constellation Orion by the three stars that make up its belt.

Note: The words *sun, moon,* and *earth* are not usually capitalized and never so when they follow the word *the.*

We should all be concerned with the ecology of earth.

How far is the earth from the sun?

Exercise 4: *Capitalizing Proper Nouns and Abbreviations*

Write the following sentences, using capitals where needed. Underline the words you capitalize.

Example

> a. The touro synagogue in newport, rhode island, is the oldest synagogue in the united states.
>
> The <u>Touro Synagogue</u> in <u>Newport</u>, <u>Rhode Island</u>, is the oldest synagogue in the <u>United States</u>.

1. Some parts of maine are located farther north than some areas of southern canada.

2. The meeting begins at 7:30 p.m. at the buddhist retreat situated on a hill overlooking the pacific ocean.

3. An enormous volcanic eruption occurred on the greek island of santorini in 1400 b.c. and completely destroyed the island.

4. Can you imagine being launched from cape kennedy one morning at 7 a.m. and then orbiting the earth in a spaceship?

5. The getty museum in los angeles is modeled after an ancient roman villa that was buried in ash after vesuvius erupted.

6. Did you know that leningrad, russia, is called "the venice of the north"?

7. The british museum in london has ancient greek statues that were taken from the parthenon in athens.

8. We joined a group called friends of the animals, which is a national organization to protect wildlife; the organization has an office in the east in washington, d.c.

9. At night in california's yosemite national park, the sky is so bright that constellations like the big dipper are clearly visible.

10. Many people living along the coast in southern france speak italian as well as french; some—especially near nice—speak a local dialect called nicoise.

Capitalize words referring to the deity, holy families, holy books of all religions, and religious terms. Capitalize personal pronouns when they refer to deities.

> The story of the Jews' exodus from Egypt is in the Old Testament.
>
> Ramadan is an important holiday in the Moslem faith.
>
> Gothic cathedrals were built higher and higher in an attempt to reach up to God and heaven.

Note: Do not capitalize the word *god* when it refers to a god of ancient mythology; capitalize the names of specific gods because they are proper nouns.

Zeus and the other Greek gods lived on Mount Olympus.

Capitalize the names of months, days of the week, holidays, and special events.

Thanksgiving is always the fourth Thursday in November.

Many people watch the Rose Bowl Game on New Year's Day.

The Wimbledon tennis matches are usually held every July in England.

Note: The names of seasons are not usually capitalized.

The first day of winter is December 21.

Capitalize the names of historical periods and events.

Leonardo da Vinci and Michelangelo were two leading artists of the Renaissance.

Capitalize the names of school subjects when they are formed from proper nouns, are followed by a number, or name a specific course.

Although there are several science courses open to sophomores, you cannot take Biology II unless you have completed Biology I.

If I take Latin and a course in American history, I won't have time to take Women in Literature. [Only the part of the name formed from the proper noun is capitalized, as in American history.]

Note: Nouns followed by a number or a letter are usually capitalized.

If you live in Election District 17, you vote at the machine in Room 24.

Are there seats available on Flight 405 to Chicago?

Capitalize the names of political parties (but not the word *party*). Capitalize the names of government departments, agencies, bureaus, and their abbreviations.

Has the Democratic party ever held a convention in Texas?

All milk products must maintain standards set by the United States Department of Agriculture (USDA).

Exercise 5: *Capitalizing Proper Nouns*

Write each of the following sentences, adding capital letters where necessary. Underline the words you capitalize.

Example

a. Dr. Franklin's course, history of art 101, meets in room 616 on thursday.

Dr. Franklin's course, History of Art 101, meets in Room 616 on Thursday.

1. Professor Rashid, who teaches religious thought 401, is an expert on the koran and the teachings of muhammad.

2. The holidays of easter and passover are not always at exactly the same time, but both are always in the spring.

3. Much of the art that we studied in our greek art course was done during ancient greece's golden age of pericles.

4. Although memorial day falls on wednesday, it will be celebrated officially on monday, may 28.

5. All final exams in literature, french, and german will be given during the third week in june.

6. On monday, october 15, the world series begins.

7. Will the banks be closed on tuesday, november 7, which is election day?

8. There will be a valentine's day party on friday night in room 725 at the elks club.

9. Because of the delay of flight 201, I missed the family's rosh hashana celebration.

10. Sometimes, we have a republican president but a democratic congress.

Capitalize the names of specific ships, trains, airplanes, and spacecraft.

617

Sailing in *The Golden Hind,* Magellan was the first explorer to circumnavigate the earth.

Everyone was astonished when *Sputnik 1* was launched into orbit by the Soviets.

Capitalize brand names of specific products.

Our car is the dark blue Spritz.

Jellfast is only one brand of gelatin dessert.

Capitalize the first word and each noun in the salutation of a letter. Capitalize only the first word in a closing.

Dear Dr. Scharf:

My dear Grandmother,

Yours truly,

Capitalize the pronoun *I* and the interjection *O.*

When should I call you?

My humble apologies, O wise one.

Note: Capitalize the interjection *oh* only when it is used at the beginning of a sentence.

Oh, I forgot my homework.

I was, oh, so weary of his idle chatter.

Capitalize the first word of each topic of an outline.

1. Popular house plants
   a. Plants needing sunlight
   b. Plants needing shade

2. Care of house plants
   a. Amount of water
   b. Special fertilizing

Exercise 6: Capitalizing Proper Nouns

Write the following sentences, using capital letters where necessary. Underline the words you capitalized. Underline words in *italics* twice.

Example

a. Visitors to Long Beach, California, can see the *queen mary*, once a luxury liner.

Visitors to Long Beach, California, can see the Queen Mary, once a luxury liner.

1. In her outline Marilyn listed seven breeds under the heading "popular cats."

2. Although all nail polish is similar, i like chelsea nail paints best.

3. When i read the greeting, "dear fellow consumer," i thought "what, oh what, are they selling me now!"

4. The *s.s. france* was a luxury cruise ship renowned for its fine food.

5. Tell me, o friend, how i might thank you.

6. Do you think "fondly yours" is too informal a closing for a business letter?

7. Lenny's sporting company sells all brands of running shoes, including zorro.

8. The *mariner* spacecraft sent back beautiful pictures of mars.

9. Yesterday i bought market basket bread, which is the store brand, and it was the cheapest of all.

10. The *concorde*—a very fast plane—flies from new york to paris in four hours; i took it last week. oh, it was fast!

Summary of Capitalization

1.	**Have** you studied dancing?		
2.	**Governor** Jones said, "**Please** be seated, **Mayor**."	*but*	The governor and the mayor were seated.
3.	I visited **Aunt** Clara.	*but*	I visited my aunt.
4.	**Ms.** Harker and Carl Morton, **Jr.**, run the shop.		
5.	It's sunny in **Acapulco, Mexico**.		
6.	The air is dry in the **Southwest**.	*but*	We drove southwest until we reached the desert.

7. All **Catholic** masses are no longer said in **Latin**.

8. Did you visit the **Fogg Museum** at **Harvard University?**

9. The **Humane Society** endorsed the **Bark Dog Food Company**.

10. The meeting was at 8 P.M.

11. Have you ever seen **Mars?** | *but* That's a picture of the earth taken from the moon.

12. The **Bible** tells of **God's** miracles. | *but* Thor is a god in Norse mythology.

13. The **Senior Prom** is on **Memorial Day, Monday, May** 31.

14. Heads rolled during the **French Revolution.**

15. When did **World War** II end?

16. **French I** and **History** 42 meet in **Room** 703. | *but* I take a history course in that room.

17. The **Bureau of Child Welfare** finds foster homes for children.

18. The **Republican** party supported the boycott.

19. **Maxwell** shoes are expensive.

20. The *Orient Express* was an opulent train.

21. **My Dear Joseph,**

22. **With** fond regards,

23. Then **I** said, "Shine, shine, **O** glorious sun."

24. 1. **Trees** of summer

25. Who wrote *Of Mice and Men?*

Review: Using Capitalization

The letter on the following page has more than fifty words or abbreviations that need capital letters. Write the letter and use capitals where needed, underlining the words you capitalize.

dear aunt irene,

we're finally settled in our new house here in hollywood, but a lot of things have gone wrong. first of all, speed-o moving company, which shipped all our belongings from detroit, arrived a week late; we didn't get anything until last saturday. our street, sunshine terrace, is very quiet; but palm shopping mall is just around the corner, and the traffic from the christmas shoppers has been nonstop! our faithful car stopped running, so we had to buy a new one. although we can walk to the shops around the corner, john has had to rely on the rapid transit company to get to his job at casablanca records.

our neighbors are friendly. ms. teng, who is principal at farley school, lives next door. her mother is visiting, and she has helped us get settled. i've also met some people from the park community center. they're having a party on new year's eve, and we're going.

well, now i have to run and pick david up at his tennis lesson at the starwood health club. then he and nancy are taking a spanish class at the ymca. tonight at 7:30 p.m. i have a meeting at the league of women voters. then i'll collapse!

give my love to uncle paul and my two favorite cousins.

your harried niece,
beverly

Writing Focus: *Capitalization*

In English, many special words and word groups are capitalized. The convention of capitalization helps both writers and readers recognize the beginning of sentences and the names of people, places, and things. Capitalize correctly to keep your writing clear and precise.

Assignment: *See the U.S.A.*

You have just won a two week vacation to any place you choose in the United States! Where will you go? What cities and states will you visit? What national parks, architectural landmarks, or spots of interest will you visit? Will you travel by car, boat, plane, or bicycle? Will you go alone or with friends? Will you visit anyone?

For this assignment, write a friendly letter to a classmate telling about your proposed trip. Include details about where you will go, what you intend to do, and whom and what you expect to see. Present

621

your items in chronological order, describing each day. Your work will be evaluated for correct capitalization.

Use the following steps to complete this assignment.

A. Prewriting

Before writing your letter, make an itinerary of people and places to visit. Select only those you could visit in a two-week period. Include specific details pertaining to landmarks, mode of transportation, activities, and people. When your itinerary is complete, number the items in the order you will visit them. You might want to use a map of the United States to help you decide the best way to proceed.

B. Writing

Use your itinerary to write a friendly letter to a classmate about your trip. Avoid merely listing the sights, people, and activities that will occupy your time. Instead, present your plans in a conversational, detailed way. Help your classmate visualize your trip and be as excited about it as you are.

C. Postwriting

Revise your letter using the following checklist.

1. Does my letter include interesting details about my trip rather than just a list of sights, people, and activities?

2. Have I used capital letters correctly?

Edit your work using the Proofreader's Checklist at the back of the book. Share your letter with your classmate.

4
Language Resources

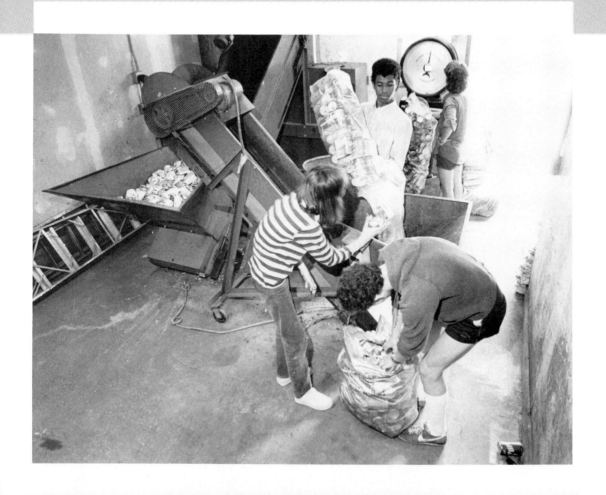

24 Library Skills

Library Resources

Library resources can be divided into two main categories: materials and people. Materials include the traditional hardcover library books, magazines, newspapers, and, more recently, such acquisitions as paperbacks, records, films and filmstrips, computers, and special equipment called *microfilm* and *microfiche readers* for reading materials that have been reduced and stored on film.

The most important library resources, however, are the librarians, for it is they who are responsible for selecting materials and for organizing them so that they can be efficiently and easily used. In this chapter you will learn the methods used by most librarians to organize materials for your easy access. As you work in your school's library, however, you may find that you have special needs or problems. If so, a professionally trained librarian or library aides are there to help you.

The Arrangement of Books

The most important division of library books is between fiction and nonfiction. Events and people in *fiction* are largely from the writer's imagination; *nonfiction* is about real-life people, objects, and events. Usually housed in separate areas of the library, books of fiction and nonfiction are also arranged on the shelves in different ways so they can be found without much assistance.

Books of fiction are arranged alphabetically, first by the last names of the authors, and then, if authors have the same last names, by first names. Books by the same author are arranged alphabetically by the first major word in the title. (The pronoun *I* is considered a major word, but the articles *a, an,* and *the* are not.) For example, Anne Tyler's books *Morgan's Passing, The Tin Can Tree, If Morning Ever Comes,* and *A Slipping Down Life* are arranged on the shelves in the following order: *If Morning Ever Comes, Morgan's Passing, A Slipping Down Life,* and *The Tin Can Tree.* In some libraries science fiction and mysteries are separated from the rest of the fiction.

Exercise 1: *Alphabetizing Books of Fiction*

On a sheet of paper numbered 1–10, arrange the following works of fiction in the order they are found on library shelves.

1. *Song of Solomon* by Toni Morrison

2. *Sula* by Toni Morrison

3. *Innocent Blood* by P. D. James

4. *Tinker, Tailor, Soldier, Spy* by John Le Carré

5. *The Spy Who Came In from the Cold* by John Le Carré

6. *Smiley's People* by John Le Carré

7. *The Dead Zone* by Stephen King

8. *A State of Siege* by Janet Frame

9. *The Edge of the Alphabet* by Janet Frame

10. *Owls Do Cry* by Janet Frame

In most school libraries, books of nonfiction are arranged according to a system developed by Melvil Dewey, an American librarian. Under this system all nonfiction is classified into ten general subject areas and assigned a range of numbers as follows:

000–099 General Works	Includes encyclopedias, periodicals, book lists, and other reference books.
100–199 Philosophy	Includes the fields of psychology, conduct, and personality.
200–299 Religion	Includes the Bible and other religious texts; theology books and mythology.
300–399 Social Sciences	Includes economics, education, etiquette, fairy tales, folklore, legends, government, and law.
400–499 Language	Includes grammars and dictionaries of different languages, including English.
500–599 Science	Includes animals, astronomy, biology, botany, chemistry, geology, general science, mathematics, anthropology, and physics.

600–699 Technology	Includes agriculture, aviation, business, engineering, health, home economics, manual training, and television.
700–799 The Arts	Includes movies, painting, sculpture, photography, recreation, and sports.
800–899 Literature	Includes poetry, drama, essays, criticism, and history of literature.
900–999 History	Includes geography, travel, history, and collective biography.

The Dewey Decimal Number

Every nonfiction book is assigned a number, called its *Dewey decimal number*, that appears on the spine of the book. For example, *Under the Sign of Saturn*, a book about art by Susan Sontag, falls into the *700–799* classification range for "The Arts" and the *700* range for books with general information about art. Depending on the size of the library, a book may have several decimals in its classification number, so that *Under the Sign of Saturn* might bear the number *700.9* or *700.904*, but it will always have the *700* number.

In addition to its Dewey decimal number, a nonfiction book is also identified by the first letter or first two letters of the author's last name and a special number (which together are called the *author number*) and the first letter of the first major word in the book's title. These letters and numbers make up the book's *call number*, a unique number assigned to no other book in the library. The following illustration of the call number for Susan Sontag's *Under the Sign of Saturn* shows how the call number appears on the book's spine.

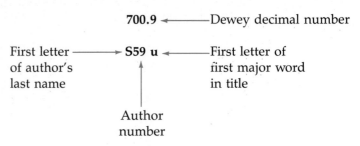

700.9 ◄————Dewey decimal number

First letter ————► **S59 u** ◄————First letter of
of author's   first major word
last name   in title

Author
number

Shelves in the nonfiction area are usually labeled with Dewey decimal numbers: *700–723.81*, for example. To find a particular book locate the shelves with the appropriate range of books. For Susan Sontag's book you would begin your search with the *700* books. Move along the shelf until you find books numbered *700.9*. If you find books numbered *701*, you know you have gone too far. The next step is to locate the *700.9* books with the letter *S* beneath the Dewey decimal number. If there are several books with the letter *S* for this particular Dewey decimal number, look next for the number and then for the final letter that indicates the first major word in the title of that book.

Exercise 2: *Applying the Dewey Decimal System to Books of Nonfiction*

On a sheet of paper numbered 1–10, write the subject area and the range of numbers assigned by the Dewey decimal system to each of the following nonfiction books. Use the table on pages 625–626 to find the required information.

Example

a. *The American Heritage Dictionary of the English Language*
   Language 400–499

1. *The New Black Poetry*
2. *A History of Latin America*
3. *The Complete Book of Cat Care*
4. *The Chicago Manual of Style*
5. *The Murder Book: An Illustrated History of the Detective Story*
6. *The Great Potato Cookbook*
7. *U.S. Energy Policy*
8. *Jim Fixx's Second Book of Running*
9. *Photography*
10. *Italian Folklore*

Exercise 3: *Understanding Call Numbers*

On a sheet of paper, list the call numbers on the next page in the order they would be arranged on library shelves.

627

1.	802.14 B23k	6.	800.24 A19m
2.	801.34 S24m	7.	804.11 B18k
3.	800.17 C13p	8.	800.09 A15b
4.	800.67 C42m	9.	801.343 S24l
5.	800.13 A17z	10.	801.23 T23m

Biography and Autobiography

In most libraries *biographies* and *autobiographies* are shelved separately from other works of nonfiction. A *biography* is an account of a person's life, written by another; an *autobiography* is a writer's own account of his or her life. These books are labeled with either the letter *B* or the number *921* and beneath that the first letter of the subject's last name: $\frac{B}{W}$ or $\frac{921}{W}$ for a biography of Richard Wright, for example. *Collective biographies*, which contain the biographies of two or more people, are usually labeled with the number *921* and the first letter of the author's or editor's last name: $\frac{921}{S}$.

Using the Card Catalogue

The *card catalogue* is a large cabinet with a series of drawers arranged alphabetically according to labels on the drawers: for example *A–Boc, Bod–Cau, Ma–Me,* and so on. Inside, most nonfiction books have at least three cards: *author, title,* and *subject. Author cards,* which are filed alphabetically by the author's or editor's last name, are useful when you want to find books by a particular writer. If you know the title of the work, looking for the *title card,* which is filed alphabetically by the first major word in the title, is the most direct approach. Especially useful for researchers are the *subject cards.* These cards are filed alphabetically by general subject headings, and there is at least one subject card for every nonfiction book in the library. A book on dieting, for example, might appear on subject cards headed *Nutrition, Dieting,* and *Weight Reduction.*

By using the card catalogue, you can quickly determine whether your library has the information you need on a given subject. The author, title, and subject cards all give basically the same information about a book: the call number, author, title, publisher and place of publication, and date of copyright. In addition, the cards may also contain information about a book's illustrations and occasionally a summary of a book's contents.

Two other important cards in the card catalogue are the *cross-reference cards* "See" and "See also." The "See" card is used to refer users to a different heading. For example, a library might file all books on dieting under the heading "Weight control," but library users are likely to check under "Dieting" first, so the "See" card refers them to the proper heading. The "See also" card is an indication that more information about a certain subject can be found under a different heading.

Exercise 4: Using the Card Catalogue

For this assignment select one of the subjects in the following list or use one of your own. Looking under at least two different headings in your school's card catalogue, determine whether or not your library has any books on the subject. If there are books listed in the card catalogue, write down authors, titles, and call numbers for at least two of them.

Subjects	Headings
Extinction of whales	Whales, Wildlife preservation, Mammals
The Aztec culture	Aztecs, South American Indians
The uses of holography	Holography, Lasers
Witchcraft in Salem	Witchcraft, Salem
The lost continent of Atlantis	Atlantis, Continents

Exercise 5: Using Author Cards

Using your school library's card catalogue, determine whether or not the library has books by any of the following authors. If you find author cards for any of the writers, copy down at least one title for each author and that particular book's call number.

1.	Sylvia Porter	6.	Pauline Kael
2.	William Manchester	7.	Leo Rosten
3.	Ann Landers	8.	Susan Sontag
4.	Joyce Brothers	9.	Will Durant
5.	Jim Fixx	10.	Carl Sagan

The Library of Congress System

The *Library of Congress system,* a newer method for classifying books, divides knowledge into certain categories designated by letters of the alphabet:

A	General Works	L	Education
B	Philosophy	M	Music
C	History	N	Fine Arts
D	General History	P	Language and Literature
E–F	American History	Q	Science
G	Geography, Anthropology, Recreation	R	Medicine
		S	Agriculture
		T	Technology
H	Social Sciences	U	Military
J	Political Science	V	Naval Science
K	Law	Z	Library

Categories are further subdivided with a system of letters and numbers, as they are in the Dewey decimal system. Unlike the older system, however, the Library of Congress classification system is used with both fiction and nonfiction. If your school library uses the Library of Congress system, ask a librarian or teacher for help in learning the divisions.

The Parts of a Book

Sometimes locating a book is only the first step. If you want to know whether or not a particular book will be helpful to you in your research, you must also be able to evaluate the book to determine its usefulness. Knowing the parts of a book will help you to do this.

1. The Frontispiece (frun'-tis-pēs')

The *frontispiece* is an illustration that faces or immediately precedes the title page. Not every book has one.

2. The Title Page

The *title page* contains the complete title of the book, the name of the author(s) or editor(s), the name of the publishing company, and the place of publication.

3. The Copyright Page

The *copyright page* is usually the other side of the title page. A *copyright* is a legal right granted to an author or a publisher to publish, sell, and distribute a work for the life of the author plus an additional fifty years. In addition, if the book is substantially updated or changed, the copyright can be renewed then. The date and holder of the copyright will be printed on the copyright page. If the copyright has been renewed, that information will also be printed there.

Information about copyright is important for two reasons. First it tells you that the work is legally owned by a person or company and that you have the right to use it only under certain restricted conditions. Second it tells you whether or not the information inside is current. For some subjects updated information is important; a book with a latest copyright of 1950 obviously would not be a source of current information.

4. Preface, Foreword, and Introduction

The *preface, foreword,* and *introduction* of a book, most often written by the author or by an expert in the field, usually contain general comments about the content, organization, and scope of the book. By skimming these sections, you can sometimes determine whether or not the material you need will be discussed in greater depth in the book.

5. The Table of Contents

In nonfiction books the *table of contents* usually shows the major divisions and subdivisions of the book. By scanning the contents, you can determine not only whether your subject is covered in that particular book but also the extent to which it is treated.

6. The Glossary

Usually appearing at the end of the book, the *glossary* is a mini-dictionary defining special terms used in the text.

7. The Bibliography

A *bibliography* is an alphabetical listing of sources the author or editor found helpful in preparing the book or of closely related sources. Usually found in the back of a book, the bibliography is sometimes divided into sections by subject headings. For example, the bibliography of Joseph P. Lash's book *Helen and Teacher,* a biography of Helen Keller and her teacher Anne Sullivan Macy, contains the following headings: *Books by Helen Keller, Books Relating to Helen Keller, Magazines and Other Materials Relating to Helen Keller.*

8. The Index

The *index* is an alphabetical listing of topics covered in the book, with page numbers. The index is more detailed than the table of contents, since the index generally covers every topic discussed in the book, regardless of the thoroughness of the coverage. To determine whether or not a book contains the information you need, look first for a general heading. If the heading is subdivided, continue looking until you find the appropriate subheading. For example, the following index entry is from Joseph Lash's *Helen and Teacher.* All the subheads in the entry are about Samuel Langhorne Clemens, better known as Mark Twain. Information about the friendship between Hellen Keller (*HK*) and Clemens is on pages 193–194, 304–306, 357–362, 380–381, and on page 439.

> Clemens, Samuel Langhorne (Mark Twain): Bacon-Shakespeare controversy and, 360–62; on HK-ASM relationship, 289–90, 450/ HK education fund and, 209–10; HK friendship with, 193–94, 304–6, 357–62, 380–81, 439; *Innocents Abroad,* 260; *Is Shakespeare Dead?,* 362; pessimism, 307; on plagiarism, 146–48, 290, 343

Exercise 6: Identifying and Using the Parts of a Book

Using this textbook as your source, answer the following questions.

1. Does this book have a frontispiece?

2. Who are the authors of this textbook?

3. What is the publishing company? The place of publication?

4. What is the date of the copyright for this book?

5. On what page of the textbook will you find a poem by Robert Hayden?

6. On what page does the table of contents begin?

7. How many chapters does this book contain?

8. What is the title of the chapter that discusses prewriting?

9. According to the index, on what pages is *brainstorming* discussed?

Using the Readers' Guide to Periodical Literature

The *Readers' Guide to Periodical Literature,* often called the *Readers' Guide,* is an author and subject index to general interest periodicals published in the United States.

Published twice a month except for February, July, and August when it is published once a month, the *Readers' Guide* consists of alphabetized subject and author entries for periodicals. (Once a year the *Readers' Guide* is published as a hardcover volume covering the months of March–February.) A separate section in the back of the *Guide* lists book reviews, arranged alphabetically by the last name of the authors reviewed. The periodicals covered by the guide are indexed in its front, where you will also find an explanation of the abbreviations used in the *Guide.* Most libraries have the *Readers' Guide,* but they may not always have the magazines you need. Your librarian may post a list of the magazines to be found in your library.

The sample column from the *Readers' Guide* appearing with Exercise 7 shows how to read the entries. Suppose you want to find information about spaniels. Since the guide is arranged alphabetically, the logical place to look would be under the subject heading "Spaniels." You could also look under the subject "Dogs," but in general the more specific you can make your subject, the sooner you will find the information you need. In the sample column, you find under the heading "Spaniels" one entry: "Are britts in trouble?" This article about the Brittany spaniel by D. M. Duffy was published in the March 1980 issue of *Outdoor Life.* The illustrated article can be found on page 164 and following pages. You may have already consulted books and other reference materials and discovered that D. M. Duffy is an authority on spaniels. With this knowledge you could also look up the name Duffy, D. M., in the *Readers' Guide.*

Two headings you will see frequently in the *Readers' Guide* are "See" and "See also." The "See" entries tell you that the subject you want is listed a different way and that you should look under another heading. The "See also" heading tells you that additional information about your subject can be found under another heading.

Exercise 7: Using the Readers' Guide

Using the sample *Readers' Guide* column reprinted at the end of this section, find the answers to the questions on the next page. Then write them on a sheet of paper.

1. What magazine contains an article about traveling in Spain?

2. Clarence Spangle is a businessman. What article was written about him?

3. Under what additional heading would you find information about tracking space vehicles?

4. Where would you find an article on shuttle engine testing in the space program?

5. Who wrote an article about the actress Sissy Spacek?

6. What article would give you information about the Spanish government?

7. Who wrote the article about Spain's naval history titled "Sailing by the Stars"?

8. How many "See also" references are there under the subject heading "Spain"?

9. What is the title of the one article about Japan's role in developing propulsion systems for space vehicles?

10. Under what heading would you look to find an article about Spanish artists?

SPACE vehicles—*Continued*

Propulsion systems

Japan pushes space launcher development. il Aviation W 112:51 Ja 28 '80

Lunar goal required huge booster [Apollo] D. Dooling. Space World Q-1-193:26-7 Ja '80

Monsters of Huntsville [test firing of Saturn rocket boosters at George C. Marshall Space Flight Center; reprint from June 1962 issue] P. O'Neil. Fortune 101:188 F 11 '80

Problem of propellant slumping delayed shuttle solid stacking. Aviation W 112:71 Ja 21 '80

Solar sailing. T. Morgan. il Astronomy 8:24-8 Ja '80

Specifications

U.S. launch vehicles: Int'l. launch vehicles [tables] Aviation W 112:108-9 Mr 3 '80

Testing

Shuttle engine test milestones nearing. C. Covault. il Aviation W 112:39-41 Mr 10 '80

Specifications

Leading U.S. & international spacecraft [tables] Aviation W 112:106-7 Mr 3 '80

Testing

Key shuttle power-on tests approach. C. Covault. il Aviation W 112:39-41 Ap 7 '80

Tracking

See also
Artificial satellites—Tracking

SPACE warfare. *See* Space flight—Military use

Secondary subject heading

"See also" reference

Subject heading ——————

SPACEK, Sissy
  Kicking free of her ankle socks. A. Johnston. il pors
    Macleans 93:55-6 Mr 10 '80
SPACELAB missions (proposed) *See* Space
  stations—Spacelab missions (proposed))

"See" reference ——————

SPACEMEN. *See* Astronauts
SPAIN
    See also
  Art and state—Spain
  Astronomical observatories—Spain
  Barcelona, Spain
  Basque Provinces
  Cultural property. Protection of—Spain
  Freedom of the press—Spain
  Santiago, Spain

        Cultural relations
          United States

"See" reference ——————

    See United States—Cultural relations—Spain
        Description and travel
  Travel/Spain. J. H. Silverman. Art News 79:56-7 Mr '80
        Diplomatic and Consular Service
          Guatemala

"See also" reference ——————

      See also
  Guatemalan seizure of Spanish embassy, 1980
        History
        Spanish American War, 1898
      See United States—History—Spanish American War,
  1898
        History, Naval

Title of article ——————

  Sailing by the stars [sixteenth and seventeenth century
    Spanish literature] J. M. Goicoechea. il Americas
    32:3-8 Mr '80
        Industries
      See also
  Airlines—Spain
        Politics and government

Name and issue of _____
magazine

  Lost momentum. il Time 115:40 Mr 24 '80
  Spain's struggling democracy. R. Alan. il World Press R
    27:23-4 + Ja '80

Subject heading ——————
Information about article ——————

SPANGLE, Clarence W.
  New boss at Memorex. K. K. Wiegner. por Forbes
    125:165 F 18 '80
SPANIARDS
    See also
  Basques
SPANIELS

Volume and page _____
numbers

  Are britts in trouble? [Brittany spaniel] D. M. Duffy. il
    Outdoor Life 165:164 + Mr '80
SPANISH AMERICAN War. 1898. *See* United
  States—History—Spanish American War. 1898.

SPANISH Americans in the United States. *See* Latin
  Americans in the United States

SPANISH artists. *See* Artists. Spanish.

SPANISH conquistadors in Peru. *See* Peru—History

25 Reference Books

Reference Books

Reference books, books containing specialized knowledge, are usually kept in special sections of the library and marked on the spine with *R* or *Ref.*

Most reference books cannot be checked out; they are for everyone's use. In large libraries a *reference librarian* is often available for users who need special help with reference materials.

The Dictionary

The reference book you probably use most often is the dictionary. The sample dictionary page on page 637 is from *Webster's New World Dictionary.* The key to the numbers printed in color on the sample page is given in the section headed "Review of Dictionary Information." Most dictionaries contain this basic information.

Review of Dictionary Information

1. Guide words are printed at the top of the page to show the first and last words on that page.

2. Word entries are printed in **boldface** type in alphabetical order.

3. Other forms of the word are also given. These forms may include plurals, principal parts of verbs, and comparative forms of adjectives and adverbs.

4. Syllables are indicated in word entries with a raised dot between syllables. These syllable markers show where words may be divided at the end of a line of writing.

5. Pronunciation is shown with diacritical marks and simplified spellings. These follow the word entry and are in parentheses.

nerv·ous (nur′vəs) *adj.* [ME. *neruous* < L. *nervosus*] **1.** orig., strong; sinewy **2.** vigorous in expression; animated **3.** of the nerves **4.** made up of or containing nerves **5.** characterized by or having a disordered state of the nerves **6.** characterized by or showing emotional tension, restlessness, agitation, etc. **7.** fearful; apprehensive —**nerv′ous·ly** *adv.* —**nerv′ous·ness, ner·vos′i·ty** (-väs′ə tē) *n.*

☆**nervous breakdown** a psychotic or neurotic disorder that impairs the ability to function normally: a popular, nontechnical term

☆**nervous Nellie** [orig. used of high-strung racehorses: in reference to *old Nell*, jocular name for a nag] [Slang] a timid person who is easily upset and is hesitant to act

nervous system all the nerve cells and nervous tissues in an organism, including, in the vertebrates, the brain, spinal cord, ganglia, nerves, and nerve centers: it coordinates and controls responses to stimuli and conditions behavior and consciousness

ner·vure (nur′vyoor) *n.* [Fr.: see NERVE & -URE] *Zool. same as* VEIN (*n.* 2)

nerv·y (nur′vē) *adj.* **nerv′i·er, nerv′i·est 1.** [Rare] strong; vigorous; sinewy **2.** [Brit.] nervous; excitable; jittery **3.** full of courage; bold ☆**4.** [Colloq.] rudely bold; brazen; impudent —**nerv′i·ly** *adv.* —**nerv′i·ness** *n.*

n.e.s. not elsewhere specified

nes·ci·ent (nesh′ənt, -ē ənt) *adj.* [L. *nesciens,* prp. of *nescire,* to be ignorant of: see NICE] **1.** lacking knowledge; ignorant **2.** *same as* AGNOSTIC —**nes′ci·ence** *n.*

ness (nes) *n.* [ME. *nesse* < OE. *næs* & ON. *nes,* akin to OE. *nosu,* NOSE] a promontory; headland: now chiefly in place names [*Inverness*]

-ness (nis, nəs) [ME. *-nesse* < OE. *-nes(s),* akin to G. *-niss,* Goth. *-nassus* (for *-assus,* with n- < end of the base of weak verbs ending in *-atjan*)] *a n.-forming suffix meaning* state, quality, or instance of being [*greatness, sadness, togetherness*]

Nes·sel·rode (nes′l rōd′) *n.* [after ff.] a mixture of preserved fruits, chopped nuts, etc., used in ice cream, puddings, pies, or the like

Nes·sel·rode (nes′l rōd′; *Russ.* nyes′sil rō′dye), Count **Karl Robert** 1780–1862; Russ. statesman & diplomat

nest (nest) *n.* [ME. < OE., akin to G. *nest* < IE. **nizdos* < base **ni-,* down + **sed-,* to sit, whence L. *nidus,* W. *nyth*] **1.** the structure made or the place chosen by birds for laying their eggs and sheltering their young **2.** the place used by turtles, hornets, fish, etc. for spawning or breeding **3.** a cozy or snug place to live or rest; retreat **4.** *a)* a resort, haunt, or den: used esp. in an unfavorable sense *b)* the people who frequent such a place [*a nest of criminals*] **5.** a brood, swarm, or colony of birds, insects, etc. **6.** a set or series of similar things, each fitting within the one next larger —*vi.* **1.** to build or live in or as in a nest **2.** to fit one into another **3.** to hunt for birds' nests: usually in the present participle —*vt.* **1.** to make a nest for **2.** to place or settle in or as in a nest **3.** to fit (an object) closely within another —**nest′a·ble** *adj.* —**nest′er** *n.*

‡**n'est-ce pas?** (nes pä′) [Fr., lit., is it not?] isn't that so?

nest egg 1. an artificial or real egg left in a nest to induce a hen to lay more eggs there **2.** money, etc. put aside as a reserve or to establish a fund

nes·tle (nes′'l) *vi.* **-tled, -tling** [ME. *nestlen* < OE. *nestlian:* see NEST & ff.] **1.** orig., to nest **2.** to settle down comfortably and snugly **3.** to draw or press close for comfort or in affection **4.** to lie sheltered or partly hidden, as a house among trees —*vt.* **1.** to rest or press (a baby, one's head, etc.) in a snug, affectionate manner **2.** to settle or house as in a nest; shelter —**nes′tler** *n.*

nest·ling (nest′liŋ, nes′-) *n.* [ME. (akin to G. *nestling:* see NEST & -LING[1]] **1.** a young bird not yet ready to leave the nest **2.** a young child

Nes·tor (nes′tər) [L. < Gr. *Nestōr*] **1.** a masculine name **2.** *Gr. Myth.* a wise old counselor who fought with the Greeks at Troy —*n.* [*also* n-] any wise old man

Nes·to·ri·an·ism (nes tôr′ē ən iz′m) *n.* the doctrine attributed to Nestorius (patriarch of Constantinople, died 431 A.D.) that the divine and the human existed as two distinct natures in Jesus: declared heretical in 431 —**Nes·to′ri·an** *n., adj.*

net[1] (net) *n.* [ME. < OE. *nett,* akin to G. *netz* (Goth. *nati*) < IE. base **ned-,* to twist together, whence L. *nodus,* a knot] **1.** a fabric made from string, cord, etc., loosely knotted or woven in an openwork pattern and used to trap or snare birds, fish, etc. **2.** anything that catches or entraps; trap; snare **3.** any of various devices made of meshed fabric, used to hold, protect, or mark off something [*a hairnet,* tennis *net*] **4.** a fine, meshed lacelike cloth, used to make curtains, trim garments, etc. **5.** *same as* NETWORK (sense 2) **6.** *Tennis, Badminton,* etc. a ball or shuttlecock that hits the net, whether or not it goes over: in full, **net ball** —*vt.* **net′ted, net′ting 1.** to make into net or a net **2.** to make with net **3.** to trap or snare with or as with a net **4.** to protect, shelter, or enclose with or as with a net **5.** *Tennis,* etc. to drive (the ball) into the net —*vi.* to make nets or network —*adj.* **1.** of or like net **2.** caught in a net; netted —**net′like′** *adj.*

net[2] (net) *adj.* [ME., trim, clean < Fr.: see NEAT[1]] **1.** remaining after certain deductions or allowances have been made, as for expenses, weight of containers or waste materials, nonessential considerations, etc. **2.** after all considerations; final [*net* loss] —*n.* a net amount, profit, weight, price, result, etc. —*vt.* **net′ted, net′ting** to get or bring in as a net; clear as profit, etc.

Neth. Netherlands

neth·er (neth′ər) *adj.* [ME. *nethere* < OE. *neothera,* akin to G. *nieder* < IE. base **ni-,* down (cf. NEST) + compar. suffix] **1.** lying, or thought of as lying, below the earth's surface [the *nether* world] **2.** lower or under [the *nether* tip of a crescent]

Neth·er·lands (neth′ər ləndz) **1.** country in W Europe, on the North Sea: 12,978 sq. mi.; pop. 12,597,000; cap. Amsterdam; seat of govt. The Hague **2.** kingdom consisting of the independent states of the Netherlands & Netherlands Antilles Du. name, NEDERLAND —**Neth′er·land′er** (-lan′dər, -lan dər) *n.*

Netherlands Antilles islands in the West Indies, constituting a part of the kingdom of the Netherlands & comprising two of the Leeward Islands & part of another & three islands off the coast of Venezuela: 394 sq. mi.; pop. 210,000; cap. Willemstad

Netherlands (East) Indies former island possessions of the Netherlands, in the East Indies: now part of Indonesia

Netherlands Guiana *former name of* SURINAM

Netherlands New Guinea *former name of* WEST IRIAN

neth·er·most (neth′ər mōst′) *adj.* [ME. *nethermest:* see NETHER & -MOST] lowest; farthest down

neth·er·ward (-wərd) *adv.* in a downward course, or direction: also **neth′er·wards**

nether world *Theol. & Myth.* the world of the dead or of punishment after death; hell

Né·thou (nā tōō′), **Pic de** (pēk də) *Fr. name of* Pico de ANETO

net national product a country's total output of goods and services during a specified period of time, valued at current market prices and after allowance for replacement of capital goods

ne·tsu·ke (net′soo kā′, -kē′; net′ skē′) *n.* [Jap.] an ornamental button or figure of ivory, wood, etc., once used to attach a purse or other article to a kimono sash

Net·tie, Net·ty (net′ē) a feminine name: see ANTOINETTE, HENRIETTA, JEANNETTE

net·ting (net′iŋ) *n.* **1.** the act or process of making nets **2.** the action or right of fishing with nets **3.** netted material

netting knot *same as* SHEET BEND; see KNOT, illus.

net·tle (net′'l) *n.* [ME. *netle* < OE. *netele,* akin to G. *nessel* < IE. base **ned-,* to twist together, whence NET[1]: from the use of such plants as a source of spinning fiber] **1.** any of a genus (*Urtica*) of annual and perennial weeds of the nettle family with stinging hairs **2.** any of various other stinging or spiny plants —*adj.* designating a family (Urticaceae) of chiefly tropical plants usually covered with stinging hairs, including the ramie and the nettle —*vt.* **-tled, -tling 1.** to sting with or as with nettles **2.** to irritate; annoy; vex —*SYN.* see IRRITATE —**net′tler** *n.*

nettle rash *same as* URTICARIA

net tom *same as* SHORT TON

net·tle·some (-səm) *adj.* that nettles or irritates

net-winged (-wiŋd′) *adj.* having a network of veins in the wings: said of insects

net·work (net′wurk′) *n.* [NET[1] + WORK] **1.** any arrangement or fabric of parallel wires, threads, etc. crossed at regular intervals by others fastened to them so as to leave open spaces; netting; mesh **2.** a thing resembling this in some way; specif., *a)* a system of roads, canals, veins, etc. that connect with or cross one another *b) Radio & TV* a chain of transmitting stations controlled and operated as a unit *c)* a group, system, etc. of interconnected or cooperating individuals **3.** the making of nets or netted fabric —*adj.* broadcast over all or most of the stations of a network

Neu·châ·tel (nö shà tel′) **1.** canton of W Switzerland, on the Fr. border: 308 sq. mi.; pop. 157,000 **2.** its capital, on the Lake of Neuchâtel: pop. 51,000 **3. Lake of,** lake in W Switzerland: 84 sq. mi.

Neu·en·burg (noi′ən boorkh′) *Ger. name of* NEUCHÂTEL

Neuf·châ·tel (cheese) (noo′shə tel′, nyoo′-; *Fr.* nö shà tel′) [Fr., after *Neufchâtel,* town in N France] a soft, white cheese prepared from whole milk or skim milk and eaten fresh or cured

Neuil·ly-sur-Seine (nö yē sür sen′) city in NC France: suburb of Paris: pop. 73,000

neuk (nyook) *n.* [Scot.] a nook; corner

neume, neum (nyoom, noom) *n.* [Fr. < ML. *neuma,* prob. ult. < Syriac *ne′mo,* a sound, tone, song, altered in form and sense by association with Gr. *neuma,* a sign & *pneuma,* a breath] any of a set of signs used in medieval church music before the invention of an exact music notation and placed over words in order to aid the memory by indicating direction of melody, manner of performance, etc. —**neu·mat′ic** *adj.*

neur- *same as* NEURO-: used before a vowel

From *Webster's New World Dictionary,* Second College Edition. Copyright © 1984 by Simon & Schuster. Reprinted by permission.

6. Usage markers show whether or not the word is used in formal English. Meanings of abbreviations for usage labels can usually be found in the front of the dictionary.

7. The part of speech is shown by an abbreviation. The meanings of part-of-speech abbreviations are also listed in the front of the dictionary.

8. Word origins are shown in brackets after the part-of-speech abbreviation. Look in the front of the dictionary for help in reading the history of a word.

9. Words that are spelled identically but whose meanings and origins differ are listed separately. The entries are distinguished by *superscript* raised numbers.

10. Definitions of the words are numbered with Arabic numerals. When a word has many definitions, the definitions are grouped according to the part of speech.

11. Phrases and compound words appear as entries.

12. Synonyms (words that mean nearly the same) often appear after definitions. *See* means "see the dictionary entry for the word."

13. Information about people, places, and events is often given.

Exercise 1: Using a Standard Dictionary

Using the sample dictionary page and the review of dictionary information, find answers to the questions on this page and the next. Write your answers on a sheet of paper numbered 1–10.

1. What is one example of a compound word or phrase given as an entry?

2. What is the synonym given for *nettle?*

3. What is a Scottish word for *corner?*

4. What is the pronunciation information given for the word *netsuke?*

5. What are the guide words on the sample page?

6. Which entry word has the most meanings listed after it?

7. How is the word *nescient* divided into syllables?

8. What is the new name of Netherlands Guiana?

9. What two words are spelled the same but are given as separate entries and have different meanings?

10. What is the adjective form of *nest?*

Special Dictionaries

Unabridged dictionaries are more extensive versions of the standard dictionary found in most classrooms. In addition to the information in standard abridged dictionaries, unabridged dictionaries give more information on word histories, usage, foreign words and phrases commonly used in English, new words, and idiomatic expressions. These reference books also detail greater distinctions between words with similar meanings. In addition, they often contain tables and charts on such subjects as constellations, crusades, and standard time throughout the world.

Use an unabridged dictionary when you want to find complete information about a word or when you need specialized information. Comparing the following two entries for the word *fate* shows the differences between the abridged[1] and unabridged dictionaries.[2]

fate (fāt) *n.* [ME. < L. *fatum,* prophetic declaration, oracle < neut. pp. of *fari,* to speak: see FAME] **1.** the power or agency supposed to determine the outcome of events before they occur; destiny **2.** *a)* something inevitable, supposedly determined by this power *b)* what happens or has happened to a person or entity; lot; fortune **3.** final outcome **4.** death; destruction; doom —*vt.* **fated, fating** to destine: now usually in the passive —**the Fates** *Gr. & Rom. Myth.* the three goddesses who control human destiny and life: see CLOTHO, LACHESIS, and ATROPOS

¹**fate** \'fāt, *usu* -ād·+V\ *n* -s [ME, fr. L or MF; MF *fate,* fr. L *fatum* prophetic declaration, oracle, what is ordained by the gods, destiny, fate, fr. neut. of *fatus,* past part. of *fari* to speak — more at BAN] **1 a :** the principle or determining cause or will by which things in general are supposed to come to be as they are or events to happen as they do **b :** foreordination by which either the universe as a whole or particular happenings are predetermined; *specif* **:** necessity as inherent in the nature of things to which the gods as well as men are subject ⟨∼ in Greek tragedy becomes the order of nature in modern thought —A.N.Whitehead⟩ — compare DETERMINISM **2 a :** whatever is destined or inevitably decreed esp. for a person **:** an appointed lot ⟨her ∼ was to remain a spinster⟩ **b :** RUIN, DISASTER; *esp* **:** DEATH ⟨the villain met his ∼ at the hands of the hero⟩ **c :** ultimate lot or disposition **:** final outcome **:** END ⟨the congress decided the bill's ∼ by a single vote⟩ ⟨the explorer's party left no trace of the ∼ that overcame them⟩ ⟨the importance of an individual thinker . . . depends upon the ∼ of his ideas in the mind of his successors —A.N.Whitehead⟩ **d :** the circumstances that befall something ⟨all human beings live as members of organized groups and have their ∼ inextricably bound up with that of the group to which they belong —Ralph Linton⟩ **3 :** one of the goddesses of fate or destiny esp. of classical times supposed to determine the course of human life — usu. used in pl. and then sometimes cap. ⟨waiting there, standing like a ∼ in the center of the carpet, a gaunt, gray, somber woman —G.W.Brace⟩ ⟨my great-aunts, formidable ∼s who sat in judgment on all the events of their time —Hugh Dickinson⟩ ⟨the ∼s . . . have smiled with an astonishing kindness on his wanderings in the jungle —*Geog. Jour.*⟩

¹From *Webster's New World Dictionary,* Second College Edition. Copyright © 1984 by Simon & Schuster. Reprinted by permission.

²By permission. From *Webster's Third New International Dictionary* © 1986 by Merriam-Webster Inc., publisher of the Merriam-Webster ® Dictionaries.

The first entry is from the abridged version of *Webster's New World Dictionary.* The second entry, from the unabridged *Webster's Third New International Dictionary,* gives more thorough explanations of word meanings and illustrates the explanations with quotations from different authors to show the word in context.

Since unabridged dictionaries are so large, libraries usually display them on a table or dictionary stand for easy use. The unabridged dictionaries your library may have include the *Webster's Third New International Dictionary* and the *Random House Dictionary of the English Language.*

Dictionaries of synonyms are also available in the reference area of the library. A dictionary of synonyms can help you improve your vocabulary and make your writing more precise and interesting. When using this aid, however, remember that synonyms do not have exactly the same meaning. The word *doom,* for example, is listed as a synonym for *fate.* The words *doom* and *fate* share the meaning of "destiny," but *doom* is always negative, while *fate* can have positive or negative overtones. When you find a synonym, always read its definition thoroughly to be certain it is exactly the word you want.

Three commonly used dictionaries of synonyms are *Roget's International Thesaurus; Funk and Wagnalls Standard Handbook of Synonyms, Antonyms, and Prepositions;* and *Webster's New Dictionary of Synonyms.* The Funk and Wagnalls dictionary organizes its words alphabetically with detailed descriptions of the variations in meaning for each synonym. Webster's is also organized alphabetically and has antonyms in parentheses after the synonyms for each word. *Roget's Thesaurus,* however, is organized differently. In this widely used resource, words are arranged by ideas rather than in alphabetical order. Words are first grouped into large classes of ideas (such as *sensation*), then into smaller categories (such as *sensation in general, touch,* and *taste*). Each of these categories consists of smaller numbered categories, as in the sample on page 641.

The words in **boldface** type can also be found under their own headings in the index.

To find a synonym in the thesaurus, use the index to locate the number of the category in which the word is grouped. The entries listed in the sample after the single word *touch* come from the index. (Notice that the first twelve entries are for *touch* as a noun; the last eleven entries are for *touch* as a verb.) What is the category number that refers to the noun *touch* as one of the senses?

The noun *touch* as it is related to *feel* has the category number 425. This is the category given in the sample from the *Roget's Thesaurus.* Notice how the category is further subdivided.

Roget's Thesaurus is a valuable tool because it contains more than a quarter of a million synonyms. However, since no definition of these synonyms is included, always use the thesaurus to refresh your memory about words whose meanings you already know, or use it in conjunction with a dictionary.

The following excerpt is from the index to *Roget's Thesaurus*.[1]

.1 NOUNS **touch,** thigmo-; sense of touch, tactile sense, cutaneous sense; taction, contact 200.5 **feel,** feeling; hand-mindedness; light touch, lambency, whisper, breath, kiss, caress; lick, lap; brush, graze, glance; stroke, rub; tap, flick 283.6; finger tip caress, tentative poke.

.2 **touching, feeling, fingering, palpation, handling,** manipulation; petting, caressing, stroking, rubbing, frottage, friction 350; pressure 283.2.

.3 touchableness, **tangibility, palpability,** tactility.

.4 **feeler,** tactile organ, tactor, tactile cell; tactile process, tactile corpuscle, **antenna;** tactile hair, vibrissa; cat whisker; barbel, barbule; palp, palpus.

.5 **finger, digit,** digiti–, dactyl(o)–; forefinger, index finger, index; ring finger, annulary; middle finger, medius, dactylion; little finger, pinkie [informal], minimus; thumb, pollex.

.6 VERBS **touch, feel,** feel of, palpate; **finger,** pass *or* run the fingers over, feel with the fingertips, thumb; **handle,** palm, paw; **manipulate,** weild, ply; twiddle; poke at, prod 283.11; tap, **flick** 283.15; come in contact 200.10.

.7 **touch lightly,** touch upon; kiss, **brush,** sweep, graze, brush by, glance, scrape, skim.

.8 **stroke, pet, caress,** fondle; **nuzzle,** nose, rub noses; feel up [slang]; rub, rub against, massage, knead 350.6.

.9 **lick, lap,** tongue, mouth.

.10 ADJS **tactile,** tactual; hand,-minded.

.11 touchable, **palpable, tangible,** tactile.

.12 lightly touching, lambent, playing lightly over, barely touching.

touch

	n.		v.
	admixture **44.7**		affect **855.16**
	communication **554.1**		beg **774.15**
	contact **200.5**		borrow **821.3**
	feel **425**		contact **200.10**
	implication **546.2**		equal **30.5**
	knack **733.6**		excite pity **944.5**
	motif **901.7**		feel **425.6**
	music **462.31**		relate to **9.5**
	sense **422.5**		sense **422.8**
	signal **568.15**		signal **568.22**
	small amount **35.4**		tap **283.15**
	tap **283.6**		

[1]Entry for "Touch" #425 (p. 325) and index for "Touch" (p. 1267) from *Roget's International Thesaurus*, 4th Edition revised by Robert L. Chapman. Copyright © 1977 by Harper & Row, Publishers, Inc. Reprinted by permission of the Publisher.

Exercise 2: Using a Dictionary of Synonyms

Select five words from the following list and find each in *Roget's Thesaurus* or another dictionary of synonyms. On a separate sheet of paper, write out five synonyms listed for each word. Indicate when the synonyms are not used in Edited Standard English by writing out *coll.* (colloquial), or *slang,* or whatever other term the dictionary uses.

1. vicious	6. oppressive
2. hardy	7. joy
3. somber	8. ideal
4. ruffle	9. frantic
5. pounce	10. exception

Encyclopedias

An *encyclopedia* is a collection of articles on a wide variety of subjects, arranged alphabetically.

Encyclopedias vary in size from thirty volumes to one volume. The multivolume sets usually have a separate volume, called an *index*, that refers the user to volumes and pages where subjects are covered. The subject of *holography*, for example, might be treated in articles headed "Holography," "Lasers," and "Dr. Denis Gabor" (credited as the inventor of holography). Only by checking the index could you be certain that you have found all the information the encyclopedia contains on your subject. Another important volume that is part of many encyclopedias is the yearbook. Published annually, the yearbook is a way of keeping information current that might otherwise become dated very quickly.

Four general encyclopedias frequently found in school libraries are *Collier's Encyclopedia* (twenty-four volumes), *Encyclopaedia Britannica* (thirty volumes), *Encyclopedia Americana* (thirty volumes), and *World Book Encyclopedia* (twenty-two volumes). The best known one- and two-volume encyclopedias are *The Concise Columbia Encyclopedia* (one volume), and *The Lincoln Library of Essential Information* (two volumes).

The *Encyclopaedia Britannica* has a relatively new approach to locating information. The first eleven volumes amount to an index with entries arranged in alphabetical order. By first looking up an article in this *Micropaedia*, the user can learn not only the various places where this subject is treated in greater depth but can also find basic reference data about the subject. The remaining nineteen volumes, called the *Macropaedia,* contain more detailed articles about many subjects and people.

Limited in their treatments of most subjects, encyclopedias can best be used as springboards to further research. By giving an overview of the subject, encyclopedias can help users identify questions to answer and particular areas to explore. Also, references at the end of many encyclopedia articles often refer users to books with more specialized information.

Exercise 3: Using an Encyclopedia

Using the index of an encyclopedia in your school library, look up one of the following subjects or another one of your choice. Then write down the volume and page numbers of at least two encyclopedia articles about the subject. Finally, read one of the articles and write a brief summary of it in your own words.

1. Comets
2. Etruscan civilization
3. Hypnosis
4. Impressionism
5. The invention of plastic
6. Madame Curie
7. The Ukraine
8. Air traffic control
9. Katherine Anne Porter
10. Spelunking

Almanacs and Atlases

An *almanac* is an annually published book of facts and figures on a wide range of subjects.

Consult an almanac when you need to find up-to-date information on current events, sports, politics, industry, arts and entertainment, and many other areas. Almanacs contain historical facts and figures. An almanac can tell you the date of the Russian Revolution, current census figures, the amount of the Gross National Product, and the names of winners of the Nobel Prize. Commonly used almanacs include the *World Almanac and Book of Facts,* the *Information Please Almanac,* and *The Official Associated Press Almanac.*

Another popular almanac, *The People's Almanac,* prints specialized information with an unusual slant. In it you will find a reprint of the world's first-known photograph, a brief history of popular inventions (such as the fork and the rubber band), and lists of everything from eleven strange postcards to the twenty-five most-written-about people of all time.

An *atlas* is a book of maps.

Standard atlases contain geographical maps of all the countries in the world, as well as maps and charts indicating a range of information from topography, climate, population, and industry to sea currents. Some of the most commonly used atlases are the *Hammond Contemporary World Atlas, Goode's World Atlas,* the *Rand McNally New Cosmopolitan World Atlas,* and *The Encyclopaedia Britannica Atlas.*

Usually the reference section also contains *historical atlases,* books of maps from various periods in history. These atlases show changing boundaries of countries, the growth of empires, and the flow of languages and cultures, as well as replicas of early maps. The *Historical Atlas of the United States,* Shepherd's *Historical Atlas,* and the *Rand McNally Atlas of World History* are all popular historical atlases that your school library may have.

Exercise 4: Using an Almanac and an Atlas

Select at least five of the following ten questions and use an almanac or atlas to find the answers. Write your answers on a separate sheet of paper and indicate the source where you found them.

1. What is the name of the current poet laureate of England?
2. How many islands compose the state of Hawaii?
3. Who is the current president of Greece?
4. What are the first- and second-largest natural lakes in the world?
5. Which coast of Australia is the most mountainous?
6. What was the site of the 1896 Olympic games?
7. What is the name of the part of the English Channel that is closest to France?
8. What languages are spoken in South Africa?
9. What is the second-largest country in South America?
10. Who was the first woman lawyer in the United States?

Biographical Reference Books

Biographical reference books are sources of information about famous people.

Webster's Biographical Dictionary presents short biographies of famous people, in one volume. *Who's Who* is an annually published British work giving current information on famous living people, primarily English. *Who's Who in America*, revised every two years, is a similar publication about famous living Americans. In addition, there are specialized Who's Who publications, such as *Who's Who in American Law*. *Current Biography* deals with prominent people in the news. Published monthly, the pamphlets are bound together in book form at the end of the year with a cumulative index for easy reference.

In addition, most arts and professions have specialized biographies for their field. To find information about writers, for example, you could consult *The Writers Directory*, *Twentieth Century Authors*, or *British Authors of the Nineteenth Century*.

Exercise 5: Using a Biographical Reference Book

Select two of the following names and look them up in one or more biographical reference books. On a separate sheet of paper, write a brief paragraph on the information you find about each person. Include the source you used for each.

1. Nancy Lopez (golfer)
2. Kahlil Gibran (poet)
3. Twyla Tharp (dancer)
4. Louise Nevelson (artist)
5. Claudio Arrau (pianist)
6. Jay Silverheels (actor)
7. Walter Lippmann (journalist)
8. Bessie Smith (singer)
9. Mark Spitz (swimmer)
10. Barbara Tuchman (writer)

Literature Reference Books

Literature reference books give information on sources of quotations and on authors and their works.

Probably the most well-known literature reference work is *Bartlett's Familiar Quotations*. This work is useful when you need to know the author of a quotation or the exact quote itself. Assume, for example, that you want to know who first said or wrote the expression "All or nothing." To find this information look in the index, where every quotation is listed alphabetically by its first major word and also by each important word. "All or nothing," then, is listed both under *all* and *nothing*. You would find that Henrik Ibsen is the author of this quotation and that it is from his play *Brand*.

If, on the other hand, you wanted to look for several of Ibsen's quotations, you would look in the author index, which comes before the index of quotations. The authors in Bartlett's are listed chronologically (with Ibsen, for example, coming before Gertrude Stein). For this reason it is often faster to use the author index.

Another reference work for quotations, *Stevenson's Home Book of Quotations*, organizes its information by subject rather than by author or first line. This is a helpful book for finding quotations on special subjects to use in your writing.

An *encyclopedia of world literature* is a useful way to find information about the history of literature, a particular writer, a genre of literature (*story, poem, play*), or a literary term (*alliteration, tragedy, symbol*). One of the best-known reference works of this type is *Cassell's Encyclopedia of World Literature*.

Cassell's Encyclopedia of World Literature is divided into three parts. Part I, titled "General Subjects," contains historical information about the literature of many different countries and regions and information on general literary topics. The latter category includes articles on genres of literature, such as the novel, short story, poem, and play; articles on movements and areas of literature, such as Classicism, Romanticism, and Mythology; and articles on general topics, such as censorship and copyright laws. Part II of the work is a collection of biographies of writers who died before August 1, 1914. Part III contains biographies of later writers.

The *Short Story Index* is useful for finding a specific story, a story by a certain author, or stories on a given subject. The main part of the *Index*, the *Index to Short Stories*, contains three types of entries arranged in alphabetical order: *author, title,* and *subject.*

The *author entry* is the most complete, containing the author and title of the story, and the author (or editor) of the title of the collection where the short story can be found, as the following sample entry shows.

Cheever, John
The season of divorce
Holmes, P. C. and Lehman, A. J. eds.
The Challenge of Conflict

The preceding entry is for the author John Cheever. His short story, "The Season of Divorce," can be found in a collection of stories titled *The Challenge of Conflict*. P. C. Holmes and A. J. Lehman are the editors of the collection.

If the story has been published in a magazine, the title and date of the periodical are given, as the sample on the next page shows.

Gardner, John
    Trumpeter
        Esquire 86: 114–16 D'76

John Gardner's story "Trumpeter" can be found in the December 1976 issue of *Esquire* magazine (Volume 86) on pages 114 through 116. The title and subject entries list only the author and title of the short story. For more information refer to the author entry.

Granger's Index to Poetry is useful when you want to find where a particular poem has been anthologized. The main entry in *Granger's Index to Poetry* is the title and first-line entry. Titles and first lines are arranged in alphabetical order by the first major word in each title or first line. When the first line of a poem is listed, the title is printed immediately after it. This entry gives information about collections or periodicals in which the poem has been published.

Exercise 6: Using Literature Reference Books

For each of the following ten questions, write the source you would consult to find the answer: *Bartlett's Familiar Quotations*, *Stevenson's Home Book of Quotations*, *Cassell's Encyclopedia of World Literature*, the *Short Story Index*, or *Granger's Index to Poetry*. Write your answers on a separate sheet of paper numbered 1–10.

1. Where would you find information on the life of the poet Gwendolyn Brooks?
2. Where would you find the name of an anthology that contains the poem "Ariel" by Sylvia Plath?
3. Where would you find the titles of short stories about the subject, adolescence?
4. Where would you find the name of the author of the short story "The Jilting of Granny Weatherall"?
5. Where would you find an explanation of the term *metaphor*?
6. Where would you find the last words of the writer Gertrude Stein?
7. Where would you find copyright information?
8. Where would you find the source of the phrase, "The salt of the earth"?
9. Where would you find the title of a poem about winter?
10. Where would you find the title of a short story by Kawabata?

26 Changes in Language

Indo-European Beginnings of English

Y ou can often tell that people are related by comparing their physical characteristics. Perhaps you have inherited your mother's hair color, your grandfather's height, or your father's jaw. In the same way, when you observe close connections between the spelling and pronunciation of words, you know that the words are probably members of the same language family. For example, the English word *night* is related to the German *nacht;* the English word *sun* is kin to the Spanish word *sol.* Noting such similarities as these, language scholars have been able to trace the origins of English and several other languages back to their roots. They have found that many languages were born from a single language spoken by a group of people, the Indo-Europeans.

The language called *Indo-European* can be considered the grandparent of the English language. When the Indo-Europeans began to form smaller groups and migrate to other parts of the world, they took with them their common language. However, over the centuries each separate group of Indo-Europeans developed variations in vocabulary and pronunciation. New words were added as the experiences of the different groups changed. Gradually, new languages grew out of the Indo-European ancestral language and developed into the languages we use today.

Germanic, which resulted from the Indo-Europeans' migration north and west out of central Europe, was one of these languages. It, in turn, eventually gave birth to English and to the linguistic brothers and sisters of English—Norwegian, Swedish, Danish, German, and Dutch.

The other offspring of Indo-European came from the movements to other geographical regions: Hellenic in Greece and its adjacent islands, Albanian and Balto-Slavic in the North and East, Italic on the Italian peninsula, Armenian and Indo-Iranian from the Iranian Plateau to the Ganges, and Celtic in western Europe. These older languages eventually evolved into the modern languages of Greek, Russian, Polish, Czech, Italian, Spanish, French, Portuguese, Lithuanian, Armenian, Persian, Hindi, Welsh, and Gaelic—all cousins to English.

Exercise 1: *Finding Word Derivations*

Each of the following English words is derived from an Indo-European base word. Use a dictionary to find the original Indo-European form of the word. (The dictionary abbreviation for Indo-European is *IE*.) Then number a separate sheet of paper 1–10 and write out each word with its Indo-European base word.

Example

a. night
   night-nekwt

1. acre
2. wheel
3. son
4. bright
5. thunder

6. daughter
7. bear
8. wind
9. father
10. gold

The Varieties of American English

The English spoken in America today varies a great deal as you move from one geographical region to another, one cultural group to another, one job to another, and even one social situation to another. The major variations within a language are called *dialects*. No one dialect is superior to the others; all meet the communication needs of their speakers in various situations. To communicate clearly with others you will find it helpful to understand how their dialects may differ from your own.

Geographical Varieties

When you plan to go out with your friend Mary, do you pronounce her name *Māry*, with a long vowel sound, or *Mǎry*, with a short vowel sound? Do you tell her that you will pick her up at *a quarter of seven, a quarter to seven,* or *a quarter till seven?* After the movie will you stop off for a *soda,* some *pop,* or a *tonic?* These variations are differences in dialect. Language scholars studying differences in grammar, pronunciation, and vocabulary among speakers of American English have isolated three major speech regions in the United States—Northern, Midland, and Southern—which may be broken down still further into more specialized dialect communities.

Spoken English varies from one dialect to another. Scholars have noted, for example, that the name *Mary* is pronounced like *merry* in the North Midland dialects but like *may-ry* in the Southern;

that Northerners say *a quarter of* while Southerners say *a quarter to;* and that carbonated drinks are often called *tonics* in the New England area but *pop* in the South.

Depending upon where you live, you may say that you had *hot cakes, pancakes, flapjacks,* or *griddlecakes* for breakfast; that you had a *mighty nice, right nice,* or *very nice* lunch or dinner at noon; and that you enjoyed *roasting ears, sweet corn,* or *corn on the cob* with your dinner or supper in the evening. Or you may pronounce words in a certain way. You may drop the *r* sound in words such as *car* and *park,* pronouncing them as *cah* and *pahk;* or insert an *r* sound in words such as *water* and *wash,* pronouncing them as *warter* and *warsh;* or you may change a *k* sound to a *t* sound in a word such as *ask,* pronouncing it *ast.*

These differences, which help to make English as varied and interesting as the people who compose the country itself, are not as great as they used to be. Many people today no longer live all their lives in only one part of the country, and television brings other dialects into areas that once were quite isolated. The result is that the language is becoming more uniform. Still, some differences continue to exist, and so long as they do, geographic dialects need to be understood and appreciated for what they are: important indicators of the richness and diversity of the American tongue.

Vocational Varieties

If you were told to "cut your lead," "try out for the lead," or "check the lead," what would you do? In each instruction the key word is *lead,* but the meaning of the word varies according to the situation in which it is used. A journalist will respond to the first command by shortening the opening, or *lead,* of a story; an actor will react to the second command by auditioning for the main, or *lead,* role; and an electrician will follow the third command by examining the main, or *lead,* electrical conductor.

Most occupations develop their own terminology. Collectively these special words and phrases are called *jargon.* Most jargon probably arose from a need to communicate specialized information quickly. It requires far less time, for example, to tell a baseball player to "steal third" than to say, "Run to third base when none of the opposing players are looking." Jargon can also reduce confusion on the job. A chef will have no problem deciding how small to cut the vegetables for a dish if the recipe calls for them to be *minced.* A writer will understand that a story needs a humorous surprise in its final paragraph if the editor calls for a *kicker* there.

Jargon can be an efficient and colorful method of communication —so long as it is understandable to those who hear or read it. Unfortunately, however, jargon is often used unnecessarily, so that meaning is obscured rather than clarified. Some people, for example, needlessly rely on jargon to express very simple ideas, thinking that such language will be more impressive. Instead of short, direct statements such as "Think before you act," these speakers prefer longer, indirect constructions filled with semitechnical terms: "Input on relevant data is imperative before operational procedures conducive toward objectification of the desired outcome can be programmed for implementation."

Exercise 2: Identifying Jargon

The fields and occupations in the following list all have their own jargon. Select two that interest you and with which you are familiar and then make a list of five words and phrases that might be considered jargon in that field or occupation. Also, write the definitions for the words and phrases. For help in identifying jargon used in these areas, look through newspapers and magazines for articles about them.

Example

a. Television
Dolly—a platform where a camera is mounted
Pan—to move a camera to achieve a panoramic effect
Peasant—audience member who waves to a camera
Track—to follow closely with a camera
Cut—to stop photographing

1. Music
2. Business
3. Sports
4. Science
5. Economics

6. Law
7. Medicine
8. Education
9. Sociology
10. Agriculture

Social Varieties of Dialect

Speaking and writing, like other kinds of human behavior, change according to circumstance. For example, when you write a letter applying for a job or write a letter to the editor to be published in the newspaper, you are communicating with a general audience that you hope to influence in some way. At such times you will use what is called *formal English.*

Formal English always observes the requirements of Standard English: (1) accurate spelling, punctuation, and grammar; (2) clearly constructed sentences; and (3) a serious tone. It avoids slang and contractions such as *don't, they're,* and *isn't.* When you use formal

English, you are, in effect, dressing up your language—being certain that it is neat, clean, and suitable to the occasion.

On the other hand, when you write to a close friend or relative, you are more likely to use *informal English.* Using informal English is like slipping into your favorite pair of jeans and T-shirt; it is comfortable language. More personal than formal English, informal English accepts contractions, slang, dialect words, and conversational tags such as *well.* Its sentences are loosely constructed and sometimes incomplete, just as they are in informal speaking situations. Informal English even allows some usages that may not be considered acceptable in Standard English, such as *It's me* and *Who did you see?*

Exercise 3: *Using Different Social Dialects*

Imagine that you are visiting a friend out of town when you run out of money. Write three letters asking for a short-term loan: (1) to a good friend at home, (2) to your parents, (3) to your local bank. As you write, pay attention to the formality or informality of your language. Be prepared to discuss the differences among your letters in class.

Avoiding Clichés

One of your most difficult tasks as a language user may be finding fresh, clear ways to express your observations and feelings. Since other people around you see the same scenes, share many of the same problems, and feel many of the same emotions, you may feel it almost impossible to find new ways to talk or write about these things. Consider, for example, the following examples.

Bitter end	Green with envy
Broad daylight	Last but not least
Clean break	Last straw
Crack of dawn	Ripe old age
Crying shame	Sink or swim
Crystal clear	Sneaking suspicion
Few and far between	Sunny smile
First and foremost	Whole new ball game

Expressions such as the preceding ones are called *clichés,* and although they are familiar and easy to use, reliance on them deadens your language. Clichés suggest to your reader or listener that you do not have anything new to say and that there is little reason to pay attention to your words.

To be an effective user of language, you must experiment with words, looking for new combinations to express your own unique perceptions of the world around you.

Exercise 4: *Varying Clichés*

Individually or as a class, list clichés you have read or heard. Select ten clichés from your list and rewrite them using your own original ideas and language. Then use each one that you have rewritten in a sentence.

Edited Standard English

While American dialect added an interesting color and richness to the language, it also created some problems. For example, in the early 1900s a major mail-order catalogue described one catalogue item as a *coal hod*, a *coal bucket*, *coal pail*, and *coal scuttle*, so that every potential customer, regardless of his or her regional dialect, would be reached. The need for a standard form for written English became apparent as businesses, newspapers, magazines, and literature developed. Such a form, called Standard English, developed to meet these needs.

In the United States today, Standard English is often referred to as the "language of the marketplace" because it is the English most accepted in business, industry, and commerce. As the English most often used by television and radio commentators, it has reached into every part of the United States, including previously isolated areas. For some Americans, perhaps those who speak a regional dialect, Standard English is a second dialect. They may speak a dialect at home and among friends and then switch to Standard English in school and on the job.

In the Grammar and Usage unit of this textbook, you can learn the written features of Standard English: subject-verb agreement, pronoun reference, and so on. Since in writing you have the opportunity to proofread, making changes that bring your writing into conformity with Standard English, the written form of Standard English is referred to by the authors of this textbook as Edited Standard English.

The Meaning of Language

The term *language* refers in general to any method of communication. For example, you have probably heard of body language, the language of art and music, and the sign language used by people who cannot hear or speak. Such means of communication are called *languages*, but what they can convey is limited in comparison with a spoken language.

While you can convey an attitude through bodily gestures, such as the raising of an eyebrow or the waving of a hand, body language alone is not able to express complex ideas. Similarly, you can convey a feeling or a general idea through music and art, but without words of explanation people may not always understand what you intend. Sign language comes closer to being a complete language, for it can communicate detailed information, ideas, and feelings, but sign language has this completeness because it is based on spoken language. The finger and hand positions of sign language represent combinations of sounds in *spoken language,* the most widely used type of communication.

Most often the word *language* refers to a specific set of sounds. All true languages are sets of voiced sounds that have essentially the same meaning for the people who make and listen to them. *Written language* is a set of symbols that stands for the sounds of spoken language. Although spoken communication probably dates back to earliest times, the first written forms of language developed only 10,000 years or so ago.

There are many theories to explain why written forms of language finally evolved. Probably written records became a practical necessity for certain cultures, or perhaps people came to feel a need to leave accounts of what they said and believed and did. Possibly they wanted to preserve their culture and history for later generations.

Whatever the reasons for their origin, the first written forms of communication were pictures representing ideas. Primitive people made records in the form of pictures like these that tell a story.

If you fill in the missing words, you can translate the story: "Home—(I) leave—(to go on a journey in a) canoe—(to be gone for) ten (days).—(I arrive on an) island (on which live) two families—(and there I meet a) friend.—We go together in my canoe—to (another) island—(where) we hunt with bows and arrows.—(We kill a) sea lion.—(We start our) return (journey—and) my friend returns in the canoe with me.—(After) ten (days—I arrive) home."[1]

While such picture stories met some of the need for communication, they were obviously limited in the amount of detail they could record. It was probably the need for increased, detailed communication that led to the development of an alphabet system. Alphabet systems contain characters that stand for, or *symbolize*, the sounds that make up languages. In this way an alphabet system allows the entire language to be recorded.

The symbols of the alphabet vary from language to language, as the sounds of the languages themselves vary. Not all alphabet systems represent individual sounds. The system used by Japanese and Chinese, for example, contains characters that stand for whole words. These characters are called *ideograms* because they express entire ideas rather than sets of sounds.

The alphabet of individual sounds and the alphabet of ideograms are both effective systems of representing spoken language. Writing does not determine how a culture uses language but rather shows how the language is used by the culture. When, for example, a society changes the ways it communicates orally, its written language reflects these changes. For this reason the written form of a language provides much valuable information about developments within a society and is a useful tool for the study of the language itself.

Exercise 5: Using Picture Language

Compose a simple picture story similar to the one given in the preceding section. If your teacher requests you to do so, exchange your paper with one of your classmates and write a translation of each other's story. Be prepared to discuss the details you could not learn from the pictures themselves.

Human Language and Animal Communication

All living creatures, human or otherwise, are born with the ability to communicate. Bees, for example, use a complicated kind of dance to signal the direction and distance of a honey source. Wolves vary their cries to let each other know when changes occur during a hunt, and whales and dolphins have highly complex communication systems.

---

[1]From *The Twenty-Six Letters*, revised edition by Oscar Ogg (T. Y. Crowell). Copyright © 1948, 1961, 1971 by Harper & Row, Publishers, Inc. Reprinted by permission of the publisher.

None of these animals, however, actually possesses language in the human sense. Many differences exist between animal communication systems and those of people. Unlike human beings, animals seem to be born with fully developed communication systems. Human beings, on the other hand, have to be taught to understand language. At birth an infant can make some sounds, but it takes a child some time to learn the specific sounds that make up its language and to associate these sounds with meanings.

Once this association process begins, however, human beings can continue to learn new words all their lives. They can also learn entirely different sound and meaning associations by studying other languages. In contrast, many scientists believe that animals are limited to the communication signals they have at birth. If they encounter new kinds of places or creatures, the scientists believe they cannot learn new signals to communicate these experiences.

As far as scientists know now, animals' signals are also limited to the expression of immediate concerns. A bee cannot tell the rest of the hive where it will look for honey tomorrow, any more than a wolf can describe to the pack the prey that got away yesterday. Only human language can deal fully with the past and the future, as well as the present.

Exercise 6: Learning About Animal Communication

Select one of the following subjects or a similar one of your own and prepare a report for class about the animal's communication system. Use the *Readers' Guide to Periodical Literature* for current information on your subject.

1. Bees
2. Dolphins
3. Ants
4. Wolves
5. Chimpanzees
6. Birds
7. Rabbits
8. Cats
9. Dogs
10. Horses

Language Is Symbolic

Language can be described as a set of sounds that humans make to communicate with each other. The characters in different alphabets stand for (or symbolize) the various sounds that people make. Furthermore, the sounds themselves are also symbolic. This means that the sounds in a language stand for things, ideas, and feelings. For example, when you say the word *shoe,* you use a combination of sounds to refer to a kind of footwear. The *word* is not a shoe itself, however, any more than a picture of a shoe in a magazine is a real shoe. The word is simply the symbol that this society has agreed will stand for *shoe*. The footwear could as easily be called a *glip* if everyone would accept that symbol instead.

Language also helps symbolize, or reflect, the person who uses it. Just as your room at home probably suggests a great deal about you, your tastes, and interests, in a similar way what you say and how you say it may tell others a great deal about you also. Your usual subjects of conversation reflect both what is important to you and what you have experienced. The way you talk about these subjects, your choice of words and how you use them, also influences the impression that you make on other people.

By examining an individual's use of language, you can learn a great deal about that person. By studying the language of a group of people, you can discover much about the ways of life of entire cultures. It is possible to know through vocabulary where the people of an ancient culture lived, by the sea or inland, in a warm climate or a cold one, how they survived, and what their way of life was like. Studies of the long-dead Indo-European language, for example, have revealed that its people lived in a temperate zone in northern or central Europe, in an area without a seacoast. Its vocabulary contains no words for *ocean* or for plants and animals native to Asia or the region by the Mediterranean. The vocabulary of different languages also reflects the nature of the people who speak them. A group of people living in the Philippines, for example, has no words to express the idea of war, and the absence of such words indicates their peace-loving nature.

Because language can reveal so much, scholars rely heavily on its study to learn about cultures that no longer exist. Scholars of the future no doubt will use written records of our own language to help determine what life was like in the twentieth century.

Exercise 7: Writing About the Symbolism of Language

In the novel *Nineteen Eighty-Four* writer George Orwell creates a futuristic society in which Big Brother (the government) controls all human activity. One of the ways it maintains its control is by inventing a language, Newspeak, that eliminates words that stand for heretical ideas—ideas the government does not support. In the Appendix to his novel, Orwell explains how Newspeak operated.

> The word *free* still existed in Newspeak, but it could only be used in such statements as ''This dog is free from lice'' or ''This field is free from weeds.'' It could not be used in its old sense of ''politically free'' or ''intellectually free,'' since political and intellectual freedom no longer existed even as concepts, and were therefore of

necessity nameless. Quite apart from the suppression of definitely heretical words, reduction of vocabulary was regarded as an end in itself, and no word that could be dispensed with was allowed to survive. Newspeak was designed not to extend but to *diminish* the range of thought, and this purpose was indirectly assisted by cutting the choice of words down to a minimum.[1]

Write a paragraph on one of the following questions:

1. Aside from *free,* what other words do you think Newspeak eliminated?

2. Do you agree that the concept of freedom, for example, could not exist if there were no words to stand for it?

3. What do you think would be the effect on society in general of diminishing the vocabulary?

The Uses of Language

All language can be thought of as an end. The language user's ends may be personal or social, private or public. Sometimes you use language simply to express yourself—you neither need nor want an audience for your words. You use language this way when you write in a journal or diary, sing when you are alone, or talk to yourself. Your purpose at such times may be to work out a problem, record your day's events, give voice to a feeling, or merely play with words.

People often devote at least part of each day to such private use of language, although most of the time they put their words to a more social, public use—to communicate with others. The most obvious use of language in public is to send and receive information. You may ask your friends about their after-school plans, explain how to work a math problem, or agree with a suggestion made by your teacher. In each case you are using language for an informational purpose.

You also use language to persuade. Whenever you try to convince others to share your point of view, to do something, or to believe in something that you do, you are using language persuasively.

Entertainment is another use of language. If you like to act in plays or tell jokes, write stories, poems, or songs, this function of language is probably very important to you.

Still another important function of language is to make verbal contact with others, to acknowledge their existence, and to signal the importance of your relationship with them. Even remarks such as "Good to see you!" and "Nice day, isn't it?" illustrate this use of language, as do the other instances of small talk you engage in with people every day.

---

[1]From *Nineteen Eighty-Four* by George Orwell. Reprinted by permission of Harcourt Brace Jovanovich, Inc. A. M. Heath & Company Ltd., the estate of the late George Orwell, and Martin Secker & Warburg Ltd.

Exercise 8: Writing About the Uses of Language

The following is an excerpt from *Hannah Senesh: Her Life and Diary*. The entry was written in 1940, when the writer was about sixteen years old. Write a paragraph describing Hannah Senesh's purpose in using language in this entry, giving examples from the passage that support your description.

> There are so many things I don't understand, least of all myself. I would like to know who and what I really am, but I can only ask the questions, not answer them. Either I have changed a lot, or the world around me has changed. Or have the eyes with which I see myself changed?
>
> I feel uncertain, undecided, positive and negative at one and the same time. I'm attracted and repelled, I feel selfish and cooperative, and above all, I feel so superficial that I'm ashamed to admit it even to myself. Perhaps I feel this way only compared to Miryam because she knows her direction, and her judgment is more positive than mine. She can penetrate more deeply to the heart of things. Or is it because she is two years older than I? I'm already making excuses for myself, afraid to face facts. I say it's being optimistic to see the good side of everything. This is an easy attitude, but it doesn't lead very far.
>
> My behavior toward others is so unnatural, so distant. Boys? I am really searching for someone, but I don't want second best. I'm kind, perhaps from habit—until I'm bored with being kind. I'm capricious, fickle, supercilious; perhaps I'm rough. Is this my nature? I want to believe it is not. But then why . . . ?
>
> Today I listened to music. Sound after sound melts into harmony, each in itself but a delicate touch, empty, colorless, pointless, but all together—music. One tone soft, one loud, staccato or long, resonant, vibrant. What am I? How do the many tones within me sound all together? Are they harmonious?[1]

Language as a Changing System

All languages have their own systems for making sounds and for putting these sounds together into intelligible words and sentences. In the English system the meaning of sounds put together to form a sentence is largely determined by word order. For example, the sentence "The bit dog man the" communicates little to a speaker of English because the words are not put together in the usual way. Once the words are rearranged into the English system's natural word order, though, the meaning becomes clear: "The dog bit the man."

---

[1]From *Hannah Senesh: Her Life and Diary* by Hannah Senesh. Copyright © by Hakibbutz Publishing House Ltd.; English edition copyright © 1971 by Nigel Marsh. Reprinted by permission of Schocken Books, Inc., and Vallentine, Mitchell & Company Ltd., London.

Not all language systems use word order to convey meaning. In Latin, for example, word order is not so important; meaning is conveyed through inflections, or changes in the form of words. It makes little difference in Latin if a sentence reads "Nero interfecit Agrippinam" or "Agrippinam interfecit Nero." In either sentence the meaning remains the same: "Nero killed Agrippina." The word endings indicate who is performing the action and who is receiving it. In English, word reversal of "The dog bit the man" could produce the sentence "The man bit the dog." This confusion does not arise with the Latin system.

No one knows for certain why language systems developed so differently. Scholars do know that in its earliest form English operated much like Latin, with a complicated set of word endings to show relationships. Over time, however, English speakers and writers dropped most of these endings, and the language evolved into its present form.

Changes are still occurring in English, for no language system is governed by rules that are fixed forever. Every language reflects the usage of its speakers and writers, and when enough people change the way they pronounce or spell a word, punctuate a sentence, or interpret a word's meaning, these changes become part of the language. Such changes do not make any language system better or worse than another. All languages are equal in the sense that they meet the needs of the people who use them.

Exercise 9: *Comparing Language Systems*

Using an introductory textbook for another language, find at least one difference between that language system and your own. On a separate sheet of paper, write down what you find and be prepared to report on it for a class discussion. Look for differences in sentence structure, punctuation, grammar, or capitalization.

Example

I found that in the Spanish language system the word order is different from English word order. In English the adjective usually goes in front of the word it describes, "the pretty child." In Spanish the adjective goes after the word it describes, "la niña bonita" ("the child pretty").

Language Is Concrete and Abstract

One way people express their perceptions of the world is through art. An artist makes an observation and then represents this observation visually with color, line, and form. Language may also be used to express perceptions, its words working in much the same way as the visual images of art.

Some artists choose to make almost exact representations of what they see. The result is a concrete visual image of the subject as it appears to the eye, almost like a photograph.

Like art, language also has concrete forms: words that refer to details in the physical world. Names of plants, animals, objects, people, and places are all examples of concrete language. When you hear the words *lily* instead of *plant, deer* instead of *animal, basketball* instead of *object, Eleanor of Aquitaine* instead of *person,* or *Times Square* instead of *place,* you are receiving concrete information.

Language also has levels of abstraction, enabling people to talk about ideas as well as about concrete details of daily life. When you talk in abstractions, you speak about things that are not *physically* present. A beautiful sunset, for example, is concrete; the ideas of beauty in general (anything beautiful—a person, painting, bicycle) are abstract.

Exercise 10: Understanding Concrete and Abstract Language

Read the following poem by Marianne Moore titled "Silence." This poet is noted for combining abstract ideas with concrete, physical details. Prepare for a class discussion on how the concrete words and the abstract words work together to communicate the poet's ideas.

Silence[1]

My father used to say,
"Superior people never make long visits,
have to show Longfellow's grave
or the glass flowers at Harvard.
Self-reliant like the cat—
that takes its prey to privacy,
the mouse's limp tail hanging like a shoelace from its mouth—
they sometimes enjoy solitude,
and can be robbed of speech
by speech which has delighted them.
The deepest feeling always shows itself in silence;
not in silence, but restraint."
Nor was he insincere in saying, "Make my house your inn."
Inns are not residences.

—*Marianne Moore*

---

[1]"Silence" from *Collected Poems* by Marianne Moore. Copyright 1935 by Marianne Moore; renewed 1963 by Marianne Moore and T. S. Eliot. Reprinted by permission of Macmillan Publishing Company, Inc., and Faber and Faber, Ltd.

27 Vocabulary and Spelling

Developing your vocabulary and spelling skills helps you to express your ideas clearly and to communicate with people whose understanding is important to you. The more words you have to work with—and the more you know about when to use those words—the more strength you have as a writer and as a speaker. In formal language situations your readers expect you to use Edited Standard English. Correct spelling and proper word usage are two important elements of ESE.

The best way to increase your vocabulary is to read many kinds of writing. As you encounter words over and over again in new situations, they become a part of your vocabulary. However, you can expand your vocabulary more easily if you know some ways to understand the new words you meet. In this chapter you will learn how clues to the meanings of words can be found in surrounding words, phrases, and sentences. You will analyze the parts of words that carry meaning. You also will study how the meanings of words can vary according to their use and how different words can express different meanings for the same idea.

Writers can learn to be better spellers by paying particular attention to spelling. In this chapter you will learn some ways to check your work and to keep yourself from making the same mistakes again. Basic spelling rules listed in this chapter will help you eliminate many errors you may make with words.

Developing Vocabulary Skills

Words in Context

The other words and sentences that surround a given word serve as its *context.*

Context clues are hints about meaning supplied by surrounding words, phrases, and sentences. These include *experience clues, definition* or *paraphrase clues, example clues,* and *comparison-and-contrast clues.*

Experience Clues

Experience with a situation can help you guess the meaning of a word. In the sentence "Sue's mother called Sue's excuse for coming home late a *prevarication*," you may not be certain of the meaning of *prevarication.* You may know, however, what could happen in Sue's situation, so you can guess the word has something to do with a *lie.* The following sentences give other examples of experience clues.

> After a *cursory* examination of the envelope, Norton tore it open and read the statement of the bill.

(People often go quickly to the contents of an envelope without reading the envelope.)

> I had been sitting in the sun for an hour, and the *incessant* buzzing of the flies was getting on my nerves.

(Your own experience with flies should remind you of the annoying way flies buzz around without stopping.)

Definition or Paraphrase Clues

Often a writer explains a word for you by defining it or by restating or paraphrasing it. The definition, or paraphrase, may follow the word and be set off by commas, or the definition or paraphrase may come later in the sentence or even in another sentence.

Definition or paraphrase clues are often found in science or social studies textbooks. Notice how the words *nucleic acid* and *nucleotides* are defined in *Biological Science: An Inquiry Into Life.*

> Only recently have biologists come to understand the importance of *nucleic* (new·KLAY·ik) *acids* and *nucleotides* (NEW·kle·o·tides) in the life of cells and organisms. Like proteins, nucleic acids are long chains of simpler units. But the units are not amino acids, as in proteins. They are nucleotides. Each nucleotide molecule is built from rings of carbon and nitrogen. Each molecule also contains atoms of hydrogen, oxygen, nitrogen, and phosphorus. Each nucleic acid is built from only four kinds of nucleotides. As in proteins, the order of the units in the chain is very important.[1]

[1]From page 70 in *Biological Science: An Inquiry Into Life,* Fourth Edition by Hickman et al. Published by Harcourt Brace Jovanovich, Inc., 1980. Reprinted by permission of the Biological Sciences Curriculum Study (BSCS).

In the following excerpt from *Men and Nations: A World History*, the word *karma* is explained by the rest of the sentence, which provides its own definition for the concept of karma.

> Buddha accepted the Hindu doctrine of karma, that the progress of the soul depends on the life a person leads, and that good is rewarded and evil punished.

Example Clues

Sometimes, the meaning of a word is indicated by examples. For instance, in the sentence "Some acronyms, such as *radar* (*radio detecting and ranging*), are a part of everyday language," the meaning of *acronym* is suggested by the example word *radar*, which is formed from the first letters of a series of words. Words like *for example, for instance, such as, like,* and *other* often indicate example clues.

> One curious *amphibian* is the newt, which looks like the land-bound lizard but can swim like the frog.

> (Frogs live in and out of water, while lizards are associated with dry environments, so the meaning of *amphibian* is hinted at by both examples.)

> There was a spirit of *camaraderie* among the construction workers. For example, during lunch two workers shared their sandwiches with a co-worker who had forgotten her lunch. By the fence four of them were singing a popular song and passing around a thermos of coffee.

> (The actions described are friendly; *camaraderie* means "friendship.")

Comparison-and-Contrast Clues

In comparison-and-contrast clues a word's meaning may be made clearer by contrasting or likening it to a more familiar word or group of words. Clues that show a similarity in meaning between one word and others are often introduced by *and, another, like,* and *as.* Clues that offer a contrast to a word often are introduced by words such as *but, however, instead, although, though, on the other hand,* and *still.*

> Jon's *petulant* voice rose above the vacuum cleaner noise and reminded father of the whine of a puppy that feels ignored.

> (The word *petulant* is compared directly with a puppy's whine.)

> Robin *quelled* his fear of the dark woods and fell asleep, but Jamie let his fears loose and could not sleep.

> (Jamie did not control his fears; this action is contrasted with Robin who *quelled,* or controlled, his fears.)

Exercise 1: Finding Clues to Word Meanings

In each of the following sentences, the meaning of the *italicized* word is suggested by context clues. On a sheet of paper, write what you think is the meaning of the word, and then write the clue on which you base your guess. Check the meaning by looking the word up in a dictionary.

1. It may be wiser to be *docile* than to show an aggressive attitude.

2. Stamp collecting may be a *lucrative* hobby for some but a waste of money for others.

3. The *turgid* river was a hazard to the troops, who were unprepared for rough waters.

4. The *nomenclature,* or system of naming, now used in botany is in part the work of Linnaeus.

5. "You'll need a bigger belt for your *girth!*" the new salesman said. Then he blushed when he realized he might have embarrassed the customer.

6. For Priscilla rock collecting was an *avocation,* but it took more of her time than her actual job in the museum.

7. When she broke the hair dryer, Rosaria tried to *mollify* her sister by buying her a new brush.

8. The lion was *satiated;* it had eaten almost the entire zebra.

9. Kiyo examined the *callus* between her thumb and finger. She wished she could exchange her chore of sweeping the steps for another one!

10. "Julio is a *braggart,*" Delia told Anna. "No matter what you do, he's done it better or faster or neater."

Connotation and Denotation

When you look up an unfamiliar word in the dictionary, you are looking for its *denotative,* or dictionary, *meaning.* For example, the dictionary meaning for *scrawny* is "lean" or "thin." *Lean* and *thin* are synonyms (words that have the same general meaning) for *scrawny.*

However, a word may also have *connotative meanings,* meanings that include the feelings people associate with it. Denotative and connotative meanings of words often differ. The dictionary, for example, assigns the same denotation to *lean* and *scrawny,* but a "*scrawny* yellow cat" may give you a different image than a "*lean* yellow cat." Although *lean* and *scrawny* are synonyms, the word *lean* is usually associated with a pleasant, attractive appearance while *scrawny* is often associated with something unpleasant.

Besides *pleasant* or *unpleasant* connotations, words can have *formal* or *informal* connotations, *modern* or *historical* connotations. For example, although the dictionary defines a *fiddle* as a *violin*, the first word is associated with an informal, usually rural setting, while the second word is associated with a more formal setting. Today you may refer to a room in your house as a *living room,* but a hundred years ago you might have called it the *parlor*. Words that lack a strong association with a feeling, that lack a formal or an informal situation, or that lack a specific period of time have a *neutral connotation.*

Using a word correctly or making the appropriate choice from several synonyms involves understanding the word's connotation as well as its denotation. For example, speakers and writers addressing the general public would probably use words with formal or neutral connotations. In a private conversation with close friends, the same individuals might be more likely to use slang or other words with informal connotations.

Understanding the context in which a word will be used will help you decide which of two or three synonyms would be most appropriate. For example, since the following sentence discusses the appearance of a famous musician at Carnegie Hall, *violin* is a better choice than *fiddle*.

She held her *violin* at her side as she acknowledged the applause of the audience at Carnegie Hall.

Exercise 2: *Using Words Appropriately*

Each of the following passages contains a word or phrase whose connotation is inappropriate for the context. On a separate sheet of paper, write each sentence, substituting a more appropriate synonym for the inappropriate word.

Example

a. With great finesse the butler started hacking the turkey with a large silver knife.
   With great finesse the butler started carving the turkey with a large silver knife.

1. My friend Phil has a new plaid waistcoat.

2. The slaughter of John F. Kennedy placed the responsibilities of the Presidency on the shoulders of Lyndon Baines Johnson.

3. Looking sternly at the defendant, the judge ordered him sent to the slammer for a period of no less than five years.

4. A dignified, fat, old gentleman walked contentedly through Central Park.

5. "When's the omnibus leaving for the wrestling match?" Jim yelled to his friends.

6. Watch out! That guy ahead of you is driving like a bedlamite.

7. The museum contains several fine examples of barbaric American paintings.

8. The League of Women Voters, who sponsored the local book exchange last Saturday, raked in several thousand dollars.

9. This report from the manager of the sales department recommends that the company hire some pushy sales personnel.

10. I admire your brother so much; his pigheadedness about going to the university has certainly been rewarded.

Word Structure

Word structure, **the way parts are combined to form a word, can provide a key to the meaning of unfamiliar words.**

For example, the words in the following list are called *derivatives* because they are formed, or derived, from shorter words. Although you may not know the meanings of all the derivatives, you should be able to identify a familiar word within the longer word. What are these "hidden" words?

collector	immortal
difference	irregularity
existence	misspell
fearsome	unfearful
illegal	unthinkable

The words *collect, differ, exist, fear, legal, mortal, regular, spell,* and *think* in the preceding list are called *roots* because each is the base, or root, to which groups of letters called *affixes* are added to form new words. For example, the affixes *un-* and *-ful* were added to the root *fear* to create the new word *unfearful.* The affix *-some* added to the same root creates the word *fearsome.* The other affixes in the preceding list are *-or, -ence, il-, im-, ir-, -ity, mis-,* and *-able.*

The following list also contains derivatives that are made from roots and affixes. Remove the affixes and decide how these roots differ from those in the first list.

conclude   transfer
presume   venerable
revolve   width

When you removed the affixes *con-, pre-, re-, trans-, -able,* and *-th,* you probably discovered that the roots were not words. Not all roots are complete words. Roots that can appear with affixes (*untruth, truthful*) and stand alone (*truth*) are called *free forms. Bound forms,* on the other hand, are roots that are not words without affixes, (*presume* and *conclude,* but not *sume* or *clude*).

Many English roots and affixes are borrowed from Latin or Greek words and keep the same meanings they had in the original language. If you learn the meanings of common Latin and Greek roots and affixes, then you will be able to determine the meanings of unfamiliar derivatives formed from these parts. For instance, knowing that the Greek root *graph* means "to write" will help you understand derivatives such as *telegraph, mimeograph,* and *graphology.* Understanding that the Latin affix *ante-* means "before" makes it easier to define derivatives such as *antebellum* or *anteroom.*

Affixes are divided into two groups. Affixes that precede, or come before, a root are called *prefixes;* affixes that follow the root are called *suffixes.*

Exercise 3: *Forming Derivative Words*

On a separate sheet of paper, write the dictionary definition for each of the prefixes and suffixes, in the list on the next page. Then combine various prefixes, suffixes, and roots until you have created ten new words (derivatives) that are listed in the dictionary. Write each derivative and its dictionary meaning.

Example

a. Prefix	Root, Meaning	Suffix
mono-	-gamy- (marriage)	-ous

mono-: one
-ous: having, characterized by
monogamy: the practice of being married to only one person at a time
monogamous: a person or group of people characterized by monogamy

Prefix	Root, Meaning	Suffix
ad-	-tech- (skill)	-able
dis-	-junct- (join)	-(n)ical
ex-	-port- (carry, way of carrying)	-er
in-	-cogn- (know)	-ure
pre-	-dic-, -dict- (say, speak)	-less
sub-	-fer- (carry)	-ment
trans-	-pon-, -pos- (place, put)	-or
un-	-spec- (look)	-ive
re-	-tract- (draw, pull)	-ion, -tion
de-	-scribe-, -script- (write)	-ation, -ition

Prefixes

The short affixes added to the front of a word are called *prefixes.*

The following list shows some of the most common prefixes in the English language and their most often used meanings.

Prefix	Meaning	Example
anti-	against	anticlimax
be-	around, about, by	bewitch
bi-	two	bifocal
cata-	down, away, thoroughly	cataclysm
circum-	around	circumlocution
de-	away, from, off	derail
dis-	not	disenchant
eu-	good	eulogize

669

Prefix	Meaning	Example
ex-	former	ex-governor
extra-	beyond	extraneous
hemi-	half	hemisphere
hyper-	excessive, over	hyperventilate
il-	not	illegible
im-	not	impossible
in-	not, into, within	indecorous
inter-	between	intercede
intro-, intra-	within	introspection
non-	not	nonporous
post-	after	post-mortem
pre-	before	prefabricate
pro-	forward, favoring	prognosis
re-	back, backward, again	revile
super-	over, above, extra	superfine
trans-	across, beyond	transport
ultra-	beyond, excessively	ultraviolet

Exercise 4: Using Derivative Words

Write the following sentences on a separate sheet of paper, supplying the appropriate words from the following list. Underline the prefix in each word you use from the list.

antibiotic	disavowed	inactive	prolong
anticipate	disintegrate	paraphrase	reactivated
biannual	illogical	posthumous	uninspired

Example

a. The club scheduled their _____ meetings for July and November.

The club scheduled their <u>bi</u>annual meetings for July and November.

1. The essay question called for a _____ of the author's main ideas.

2. Jorge thought studying so much made him _____, so he joined the swimming team.

3. The mayor angrily _____ any knowledge of the budget scandal.

4. Although they selected beautiful pieces, the orchestra's playing was _____.

5. One blast from the ray gun caused the whole spaceship to _____.

6. The doctor tried a new _____ to bring down the sick child's fever.

7. Not wanting to _____ the students' anxiety, the teacher passed back the tests.

8. The candidate's argument was so _____ that no one could make sense of it.

9. In storage for many years, the ship was _____ and took its place once again in the fleet.

10. The committee made a _____ award to the famous painter whose premature death had saddened everyone.

Suffixes

Affixes that follow root words are called *suffixes*.

You are already familiar with how suffixes are used grammatically to show number and tense. For example, you know that adding the suffix *-ed* to the verb *paint* (*painted*) shows that the action occurred in the past. You also know that the *-s* or *-es* suffix is used to form plurals: (*girl, girls*). However, suffixes are also used to create new derivatives or to change the part of speech to which a word belongs. For instance, when the suffix *-er* is added to the verb *photograph*, the noun *photographer*, meaning "one who photographs," is formed. When the suffix *-ology* is added to the root *-graph-*, meaning "to write," the derivative *graphology*, meaning "the study of handwriting," is created. If the root *-bio-* means "life," what does the derivative *biology* mean?

The list on the following page shows some of the suffixes used most frequently in the English language and the meanings they usually carry. Since these endings often determine the part of speech for words, the suffixes are classified by the part of speech they form.

671

Noun-Forming Suffixes	Meaning	Example
-age	process, state, rank	lineage
-ance	the condition of, act of	dominance
-ation	action, state of	demonstration
-dom	state, rank, condition	serfdom
-hood	state, rank, condition	parenthood
-ism	act, manner, doctrine	barbarism
-ist	doer, believer	monopolist
-ment	means, result, action	bedevilment
-ness	quality, state	pretentiousness
-tude	quality, state, result	fortitude

Adjective-Forming Suffixes	Meaning	Example
-able	able to	sociable
-en	made of	ashen
-ful	having qualities of	purposeful
-ish	suggesting	fiendish
-less	lacking	graceless
-like	like, similar	lifelike
-some	apt to, showing	loathsome
-ward	in the direction of	windward

Verb-Forming Suffixes	Meaning	Example
-ate	become, form, treat	designate
-en	cause to be	enlighten
-esce	become, continue	coalesce
-fy	make, cause to have	amplify
-ize	make, cause to be	dramatize

Exercise 5: *Defining Derivative Words*

Each of the following words combines a root and a suffix. On a separate sheet of paper, write the definition of each word, including the meaning of the suffix. Underline the suffix in each word.

Example

a. Freedom
    Freedom: the state or condition of being free

1. Suffrage
2. Forbearance
3. Industrialization
4. Christendom
5. Statehood

6. Activism
7. Rightist
8. Wonderment
9. Righteous
10. Marketable

Review: *Developing Vocabulary Skills*

In the following passages from *Last Flight,* Amelia Earhart describes some of her experiences as an early aviator and world traveler. On a separate sheet of paper, write a definition for each underlined word, using context clues or word structure to help you. Briefly explain how the clues or structure led to your definition. Finally, check your definitions with those in the dictionary.

Example

a.   After midnight the moon set and I was alone with the stars. I have often said that the lure of flying is the lure of beauty, and I need no other flight to convince me that the reason flyers fly, whether they know it or not, is the esthetic appeal of flying.

esthetic: appreciating beauty
The "lure of flying is the lure of beauty," so esthetic must have something to do with appreciating beauty.

1. In addition to enjoying its beauty, that dawn over the Pacific was disconcerting. For the sun made its appearance well to the right of the course I was following. It seemed to me I should be flying much more in its direction than I was. For a brief moment I wondered if all night long I had been headed for Alaska! I checked my charts and I checked my compass and everything

seemed to be as it should—so I could only conclude that the sun was wrong and I was right!

2. Here are verbatim extracts from my log book as they were penciled in it that night over the Pacific:
Clipper ship 2 photographs.
1:15 rainbow
1:30 ship
Ice in carb. Rt engine in and out.
Leaned too much. Then rainbow.

From a pilot's standpoint that was an interesting journey. The start made before midnight was lit by a generous moon which
3. gilded the hills gloriously, but by the time I had reached the arid stretches of the Gulf of California there crept up a white haze which made it difficult to tell what was water and what was sand ahead. Only when I could catch a glimpse of the moonlight on the water or see the black shadows of crinkled sand directly below, could I tell which was which. Even the mechanical difficulties which beset the early hours of the flight—chiefly an engine which overheated because of a faulty propeller setting—
4. could not mar the rare loveliness of the night and of the far-flung countryside which slumbered beneath.

I circled the ship several times, wanting the Captain to be sure to
5. notice me. Then I lined myself up with the wake of the vessel, which I could see for more than a mile behind it, and found that
6. the course I had been flying coincided exactly with the track made by the ship, which was a very good check on direction. I could not talk directly with the steamer, so I radioed San Francisco asking for its position and within fifteen minutes received word that I was then three hundred miles off the coast of California, exactly on my course.

Being fairly sure they could hear little of what I said, I became slightly careless with words. I commented on the scenery, which wasn't much, and made other remarks. After flying over
7. this monotonous fog—you have no idea how wearying it can be—for one hour, for two hours, for three hours, I remember saying into my little hand microphone: "I am getting tired of this fog." My message was picked up "I'm getting tired." So a nurse and physician were dispatched to the airport at Oakland to
8. revive the exhausted flyer when and if she arrived. Of course I wasn't tired at all.

9. Just about then an insect, or possibly some infinitesimal speck of dirt, lodged in my eye. In addition to being extremely painful,
10. that minute accident played havoc with my sight. So, with the

maps, such as they were, blurred even to my "good eye," which at once went on strike in sympathy with its ailing mate, and having the feeling of being lost anyway, I decided to set down and ask the way.

We had picked mid-March as about the best time for the flight from the standpoint of weather—so far as one could expect consistent "bests" on such a long route. Setting back the date three months would see seasons relentlessly progress. In some places progress would be with benefit to pilots, in others the

11. reverse. Here rains began, there they <u>abated</u>, here winds were favorable, there monsoons and choking dust storms were due. So we set to studying again the weather maps of the world and

12. consulting with <u>meteorologists</u> who know the habits of fogs and rains and temperatures around the long equator.[1] [Underscores added.]

Developing Spelling Skills

Spelling Correctly

Many writers think the ability to spell correctly is a mysterious gift, but nothing is further from the truth. The key to successful spelling involves proofreading carefully, correcting individual spelling errors, and learning the basic spelling rules about sounding out the letters and understanding exceptions to the rules.

Proofread carefully.

Even the very best writers make some mistakes, but good writers always check their work carefully. Proofreading for spelling errors will be easier if you start at the bottom of the page. Use a ruler to mark the line you are proofreading. As you move up the page, read backwards, from right to left, and look at each word separately so you are not just assuming how the word should be spelled. If you are not certain that a word is spelled correctly, circle it lightly in pencil and check its spelling in the dictionary.

[1]From *Last Flight* by Amelia Earhart. Copyright 1937 by George Palmer Putnam; copyright 1965 by Mrs. George Palmer Putnam. Reprinted by permission of Harcourt Brace Jovanovich, Inc.

Use your dictionary as a spelling aid.

When you are uncertain about how a word is spelled, do not guess. Once you are familiar with the dictionary, it takes only a moment to check a word's spelling. If a word does not appear as you have written it, try alternative spellings.

Keep a record of your spelling errors.

Many students record the words they have misspelled on a special page in their notebooks. Divide the page into three columns. In the first column write the correct spelling of the word and underline the letter or letters that are causing you to misspell it. In the second column write the word again, but this time divide it into syllables and show the accent. In the third column write down any information that will help you learn the word. For example, you may misspell the word because you pronounce it incorrectly. Noting this fact beside the word will help you remember that correct pronunciation is the key to spelling this word correctly. Consider the following examples.

library	li'brar·y	Pronounce the *r* in the second syllable.
science	sci'ence	An exception to the *ie* rule.

Another good idea is to write the correct spelling of each problem word on a card. To study the word, take the card and look closely at the letters and their order. Then turn the card over and write the word on a piece of paper. Check what you have written with the spelling on the card and keep practicing until you have mastered each problem word.

Learn the basic spelling rules.

Students sometimes discover that many of their spelling errors occur because they do not understand the basic spelling rules. For example, they may frequently misspell words containing the *ie* or *ei* combination. Learning the rules for these words will help eliminate errors with many words. Even though there are some exceptions to the rules, mastering them saves time and worry.

Use the *see-say-write* method.

For difficult words that follow a rule, use the *see-say-write* method. Most good spellers see a word in their minds before they spell it. Try to develop this habit, perhaps picturing the word written on a mental blackboard. Then say the word to yourself but be certain you pronounce it correctly. Finally, write the word and compare your spelling with the correct one.

Learning Spelling Rules

The following spelling rules cover the spelling of hundreds of words. If you master these rules, you will avoid some of the most common spelling mistakes; but remember that there are some exceptions to these rules. Once you know each rule, work on learning to spell the few words that are exceptions.

Words with ie *or* ei

If a word is spelled with an *ie* or *ei* combination that sounds like long *e*, write *ie* except after the letter *c*.

ie sounded as long *e:* belief, thief, yield, retrieve

ei after *c:* conceive, ceiling, receipt

Exceptions: neither, either, leisure, sheik, seize

If a word is spelled with an *ie* or *ei* combination and is not pronounced with long *e*, write *ei*, especially when the sound is a long *a*, as in *weigh*.

ei sounded as long *a:* weight, reign, eight

ei not sounded as long *e:* heir, foreign, sleight

Exceptions: mischief, friend, handkerchief, science

The -seed *Sound*

Words with a syllable that is pronounced like the word *seed* are spelled in one of the following three ways.

1	*2*	*3*
supersede	exceed	accede
	proceed	concede
	succeed	intercede
		precede
		recede
		secede

Supersede is unique; it is the only word in English with a *-sede* ending. Notice that only three words (*exceed, proceed*, and *succeed*) are

677

written with a *-ceed* ending. However, because these three words are used so often, you should concentrate on learning the correct ending for this threesome. All the other words with a *seed* sound have a *-cede* ending.

Exercise 6: *Spelling Words with* ei *or* ie, *or the* -seed *Sound*

Write each of the following sentences and add the correct *ei* or *ie* combination or ending for the *-seed* sound that is missing. Underline the complete word. Your teacher may ask you to explain which rule you used to decide the correct spelling.

Example

a. Although she lost her sight in an accident, our n___ghbor continued to study and completed her degree in computer programming.

Although she lost her sight in an accident, our neighbor continued to study and completed her degree in computer programming. (*Neighbor* has a long *a* sound.)

1. In the course of her research about her family, Amy discovered that her great-grandfather was a Blackfoot ch___f.

2. My aunt won't con___ that Uncle Ramon is a better cook.

3. During his l___sure time Eduardo works as a volunteer at the children's hospital.

4. On his job as welder, Mr. Jones wears a metal safety sh___ld.

5. Your grandfather should ___ther close the windows or turn off the air conditioner.

6. Inspecting d___sel engines is one aspect of her job Rosaria really enjoys.

7. Karim gained valuable exper___nce from his br___f summer job working for a gardener.

8. The w___ght of the baby beluga whale at the county zoo now ex___s 300 pounds.

9. After the drum and bugle corps demonstration, the parade pro___ed down Michigan Avenue to the park.

10. Thurgood Marshall suc___ed in winning over thirty of the civil rights cases he tried before the Supreme Court.

Adding Prefixes

If a prefix is added to a root word, the spelling of the root word does not change.

Prefix	+ Root	
il	+ legible	George had trouble typing the report because his employer's handwriting is almost *illegible*.
un	+ certain	If you are *uncertain* about the wiring safety in your house, have an electrician check it.
re	+ commend	I *recommend* Mrs. Sakudo; she is an excellent accountant.

Adding Suffixes

If a root word ends in an *e*, drop the *e* before adding a suffix that begins with a vowel.

Root Word	+ Suffix	
care	+ ing	Georgette is a responsible and *caring* first-grade teacher.
believe	+ able	*Maud Martha* is an interesting and *believable* novel about a girl growing up in Chicago.
please	+ ant	Jenni's grandfather took her on a *pleasant* canoe trip down the Fox River.

If the suffix begins with a consonant, do not drop the final *e* from the root word.

Root Word	+ Suffix	
care	+ less	Proofreading will help you eliminate *careless* errors.
hope	+ ful	She is *hopeful* that their relationship will last.

Exercise 7: Adding Suffixes to Words with Final e

Write each of the following sentences. For each blank, insert the correctly spelled combination of the root word and suffix given in parentheses. Underline the new word.

Example

a. Maria is especially _____ when she uses the radial arm saw. (care + ful)

Maria is especially <u>careful</u> when she uses the radial arm saw.

1. Mrs. Garcia, our neighbor, showed us how to eliminate the annoying _____ on our brand new stereo system. (interfere + ence)

2. Ali carefully read the _____ _____s for the new toaster he got for his birthday before he used it. (safe + ty) (regulate + ion)

3. Dr. Ernest Just, a Harvard University professor, was an early _____ of cell structure. (investigate + or)

4. Mrs. Hopkins is the _____ bus driver in our school district. (nice + est)

5. As a child, Duke Ellington often composed skillful musical _____s from the songs he learned during his piano lessons. (arrange + ment)

6. My grandfather skillfully mended the rip in the tent _____. (line + ing)

7. To save money Mrs. Lowery repaired the garbage _____ herself. (dispose + al)

8. James Weldon Johnson's _____ prepared him to teach, but he achieved his greatest fame as a _____. (educate + ion) (write + er)

9. Ralph Bunche attended the University of California on an _____ scholarship but worked as a janitor to pay his other expenses. (athlete + ic)

10. On her first job as a journalist, Ann Petry wrote _____s for a Harlem newspaper. (advertise + ment)

If a root word ends with a *y* preceded by a consonant, change the *y* to *i* before adding a suffix that begins with a letter other than *i*.

Root Word	+ Suffix	
worry	+ ed	The whole neighborhood *worried* until it was learned that none of the large maple trees would be cut down when the street was widened.
hasty	+ ly	If you shop *hastily*, you will not shop wisely.

Note: Words that end in a *y* preceded by a vowel usually do not change their spelling when a suffix is added.

joyful (joy + ful)   coyest (coy + est)   boyhood (boy + hood)

If the suffix begins with an *i*, do not drop the final *y*.

Root Word	+ Suffix	
worry	+ ing	*Worrying* is not a solution to the problem.
study	+ ing	As a carpenter's apprentice, Felicia combines *studying* and working.

Exercise 8: *Adding Suffixes to Words with* Final y

Write the following sentences. In each blank, insert the correctly spelled combination of the root word and suffix given in parentheses. Be sure to underline the word you form.

Example

a. The cold, _____ wind blew in our faces. (pity + less)
   The cold, <u>pitiless</u> wind blew in our faces.

1. Mrs. Kim _____ about her horticulture exam, but she did very well on it. (worry + ed)

2. Although he didn't catch any fish, Dad _____ the ones Mom caught. (fry + ed)

3. My great-aunt is always at her _____ when she starts one of her remodeling projects. (merry + est)

4. _____ my brother does all the family laundry, but this week he's out of town. (Ordinary + ly)

5. Wayne, the _____ pinochle player I know, is teaching me to read the Braille on his deck of cards. (lively + est)

6. JoAnne is the most _____ and _____ student in the new nursing class at the hospital. (rely + able) (industry + ous)

7. Lou talked _____ about the committee's plans for the African Folk Arts Festival. (happy + ly)

8. The _____ of the politician's speech did not impress the audience, who wanted clear answers to their questions. (wordy + ness)

9. Role-playing scenes from the book made our small group discussions much _____. (easy + er)

10. The President believes the nation's _____ on a limited supply of energy will lead to serious problems. (rely + ance)

Double the final consonant before a suffix beginning with a vowel when both of the following conditions exist: (a) the word has one syllable, or the accent is on the last syllable, and (b) the word ends in a single consonant preceded by a single vowel.

Root Word	+ Suffix	
plan	+ ing	*Planning* the truck's route is part of Mr. Smith's job. [one-syllable word]
for·get'	+ ing	*Forgetting* to feed the cat was a thoughtless mistake. [accent is on the second syllable]

If both of these conditions are not met, the final consonant is not doubled before a suffix.

cook	+ ed	Jane *cooked* a Mexican meal for us last week. [a single consonant preceded by a double vowel]
con·fer'	+ ence	Margarita thought the *conference* on soil conservation was valuable. [The accent shifts to the first syllable when a suffix is added.]

Exercise 9: *Doubling the Final Consonant*

Write the correct words for the following root-and-suffix combinations. Your teacher may ask you to explain why you did or did not double the final consonant. Use a dictionary to check the accent in words of more than one syllable.

Examples

a. hit + er   hitter (one-syllable word)
b. dif·fer + ence   difference (accent on the first syllable)

1. shop + er
2. con·trol + ed
3. hop + ed
4. soak + ing
5. plan + ed

6. re·fer + al
7. de·vel·op + ed
8. re·mit + ance
9. con·fer + ed
10. shov·el + ed

Review: *Developing Spelling and Usage Skills*

Thirty words are misspelled or misused in the following paragraphs from a student's report. Write the corrected words on a sheet of paper numbered 1–30.

As a teenager in Connecticut, Ann Petry thought of her writeing only as an amuseing hobby for her liesure time, since she planed to attend college and become a pharmacist. She studyed at the University of Connecticut and graduateed in 1934. Then she worked for a breif time in her family's drugstore, but gradually writing became her principle interest.

In 1938 she married George Petry and moved to New York City. Their she excepted a job with a Harlem newspaper to gain some expereince as a reporter. In the begining Ann simply wrote ads and sold advertiseing copy. She also was involved in organizeing a nieghborhood recreational program for poor children.

In 1943 she succeded in haveing one of her stories published in *Phylon*. Latter three of her stories appearred in the magazine *Crisis*, and an important editor adviced her to write a novel. Mrs. Petry adaptted some of the short peaces she had writen about the greifs, joys, and troubles of her knew friends on 116th Street in Harlem. She new if she put these altogether, they might work as a small book. Within two years Mrs. Petry had finished *The Street*, her first novel. The book's popularity exceded all her hopes.

28 Speaking and Listening

Anyone who has ever experienced the unity behind a team's winning effort knows how rewarding it can be to participate in an effective, successfully functioning group. On the other hand, how frustrating it is to be in a group whose members seem to be acting in opposition, whose energy is scattered, and whose purposes are uncertain! But what is it that makes some groups succeed, while others fail?

Sociologists who have studied the functioning of groups have identified a number of factors that are critical to the successful operation of task-oriented groups. All of these factors arise out of one underlying issue: the type of interaction, or communication, that is established by group members working together.

In this chapter you will learn the various discussion techniques to use in order to be an effective member of a task-oriented group.

The Types of Groups

Once you find yourself involved with different groups of people, you become aware of the various purposes and procedures these groups have. The "Let's-Get-Together-at-Lunch" group may differ greatly in its agenda, format, and interaction from the "Let's-Get-Down-to-Business, It's-Time-to-Plan-the-Fall-Play" group.

A group's purpose often dictates the way people behave and communicate within the group.

If the group consists of good friends, the members may be informal, flexible, and spontaneous about what they do and say. If the group is meeting for the first time to establish a new student discipline code, the group atmosphere may be more formal and structured. This atmosphere will in turn affect the way people interact.

Group purposes can be plotted on a continuum, or line, that ranges from *task-oriented groups* on one end to *social-oriented groups* on the other with task/social-oriented groups falling directly in between.

Task	Task/Social	Social

Task-oriented groups are formed when there is a problem to be solved or a goal to be achieved that can only be accomplished with a group effort.
Social-oriented groups, on the other hand, originate because the members just enjoy being with each other.

Even though group members may be influenced by one purpose more strongly than another, somewhere in between these two ends are all of the groups that are influenced by both purposes. A student council, for example, may be mostly task-oriented, even though its members socialize, too. In comparison, your softball buddies play mostly for fun except for the task they undertake when they organize a game against their parents.

These group labels can help you understand that different groups demand different types of discussion skills. The organizational skill needed to make a task-oriented group work may never be needed in a social-oriented discussion, yet people who know how to make supportive statements are needed in all group types.

In the rest of this section on discussion, you will learn about many discussion skills and specifically about those that pertain to task-oriented groups.

Exercise 1: Using Group Labels

On a sheet of paper, label three columns with the words *GROUP*, *TYPE*, and *PURPOSE*. Under the *GROUP* heading, list all of the groups to which you belong. Some may actually have names like *Wrestling Club* or *Band*. Even within these groups, however, you might be in subgroups that you will need to label. You may even find that the number of different social groups to which you belong is greater than you realize. Under *TYPE* determine whether the group is *task, task/social,* or *social.* Under *PURPOSE* try to describe exactly why the group exists.

Exercise 2: Comparing Groups

Describe in writing two groups to which you belong by comparing the differences between the two. You might want to compare the atmosphere, interaction among group members, and the expectations for behavior. Finally, describe why you think these differences exist and why you belong to both groups.

Discussion Techniques for Task-Oriented Groups

In a successful task-oriented group, the group *discussion* becomes the pivotal point for group direction and group action. Discussion is the cement that holds the group together. When a group can build a bond of common understanding within the group discussion, its members will act with unity and solidarity. Without this, members may go off in different directions and try to accomplish their individual goals in their own ways.

The following guidelines will help generate successful discussion in a task-oriented group.

Develop an attitude of cooperation.

Cultivate a cooperative attitude. This involves recognizing that every member's opinions and beliefs are equally important. Express your views, and allow others to express theirs. Then, be willing to compromise and cooperate to meet the needs and desires of the group as a whole.

Work to establish an open-channel network.

Every group develops a communication network within itself, and those lines of communication can affect the way a group works. If you have a network where all communication is channeled through just one person, you may get things accomplished quickly, but you might not have a unified group that feels good about itself.

The best kind of communication network for discussion groups is known as the *open-channel network.* All lines of communication between people are completely open, and all group members feel free to speak up whenever they so desire. Communication flows freely from one member to another with all comments directed to the group as a whole rather than to a selected few.

This type of network does not just magically happen. Group members have to work at making certain that everything they say is group-centered and that they are allowing others the same opportunity to speak and be heard as they claim for themselves. The minute you find yourself in a group speaking only to one other person is the minute you are creating a different type of network. Not every group can develop an open-channel network one hundred percent of the time during a discussion. If it is not the predominant network most of the time, however, a group will find itself facing problems that undercut its effectiveness.

Determine the leadership needed by the group.

Groups do not function well if everyone in the group goes off in a different direction. Somehow a group must be encouraged to stay with the task at hand until it is completed. This need for direction is often fulfilled by a group leader, although in small groups it is often possible for members to share leadership duties without having to single out any one person.

When a leader emerges, it is because the group needs someone to help guide the discussion. The leader may be appointed by someone from outside the group, may be elected by the group members, or may naturally emerge as the discussion calls for one. Encouraging members to participate and making certain that all members have an equal chance to speak are two of a leader's major responsibilities.

Asking questions, resolving disagreements, clarifying and summarizing ideas, promoting good feelings among members, listening to all contributions, being tactful, and avoiding the tendency to dominate a group are skills of the democratic leader who helps a group to stay group-centered and cooperative.

An *autocratic* or a *do-nothing* leader will hinder the group's functioning. The autocratic leader is the total take-charge type of person. This leader dominates the group and totally determines all group decisions. The autocrat may actually bully people or try to manipulate them. On the other hand, the do-nothing leader provides no guidance in a group. When the do-nothing leader does not exercise the leader's power, the group may then flounder and accomplish very little.

Choose a group-centered decision-making process.

Closely related to the idea of leadership is the idea of decision making. When a group has an autocratic leader, that leader is the group's decision maker. When a group has a democratic leader who promotes cooperation and an open-channel network, the group generally will choose one of two decision-making processes: majority vote or consensus.

When a group is split over what should be done, often a simple show of hands is used. The side with the most votes determines what the group as a whole will do. *Majority vote* can be very beneficial in helping a group to arrive at decisions quickly, especially when there are a variety of opinions and a lack of compromise. Its drawback, though, is that the group is left with a minority that may not feel totally committed to the group's decision.

A better group-decision-making process is *consensus*. Very simply, consensus means that everyone agrees to the group's decision on an issue. That decision can be a very strong one since it is fully supported by all group members. Consensus, however, is not easy to reach and often is very time-consuming. To reach a consensus the group must work out compromises that in some way satisfy everyone at least a little. For a consensus, group members must remember to approach a decision on the basis of logic and to avoid stubbornly arguing for their own way.

Exercise 3: Reaching Consensus

Read through the following problem.

> You are in a space crew originally scheduled to rendezvous with a mother ship on the lighted surface of the moon. Mechanical difficulties, however, have forced your ship to crash land at a spot some 200 miles from the rendezvous point. The rough landing damaged much of the equipment aboard. Since survival depends on reaching the mother ship, the most critical items available must be chosen for the 200-mile trip. The fifteen items left intact after landing are in the following list. Your task is to rank them in terms of their importance to your crew in its attempt to reach the rendezvous point. Copy the list on a sheet of paper and then complete it. Place number *1* by the most important item, number *2* by the second most important, and so on through the least important, number *15*.

_____	Box of matches
_____	Food concentrates
_____	50 feet of nyion rope
_____	Parachute silk
_____	Portable heating unit
_____	Two .45 caliber pistols
_____	One case dehydrated milk
_____	Two 100-pound tanks of oxygen
_____	Stellar map of the moon's constellation
_____	Life raft containing CO_2 bottles
_____	Magnetic compass
_____	5 gallons of water
_____	Signal flares
_____	First-aid kit containing injection needles
_____	Solar-powered FM receiver-transmitter[1]

After you have done the individual ranking, break up into groups of five to seven people. As a group, rank the fifteen items and record your answers on a separate sheet of paper. You should arrive at your answers by using the consensus method of decision making. In other words, do not make a final decision about each item's ranking until *every* group member agrees to that ranking.

---

[1]"Lost on the Moon Game" by Jay Hall from *Learning Discussion Skills Through Games* by Gene and Barbara Dodds Stanford, copyright © 1969 by Scholastic Inc. Reprinted by permission of Scholastic Inc. Originally published by Citation Press, 1969.

Next, compare your group's ranking to the answers determined by the space survival unit of the National Aeronautics and Space Administration found at the end of this chapter. Score your group's answers by finding the difference between NASA's ranking and the group's ranking. For example, NASA may say that an item's rank is *15* while the group's rank for that item is *10*. Subtract the difference between *15* and *10* and record that number (5). Then total up that group of numbers. The lower the total, the better the group did.

After all of the groups have completed the task, discuss as a class the following questions.

1. Did group members cooperate? Why or why not?

2. Was there an open-channel network? Why or why not?

3. Was there a leader in the group? How was this leader chosen?

4. What type of leadership was displayed? How did the leader exhibit democratic leadership?

5. How did the group resolve conflicts and disagreements?

6. Was there a spirit of compromise by most group members? If not, how did this affect the group?

7. Were there any group members who did not participate or voice their opinions? If so, what could have been done to encourage them to participate?

8. Would the majority-vote method of decision making have been easier? Would it have been better for the group to have used majority vote? Why or why not?

Develop a plan for discussion.

A common complaint about group discussion is that people become sidetracked too easily. Outward symptoms of the disorganized group can range anywhere from group members talking all at once because they lack direction to no group members talking because they lack direction. The most common symptom, though, is the helter-skelter effect where the talk is excited and spontaneous but often unrelated. Members do not respond to each other's comments, and there may be no discussion of an idea before another idea is introduced. Time is wasted; topics are not explored completely; the same material is raised over and over again as people spin their wheels; and meaningful discussion is never achieved.

If your discussion group is plagued by any of these symptoms, you need to develop a plan for discussion. The best plan for a task-oriented discussion group to follow is known as the problem-solution format of discussion.

Step One: Diagnose the group's task. Before group members can achieve a meaningful goal, they must first clearly understand the task—the obvious sides as well as the not-so-obvious sides. If the task is to solve a specific problem, they must be able to completely diagnose the symptoms before they can suggest a cure. This diagnosis begins when members first try to gain information by discussing among themselves questions like the following ones.

Can we define exactly what we need to do?

Are there issues raised by this task that are not obvious?

Who seems to be most affected by this problem and why?

How does this problem affect people?

What causes this problem to exist in the first place?

Is the cause obvious?

How widespread and serious is this problem?

What information do we need to know to solve this problem?

How can we get this information?

Has anything already been done toward solving this task?

Step Two: List all possible solutions. Once everyone has a clear understanding of the problem, the group members then begin to seek answers. Discussing what might be done to solve the problem should be your next organizational step. At this point in the discussion, group members should be inventing as many solutions as possible without discussing them. Your purpose is to suggest all possible treatments. The actual prescription will come later.

Step Three: Discuss the pro's and con's of each suggested solution. Evaluation is implied in this step because you will take each listed solution and decide its good and bad points. You will be judging how well each solution will solve the problem you discussed at the beginning. For instance, if your committee is responsible for selecting an off-campus prom site, then your committee must discuss the merits of each possible site. To do so you might consider the initial problems you discussed—money, decorations, space, time limit, traveling distance—to see which place best suits your needs.

Step Four: Select a solution. Step Four is a natural outgrowth of Step Three. If your group has weighed all of the information concerning the problem and solutions, then it must come to an agreement about what to do. Maybe group members will choose only one idea, or maybe they will opt to combine several ideas for their final recommendation. In any case the group is ready to prescribe a remedy because it has examined all aspects of the topic in an organized, thoughtful manner.

Step Five: Put the solution into effect. Sometimes, it is necessary to discuss who will do what and when. A plan for action must be drawn up by the group that ensures that the solution is carried through. The group's task is not completed until the group has carefully considered these details, too.

Exercise 4: *Using the Five-Step Method*

Select a problem that your school or community now faces and provide a solution to it by organizing your discussion around the five-step method. You may want to break down into smaller groups, or you may want to hold the discussion with the entire class participating.

Learn to use positive group-centered behaviors.

Where self-centered behaviors may undermine the group process, positive group-centered behaviors actually promote it. The following list specifies some of the positive group-centered behaviors that members can assume at various times during a discussion.

a.   *The Initiator.* This member proposes new ideas, raises new questions, starts the group down a yet-to-be-explored path.

b.   *The Supporter.* When you say "I agree," nod your head, or indicate in some way your praise for another member's ideas, you are helping to establish group cohesiveness.

c.   *The Clarifier.* Anyone who asks for facts, who asks for additional information, or who tries to clearly define issues or ideas is acting as the group's clarifier.

d.   *The Gatekeeper.* This person brings in members who have not spoken and makes certain that all members get a fair chance to speak.

e.   *The Mediator.* When differences of opinion do arise, someone needs to act as a go-between.

f.   *The Energizer.* This person tries to keep the group on track during the discussion by gently urging on group members.

g.   *The Summarizer.* This group member helps the group to stand back for a minute to see what has been accomplished. The summarizer may give the group a progress report, may point out the areas that still need to be discussed, or may summarize areas of agreement and disagreement.

Exercise 5: *Participating in a Task-Oriented Group*

Divide the class up into small groups of five to six people to solve the following task. Your group should follow the five steps of the problem-solution format and should appoint a secretary to take notes about what your group discusses under each step. These notes should include your group's final decision and then be handed in to your teacher.

C.H.S. Senior Ditch Day

Senior ditch day is not officially recognized at Capital High School, even though it is tolerated every year by the administration and faculty. This year, however, major problems existed that make it necessary for the administration to take action and stop senior ditch day. It seems that over $300 worth of damage was done to the school and surrounding community as seniors "cut" the entire day. The school and community homes were egged and toilet-papered, air was let out of car tires on the school parking lot, and ruts were made in lawns as some seniors jumped curbs with their cars. No one was hurt during this day, and all of the damage was of a prankster nature. This day was dubbed "Senior Ditch Day."

Facts in the Case

1. Community members were able to identify some of the seniors who were hot-rodding around the neighborhood.

2. Four members of the senior class were identified as the ringleaders. Even though all four of them tend to be class clowns, they have never gotten into serious trouble before.

3. When questioned about Senior Ditch Day, these students admitted to their leadership role in the day's activities. They readily accepted their guilt, but they did not mean any harm.

Your Group's Task

1. Your committee is responsible for a decision that would be fair and just, but that would also punish the offenders and pay for the damage.

2. Your committee is also responsible for coming up with a plan to eliminate Senior Ditch Day.

3. Your plan may include an alternate solution.

4. Your solution should be written out.

5. When each group has completed the task, a spokesperson or group leader should share the solution with the class as a whole.

Answers to Exercise 3

1. Two 100-pound tanks of oxygen (fills respiration requirement)

2. 5 gallons of water (replenishes loss by sweating, etc.)

3. Stellar map of moon's constellation (one of principal means of finding direction)

4. Food concentrates (supplies daily food requirement)

5. Solar-powered FM receiver-transmitter (distress signal transmitter, possible communication with mother ship)

6. 50 feet of nylon rope (useful in tying injured, help in climbing)

7. First-aid kit containing injection needles (oral pills or injection medicine valuable)

8. Parachute silk (shelter against sun's rays)

9. Life raft (CO_2 bottles for self-propulsion across chasms, etc.)

10. Signal flares (distress call within line of sight)

11. Two .45 caliber pistols (self-propulsion devices could be made from them)

12. One case dehydrated milk (food, mixed with water for drinking)

13. Portable heating unit (useful only if party landed on dark side)

14. Magnetic compass (probably no magnetized poles, thus useless)

15. Box of matches (little or no use on moon)

Glossary of Terms

Absolute phrase A phrase, usually consisting of a noun or pronoun and a participle, related in meaning to the sentence in which it is inserted but not modifying a specific word in the sentence

Abstract noun A noun that names a quality, thought, or idea

Action Any physical or mental thing that has happened or is happening

Action verb A verb that shows either physical or mental action

Active voice The form of the verb when the subject performs the action

Adjective A word used to modify a noun or pronoun

Adjective clause A group of words with a subject and verb functioning as an adjective

Adjective phrase A prepositional phrase that modifies a noun or pronoun

Adverb A word that modifies a verb, an adjective, or another adverb

Adverb clause A subordinate clause that modifies a verb, an adjective, or an adverb

Adverb phrase A prepositional phrase that modifies a verb, an adverb, or an adjective

Affix One or more letters added to the front or back of a word to modify or to change its meaning or to change its part of speech

Alliteration Use of words in poetry that begin with the same sound

Almanac An annually published book of facts and figures on a wide range of subjects

Antecedent A noun or another pronoun that a pronoun replaces or refers to

Apostrophe Punctuation mark (') used to show the omission of letters or numbers, to form the plural of letters or numbers, and to form possessive nouns

Appositive A noun or pronoun that follows or precedes another noun or pronoun to identify or clarify it

Argumentation Persuasion through logical reasoning

Article One of the frequently used adjectives—*the, a,* or *an*

Assonance The repetition of vowel sounds in poetry to create a rhyme

Atlas A book of maps

Autobiography A writer's own account of his or her life

Bandwagon appeal An appeal to the emotional need to be like everyone else

Begging the question The fallacy of arguing that a conclusion is true without offering any evidence or reasons

Biography An account of a person's life, written by another

Brainstorming Stimulating creative thinking by letting one's mind wander freely over a subject

Call number A group of numbers and letters placed on a book to indicate its location in the library

Card catalogue A cabinet containing, in alphabetical order, title, subject, and author cards

Card-stacking Withholding information in order to persuade

Clause A group of words that contains a subject and a predicate and functions as part of a sentence

Cliché A trite or overused phrase or expression

Clustering system A system to encourage a flow of ideas and to group ideas as they come

Coherent writing Writing in which the logical relationships between ideas are apparent

Collective noun A noun that stands for a class of items

Colon Punctuation mark (:) used to separate elements within a sentence to call attention to the word, phrase, or list that follows it

Comma Punctuation mark (,) used to separate words, phrases, or clauses within sentences

Common noun A noun that does not specify a particular person, place, thing, or idea

Comparative degree The form of an adjective or adverb that compares two persons or things

Complement A word or group of words that completes the meaning of the subject and the verb

Complex sentence A sentence that contains one independent clause and one or more subordinate clauses

Compound sentence A sentence that contains two or more independent clauses and no subordinate clause

Compound-complex sentence A sentence that contains two or more independent clauses and more than one subordinate clause

Concluding sentence Final sentence in a paragraph that restates the central idea in a new and interesting way or that sums up the information presented

Concrete noun A noun that names something that can be perceived through the senses

Conflict A struggle either within a person or between one person and some other person or force

Conjunction A word that connects other words or group of words

Connector A word used to make effective connection between sentences

Connotative meaning The meaning of a word that includes the feelings associated with it

Consonance The repetition of consonant sounds in poetry to create a rhyme

Context The other words and sentences that surround a word

Context clues Hints about the meaning of a word supplied by surrounding words, phrases, and sentences

Coordinating conjunction A connector that joins two statements of equal importance by indicating a relationship between the two

Copyright Legal right of an author or publisher to publish, sell, and distribute a work

Dash Punctuation mark (-) used to call attention to the word or word group that precedes it

Declarative sentence A sentence that states a fact

Deductive reasoning Reasoning that begins with a general statement, adds supporting evidence, and ends with a conclusion based on the data

Definite article The adjective *the* that refers to a definite person or object

Demonstrative pronoun A pronoun that points out a specific person, place, thing, or idea

Denotative meaning The dictionary meaning of a word

Derivative word A word formed, or derived, from a shorter word

Description A word picture that helps the reader form a mental image of the subject

Dewey decimal number A number assigned to a nonfiction book filed under the Dewey decimal system

Dialect A major variation within a language

Dialogue Words said by two or more people having a conversation

Direct object A word or group of words that receives the action of the verb

Double negative A construction when two negative words are used where only one is necessary

Edited Standard English The written form of Standard English

Exact rhyme Repetition of almost identical sounds

Exclamation point Punctuation mark (!) used to end exclamatory sentences

Exclamatory sentence A sentence that expresses surprise or strong feeling

Expository writing Writing to present factual information or to explain ideas and feelings

Factual detail Detail used in objective description that does not include the writer's thoughts and feelings

Factual statement A statement that can be proved or disproved by measurement, experiment, or research

Fallacy An error in logical thinking

Faulty parallelism The incorrect use of conjunctions to join dissimilar parts of speech

Fiction Books in which events and people are from the writer's imagination

Final bibliography A list of all the sources actually used in writing a research paper

First-person pronoun A pronoun used when speakers and writers refer to themselves (*I*)

Footnote The sources of information or of direct quotations used in a research paper

Formal outline An outline showing the relationship of major and minor ideas in a research paper using Roman numerals, capital letters, and Arabic numerals

Formal poetry Poetry that follows a standard form

Free verse Nonformal poetry that does not use all the formal elements of rhyme, regular meter, and stanzas

Frontispiece   An illustration that immediately precedes the title page of a book

Future perfect tense   A verb tense that describes a future action that will be completed before another future action

Future tense   A verb tense that describes an action that will happen in the future

Gerund   A word ending in -*ing* that is formed from a verb and that functions as a noun

Gerund phrase   A verbal phrase consisting of a gerund and its modifiers and complements

Helping verb   A verb that helps the main verb express action or state of being

Hyphen   Punctuation mark (-) used to link the parts of some compound words or to link the part of a word begun on one line with the part finished on the next

Imagery   The use of language to appeal to the senses

Imaginative writing   Stories, novels, plays, and poetry

Imperative sentence   A sentence that gives a command or makes a request

Incomplete construction   A sentence with part left for the reader to complete

Indefinite article   One of the adjectives *a* or *an* that does not refer to a specific person or object

Indefinite pronoun   A pronoun that does not refer to a specific person or thing

Independent clause   A clause that can stand on its own as a sentence

Index   An alphabetical listing of topics covered in a book, with page numbers

Indirect object   A word that tells *to whom* or *for whom* the action of the verb is done

Infinitive   A verb form preceded by the word to and used as a noun, adjective, or adverb

Infinitive phrase   An infinitive plus its modifiers and complements

Informal outline   An outline that uses neither numerals nor letters; subheads are identified by indentions

Intensifier   An adverb such as *very, quite, rather*, or *too* that answers the question *to what extent?*

Interjection   A word that expresses strong emotion, or surprise

Interrogative adverb   An adverb used to ask a question

Interrogative pronoun   A pronoun used in asking a question

Interrogative sentence   A sentence that asks a question

Intransitive verb   A verb that does not take a direct object

Jargon   Special words and phrases used within a specific occupation

Letter of adjustment   Letter in which the writer is trying to convince a company or individual to replace damaged merchandise, refund money, or correct an error in billing

Letter of application   A letter written to apply for a job

Letter of appreciation   The business letter counterpart of a thank-you note

Letter of request   Letter in which the writer is asking for something

Library of Congress system   A method of classifying fiction and nonfiction books using twenty-one categories designated by letters of the alphabet

Linking verb   A verb that links the subject of the sentence with a noun, a pronoun, or an adjective in the predicate

Logical organization   An ordering of thoughts and ideas that makes sense

Main verb   Usually the last verb of a verb phrase; the part of the verb phrase that is not a helping verb

Marginal note   A note printed in the margin to the left or to the right of the page's main text

Metaphor   Figurative language that makes a connection between two different types of items

Meter   A formal rhythmic pattern of sound in poetry

Modifier   A word that describes another word

Nonfiction   Books about real-life people and events

Noun   A word that names a person, a place, a thing, or an idea

Noun clause   A group of words that contain a subject and verb and that function as a noun

Object complement   A noun or an adjective in the predicate that identifies or explains the direct object

Omniscient narrator A narrator who is not a character in the story but knows everything that happens, and can describe what each character thinks and feels

Only-cause fallacy The fallacy of naming a single cause for a complex situation

Order letter Letter in which the writer is requesting that a company send merchandise

Paired connectors A set of connectors used to make a connection between two sentences of equal importance

Paraphrase To restate words in a different way without changing the meaning

Parentheses Punctuation mark used to enclose elements that interrupt a sentence

Participial phrase A participle plus its modifiers and complements

Participle A word formed from a verb that is used as an adjective

Passive voice The form of the verb when the subject receives the action

Past perfect tense A verb tense that describes an action that took place in the past before another action

Past tense A verb tense that describes an action that happened in the past

Pentad A method of organizing writing by asking five questions (about *action, actors, scene, method,* and *purpose)*

Period A punctuation mark (.) used as an end mark to separate sentences or as a mark to show the omission of letters in abbreviations

Personal detail Detail shaped by the writer's thoughts and feelings and used to describe the subject as it appears to the writer

Personal pronoun A pronoun that refers to the speaker or writer, to the person or people being addressed, or to a third person or people

Personal writing Writing that is about the writer's thoughts and feelings

Persuasive essay An essay that makes an argument

Persuasive speech Use of the spoken word to influence others

Persuasive writing Writing whose purpose is to convince readers to think, believe, or act a certain way

Phrase A group of words, without a subject and its verb, that functions as a single part of speech.

Phrase modifier A string of words with no subject or verb that acts as an adjective or adverb

Plot A story-line or plan of action that centers on a conflict and is brought to a conclusion

Positive degree The regular form of an adjective or adverb that describes a quality

Possessive noun The form of a noun that indicates ownership or relationship

Predicate The part of a sentence that says something about the subject and contains a verb or verb phrase

Predicate adjective An adjective that follows a linking verb and modifies the subject of the sentence

Predicate nominative A noun or pronoun that identifies or renames the subject and is joined to it by a linking verb

Prefix A letter or letters added to the front of a word to change or modify its meaning

Preposition A word that shows a relationship between a noun or pronoun and another word or words in the sentence

Prepositional phrase A phrase that consists of a preposition, its object, and any modifiers the object may have

Present perfect tense A verb tense that describes an action begun in the past that may continue to the present

Present tense A verb tense that describes an action happening now or an action that is habitual or repeated

Progressive verb A form of a verb that expresses ongoing action

Pronoun A word that takes the place of one or more nouns or other pronouns

Proofreading Checking writing for errors in spelling, grammar, and mechanics

Proper adjective An adjective formed from a proper noun

Proper noun A noun that names a specific person, place, thing, or idea

Question mark A punctuation mark (?) used as an end mark for an interrogative sentence

Quotation marks Punctuation marks ('') used to enclose a word or group of words and separate them from the rest of the sentence

Reference books Books containing specialized knowledge

Relative pronoun A pronoun that introduces an adjective clause and that has a function within the clause

Research paper An extended, formal essay presenting specific information gathered from several sources

Résumé A summary of personal data, background, and experience in outline form

Revising The process of making changes in the content and style of a piece of writing

Rough draft The first draft, or copy, of a composition

Run-on sentence A group of words that result when two or more sentences are joined together with a comma or with no punctuation at all

Semicolon Punctuation mark (;) used to signal a more definite break in thought

Sensory detail Details of sight, sound, taste, smell, and touch

Sentence A group of words that expresses a complete thought

Sentence fragment A group of words that does not express a complete thought

Sentence outline An outline in which the headings are stated as complete sentences

Simile A comparison between items using words such as *like, as, than, seems,* and *appears*

Simple sentence A sentence containing one independent clause and no subordinate clause

Single quotation marks Punctuation marks (') used to enclose a direct quotation that occurs inside another quotation

Six basic questions A method of organizing writing by asking *Who? What? When? Where? Why?* and *How?*

Standard English The form of English most accepted in business, industry, and commerce

Stanzas Patterns of repeating lines in poetry

Statistic A fact containing a number

Stressed syllables Accented or spoken more loudly

Subject The part of a sentence that is the person, place, thing, or idea that the sentence is about

Subject complement A noun, pronoun, or adjective that follows a linking verb and that describes or explains the simple subject

Subordinate clause A clause that does not express a complete thought

Subordinating conjunction A word that links a lesser statement to a major statement by indicating the relationship between the two

Suffix One or more letters added to the end of a word that change its part of speech or its meaning

Superlative degree The form of an adjective or adverb that compares three or more persons or things

Synonyms Words with nearly the same meanings

Tense A verb feature that indicates the time of the action or state of being

Thesaurus A dictionary of synonyms

Thesis statement A sentence that states the thesis, or topic, of the composition

Topic outline An outline in which only words and phrases are used as headings

Topic sentence A sentence in a paragraph that introduces the central idea or topic to be developed

Transitive verb A verb that can transmit its action to the direct object

TRI pattern A method of paragraph development using Topic, Restriction, and Illustration

Verb A word that expresses action or a state of being

Verb phrase A group of words composed of a main verb and one or more helping verbs that together act as the main verb in a sentence

Verbal A word formed from a verb but used in a sentence as an adjective, an adverb, or a noun

Verbal phrase A verbal with its modifiers and complements used as a single noun, adjective, or adverb

Working bibliography A list of all the possible sources for a research paper

Writer's Notebook A record of the writer's experiences, thoughts, and observations

Index of Authors and Titles

Index

Bold numbers feature basic definitions and rules.

E

Each, number of, **331**
Edited Standard English, **653**
Ei, ie, **677**
Either, number of, **331**
Either-or argument, **188**
Either . . . or, 461
-Elect, hyphenation of words ending with, **595**
Emotions, appeal of persuasive writing to, **178**–179
Encyclopedia Americana, 642
Encyclopaedia Britannica, **642**–643
Encyclopaedia Britannica Atlas, 644
Encyclopedias, **642**–643
  of world literature, **646**
End marks
  exclamation point, **576**–577
  period, **573**–575
  question mark, **575**
English language
  American English, **649**–653
  dialects, **649**–652
  Edited Standard English, **653**
  formal, **651**
  history, **648**
  informal, **652**
  jargon, **650**–651
  social varieties, 651–652
  Standard English, 651, **653**
English language. *See also* Language
Entries
  bibliography, format for, 141–143
  in Writer's Notebook, **29**–31
Envelope, addressing, **268**
Essay, expository, **94**–130
  body, **105**, 111
  coherence in, **118**
  comparison-and-contrast, 120–121, **127**
  conclusion, **105**, 112
  examination, **120**–129
  explain items, **121**
  focusing subject, **95**–96
  gathering information for, **96**–98
  illustrations in, **111**
  informal outline for, **103**–104
  introduction, **105**, 110–111
  logical organization in, **111**

organizing notes for, 100–102
planning, 94–104
process analysis essay, **114**–116, 119
recording information for, **99**–100
revising, checklist for, **114**, **119**
thesis statement for, **102**–103
trace items, **121**
unity in, **111**
writing, 105–113
Essay, persuasive
  audience for, knowing, **194**
  body, **203**
  conclusion, **204**
  introduction, **202**
  planning, 193–194
  revising, checklist for, **205**
  sample of, 189–192
  thesis statement for, **198**–199
  topic outline for, **201**
  writing, 202–205
Essay tests. *See* Examination essay
Essay, titles, quotation marks enclosing, **602**
Essential adjective clause, **548**–**549**
Essential participial phrases, no commas with, 523–524
Essential phrases, 523, 584
  no commas with, 584
Events in chronological order, **42**–43
Every, verb form with, **385**
Every or *many a,* agreement with, **385**
Everybody, number of, **331**
Everyone, number of, **331**
Ex-, hyphenation of words beginning with, **595**
Exact rhyme, **215**
Examination essay, **120**–129
  comparison-and-contrast, **127**
  explain, **121**
  organizing, **125**–126
  planning writing time, **122**–**123**
  reading directions, **123**–124
  trace, **127**–128
Example clues, **664**
Examples, paragraph development with, **78**–79

Except, accept, **443**
  not used as conjunction, **462**
Exclamation point
  with interjection, **467**, **576**
  with quotation marks, **601**
  uses of, **576**
Exclamatory sentence, **481**
  ending with exclamation point, **481**
Experience clues, **663**
Explain essay, writing, **121**, 128–129
Explain items on examination, **121**
Explanation
  colon separating from introductory statement, **590**
  dash separating from introductory statement, **592**
Expletive, *here* or *there,* **487**
Expository paragraph. *See* Paragraph
Expository writing, **94**–130
  body of, **105**, 111
  checklist for revising, **114**
  choosing and limiting subject, **94**–**95**
  coherence in, **118**
  conclusion, **105**–**112**
  examination essays for, **120**–129
  finding subject, 94–**95**
  focusing subject, **95**–96
  gathering information for, **96**–98
  illustrations in, **111**
  informal outline for, **103**–104
  introduction, **105**, 110–111
  logical organization in, **111**
  model, expository essay, 105–109
  model, informal outline, 104
  organizing notes for, 100–102
  planning, 94–104
  process analysis essay, **114**–116, 119
  purpose of, **94**
  recording information for, **99**–100
  revising checklist for, **114**, **119**
  thesis statement for, **102**–103
  unity in, **111**
  writing, 105–112

Loaded words (appeal to emotion), **178**–179
Logical fallacies, **186**–189
Logical organization in expository essay, **111**
-Ly ending, **423**–424

M

Magazine articles, finding in *Readers' Guide*, **633**–635
Magazines. *See* Periodicals
Main clauses. *See* Independent clauses
Main idea. *See* Thesis statement
Main verbs, **359**–361
Major premise, **183**–185
Making connections (clustering), **6**–7
Many, number of, **331**
Many a, every, verb form with, **385**
Metaphors, **231**–232
  combined with similes, 232–233
Meter, **217**
Method, questions about, **13**
Methods of paragraph development. *See* Paragraph
Microfiche, **624**
Microfilm, **624**
Micropaedia, **642**–643
Midwest, dialect of, **649**–650
Minor premise, **183**–185
MLA form for parenthetical documentation, **150**–151
Modes of writing, 10–**11**
Modifiers
  adjective clauses, **171**
  adjectives, **396**, **399**–400
  adverbs, **418**
  appositives, **206**
  of appositives, **521**
  bad, badly, **430**
  expanding sentence pattern, **497**
  good, well, **430**–431
  infinitive phrases as, **519**
  of gerunds, **517**
  inserting, **131**–132
  intensifiers, **403**
  introductory participial phrases as, **525**
  participial phrases as, **525**–526

participles as, **477**
  of participles, **515**
  phrases as, **134**–135
  predicate adjectives, **494**–495
  slow, slowly, **431**–432
  prepositional phrases, **438**
Mood
  in descriptions, **34**
  establishing, **36**–37
More and *most*, **423**, **427**–428
Most, number of, **332**
Moreover, **88**
Myself, ourselves, yourselves, etc., **333**

N

Name calling, **180**
Names
  abbreviations, **573**–574
  capitalizing, **299**
  of countries, singular verb form with, **384**
  geographical, commas separating parts of, **586**
  personal, comma separating from degree, title, or affiliation, **587**
Narrative, personal, **41**–43
Narrative writing, purpose of, **41**–42
Natural writing voice, **24**–26
Near rhyme, **215**–216
Negative adverbs, **420**–421
Negatives, double, **433**
Neither . . . nor, **461**
Neither, number of, **331**
Nevertheless, **88**
Newspapers. *See* Periodicals
Nicknames, with quotation marks, **602**
No, adjective and adverb, **420**–421
  set off by comma, **581**
No, nothing, none, **433**
No one, number of, **331**
None, number of, **332**
Nominative case, **344**
Nominatives, predicate, **385**, **507**
Nonessential adjective clauses, **549**
Nonessential appositives, **584**–585
Nonessential clauses, **584**

Nonessential phrases, **584**
Nonfiction, arrangement in library, **624**–627, **630**
Nonformal poetry, **221**–225
  line breaks in, **224**–227
Nonrestrictive clauses. *See* Nonessential clauses
Nonstandard English, **649**–653
Nor, neither, **461**, **579**
Not
  commas preceding, **581**
  in double negatives, **433**
Note cards
  for expository essay, **99**–100
  for research paper, **144**–145
Note-taking. *See* Note cards
Noun clauses, **253**, **545**
  inserting, **253**–254
  introductory word dropped from, 545–**546**
Nouns, **298**–319
  abstract, **300**
  as adjectives, **399**
  adjectives modifying, **396**
  as adverbs, **421**
  changing to possessive, **311**–312
  classifying, **299**–300
  collective, **381**–382
  common, **299**–300
  compound, **300**, **310**–311
  concrete, **300**
  of direct address, comma with, **581**–582
  features, **301**–303
  gerund, **472**–473
  gerunds acting as, **473**
  infinitives functioning as, **519**
  with no singular form, **384**
  as object complement, **504**–505
  with plural form and singular meaning, **384**
  plurals, **302**, **304**–311
  plurals, spelling, **304**–311
  possessives, **302**–303, **311**–312
  proper, **299**–300, 307, **313**–315, **398**
  singular, **302**, **309**
  suffixes forming, **302**
Number
  of pronoun and antecedent, **338**

Skills Index

Writing

Business Writing

addressing envelopes, 268–270
adjustment letters, 278–280
application letters, 284–285
appreciation letters, 280–284
filling out forms, 287–288
folding, 266–267
forms of, 260–264
order letters, 276–278
request letters, 274–276
résumés, 284–285
styles, 264–265

Expository Writing

body, 111
checklist for revising, 114
coherence in, 118
conclusion, 112
examination essays, 120–130
focusing subjects, 95–96
gathering information, 96–99
informal outlines, 103–104
introduction, 105–111
note-taking, 99–102
planning, 94–104
process analysis, 114–117, 119
thesis statement, 102–103

Fiction and Drama

checklist for revising a short
   story, 246
creating characters, 240–241
dialogue, 241–243, 248–252
drama, elements of, 247
fiction, elements of, 235
plot, 237–240
point-of-view, 243
settings, 236–237, 247

Paragraphs

central impression, 32–41
coherence in, 66–73
descriptive, 31–41
order, types of, 66–69
question-answer, 58–61
topic sentence 52–56
TRI pattern, 52–56
transition words, 69
unity in, 61–65
using a combination of methods
   to develop, 67–68
using comparison and contrast
   to develop, 65–67
using descriptive details to develop, 73–76
using examples to develop,
   78–79
using facts and statistics to develop, 76–78
using reasons to develop, 80–81
varying patterns, 56–58

Persuasive Writing

conclusion, 205
body, 203–204
emotional appeal, 178–180
introductory paragraph, 202
knowing audience, 194–196
logical reasoning, 183–185
point of view, 193
recognizing facts and opinions,
   176–177
recognizing false reasoning,
   186–189
thesis statement, 198–199
topic outline, 201

Poetry

elements of, 214
figurative language, 228–235
free verse or nonformal, 221–228
meter, 217–221
rhyme and alliteration, 214–217

Prewriting

brainstorming, 4–6
clustering, 6–8
determining audience, purpose,
   and mode, 10
free writing, 9
methods, 4
questioning, 12–13

Proofreading

business letter, checklist for, 286
checklist, 19–20

Research Writing

bibliography, 161–162
bibliography card, 141–144
checklist for revising, 163
choosing and limiting topics,
   138–141, 145–147
controlling idea 145–146
final draft, 162–163
   149–152, 158
formal outline, 147–148
gathering information, 141
parenthetical documentation,
   149–152, 158
rough draft, 148–149
taking notes, 144–145
using quotations, 149

Revising

autobiographical narrative, 26
checklist for revising, 17–18
checklist for short story, 246
editing symbols, 16
journal entries, 20
expository writing, checklist for,
   114
personal writing, checklist for,
   40–41, 46
persuasive essay, 205
research report, checklist for,
   163

Mechanics

Capitalization

to set off groups of words,
608–611
to set off single words, 611–620

Punctuation

apostrophes, 598–600
colons, 590–592, 601
commas, 577–588, 601
dashes, 592–594
exclamation points, 576–577, 601
hyphens, 595–598
parentheses, 594–595
periods, 573–575, 601
question marks, 575, 601
quotation marks, 600
semicolons, 588–590, 601
using, 572–573
writing dialogue, 604

Language Resources

Library Resources

almanacs and atlases, 643–645
arrangement of books, 624–628,
636
dictionaries, 636–642
encyclopedias, 642–643
literature reference books, 647
parts of a book, 630–631
Readers' Guide, 633–635
using the card catalogue,
628–630

Speaking and Listening Skills

discussion techniques, 686–693
types of groups, 685

Spelling

rules for, 677–683
ways to improve, 675–676

Vocabulary

changes in language, 659–660
connotations and denotations,
665–667
concrete and abstract language,
660–661
context clues, 662–665
history of language, 648–649
meaning and uses of language,
653–659
meaning through structure,
667–673
variations, 649–653

Proofreader's Checklist

1. Have I indented each paragraph?

2. Did I capitalize the first word of each sentence, all proper nouns, and the word *I*?

3. Did I punctuate each sentence correctly?

4. Are there any sentence fragments or incomplete sentences?

5. Do related verbs, nouns, or pronouns in each sentence show agreement in kind and number?

6. Are all words spelled correctly?

7. Is my writing easy to read?

Acknowledgments

Credits

Key: (t) top, (c) center, (b) bottom, (l) left, (r) right.

Page 1, Gregg Eisman; 2, Thomas Hooke Photography; 3(l), Bruce Powell; 3(r), Culver Pictures, Inc.; 5, Jim Whitmer; 8, V. Lee Hunter; 11, Jean-Claude Lejeune; 13, Vito Palmisano; 17, Thomas Hooke Photography; 21, Bruce Powell; 23, Thomas Hooke Photography; 24, 25(l), 25(r), Jean-Claude Lejeune; 27, Nicholas Sapieha/Stock, Boston; 28, Bruce Powell; 30, Jean-Claude Lejeune; 33, Vito Palmisano; 35, Frank Loose; 36, Thomas Hooke Photography; 39(l), Bruce Powell; 39(r), Vito Palmisano; 41, Thomas Hooke Photography; 43, Vito Palmisano; 47, Jim Whitmer; 48, Bruce Powell; 49, 51, V. Lee Hunter; 52, Thomas Hooke Photography; 53(l), Steven E. Gross; 53(r), Steve Kiecker; 55, 57, Thomas Hooke Photography; 59, 60, Jean-Claude Lejeune; 63, Vito Palmisano; 65, Jean-Claude Lejeune; 67, V. Lee Hunter; 70, Peter Vandermark/Stock, Boston; 72, 77, 79, 82, Vito Palmisano; 85, Thomas Hooke Photography; 87, Jean-Claude Lejeune; 89, Vito Palmisano; 91, Frank Siteman/The Marilyn Gartman Agency; 93, Jean-Claude Lejeune; 94, Thomas Hooke Photography; 95(l), NASA; 95(r), 97, Steven E. Gross; 98, Vito Palmisano; 101(t), Jean-Claude Lejeune; 101(b), Frank Siteman/The Marilyn Gartman Agency; 109, Bruce Powell; 111, 112, Vito Palmisano; 114, Jean-Claude Lejeune; 115, Philip Bailey/Stock, Boston; 117, Frank Siteman/The Marilyn Gartman Agency; 120(l), John Weinstein; 120(r), Bruce Powell; 124, Andrew Rakoczy; 130, Jim Whitmer; 133, Thomas Hooke Photography; 137, D. Donne Bryant/Art Resource; 138, Thomas Hooke Photography; 139(l), Culver Pictures, Inc.; 139(r), 146, Springer/Bettmann Film Archive; 149, Culver Pictures, Inc.; 152, Strix Pix; 154, Culver Pictures, Inc.; 155, 156, 160, Springer/Bettmann Film Archive; 164, Bruce Powell; 167, John Weinstein; 172, Kamila Kiecker; 173, UPI: 175, Jean-Claude Lejeune; 177(l), 177(r), UPI; 178, Jean-Claude Lejeune; 179, Bruce Powell; 180, Thomas Hooke Photography; 181, Jean-Claude Lejeune; 182, Thomas Hooke Photography; 183, Vito Palmisano; 184, UPI; 185, Jim Whitmer; 187, 190, Bruce Powell; 194, 197, Steve Kiecker; 204, Jean-Claude Lejeune; 206, Thomas Hooke Photography; 207, 208, Vito Palmisano; 211(l), Bruce Powell; 211(r), Jean-Claude Lejeune; 214, Thomas Hooke Photography; 215(l), Jean-Claude Lejeune; 215(r), V. Lee Hunter; 217, 219, 220, Jean-Claude Lejeune; 225, Vito Palmisano; 226, 227, Thomas Hooke Photography; 229, Jim Whitmer; 238, 242, 251, Vito Palmisano; 252, Bruce Powell; 255, Jean-Claude Lejeune; 259, Frank Siteman/The Marilyn Gartman Agency; 260, Thomas Hooke Photography; 261(l), Jean-Claude Lejeune; 261(r), Gregg Eisman; 263, Jean-Claude Lejeune; 270, Thomas Hooke Photography; 272, Gregg Eisman; 276, D. Shigley; 277, Gregg Eisman; 278, 291, 293(l), Thomas Hooke Photography; 293(r), Jean-Claude Lejeune; 294, 295, Bruce Powell; 297, Gregg Eisman; 319, Vito Palmisano; 357, Frank Siteman/The Marilyn Gartman Agency; 395, Peter Menzel/Stock, Boston; 415, Jean-Claude Lejeune; 416, Chicago Historical Society; 417, Bruce Powell; 437, Julie O'Neil/Stock, Boston; 451, Jean-Claude Lejeune; 464, Gregg Eisman; 465, Jim Whitmer; 469, Gregg Eisman; 479, The Association of Universities for Research in Astronomy, Inc., The Cerro-Tololo Inter-American Observatory; 510, Jean-Claude Lejeune; 532, 533, Brent Jones; 555(l), John Weinstein; 555(r), Thomas Hooke Photography; 570, Bruce Powell; 571, Gregg Eisman; 607(l), Bruce Powell; 607(r), Jean-Claude Lejeune; 622, Vito Palmisano; 623, Gregg Eisman.

1 2 3 4 5 6 7 8 9 0—93 92 91 90 89 88 87